WHAT CAN WE DO FOR OUR COUNTRIES?

The Contribution of Universities to National Development

The Report of Proceedings of the Fourteenth Congress of the Universities of the Commonwealth Perth, February 1988

THE ASSOCIATION
OF COMMONWEALTH UNIVERSITIES
JOHN FOSTER HOUSE, 36 GORDON SQUARE, LONDON,
ENGLAND WC1H 0PF
1988

Editor of Congress Proceedings
T. CRAIG, MA

Deputy Editor
EILEEN A. ARCHER, MA

This report is published for information purposes only. All reasonable efforts have been taken in the collation of the material it contains, and in the editing thereof; and no liability is accepted for its contents by the Association of Commonwealth Universities.

Price £9.80

Printed in Great Britain by Hobbs the Printers of Southampton
Copyright © The Association of Commonwealth Universities, 1988
ISBN 0 85143 116 X

FOURTEENTH CONGRESS OF THE UNIVERSITIES OF THE COMMONWEALTH
1988

Ministry of Education, Ontario
Information Services & Resources Unit,
13th Floor, Mowat Block, Queen's Park,
Toronto M7A 1L2

The Congress Symbol

For a list of ACU publications, see end of volume.
Reports of some previous Congresses are also available.

FOREWORD

This Report contains
- *papers* (or shorter versions thereof) presented by the speakers who introduced each of the discussion sessions held during Congress week. Also included are several papers provided by designated speakers who were at the last moment unable to be present; and mention of other papers circulated during the Congress;
- *summaries* of the discussions that followed the presentation of the papers;
- a *commentary* by each of the seven Topic Chairmen on the nature and outcome of his own group's meetings;
- *addresses* given at the opening of the Congress, at the first plenary session, and at the closing ceremony.

Speakers and rapporteurs were asked to provide for inclusion in the Report texts within specified maximum lengths and in some cases it has been necessary, in the interests of balance, to edit the original text so as to bring it within the suggested format.

The Preface contains an overview of the Congress as a whole—its planning and organisation, and the major events and other meetings associated with it.

CONGRESS ORGANISING COMMITTEE

Professor L. M. BIRT, *Chairman*
Professor A. O. ADESOLA (until 4.11.86)
Mr. F. S. HAMBLY
Professor J. MANRAKHAN (from 4.11.86)
Professor Dato' NAYAN BIN ARIFFIN (5.11.85–3.11.87)
Mr. M. R. ORR
Professor G. D. SIMS
Sir ALBERT SLOMAN (28.2.85–3.11.87)
Professor T. H. B. SYMONS
Professor S. WIJESUNDERA (until 5.11.85)

Dr. A. CHRISTODOULOU, *Secretary General, ACU*
Mr. T. CRAIG, *Editor of Congress Proceedings* (*Deputy Secretary General, ACU*)
Mrs. BLANCHE GUBERTINI, *Personal Assistant to the Secretary General, ACU*

CONTENTS

	Page
PREFACE	9
OPENING CEREMONY	17
Mr. D. H. Aitken	17
Professor L. M. Birt	17
H.E. The Rt. Hon. Sir Ninian Stephen	21
The Hon. D. C. Parker	22
Professor R. H. T. Smith	24
Professor J. Manrakhan	27
FIRST PLENARY SESSION	33
The Contribution of Universities to National Development	
Professor L. M. Birt	33
Keynote Address: The Hon. Justice G. J. Samuels	35
The Rt. Hon. Lord Flowers	48
GROUP DISCUSSIONS	
Topic 1: The University as Critic	53
Topic 2: The University as a Knowledge Factory	105
Topic 3: Universities and Continuing Education	173
Topic 4: Universities and National Administration	255
Topic 5: Universities and Culture	291
Topic 6: Universities and the Social Impact of Technology	369
Topic 7: Universities and Rural Development	455
SECOND PLENARY SESSION AND CLOSING CEREMONY	503
H.R.H. Prince Ado Ibrahim	503
COUNCIL OF THE ASSOCIATION	505
MEMBERS OF THE CONGRESS	507
CONGRESS COMMITTEES AND SECRETARIAT	529
APPENDIX: Message from UNESCO	531
NAMES INDEX	533

PREFACE

The fourteenth in the series of quinquennial ACU Congresses of the Universities of the Commonwealth was held at the University of Western Australia, Perth, from 7 to 12 February, 1988, with the Australian universities acting as hosts. The series began with the 1912 Congress in London, out of which the Association of Commonwealth Universities (the Universities Bureau of the British Empire as it was then called) was born, and has continued without interruption except during the two world wars. After world war II the decision was taken that Congresses should be held alternately in Britain and another part of the Commonwealth; and thus the eighth Congress was held in Montreal in 1958, the tenth in Sydney in 1968 and the twelfth in Vancouver in 1978. The thirteenth in the series was held at the University of Birmingham in August 1983. The fourteenth was particularly significant since 1988 marked the 75th Anniversary of the Association, the 75th Anniversary of University of Western Australia where it was held, and the bicentenary year of Australia.

A General Meeting within the week before or after the Congress is required by the Association's Statutes, and around it is arranged a Conference of Executive Heads of member institutions; it is customary also for the Council to meet, in the same country, before or after the Congress. The meeting of the Council was held on Wednesday, 3 February, and was followed that evening by an informal dinner given, at his home, for Council members and accompanying partners by the Vice-Chancellor of the University of Western Australia, Professor R. H. T. Smith.

ACU Conference of Executive Heads

Attending the Conference were 227 participants accompanied by 113 family members. The participants gathered during Wednesday, 3 February, and spent Thursday, 4 February in intensive discussions on 'Issues in the development of a national university system' based on the October 1987 report of the New Zealand Universities Review Committee entitled *New Zealand's Universities: Partners in National Development*. The discussions were organized by the vice-chancellors of the New Zealand universities under the chairmanship

of Dr. W. G. Malcolm, Vice-Chancellor, University of Waikato, and their presentation was made at a plenary session, after which the meeting divided into four parallel discussion groups:
- 'The operational structure of a national university system' chaired by Professor B. G. Wilson, University of Queensland, with Dr. A. J. Earp, Brock University, Professor C. Ikoku, University of Nigeria (Nsukka) and Sir John Kingman, University of Bristol, as speakers
- 'Access to universities' chaired by Professor J. F. Scott, La Trobe University, with Professor Dato' Abdul Hamid Abdul Rahman, Universiti Kebangsaan Malaysia, Professor H. J. Hanham, University of Lancaster and Professor R. Panabokke, University of Peradeniya, Sri Lanka, as speakers
- 'The accountability of a national system' chaired by Professor R. H. T. Smith, University of Western Australia, with Professor G. J. Davies, University of Liverpool and Professor W. J. Kamba, University of Zimbabwe, as speakers, and
- 'The funding of a university system' chaired by Professor L. W. Nichol, University of New England, with Professor J. M. Ashworth, University of Salford, Dr. A. A. Lee, McMaster University and Professor M. W. J. G. Mendis, University of Moratuwa, Sri Lanka (replacing Professor S. Wijesundera, University of Colombo, whose arrival was delayed).

At a final plenary session each chairman reported briefly on the discussions of his group and a panel discussion on 'Universities from the national perspective' was held, chaired by Dr. Malcolm. The panel comprised Dr. T. L. Johnston, Heriot-Watt University; Dr. A. Naimark, University of Manitoba; Professor A. N. Mohammed, Ahmadu Bello University; and Professor Moonis Raza, University of Delhi.

The statutory General Meeting was held on Friday, 5 February, the main items on the agenda being the Secretary General's quinquennial report on the activities and affairs of the Association; the Honorary Treasurer's report on the work of the Special Group on Future Developments of the Association; and recent developments about student mobility between Commonwealth countries. Consideration of the latter led to the adoption of a resolution for transmission to the Commonwealth Secretary-General urging Commonwealth Heads of Governments to support measures leading to the freest possible interchange of students within the Commonwealth. The Honorary Treasurer reported on the progress of the 75th Anniversary Appeal, due to close at the end of 1988, for funds to set up a new programme of development

PREFACE

fellowships. Already half the total target of £3 million had been reached.

At the Meeting the Symons Award for 1987, for services to the Association, was conferred upon Professor Akin Adesola, Vice-Chancellor, University of Lagos.

The Conference's social programme included a river cruise and barbecue at the Royal Freshwater Bay Yacht Club, a lunch reception at the City Council House by the Lord Mayor of Perth, a reception by the Chancellor of the University of Western Australia at St. George's College, and an all-day tour to Rottnest Island.

Preparations for the Congress

The Congress Organising Committee consisted of the five currently serving officers of the Association, together with Professor L. M. Birt, Vice-Chancellor of the University of New South Wales; Mr. F. S. Hambly, Secretary of the Australian Vice-Chancellors' Committee; and Mr. M. Orr, Registrar, University of Western Australia. The Committee held its first meeting on 9 November, 1984, when Professor Birt was appointed its Chairman.

During their periods of office, the following officers of the Association served on the Committee: Professor T. H. B. Symons (Canada), Professor G. D. Sims (Sheffield), Professor S. Wijesundera (Colombo), Professor A. O. Adesola (Lagos), Professor Dato' Nayan bin Ariffin (Pertanian Malaysia), Professor J. Manrakhan (Mauritius), Sir Albert Sloman (Essex). The secretariat were represented by the Secretary General, Dr. A. Christodoulou; Mr. T. Craig, the Deputy Secretary General; and Mrs. Blanche Gubertini, P.A. to the Secretary General.

The Committee held its first, second and fourth meetings in London, and the third in Penang during the Executive Heads' Conference of 1986.

The Australian universities set up a local organizing committee under the chairmanship of Professor Birt, comprising Mr. F. S. Hambly; Professor P. J. Boyce, Vice-Chancellor, Murdoch University; and Professor R. H. T. Smith (Vice-Chancellor), Mr. M. R. Orr (Registrar) and Mrs. Margaret Shellam-Harper (Executive Director, Conference and Development Office), all three of the University of Western Australia. Mrs. Shellam-Harper was the Congress administrator. The Secretary General attended meetings of the local committee in February 1986 and April 1987. A hospitality committee, under the leadership of Mrs. Margaret Aitken, wife of the Chancellor of the University of Western

Australia, was set up to arrange a programme for accompanying persons.

A first circular, giving dates of the meetings, was sent out in April 1986. A second circular with more details, together with an invitation to member universities to nominate up to four delegates each and to a wide range of other organizations to send a representative, was issued in October 1986. The final circular and registration forms were sent out in June 1987 and a bulletin giving the latest information in October 1987. As usual, executive heads of member universities and secretaries of Commonwealth inter-university associations were invited to attend the preceding Conference.

Membership of the Congress

Attending the Congress were 475 official delegates (comprising 415 nominated by 222 member institutions together with 60 representatives of other organizations and specially invited guests), about 250 of whom were accompanied by one or more members of their families. The total number attending was 728. His Excellency, the Right Honourable Sir Ninian Stephen, Governor-General of Australia, graciously consented to be the Patron of the Congress. Other invitees included the chairmen of various university grants committees and equivalent bodies, representatives of a variety of other Commonwealth and non-Commonwealth and international organizations concerned with university education, including university representatives from the USA.

The Congress

Members of the Congress and their families assembled on Sunday, 7 February, and were accommodated in halls of residence of the University of Western Australia or in hotels in Perth according to their choice. The University organized an Asian Banquet on its campus that evening which included Chinese dragon dancing and a welcoming address from the Chairman of the ACU, Professor Michael Birt. The business meetings of the Congress were held on campus.

The Congress was formally opened in the University's Winthrop Hall on Monday, 8 February, with a ceremony, preceded by an organ recital and aboriginal music, at which the Council of the Association processed in academic robes accompanied by the Chancellor and Vice-Chancellor of the University of Western Australia and the Vice-Chancellor of Murdoch University. Special guests

PREFACE

included the Hon. David Parker, Minister for Minerals and Energy, Economic Development and the Arts (representing the Premier of Western Australia) and the Hon. Norman Moore, representing the leader of the State Opposition.

The Chancellor of the University, Mr. Donald Aitken, gave a general welcome; the Chairman of the Association, Professor Michael Birt, welcomed participants to the Congress; and H.E. The Hon. Sir Ninian Stephen, Governor-General, welcomed the Congress to Australia. The Hon. David Parker welcomed the Congress to the State of Western Australia and the Vice-Chancellor, Professor R. H. T. Smith, to the University. The formal vote of thanks to the speakers was given by Professor J. Manrakhan, Vice-Chancellor, University of Mauritius, and Immediate Past Chairman of the Association.

After the formal opening, the first plenary session was held under the chairmanship of Professor Michael Birt. A keynote address on the overall Congress theme 'The contribution of universities to national development' was given by the Chancellor of the University of New South Wales, the Hon. Mr. Justice Samuels. The seven topics under this theme—'the university as critic', 'the university as a knowledge factory', 'universities and continuing education', 'universities and national administration', 'universities and culture', 'universities and the social impact of technology' and 'universities and rural development'—were then discussed in groups on Monday afternoon, Tuesday morning and afternoon and Thursday morning and afternoon, after addresses from lead speakers drawn from universities throughout the Commonwealth. On Friday morning the second plenary session of the Congress was held, at which summary reports on the discussions were given by the chairmen of the seven topics: Dr. Wang Gungwu (Vice-Chancellor, University of Hong Kong); Sir John Kingman (Vice-Chancellor, University of Bristol); Dr. J. Daniel (President, Laurentian University, who had taken over at short notice from Professor G. Ram Reddy, Vice-Chancellor of Indira Gandhi National Open University, who was unable to attend); Professor P. J. Boyce (Vice-Chancellor, Murdoch University); Professor L. C. Holborow (Vice-Chancellor, Victoria University of Wellington); Dr. J. Downey (President, University of New Brunswick); and Professor D. Odhiambo (Vice-Chancellor, Moi University). This was followed by the closing ceremony at which Prince Ado Ibrahim (Nigeria) delivered a goodwill message from the President of Nigeria, and Professor B. Clarkson, Vice-Chancellor, University of Wales and Principal, University College of Swansea, expressed the thanks of the participants to all who had contributed to the success of the Congress.

The main social events of the Congress were the Asian Banquet (see above); a reception and banquet at Murdoch University enlivened by an open-air performance of the ballet 'Picnic at Hanging Rock'; a reception given in the grounds of Government House by the State Government of Western Australia; an evening on the Swan River; and a visit to Curtin University of Technology. The last event of the Congress was the customary banquet on Friday, 12 February, at which Professor Michael Birt, Chairman of the ACU and of the Congress, proposed the loyal toast. The Federal Minister for Employment, Education and Training, the Hon. John Dawkins, gave the after-dinner address, and was replied to by the ACU's Honorary Treasurer, Professor T. H. B. Symons. Mr. Dawkins was introduced by Professor J. F. Scott, Vice-Chancellor of La Trobe University.

For persons accompanying the delegates there was a special daily programme, including a fashion show and visits to art galleries and exhibitions and to the cities of Fremantle and Perth.

The Association is much indebted to the University of Western Australia and its staff of whom special mention can be made here of only a few: the Chancellor, Mr. Donald Aitken and his wife Margaret (who organized the hospitality committee); the Vice-Chancellor, Professor Bob Smith and his wife Liz; Mr. Malcolm Orr, the Registrar (who had charge of the whole operation) and his wife Jeanette; and Mrs. Margaret Shellam-Harper, Executive Director of the Conference and Development Office. The enthusiasm and commitment of all their staff, and the staff of the Colleges of the University, contributed enormously to the success of the Congress.

Mention must also be made of the WASPS—the Western Australian Student Participants—who helped with all aspects of the running of the Congress, and coped cheerfully with every eventuality.

To all of them the Association expresses its deepest gratitude.

September 1988   A. CHRISTODOULOU
Secretary General

ACKNOWLEDGEMENTS

Sincere thanks are expressed to the many persons, companies, institutions and other bodies which so generously contributed, in both money and kind, to the successful operation of the conference and Congress.

The Western Australia State Government
The City of Perth
Westpac Banking Corporation
Bond Brewing
Australian Development Assistance Bureau
The Myer Foundation
The Potter Foundation
The British Council
The Commonwealth Foundation
Carnegie Corporation of New York
International Development Program of Australian Universities and Colleges
The Australian Wool Corporation
Qantas Airways Ltd
Australian Airlines
Tony Barlow Menswear Pty Ltd
Shiseido
Campus Pharmacy
Pacific Film Laboratories Pty Ltd

OPENING CEREMONY
Monday, 8 February

Mr. D. H. AITKEN (*Chancellor of the University of Western Australia*): It is my privilege and very great pleasure as Chancellor of the University of Western Australia, and on behalf of its Senate, to welcome you all to our campus for this important occasion. We are particularly pleased and indebted to his Excellency the Governor-General, Sir Ninian Stephen, for being with us, and delighted that Lady Stephen is able to return to her alma mater for the occasion.

Very few universities have the privilege of hosting a Quinquennial Congress of the Association of Commonwealth Universities. A university chosen for such an event is not likely to be the venue again for centuries, if at all. That is why it is such an important and proud occasion for us to be the hosts for the fourteenth Quinquennial Congress. It is therefore a unique honour for us to be able to welcome representatives of over 300 universities from throughout the Commonwealth to the University of Western Australia and no doubt the Vice-Chancellor, Professor Robert Smith, will expand on this later in his welcoming address. It is also fitting that the Association should be having its Congress at this University which, like the Association of Commonwealth Universities, is celebrating its 75th Anniversary in 1988. We are all bound to be enriched by the experience of having attended a Congress and I hope you all enjoy the many facets of it. I wish it well.

It is now my pleasure to introduce and hand over proceedings to Professor Michael Birt, Chairman of the Association and also of the Organising Committee for this Congress. He is Vice-Chancellor of the University of New South Wales and has been the Chairman of the Organising Committee since November, 1983. He has a wide reputation for his great academic and executive skills and for his energy.

Professor L. M. BIRT (*Vice-Chancellor and Principal of the University of New South Wales and Chairman of the Association of Commonwealth Universities*): May I extend to you *all* a warm welcome to this, the

Opening Ceremony of our Quinquennial Congress. It is a particular pleasure to welcome as delegates their Excellencies, Sir Hugh Springer and Lady Springer—Sir Hugh is a former Secretary General of the Association; His Royal Highness Prince Ado Ibrahim; the Honourable Robert Pearce, Minister for Education in the State of Western Australia; and Mr. Jean Fournier, Under Secretary of State in the Canadian Federal Government.

As you know, this Congress marks the 75th Anniversary of the founding of the Association of Commonwealth Universities in 1913. The Association was established to promote contact and co-operation between its member institutions throughout the Commonwealth, by promoting the movement of academic and administrative staff and students from one country of the Commonwealth to another, thereby assisting their personal development and that of their institutions; to disseminate information about Commonwealth universities; and to organize meetings which assist those universities to share their experience and deal with emerging problems. Most recently it has launched a '75th Anniversary Appeal', to enable the universities of the Commonwealth to develop the human resources of their countries through the interchange of people, knowledge, skills and technologies. The Appeal funds—now standing at about £1·5 million, with a target of £3 million—will support a number of 'development fellowships', to permit the movement of people in mid-career between countries of the Commonwealth, and between industry, commerce, the public services, and the universities, in order to develop the human resources of those countries. The Association is conducting this Appeal in the belief that the most important asset available to Commonwealth countries (especially, but not exclusively, the developing countries) is their pool of highly-trained men and women—for it is on the understanding and work of these people that effective action in national development finally rests. The launching of the Appeal is the most recent re-affirmation of the conviction of the Association's members that it can assist in a very significant way the development of Commonwealth countries, and the forging of strong links between peoples and nations, by providing opportunities for higher education and training to the best young minds and future leaders of each generation.

Since its establishment the Association has grown to become a family of 327 member institutions, serving some 48 countries of the Commonwealth, and providing university education for about 5 million students. As a family, it has sprung from, and continues to recognise, a common heritage: the tradition of university education which has evolved, over the last 1000 years or so, from the great universities of Europe. This is a tradition based on a deep respect for scholarship, which is expressed in training and exercising the intellectual powers of men and women, and in the enlargement and application of knowledge. As an *extended* family, the Association has developed local variants of university life and work, to meet particular local or temporal demands, in the service of the many different societies and cultures which make up the Commonwealth. And as it has grown it has been enriched by the insights gained from the educational traditions of many cultures.

The Australian universities are proud indeed that the Congress is being held in our country in 1988, the year in which *we* celebrate our own Bicentenary as a modern nation. Ladies and gentlemen, you honour us, as a national university system, by joining us in Perth now—and at a University, the University of Western Australia, which also celebrates its 75th Anniversary this year. Chancellor, may I express the Association's congratulations to your University, and thank you for offering it as a venue for our Congress and for your welcome this morning. This coincidence of important anniversaries makes it especially fitting that the Association should reflect, during the Congress, on the ways in which its university members have contributed, or could contribute, to the development of the countries in which they work.

It is no new thing to suppose that universities should serve their societies: they do it, primarily, by the cultivation and application of the intellectual powers of each succeeding generation, and have done since the earliest days; but in Europe the universities undertook, from their inception, vocational teaching in medicine, law, theology and the arts; and they were proud to contribute to the shaping of their nations over the centuries. It was that tradition of service to society which led Sir Thomas More in the fourteenth century to remark that 'the end of education is utility'—'useful' to its members, in that it provides them with a means for the development of their personal understanding, skills and interests; useful to society, in that it prepares men and women for citizenship and for highly-skilled work. Each new generation needs to define how the universities can best serve their countries—there is no abiding prescription, as knowledge broadens and deepens.

Hence our Congress theme: 'the Contribution of Universities to National Development'. I hope that you will find, in the working sessions, opportunities to increase your perception of the breadth and scope of that contribution, to enhance your understanding of the place of the university in society, and—most important—to exchange ideas and arguments with long-standing friends and colleagues, and those newly-met.

With that hope in mind we have arranged for the discussion of the Congress theme to proceed through the consideration of a number of sub-themes. The first of these, 'The University as Critic', will examine the ways in which the university might usefully serve society by standing back from it, as it were, and engaging in a critical analysis of national economic, political, socio-cultural and intellectual activities—in a way acting as the 'gadfly of the state', in the tradition of one of the first academics! The second deals with the responsibility of universities to generate, transmit and apply new knowledge gained through research. The third explores the role of universities in ensuring that the citizens of Commonwealth countries have adequate opportunities to update and upgrade their knowledge and qualifications, through continuing education and distance education. The fourth explores the contribution made by the universities to the administration of individual countries, to the formation of national consensus about action on important issues and to improving public accountability. The fifth considers the relationships between national cultures and the universities, and the problems of providing university education in multi-cultural societies. The sixth examines, or rather re-examines, a question which was dealt with in the Birmingham Congress of 1983, namely, the ways in which the universities can assist society to cope with technological change. We return to it in 1988 because we all recognise that there are many aspects of this issue which still await clarification and resolution. The seventh, and last, deals with the special contributions which universities can make to rural development. Each topic will be addressed by a group of speakers drawn from different countries of the Commonwealth, and will then be opened for general discussion—which I hope will be relevant and lively. Our programme will end with the summary reports of rapporteurs dealing with the material presented in each of the separate discussions.

In a Congress devoted to considering the manifold interactions between the universities and the societies which support them, it is particularly fitting that our proceedings should be opened by the *representative* of the Head of the Commonwealth, Queen Elizabeth II, who is the Patron of the Association. We are delighted, therefore, that their Excellencies have consented to be with us at this ceremony, and for that purpose. The Governor-General is a distinguished Australian lawyer—a member of a profession which has a history firmly linked with that of the universities since their inception. Sir Ninian served for a number of years on the Council of the University of Melbourne (indeed he was Pro-Chancellor at the time of his appointment as Governor-General) and we were

OPENING CEREMONY [*Stephen*]

honoured when he agreed to become the Patron of this Congress; so that, in a very real sense, we can regard you, Sir, as 'one of us'! Your Excellency, may I invite you now to open the fourteenth Quinquennial Congress of the Association of Commonwealth Universities.

H. E. the Rt. Hon. Sir NINIAN STEPHEN (*Governor-General of the Commonwealth of Australia*): What a pleasure today it is to welcome to Australia, in this, its Bicentennial year, so many distinguished visitors from overseas to this Congress here at the University of Western Australia. Australia and, in particular, its universities, are both honoured and proud to play host to this Congress of the Association of Commonwealth Universities, now for only the second time, after an interval of 20 years, being held in this remote southern continent of ours.

Your Association, like our nation, is celebrating an important anniversary this year; for the Association it is its 75th year of existence. Incorporated by royal charter in 1913, your Association is the oldest international association of universities in the world, with, I read, 327 member institutions spread throughout 29 Commonwealth countries. In truth this Congress is a very Commonwealth Heads of Government Meeting (CHOGM) unto itself, although bereft of that atmosphere of what has come to be called charisma, associated with meetings of the great and powerful. Indeed, in the perennial debate about the continuing worth of the Commonwealth of Nations, the existence and work of your Association is one of the cogent arguments in its favour. The close operational links which, over the years, you have forged and now maintain between the universities of the Commonwealth are of unique value, as are the encouragement and assistance which you give to tertiary education, especially in developing countries of the Commonwealth. Your Association has demonstrated that it can transcend political and, of course, racial and religious differences in its promotion of the cause of tertiary education throughout the Commonwealth.

Universities at their best have, since their earliest days, been places where scholars from many cultures might find common ground and share in common discourse. This tradition, sometimes sadly lost sight of over the centuries, your Association has nourished throughout its 75-year-long existence. In doing so it has, at the same time and almost as a by-product of its main endeavours, been a potent force for better understanding between member nations of the Commonwealth. Now one of the three major projects initiated to mark the Association's 75th anniversary year is, by a happy choice, concerned with this very matter of international scholarly intercourse—the creation of a fund to endow a new fellowship scheme that will encourage staff movement between universities. Interestingly, it will extend beyond the campus and will aim, too, at interchange between universities on the one hand and private and public sectors generally on the other. This is an imaginative development that, at least to me, very much a layman in these matters despite the finery I wear tonight, seems capable of great and numerous benefits both to academia and to the community at large.

The theme for this year's conference—'The Contribution of Universities to National Development'—has, for all Australians, great relevance today as we confront a changing world economy. We must increasingly look for our future economic and social well-being to products of the human intellect rather than solely to products which our soil can be made to nourish or produce, or our ore-bodies to yield up.

Hence the topics of your discussion groups this week promise to be, from a purely domestic, Australian, viewpoint, of great community value, opening up for scrutiny whole fields of interest in which universities can play a vital role in national development. I would be surprised if overseas visitors find the topics of any less immediate relevance. So you are going to have a stimulating and rewarding, and perhaps at times provocative, week. I now take great pleasure in declaring open the Fourteenth Quinquennial Congress of the Association of Commonwealth Universities.

The Hon. D. C. PARKER (*Minister for Minerals and Energy, Economic Development and the Arts, State of Western Australia*): On behalf of the government and people of Western Australia, it gives me great pleasure to welcome such a distinguished gathering to Western Australia. I cannot remember Perth playing host before to such an impressive, if not daunting, array of academic achievement.

It is now 20 years since your Association last met in Australia, in Sydney in 1968. Many changes have taken place since then and nowhere more so than in Western Australia. In the 1960s the state was emerging from its 'long sleep' and being transformed from a

OPENING CEREMONY [Parker]

rural backwater to a dynamic and thriving mainstream community, a leader in the world mining scene. We were at the threshhold of a spectacular wave of resource development and few could have foreseen just how far the industry would have progressed in the following 20 years. We have become a major producer of such essential commodities as iron ore, gold, alumina, mineral sands, nickel, diamonds, salt and so on. From next year we will become an exporter of energy in the shape of LNG (liquefied natural gas), from the giant Northwest Shelf project, and LPG (liquefied petroleum gas). Over the period, the income generated by mining has risen almost 20-fold in real terms.

Today we are embarking on the next stage of our resource development programme, that of secondary processing, by utilising our abundant energy supplies and our equally abundant brain-power, to add greater value to our basic mineral exports.

Those of you who passed through Perth on your way to or from Sydney 20 years ago will have noticed enormous changes in the city itself. Perth has made the transition from a large country town to attractive, efficient, modern city. At a personal level, I was still a student at school in 1968 with my sights set on attending this University and already interested in the protest movement then sweeping across campuses around the world against the war in Vietnam.

Then, this was Western Australia's only university. Now we have three. While university enrolments in Australia as a whole have nearly doubled over the past 20 years (from 101,000 to 196,000), here in Western Australia they have quadrupled (from 6500 to 27,000). Additional universities, more students and changing circumstances have brought other changes such as the introduction of new disciplines and the demand for multi-disciplinary studies. The fields of biotechnology and materials technology are obvious examples. It is clear that the next 20 years will produce an even wider range of new courses in response to the demands of the times.

Another interesting development, which is still in its fledgling stage, is the establishment of Australia's first private university, the Bond campus in Queensland under the direction of our old friend, Dr. Don Watts.

As in other countries, universities in Australia are having to contend with severe economic restraints. In an effort to generate income and utilise facilities more efficiently, much attention is being focused on attracting fee-paying students from overseas countries. Western Australia is in the forefront of this marketing drive. In all walks of life people are being expected to achieve more at lower cost, to raise their productivity, to make more efficient use of available resources. While some academics might recoil in horror from such shop-floor concepts of productivity, I think there would be a general appreciation that universities cannot be immune from such concepts if we are to maintain and improve participation rates and provide even better access to a first-rate education. This must be the primary goal.

The working theme for this conference—'The Contribution of Universities to National Development'—could not be more appropriate for Western Australia. The growth of this state's great resource industries owes much to the Australian university system. The universities have produced the bulk of the agricultural scientists who have made us amongst the most efficient agricultural producers in the world. They have trained a majority of the geologists, geophysicists and engineers responsible for our mining and petroleum discoveries and developments. The universities have ensured that Australian graduates in these disciplines have been equal to the best in the world. Indeed in many cases companies operating here are at the forefront of global science and technology. In an increasingly competitive world we must continue to train high-calibre and innovative professionals if we are to reap the benefits of our potential wealth. As always, education is the key to the future.

The government is very conscious of the enormous and practical contribution that our universities have made in the shaping of present-day Western Australia. If anything, the demands in the future will be even greater. I derive great satisfaction from the knowledge that our universities not only have been instrumental in assisting Western Australia to meet the material needs—mineral and agricultural—of our region, but will be playing an increasingly important role in preparing the region's young people for the challenges of the twenty-first century.

May I take this opportunity to wish you well in your deliberations.

Professor R. H. T. SMITH (*Vice-Chancellor of the University of Western Australia*): I take genuine pleasure in welcoming each and every one of you to the University of Western Australia. We are proud and honoured to be the host institution for this Congress. We very much hope that the time you spend with us will be memorable and rewarding. I trust you will not think it in poor taste if I declare that this is arguably the most attractive university campus in Australia. I invite you to explore it and enjoy it.

This is only the second Congress to be held in Australia since the founding of the Association in 1913. The year 1988 is rather special, marking as it does the 200th anniversary of European settlement in this country. It is special for at least two other reasons: first, it is the 75th anniversary of the founding of the Association of Commonwealth Universities; and second, it is also the 75th anniversary of the University of Western Australia. We are therefore delighted that we can share our year of celebration in this very personal way with the Association of Commonwealth Universities. We congratulate the Association on this significant milestone and I assure you, Mr. Chairman, of our support for the activities of this most plural of international bodies.

When the University of Western Australia was established in 1913 it was Australia's sixth university. While it resembled its five distinguished Australian predecessors—the universities of Sydney, Melbourne, Adelaide, Tasmania and Queensland—in its state capital location, it was unique in at least one respect: no tuition fees were levied on its students. This commitment to tuition-free education persisted until 1963 when federal/state financial arrangements dictated that it be abandoned. There was a strong thread of egalitarianism running through the founding act, exemplified particularly by several paragraphs in the preamble to that act. Let me quote two of them:

'and whereas it is desirable that provision should be made for further instruction in those practical arts and liberal studies which are needed to advance the prosperity and welfare of the people'

'and whereas it is desirable that special encouragement and assistance should be afforded those who may be hindered in the acquisition of sound knowledge and useful learning by lack of opportunity or means'.

The reference to 'the prosperity and welfare of the people' clearly established the University's responsibility to *all* of the citizens of the state. And the words 'who may be hindered in the acquisition of sound knowledge and useful learning by lack of opportunity or means' indicated a sensitivity to some of the issues of access that so bedevil us today. Indeed, there are strong overtones in those words of what have been seen as distinctively Australian values and ideals.

This is a University that has pursued diligently its opportunities and obligations for service to its many communities throughout its short history, whether in the form of pioneering research on trace elements in the soil; of the presentation of a summer school for each one of the last 60 years to a predominantly lay group which this year numbered over 2000; of a joint venture with Telecom Australia to develop an electronic switching device that could well revolutionise modern communications; or whether in the form of the maintenance of a remarkably comprehensive collection of social and cultural Aboriginal art materials constituting an immensely rich research resource—all the while offering quality undergraduate and postgraduate degree programmes across a wide range of generalist and professional faculties.

We take pride in the fact that many of our graduates have held and now hold political office at the local, state and federal government level. They are also to be found in leadership positions in large and small corporations in the public and private sectors as well as in trade unions and in the community at large. Our graduates may be found on the academic staff of many of the universities represented here today. And of course they are scattered far and wide in this vast country, making their distinctive contributions to the national life.

It is fitting that we have chosen the theme 'Campus in the Community' for our 75th Anniversary year. It reflects our history of achievement to the present and also our commitment to the future. Just as there have been many communities in our past, so there will be many in the future. Of particular significance is the Southeast Asian community of which we are, if only by virtue of geography, inextricably a part: we are no further in flying time from Singapore than we are from Sydney. These links of proximity have been the foundation of an enduring set of relationships through our alumni—our graduates and former students—and they will become increasingly important in the years ahead.

We are a fortunate university, having benefited from what might be described as the astonishing foresight of those who drafted and passed into law the University Endowment Act of 1904. We have also enjoyed the support of many in the private sector. In the early days of the University, Winthrop Hackett of West Australian Newspapers—the University's first chancellor whose name this magnificent hall bears—was a tireless advocate and also a generous benefactor. More recently there were and are many in this community who have supported a public appeal for funds to construct a permanent home for our impressive collection of modern Australian paintings. Of them, may I recognise Lawrence and Dorothy Wilson whose names the gallery will bear.

It is in this context of earned public and private support that I say we face the future with confidence and enthusiasm. I prefer to see opportunity rather than threat in the current environment of assessment, evaluation and questioning that has been created by the policy discussion paper on higher education issued by the Federal Minister for Employment, Education and Training, the Hon. John Dawkins—himself a graduate of this University. I have long felt that universities and other higher education institutions should be funded for what they do and how well they do it, and during the brief two years that I have been privileged to serve this fine University I have encountered little in the way of argument or evidence to persuade me otherwise.

This University reaffirms its commitment to the service of its many communities, and especially the community represented here today, in a context that sees the creation and preservation of an environment in which the scholarly values of curiosity, experimentation and critical appraisal can flourish, as the most noble of callings.

Once again I welcome you to the University of Western Australia; I commend to you this superb campus of which we are the privileged custodians; and I wish you well during your stay here.

Professor J. MANRAKHAN (*Vice-Chancellor, University of Mauritius, and Immediate Past Chairman of the Association of Commonwealth Universities*): It is indeed an honour, and privilege, for me to have been invited to propose a vote of thanks to Your Excellency and the other speakers at this Opening Ceremony, to reflect on past Congresses and conferences of the Association of Commonwealth Universities (ACU) and to comment on the importance of continuing such functions.

On behalf of all of us, I have great pleasure in expressing our profound gratitude and warm appreciation to Your Excellency, both for your most welcome presence in our midst and for your stimulating address. You have enlightened us on the problems, hopes and prospects of Australia, celebrating this year the bicentenary of Euopean settlement. We must also thank you for your kind words regarding the ACU which is celebrating its 75th Anniversary of a unique world-wide inter-university service—one which Dr. John Foster, Australia's own gift to the ACU, described as of 'much closer mesh than can be provided for by international organisations in the world at large'. Your speech, Excellency, characterised by deep reflection and constructive comment, will certainly be invaluable to us in our deliberations.

We are also honoured by the presence of the Hon. David Parker, representing the Premier of Western Australia. Your speech, Minister, has highlighted the importance which Western Australia attaches to this ACU gathering; it has also provided us with useful insights on your educational policies, especially in higher education and interrelationships between the latter and general development. We can assure you that we need no encouragement to do our utmost to remove any feeling of isolation, academic and otherwise, this part of the world is supposed to suffer from.

In expressing our congratulations to the University of Western Australia for its 75th Anniversary, and our thanks to the host Vice-Chancellor, Professor Robert Smith, his colleagues and the 'white brigade' for their cordial welcome, generous hospitality and excellent organisation, we wish to point out just how deeply impressed we all are with the standing and achievements of the University of Western Australia.

In expressing our appreciation to Professor Michael Birt and his colleagues of the Australian Vice-Chancellors' Committee in connection with this ACU gathering, we would like to say how valuable we regard the contribution of Australian universities to the world of learning and to the world of work. Criticisms to the contrary can, in my view, only firm the resolve of Australian universities for ever greater endeavours and successes to add to an already impressive record by world standards, in fields ranging from agricultural science and astronomy, through distance education and medical science, to oceanography and zoology. Over the next 200 years Australian society must become far more knowledge-based rather than one predominantly dependent on materials, and stronger interactions between the university and such institutions as the Australian Commission for the Future should develop—to enhance further the role of the university in national development in Australia, and elsewhere.

In Sydney, 20 years ago, the Commonwealth of Australia generously hosted, for the first time, a Quinquennial Congress of the universities of the wider Commonwealth. Today we gather 'twixt majestic river and superb parkland on the magnificent Perth campus, possibly the finest in this island continent.

Whilst the tenth Congress in 1968 had student unrest in the background, the backcloth to the fourteenth Congress opening today is one of general university bashing—the 'unibash' process—unprecedented in scale, duration and intensity, about which our Secretary General, Dr. Anastasios Christodoulou, had forewarned us in 1980 when he used phrases such as 'the quintessential suddenly becomes dispensable' and 'the questioning begins with a vengeance'.

The twin themes in Sydney, namely the roles of the university in contemporary society and in higher education systems, spanned professional training, technology research and postgraduate training. The Perth Congress, on the very opposite theme of the contribution of universities to national development, aims to cover (as Professor Michael Birt, Chairman of the ACU and the Congress Organising Committee, has so ably described) such topics as socio-politico-economic development, advancement and dissemination of knowledge, continuing education, national governance, cultural development, social impact of technology and land in rural development.

In 1983, at Birmingham, we looked at university roles in technological innovation, comprising social, cultural and economic aspects, integrated rural development, technology transfer, continuing education and industry-university partnerships. Ten years ago, at Vancouver, it was the theme of pressures and priorities in the university world that came under scrutiny, with food, energy, population and health interrelationships; higher education systems; reconciliation of equality and excellence; and the public view of universities. At Edinburgh, in 1973, the environment and culture dominated the agenda.

Meanwhile executive heads' meetings—in Melbourne (1968), Legon ('71), Exeter ('73), Wellington ('76), Western Ontario ('78), Hong Kong ('81), Birmingham ('83), Penang ('86) and Perth ('88)—have also picked up many of those themes, not least concerning student mobility, besides more mundane ones involving university governance and operating structures, relevance and accountability, funding arrangements and inter-institutional collaboration, neatly subsumed under the label of 'Issues in the Development of a National University System' for the Perth deliberations of last week.

If the themes and topics are evergreen, of continuing relevance, the deliberations and outcomes of the discussions, like answers to certain examination questions, vary widely over time and circumstances.

In addressing the Sydney Congress, Excellency, your predecessor, the Rt. Hon. Lord Casey, made the very pertinent point, that universities are set on a journey into the future. They have, at any given moment, a certain amount of equipment, which might not be the most appropriate for the next generation. One possibility would be to pick up new and more appropriate equipment on the way as more information accumulates. But, Lord Casey went on, 'it is more useful, though very difficult, to try to estimate in advance the equipment you are likely to need in the future, with the curve of the recent past and your own intelligence to guide you. Indeed, I need hardly say, this is largely what your conference is about'. Therein lies the fundamental justification, in a fast-changing world, for continuing with periodic Congresses and conferences of executive heads of the ACU, which as the Commonwealth Secretary-General, H. E. Shridath Ramphal, has rightly argued, 'stands for a wide and more liberal version of the world, in which the intellectual contact and exchange are fundamental imperatives rather than dispensable luxuries'.

In this delightful *Australian Universities: A Descriptive Sketch*, published for the Sydney Congress, David Macmillan wrote: 'To retain the essential best of the old, while being receptive to the novel, the unfamiliar and the daring, is surely the aim'. That aim is true not only for Australian universities but also for the universities of the wider Commonwealth, and of the world. That has been, and continues to be, the aim of the Association of Commonwealth Universities in the planning of its activities—Congresses, conferences, council meetings, studies and publications, scholarship and fellowship schemes and the like—with a highly efficient secretariat headed, in turn, by personalities of the calibre of Dr. John Foster, Sir Hugh Springer and our present Secretary General with a renewed mandate. And that aim is also true of countries.

From *The Recruiting Officer*, the first play produced here and performed by an all-convict cast in 1789, to the bicentennial production of a musical based on a monumental and controversial *History of Australia*, and that of a dusk-to-dawn staging of *The Mahabharata*, Australia has travelled very far in terms of cultural and other efforts. But precisely when, during the past 200 years, the authentic spirit of things Australian emerged, is a moot point. The poet Henry Lawson is deemed by many to have been the first articulate voice of the real Australia. For the solace and comfort and guidance of the representatives of the universities of the wider Commonwealth, I would like to quote the opening and closing lines from his poem *The Wander-Light*, written in 1903:

'Oh, my ways are strange ways and new ways and old ways,
And deep ways and steep ways and high ways and low;
I'm at home and at ease on a track I know not,
And rest-less and lost on a road that I know.
. . . .
'And my dreams are strange dreams, are day dreams, are grey dreams,

And my dreams are wild dreams, and old dreams and new;
They haunt me and daunt me with fears of the morrow—
My brothers they doubt me—but my dreams come true.'

May all our nightmares concerning the university vanish as we proceed towards, and into, the twenty-first century with Perth, New Delhi and Swansea witnessing the laying of additional foundations to enable the university to re-emerge as a trustworthy, valuable and effective societal instrument, accepted by governments and society at large as having many appropriate features to be advantageously utilised in the processes of national and international development, short-term *and* long-term. And may that dream come true.

FIRST PLENARY SESSION
Monday, 8 February

Professor L. M. BIRT (*Vice-Chancellor and Principal of the University of New South Wales and Chairman of the Association of Commonwealth Universities*): During the opening ceremony of our Congress I referred briefly to the Congress theme—'The Contribution of Universities to National Development'—and the way in which our examination of this theme was to be approached, through discussion of a number of sub-themes. In this plenary Congress session we are to hear the Keynote Address which will set the scene for the more specific deliberations that follow. It is to be delivered by the Chancellor of the University of New South Wales, the Hon. Mr. Justice Gordon Samuels. Mr. Justice Samuels was educated in the United Kingdom, at the University College School and Balliol College, Oxford. He is now a judge in the Court of Appeal, a position he has held since 1974, having been a judge of the Supreme Court of New South Wales since 1972. These appointments followed a distinguished career as a barrister. He was called to the English Bar (the Inner Temple) in 1948, admitted to the New South Wales Bar in 1952, and became Queen's Counsel in New South Wales in 1964 and in Victoria in 1965. His recreational interests are centred on the arts, especially music (he has for some years been chairman of the Australia Ensemble Management Committee, and has led that group to achievement of both national and international prominence) and the theatre. He has been a member of the Council of the University of New South Wales since 1969 and its Chancellor since 1976, and was made a Companion of the Order of Australia in 1987.

You may think it a little surprising that the two of us, from the same stable, come together on this platform—a clear case, you may be tempted to say, of the misuse of influence by the Chairman of the Association of Commonwealth Universities? Let me assure you that this is not the case. My Chancellor is the Keynote Speaker by the unanimous choice of my colleagues in the Australian Vice-Chancellors' Committee, a choice which was made for two reasons: first, because some of them have gained both enjoyment and edification from hearing him speak elsewhere; and second (and perhaps more importantly) because of a letter. The 'letter' to which I refer was penned in the following circumstances.

[*Birt*]   FIRST PLENARY SESSION

Some 18 months ago the chancellors of Australian universities made representations to the Australian government for an adjustment—an upward adjustment, I hasten to add—of the salaries of their vice-chancellors. Clearly it was a cause well worthy of the fullest and most dedicated support, one which commended itself properly to both legal chancellors and illegal (I am sorry) non-legal chancellors alike. As was only right and proper, the chancellors were successful in their endeavours; and so efficient and effective had they been (a shining example to their universities) that they did not use all the funds available to them—a small sum remained. Thus it was that Mr. Justice Gordon Samuels was able to write to the chairman of the Australian Vice-Chancellors' Committee in the following terms:

'Since it seems hardly worth while to divide this (small sum) up 18 ways and distribute it to various Chancellors and Vice-Chancellors, I have proposed to my fellow Chancellors, and they have accepted, a more constructive course. We propose to bestow the money upon the AVCC asking you to invest it . . . desiring that you use the interest to obtain the means of drinking your Chancellors' health in decent champagne at your first meeting in every calendar year. The occasion will be known as 'The Chancellors' Libation' and will be designed to bring down blessings upon the tasks ahead. The contemplated income should be sufficient to obtain six bottles of non-vintage French champagne or rather more of acceptable Australian sparkling wine. We feel confident that we can leave to the Vice-Chancellors' conscience the option to be preferred.'

You will understand why the vice-chancellors warmed to the prospect of being addressed by such a man. He exhibits clearly in this brief passage so many of the virtues which one looks for in a senior member of the university. I have mentioned effectiveness and efficiency; but in addition there is the concentration on the most important issues; the desire to promote excellence of performance; the recognition that special steps must be taken to bless the endeavours of vice-chancellors; the quantitative approach to the definition of actions to be taken and in the selection of alternatives; clear recognition of the need of an international scope in the activities of senior members of the university; a willingness to delegate; and, most important of all, a recognition that it is the vice-chancellors who should make the really important decisions in the internal affairs of the universities. I am sure that at least half the audience before me would endorse those sentiments with acclaim, and that the entire audience will do the same about the choice of Chancellor Samuels as our Keynote Speaker.

THE CONTRIBUTION OF UNIVERSITIES TO NATIONAL DEVELOPMENT
(Keynote Address)

The Hon. Justice G. J. SAMUELS (*Chancellor of the University of New South Wales*): I am greatly honoured to have been given the opportunity of speaking at this first plenary session of the fourteenth Congress of the Association of Commonwealth Universities. Sir Adrian Cadbury, then Chancellor of the University of Aston, who delivered this address at the last Congress noted that the selection of Birmingham as the venue honoured his home town. I cannot lay any direct claim to Perth but venerate it by marriage, as it were, since my wife was born here and is a graduate of this University. Sir Adrian also observed that it was extremely broad-minded of the organizers to invite a chancellor to speak whose more accustomed role was to be seen and not heard. He, however, was heard to such purpose and with such approval that an invitation was directed on this occasion to another of the same species.

I must in turn, therefore, court the hazards involved in repudiating the convention of silence. I trust that they are not as stringent as those conventionally entailed for breach of the Sicilian vow of Omerta. University administrators are sometimes said to resemble the Mafia, it is true; but in point of cohesion rather than discipline, I think. I can always, of course, seek refuge in my amateur status and in the ambiguities of 'chancellor-speak' in which you pretend to know what you do not and not to know what you do. By this means, and at smaller cost, you may rival the omniscience of your vice-chancellor. On reflection, I must add that it now occurs to me to regret my glancing reference to the Mafia lest some wholly indefensible connection be suggested between my vice-chancellor's role as chairman of the Congress and my appearance here this morning.

My task in delivering the Keynote Address is, I understand, to establish the basic subject matter of our conference. It thus allows that large measure of flexibility striven for by academic speakers (a status which I may perhaps borrow for this occasion), exemplified by the popularity of the titular adjunct 'revisited' which can be attached to a named subject matter without revealing any indication of opinion or of the duration of the speaker's stay.

The selection of the theme owes a good deal to the fact that this year marks the 200th anniversary of European settlement in Australia. It is appropriate, therefore, for Australians at all events, noting the part played so far by the universities in the development of their nation, to assess the nature of the mission ahead; and the organizers evidently thought (as I do) that reflections of a similar kind would constitute a topic of general interest and importance for all the members of our Association. The theme, and the variations revealed by the group Topics, invite us to consider the variety of roles and responsibilities which, if undertaken by the universities, would contribute to national development; that is, would enhance the social and cultural life of their communities and advance their economic capacity. Plainly the imperatives and priorities of national development will differ markedly from country to country. In developing nations the eradication of poverty, ignorance and disease may constitute the key targets. In more developed countries the primary objective is usually seen as an increase in economic competitiveness; and in that context there is a gathering inclination to view the universities as a vast cohort of carborundum wheels marshalled to whet the cutting edge of the nation's economic capability. That is a matter, central to this debate, to which I will return presently.

The theme, and the variations, seem to me to focus on the topic rather from the standpoint of the universities than of the community. However what I propose to examine is essentially the relationship between the universities and their communities; or, to frame the subject in a more manageable singular, between the university and its community, noting that it is the national community and not the local or regional one which the subject contemplates. Perhaps it overstates the case to suggest that our topic covers the whole of that relationship. But at least it comprehends the manner in which the university deploys its resources in satisfaction of the needs of its community. Let me say at once that I do not intend by that proposition to assume, or to ask you to accept, that the overall needs of the community may be readily identified, measured and assessed; or that the phrase, popular though it is, commonly represents anything other than an abstraction often more misleading than useful.

Interests may be advanced by sections of the community and the community as a whole undoubtedly has basic needs for food, shelter and the like, whether they are articulated or not. In areas of greater sophistication demands are often made by different interest groups and attributed to the community. Demands upon the university are usually denunciations of present practice coupled with exhortations for future improvement made by ministers for education or educational administrators and said to represent the profound convictions of the people. Ministerial clairvoyance of this sort is singularly implausible, but it is, I suppose, an acceptable convention of democracy to pretend that every policy gambit of a minister is authorized by the majority (not always a majority of course) that elected her or him—or, to be precise, elected the party which made the appointment to office. I recognise that questions of interpretation feed the lawyer's passion for explaining the meaning of tolerably clear words in language of impenetrable obscurity. I take the exercise no further, merely emphasizing that although I will no doubt employ it, the traditional phrase, the needs of the community or of society, tends to conceal more than it reveals.

Let me turn then to the relationship between the university (to retain the singular) and its community. Every relationship is influenced by the complex of perceptions which it engenders, including not only the participants' view of each other but their own views of themselves. For present purposes I can confine myself to the university's own perception of its role in this relationship, and the community's perception of what the university's role ought to be. I recognise the difficulty of personifying the university and the community in this way; but I don't think that it need delay us.

More to the point is that I have assumed that the university will acknowledge that it does have some role with regard to the community. I do not think that any university of our number would now deny that assumption or, indeed, repudiate the role I have implicitly chosen for it; that is, of making some contribution to the advancement of its society. I do not desire to encourage the prospects of any who might still adhere to the romantic notions of Von Humboldt, and the intrinsic beauties and societal benefits of his Academy. Indeed it is probable that the concept of the university as an harmonious community of scholars wholly detached from the pressures and realities of the world was always a myth. Certainly it could scarcely have survived the dilution of governing bodies by the appointment of external members or, in more recent times, the unionization of academic staff. And I understand that the University of Paris, whose charter was the matrix for the statutes of Oxford and Bologna and of those foundations which followed, was accorded its privileges in the hope that an element of self-government might curb the riotous behaviour of competing lecturers and their tumultuous clients.

Our tradition, however, the tradition which forms our common heritage although in many respects modified and in some respects rejected to accommodate local needs, is largely formed by the practice and attitudes of the England of the nineteenth century. A head of house at Oxford then might have had some trouble with the concept of national development, but would have been quite clear that his task, and that of his colleagues, was to train their young men (and they were all young men in those days) for the service of their society. The Balliol bidding prayer gave thanks to its benefactors for enabling the College to produce graduates 'to serve God in Church and State'. I am doubtful whether Benjamin Jowett, its great Master, can be regarded as entirely typical for this purpose, but he once frankly admitted that he had 'a general prejudice against all persons who do not succeed in the world'. The undergraduates of that day were taught to succeed in the world and success was expected of them. The world from which they came, and the world of leadership for which they were being educated, was in each case narrow and difficult of access. The curriculum to which they were exposed was narrow, too. By the critical study of classical language, literature and philosophy, sound minds were prepared (as a Canadian professor—a scientist too, incidentally—has put it) 'for the subsequent advancement of knowledge in any discipline'.

I do not think it open to dispute that universities accept—and have long accepted—that they have a responsibility to educate students for the many professional and vocational callings for which a trained body of practitioners is required. But it is legitimate to go further because in many other respects than this the university exists to serve its community; a function which it undertakes without any compulsion exerted by the manipulations of its funding body. The general proposition seems to me to be unarguable, and I will not pause to embellish it.

So, on the footing that the university I have hypothesized accepts the responsibility to provide a large measure of service to its community, how does it see its more detailed role in that relationship? In order to attempt a preliminary answer to that question I need some definition of the mission of a university. I am reluctant to revisit this well-trodden turf, for reasons with which those who have recently grappled with the task of formulating forward plans or the public articulation of their university's objectives will be only too familiar. To some, such definitions need only satisfy the criteria enunciated, in a different context, by a character in a novel by Muriel Spark; that is, they 'need not be plausible, only hypnotic, like all good art!' Others find their satisfaction in reasoning too metaphysical to be worth pursuing.

B. R. Clark in his book *The Higher Education System* quotes a statement in these crushing terms:

> 'Almost any educated person could deliver a lecture entitled "the goal of the university". Almost no one will listen to the lecture voluntarily. For the most part, such lectures and their companion essays are well intentioned exercises in social rhetoric, with little operational content. Efforts to generate normative statement of the goals of the university tend to produce goals that are meaningless or dubious'.

Nevertheless, I must persist in formulating my definition and, putting aside hypnosis, metaphysics and as much social rhetoric as I can discard, I imagine that I can safely suggest that the broad mission of a university is to preserve, advance and transmit knowledge (including responsibility for professional certification) and to promote the search for objective truth. Hence, the hypothetical vice-chancellor of my hypothetical university (its chancellor having wisely preferred the option of silence) might well assert that by acting as its society's memory, its vehicle of basic research, its provider of general and specialized postgraduate education and its trainer of professionals, and in pursuing these functions with scrupulous regard for scholarly reason, detachment and scepticism, the university, by these means and without more, confers benefits upon its community and thus contributes to the development of its nation.

Now, how does the community's view and expectations of the university compare with that account of the university's own perception of itself? My hypothetical community representative might well accept as substantially accurate the university's statement of its mission. But I imagine that approbation would be qualified in, at least, one major respect. The mission statement, as my hypothetical vice-chancellor has advanced it, appears to contemplate, as indeed it should, that the university will itself be sole arbiter of what it does and therefore of the nature and scope of its research and the content of its courses. But the statement does not expressly include any provision for consultation between the university and agencies of its community, or for transmission to the university of what the community perceives its educational needs to be. As a result, the complaint would continue, there might be a profound gap between what the university did and what the community needed.

Perhaps I may continue to act as manipulator of my hypothetical vice-chancellor, an opportunity never likely to befall any chancellor in real life. There are probably three answers to the criticism just suggested. First, the university accepts a duty to take account of the changing demands and expectations of its society, and is astute to identify and assess them so far as it can. It is, however, sceptical (as I have earlier indicated) of the authenticity of so-called demands and expectations, realizing that the common condition of society is one of flux in which many inconsistent demands are made, not all of which can be harmoniously satisfied. Secondly, the problem for the university is not only that of the rational absurdity of providing mutually contradictory solutions without assessing which of the complaints is more worthy. It also involves the university's requirement that it maintains the integrity and excellence of its own operation, and must therefore avoid commitments inconsistent with its standards or incompatible with the retention of other and essential areas of its undertaking. The university's responses must be consonant with its mission. Thirdly, its duty to serve and to respond to the needs of its community, so far as they can be ascertained, may be viewed as the university's consideration for the autonomy which the community accords to it. That autonomy enables the university to pursue its legitimate activities without external interference, and, in the last resort, affords it immunity from any of the community's demands which offend those imperatives.

Let me now interrupt this dialogue, as it has become, which has established the context for the critical aspects of the relationship between the university and its community which I wish finally to consider. That relationship, we may agree, secures to the community the benefits which flow from the performance by the university of its own mission. That mission includes the university's responsibility to satisfy certain of the demands which the community may make upon it, assuming their pedigree can be established. But which demands? The answer must be, as I have already suggested, those demands which the university can satisfy consistently with the maintenance of the integrity of its commitment to its primary purposes. The report *Universities under Scrutiny* made by the Organization for Economic Co-operation and Development in 1987 emphasizes that some non-traditional programmes may be justified on educational and social grounds but may yet not be a legitimate part of the responsibilities of a university. The report continues:

'Indeed, their existence in university settings endangers the central core of values that universities can uniquely sustain and protect—excellence, the life of the mind, a critical standpoint vis-à-vis the State and the culture of the wider society, the pursuit of pure, curiosity-oriented research and scholarship. For some, the university has endangered itself by being too responsive to ephemeral "needs"'.

We are all familiar, I think, with the insistence upon relevance in university teaching aimed particularly at programmes in the humanities. This produced demands for courses which were often of astonishing and bizarre irrelevance to the requirements of scholarship and the cultivation of the mind. If such demands represented needs at all they were no doubt ephemeral and ought to have been rejected, as many were and have not been revived. But there have also been solid demands not only articulated by sections of the community or by government, but plainly the product of important movements in social circumstances. I refer, for example, to considerable changes in the number and composition of the university's clientele, to great increase in those wishing to undertake part-time courses of many kinds, to the added emphasis upon continuing education, to recognition of the needs of disadvantaged students and to other phenomena which the universities have in general rightly acknowledged and endeavoured to accommodate.

So, if I may pause at this stage, I can say that the university perceives its role in the relationship under discussion to be to contribute to its community by maintaining the integrity and efficiency of its mission, which is essentially one of service, in the course of which it will be astute to identify the legitimate needs and expectations of its community and will respond positively to those which it can satisfy consistently with the pursuit of its own objectives.

That statement assumes, of course, that the university remains free from compulsion either because its autonomy protects it or because no attempts at direction have been mounted. Now, attempts at direction assume dissatisfaction, which is usually their precipitant. And undoubtedly over recent years considerable criticism has been levelled at the university system for its failure to respond rapidly enough to changes in the social and economic climate, particularly the latter. In particular, universities have been urged to commit a larger proportion of their effort to addressing the economic difficulties which have beset us all, and have year by year eroded the universities' share of the national budget. Since governments of both more and less developed countries see the solution to their problems in an increase in economic competitiveness achieved by innovations in science and technology and in a better educated workforce, considerable pressure has been exerted to emphasize the need to encourage applied research, if need be at the expense of basic research, and managerial and vocational training. For example, the Australian Minister of Education, in his policy discussion paper 'Higher Education' issued in December 1987, stressed that 'the higher education system has a critical role to play in restructuring the Australian economy' by the development of internationally competitive manufacturing and service industries. Much the same message was conveyed in the United Kingdom White Paper of April 1987 which asserted that: 'Higher education has a crucial role in helping the nation meet the economic and social challenges of the final decade of this century and beyond'; and identified one of its aims and purposes as 'serving the economy more effectively'.

Those statements presaged events in both Australia and the United Kingdom which have lent our theme additional point. But in order to appreciate the potency of the ministerial directives which I will summarize in a moment, it is essential to remember that in each country and alike in the others represented here either the whole or a most substantial part of university funding is provided by the government which, in the absence of intermediate advisory bodies such as the University Grants Committee or the Tertiary Education Commission (both of which seem to be not long for the world), itself makes or will make the direct allocation.

In both the United Kingdom and Australia a proposed restructuring of the funding base of the universities is designed, it is said, to enhance their efficiency and to improve their response to the economic needs of the nation. In each case, apart from projected variations to the employment conditions of academic staff, the objectives are to be achieved primarily by selective methods of funding research. In short, research which has prospects for commercial exploitation, or is considered by the government to be of national economic and social importance, will receive high priority in the allocation of available funds. Both approaches expressly abandon the concept that all universities should be funded for both teaching and research. Although the prescriptions differ, each intends by use of the funding power to ensure institutional acceptance of the national educational priorities identified by the government. In the United Kingdom these proposals have been reinforced by an Education Bill which, so far as the universities are concerned, provides for a new mode of allocating funds and for the abolition of academic tenure.

Understandably these intentions have been greeted with alarm and not only by academics. *The Guardian*, a journal not ordinarily prone to hysteria, spoke of 'the menacing shadow over British universities' and of 'demoralised Dons in search of a champion'. Lord Beloff, in *The Times* and a contributor to 'Viewpoint' in *The*

Tablet, drew parallels betwen the proposed legislation and the dissolution of the monasteries. Australian leader-writers, apparently unable to deploy such rich historical material, were more restrained; even, in the case of our national daily newspaper, approving, on the footing that the Australian proposals restored credibility to our educational system. *The Australian* dismissed fears of interference with academic freedom by assuring its readers that the ministerial statement envisaged 'an acceptable degree of autonomy within universities . . . so long as the institutions accept overall government priorities'. This circuitous gem seems to me to reveal no more than a tenuous grasp of the issues. But the commentators here have also raised the alarm, though preferring to invoke Von Humbolt, John Maynard Keynes, Shakespeare, Santayana and Aristotle rather than the depredations of the Tudor monarchy. Only universities in the United Kingdom and Australia are directly affected by these proposals. But the principles involved are, I venture to suggest, of great importance to all the members of our Association. They are fundamental to any consideration of the relationship between the universities and the community and form an essential part of our theme.

I have not attempted to do more than briefly indicate the essential nature of the proposals to which I have referred. Since it is not within the scope of this address, or the reach of my amateur status, to examine them in detail, I need only describe both sets of measures as designed to achieve the following objectives, amongst others: first, to establish direct ministerial control over funding by, amongst other means, eliminating any advisory body standing between the universities and the government; secondly, to establish the principle that priority in funding both teaching and research will be given to those programmes which advance national objectives identified as such by the government; thirdly, to ensure that applied research will have a clear advantage over basic research; fourthly, although this aspect is unclear in each ministerial statement, to establish a system by which a university will tender to the minister for a contract to provide a specific programme. Many of you will be more familiar than I with the details of these proposals. I merely mention them to the extent necessary to indicate the basis upon which I approach them.

There are plausible professional academic objections to what is suggested. Academics fear their potential to dislocate traditional institutional balance, the likely diminution in the influence and importance of humane studies and, in particular, the rejection of the concept that the university ought to provide the fundamentals of a general, liberal education. They argue that the shifts in the deployment of resources necessary to engage urgent but perhaps short-term problems may have long-lasting and detrimental effects upon the systematic regulation of teaching and research. Moreover any bias away from basic research to applied research combined with a diversion of available funds will not only reduce the knowledge base indispensable to further mission-oriented and applied advances but will disrupt the essential link between teaching and research with predictable damage to the teaching function.

There are other points of substance advanced in both governments' discussion papers, and other arguments may be advanced against them. It may be that the selection of technology as a panacea is not well-advised. As the OECD pointed out in the report to which I have referred: ' . . . the relationship between technological innovation and economic growth is not simple'. Barry Jones, the Australian Minister for Science, in his book *Sleepers Wake* put the matter in terms to which our educational administration might have paid more regard. He said this:

'We face an extraordinarily ambiguous future. Technology can be used to promote greater economic equity, more freedom of choice, and participatory democracy. Conversely, it can be used to intensify the worst aspects of a competitive society, to widen the gap between rich and poor, to make democratic goals irrelevant, and institute a technocracy. We must evolve policies in response to the current era of rapid technological change. However, we must first attempt to understand what is going on'.

And the author observes that the technicalities are easier to solve than the human and social problems which rapid technological change precipitates. Hence advances in technology must be accompanied by studies designed to put those advances in their proper social context; studies, that is, concerned with judgement and social control.

I do not wish to advocate a reversion to the situation which C. P. Snow described in *The Two Cultures*. But Sir Peter Medawar in *The Limits of Science* 'roundly declared', to use his own words, 'that political and administrative problems are not in general scientific in character, so that a scientific education or a successful research career does not equip one to solve them'. For my own part I merely make the point that it may well be an act of unsound judgement to upset the academic equilibrium so profoundly as these recent initiatives appear to propose. Certainly, the Australian discussion paper includes ritual genuflections towards preservation of humane studies. But what is one to make of a formal response by the Commonwealth Tertiary Education Commission to a report of a review of Australian law schools which contains this observation: 'For the time being, therefore, it is likely that, given present Commonwealth priorities, any research funds provided to advanced education institutions will continue to be for applied research activities in areas relevant to national development rather than in disciplines such as law'. The message was twice repeated. I am not making a specific case for law. I indicate simply that it is easy to see how humanities, widely categorized, may now be not merely permitted but encouraged to wither.

As I have said, there are many submissions to be made on both sides of the argument. But in my opinion they do not include, on the academic side, any appeal to the principle of university autonomy. University autonomy, I think, must be taken to mean the university's right of self-government, and, in particular, its right to conduct its legitimate activities of teaching and research without interference from any other authority. The point has been well put by the Education Commission of India in this way:

'The case for autonomy of universities rests on the fundamental consideration that, without it, universities cannot discharge effectively their principal functions of teaching, research and service to the community; and that only an autonomous institution, free from regimentation of ideas and pressure of party or power politics, can pursue truth fearlessly and build up, in its teachers and students, habits of independent thinking and a spirited enquiry unfettered by the limitations and prejudices of the near and the immediate which is so essential for the development of a free society.'

Autonomy of government may be secured by charter or statute; it is not otherwise a right secured by law. Restrictions upon self-government may be imposed by charter or statute, and sometimes are. Autonomy is a privilege essential to the effective functioning of the university. It is also essential to the life of a free society. It protects the role of the university as a fearless critic and commentator. Or, in deference to technology, it establishes the university as a litmus paper designed to detect social abuse. These functions protect the community, it being essential for society's well-being that it should preserve a focal centre for the free discussion of ideas. Hence the privilege of autonomy is not granted only to protect the university and to facilitate the pursuit of its individual objectives. Rather there is a general social or public interest in the preservation of the universities' independence and self-government for the benefit of all.

The banner of autonomy is to be proudly unfurled in the defence of great issues. Excessive exposure tarnishes its lustre. I do not think, on balance, that it has a legitimate place in this controversy. First, the proposals do not involve any direct interference with the independence of the universities, although they will exert considerable pressure to conform to the pattern which the governments intend to establish. But I can see no valid objection to the funding body deploying available money in accordance with its own plan. I do not think that autonomy enables a university to demand funding for such courses as it desires to teach or for such research as it determines to undertake. Secondly, it is a prerogative of a democratically elected government to determine national economic priorities and how they are to be achieved. There is much room for individual disagreement; but there is no room in the matter for institutional dissent which would entail a political judgement. Universities as such have no politics; they must be taken to eschew any corporate political stance as another part of the consideration for the privilege of autonomy. I do not consider that the proposals in question do infringe that autonomy, or that, consistently with what I have taken to be the universities' own perception of their role in their relationship with their community, they could justify limited opposition on that ground. Individual institutions, at least under the Australian proposals, could decline to participate.

It is, of course, regrettable that discussions between the government as funding body and the universities so often take place in an atmosphere of confrontation. It often appears that little attempt is made to understand the way in which universities are governed and structured or even the nature of their aspirations. In particular, universities exist to conserve as well as to advance knowledge. They are not designed for the role of instant problem-solving. They are inclined to cherish the long view rather than to adopt short-term frames of reference. And of course, as I have indicated, academics by the nature of their calling are critical and sceptical. Politicians, on the other hand, are inclined to manifest optimism since any world of their making must be the best possible in which everything is necessarily for the best. The celebrated social critic and reformer A. P. Herbert once observed through the mouth of one of his perceptive lawyers, that the assumption of the common law that citizens who took their own lives were mad was partly due to the conceit of the state, that is, the government, 'which likes to think that it so well disposes the lives of the citizens that anyone who wishes to leave it *must* be mad'. Moreover, politicians' principal preoccupation being with the retention of office, their minds are mainly directed to the next election and their aspirations thus coloured by the exigencies of the short term.

It is evident that direct dealings between politicians and academics, even vice-chancellors, are unlikely to be free of stress. Moreover it is, I believe, inappropriate for governments, as funding bodies, to engage directly in the allocation of funds. It was for this reason amongst others that in both the United Kingdom and Australia a buffer body with power to advise has long existed (but probably not for much longer) between the government funding body and the universities. Such an arrangement of course diminishes the possibilities of tensions betwen the directions which the government's economic priorities are seen to require and the autonomy and academic freedom of the universities. The experience of Ghana and Nigeria upon this question is instructive. It seems to me that a body of both academics and non-academics required to investigate the universities' financial requirements and advise the funding body is indispensable.

It is evident that financial stringency and the determination of governments to back advances in technology as the primary solution to their economic problems has placed the relationship between universities and the community (synonymous for government in this context) under considerable strain. It is ironical that recent invitations (of a type, it is true, which brook no refusal) to the universities to make what the government regards as essential contributions to national development (indeed, almost to national survival) have been greeted with apprehension and doubt.

In response to the criticisms of recent times, many of them, but not all, ill-deserved, universities have tended to fall into an inappropriately defensive posture. I have no doubt that morale has suffered, and that we no longer see sharply enough the main objects which the system ought to pursue. There has often been too negative a reaction to claims for increased accountability and demands that the universities should submit themselves to assessments of performance. These are, I know, slippery concepts. But in principle universities should be prepared to open their society to any reasonable scrutiny and adopt the need to examine those aspects of their management and government which allegedly fail to reach acceptable standards of efficiency.

I appreciate the problems inherent in the formulation of mission statements and the like, and the beguiling temptation to lie down with soothing platitudes. But we can be sure at least that our mission is to serve our nations by preserving, advancing and transmitting knowledge. Since we therefore represent one of our nations' vital resources we must keep ourselves under constant scrutiny to identify and remove complacency and to modify restrictive employment and other practices which can no longer be justified. We must preserve our independence without exaggerating the extent of its frontiers. We need that degree of autonomy essential to maintain our liberty of intellectual choice, discussion and criticism, and which is a vital ingredient in preserving the freedom of the nation. We must recognise the responsibilities that accompany our mission of service. We must be responsive to the pressures and demands imposed upon us within the limitations that the maintenance of standards and a long-term perspective entail. We must pay careful heed to the needs of our clientele, the students, and to the necessity for co-operation with government in order to advance what are, of necessity, shared interests and aspirations.

I do not intend that to be an exclusive check list of objectives; but any more invites, or confirms, a descent into social (or academic) rhetoric. Above all, the contribution we make will ultimately depend upon the extent of our confidence in ourselves.

The Rt. Hon. LORD FLOWERS (*Vice-Chancellor of the University of London*): As one of the first visitors invited to speak at this Congress, perhaps I may be permitted to express the gratitude and admiration we all feel for our reception these past few days. We have already been shown many kindnesses. We know there is much yet in store, and we need no persuasion that it will all be immensely stimulating and enjoyable. And, of course, there will be many expressions of gratitude during the course of it all. May I therefore start by offering my own thanks to Professor Michael Birt, our Chairman, and to Professor Robert Smith, our friendly local Vice-Chancellor, who with their wives and their various staffs, and a colossal effort on the part of all concerned, have put before us such rich provender.

Mr. Chairman, you may not have expected these words from me at this time. They were not foreseen in the programme. Please regard them more as an irrepressible eruption of thankfulness than as mere misconception of duty. My duty today—and it is one I am greatly honoured to perform—is to respond to the Keynote Address—careful, thoughtful, wise and witty—to which we have just listened, enthralled, of the learned Chancellor of the University of New South Wales, Mr. Justice Samuels.

Now, Professor Birt and I happily share many things in common. One came to mind as the judge was speaking. It is the motto we both bear upon our escutcheons: non carborundum illegitimi. (For those who do not speak European Aboriginal that means: don't let the bastards grind you down.) Another, however, is that we have both been hired, and can just as readily be fired, by the senior judges who preside over our respective councils. The mafia of vice-chancellors is a palpable myth; the mafia of judges, however, is quite another matter, and I must choose my words with care.

Mr. Justice Samuels has given us a brilliant, and on the whole encouraging, analysis of the university in relation to its community—and I, too, like the singular, because there is, necessarily and desirably, much diversity among us. Many of us, in the older Commonwealth especially, have been inclined to see the new demands being made of us as a threat to the established contributions we make to the community, rather than as an invitation to make further contributions more directly concerned with economic development—as a cry for our help, if you like. However the judge has wisely been at pains to emphasize that it is well to draft a clear and simple statement of the mission of the university, and to see that the contributions it attempts to make are compatible with that mission. Some of us will insist that our missions are different, and our contributions distinct, and that is also as it should be.

We hear much nowadays about the four As—of access, academic standards, accountability and autonomy—all of them reflecting legitimate public interest in our affairs. We have no problem in principle with increased access, except that it is difficult to maintain academic standards unless resources are increased to match. We have increased the load on our teachers and tried to improve their methods of teaching, but that cannot be extended into the indefinite future.

Accountability is more of a problem, because we are mostly ill-prepared for the business methods we are nowadays being expected to adopt. We do not deny the need nor the value of the discipline of having to show that we have spent our monies effectively and efficiently. But I have yet to see criteria designed for business management which are compatible with the mission of a university, and we ourselves—it must be said—are not always plausible when we devise our own set of performance indicators. For example, the annual telephone charge per full-time equivalent student has been proposed as an indicator combining the best of academic and business considerations. (But should it be high or low? Think carefully before you answer!) And the closer one comes to the academic process the more it seems that traditional judgements of the quality of the grey matter must be abandoned in favour of measuring the distance between the ears. In these circumstances management consultants flock to help: but beware, they only borrow your watch to tell you the time, and charge a fat fee for the service.

A better remedy, it seems to me, is that real business men and women become conversant with our affairs to help us in our task, and this is happening everywhere. Personally I would rather rely upon their qualitative, but locally knowledgeable, judgements than upon distantly generated, quantitative measures of dubious applicability. There is a proper contribution here to be made by the community to its university.

Then, finally, autonomy—to which Mr. Justice Samuels devoted much of his very careful analysis. He spelled out the essence of the proposed Australian and British legislation with great clarity, and I find no need to comment upon it—except, perhaps, to say that in seeking to establish ministerial control over the teaching and research of the universities—and therefore over the interpretation of their missions—it is as well to remind ministers, as the judge has reminded us, that they should rely less on clairvoyance and more on consultation with those best qualified to express an opinion.

I am, for instance, greatly encouraged that senior industrialists in Britain are now speaking with alarm of the weakening of the basic research of the universities due to continuing government insistence that we concentrate more effort on applications. I wish the government would listen to and understand those who are predominantly their own supporters.

The question is whether the new legislation, and equivalent processes taking place elsewhere, threatens university autonomy in the sense we have just heard so carefully defined, or not. Mr. Justice Samuels has considered the proposition and has concluded that on balance it does not. I am sorry to say that here I do not agree with him and I shall shortly be appealing to parliament itself—if not for a reversal of the verdict, at least for a handsome remission of the sentence. I beg forgiveness for making a particular British point, but in the words of Sylvanus P. Thompson, in his celebrated book *Calculus Made Easy*, 'what one fool can do, another can'; the mafia of politicians is the strongest of them all.

The British government clearly intends to take powers which would enable it, if it so chose, itself to control the manner in which individual courses are given and particular researches pursued. That it is beyond the capacity of government to do anything of the kind across the board is undeniable; but that it has already tried unsuccessfully to do so in the past, in a few cases which have caused it political vexations or other inconveniences and annoyances, leave us in no doubt of the general intention and of the consequent threat to university autonomy. Without that autonomy we shall be unable to make so readily or so effectively the new contributions that the community expects of us.

Whether or not we accept Mr. Justice Samuels' judgement on that particular score, we have been greatly stimulated by his Keynote Address, which has opened wide our minds as well as our mouths; and we thank him for it.

Group Discussions

TOPIC 1

THE UNIVERSITY AS CRITIC

The Role of Universities in Analysing and Evaluating Political, Economic and Social Development of their Country or Region

Chairman: Dr. WANG GUNGWU
Vice-Chancellor of the University of Hong Kong

Chief Rapporteur: Mr. D. D. NEILSON
Vice-Principal of La Trobe University

		Page
Sub-Topic 1(a)	THE UNIVERSITY AND THE NATIONAL ECONOMY	
	Speaker	
	Professor M. W. J. G. Mendis	55
	Discussion	58
	Paper by Dr. G. R. Weller and Dr. R. G. Rosehart	59
Sub-Topic 1(b)	IS THERE A POLITICAL ROLE FOR UNIVERSITIES?	
	Speakers	
	Professor W. J. Kamba	62
	Professor P. N. Tarling	68
	Discussion	74
Sub-Topic 1(c)	THE SOCIO-CULTURAL ROLE OF UNIVERSITIES	
	Speakers	
	Professor W. Taylor	75
	Professor G. F. A. Sawyerr	82
	Discussion	86

			Page
Sub-Topic 1(d)	THE UNIVERSITY'S ROLE OUTSIDE NATIONAL BOUNDARIES		
	Speakers		
	Professor Yue-man Yeung		87
	Dr. D. W. Strangway		93
	Discussion		98
Final Session			100
CHAIRMAN'S REPORT ON THE GROUP'S DISCUSSIONS			101

For index to names, see p. 533

Sub-Topic 1(a)

THE UNIVERSITY AND THE NATIONAL ECONOMY

Monday, 8 February

Professor M. W. J. G. MENDIS (*Vice-Chancellor, University of Moratuwa, Sri Lanka*): By convention and tradition the universities have been perceived by the community as centres of excellence. Their concentration of expertise, facilities and a variety of activities has been recognised as vital for the economic development of a nation. Accordingly, universities have been regarded as places wherein the nation's most talented youth is trained by well-qualified teachers to provide the academic and professionally qualified graduates required for the managerial and professional jobs necessary for economic development. Furthermore, the nation's efforts in innovation, discovery and invention are also looked for from the universities through their research programmes. In such a context, as previously stated, the universities have always been respected and regarded as storehouses of knowledge.

In these circumstances the governments of all nations have always granted the universities, in varying degrees, freedom and autonomy in the pursuit of their activities, while being also the providers of the funds that maintain those universities. The funds have, however, been under closer monitoring in recent times in some Commonwealth countries, whose governments have been seeking 'value for money'. This has resulted in a great deal of concern, as it constituted a new dimension in university affairs. Consequently attempts are being made to understand this factor and to integrate it into the mainstream of university culture.

Meanwhile the universities have not lost their traditional role, although the above-mentioned interventions have probably altered the scope of their activities. The pursuit of knowledge (and of truth) continues to flourish in them. There are increases in student intake, staffing, research and publications, by comparison with the situation in the Commonwealth ten years ago. Further, there is even greater inter-action between universities in the Commonwealth and elsewhere. The mobility of staff and students has vastly enhanced the capacity and capability of universities to contribute to national (and global) economic development.

It is also a fact that in all nations the total resources available to universities (from governmental and other sources) have increased and continue to increase. This represents an expression of faith in the universities as providers of advanced knowledge. In this connection in some Commonwealth countries universities have forged links with the 'direct contributors' to economic development, *i.e.* manufacturing industry and agriculture. Consequently 'science parks', 'business parks', etc., have been established as complementary institutions with strong inherent relations with governmental and private sector institutions, and without loss of the principal aims of the universities as such.

The pace of economic development required in the countries of the Commonwealth, especially in its less prosperous nations, would have greatly suffered had it not been for the increased number of university graduates available to them. The graduates have formed the backbone of the leadership in both public and private sectors. The reliance on them to play a vital role in major decision-making has been another expression of the confidence in the universities as pivots in fostering economic development. In several countries, however, economic development has not been able to absorb all the graduates. The imbalance between the output of certain disciplines and what the economy required has to some extent diluted the impact of universities on development. In nations with this situation a conflict has arisen between the governments and the products of the universities. In the search for a solution to the problem the weaknesses in both institutions have emerged, with the universities being called upon to focus attention on reforms which would facilitate the employability of their graduates without necessarily depending upon the governments to provide secure wage-earning jobs for all of those graduates.

The inter-action between governments, universities and the economic sectors has thus increased significantly. It has been accompanied by a simultaneous thinning of the interface between them. Hence each is seeking levels and modes of relationships which will enhance one another's contribution to development. In such a context differences of views are likely to result and have resulted. Consequently misunderstandings and confrontations have occurred, especially between universities and governments. In these circumstances the convention that universities should be exclusively places of training and research has been lost sight of. The outcome

SUB-TOPIC 1 (A): THE NATIONAL ECONOMY [*Mendis*]

of criticism as the means of establishing a different path towards national development has significantly affected the role of universities as a critic. This has become evident in the grave and unsettled conditions of universities in many countries of the Commonwealth, and is the situation that has caused the governments to seek value for money from these institutions.

A significant feature in the above scenario is that the university community has sustained its role as a critic. The role now involves the student body, which constitutes an important segment of the total community. Their perceived role as agents of change has prompted them to seek it both within and outside the bounds of academia, causing concern to some sections of the external community and even to the governments, especially about their modalities of criticism. There is a danger that the universities could become the entry point for forces of destabilization which could lead to a damaging conflict between them and governments, with opportunists exploiting the vulnerability of the youth population in the universities. The students as a constituency have now become the vanguard of the university as a critic in some Commonwealth countries. In others they hold levels of responsibility which ensure their role as critics. Accordingly the traditional role of universities as passive critics has changed to the opposite.

The harnessing of criticism into the mainstream is now an area which requires consideration. The fostering of fairness and objectivity in criticism and its modelling into the most appropriate form of organisation is necessary. It is desirable to retain the scientific and objective approach to knowledge in the universities, while some degree of refinement will be required in the formula for relations with governments and societies. The university as critic will then play its envisaged role as a signpost for policy-making in the sphere of economic development. This, however, implies that the universities must be incorporated as integral parts of the developmental structure of the nation. Their role is then seen in the widest meaning of centres of excellence—not confined to the art and science of an activity in a vacuum, but directly related to reality itself.

The identity and relevance of the university as a critic is greater now than in previous times. It is an era in which changes are rapid in a variety of spheres, especially technological. The impact of technology in socio-economic development relies heavily on many unknowns and least-knowns. In such circumstances the universities become the centre-points for the generation of thought processes. Consequently their relevance as critics becomes extremely meaningful.

TOPIC 1: THE UNIVERSITY AS CRITIC

It can thus be concluded that the continued reliance of universities on government funding has not necessarily meant departure from their perceived role as critics.

DISCUSSION

(*Rapporteur:* Mr. N. W. KINGSBURY, Registrar, University of Waikato)

Professor Mendis had outlined a model showing the relationship in the developing countries of a development process of a national economy, between the university and the government, and between the university and the society. He expanded on knowledge, specialization and the student body as elements in the development process. The expectations of government were canvassed, and the tension noted between an immediate requirement for specialists and the longer-term university production of generalists, which demonstrated the difficulties in determining the appropriate balance for university programmes and the link with government allocation of resources.

A number of issues were raised in discussion based on experiences in several countries including—

(1) The reaction of government and business leaders to 'student', which was often equated with 'university', behaviour.

(2) Accountability to the society, especially where the university might be the only one in the region or country.

(3) The problems associated with universities operating in an economic or socio-political climate over which they have little or no control.

(4) The extent to which universities can justify their use of scarce national resources.

(5) The importance, in a number of countries, of universities providing extension services to the wider community.

(6) There is no longer a consensus in society about the value of the traditional role of universities.

(7) Whether universities should be taking greater initiatives in determining their own futures, rather than responding defensively. In this context it was agreed that universities should make much greater effort to communicate to society at large and to the members of the government the worth of what they are doing.

(8) It was suggested by some delegates that the universities' present predicament is because their members (or the institutions themselves?) have failed as public critics, and/or failed to provide leadership as 'thinkers' in society.

(9) Too often comment from university members, in a variety of roles, is seen as being destructive; that is, long on condemnation and short on constructive alternatives or proposals.

SUB-TOPIC 1 (A): THE NATIONAL ECONOMY [*Weller/Rosehart*]

(10) More attention should be paid to fostering closer relationships between staff and students and providing support to students as people.

(11) The possible limitation on staff acting as dispassionate critics was noted where special funding and project links exist with university staff. Independence in funding was seen to be an important prerequisite to independence in criticism.

Note.—The authors of the following paper, who were also to have spoken on Sub-Topic 1(a), were at the last moment unable to attend the Congress but have provided their text for inclusion in the Report of Proceedings.

Dr. G. R. WELLER and Dr. R. G. ROSEHART (respectively *Vice-President (Academic)* and *President, Lakehead University*): Historically, universities have been thought of in terms of old arched buildings, vines, and institutions where the creative thought process is cultivated—the so-called ivory tower. Nearing the end of the twentieth century, almost all universities have, to some extent, accepted the fact that they need to relate also to *today's* societal needs and pressures while, at the same time, not sacrificing traditional scholarship and research freedoms. In fact many research intensive universities have developed strong identities with economic spin-off related ventures—the University of Waterloo in Canada and MIT in the USA are prime examples.

Yet throughout the Commonwealth another type of institution exists—a regional university. What are the roles of regional universities? To some extent this depends on the state of development of the host country or province but, generally, one could look at regional universities in either a narrow or an expanded format. In the narrow focus the regional university serves strictly as a regional access point for post-secondary education from a given territory or region. Typically such an institution is small, has a limited range of programmes, and very few research thrusts primarily due to lack of graduate studies.

In the wider context, a regional university can serve numerous roles which can have a significant impact on the social, cultural and economic development of an area. Specifically, such a regional university would have several roles including:

(i) *Regional access point.* A primary rule has to be the provision of 'local access'. However, there is a role for the development of programmes that attract students from outside the region. Particularly in professional fields, it is often difficult to recruit staff to non-urban areas and viable programmes can exist at regional centres by drawing enrolment from larger centres. The positioning of medical programmes at regional universities in Sweden and Finland has been a dramatic example of the success of such an approach.

(ii) *Regionally-related programme development.* Programmes can be devised that exploit the uniqueness of a given region. At Lakehead University, for example, we have a unique programme in outdoor recreation which attracts most of its enrolment from the urban part of our province. The development of such programmes not only draws students to the region and promotes the region but also enhances the viability of typically small regional institutions.

(iii) *Direct economic impact.* Typically, geographically distinct regions have limited or narrow focus economic foundations. In such contexts post-secondary education facilities can be a *major* industry and tool for economic development. In the Ontario context, every 100 students of additional enrolment that are fully funded represent an additional $1 million of operating income. Almost all of this money is spent in the local labour/marketplace and the multiplier effect from such employment is significant.

(iv) *Regional promotion.* Most geographically distinct regions have difficulty attracting professionals and other specific employment skills to an area. This is partially true in the Canadian (and Ontario) north. The presence of a regional university with its associated and related cultural umbrella is usually significant in rounding out the social-cultural maturity of a regional university community. It is interesting, in northern Sweden, that the communities blessed with a regional university seem to be prospering, and that communities that are not so fortunate from an economic development perspective point to the lack of a university. The movement of non-regional origin students through a regional university over time will build up a better understanding of a particular area. From a long-term political perspective, this has to be significant and positive.

Lakehead, as one of two major regional universities in northern Ontario, owes its roots to a technical school that was established over 40 years ago. Lakehead became a university in 1965 and immediately aspired to be not a 'true regional university' but rather a 'little Oxford or Cambridge of the North'. Although nicely achieving this objective by the early 70s, this role really did not suit either the region or the development philosophy of the builders of the institution. Driven by regional demand over the past 15 years, the University has developed and continues to develop programmes of a professional nature significant to the region. Also, basic and applied research efforts have evolved as well as associated infrastructures that allow Lakehead to be a university both 'in and for' the region of northwestern Ontario. Examples of recent developments include an innovation centre, a centre for entrepreneurship and a centre for northern studies.

Has Lakehead reached the ultimate pinnacle in terms of a northern (and regional) university? The answer is very clear: 'No'. Although government which tries to cope with regional social and economic disparities increasingly sees the value of the regional university role, the political will only goes so far. The development of the new universities in northern Sweden, at Umeå, and at Oulu in northern Finland, for example, include medical and dental schools which are very important in a regional context. If one has to calculate capital and operating grants to a regional university on the same basis as other institutions in a university system, then the concept is doomed. The public and political support must be there at the highest levels to view regional and northern universities as the 'first cogs' in the social, cultural and economic development of a region.

Although this paper relates to northern Ontario, it would apply to most unique and developing regions of the Commonwealth. It is a suggestion that, perhaps at future conferences, a meeting could be held of all institutions with a similar vision.

Sub-Topic 1(b)

IS THERE A POLITICAL ROLE FOR UNIVERSITIES?

Tuesday, 9 February

Professor W. J. KAMBA (*Vice-Chancellor, University of Zimbabwe*): Taken in its baldest, most direct sense, there can be only one answer to the question posed in the title assigned to me. By their social location, by their dependence (either direct or oblique) on the power structures of their environing societies and, *a fortiori*, by their claims to a unique stance in the acquisition and transmission of systematized knowledge, universities are political institutions and their role is inherently and necessarily political.

Let me begin with a few observations about context. Too often this issue is conceptualized in an over-simplified, bi-modal formulation, linked with the concept of 'academic autonomy'. In this conceptualization there are, on the one hand, those 'liberal-democratic' contexts which afford university institutions and the intellectual community that they represent the opportunity to assume a critical stance to the socio-political *status quo* with relative impunity. On the other hand there are those 'totalitarian' contexts which suppress dissent and prohibit debate in the open market-place of ideas. Academic freedom—and by extension the genuine university—can, it is suggested, only exist in the former.

Past and present societal realities provide no basis for such a clear-cut binary typology. They suggest rather a broad spectrum of degrees of academic autonomy on which the actualities of university experience are located in response to a constantly shifting configuration of socio-political dynamics. Clearly our academic ethos seeks a location on this spectrum which is close to polarity of autonomy; it is equally clear that we are all differentially placed on this spectrum, with no assurance that what pertains today will hold tomorrow. The lesson to be derived from this is that, while socio-political context is clearly important, it cannot, in itself, define our enduring political role. Nor can we allow it to become the definitional criterion for what we designate as a university.

SUB-TOPIC 1 (B): A POLITICAL ROLE? [Kamba]

Some university institutions may well exist in repressive socio-political contexts which lower the public profile of their political role and mute the vocality of their critical function. Such indices may denote a loss of the intellectual integrity which must be the hallmark of our enterprise; they may however also indicate the adaptive tactics which are also characteristic of the university tradition. 'Silence' on the part of the academic community can itself be a political statement and it can be cogently argued that in certain circumstances the 'low-profile' mode of expression is the best discharge of its political role that a university can engage in. This is true as long as an important qualification is observed—that the tactic remains a means and is not allowed to become the end, that the survival in form of an academic institution (or career) does not supplant the political role which is an integral dimension of the academic ethos.

What is this end, this role? The paragraphs above have taken me from context to content, to the issue of what, in essence, the political function of a university is. The answer to this question derives from the nature of the academic ethos itself, the particular and distinctive nature of the academic approach to knowledge which sets it apart from technocratic, religious and political modes of dealing with the same subject. Like these other institutionalized forms of human behaviour, universities are concerned with knowledge: its discovery, acquisition, systematization, transmission and application. To this extent universities share a common objective with the priest, the politician and the technocrat. What sets the academic enterprise apart from these other modes is the conditionality which it attributes to the status of knowledge in given time and place. The primacy which it assigns to the logic of enquiry, its pursuit of the directions of logic wherever they may lead, its willingness to re-open debate on first principles and axiomatic propositions—all these give a distinctive character to the academic pursuit of knowledge, which in this formulation can be termed 'contingent cognitive truth'.

The assertion of the contingent nature of cognitive truth is a profoundly and pervasively political statement. It places the academic in a potentially or actual oppositional stance to the assertions of received dogma, be they of a religious or ideological kind. But the actual or potential conflict is not simply of a cerebral kind; the political salience of the academic ethos lies in its implication that socio-political structures rationalized by these religious or ideological assumptions are also contingent, subject to constant re-evaluation and revision. Politics generally (and here I coalesce politics and religion—our past and present experience show how

63

close these two can be) dislikes this implication. The political mode erects and maintains socio-economic structures on the premise that they are the best possible, and on the grounds that policy and practice are based on sound and enduring principles. To question these principles, or the details of their application, can be politically dangerous or subversive.

In view of this potential for conflict, one can ask why the academic ethos has been allowed for centuries by its environing political power structures to continue to exist and indeed in many instances (including, happily, most of the contexts we represent here today) to flourish. In part the answer lies in the tactical adaptability of universities, which I have already touched on. Part of the answer lies in the teaching and technological services which universities provide, and for which politicians are willing—up to a point—to pay the price of an inconvenient cognitive subversion. But a more important part of the answer lies, I believe, in a general and diffuse but nevertheless enduring acceptance in most of the cultures we represent of the importance for progress in knowledge of the academic ethos which I have described. The socio-economic concerns which occupy the day-to-day attention of our constituencies demand immediate, applicable certitudes, a demand to which politics is responsive. Balancing, however, this imperative is the perception of contingency, fed by our current cultural emphasis on societal change and the denial of stasis. This perception provides its own imperative, a demand for the scrutiny of current certitudes, for the existence of an independent 'court of inquiry' providing a continuous evaluation of the premises and policies which direct our societal histories. It is to this imperative that the academic ethos is responsive, and the strength of this imperative is of such importance that political structures are willing, sometimes grudgingly, to allow the universities to perform this role.

But what, we may ask, gives the universities the claim to act as such independent 'courts of inquiry'? What has produced the persistent (and often misplaced) public faith in their capacity to do so? Much of this faith stems from the mystique surrounding specialized knowledge, often abetted by the esoteric idiom in which it is couched. Who, outside the university community, is likely to contest the conclusions of the biochemist based on his algebraic formulae or those of the sociologist stated in his convoluted neo-logistic prose? But the specialized competencies of the biochemist or sociologist in handling the theoretical, methodological and idiomatic conventions and concerns of their respective disciplines *per se* provide little basis for, and no guarantee of, competence

SUB-TOPIC 1 (B): A POLITICAL ROLE? [*Kamba*]

when they move outside these specialisms to take up the political role we have discussed. That guarantee rises rather from an adherence to the cannons of scientific and scholarly truth: an intellectual rigour which consistently subjects premises and analyses to the judgements of one's peers, an intellectual integrity which pursues implications however unpalatable, an intellectual probity which circumscribes one's claims to the scope of knowledge and an intellectual holism which contextualizes specialist knowledge within larger contexts. It is this configuration of cognitive truth-seeking that provides the charter for a political voice on the part of academics and universities and provides (where present) the guarantee of competence which our constituencies rightfully demand. As Shils has remarked regarding the outputs of scientific advisers, the safeguards which the society has lie in their 'scientific conscience . . . in their inhibitions about saying more than they know, and in their self-discipline in not asserting as true propositions which have only the merit of supporting a desired policy'.[1]

The configuration of cognitive truth-seeking which has been discussed above has running through it a strong thread of moral obligation—moral in the sense that adherence to the academic ethos has become an internalized value, integral to the process. Intellectual morality is not a popular phrase in our contemporary positivist and utilitarian academic culture, yet it remains an essential element in the academic ethos and an expectation which continues to be held by the societies in which we exist. Without it the basis for our political role is eroded. Intellectual morality is not, however, the only check which the academic community imposes upon itself. Peer surveillance, with its sanctions and rewards, is an integral part of the university routine. As Shils has also commented: 'The advantage of the academic lies in the public character of scientific procedure and the public status of his results'.[2] Our emphasis on public debate, on refereed publication, the criteria we use for appointment and promotion—all are part of the process. While some may escape the net, most intellectual cheats are caught out. And what goes for individual academics also applies to universities corporately. Here the international character of the academic community becomes particularly important, providing an external referent for the university, which in so many other ways is encapsulated in a national context. Indeed it is through this link that the university's status to be an independent 'court of inquiry' is considerably enhanced, since its judgements can claim this broad, non-parochial location.

I have said enough about the nature and content of the university's political role to make clear my response to the proposition that it should 'be scientific and objective about knowledge and also directly critical of societies and governments'. Scientific objectivity in the pursuit of knowledge, by its intrinsic character, demands a critical stance. What the nature of this critical stance is—confrontationist or accommodative, reformist or revolutionary—will be determined by a range of variables relating to both the university and the society including, importantly, a sense of historical perspective. Universities corporately, and in contrast to segments of the academic community which they incorporate, are rarely revolutionary in their critical stance. Yet, under certain circumstances of generalized historical perspective which situates societal revolution in the future, they too on occasion have become revolutionary in an oppositional, confrontative role. This, however, is rare; most of our universities exist in societal contexts where our revolutions are notionally located in the past—for those of us in the post-colonial states of the third world, in the immediate past. Our stance is therefore likely to be 'reformist', a position defined by Raymond Aron as the 'approval of the whole and criticism of the parts'.[3] This leads me back to the words of our programme directive, and particularly to the phrase 'directly critical of societies and governments'. This phrase could be interpreted to infer that the critical stance which, I have argued, is integral to the academic ethos is necessarily confrontative and oppositional. However the reformist mode in which most of us operate suggests no such necessary conclusion. Indeed the governments of many of the societies in which we operate invite our universities to play a political role which is supportive in their efforts at nation-building and is in no way a negation of the critical stance which is an essential component of our scholarship.

This invitation characteristically comes to us in two forms. One is to augment the store of scientific and technological knowledge held by the society, itself an important dimension of political power. Universities are well placed to perform this task by virtue of their location in an international academic community of which I have already spoken in another context. Through their membership in this community, functionally active in a manner not often found in other international networks, universities can serve as 'information terminals' within the state which can act as a conduit for global perspectives and knowledge, contextualizing this global intellectual property in a manner appropriate to local concerns.[4] This task of transmitting and interpreting intellectual property from the international 'centre' to the national 'periphery' is not as easy as the term 'information terminal' might imply, requiring as it does that our scholars 'possess both the cultural competence to perceive national needs and social demands ... and have sufficient social and cognitive authority for active participation in the scientific discourse at the centre'.[5]

The second form comes in the invitation to academics to participate with the politicians in a massive effort in political and cultural engineering which defines societal goals and integrates the dynamics of human potential with the material and technological resources available. In other words, our universities are invited to organize an enterprise in intellectual activity which viably synthesizes ends and means.

This invitation, often immediate and explicit in third-world contexts, in some ways parallels the growing interpenetration of relationships between intellectualdom and the sphere of political authority in the west. On this Lipset and Basu comment on 'the fact that the complexities of "running" an advanced industrial or postindustrial society forces laymen, both political and economic leaders, to seek advice in depth, to defer to the scholarly-scientific community'.[6]

This has not, however, meant that intellectuals in these countries have developed an adequate forum in which to give their reflective insights effective political expression. As Nettl has observed: 'The very processes that enhance the worth of scholars to the powers, the growth of needed arcane knowledge, have resulted in a variety of highly minute particularistic specialities, thus reducing their potential to behave as intellectuals in the political arena, to be concerned with structural arrangements according to universalistic principles'.[7] The same processes are operative in third-world contexts. By virtue of their invitation to participate with politicians in nation-building, academics apparently gain access to the 'corridors of power' only to be pushed back into the role of 'experts' rather than social innovators, called upon to solve 'problems' rather than to define social goals. Much of this is a result of the unjointed disciplinary and specialist fragmentation which has been allowed to develop within our universities, rather than by political design. This has been at the expense of our integrative task in the search for cognitive truth and the efficacy of our political voice.

The corrective to this trend is a renewed attention to the etymology of the title which we, with more than a touch of arrogance, assign to ourselves, a title which implies that each is a *universitas* of knowledge and understanding, a microcosm of the accumulated wisdom and experience of our societies and cultures. Few, if any, of our universities approximate this comprehensive ideal. Perhaps comprehensiveness is not essential, as long as our scholarship ranges over a spectrum sufficiently broad to be responsive to societal needs and to permit the synthesizing function which we are called upon to perform. More important is a deliberate effort to foster an interdisciplinarity in our scholarship which not only permits but also produces the required synthesis between ends and means. Our search for cognitive truth must, if it is to have enduring meaning, include this synthesis as a prime objective. Our political voice, if it is to bear its proper salience, must speak to this goal.

REFERENCES

1. E. Shils (1977): 'The Academic Ethos' in *The Future of the University in Southern Africa*; H. V. van der Merwe and D. Welsh, eds. Cape Town: D. Philip, p. 21.
2. E. Shils (1977), p. 11.
3. R. Aron (1965): *Main Currents in Sociological Thought I.* Harmondsworth: Pelican Books, p. 11.
4. *cf.* W. J. Kamba (1985): 'The Role of Universities in South-South Cooperation'; paper presented to the South-South Conference, Harare, pp. 17–18.
5. V. Stolte-Heiskanen (1987): 'The Role of Centre-Periphery Relations in the Utilization of the Social Sciences'. *International Sociology*, Vol. 2, No. 2, p. 192.
6. S. M. Lipset and A. Basu (1975): 'Intellectual Types and Political Roles' in L. A. Coser, *The Idea of Social Structure*. New York: Harcourt, Brace Jovanovich, p. 457.
7. J. P. Nettl (1969), paraphrased by Lipset and Basu, *op.cit.*, from 'Ideas, Intellectuals and Structures of Dissent' in P. Rieff, ed., *On Intellectuals*. Garden City: Doubleday, pp. 80–82, 118–119.

Professor P. N. TARLING (*Professor of History and Deputy Vice-Chancellor, University of Auckland*): There is necessarily a political role for universities. They are engaged in teaching citizens; they are engaged in research; they are preserving, expanding and disseminating knowledge. They are financed by citizens, by fees, by taxes. They cannot avoid being in politics, since all these issues have political overtones. Which citizens shall they teach? What shall they be taught? What research should they foster? Is their funding more a private or more a public responsibility? Determining such questions involves political considerations. The question is not whether there is a political role for universities, but what that role is.

SUB-TOPIC 1 (B): A POLITICAL ROLE? [*Tarling*]

To define that role requires some definition of a university: the role it might play will vary with its nature. In, say, a totalitarian state, the citizens it may teach will be prescribed by a political test, and the research it may attempt confined by ideological criteria. But an institution in such a plight, we may conclude, falls outside the definition of a university. Nor would that definition subsume institutions in non-totalitarian societies which were substantially or exclusively devoted to training, even at the tertiary level, and the research in which was substantially or exclusively of an applied nature. This paper indeed proceeds on the assumption that the universities with which we are concerned are defined by features which, though not of divine origin, have come, as a result of a long historical process, to include

(*a*) higher professional education, in the sense, not of imparting strictly specific professional skills, but of providing students with theoretical, factual and logical knowledge and skills that enable them 'to attain an intellectual mastery of a certain domain of culture and to exploit their skills in different professions', normally after additional training;

(*b*) 'the continued transmission of human culture';

(*c*) 'the enrichment of our knowledge about the world';

(*d*) 'the teaching and spreading of certain values that are applicable not only in scientific matters but in all fields of social life, including the political, including impartiality in judgment, tolerance, criticism, obedience to logical rules'.[1]

You might say that this attempt at definition aims to outline the tasks of the university in the classical liberal sense, an amalgam of the concepts of Newman and the German-American research tradition. 'Without intellectual autonomy—freedom of the mind—there could be no institution that we would recognise as a university. . . .'[2]

If such universities have a political role—and in fact they cannot avoid it—that role is to defend themselves. That may at first appear to be too limited and too selfish a role. In my view it is a large task and a widely important one, requiring all the wisdom and wit, clarity and conviction, tenacity and adaptability, patience and perception that mere professors like me assume is possessed in full measure by the vice-chancellors and principals represented at this conference.

Those who initially think that the role I offer to the universities is too negative or limited a role may point out, for example, that the values a university seeks to foster and inculcate are important in other fields of endeavour. Should a university not play its role in scenes where larger social and political struggles are acted out?

Should it not merely defend itself but, adopting what is sometimes called the best mode of defence, attack social and political forces that are inimical to the values it must itself endorse? Should it at the very least determine to set examples to the societies in which it exists, say of 'equal opportunity' or 'preference' or 'social responsibility'? Should it take part in movements designed to criticize or reform social and political trends in community or government? My answer is yes and no. These are scenes in which a university may appear, but it cannot be a main protagonist. It must frame what it does within its essentially defensive mode. Only at times of extreme crisis for state or society should it throw aside that limitation, joining with other social forces, say, to resist the onset of a totalitarian regime. Even then, of course, it would be acting to preserve the conditions under which alone it might play its full and proper role.

Why insist that the universities play a role in politics that is defined by defending themselves? First, they represent something that is worth defending. They are places the characteristic feature of which is open-endedness of debate, and often, maddening to some, inconclusiveness of outcome; of certainty qualified by uncertainty and tried by argument and research; places where statements can be tested by the dialectic of discussion. Where the truth cannot be challenged by free discussion, as Mill put it, 'instead of a vivid conception and a living belief, there remain only a few phrases retained by rote; or, if any part, the shell and husk only of the meaning is retained, the finer essence being lost'.[3] But in these places, where men and women have these tasks, objectivity is valued and inculcated; tolerance, sometimes lost, regained; prejudices and presumptions seen for what they are.

Second, the universities need defending from others and from themselves. In earlier centuries they defended themselves more readily because they cost less, and cities valued their custom. Now they are costly institutions: research and teaching are for the most part costly endeavours. And indebtedness implies dependence. In my 30-year association with universities in the liberal tradition, they have undergone two crises, in a sense separated by a generation, but also in a sense linked; the student revolts of the late 1960s; the right-wing assaults of the 1980s. The students sought for greater 'relevance' in teaching, though they also wanted to be sure that research was not directly relevant to the needs of defence ministries or counter-insurgency programmes. The right-wing critics use radical criticisms of the universities—they have been captured by the middle-class, they say—as a means of changing their role. That role, they stress, is to train those that the economy needs, and that training can be paid for by the individuals who will benefit by undertaking it. The larger aims are difficult to quantify, and risk being passed by with a distant nod of recognition. Should those old bits of bric-à-brac be on the stage at all? Are they mere trompe l'oeil?

If there are critics without, there are critics within, too. There will, quite properly, be those who are exploring or evaluating the concepts of 'relevance' or 'user pays'. But there will also, more dubiously, be those who are tempted—by the media, by passing fads and enthusiasms, by money or by mistake—to go along with criticisms that are in the end at odds with the prospect of sustaining the open-endedness of universities, using the stage as a platform for other purposes or taking the juvenile lead. To argue, as radicals might, that because objectivity cannot be obtained it is not worth seeking is to deny that there are degrees of objectivity, that some is better than none, and more than some. To argue that the only relevance is market value imparts another ideology that should undergo testing rather be granted the immediate accolade of application. It is likely, as so far conceived, to be narrowing, and runs the risk not only of restricting the universities to training professionals but of restricting the training the professionals get.

The third reason for taking a defensive role is that this will be hard enough. Possibly, indeed, it is as much as, if not more than, weak institutions like universities can reasonably contemplate. Universities are weak, and necessarily so, since they are designed to allow opinion to rub against opinion, truth against truth. Directly to intervene in society and politics, in order to promote the values a university holds dear, is not of course inconsistent with those values. But the outcome may undermine them. Fully in the political arena, the universities may lose their special role. They have no normal political constituency: their critics and opponents would take the opportunity to destroy them. Their interventions must be designed not to reorder society, but to ensure that society does not so reorder them as to prevent them fulfilling their role.

The defensive role is one designed to ensure the neutral ground, or sustain the non-alignment, in which the open-ended activities of a university can be pursued. It is not in fact a negative role, and it may indeed require intervention to try to ensure that 'the structures of action and opinion in the wider community are favourable to the independence and political neutrality of a university. . . . one has to assume, with or without some sense of paradox, that a university, seen as a sponsor of a free, creative activity, cannot remain neutral in the defence of its essential interests, one of which is the preservation of its political neutrality.'[4] Seeking funds from government or corporation, it must not yet be so tied as to undermine its non-alignment or destroy the conditions for open-minded enquiry and instruction. The task may be hard enough in itself. Pursuing its objectives may after all be not only as much as it can realistically do, but a striking act in itself. The cynics—and too many of our students are among them—may wonder what example a university sets. Its members seem to be engaged in their own politics, pursuing their own ambitions, working or agitating for promotion, like those of any other organisation. But there is more than a mere residue of open-endedness, of objectivity, of discovery, of intellectual excitement, to undermine the cynicism that often their no more than half knowledge brings.

If attack is not the best form of defence—except in a limited sense, targeting particular snipers or avoiding ambushes rather than getting involved in campaigns at large—should the universities take hostages or seek allies? They may indeed take on additional roles, offer to perform additional functions. But they must beware of taking on too much, and thereby exposing themselves to attack. If a university takes on tasks that are not by definition its proper tasks it may be taking on liabilities. If it seeks funds for narrow training or tied research it may pay heavily for them. If it tries to serve the community too closely it may serve it too narrowly.

The idea of community service was added to the functions of the university with the Wisconsin idea of the late nineteenth century. Clearly, indeed, a university will function more effectively if it takes account of the interests and problems of its city, its region and its country. But it must always reckon also with the wider interest that it serves, the preservation of certain values that have been nurtured with difficulty through the centuries and are not to be readily discarded. A state may look to the universities, for example, to train future leaders. But to produce them should not be the immediate aim of the universities. It is to initiate them into a tradition of enquiry with its own internal demands. One technique of initiation, though only one, might involve practical problems, but their discussion would relate to the issues within the tradition of enquiry. It would 'spill into' issues of social and political relevance, but they would not be the only issues to be discussed.[5] The academic is engaged in the pursuit and communication of knowledge. 'This function is a community service. . . . It is a service to his country, a service to civilization, a service to mankind. . . .'[6]

If there is an attack to be mounted that is a form of defence, it is to endeavour not only to sustain this view but to make it understandable and acceptable to society, to governments, to those who form opinion and control treasuries. The universities have found this difficult. But it may be that all the reviews and the doctrines of recent times will ultimately have helped the universities, if they have made us define our purposes so clearly that we can defend them more effectively. Their best service to the community is to remain themselves. At the same time they must recognise that they are not perfect. Pressure from outside may also be welcome if it induces those within to reform, the better to defend. The direction of the reforms must clearly be towards reasserting the fundamental purpose of the universities. For that, it has been suggested, they must be 'constitutionalised'.[7]

But what relations does the member of the university community have as an individual with the wider community? If a university should not positively take on the reform of society as a whole, does that mean its members must be silent on the public issues of the day? The answer is clearly in the negative. But conditions within the institution must be such as to encourage a sense of responsibility to its values—'a decent regard for the obligations of academic citizenship'; while outside the institution the distinction is to be drawn between the institution and its members, a task that adds to the task of effectively defending the universities but again suggests that that is their proper role in politics.

The future of the university depends upon articulating and propagating an idea of the university that is valid and compelling: that, as Nikolaus Lobkowicz has suggested, can only be the concept of the university as 'institutionalised truth-seeking'. 'We may have efficient training schools, devoted to excellence, but the true university is not a technocratic institution, any more than it is a political institution. The central virtue of the university . . . is thoughtfulness, pensiveness, the recognition that truth is always more complex and elusive than we are tempted to believe.'[8] It is of the world, but not in it; it serves society by avoiding subservience to it.

REFERENCES

1. Kolakowski, Leszek: 'Neutrality and Academic Values' in A. Montefiore, ed., *Neutrality and Impartiality*. Cambridge University Press, 1975, p. 76.

2. Introduction to John W. Chapman, ed., *The Western University on Trial*. Berkeley and Los Angeles, University of California Press, 1983, p. 7.

3. Mill, J. S.: *On Liberty*. Penguin Classics, p. 101.

4. Weinstein, W. L.: 'The academic and the political' in Montefiore, pp. 165-6.
5. Ten, C. L.: 'Politics in the Academe' in *ibid.*, p. 161.
6. MacIver, Robert M.: *Academic Freedom in our Time*. New York, Columbia University Press, 1955, p. 10.
7. Chapman, pp. 12, 19-20.
8. Lobkowicz, Nikolaus: 'Man, Pursuit of Truth, and the University' in Chapman, pp. 31,35,37-38.

DISCUSSION

(*Rapporteur*: Mr. W. B. NICOLL, Registrar, University of Auckland)

In general, discussion on this sub-topic supported the themes of the two papers, and delegates agreed that the political role of the institution depended on the dramatically different political and socio-economic circumstances prevailing in individual countries. It was suggested that a government's view of a university may depend on the stage of development of the country, *e.g.* in small developing countries universities may be seen as prestigious institutions bringing international and social acceptability.

Other points discussed included—

(1) Government criticism in the more developed countries was often levelled at the time taken by universities in meeting the changing needs of society.

(2) Several speakers suggested that governments represent only current society, and that universities were much more stable institutions than governments.

(3) Many issues raised by universities over the past 10-20 years on such matters as the environment are only now being addressed by governments.

(4) The need to defend the university and increase its public profile may in some extreme cases, however, not be appropriate and it may be preferable for the university to be silent.

(5) Whatever the strategy, preservation of the integrity, the autonomy, the central core of the institution was essential.

(6) Limitations which might be imposed by charter or legislation on the activities and political role of the university.

(7) What in fact comprises 'the university'—the governing body, the chief executive, the staff of all kinds, the students, or the legal entity?

Sub-Topic 1(c)

THE SOCIO-CULTURAL ROLE OF UNIVERSITIES

Tuesday, 9 February

Professor W. TAYLOR (*Vice-Chancellor, University of Hull*): There is no more important topic for consideration at this or any other academic gathering than that of relations between the university and civil society, a topic which subsumes the role of the university as critic and its social/cultural function.

Intelligence, our self-conscious ability to use tools, to exercise foresight, to create and to communicate culture, are the marks of human uniqueness—not only among the other species with whom we share this world but perhaps also within the universe itself. Only one institution is comprehensively charged with the nurture and development of intellect, and that is the university. The maintenance and support of universities is a crucially important task for any society that does not wish to return to barbarism. We must show no modesty in asserting the importance of the university as producer, guardian and disseminator of those manifestations of intellect that make us human and enhance the possibilities of civilization. There is nothing culture-bound or relative about the processes involved, or the conditions needed to enable them to flourish.

Sadly, however, dependence on public funds, industrial support and the favour of politicians; guilt induced by the misuse of technology; the diversification of educational and research functions among other organizations; and the realities of governing pluralist societies and institutions dominated by single-interest politics; have combined to sap the confidence of the university in its mission and hence in the claims it can rightfully make upon society.

If there need be no modesty in our claim to uniqueness, neither must there be arrogance. Our role imposes upon all of us who work in universities responsibilities at once both awesome and exhilarating. That we constitute an elite demands no apology, providing it is sustained by the quality of our intellectual output. Nor do we have to be defensive about maintaining the necessary conditions for productive intellectual labour, providing again that these are not merely the unjustified sequestering of traditional privilege.

Academic employment is not just a job, with similar demands to those which fall upon the increasing number of men and women in modern societies who work with brain rather than with hand. It cannot be performed to a specification (although that is no excuse for neglecting duties and deadlines); it requires, at every level, a large measure of personal autonomy in the deployment of time and attention; it essentially demands freedom to pursue and publish truth as the individual sees it, without fear of penalty (but subject always to reasoned public assessment by professional and disciplinary peers, and without any right to use the university as a base for direct political and social action based on one's beliefs, however sincerely held). (*See* Bok (1982)).

Ironically, that many governments (even some in liberal democracies) do not now give sufficient attention to such simple and obvious propositions is in part at least our own fault. Our reflexive consciousness has become too sophisticated for our own good. Oversimplified ideas attributed to Darwin, Freud and Marx are now part of the fabric of popular and political discourse. We have become so culturally relativistic, so sensitive to anything that might smack of chauvinism, so aware of the fragility of any form of inter-group agreement, so knowing in our analysis of motives and self-interest, that we have gone a long way towards emasculating reason and thus denying the university its essence.

The post-Enlightenment university exists to propagate the life of reason, not to serve the purposes of a particular political or cultural ideology or economic system. The core social/cultural role of any university worthy of the name is to establish, to cherish and to perpetuate processes which extend the realm of reason in human affairs. It is against this standard that all the quotidian activities and responses of the university must be judged. The use of the referee system; the grounds on which a member of staff may be dismissed; willingness to enter into contracts with or accept funds from industrial and commercial undertakings in support of particular projects; internal resource allocations to teaching, research and service in each of the university's areas of academic activity; the setting up of new departments or interdisciplinary centres; whether to respond to a local community's request for an extra-mural course in a particular subject—every such decision, however apparently unrelated to any point of principle, must be consistent with the university's overall obligations to the life of reason.

The university's role as critic is thus central to its functions in a free society, and to its interaction with the social and cultural forms of that society. At a descriptive level the reality of such interaction is almost too obvious to require elaboration. Most of those who govern and administer, at national and regional if not yet at local levels, have been educated in universities; this is often as true in developing as in developed countries. An increasing proportion of the men and women who possess economic power, as owners, managers and trade union officers, are the products of universities. So are a very high proportion of professional cadres in the public service, in teaching and in all aspects of medicine. University graduates are becoming more prominent in the ranks of media people, actors, musicians and other artists. If three or more years at university has a distinctive impact upon the subsequent development of personality, attitudes and behaviour, then given the destinations of graduates there can be no denial of the importance the university plays in the social and cultural life of society.

There are, of course, many other ways of looking at the university's social/cultural role. One would be to examine the effects of university education on subsequent life chances, in relation to the socio-economic composition of student populations. For many years such questions of access were pre-eminent in policy discussion (OECD, 1982). More recently the focus has shifted; relations with industry and improved 'effectiveness' tend to be the preoccupation in many quarters (Taylor, 1987).

Another approach—and the core of many biographies—would be to identify the influence that prominent individuals have exercised on the social and cultural lives of their respective countries, and to relate this to their experience of the university. A variation is to examine the sway exerted by a particular group of like-minded individuals, such as the Cambridge Apostles (see Deacon, 1985).

In all this it has to be remembered that universities not only interact with the social and cultural life of whole nations, but also and importantly with that of their region and locality. The extent to which universities are actively involved in the social and cultural life of their regions and localities varies markedly, however, with both time and place.

In the United Kingdom the civic universities established between the mid-nineteenth and mid-twentieth centuries were rooted in local enthusiasm and local need. Their efforts to achieve national and international recognition won local support as reflecting back on the communities of their origin. It has been argued that such efforts often went further than was at first envisaged:

> 'It would be an interesting study to collate the evidence of the process by which the new universities of the early twentieth century began to rid themselves of the vestiges of their origins as "local colleges" . . . As far as their internal social and educational environment was concerned the civic universities aspired to be less and less civic. In the search for dignity they renovated significant parts of the regime of the old, socially exclusive universities. The model of real university provision was seen . . . in the intensive training of a captive group of late-adolescent students who would be brought into several years of continuous residence, who would have no necessary connection with their university's locality, and who would be insulated from the regular business of life' (Marriott, 1983, p. 2).

The so-called 'green field' or 'plate glass' universities established at the beginning of the period of expansion in the 'sixties, although also commanding local support and distributed widely throughout the country, were all located away from city centres. In contrast, most of the former colleges of advanced technology, upgraded to university status in the mid-'sixties, retained their urban locations.

Although the regional and local impact of universities, even those located on 'green field' campuses, was never insignificant it received a new emphasis almost everywhere with the financial exigency of the 'eighties. Universities were able to demonstrate the substantial employment effects of their presence in a particular locality. A study contributed to an OECD workshop in 1984 (O'hEocha and Watson, 1984) argued that when a new university is established in a region

> '. . . it has an immediate impact which can be accurately quantified. In addition to the immediate employment effects there is the demand for goods and services and student expenditure which creates other jobs in the region. A 1977 German study estimated that for each 10,000 students there were 3000 highly qualified university jobs while spin-off employment amounted to 4300. This multiplier of 1·43 is more than that of industrial development.'

In some countries there are whole communities almost completely dependent on a university for their economic survival, towns where the population is reduced by half during the vacation periods in which students return to their own homes. It is not unknown for a university to be the largest single employer of local labour. The running down or closing of an academic institution is a threat to the jobs of many more than the directly employed academic, administrative, technical and support staff. For locally elected members of national or regional legislatures these wider employment consequences of contraction or closure can be a more compelling source of interest and support than the possible loss to scholarship and science of the teaching and research that the institution undertakes.

In some cases a decision to establish a university in an otherwise 'underprivileged area' has been part of a regional development policy, designed to foster economic and cultural development, to increase local participation rates in higher education, to make available larger numbers of trained personnel who as a consequence of the presence of the university are drawn in (with their families) from elsewhere. As well as affecting the economic prospects of a locality or region, the presence of a university makes services available to agriculture, industry and commerce that might otherwise be unobtainable commercially.

Many academics welcome such contacts with local industry, especially when their research and scholarly activity require proving grounds, industrial trials and other facilities for 'action research'. The importance of such relations, and of the capacity of the university to link regional and local interests with national and international networks of knowledge and experience, has grown as economic competition has increased. However, as Blume (1985) has pointed out, what local industry asks of its university can be very different from the demands of multi-nationals and large firms. The latter depend for major innovations more upon the fundamental research activity of major institutions with high levels of equipment and resource than on the type of applied and development expertise available locally. This may, in any case, be more sensibly provided in diversified systems by other non-university institutions of higher education.

The presence of a university can also have consequences for local or regional government. The political life of some municipalities can be much influenced by participation in local affairs of university staff resident in the locality. There are many kinds of academic expertise of great value to bodies like regional hospital boards, economic development councils, the magistrates' bench and the school board.

Important as all these are, a university does much more than this for the social and cultural life of its region. It offers a direct model of what such an institution is, of what it means to pursue studies in higher education, of the nature of academic life, about which citizens and potential students might otherwise have only an indirect and less concrete impression.

There is no reason in principle why a university's research and teaching activities should not contribute to the social, cultural and economic development of its region without prejudicing the national and international recognition that comes from significant additions to knowledge. But achieving the right balance is not always easy. Staff time and attention are scarce resources. They need to be distributed in accordance with an ordered set of priorities. Anxieties persist about the effects on the central mission of universities of their acting as what Asa Briggs has called 'service stations', devoting too much time to politically or financially lucrative short-term contracts at the expense of their distinctive teaching and research roles.

How does the university, in the words of an OECD report of 1982, '. . . combine commitment with neutrality, scientific objectivity with involvement in social problems and hence in social conflicts, and, in the final analysis, independence with participation?' (p. 44). Some critics of contemporary trends in university development take the view that this question is today being answered in ways that not only undermine the core values of the academy but bode ill for the longer term prospects of the very activities to which university men and women now devote so much of their time—obtaining research support, soliciting development contracts, training professionals, and rendering service in applied fields as diverse as engineering and education.

The reality is that universities are not the homogenous entities implied by generalizations about their role. Few have departments, schools or faculties uniform either in distinction or in the balance of their activities. Some academic units are home to individuals and groups recognised as playing major critical roles in their disciplines and professions. Other units in the same institution may be better known for their teaching, applied research and a variety of forms of service.

Whilst many of the ideas that spark off fundamental revisions in our concepts of ourselves and of the physical and social world are the product of the physical and life sciences, the social sciences and the humanities, individuals and departments in applied and professional subjects can also perform important critical functions in their own areas of responsibility. In all these fields what matters is whether the academics and researchers concerned are able to pursue their enquiries and to publish their results without the irrelevant constraints of ideology, orthodoxy or political expediency. The terms and conditions on which they hold their appointments, the basis on which their departments receive resources from the university, and the nature of the support that the university receives from the state and from private sources, can safeguard or deny the freedom and independence without which no university makes its proper contribution to the life of reason.

Which being said, leaves important questions still to answer. What sort of individual contract is consistent with these values? At what point does a university become so dependent on industrial funding as to prejudice its essential critical function? Which kinds of strings attached to private benefactions are acceptable, and which unacceptable? What should be the balance of local, regional, disciplinary, professional and national interests on a university's governing body? What part, if any, should national authorities play in the appointment of staff? Do the external political activities of Dr. X now impinge to such an extent on his teaching and research as to invalidate his academic role?

No general discussion of the critical, social and cultural role of the university can itself answer such questions. What it *can* do is help us recognise the common principles that must apply to the resolution of these and the many other issues that today confront the vice-chancellor and governing body of any institution worthy to bear the title of university.

REFERENCES

Blume, S. (1985): 'After the Darkest Hour: Integrity and Engagement in the Development of University Research' in Wittsock, B. and Elzinga, A. (eds.), *The University Research System*. Stockholm.

Bok, D. (1982): *Beyond the Ivory Tower*. Cambridge: Harvard University Press.

Deacon, R. (1985): *The Cambridge Apostles: A history of Cambridge University's elite intellectual secret society*. London: Robert Royce.

Marriott, S. (1983): *Extra-Mural Empires: Service and self-interest in English University Adult Education*. Nottingham: Department of Adult Education, University of Nottingham.

O'hEocha, C. and Watson, J. A. (1984): 'The Regional Role of the University', *International Journal of Institutional Management in Higher Education*, 8:2.

Organisation for Economic Co-operation and Development (1982): *The University and the Community: the problems of changing relationships*. Paris: the Organisation.

Taylor, W. (1987): *Universities Under Scrutiny*. Paris: OECD.

Professor G. F. A. SAWYERR (*Vice-Chancellor, University of Ghana*):

A FRAGMENT ON THE SOCIO-CULTURAL ROLE OF THE UNIVERSITY IN COMMONWEALTH AFRICA

As a result of their functions and composition universities influence their societies in a variety of important ways. But the precise character of this influence turns on a range of specific historical and local factors. For this reason I will confine my discussion essentially to the universities of Commonwealth Africa, which, while sharing the core characteristics of all universities, differ sufficiently to justify separate treatment.

Among the core characteristics of any university—we speak here of the university not as a corporate entity but as a community of scholars engaged primarily in research and teaching—are the following:

- internationalism—in what and how its members study and teach, and the contacts they maintain;
- an ethos of scholarly objectivity in the pursuit of truth through research and reflection;
- freedom for its members—not only from outside agencies, but also from their 'superiors' and their peers—to conduct research, to teach and to express themselves; and
- autonomy from the direct control of government and other agencies external to itself.

The corporate form and guiding conventions of the typical university have been devised precisely to promote, protect and provide institutional supports for this freedom to pursue the truth and all its implications.

The degree to which any university attains all these ideal conditions clearly depends upon its specific history, the general conditions of its society and its location within it, and is nowhere unchanging. What is certain is that in almost all societies the university enjoys more of these features than other comparable institutions.

One of the consequences of this dedication to the truth is that in the search for answers to fundamental questions all 'truth' is regarded as contingent, and therefore subject to challenge. This leads to a chronic questioning of 'what *is*', and its constant measurement against 'what *used to be*', 'what *could be*', or 'what *should be*'. This posture, always measuring present reality against an 'ideal' alternative, and arising necessarily out of the investigative or reflective work of the university scholar, especially in an atmosphere of free expression and debate, poses a potential challenge to the established order, whether this be political, social or ecclesiastical. How far this challenge is made explicit by the advocacy of specific positions is conditioned by the particular circumstances, including the institutional and individual interests and judgements of the university and its members. But whether explicit or implicit, the very nature of unfettered intellectual work results in a critical stance towards the established order.

While this is true of universities in general, a grasp of the specific role of the university in Commonwealth Africa requires the identification of such of its special features as relate to this role. Notable among these are the fact that:

- the typical Commonwealth African university is a very young one—with the exception of a few established before 1960 (including Fourah Bay College, 1827), the typical university is less than 27 years old;
- it was established at the end of the colonial period or soon thereafter, usually in a 'special relationship' with a metropolitan university;
- it is the sole university, or one of at most three universities (except Nigeria, with 24), with a limited number of students, resulting in a heavy concentration of national intellectual talent—both faculty and students;
- restricted/selective access, and a small output of graduates as a proportion of the relevant age-group;
- a nationwide catchment area, drawing students and staff from a wide variety of ethnic, regional and class backgrounds;
- it constitutes the predominant source, or one of the few sources, of high-calibre cadres, new knowledge and modern ideas;
- it has an exclusively, or almost exclusively, residential campus arrangement;
- it constitutes a mini-municipality, providing the full range of services—housing, transportation, health, sanitation, etc.—to a community of lecturers, students and workers, and their families; and
- it is wholly state-supported.

Turning to an assessment of the characteristic social effects of these special features one notices, first, that the small number of universities and the nation-wide catchment area create a 'melting pot' effect in the universities. Thus the university community and its products tend to develop a trans-ethnic outlook and a heightened sense of nationhood—a matter of great consequence to societies in the process building a nation out of a collection of ethnic and regional groupings. Secondly, the residential campus arrangement, the special treatment of university members, the nature of their academic preoccupations and their non-involvement in directly productive activity tend to set the university community apart from the rest of society.

Thirdly, in the specific context of Africa, the necessarily international dimension of the university imports a foreign/European bias and a departure from traditional ways, thereby exacerbating the social distance between the university and the wider society. A communication gap, greater than in other parts of the Commonwealth, thus develops between the two, through diminished comprehension one of the other. It is not so much a case of the university failing to 'sell' itself to society, as of the university in Africa working in a manner that is intrinsically mysterious to the rest of society. In spite of the foregoing it is the case, finally, that as the pinnacle of an educational system cherished by all, the hoped-for destination of everyone's children, the predominant source of new knowledge and highly-qualified professionals, and indeed because of the very mystique surrounding it, the typical African university enjoys enormous prestige, and its views and the actions of its graduates exercise a major influence on national affairs.

How does all this relate to the position of the university as a critic of society? We have already noted the unavoidable tension between thoroughgoing intellectual enquiry and the established order. The explosive potential of this tension is most often realised through the activism of students, who are in general less 'socialised' into accommodation with the existing order, and less tactically inclined in the face of what they consider to be clear issues of principle. The resulting challenge to both university and state political order by university students is particularly evident in Africa, where the prevailing political cultures barely understand and rarely tolerate free expression and debate, and where university students often constitute the only organised body able to articulate popularly-held views against specific government measures, or indeed against the government itself. All this finds dramatic expression in the all-too-frequent and sometimes violent campus disorders and closures in Africa.

Note should be taken of the contradictory tendencies engendered in the typical university student by all the factors outlined above. On the one hand his relative trans-ethnicity, westernisation and privileged status tend to alienate him from the rest of society. On the other hand his increased social consciousness, awareness of nation, relative objectivity and relative immunity from the direct consequences of his actions, predispose him, while in university at least, to espouse popular democratic causes and take nationalist positions. Though this posture does not survive in every student in quite the same form after graduation, its effect, as generation succeeds generation of university graduates, is arguably to help reinforce the democratic/progressive tendency in society.

In a less confrontationist stance the university can, by its mode of organisation and the outcome of its work, constitute a standing criticism of the wider society. For instance, the typical Commonwealth African university community is severely hierarchical in its organization—from the gradations of academic and administrative staff, through students to wage workers. At the same time the notions of freedom of association and of expression, and the devotion to truth and fair play, generate a democratic current which can temper the rigidities of hierarchy. Thus in recent years some African universities have moved to the position where representation of students and workers on their governing and management bodies has reinforced the democratic tendency on the campuses. The strength of this tendency varies from place to place, and can be exaggerated. But even in its mildest form it enables the university community to exhibit an alternative organizational mode in essentially anti-democratic African polities.

Again, because of its privileged access to advanced and specialised knowledge, its broader comparative perspective and its devotion to scientific enquiry, the African university community has the potential for throwing up alternative views and different approaches to the solution of society's problems. This invariably implies a calling into question of some aspect or other of existing society. These alternative views are sometimes expressed as criticism, and occasionally form the basis of explicit advocacy or even political opposition. The fact that more often, even without explicit advocacy, these alternative positions are accepted, in the sense that they lead to changes in society, does not remove the element of criticism implied in their formulation. Indeed it can be argued that this insidious, non-confrontational form of criticism, arising naturally from its character and mode of enquiry, is the principal *modus operandi* of the university as critic of society. For in the absence of the most exceptional circumstances the African university, despite its chronically critical stance, is not an agent of revolution.

TOPIC 1: THE UNIVERSITY AS CRITIC

DISCUSSION

(*Rapporteur*: Ms. L. ANNE HIGGOTT, Academic Secretariat, Murdoch University)

During discussion of this topic further factors were identified as affecting the interrelationship of universities and their societies. These included historical circumstances, location and relation to other universities in the area, the level of active participation of the community in the affairs of the university, the composition of the student body, the needs of the society (locally, regionally, nationally) and the institutions' size and status. The impact on developing countries of universities modelled on western concepts was identified in terms of creating tension and potentially divisive elitism.

Major points raised by delegates included—

(1) Only by a process of an ongoing self-analysis could universities avoid ossification.

(2) Universities were not perfect entities, as they were essentially human institutions associated with human failings.

(3) Chief executives had a special responsibility to explain, to both the university and the wider community, the role and objectives of their respective institutions.

(4) Lay members on governing bodies had an important role to play in propagating the view of the university outside the institution. However universities did not generally provide these members with appropriate tools and training to carry out this role.

(5) Non-academic staff were often undervalued as an essential link forging relationships with the community in which they lived and worked.

(6) Movement of students between educational institutions and locations, at different stages of their careers, was highly desirable to avoid parochialism.

(7) In general universities should not be seen to have discrete local, as distinct from international, roles, but should act as mediators by translating international knowledge to the local area.

(8) The dangers inherent in current world-wide proposals to stratify universities by establishing a classification of institutions giving each an identifiable role in research, research and teaching, or teaching only. (There were a number of strong statements made opposing this development). In this context it was noted that academic offerings may nevertheless be limited in various institutions, and differing areas of strength properly acknowledged.

Sub-Topic 1(d)

THE UNIVERSITY'S ROLE OUTSIDE NATIONAL BOUNDARIES

Thursday, 11 February

Professor YUE-MAN YEUNG (*Registrar and Professor of Geography, Chinese University of Hong Kong*):

REFLECTIONS ON THE SOUTHEAST ASIAN EXPERIENCE

In Southeast Asia, where the overwhelming majority of universities was established after world war II, national priorities emphatically take precedence over international concerns. However the first university in the region, the University of Santo Tomas in the Philippines, was founded as early as 1619, and a handful of universities were already in existence in the early part of the present century. All these and later-founded universities have had an international dimension to their work, for even more than two decades ago Silcock (1964:30) observed that: '. . . it is at least desirable that university administrators and leaders should recognize international university extension as something with far more intellectual challenge than extension work within any one country'. This paper will therefore attempt to reflect on the experience of the universities in Southeast Asia in the ways they have affected the affairs and development outside their own countries.

It would be instructive to begin this review with several specific examples. The best example of a university designed to serve a wider purpose other than fulfilling local needs is the University of Hong Kong (HKU). The university was brought into being by Ordinance No. 10 of 1911, which included in its preamble 'the maintenance of good understanding with the neighbouring country of China' as one of HKU's main purposes. This political objective remained part of the legislative instrument until the ordinance was amended in 1958. The idea of HKU serving as a centre of British-inspired education for China persisted. In 1937 a committee reviewing the university's state re-affirmed that 'the true vocation of the University is . . . the training of students from China'. Even after the war the question of whether HKU was to serve local needs alone or to play a wider regional role was raised in proposals to rehabilitate the university. Only financial stringency prevented a more ambitious design to serve the region. However even by 1952 the international role was patently revealed by the distribution of its student population: of its 932 students, 540 came from Hong Kong itself, 158 from Malaya, 177 from China and the rest from 20 different countries (Maxwell, 1980:64, 319–335). Although founded with the maintenance of British prestige in the Far East as a major objective, HKU gradually shifted after the 1950s away from this design and became more firmly rooted in the aspirations and needs of the local community whose capacity for rapid economic growth has been accompanied by an ever-increasing need for expanding higher education.

The National University of Singapore and the University of Malaya can be traced in their formation to a time when co-operation mattered a great deal across national boundaries. When discussion for a new university was in earnest in the 1950s, Singapore was a British colony and Malaysia was a federation of Malayan states who shared the goal of a common university to serve the two lands. After the false start of a new university to be located in Johore Bahru, further consideration of sensitive issues finally led to the establishment in 1957 of a single university, called the University of Malaya but based in Singapore. This was followed by the decision, in view of the imminent grant of internal self-rule to Singapore, in 1959, to create a new University of Malaya in Kuala Lumpur, forming in effect a federal university with the same name in two campuses. The Singapore division was renamed the University of Singapore in 1962. Co-operation between the two universities has since been close but has had its ups and downs as Singapore and Malaysia became a nation in 1963 under the new Federation of Malaysia, only to witness Singapore become an independent nation in 1965 (Maxwell, 1980:291–303). Academic links and exchange cannot be entirely divorced from politics, which is inevitably reflected in the nature and level of co-operation. To quote one example, the well-established *Journal of Tropical Geography* that was launched in 1953 had to be splintered into two separate journals of the same title preceded by their country name in the late 1970s.

However, for a university by design to serve a wider area than a country, one has to cite Nanyang University, which was founded in 1953 with the purpose of providing the Chinese in Southeast Asia with tertiary education in their vernacular. The idea of a Chinese university in a region of vast cultural and ethnic diversities accounted for its rocky start from the very outset, despite strong financial and emotional support by the Chinese in the region. Two commissions in 1959 and 1965 scrutinized academic standards, the curriculum and other issues confronted by the university. In 1968 its degrees were finally recognised by the Singapore government. This achievement notwithstanding, the university's lagging status and falling standards eventually led to its being integrated with the University of Singapore to form the National University of Singapore in 1980. Nanyang University thus was a failed experiment for the purpose it was set. Silcock (1964:67) concluded that: 'Possibly the colonial government ... showed some sense of academic values that need safeguarding. But it showed both too little adaptability to the special needs and pressures of the region'.

If universities themselves proved to be not ideal units to extend co-operation across national boundaries, there has been no dearth of international associations dedicated to this objective. The Association of Southeast Asian Institutions of Higher Learning (ASAIHL) was established in 1956 for the promotion of research and exchange of staff among universities in the region. The Regional Institute of Higher Education and Development (RIHED), formed in 1971 and based in Singapore, has been supporting a series of flourishing inter-university administration workshops. At another level, the Southeast Asian Ministers of Education Organization (SEAMEO) has also been active in promoting research and learning through practical approaches to promoting education. For example Project Impact (an acronym for Instructional Management by Parents, Community and Teachers) was innovated in the Philippines as a viable delivery system for primary education and disseminated in the region, with the administrative support of SEAMEO and funding by the International Development Research Centre (IDRC) for research and training. Another similar activity for the advancement of training and research with the participation of multiple actors has been the very successful training-cum-research awards programme on population called the Southeast Asian Population Research Awards Programme (SEAPRAP), funded jointly by IDRC and the Ford Foundation between 1974 and 1978. In that period a total of 90 researchers had been trained or benefited in other ways from the programme. Finally, in view of the difficulties of creating regional centres of excellence (Maxwell, 1980:80), Singapore went ahead to set up the Institute of Southeast

Asian Studies (ISEAS) in 1968, entirely on its own resources but with an unmistakable orientation towards the affairs of the region. It has now grown to be a throbbing centre of research and academic activities in the region.

There are other geographically more widely-based organisations to which academics and university administrators from the region contribute. Some of these broadly Asian bodies include the Association of Development Research and Training Institutes for Asia and the Pacific (ADIPA) that was founded in 1973 with critical initial funding by IDRC. Its membership grew from 30 to 130 within six years. The Council for Asian Manpower Studies (CAMS), also funded by IDRC, is a grouping of Asian scholars interested in economics and demography, particularly as they bear on manpower and employment issues. The Pacific Science Association is also active in the Asian Pacific rim, where congresses and inter-congresses have been hosted. Almost every major international funding and development agency, such as the Ford Foundation, the Rockefeller Foundation, the Population Council, IDRC, the World Bank, UNICEF, ILO, WHO, etc., has its representative office in Southeast Asia. The Asian Development Bank and the Economic and Social Commission for Asia and the Pacific (ESCAP) are, of course, headquartered in, respectively, Manila and Bangkok. The universities and their staff contribute in various ways to the activities of these international bodies and, in so doing, have extended their influences beyond their national boundaries in indirect but significant ways.

Indeed, if the production of knowledge and scientific innovations are viewed as the central feature of the university, its real environment is the international academic community. It is for this community that the university produces knowledge and it is by that community it wishes to be judged (CERI, 1982:152). In this respect it must be admitted that the universities in Southeast Asia have made significant strides over the past few decades, but progress is understandably uneven across disciplines and countries. There has been a creditable number of new academic journals in the region, but academics still seek, by and large, publication of their quality papers in foreign journals in developed countries. It is perhaps upon this critical need for the production of knowledge and its dissemination and application within and beyond the country of production that future efforts of Southeast Asian universities should focus.

On university research and its potential application, a recent OECD (1984:24) study noted:

'. . . the university of the less industrialized countries tends to be rigid, hierarchic, traditional, and lacking autonomy with respect to their Ministries of Education. University research groups are often so small as scarcely to be viable. There is little or no external demand for academic research, since firms make little use of R and D and lack the capacity to absorb its results'. This verdict is certainly true of many small regional universities outside metropolitan centres, but several of the best universities in Southeast Asia have been making noticeable headway in strengthening industrial liaison, establishing formal and informal networks with firms, and transforming new knowledge into new products, services or processes. The same OECD article reported a wide variety of models in its member countries in which 'matching' opportunities between universities and industry are capitalized, university research is transformed into commercializable knowledge, and patent legislation is enacted to protect inventors. In short the university, together with its wider environment beyond its national boundaries, is managing the change in technology, life and society.

The management of change can be effected across nations through, among other means, international conferences, seminars, workshops, short courses and other non-degree oriented upgrading and training for government officials. To a degree these kinds of activities are being promoted and held all the time, with national and international sources of funding. More work in this direction should be done. As a first step existing centres of excellence must be identified and strengthened, to a point where they can devote some of their efforts and energies to meeting extra-national obligations. The Chinese University of Hong Kong (CUHK), for example, has through its faculty of business administration been helping universities and other bodies in China to train manpower in the latest philosophy and techniques of the discipline.

Academic interchange, not only between universities within a region but between such universities and those in the highly developed countries, has much room for further support and expansion in Southeast Asia. More than two decades ago, when university heads met in Hong Kong in 1966, the then Vice-Chancellor of HKU, Dr. Kenneth Robinson, put forth a convincing case for increased direct and continuous staff interchange links between departments or research centres in two universities, rather than haphazard placing, to promote better informed exchange of ideas and dialogue (Pierson, 1967:26). We are not a great deal better off now in spite of increased support through the Commonwealth Academic Staff Scholarships, the Committee for International Co-operation in Higher Education (CICHE) of the British

Council, ASAIHL, the Luce Foundation, Pearson Fellowships (IDRC) and other awards. Paired university interchange on a sustained basis is yet to be developed but financial constraint is a major limitation.

Taking the role of universities outside national boundaries to its logical extreme, one may suggest that the university should be concerned with transnational approaches to world problems. The university should then be dedicated to finding solutions to major problems plaguing mankind at this time: war, poverty, environmental pollution, maldistribution of natural and human resources, and so on. The role of the university will be a resource centre for non-violent political, social and intellectual change, and political and social revolution of world-wide significance. This train of thought eventually led to the founding of the United Nations University (Smallwood, 1973). Within Southeast Asia a regional university serving the Association of Southeast Asian Nations (ASEAN) was mooted in the late 1970s, with even a large-scale international conference convened in Kota Kinabalu of Sabah, East Malaysia, to consider the proposition. There was considerable initial interest but the practical difficulties were so enormous that the idea was soon dropped. However the closest to being a regional university for Southeast Asia is the Asian Institute of Technology (AIT), located on the outskirts of Bangkok. The beginnings of the Institute can be traced to the time of the Southeast Asian Treaty Organization (SEATO) and it hence has had substantial technical assistance from developed countries. This pattern of financial support remains, although AIT has established a respectable reputation in its delineated fields of specialization, serving the wider Asian region.

Perhaps this essay should be concluded with an insight of Silcock (1964:17) who commented thus about inter-university co-operation:
'Universities exist primarily to propagate the fundamental values of learning by institutions and codes that will insure their survival in different environments. The relations, and the communications, between universities need to be related to this objective; appraisal must be based on sympathetic understanding of different conditions, for only such appraisal will enable the different universities to combine mutual support with flexibility'.

REFERENCES

Centre for Educational Research and Innovation (CERI) (1982): *The University and the Community: The Problems of Changing Relationships*. Paris: OECD.

SUB-TOPIC 1 (D): OUTSIDE NATIONAL BOUNDARIES [*Strangway*]

Maxwell, I. C. M. (1980): *Universities in Partnership: The Inter-University Council and the Growth of Higher Education in Developing Countries 1946–70.* Edinburgh: Scottish Academic Press.

Organisation for Economic Co-operation and Development (OECD) (1984): *Industry and University: New Forms of Co-operation and Communication.* Paris: OECD.

Pierson, Harry H. (ed.) (1967): *University Cooperation and Asian Development* (Proceedings of a Conference of University Heads organized by the Asia Foundation and held at the University of Hong Kong, December 18–21, 1966). San Francisco.

Silcock, T. H. (1964): *Southeast Asian University: A Comparative Account of Some Development Problems.* Durham, North Carolina: Duke University Press.

Smallwood, Osborn T. (ed.) (1973): *Universities and Transnational Approaches to the Solution of World Problems.* Columbus: Office of International Programs, Ohio State University.

Dr. D. W. STRANGWAY (*President, University of British Columbia*): These may be difficult times, but they are also exciting times. The world around us is changing rapidly. We in the universities are contributing to much of the change and are among the major institutions in society that are available to help individuals to deal with change.

In the last few decades we have achieved a great deal. Perhaps as significant as any achievement is the now widespread recognition of the interdependency of the world. A major step was the launching of the first artificial satellite in 1957. A second was man leaving the earth in space vehicles and looking back on our fragile home from the perspective of outer space. Suddenly we all had to recognise that we lived on just one of several planets, a very special one of course, which happened to be located at the appropriate distance from the sun, with water in large quantities above the freezing point, and a gravitational pull 'just right' for development and retention of an atmosphere to provide an environment in which plants and animals could flourish.

Even in this benign environment our condition has not remained static. It has changed over time, life has changed, temperatures and climates have changed. Always there have been natural disasters—earthquakes that damage major parts of the earth; volcanic eruptions that create rich soils, but also block out the sun for months and years at a time; asteroids that have collided with the earth from time to time causing rapid changes in life such as the extinction of the dinosaurs. Continents 'drift' as the giant plates that cover the earth's molten core slowly collide. Our oceans have changed their circulation patterns and our atmosphere is in a constant state of change. Today we understand these processes as never before, as we study the process of global change. Some of the changes are natural and some are of our own making. It is in the universities of the world where much of the study and analysis of these phenomena takes place. It is abundantly clear that we have a challenge of international scale in order to understand such phenomena and to develop the necessary approaches to ensure that we do not irreversibly damage our fragile environment.

Increasingly one of the challenges facing universities is to monitor and to understand our environment and its changes, and to advise our respective governments of these issues. It is largely from university scholars that environmental issues became part of the national and international agendas as we challenge the conventional wisdom. But, of course, it is also the universities that have produced the geologists, the engineers and the chemists who have developed our forest industries, our mines and our great manufacturing complexes. We now know that our industrial processes can affect the upper atmosphere and that this can lead to changes which may not be contained. We have the obligation in our global community to monitor these effects, to understand how they work and to advise on the steps necessary to ameliorate the problem. Universities and governments of many nations must work together to establish national and international policies permitting environmentally responsible development.

Today we have ready access to remote sensing data from satellites that are continually monitoring the vegetation—both natural and cultivated. Information from these satellites is readily available to anyone wishing to acquire access to read-out stations. One university I visited recently in Japan has just such a station of its own and can compile global data. We can all do this and through this means we can expand our capacity to work together toward a more common understanding of the nature of our globe.

The terrible consequences of earthquakes can only be mitigated if we understand them. We can understand them only if we have global networks providing us information on an increasingly reliable basis. Perhaps we will never be able to predict them with a high degree of confidence, but surely we will come to know and understand them better and to learn how to design and to build earthquake-resistant structures in the man-made part of our world.

Wherever we are in the world today we can turn on the television set and get reasonably good weather forecasts. We see satellite

SUB-TOPIC 1 (D): OUTSIDE NATIONAL BOUNDARIES [*Strangway*]

pictures of weather centres moving across the Pacific or the Atlantic or across various land masses. Even this, it seems to me, reminds us that the processes of the earth know no national boundaries. To know what is happening to us we must know what is happening elsewhere. We must have both national and international commitments in studying these large-scale processes. And surely we must come to understand the basic phenomena that lead to these patterns and predictions. This requires international co-operation at an academic and technical level. The role of the international community of scholars is surely a key to this understanding. We are totally interdependent if we are to understand those factors that affect our globe and hence those that affect us. As scientific observing facilities become increasingly costly and complex we must learn to share facilities that cannot possibly de duplicated.

In our country the problem of industrially triggered acid rain is a problem of major proportions as we see lake after lake die in our Precambrian shield. These lakes are already naturally vulnerable due to the presence of acid-rich rocks. This problem affects equally the northeastern United States as we exchange acid-rich industrial pollutants across our border. Resolution of this question is but one example of many similar issues. Governments must be advised by those in the international community of scholars at the technical, the political and the diplomatic levels.

In this way we become critics of government and require them to follow up on the issues we lay out and identify. Frequently governments will seek people from our community to serve on senior panels or advisory boards as they formulate new plans of action. In these groups many diverse and conflicting view-points are present, often struggling with problems that have no simple answer. We talk of responding to the pressures of governments. But I believe the situation is more frequently the reverse, as we develop new approaches, new techniques and require new facilities. Governments must respond to the changing imperatives. We surely demand that governments must be accountable.

There are similar issues as we study and learn more about our oceans. The oceans have global circulation patterns that affect our climates and our way of life. They distribute nutrients which are essential for the chain of natural production that culminates as seafood for human consumption. But these supplies are not unlimited and they can be damaged by our interventions. First, how can we estimate the productive capacity of fish stocks and, second, how can we establish an international approach to ensure that the actions taken are in everyone's interests? When we consider the age-old traditions of fishing far from one's own land mass, reinforced by the modern technology of fish processing and freezing factory ships, we realize that the game has changed. International agreement is essential for wise use of the ocean's living resources.

If we are to understand the biosphere and how it works we must collaborate far beyond our own national boundaries—for without this we cannot come to know our environment and to ensure that it will be sensitively exploited.

There are many dimensions to the questions of universities' roles beyond national boundaries. I have been informed that the increase in life expectancy around the world, for example, is almost entirely due to public health and preventive medicine. On a global basis medical intervention in response to a crisis does a great deal for the individual, but in and of itself clinical practice has scarcely changed life expectancy. Instead improved nutrition, methods of purification of water, preventive drugs and sharply improved methods of sanitation and refrigeration have been responsible for alleviating much human suffering. These again are issues that know no national boundaries. They require study and understanding of the kind that takes place in universities around the world. This study in our institutions is the prerequisite for appropriate national and international action and policy-making. As we come to understand problems we put pressures on our governments. They have no choice but to respond whatever the local fiscal circumstances.

The geological history of our globe is one of environmental change. Today we are the cause of much of the change—some of it beneficial, some of it detrimental, and much of it both. The predictions of the Club of Rome have proven to be hopelessly and unbelievably wrong. How is it that a few short years ago we foresaw the day when we would run out of resources? Were our intellectuals so misinformed or was it that they simply did not understand the interdependency of today's globe? Did we not recognise that man would be inventive enough to find substitutes, that in many cases resources are a question of supply and demand and that lower-grade materials could often be substituted as technology improved? Today we concern ourselves with environmental causes and disasters. The earth can tolerate much environmental insult. It always has—whether natural or man-made. *But* there are some environmental consequences of some of our actions that are dangerous and intolerable. We must work internationally together to establish which these are and develop ways of dealing with them. We must ensure that our respective governments respond to these imperatives.

Increasingly we find reminders that the world is interconnected in many ways. International competition for business is a remarkable example. The invisible hand of commerce is truly international. In the last few years the computer has linked the money markets of the world and changed the ways our offices and our businesses are run. More money is exchanged by computers in fractions of a second than in all the conventional global trading in a day. October 19, Black Monday, was a remarkable example of what the electrical engineers call positive feedback. The very act of creating an interdependent network without appropriate controls and damping leads to instabilities. Is it possible that our economists and our business schools can study this problem and develop methods to advise governments on how to develop stable systems? These are issues that are not unique to any one country. They are no longer even dominated by one or two countries, as money moves around the world to an increasing number of locations with increasing speed. Vancouver seeks to become an international finance centre simply because it can do business with Tokyo, New York and London on the same business day.

All of our countries are increasingly becoming trading nations. This is a necessity in the world of increasing information, of easy transportation and instant communication. As we move more and more to commerce with other countries, it seems to me that we must increasingly understand one another and be able to communicate. More and more we in the universities will become a resource for the study of language and culture of other countries and other societies. More and more this will encompass a knowledge of language and culture beyond parochial boundaries as we become increasingly internationalized.

Exchanges of faculty and students will increase the international network, which will in turn become a major resource for our governments. Governments come and go and change and cannot provide continuity for these international networks. It is to us that they will increasingly turn and deal with on our terms. This is at the core of what universities are about. I fully believe that we will see an ever-increasing role for the humanities and the social sciences as the key to international co-operation and understanding and as the key resource in our national settings.

It is only in the last two or three years that the various provincial and federal governments in our country have come to understand this. After years of squeezing and pressuring us and telling us how irrelevant international students were and that international studies did not matter, they are today recognising our significance and role and are seeking our advice and input in areas that three years ago they considered irrelevant and unnecessary.

Today, at my university, for example, we are building and

strengthening our role in the study of the Pacific nations but this is based on a long tradition that goes back nearly 60 years. Our economics development minister has asked us to provide lists of our international graduates and they are organizing meetings and receptions for them in different countries. We are all also reinforcing our studies of other nations. It is my perception that we will see increasing co-operation and collaboration among universities around the world. It will be necessary if our respective societies are to continue on the present path of internationalization and globalization. It will continue to be our commitment that will be the base for many needed government actions and form the policy base as we interpret and analyse the world not only within national borders but beyond.

DISCUSSION

(*Rapporteur:* Mr. F. T. MATTISON,
Registrar, University of Hull)

In consideration of the universities' role outside national boundaries, four main issues or themes emerged.

(1) The development of inter-institutional links represented one of the most important portrayals of the external role. The impact of these developments on the Commonwealth was considered, and reference was made to the changing pattern of trading partnerships, and the possible weakening of Commonwealth links. However it was suggested that the bond of sentiment remained strong, and membership of a range of different communities was not contradictory. It was further considered that student movement between members of the Commonwealth should be two-way and not, as it rather tended to be, a one-way movement from developing to developed countries. It was noted in this regard that governments expected credits to be transferred, and the failure of universities to introduce a working scheme impaired their credibility.

(2) Should consideration be given to the development of courses for students specifically dedicated to the development of international understanding?

(3) The need for, and difficulty of, determining priorities in research. The expense of some research even renders it necessary to consider the development of specialization on an international level; and co-ordination and management of such programmes is expensive. Who would provide the international co-ordinating agency? While no simple answer was forthcoming, it was important for the universities to be involved in the determination of priorities and the process of specialization.

(4) Interaction of government and university in a research context was not always beneficial. Governments tended to regard scientific objectivity

SUB-TOPIC 1 (D): OUTSIDE NATIONAL BOUNDARIES

and disputes as unacceptable reasons for delay. While cross-national co-operation could become easier through technological advances, the closer meshing of scientific enquiry with industry raised problems of handling intellectual property rights and questions of commercial confidentiality. The pressure for short-term financial gain in relations between universities was recognised and regretted, and the desirability of considering relations in their longer-term setting emphasized. The influence of new technology, especially on distance learning, where there might be a university role outside national boundaries, was stressed.

Topic 1

FINAL SESSION

Thursday, 11 February

During the final panel discussion several issues were examined in greater depth against the background of a question posed by the chairperson: 'Are we trying to regain a nostalgic past-position, or to adjust to a new position? If the ground rules change, does the role of the university as critic change, and do we need to review what we understand a university to be?'

Issues included—

(1) The belief that we can still be a critic even when we depend on others for resources. But we may need to redefine how we do this.

(2) Universities as institutions are to be distinguished from their members—who are intellectuals, academics, experts and citizens.

(3) What are the essential conditions of intellectual freedom? In answering this it is profitable, rather than focusing on generalizations, to consider the 'minute particulars' which will differ from system to system.

(4) In being a critic universities need to give credit as well as blame, and to criticize in such a way that they address possible outcomes and alternatives.

(5) Universities must exercise the highest standards of criticism of themselves.

Topic 1

THE UNIVERSITY AS CRITIC
The Role of Universities in Analysing and Evaluating
Political, Economic and Social Development of their Country or Region

CHAIRMAN'S REPORT ON THE GROUP'S DISCUSSIONS

Second Plenary Session
Friday, 12 February

Dr. WANG GUNGWU (*Vice-Chancellor, University of Hong Kong*): The topic originally had a longer title: 'The role of universities in analysing and evaluating political and economic developments, and social developments, in the countries where these universities are located', but was shortened to 'The University as Critic'. And that, of course, provided us with a bit of a focus and we focused on universities being scientific and objective about knowledge, but at the same time prepared to be directly critical of societies and governments. It is a great idea but there was a question whether this was still a manageable or definable idea that only needed some redefining to meet the needs of our times, or whether this old idea was now at best a meaningless ideal or at most a formula which could lead to dangerous conflicts between universities and governments and the community.

The sessions brought forth many diverse questions, too many for me to try to summarize here. I will simply limit myself to brief comments about each of the sessions.

As usual with academics, the first session gave some time to defining the responsibilities of universities, making it quite clear that the most important factor was that we continue to do valuable research and that we educate and train graduates for our countries.

But of course we recognised that things are changing and that we cannot afford to take anything for granted. Universities are, as we are constantly being reminded, accountable to society and to governments, and at the same time we need to be reminded also that universities should be more directly involved in the community. I think that our staff in particular should be closer to our students, that at the same time we should be providing extension services to the community at various levels and make every effort to communicate to the community the value of what we are doing. And that process of communication would need universities to take more initiatives to demonstrate their worth and educate the community to understand what universities stand for, why their work is essential to a developing, progressive and modern society.

We really got going at the next session on the universities' political role. As you can imagine, this was a little bit more complicated and we recognised that a political role could often be very difficult and very easily misunderstood. There was nevertheless agreement that universities should and do produce citizens, leaders, experts, specialists, and therefore are valuable political institutions in themselves, and their political role should include efforts to preserve qualities like the integrity of a university and its autonomy, a quality which we all agreed was essential for the survival of a university as a university. We all must learn how to do that, and as times change and circumstances change we need to be more alert and certainly not complacent in order that we may defend what is worth defending. And I think in more recent years we have all begun to discover how difficult this is when the old easy confidence, easy trust, between universities and their communities, seem to have been eroded in many countries.

Our third session focused on the social/cultural role of universities and we agreed how important it still is for each university to know its locality and the specific community it serves, and this would certainly include closer identification with the needs of time and place, not simply to be pale imitations of great and famous universities. Each university should invite active local participation particularly of those lay members of our councils. The local community could be helped fully to understand the particular requirements of university students, university graduates and university staff. Certainly the lay members should be more directly involved than has been the case in some places. And of course in places where the university itself is the major industry in the town or the city, bringing employment to people and itself offering distinctive social and cultural values to that locality, the university has an additional responsibility to avoid parochialism or provincialism and also to avoid being too dominant. It has a role to act as a mediator, translating international knowledge to the local area. It was also conceded, a bit reluctantly, that not every university can do everything and that some simply must focus on their areas of strength. But at the same time we also heard very strong statements against the idea that institutions should be graded in some way, divided into those largely for research, those largely for teaching and those somewhere in-between.

Our next session was on the role of universities crossing national boundaries. It centred on how this international role could rise above simply pious hopes and mere expressions of good intentions. The practical problems I think are much more difficult than before but we all acknowledged, without any doubts at all on this one, that the most important thing was to continue to develop strong inter-institutional links across national boundaries. There is a great need to make these links, particularly where staff and student movements are concerned. That is a very good example, I believe, of the kind of need that we must support, and the ACU has done well in this, but we need much more two-way traffic in staff and student exchange. There seems to be a tendency for one-way traffic from developing to developed countries. That is probably unfortunate and we paid particular attention to this point.

We also need, I think, a workable scheme for credits to be transferrable; that is another example of the kinds of problems we still face. We also talked about research. I think that too is an area where international and inter-institutional links are very important. That is very obvious; but this is related, I think, to Topic 2 where research priorities, which we touched on, has been given special attention, so I won't say any more about this.

International co-operation, of course, is vital to researchers in our universities to enable them to analyse and evaluate developments of common concern to everyone. But we were quite realistic in recognising problems of expense and funding, problems of rivalry and competition between institutions, between countries, in fact, and problems which are much more complicated and sophisticated today, problems of the ownership of intellectual property; and for none of these are there any easy solutions. Nevertheless we did believe that universities should be out front there, trying to reduce the obstacles to such kinds of scholarly co-operation.

There was one area, though, where we were quite optimistic. It has been raised elsewhere, I think, and in fact serious planning is being done already to have it implemented. That is in the area of distance learning, in our era of new technology, where the new technology could be employed to overcome some of the traditional obstacles to this form of transmitting skills and knowledge across national boundaries and teaching in new and revolutionary ways for the future. This is being explored. We commend that very strongly and recommend that more ought to be done about this.

In our final session we reaffirmed, as you would expect, that universities should continue to be places where their members could play the role of critic. However, we should be more sensitive and we really need to do a better job and not just carp and scold and be merely negative. Instead we should show ourselves to be knowledgeable, scientific, objective and informative. In short as critics we should not be afraid to write good reviews when they are deserved, and not least, as we ended our sessions, we realized we must be ready to criticize ourselves too, and there are many ways we can do this which have not been tried before.

Let me end on a personal note. I wish to thank the ACU for the opportunity to take part in this excellent Congress. I have learnt a lot personally and am very grateful. Although most of us have never met before, and come from very different parts of the world with very different circumstances, what impressed me most of all when we sat down and started to talk was that we discovered that we talked the same language; not just English, but the same language of universities. We understood each other almost immediately and we found we were talking about the same things; and when we disagreed we disagreed because we valued the same qualities that universities stand for; and I came away much refreshed and encouraged.

Group Discussions

TOPIC 2

THE UNIVERSITY AS A KNOWLEDGE FACTORY

The Role of Universities as Centres for the Advance and Dissemination of Knowledge and for its application in support of National Development

Chairman: Sir JOHN KINGMAN
Vice-Chancellor of the University of Bristol

Chief Rapporteur: Mr. E. C. WRIGHT
Registrar and Secretary of the University of Bristol

		Page
Sub-Topic 2(a)	ACADEMIC LEADERSHIP AND THE MANAGEMENT OF RESEARCH	
	Speakers	
	Professor A. Lazenby	107
	Professor Sir David Smith	112
	Discussion	118
Sub-Topic 2(b)	THE ESTABLISHMENT OF RESEARCH PRIORITIES	
	Speaker	
	Professor Rosie T. T. Young	121
	Discussion	127
	Speaker	
	Professor Don Aitkin	129
	Discussion	133

		Page
Sub-Topic 2(c)	THE DISSEMINATION AND APPLICATION OF THE FRUITS OF RESEARCH	
	Speakers	
	Professor Lydia P. Makhubu	137
	Professor B. J. Ross	142
	Discussion	148
Sub-Topic 2(d)	THE POTENTIAL FOR FURTHER INTERNATIONAL CO-OPERATION OF UNIVERSITIES IN RESEARCH	
	Speakers	
	Professor L. S. Srinath	152
	Professor G. Benneh	158
	Discussion	164
Final Session		167
CHAIRMAN'S REPORT ON THE GROUP'S DISCUSSIONS		170

For index to names, see p. 533

Sub-Topic 2(a)

ACADEMIC LEADERSHIP AND THE MANAGEMENT OF RESEARCH

Monday, 8 February

Professor A. LAZENBY (*Vice-Chancellor, University of Tasmania*):

Leadership and Management

In simple terms leadership involves those qualities needed in formulating a vision or goal for an institution, persuading one's colleagues to embrace it and maintain enthusiasm to work towards the goal even when the going looks impossibly hard. Good management—at least of continuing programmes—requires effective and efficient administration, making the best use of all the resources available, and delivering the goods at the end of the day. Every institution needs both, but the head must provide leadership whilst management of on-going projects can be undertaken by a deputy.

It is stating the obvious to say that universities are passing through a period of considerable and continuing change—*e.g.* in funding levels, and attitudes of government and the wider community to higher education. Increasing intervention with demands for accountability and relevance in the use of funds are now the order of the day. It is important therefore to look at academic leadership and research management in the context of the need for change. *Management for change* demands considerable qualities of leadership.

Leadership style is fundamental to the way things are done; any institution (or department) reflects in one way or another the leadership style of its head. Style is also fundamental to success or failure in reaching objectives. My style is more that of a doer than a fundamental thinker, more concerned to respond to challenges than with underlying concepts and philosophies. In that sense I am an unashamed pragmatist, trying to decide, of the things which seem important at any time, which problems can be solved and where there are real opportunities. I then attempt to take whatever steps are needed to make the most of these opportunities.

To me three things are basic to successful leadership—namely people, teamwork and judgement. People with ideas are fundamental for any good university teaching and research, and I at least believe in backing individuals. Whilst academic leadership involves trying to persuade established staff to work together, it would be a missed opportunity if the head of a university department or a vice-chancellor did not take every chance to appoint individuals at least sympathetic with his general objectives and compatible with his style. It goes without saying that senior staff play a key role in academic and research leadership and I have no doubt that the biggest long-term effect of a vice-chancellor on his university still comes through his influence in appointing professors.

I think it important that individuals feel part of a team, working *with* rather that *for* its head, that each has a clearly defined role in a broader goal and is given his head to use his own style. *But* for continuing support it is necessary that individuals perform. No one has a monopoly on ideas, and an open environment—where people are encouraged to contribute their ideas to the improvement of the overall programme—is likely to lead to an atmosphere of intellectual stimulation and the development of mutual creativity and trust. It is often important for the team to come to the right decision rather than its leader being precommitted to a particular solution. However I've no doubt that the team leader must be not only willing to listen but capable of making a difficult decision and sticking to it.

All of us need encouragement and support, which can be demonstrated in a range of ways from genuine interest in the progress of an individual to the head of the institution doing his utmost to obtain the resources needed for teaching or research activities to be undertaken properly; this may require an initiative either through or outside established channels. It is vital that funds should be available to a vice-chancellor to demonstrate self-help and commitment in the initiation of a project of real opportunity. Further, I believe it is fundamental that institutions have sufficient seeding funds to provide support for an individual or a project of real research potential.

Good judgement is also integral to successful leadership, *e.g.* in deciding which individuals to back, what stance to take on a controversial issue, which potential opportunities to pursue, and which battles to fight and which are a waste of time and energy.

SUB-TOPIC 2 (A): LEADERSHIP/MANAGEMENT [*Lazenby*]

Higher Education in Australia

Reduced government funding, altered patterns of student enrolment, other outside pressures and the recent publication of the green paper on higher education combine to make challenges now facing Australian universities greater than any experienced in my time. The government is clearly determined that Australian universities should make a bigger contribution to the solution of our economic problems, both by increasing the enrolment of students in areas seen to be critical to the achievement of national objectives—engineering, computing and business studies—and by greater emphasis on research said to be more relevant to such objectives.

Whilst not accepting the proposition that it should act the part of the piper having a right to call the tune, I do think that a democratically elected government should be able to use public funds to help choose the music. I am one who endorses the general proposition that universities should play a greater role in helping our national economy.

As to research, I believe that its funding should be on the basis of achievement and that there is some need for specialization and concentration. Greater competition could result in some redistribution of research funds amongst the institutions, and though my own university is not large I am prepared for the research undertaken there to be judged on merit. I am confident that the Australian Research Council will use proper quality criteria as well as relevance to make fair and proper decisions. However I would want to insist on universities having some untied resources to provide seeding funds for new staff and projects with outstanding potential—even in areas not provided with infrastructure funding. I could *not* accept the proposition that some areas in a university be denied for all time the chance to undertake research.

It is clear there are going to be changes. The binary system will come to an end; there will be more competition for research funding; so-called educational profiles will be established for each university—listing courses to be offered and research to be undertaken—and used as the basis of government funding; there will be some concentration and specialization in research; pressures will continue for universities to develop closer collaboration with industry and for industry to assume a greater financial responsibility for funding university activities, especially research. However I for one believe that any change also brings opportunities.

Although firmly believing that as many as possible of the decisions on higher education should be taken within individual institutions, it is a waste of time to fight against changes which are inevitable. However it is a different matter when it comes to *how* such changes should be implemented: it is there where I am convinced that there is a great opportunity to exercise academic leadership both nationally and within individual institutions.

The past few weeks have seen changes both in the organisation of funding for higher education and in the personnel involved. The Tertiary Education Commission has been abolished and all personnel previously involved at a policy level, both in the Commission and in the Department of Education, have now either departed the scene or are about to do so. The loss of their main buffer body, providing independent advice to government, poses a real threat to universities; it is obvious that critical decisions could be made either in ignorance or on purely political grounds. But the situation also provides opportunities. I don't believe there has ever been a better opportunity for the Australian Vice-Chancellors' Committee (AVCC) to exercise national leadership for Australian universities. A constructive, full and united response by the AVCC to the Green Paper, broadly sympathetic with the general objectives of government but with well-argued positions on matters such as funding, participation and access, and research, could have a far-reaching influence. When all is said and done, the minister must take the universities with him if he is to achieve his objectives for higher education.

It is clearly in the interests of individual universities to improve their flexibility by obtaining non-government funds, *e.g.* through co-operative ventures with industry, from full-fee-paying overseas students, for professional upgrading and other fee-for-service courses, and the commercialization of their innovations and inventions. It goes without saying that universities should also take whatever steps are possible to free up some of their resources, *e.g.* by encouraging early retirement and making fractional appointments. However the effects of these measures in providing extra funds will generally be relatively minor—at least initially—and I would be surprised if there are many Australian universities which don't have the task of redistributing part of their funds for priority activities.

The hardest of any university change to make is one involving the redistribution of resources for academic activities. Perhaps the biggest hurdle is to convince staff to admit that there is a problem and that some changes are necessary. I have no doubt that the present changed conditions demand some changes in the way decisions are made and resources are managed—at least in my university, where simplifying academic decision-making, streamlining the implementation of such decisions and evaluating performance all need to be tackled; they all require changes in established patterns. I believe that part of the leadership role of a vice-chancellor is to be the driving force in stimulating, effecting and implementing these changes. A vice-chancellor undertaking these tasks would be unwise to expect too much support from his academic colleagues! Indeed, any vice-chancellor taking an active role in seeking changes can expect a lot of personal criticism: he shouldn't take such criticism too seriously. A sense of humour is helpful and it is important that he always retains his optimism—at least in public.

Producing a long-term plan for a university—determining the balance of resources it wants to put into teaching, research and relations with the wider community and deciding on its strengths and priorities for development—is not too difficult when written in general terms. The problems arise when the proposals become more specific and when it becomes clearer who are likely to be the winners and the losers in the resource distribution. It is surprising then how many arguments can be produced against the need to plan; how difficult it becomes to convince staff that changes in emphasis are necessary. But this is not entirely surprising in an institution where traditionally everyone has been encouraged to do his own thing, and thus where every individual or group is competing with everyone else for money and influence. Those who do best out of the present system are naturally its greatest defenders; further, it is hardly common for staff—even senior academics—to take a university-wide view. In addition it is surprising how many eminent people outside the university can be persuaded to write letters opposing any reduction in their areas of special interest.

Traditionally, in my university, academic decisions have been left essentially to departments with allocation of the resource determined centrally. Currently we are in the process of structural change involving the devolution of responsibility; a small number of resource groups, each headed by a senior member of the university, are planned. This would enable the bringing together of academic and financial decisions and give staff a better chance of seeing and helping determine their own role in the broader context of a university goal; I am hopeful that this, in turn, will encourage a greater commitment of such staff and better implementation of decisions. I believe that by making departments work closely together they would be more inclined to co-operate rather than compete and to take initiatives enabling better use of the resources in teaching and research. Whilst there has been some difficulty in convincing many academics of the need for such structural change, there is now greater realization that some such change is needed.

I am sure that a vice-chancellor has to stress consistently, and often, the positive effects of change and there is no doubt in my mind that arguments have to be backed up by facts and figures. In attempting to manage for change a vice-chancellor needs all the help he can get, inside and outside the university. The use of *ad hoc* groups and committees where he has the majority are not enough when faculties and professorial (academic) boards need to be convinced. In the present climate change is essentially a political exercise for which a political strategy is needed. Not only is it important to have key people on committees but lobbying of those who are influential in decision-making is even more important.

Professor Sir DAVID SMITH (*Principal and Vice-Chancellor, University of Edinburgh*):

Introduction

This paper explores the role of the head of a university in improving and maintaining the quality of the research output of his institution. It is presented from a United Kingdom perspective and deals primarily with scientific research, but it concerns a problem of significance to many Commonwealth countries. The problem derives from the interaction of a number of political and other factors.

(i) As part of its economic policy, the UK government gives unprecedently high priority to reducing the burden of public expenditure.

(ii) The government believes that British universities are very good at basic research, but bad at translating the results into profitable applications which improve national wealth. Funding of basic research does not therefore need to be increased, but universities must be compelled to work much more closely with industry.

(iii) The University Grants Committee (UGC), by means of expert committees, recently assessed the research quality of universities, grading each department into one of four categories: outstanding, above average, average, or below average. These assessments are incorporated into the complex formulae used by the UGC to calculate the amount of grant given to a university. The views of research councils were influential, and especially the number of research council grants awarded to a department. The views of industry were not sought, and income from industry was given little account. This was because research council awards are highly competitive and subject to rigorous peer review, while industrial research money was believed to be less competitive and not such a good indicator of quality. The assessments were widely publicized, but the criteria on which they were based were not. The assessments therefore affected the external perception of *all* activities of a department, *including* its undergraduate teaching, with sometimes unfortunate consequences for academic staff morale.

(iv) Last year, the Advisory Board for the Research Councils published a report entitled *A Strategy for the Science Base*. This took into account a situation in which the demands on the science budget were increasing, but the amount of available resource was contracting. If the UK were to remain internationally competitive, large-scale research groups were required in a growing number of fields. Selectivity and concentration in the allocation of research resource was of paramount importance. The report envisaged that entire universities would be graded into three kinds: type 'R', with substantial research activity and offering postgraduate teaching across most fields; type 'X', with substantial research activity in only particular fields; and type 'T', very largely devoted to teaching and only offering some postgraduate courses with associated research activity but without advanced research facilities. Ominously, the report commented: 'there is a lack of purposeful direction in the redeployment of university research effort, both between and within institutions'. It suggested that the resource which the UGC allocates to universities for research should be transferred to research councils. Type 'R' universities would thus lose their ability to control the strategic direction of their research. The proposed classification has been rejected by the university community, but the competition for research grants is now so severe that there is a slow drift towards a *de facto* classification of this kind, at least at departmental level. The UGC is currently carrying out national reviews of scientific subjects, and this is likely to accelerate the segregation into research and non-research. The report envisages that 'teaching only' institutions would be as well regarded as the major research universities, but the universal belief of the academic community is that some institutions would be considered third-rate, with a consequent loss both of morale and of the better members of staff.

Thus UK universities have become faced with the reality that the quality and quantity of their research output, as assessed in close detail by external agencies, will determine their overall status and have a significant impact on their funding. There are the further pressures to develop extensive research collaboration with industry, accompanied by concern as to how this will affect the traditional role of universities as the principal centres of basic scientific research.

Scientific research in universities is carried out largely by young people at the laboratory bench; they are at their most creative if they are in an exciting research environment where there is the free and rapid interchange of stimulating ideas—the kind of vibrant atmosphere found in a first-class research group. But such atmospheres are delicate, and do not easily survive outside interference by anyone above the level of a head of department. How can the head of a *university* exercise any influence?

In exploring this question I will distinguish between *academic leadership*, which is concerned with strategic issues, and *research management*, which is concerned more with the tactics of achieving the strategy.

Academic Leadership

Some key aspects include the following—

(i) *Making contacts with a view to obtaining substantial increases in external income*. This has always been a traditional role, but it has recently become a lot sharper as the competition has intensified. The vice-chancellor has to become more familiar with the technical details of the research expertise that the university is trying to sell, having to present a convincing image that the 'man at the top' of the university is knowledgeable and enthusiastic.

(ii) *Preserving the autonomy and independence of his institution*. Priorities in university research are being increasingly determined by external bodies which are often primarily concerned with topics believed to have potential application. But universities *are* the principal centres of basic scientific research, and we all *know* that useful innovations cannot be planned and foreseen in the external setting of research priorities. It therefore becomes a prime duty of universities to try to create conditions in which genuinely excellent academic staff can follow their own ideas. But universities can only do this if they have adequate private resources of their own. And this highlights the major importance of building up endowments and other sources of non-government income which are not committed to specific and narrowly defined academic purposes.

(iii) *Clarifying the relationship between teaching and research*. It is a widely accepted dogma of academic life that teaching and research are inseparably linked. We argue that teaching conducted in the ethos of a research environment is somehow better than teaching which is not. However these arguments are becoming less and less convincing to those outside universities (hence the suggestion that universities become classified into 'R', 'X' and 'T'). What is the *evidence* that teaching is better in a research environment, and that it produces graduates better suited to national manpower needs? Most science graduates do not go into research, and most university lecturers spend most of their teaching time on subjects in which they do not research. Few scientists, when they graduate, have detailed awareness of the full spectrum of research carried out in the departments which taught them. Unless we can produce much more convincing arguments that research and teaching are inextricably linked, then university research is at further risk. But we must also be honest: if there really is no close linkage then we must ourselves change our research strategy (or it will be changed for us).

(iv) *Getting the right balance between government- and industry-funded research.* In my own university the total research capacity is becoming saturated. Edinburgh has the fourth largest external grant income in the UK—but the balance is heavily towards government-funded research, which is unprofitable because no overheads are paid. Indeed it can be a financial penalty—last year my university increased its grant income by £5m. but its cash position at the end of the year was £3m. worse off. This is because you can only claim for a grant after you have spent the money, so that one is acting as a temporary banker to the research councils. If we switched more of our research effort towards industry we would make more money, and we would earn some government praise—but would it affect our research assessments, and would it dampen the enthusiasm of the brighter researchers who are attracted by the glamour of basic science and its intellectual prizes (*e.g.* Fellowships of the Royal Society)? Is industrial research, frequently for short-term objectives, good for the long-term advancement of scientific knowledge?

(v) *Interdisciplinarity.* One of the most potent factors stimulating true innovation is interdisciplinary research. Traditional departmental boundaries militate against this, so the breaking down of them is an important tactic for improving the internal climate for innovatory research. Indeed one of the research areas for which my own university enjoys an international reputation is artificial intelligence, which now depends not only on inter-departmental but even inter-faculty collaboration.

Research Management

Five examples of tactical issues in research management will be mentioned.

(i) There must be satisfactory mechanisms for selecting good research. This is achieved in some universities by establishing a central research committee. This mechanism probably operates effectively only up to a certain size of university, and best of all in those with a concentrated, campus-based structure. My own university is large, geographically dispersed over a large area of the city, and with a very diverse range of academic disciplines. A very high degree of budgetary authority is delegated downwards to faculties and it becomes their responsibility to exercise research selectivity. Accountability for this is by private meetings of individual deans with the principal and vice-principals, in which frank and confidential reviews are given of the strengths and weaknesses of each department. Such confidential discussions can be far more useful than the public debates of a research committee.

(ii) Linked with selectivity must be mechanisms for the efficient allocation of money. Some universities use rigid formulae, with factors for numbers of graduate students, technicians, postdoctoral workers, laboratory area, complexity of equipment, etc. Too rigid an application of such formulae may deny the flexibility needed to back quality. Sometimes the use of a formula is balanced by the existence of some type of 'seedcorn' or 'initiative' fund to which all academic staff can submit bids for novel research ideas.

(iii) Facilitating technology transfer and the exploitation of research results. As industrial funding assumes increasing importance an efficient way of interfacing with industry must be developed. In particular good mechanisms are needed to profit from marketable discoveries or the sale of other functions. Some universities put great effort into science parks; others allow companies to arise and proliferate wherever serendipity determines; and some, such as my own, set up a master company to give professional advice and supervision to the establishment of smaller campus companies—and especially to ensure that a reasonable financial return is gained from commercial contracts. There is also a rapid growth of venture capital companies established in various kinds of relationships with universities to exploit campus-based inventions. Edinburgh, for example, has established its own venture company, the university contributing 25% of the capital while three financial institutions subscribe the rest.

(iv) Mechanisms for motivating staff towards all kinds of research must be improved. Promotion procedures should recognise not only the conventional research papers in learned journals but also patents and inventions. Here the greatest obstacles are often senior scientists convinced that weight of publications alone should be the main criterion for promotion.

(v) The research budget must be protected against the demands of teaching when resources are declining. Although academics are, in theory, equally devoted to research and teaching, many departmental committees choose to direct resource towards keeping the full teaching load at the expense of research. A vice-chancellor can benefit research indirectly by emphasizing the need to 'radically reassess teaching methods to make more economic use of the available resource'. In particular, as staff numbers decline, heads of department must be encouraged to protect research time by ensuring that the teaching load of remaining staff is not increased.

Research in Non-Scientific Subjects

Research in non-scientific subjects is faring even worse than scientific research. Universities must not forget their duty as the custodian of cultural heritage, and this is far more often vested in the humanities, social sciences and arts than in the sciences. There is the myth that research in the arts is 'cheap', requiring only libraries, pencils and paper. The reality is that modern techniques, and especially information technology, are spreading rapidly throughout research in the arts faculties. But the available support, in terms of resource, is even proportionately worse than in science. In the UK there are far fewer postgraduate studentships in the arts and humanities, and many are for two years and not three. We have no humanities research council—only the British Academy which, although of great academic prestige, is far poorer than the corresponding scientific body, the Royal Society. A few years ago the Economic and Social Science Research Council became spitefully downgraded by the removal of the word 'Science' from its title, and, more sadly still, by the emasculation of its budget.

One of the most important cultural responsibilities of universities is to ensure the survival of research in the arts and humanities, and especially the preservation of the smaller subjects.

TOPIC 2: A KNOWLEDGE FACTORY

DISCUSSION

(*Rapporteur:* Mr. G. G. WILLIAMS, Secretary and Registrar, Queen Mary College, University of London)

1. *The Need to Clarify the Relationship between Teaching and Research*

Several contributors stressed the inter-relationship of teaching and research and the dependence of one upon the other. Universities blend teaching, pure research and applied research, and therefore it is important that pure research is continued—this distinguishes research undertaken in universities from that in industry (Dr. P. Kenniff, Concordia).

Research work in universities benefits from young, innovative research students working with academic staff—this again is less likely in industry. Teaching enriches research and research improves the content of what is taught (Professor M. W. Thompson, Birmingham).

Sir Alastair Pilkington (Lancaster) said that he recognised that a department's standing would decline if it did not undertake research, but he said some members of staff were good at research and deserved funding, whilst others were poor and consequently deserved little support.

Professor P. L. Wahi (Postgraduate Institute of Medical Education & Research) said that teaching, research and service were all essential ingredients if a medical institution was to flourish in India. Several members stressed the need to make the public aware of the relationship between teaching and research and the importance of research to the advancement and dissemination of knowledge.

Mr. R. M. Mawditt (Bath) said that the universities needed to improve their image and should exert more influence on their local community, industry and clients.

2. *The Need to Examine the Universities' Relations with Industry*

The governments of several countries were demanding closer associations between universities and industry, the increase in research grants from industry and commerce, and more applied work in universities. Some members felt that a stronger challenge should be made by the universities against governments which wished to reduce public expenditure and therefore expenditure on higher education—this point was stressed by Professor H. W. Arthurs (York, Canada).

Concern was expressed about more research funds being routed through the research councils, which could determine national priorities and research being determined by short-term objectives (Professor D. G. Penington, Melbourne). Several contributors expressed the need for a balance to be established between research sponsored by research councils and that sponsored by industry.

Professor C. K. Kao (Chinese U. of Hong Kong) stated that industry was contributing more than ever to research in universities, because it could not cover all areas in-house and because it did not always obtain the most reliable results from ideas generated totally from within its own organization. Sir James Lighthill (University College London) stressed

SUB-TOPIC 2 (A): LEADERSHIP/MANAGEMENT

that interaction between universities and industry was of benefit to both parties and that much effective research resulted from links established with multi-national companies. Sir James said that universities were devoted to establishing the truth, even if on occasions the results of research lead to governments spending more money to remedy a situation.

Several speakers referred to methods used in various countries for judging research and one contributor made a plea for greater recognition to be given to industrial research grants when research assessments were undertaken in future in the UK.

3. Cost of Research

Several points were made in the discussion relating to the cost of research. Sir Alwyn Williams (Glasgow) said that 'death' was in the air for the binary system because the majority of UK degree students were now in polytechnics, where the unit costs for training undergraduate students were 30%-80% (dependent on subject) lower than those in universities. Within 18-24 months universities would be required to determine the cost of research and this could put the dual support system under challenge—money could be transferred from the UGC to research councils.

Dr. R. O. H. Irvine (Otago) noted the situation in the UK but hoped that the two sectors of higher education in New Zealand would remain separate, but that there would be greater co-operation between them in future.

Professor D. W. Watts (Bond) stressed the need for all research to be fully costed and for full overheads to be charged. In response to Sir David Smith's observations that some departments had taken on so much applied research that they had run out of capacity, he stated that this might be because the sponsoring organization had not contributed towards costs of buildings, laboratories, equipment and consumables at the proper rate. Another speaker said that universities often failed to take decisions relating to termination of research projects, so that the resources could be deployed for more useful work.

4. Management of Research

Several contributors stressed the points made by the lead speakers relating to the management of research. They supported the view that research management required the ability to motivate and encourage the creativity of individuals and at the same time to determine the resources that could be made available for various areas which required careful judgement. The need for seed funds to support specific research workers or projects was recognised.

Several speakers said that the most important role in managing research was deciding which areas to develop and which to run down or stop. Reference was made to factors influencing such decisions, *e.g.* national demands, strength of existing research, new professorial appointments.

Professor A. Sale (Tasmania) referred to the fact that industry regularly terminated research projects, yet universities often shirked from making judgements on individuals' performances in research areas. He questioned whether universities were positive enough in this respect and were redirecting sufficient resources to other areas where they could be better used.

Reference was made by Professor M. G. Pitman (CSIRO, Australia) to the need for training in project management, so that research projects and teams were better managed, but it appeared that little attention had been given to this topic in UK universities.

5. *Technology Transfer*

Reference was made by the lead speakers and several contributors to the debate on the development of science parks, university companies, etc., to strengthen links between universities and industry and to promote technology transfer. Mr. J. L. Schlosser (Alberta) doubted the wisdom of universities entering this field—he said that universities were not structured to operate companies in the business world and that they could assume liabilities in fields such as medical research that could damage them financially.

Another speaker agreed with Professor Sir David Smith's view that ventures of this kind did not bring any immediate financial benefits to the institution and in most cases not much money came to central funds.

Although many such companies were being established, Professor H. W. Arthurs (York, Canada) felt that it should not be assumed that technology transfer was the way ahead—all projects should be examined very carefully.

6. *Problems experienced by the Developing Nations*

Professor L. R. B. Robinson (West Indies) said that one of his country's major problems was finding staff of the right calibre to fill the vacant professorial posts and he appealed to the universities in the developed countries to support his university's development through secondments, visits and attachments of staff. He referred to the point raised earlier in the discussion that some staff were active in research whilst others were not, and he raised the question as to whether a heavier teaching load should be given to the latter group of staff.

Dr. J. M. Dubbey (Malawi) said that the problems confronting many of the developed nations were not the ones affecting Malawi. He said that his university was responsible for the national direction of research and that funding was available from international agencies for good projects in the fields of agriculture, health, education and technology. He said that there were only 150 persons with PhDs working in the country and 100 of these were in the university. He said one of the major tasks was to co-ordinate the research work of the academic staff and to encourage the best persons to concentrate on research.

Sub-Topic 2 (b)

THE ESTABLISHMENT OF RESEARCH PRIORITIES

Tuesday, 9 February

Professor ROSIE T. T. YOUNG (*Pro-Vice-Chancellor and Professor, Department of Medicine, University of Hong Kong*):

TO SET PRIORITIES WITHIN A LIMITED RESEARCH BUDGET

A university has two basic functions—teaching and the pursuance of truth through research. Most universities are public institutions and have a third function of providing public service and contributing towards national development. They must respond to the national needs and social changes and be accountable to the community which provides the funding. One may argue that at times of financial stringency it may be necessary for the research function of the university to subsume to that of teaching and that service to the community should take priority over the pursuance of truth. But active research is fundamental to good teaching, and advancement of knowledge will in the final analysis benefit the community. An adequate research base is necessary in order to maintain a lively enquiring academic community which is vital if we wish to cultivate in our students an enquiring mind and a capacity for independent thinking. The existence of good research opportunities will attract able staff. Research also provides an environment suitable for the training of the next generation of high-calibre manpower needed for administration, education, industry and commerce. The fruits of research will produce new knowledge and high technology required for the development of industries and the strengthening of national defence. At times of financial stringency the question is therefore not whether research activities should be curtailed or research budget cut but which type of research should be given more encouragement and support and how the limited human and financial resources can be redistributed to maximize their benefit.

Research activities can be classified into three types:

(1) basic (fundamental) research—undertaken in a free spirit of enquiry, primarily to acquire new knowledge and with no specific application in mind;

(2) strategic research—which is a focusing or intensification of basic research with the objective of developing expertise and/or knowledge in certain areas which it is thought will be required in a practical way; and

(3) contract (developmental) research—which is supported by commercial or government agencies and which aims to employ available expertise, knowledge and other resources in the development of practical applications from the findings of basic research. Nevertheless the three types of research are interrelated.

Basic research is pursued by all departments in a university but more so in the humanities and natural sciences than in the professional disciplines. It contributes towards the intellectual development of staff and students although no immediate benefit is evident from the fruits of research. Initiatives for basic research are usually taken by the individual academic staff and the nature of the research depends very much on the tradition of the university, the interest and quality of the staff recruited as well as the resources available, such as library collection for the disciplines in humanities or laboratories and equipments for the science departments. Support for basic research is the responsibility of every university and this is achieved by the provision of support staff, accommodation and recurrent expenditure from the university general budget as well as a specific budget for research.

By their applied nature strategic research and contract research are mainly undertaken by laboratory-based science and technology departments or professional departments. Contract research is undertaken by agreement between the university on the one hand and the government, industry or business on the other. Its funding is external and excluded from university financial consideration. Very often the expertise required for contract research is only available within the universities. Although the type of research to be pursued is a matter of demand and supply and depends on the 'market' of the time, a comprehensive data base is required for accurate evaluation of the current demand and reliable prediction of future trends. Funding does not come directly from the public but it is generally agreed that government should play a pivotal role to bring the universities and private sector together, to co-ordinate their research activities and provide a forum to establish a comprehensive data base and long-term strategy. It is also desirable that government provides financial assistance to support selective types of contract research to help industries compete in the international market.

Strategic research is a bridge between basic and contract research. It should be supported by government or public funds. Considerable expertise is required to identify the potential areas of strategic research in any locality and to match them with the research strength of the universities therein.

In the unlikely event that universities are adequately funded, it would be an easy task to allocate a generous proportion of the budget to enrich every area of research and to satisfy the healthy appetite of enquiry of the academia. But in real life this can never by achieved and priorities must be set. To search for a better quality of life in an era of high technology, there are good reasons to give preference to applied or strategic research in science and technology. But it would be short-sighted and irresponsible if universities were to lose sight of the importance of basic research in the humanities and natural sciences which is essential for the intellectual development and socio-cultural growth of mankind.

In Hong Kong there are five institutions of tertiary education including two universities* (the University of Hong Kong and the Chinese University of Hong Kong), two polytechnics and one post-secondary college. The University of Hong Kong is the older of the two existing universities. Funding for tertiary education comes almost exclusively from the government through the University and Polytechnic Grants Committee (UPGC) which is the equivalent of the University Grants Committee in United Kingdom.

Research Policy and Provisions at the University of Hong Kong

The University regards the development of research as of prime importance. It encourages the initiative of academic staff to engage in research and supports defined projects, whether the work be basic research or studies of a more applied nature, with specific grants administered by a Committee for Research and Conference Grants (CRCG). But research is not always and at all stages capable of being formed into distinct projects with finite objectives. Departmental budgets for general expenses and equipments are therefore the prime source of funding to support research before the projects take shape. Because of its limited budget the CRCG cannot give substantial funding to any single project. With the additional allocation of a strategic research grant of $20 million

**Editorial note.* A third university—the Hong Kong University of Science and Technology—came formally into being on 10 April 1988.

(US$2·564 million) by the UPGC in the present triennium (1985–88), it became possible to encourage the formation of groups of related projects and to that extent introduce an element of academic directive. Every attempt is also made to attract donations from private sources and external funding from WHO, the International Atomic Energy Agency (IAEA) and Croucher Foundation for specific projects.

(1) *UPGC block grant*. The UPGC block grant provides teaching departments with the infrastructure and 'hidden' cost for research which is difficult to quantify. This includes staff time, salaries for support staff and postgraduate students, general expenses, equipments, library books and journals and accommodation. This is in addition to a small budget administered by the CRCG for defined research projects. For 1986–1987 the CRCG budget was HK$2·86 million (US $0·367 million). Awards were competitive, based on academic merit and feasibility of the project. Because of the limitation of funds projects costing more than HK$100,000 (US$12,820) could only be supported in part and no guarantee for continued support could be given for projects lasting longer than a year. In medicine the projects supported by CRCG in recent years include basic research such as cloning and sequencing of restriction fragments from human long foldback DNA, molecular genetics of thalassemia to more applied studies such as epidemiology of hospital infection in Hong Kong and HLA-typing in Chinese.

(2) *Indicated grant from UPGC for strategic research (1985–88)*. This was a new allocation to enhance research in the universities and polytechnics in Hong Kong and was made in response to Lord Flowers' report on 'Basic Research in Hong Kong's Institutions of Higher Education' (1983). The budget of $20 million (US$2·564 million) for this triennium is used to fund projects which meet the 'strategic research' criteria described above.

A strategic research committee was established in the University in 1985 to set the objectives, receive applications, assess and decide the grants to be made and to monitor progress. The committee works in conjunction with two specialist panels—laboratory based and non-laboratory based—in the allocation of grants. Each proposal is subjected to vigorous scrutiny, evaluated both on academic merit and on adherence to the University's established criteria for strategic research. Projects satisfying these criteria are sent for external assessment, often overseas, by recognised experts in the field. Since its inception the committee has considered a total of 75 applications and approved 35 grants. In 1985–86 projects related to manufacturing industries received 32·8% of the total allocation, environmental studies and geotechnics 31·6%, biotechnology and health 21·9%, education 7·4%, linguistics 2·9%, international business studies 1·8% and political science 1·6%.

In 1986–87 the distribution is: health and biotechnology, 35%; computer and computer-aided design and manufacturing, 33%; ergonomics, 16·7%; environmental studies, 6.6%; comparative economic studies, 4·2%; public administration, 2%; historical studies, 2%; and sociological studies, 0·5%.

(3) *Private donations*. The University has been fortunate to receive substantial donations from private individuals, and organisations from time to time. The donations are invested by the University and the income generated is used to support research. More often than not the donors specify fields of research for which the donation is intended. Despite this limitation private donations have not only strengthened research in these specific areas but also released funds to supplement the inadequate UPGC funding for research in the University as a whole.

(4) *External funding*. This includes grants made by external organisations such as WHO, IAEA and Croucher Foundation for specific projects.

(5) *Contract research with government, industry, business*. Regrettably there has been very little large-scale contract research going on between the universities and the industries in Hong Kong. Earlier this year the government, on the advice of Industry Development Board, awarded a grant of $4·2 million (US$0·54 million) to the two universities for the development of CAD/CAM programme for the local manufacturing sector. A committee for science and technology is being planned with the aim of identifying potential areas of research and development in science and technology which will benefit industries in Hong Kong. This will increase the opportunities for collaborative research between the universities and industries.

In the next triennium, 1988–91, the strategic research grant allocation by UPGC will be replaced by a research budget of HK$120 million (US$15·385 million) to be administered by a UPGC research subcommittee. It will support both basic and strategic research and awards will be made to projects submitted by the five higher institutions in Hong Kong on a competitive basis. This will establish for the first time a 'dual support' system for research in Hong Kong.

The teachers in the University respond to this new scheme with unsurpassed enthusiasm. Most faculties have established research committees to (*a*) identify areas of research strength or development in the faculty and encourage the formulation of appropriate projects and (*b*) advise staff members on the preparation and presentation of research proposals to meet the standards expected by funding bodies. I am confident that the injection of $120 million (US$15·385 million), though modest by international standard, to support basic and strategic research in Hong Kong will enable the universities to strengthen further those areas of research already identified as excellent, as well as embarking on new projects in which the universities see a clear potential for development.

With the exception of contract research, whatever the source of funding and whatever the disciplinary focus, grants should be made on the basis of the academic worth of a proposal, the soundness of methodology and the potential significance of the results to the world of scholarship. When funds were extremely limited only less expensive and short-term projects could be supported to permit staff development in the subject and to encourage a spirit of active enquiry in the University. With recent increase in research funds it has also been possible to introduce an element of academic directive to encourage the formation of groups of related projects, to allocate seeding money to research in entirely new fields and to encourage an extension of the scope of work undertaken in the University. While a number of the on-going research projects are collaborative efforts with other organisations, hitherto there have not been many occasions of collaborative research with other tertiary institutions in Hong Kong. To maximize the effective use of public funding more efforts must be made to establish interdisciplinary as well as inter-institutional collaboration in research.

At all times the University must put a high priority on research, basic and strategic, in the humanities, natural sciences and professional disciplines. It must identify its strength and potential in research and build on its areas of excellence. It must search out areas of potential growth and strategic importance to the community and nation to which it belongs. It must encourage academic freedom and not stifle individual initiatives. But at the same time it should introduce an element of 'academic directive' where appropriate and be prepared to give guidance to the academics to focus on selective areas of research. Even with a limited budget it is possible for a university to encourage its staff to build up their research experience and at the same time concentrate on a limited number of areas for substantial development.

SUB-TOPIC 2 (B): RESEARCH PRIORITIES

REFERENCES

The Future of University Research. Organisation for Economic Co-operation and Development, 1981.

Report of a Joint Working Party on the Support of University Scientific Research. Advisory Board for the Research Councils/University Grants Committee; H.M. Stationery Office, London, 1982.

Session 1986-87: *First Report on Civil Research and Development.* Select Committee on Science and Technology; H.M. Stationery Office, London, 1986.

Report of the Research Working Party on 'Basic Research in Hong Kong's Institutions of Higher Education.' Lord Flowers (unpublished), 1983.

DISCUSSION

(*Rapporteur*: Ms. CHRISTINE SHERVINGTON, Archivist, University of Western Australia)

Dr. D. J. E. Ingram (Kent) voiced the need to stress to politicians the fact that universities do produce better trained people generally, not just researchers.

Sir Edward Parkes (Leeds), in commenting on Professor Young's paper, questioned whether Hong Kong as a paradigm of a small country with a number of tertiary education institutions is self-sufficient. He made the points: (i) that as 1997 approaches it appears that Hong Kong, by trying to improve the standard of English, is acknowledging the value of links with English-speaking countries; and (ii) that as a small country with a large population and six tertiary institutions, three of which are universities, the economy needs to encourage inter-institutional co-operation.

Dr. C. E Young (California, Los Angeles) expressed concern at the thrust of discussion, relating back to the topic and sub-topic titles, stating that in the context of the discussion this implied a difference of approach between the universities and the environment that supports them, with consequences for the autonomy of the university. He believed the attempts to use the universities as mechanisms primarily directed to the production of an end product usable by industry for the economic development of a country is destined to failure. The danger is, if the production of 'products' becomes the main aim, universities will be judged to have failed. Universities currently contribute to the economy as educators training graduates such as engineers who go out into the economy to undertake the applied work and produce the 'products'.

Professor L. Finkelstein (City) supported Professor Young's argument. He made the following points: (i) it is only in universities where free interaction exists that interdisciplinary projects can be explored; and (ii) the results from fundamental research are different from the results of applied research.

Dr. Chia-Wei Woo (Hong Kong U. of Science and Technology), in

TOPIC 2: A KNOWLEDGE FACTORY

supporting Professor Young warned, however, that it is important to take into account the stage of development of a country when discussing the relationship between universities and government. For instance the USA is different from Hong Kong where the public sector and universities can work closely together because of geographical and historical differences.

Dr. M. Horowitz (Alberta) expressed disappointment at the fact that, as a group, the ACU had lost the passion that it demonstrated at the 1981 conference; it is not exhibiting the kind of leadership it should be exhibiting, rather is too busy worrying about what politicians expect of it. The aims of the group have not changed, nor should they.

Professor C. K. Kao (Chinese U. of Hong Kong) referred back to the discussion on Hong Kong, and stressed that the country does have lots of talent, and in its function as a service centre for the world and its increasingly important role as the gateway to the Pacific region has demonstrated that it does want to be much more involved with the external world.

Professor J. M. Ashworth (Salford) commented on the fact that the university sector still exhibits passion at the point when change is about to occur. For example, in the United Kingdom the value of a centrally planned bureaucratic research funding body is now being questioned, and the government is favouring a situation where market forces determine research priorities. He pointed out that this has aroused passion because universities are worried about how they will adapt to the new system.

Professor D. G. Penington (Melbourne) in commenting on the Australian situation made the point that it is an Australian trait to cut down tall poppies and to place no great emphasis on intellectual endeavour. Owing to the current major balance-of-payments crisis in the country the new Australian Research Council will be heavily weighted towards industry, not towards academic endeavour. Reaction from within the university sector against this situation carries no weight. There is a need to shape priorities via public opinion and a need to speak to the community in terms they can understand to force this to happen. There is also a need to look to longer-term solutions, something that is a problem with short-term governments.

Colonel G. S. H. Dicker (East Anglia), as a lay member of his council, agreed with this need to educate the general public, and another delegate stressed the need to instil in graduates pride in their education and institution.

Dr. D. Harrison (Exeter) reminded the meeting that this session was about research not undergraduate study.

Dr. R. C. Atkinson (California, San Diego) commented on the fact that much time in the 1970s was devoted to selling research to industry, and, while there was no question about this link between universities and industrial research, this emphasis did raise the problem of universities being viewed as 'job shops' and created an uneasiness that universities will be judged on external criteria.

Professor J. F. Scott (La Trobe) agreed that this feeling of unease exists and that there was a need to change the image of universities and a need to look for new ways to fund universities and research. He believed it was a time to question: he did not blame governments for questioning where the money is spent; and questioned whether the PhD

SUB-TOPIC 2 (B): RESEARCH PRIORITIES [*Aitkin*]

degree by research is the best way to train students for research in commerce.

Dr. W. A. Pullman (Western Australian Post-Secondary Education Commission) questioned the origins of the advice to governments regarding the allocations of money for research, and offered several amusing hypotheses in answer.

Thursday, 11 February

Professor DON AITKIN (*Interim Chairman, Australian Research Council*): From the perspective of a national government the setting of priorities is a normal, daily, routine affair. Indeed the central business of government *is* the setting of priorities—choosing between alternative ways of achieving public goals, putting 'today', 'tomorrow' or 'sometime' against proposals all said to be of great urgency, rationing scarce resources. From a government perspective research is simply another resource-consuming activity, whose proponents advance strong but incommensurable arguments for every kind of research: medical research comes with a life-or-death implicit choice; energy research foreshadows the exhaustion of national fossil fuel reserves; humanitites research, like astronomy, addresses fundamental questions about our existence and stops us lapsing into materialism and barbarism; biological research may enable us to solve the problem of how to feed the world; research in physics helps us unlock the nature of matter; social science research may in time provide better functioning economies, more democratic policies and more humane and efficient criminal justice systems. All these research activities cost money, the great bulk of it public money. On the whole, and understandably, governments prefer to fund research that is likely to have some kind of tangible return. But even then resources are limited, and research is always a gamble—otherwise it would not be interesting.

When research was a minor activity, governments were not much involved in its funding. Since the second world war its importance has grown to the point where in a number of countries around 3% of gross domestic product is employed in research and development; by the end of the century the proportion may be past 5%. Governments everywhere provide a major proportion of the funds, and are asking, and will go on asking, for better systems of financial control and for some kind of workable system of research priorities.

For the university world requests of this kind are hard to respond to, for a variety of reasons. First, universities do much of the 'basic' or 'fundamental' or 'curiosity-led' research (these terms are essentially synonymous) that goes on in any society; such research usually has no immediate pay-off, and in general if there is one you can only point to it after the event, sometimes long after the event. Imposing priorities on basic research is not a straightforward business. The most widely used one is the excellence of the researcher and his or her proposal, judged by a peer group or other researchers. But peer-group assessment has obvious weaknesses and its greatest asset is credibility within the research community.

Secondly, universities practise parity of esteem. Officially, and necessarily, research inside the university walls is of equal importance so long as it is equally excellent. Of course, research in engineering or physics or chemistry costs more than research in history or classics, but it is not thought to be more important for that reason. In Australian universities, and commonly in those elsewhere, salaries, appointment levels, promotional criteria and honour are related to excellence in research performance, but not at all to the research field itself. Even in the United States, the metropolis of free enterprise, the size of the research budget does not greatly affect the size of the researcher's salary.

Thirdly, in most universities research is now an activity that is hard to separate from teaching. Although I do not myself believe that good teaching *requires* a lively research activity, let alone that good research requires a body of undergraduates close by, I concede that a university teaching activity that was known to be quite unrelated to research would be generally regarded as intellectually inferior. Whatever discipline or area a university is prepared to offer to students, therefore, it will feel constrained to encourage research in it.

The understandable urge by governments to establish priorities in research has, therefore, been met by reluctance and even hostility on the part of universities. In Australia, as in Britain, the resulting hostility has been exacerbated because of the fact that the universities' funding includes a large but not precisely identified element for research: discussions about research priorities, when the university world is involved, quickly become discussions about university funding and university management. University people tend to take up intransigent positions on these matters: teaching cannot be separated from research, even conceptually; performance indicators for research are hopelessly flawed; national priorities require national goals and national goals are intrinsically vacuous;

if priorities are to be set the mechanism must be 'bottom-up' because only researchers know where the possibilities lie; and so on. The consistent message is 'touch me not!'.

Yet touched the universities are, and will continue to be, so long as they depend on the government for the greater part of their income. A sensible ordering of priorities in research is not beyond the wit of man, and I have no doubt that we will achieve one in Australia before very long. Nor is it hard to see what the elements of such an ordering might be. I offer the following as a possible conspectus.

(1) Since Australia is getting relatively poorer rather than relatively richer, government is naturally interested in research that would quickly improve our balance of payments or our competitive position in international markets. Such research would relate to our plant and animal industries and to mining and mineral processing. Given our heavy imports of electronics, it would also relate to the information sciences. As it happens we are much more conspicuous in the world for our research in biology than for our research in, say, physics. From the perspective of national priorities, a relative prominence in the biological sciences is appropriate.

(2) No university can unilaterally adapt itself to national research priorities by an act of imagination. For one thing a national research policy is built on knowledge of what is being done, and not being done, right across the nation. In Australia the problem is compounded by great distances and a federal political system. There will be more duplication in Australia in research activities than might be thought necessary in a small, unitary nation, and that should be accepted rather than resisted. Nonetheless universities need to emphasize their particular strengths rather than endeavour to be excellent at everything. Only then will it be possible for those developing a national research policy to see where the strengths and the weaknesses of the whole country are, and propose policies to build on the first and overcome the second.

(3) It will be important both for government and for the universities not to pay so much attention to present national needs and presently strong performers that the future is overlooked. Australia needs to overcome its historic economic dependence on unprocessed primary products and minerals. It must once again become decently strong in manufacturing—but manufacturing what? And if—as is urged—that 'what' is in the high tech area, what kinds of research will be needed to support it? Our current research funding arrangements favour the proven performers and the established research fields, and that remark applies to universities no less than

it does to external research-funding organizations. We need new mechanisms for paying attention to the future, making decisions about areas, and backing those decisions with funds. Given the importance of young researchers in changing research directions, we need to be able to fund the best young researchers even when what they want to do is tangential to current research programmes and they themselves lack track records.

(4) In all of this the role of the newly established Australian Research Council (ARC) will be central. One half of its task will be research granting, the other half research strategy. The first requires expertise that is readily available through the granting bodies subsumed in the ARC. The second requires the development of a partnership between the ARC and the universities, in which selectivity and concentration will be the key concepts. A national research strategy will affect all aspects of research in universities, including the location of expensive facilities, the provision of postgraduate training, and of course the availability of research funds. It will involve a great measure of 'bottom-up' contributions and plans, but the final decisions, particularly where concentration is involved, have to be made at the top.

(5) In all of this I have been talking essentially of basic research, for that is what universities principally do: applied research is usually an add-on, undertaken because there is someone outside who is prepared to pay for it. The role of the ARC is not to turn basic researchers into applied ones but to achieve a measure of planning in the field of basic research. Are there important areas of basic research where we are weak, and should be stronger? Are there other areas where our work, though of good quality, is less important than it once was? I am not talking about turning people trained in one discipline into practitioners of another, though it would be generally useful if retraining and mobility were in greater provision than they now are. But in the era of growth heralded by the Green Paper some areas of basic research are likely to advance rapidly, others to be held relatively constant. The Council has the task of advising what those areas ought to be.

(6) The balance in funding between research which is thought to be of national priority and that which is supported because of its intrinsic merit will have to be determined. At least in the beginning it is likely that the ARC will follow a common overseas model, and keep national priority research funding to about 15% of available funds, the remainder going, as hitherto, to research projects and programmes whose excellence is attested to by experts in the fields. One reason for doing so is that priority research can have an imitative air to it: a number of European countries have

SUB-TOPIC 2 (B): RESEARCH PRIORITIES

priority programmes in alternative energy sources or biotechnology or information science. It is hard to see how any of them can derive comparative advantage by doing so.

A second reason is that we do not know where the next scientific breakthrough will occur. We did not predict superconductivity, and are not likely to be wiser in these matters than our colleagues overseas. A heavy emphasis on national priority areas for research might be an act of national hubris, no matter how well-intentioned or well-argued it is. A third reason supports the first two: we want to attract the best researchers and the best students to national priority areas. We cannot do this if there are too many such areas, or if the designated areas are less intrinsically interesting than mainstream areas. And of course basic research supplies the training and the breadth that applied researchers need to bring to their task.

In short, the policy needs to be one of 'little by little' and learning through experience. We have had for the last few years a national priority area in marine science and technology; it will be useful and instructive to explore what has been learned in this area about the business of priority research.

It would be easy to caricature this process, and assert that nothing whatever should be done until the question of national research priorities has passed a serious intellectual scrutiny in which all interested parties will have had their say. And indeed there have been calls of this kind already. But that won't do at all. It presumes that the current dispensation is satisfactory—that the pattern of research in Australia's universities, which is in large part an artefact of the courses that universities have decided that their undergraduates should take, is somehow close to a national optimum. It isn't, of course, and that is why the search for a priority policy is under way, and why a successful outcome needs the kind of partnership I have described. I believe it will be possible to achieve that partnership, and to do so much more quickly than has been expected.

DISCUSSION

(*Rapporteur:* Dr. A. W. ROBERTS, Registrar and Secretary,
University of Wales College of Medicine)

In his presentation Professor Aitkin had stressed four points: first, that there had hitherto been no tradition of establishing research priorities on a national scale; that the new Research Council of Australia would seek to do so in the future; that the task would be difficult because priorities were not immutable; that the Council's policy would therefore be to advance 'little by little' and learn by experience; and while some priority would be given to supporting those research areas most likely to enhance the country's economic performance, most of the funds at the Council's disposal (about 80%) would continue to be devoted to 'curiosity value' research, subject to peer group assessment.

In the discussion that followed two issues predominated: the determination and implementation of research priorities; and the relationship between teaching and research in universities.

(a) The Determination and Implementation of Research Priorities

Sir Alwyn Williams (Glasgow) reported on recent attempts to tackle these issues in the United Kingdom where the emphasis was on the creation of a relatively small number of centres of excellence within the university system rather than attempting to spread expensive research facilities across the board. Using a UGC review of the earth sciences as a prototype, the Advisory Board for the Research Councils had produced a 'Strategy for the Research Base', one of the main features of which was the classification of whole universities according to what might be considered the level of research effort appropriate to them. This approach had, inevitably, aroused considerable controversy during which fundamental questions on the nature of universities were posed.

Professor Joan Foley (Toronto) offered an alternative approach which had been adopted with some success in Ontario. Here the government had encouraged universities to collaborate in the submission of joint proposals for research funding thereby exploiting the strengths of individual institutions to best effect. While few universities could be expected to be excellent in everything, most had acknowledged strengths in some areas.

For Professor J. M. Ashworth (Salford) the problem with what he had so far heard that morning was that accounts had been given of how research priorities were being determined centrally, in a bureaucratic system the prime instinct of which was inevitably to act conservatively. He welcomed the impact of market forces on the formulation of priorities and referred to a major initiative in the field of robotics in his university as an example of what could be achieved with a combination of public and private funds.

Dr. G. J. Hills (Strathclyde) expressed doubts about universities becoming over-committed to market-forces-led research because the 'shelf-life' of knowledge was relatively limited and priorities were bound to change. Others, including Professor M. G. Pitman (CSIRO, Australia) and Professor D. W. Watts (Bond) had no such fears about the effects of applied, or mission-orientated, research on the university community, particularly if proper feasibility studies were conducted beforehand and provided that academic standards were not compromised. Such research

SUB-TOPIC 2 (B): RESEARCH PRIORITIES

still enabled universities to perform one of their fundamental roles, that of education and the transmission of research skills.

Referring back to Professor Aitkin's presentation Professor P. D. Hajela (Doctor Harisingh Gour) commented that basic research had to be geared to the industrial and economic environment of the country in which that research was being carried on. In the Indian context therefore, although space research and other high technology research was being pursued, the vital need was for research relevant to India's demographic situation. In other words what was required was research the effect of which would be to employ a vast population, 70% of whom were involved in agriculture.

In his description of the various research-funding agencies in India Dr. K. H. Cheluva Raju (Gulbarga) referred to current demands for more decentralization of research funding to the regional or state levels to ensure that funds were used to best effect.

Professor L. Finkelstein (City) was concerned that in their quest to identify research priorities and to emphasize the relevance of universities within their communities the group might lose sight of what he believed to be the primary role of universities. The priority that every university should fix for its own research was the creation of teachable subjects. It was through the creation of teachable subjects, the acquisition, interpretation and systematization of knowledge and its transmission to students, that universities made their greatest contribution.

(b) The Relationship between Teaching and Research in Universities

As an introduction to this theme Professor Sir David Smith (Edinburgh) reviewed some of the arguments in favour of, and against, the general proposition that teaching and research were indissolubly linked in the university context. He stressed that some of the arguments for linkage were stronger than others and if, as he believed, teaching and research at university level were indeed inseparable, the universities had to be prepared to defend the proposition.

There was, within the group, general agreement with the proposition articulated by Dr. Chia-Wei Woo (Hong Kong U. of Science & Technology) that universities should be environments of learning, where teaching and research were pursued hand in hand.

That did not mean that every university teacher should be actively pursuing research all the time. Indeed some teachers did not pursue research in the accepted sense but their teaching was, as Mr. G. J. G. Vines (Deakin) suggested, enriched by personal experience of the subject they taught (*e.g.* management, civil engineering). Others, in the view of Professor J. M. Ashworth (Salford), might have run out of steam in the research sense but were still able to contribute very effectively as teachers.

A number of Canadian members of the group reported on the high priority placed on excellence in teaching in the universities of their country. Dr. M. Horowitz (Alberta) referred to the establishment of a Centre for the Improvement of Teaching and Learning at his institution.

Nevertheless it was accepted by all participants that the pursuit of basic research and scholarship must be an essential feature of every university, not necessarily to produce results of immediate relevance to the domestic economy but because it would inculcate in its members, staff and students alike, an appreciation of the importance of acquiring a spirit of independent and critical enquiry, a point made by Professor Lim Pin (Singapore) among others.

Moreover Dr. D. J. E. Ingram (Kent), Mr. H. W. Try (Brunel) and others emphasized the need to convince the community of the importance of the universities fulfilling these roles. It was vital to get over to the students, many of whom would be the opinion-formers and decision-makers of the future, the extent to which the teaching received from their teachers was nourished by involvement in research (though this might not immediately be apparent). The lay members of university councils had an equally heavy responsibility to sell the virtues of the university system to the outside world.

However, as Sir Alwyn Williams (Glasgow) pointed out, if it was generally agreed that students were the better for being nurtured in a research environment one should not dismiss the claims of non-university institutions of higher education to a share of the resources required to pursue effective research. Apart from Professor E. P. Bachelard (Australian National) who opposed any blurring of the binary line, no other member of the group pursued Sir Alwyn's challenging proposition.

Sub-Topic 2(c)

THE DISSEMINATION AND APPLICATION OF THE FRUITS OF RESEARCH

Tuesday, 9 February

Professor LYDIA P. MAKHUBU (*Acting Vice-Chancellor, University of Swaziland*):

Introduction

This paper presents activities of many research and development institutions in Africa in the past three decades and discusses factors which have influenced their efforts to reach the end users of their research results. Although the observations are based on the areas of science and technology they are sufficiently general to apply to the human and social sciences.

The potential of research to provide solutions to problems in the key sectors of agriculture, health, rural development, industry, etc., was long acknowledged by African governments[1,2]. Despite limited resources many countries have set up bodies to monitor and direct research and also built institutions to focus on designated priority areas. Universities, which in many countries represent the highest concentration of research competence, have accepted the mandate to conduct both basic and applied research of relevance to their countries and region[3].

What is of greatest concern to governments and researchers alike is how to provide adequate resources to create dynamic research programmes and how to utilise the results of research in the effective solution of the urgent problems which are plaguing the continent. In addition there are large amounts of research data accumulated in other parts of the world, especially in developing countries with similar problems, which could be translated and adapted for dissemination and utilisation under local conditions. The question is how to adapt, disseminate and utilise this information. Before examining these issues it might be useful to discuss briefly the status of research in Africa.

Research in Africa

There are many obstacles to the growth of healthy and stable research programmes in Africa, and these reduce the amount of research results that can be generated and also weaken the process of dissemination and utilisation. In spite of this general problem some countries have managed to build research institutes of high calibre, which demonstrates that the potential for excellence exists in the continent when the right approach has been followed and the necesary inputs provided.

The following are some of the key inhibitors of progress in this area:

1. *Inadequate funding*. In terms of global statistics the African continent shows the lowest investment in research and development (R&D) by national governments[4]. Many research projects of direct relevance to development are externally funded and even co-ordinated by foreign experts, factors which can limit national influence on the appropriateness and direction of research. This low level of investment in R&D is translated into poor remuneration and conditions of work for researchers, which diminishes chances of attracting and retaining high-calibre personnel who are prerequisite to the creation of a dynamic research environment[5].

2. *Manpower for research and development*. Recent statistics show that although many countries have made great strides in the training of scientific and technical manpower in the past 30 years much still remains to be done to develop a strong research cadre which will make research a full-time occupation. A large number of those engaged in research are either university employees or hold other positions. The statistics also show that there are more researchers in the natural sciences, agricultural sciences and social sciences than in engineering and technology, the two areas most vital for the application of the fruits of research[6].

Data on sectoral employment indicates that higher education is the largest employer of scientific personnel in many countries and that of those employed in the productive sector few are engaged in research which is linked to production. These facts are a few indicators of the problems of manpower for research and development which hamper the utilisation of research results.

3. *Technological dependence*. Dependence takes various forms.

(i) Dependence on approaches of industrialized world in setting up institutions has been cited as a crippling factor which has caused the isolation of the research establishments from the concerns of the majority of the population. Once the institutions have been built, sometimes with considerable international assistance, a theme selected, they are supplied with equipment and personnel and then conduct research which does not influence the people in any significant way[7].

(ii) Dependence on the importation of equipment and spare parts, often at high cost, places severe strain on already meagre resources and limits the type and pace of research that can be undertaken. In addition lack of essential analytical equipment sometimes necessitates the sending away of samples for simple routine analysis so that rate of production of results is generally slowed down.

(iii) Publications of all types can be a definite handicap where a researcher must await the arrival of a reprint before following a procedure that is crucial to the whole experiment. This is an important consideration because many researchers work virtually alone in their areas of specialization and cannot depend on peer support.

4. *Inappropriate research and development.* One of the reasons frequently quoted for the poor dissemination and utilisation of research results is the failure properly to identify the needs and conditions of the users. The problem is exacerbated by the diversity of the users who are to be found in the 'modern' and 'traditional' sectors, as well as in the rural areas where the majority reside. All of these are set in different conditions and exhibit different concerns and patterns of consumption.

Research in its present state is said to address mainly the modern sector and barely to address the issues affecting the majority. It therefore fails to make the necessary impact on governments and to stir popular understanding and support[9].

From these few observations it may be concluded that priority must be to strengthen the status of research in Africa if it is to generate results on a stable and continuous basis. However while this long-term process is proceeding existing institutions could contribute to its success by initiating active and aggressive campaigns to disseminate their objectives in order to stimulate the interest of governments, industry and the public. Although the following suggestions have been discussed in many fora they remain valid and will be explored in the remainder of this paper, in the context of the topic.

1. *Creating an awareness of the potential of research*[8,9]. In times of scarce resources, research, which is often long-term and costly, is forced to compete for funds with projects which offer quick answers to urgent problems. Research institutions must make the raising of awareness of the importance of research a part of their activities.

This means acquiring a clear understanding of the problems that require research, assessing the needs of the end-users and demonstrating their own capability to offer solutions to the problems.

This exercise could be done as follows:

(i) RESEARCH EXTENSION OFFICERS. Extension officers in agriculture, nutrition, public health, social welfare, have been very effective in disseminating the results of research to all levels of society and in obtaining a feedback on end-user reactions. Perhaps the 'extension officer' should become a member of every research team. Such an officer could be a highly skilled individual who could provide 'on-the-spot' solution of problems for end-users, a service which could enhance the users' confidence in the researcher's capabilities and facilitate dissemination and eventual utilisation of results.

Such an activity could also have the advantage of providing 'on-the-spot' reactions on other aspects of an innovation. For example many research findings designed for rural people have been rejected because the researchers had failed to take into account conditions such as technical proficiency, capability to purchase innovation and numerous others which a research extension officer can determine on a face-to-face contact.

(ii) RESEARCH PROMOTIONS' GROUPS.

- Interdisciplinary research groups. While science and technology may be key to development, success in applying them is usually determined by socio-cultural factors, making interdisciplinary interaction important in the design and execution of research projects as well as in the dissemination of results. The groups could incorporate influential members of society who may assist in the dissemination of the objectives of the research.
- Liaison groups. These may be more valuable where large industries are concerned. Their main role will be to provide a forum for a continuous exchange of information on new processes, new approaches, new technologies, etc., between industry and the research centres. The same groups could arrange staff exchange to enable industry and research establishments to gain greater insight into each other's expectations. It has also been suggested[8] that this liaison could be strengthened by planned periodic assessment of industrial needs by research centres as way of maintaining contacts already made and of establishing new trends so as to redirect activities towards new challenges.

(iii) DEMONSTRATION PLANTS. Universities and other research centres are often criticized for failure to translate bench results to production. Demonstration plants set up with small industries have been suggested as a way of promoting the use of research results. Strong government financial support would be required where the researchers were seeking to form partnership with small, poor organizations in the rural areas. This mechanism lends itself to studies of economic feasibility, consumer, acceptance of products, and could be a powerful tool for the training of students if universities were involved.

Research establishments tend to assume that it is their results that can solve the problems of rural communities. However some members of these communities have been known to be highly innovative and to command a lot of respect from their fellows for their skills in producing innovation to address efficiently specific problems. It has been suggested that universities and other research centres could stir considerable popular interest and support if, as part of dissemination, they collected rural innovations and organized demonstrations to promote their wider use. This undertaking might be coupled with the production of practical manuals in the local language for use by those who can read.

(2) *Technical information dissemination*. The scope for collecting technical information has now been enhanced by the emergence of the technologies for storing and retrieving information. Universities and research institutions can serve not only as depositories of such information from all over the world but also as centres for sorting out what is relevant and translating it into a manner appropriate to the local conditions. This information can also be directed to research scientists who often have to work in isolation and whose progress can be severely hampered by the shortage of current publications in their fields.

(3) *Government support for research*. Any of the above suggestions for strengthening the dissemination and utilisation of research results require finance. Substantial government investment is imperative if stable and continuous research activities which are dependent upon indigenous thinking and innovation are going to emerge and give results which will influence the direction for development[5,9].

(4) *Regional co-operation*. This topic has been explored with respect to other sectors. There is general consensus that although co-operation may be difficult it is important where manpower and other resources are in short supply and where there is such a wide array of common interests and problems.

The foregoing suggestions are by no means exhaustive. Classical methods of dissemination such as publications and movement of scientists, seminars, were not mentioned. It is hoped however that the presentation exposes sufficiently the problems involved in the dissemination and utilisation of research results, using the African situation as an example.

REFERENCES

1. UNESCO/ECA, Final Report of the Lagos Conference: *Organization of Research and Training in Africa in Relation to the Study, Conservation and Utilization of Natural Resources*. Paris, UNESCO, 1964.

2. UNESCO/ECA, *Final Report:* Conference of Ministers of African Member States Responsible for the Application of Science and Technology to Development held in Dakar, Senegal. Paris, UNESCO, 1974.

3. Yesufu, J. M. (ed.): *Creating the African University: Emerging Issues of the 1970s*. Oxford University Press, Ibadan, 1973.

4. UNESCO, Second Conference of Ministers Responsible for the Application of Science and Technology to Development in Africa: *Statistics on Scientific and Experimental Development in Africa*. Arusha, 1987.

5. Odhiambo, T. R.: 'Establishment of Reward System for Scientific Activities and Technological Innovators'; paper delivered at the Second Symposium, Science, Technology in Africa, convened by the Special Committee on Africa. 1985.

6. Wad, Atul and Radmor, Michael: *Science and Technology in Africa: Priorities and Implications for International Co-operation*. National Science Foundation, Washington, D. C., 1983.

7. Adubifa, Akim: 'Obstacles to Linkages between R&D Activities and the Production System in Research and Development'. *Linkages to Production in Developing Countries*; (ed.) Mary Pat Williams Silveira. Westview Press, 1985.

8. Blackledge, J. P.: 'The Potential for Contribution of R&D to the Production System in Research and Development'. *Linkages to Production in Developing Countries*; (ed.) Mary Pat Williams Silveira. Westview Press, 1985.

9. UNESCO, Conference of Ministers Responsible for the Application of Science and Technology to Development in Africa: *The Role of the Human and Social Sciences in the Application of Science and Technology to Socio-economic Development in Africa*. Arusha, 1987.

Professor B. J. Ross (*Principal, Lincoln College*): The extent to which universities have come to be regarded as agents of national development has highlighted questions relating to the efficiency with which they discharge this role. Growing numbers of graduates, or at least an increasing proportion of school-leavers attending universities in most countries, suggests that universities are facing up to their responsibilities for producing the highly educated people

SUB-TOPIC 2 (c): THE FRUITS OF RESEARCH [*Ross*]

which advanced growing societies need. The world-wide explosion in the amount of material being published in almost all disciplines, with a large proportion of it coming from universities, suggests that the universities are also carrying out their research function. On the other hand there is evidence that the results of work carried out in the universities are not always being transferred to the possible users of that work as fast as they could be, and this lag in the utilisation of university research must be regarded as an inefficiency in the system which should be reduced as much as possible.

Undoubtedly universities have their major impact upon society through the influence of their graduates during the course of their careers. One hopes that it is a mode of thinking they have acquired during their time at university which chiefly characterizes the difference between graduates and non-graduates in society. Nevertheless graduates usually take with them from their university an amount of knowledge which they have acquired through their studies, and part of their contribution to society is the application and dissemination of that knowledge. One assumes that senior undergraduate students will have been given some idea of the research being carried out by their teachers in the disciplines in which they have majored, and postgraduate students will usually have carried out some research themselves. Part of the success with which the fruits of a university's research are disseminated and applied will therefore depend upon the actions of its graduates in their careers.

New graduates often complain about being under-employed or under-utilised, saying that their new employers do not appreciate the skills and knowledge which they bring to their new positions. Employers, on the other hand, sometimes complain about the bumptiousness of young graduates who arrive fresh from business school only too willing to undertake tasks normally left to managing directors. The truth is that there is probably much to be gained if we can learn how to harness the knowledge and skills of the young graduates in ways which are tempered by the wisdom and experience of those who have been in their respective fields for many years. Part of the problem may lie in the failure of the young graduates to communicate effectively with their superiors. Universities everywhere should stop from time to time and ask themselves whether they are really equipping their graduates with the skills to communicate their knowledge and ideas when they leave the university. The ability to communicate involves being able to get a feel for one's audience, to adapt one's message to that audience and then really to sell the idea one is trying to communicate. Knowledge alone is not enough for the young graduate; he or she must be able to communicate that knowledge to others. More and more professional schools are including communications courses in their offerings, and it is to be hoped that this trend spreads and that communications courses become available to all students. Where the courses are options they themselves need to be sold to the potential customers.

My own institution, which has had a long history of dealing directly with farmers and of training graduates who will take up careers as extension officers, has a mixed history with regard to communications courses. Full-length extension or communications courses have always been optional but some exposure to communications methods has always been a core, or compulsory, part of our agricultural science degrees, sometimes as part of major subjects such as farm management. Every time our degrees are revised there is general agreement that a much greater emphasis must be placed on communications, but as is usual with semi-professional degrees we generally have a problem to find the time to slot in a subject which does not have a strong department pushing for its inclusion or expansion. I am therefore very ready to admit that it is not easy but, I repeat, if our graduates are to make an early contribution by persuading their superiors of the value of their knowledge and ideas they must be able to communicate to those superiors, and their ability to do this is likely to be greatly enhanced by some formal training in the art of communication.

Staff members of universities have traditionally used the publication of papers in professional journals as the way of presenting their research results to the world. The reading audience of such journals can be very limited, however, and there must be doubts about this form of publication as a means of transferring information from the universities to industry, government and other potentially interested institutions. Many of the stories one hears about discoveries being published and neglected until being rediscovered years later probably relate to discoveries the potential uses of which could not be foreseen by anyone, but there must be some where potential users are just unaware of the discoveries that have been made. This suggests that the dissemination of the fruits of research could be accelerated if academics took communications more seriously, and worked to ensure that information gets to those who can use it. It is my impression that in recent years universities have generally been making bigger efforts to help academics promote their work, in the interests of promoting the institutions for which the academics work. The communications skills of researchers are now often supplemented by the skills of

SUB-TOPIC 2 (c): THE FRUITS OF RESEARCH [Ross]

university-employed journalists and public relations experts.

Communication skills are also at the heart of the extension programmes which many agricultural universities around the world use to convey the latest in agricultural technology to the farmers in their regions. These extension programmes are often an excellent vehicle through which top-level researchers can communicate their latest research findings and something of their current research efforts to potential customers. Over the years such programmes run by universities have been extraordinarily successful in a number of countries in inducing the uptake of modern methods of farming. More recently some universities have extended such programmes into a much wider range of industries from medicine to electronics in the attempt to speed up the introduction and acceptance of new technology.

The term 'extension' can be used to describe any method by which people try to transfer ideas to another group, and the extension programmes run by the universities can be very diverse. They can range from the organization of formal conferences, or seminars at the university or at another locality designed to appeal to the potential audience, to field days on farms and factories, or laboratories, or a range of media presentations through newspapers, magazines, radio or television. Extension can also take the form of support of a variety of outside groups, whether it be professional groups where university scientists talk to their peers, farming or industry groups, or some method by which the university staff members communicate with the public in general.

For many universities the problem with extension of all or many varieties is that the university is not specifically funded to carry out extension activities. Thus some forms of extension will require expenditure to be diverted by the university from some other use or will require individual staff members to commit themselves to extension for possibly no tangible reward. Perhaps promotion criteria need to put greater emphasis on this sort of activity.

A number of the other ways in which the universities can become involved with business sectors can actually involve net increases in the resources available to universities, although there may well have to be initial investments by the universities. Probably one of the oldest forms of commercial relationship between universities and business enterprises has been the granting, by the universities, of rights to business enterprises to exploit patents held by the universities. The spectacular successes of a few university patents, coupled with the increasing pressure on resources in universities in most countries, has led many universities to formulate policies with regard to patents in the hope that their staff will develop products or processes which can be patented to the eventual financial benefit of the university. Much time and effort has been spent in some institutions in developing policies by which the benefits of licensing patents can be shared between the institution and individual staff members, so as to provide an incentive within the university to work in areas from which patentable ideas might emerge.

The potential profits to be made are not the only reason for pursuing patents, however, as they can have a positive role to play in accelerating the uptake of developments coming from the university. My own institution has had a rather indifferent financial experience with patents. They are relatively expensive to take out and, on average, the financial returns have been rather meagre. On the other hand once a product has been patented it is possible to grant exclusive rights to the manufacturer of that product, and we have found that in some cases it is necessary to give a manufacturer such rights before he will be willing to undertake production. I have the impression that concentration on the possible financial benefits for the university to be obtained from patenting may have obscured the real role that patenting may have in ensuring uptake of a particular product or process.

In similar vein I think it can be argued that whereas contract research has been viewed as a way of increasing the resources available for research within the university, it also has a role in the dissemination of the results. Where a company has paid for a research project it will take a keen interest in the results, and in a market economy the ability to attract contracts should be seen as a major test of the usefulness of any research which is likely to have benefits that could be captured by a single client. Other research should be judged in other ways.

In parentheses, a comment on a couple of the points raised yesterday and this morning. Much of the research conducted in universities is related to postgraduate teaching, *i.e.* the research is largely undertaken by PhD students. The fact that there is a teaching component in the total cost of the research means that it may not be appropriate to apply full-cost recovery to contracts which enable PhD students to undertake projects that might otherwise have been too expensive. In a sense, any contribution to such a project should be gratefully received! On the other hand it may be difficult to justify wildly different charging policies within an institution simply on the basis of the degree of staff involvement in a particular project. Charging policies are not easy to get right!

Some universities have taken a further step towards the commercial world by, in a sense, joining it, with the establishment of their own venture companies. Through such companies universities can form joint ventures with other companies to exploit particular developments or, less commonly, can undertake the full development of a product or process themselves. The company concept is seen to have a number of advantages, such as helping to ensure earlier uptake of ideas by actively participating in their commercial development. The active involvement ensures that the idea is likely to be promoted more as the developers anticipated (although it should be noted that this may not be the most commercially rewarding avenue) and the involvement is seen as being potentially more profitable if an idea should really pay off. The formation of venture companies may be more expensive to universities than simply licensing patents which they have taken out, but in some instances the universities have participated in joint ventures by accepting the issue of shares in the joint venture in return for the rights to exploit the university-held patent.

Another form of involvement of university staff members with the potential users of their research is in the provision of consultancy services of one form or another. Many universities allow, or even encourage, staff members to undertake consultancies on a private basis. The dual objective from the point of view of the university is to allow university expertise to be put to use in other sectors of the economy, and at the same time enable the university staff members involved to obtain additional practical experience, which is likely to be beneficial in their teaching and research.

Somewhat akin to the general idea of consultancy services is the idea that universities are pools of expertise and talent and knowledge which would be tapped more often by government and commerce if the availability of the expertise were better known and more readily accessible. It is with this thought in mind that many universities have recently established liaison groups or applied research offices which provide contact points through which people from outside the university who seek help of some sort can be put in touch with the appropriate members of university staff. The importance of the universities making their capabilities known to all potential users was highlighted by one of the items in the 1987 report of the Universities Review Committee in New Zealand. The Committee commissioned a study of the attitudes of businessmen towards the universities and found that those businessmen who had been involved in linkages with the universities were generally satisfied with the arrangements which they had, whilst those who had not had an involvement were reluctant to become involved and were sceptical about the payoff from such closer ties. I would like to think that they simply did not know what they were missing.

The message is that, if universities are to reach their full potential as agents of national development in a rapidly changing world, they will have to sell their wares more aggressively. The production of good graduates and the publication of the results of good research in high-quality journals will remain the key functions of any university and the chief preoccupations of most academics. In addition, however, more academics will have to reach out into the community in different ways. For this to happen universities will have to recognise, and give credit for, efforts which are made. In some quarters there has been a tendency to look down on academics who have been successful 'popularizers'. Despite the presence of some brilliant people among their ranks, 'popularizers' have sometimes been decried as playing to the gallery, whereas they should have been seen as gifted educators who could communicate difficult concepts to non-specialists. The ability to communicate like this, by any of the means I have described, must be seen as a skill to be fostered by the universities. The universities must also study all the various ways in which they can make formal contacts and arrangements with the potential users of university research, and follow up those which seem applicable in each individual case.

Attitudes and actions are changing, and will have to change further, but the signs are that in many countries universities are changing themselves to ensure a great improvement in the rate of dissemination and application of the fruits of their research in the interests of national development.

DISCUSSION

(*Rapporteur*: Mr. D. Bowes, Assistant Registrar,
University of Western Australia)

Discussion in this session covered not only the dissemination of the fruits of research but also matters of a more primary nature related to ensuring a high level of research activity, diversity and freedom. The latter required universities to explain convincingly to governments, and the wider community, the value of research and scholarship in all areas of activity, not only in applicable science, technology and business, but also in the basic sciences, social sciences and humanities. Several speakers referred to the fact that advances in science and technology had outstripped our ability to solve social, political and economic problems on both the national and international scales, and that there was a consequent need for much greater emphasis to be placed on research and scholarship in the social

SUB-TOPIC 2 (c): THE FRUITS OF RESEARCH

sciences and humanities as an important resource in the search for solutions. Yet it was these very areas which found themselves embattled in the current thrust to channel funds into activities which were seen by governments to be of immediate economic benefit. Because of this the suggestion was made that the social sciences and humanities and, to some extent, the basic sciences had a special claim on the recurrent funds of universities.

It was recognised that there was a conflict between the wish of funders, whether government or private, to control research directions in the pursuit of relatively short-term objectives, and the conviction of most academics that freedom to follow their own research interests and to increase the general fund of knowledge was of paramount importance for the future of mankind. Some speakers went even further and said that an important function of universities was to pursue and disseminate knowledge for its own sake, rather than involve themselves directly in its practical application which should be left to other facilitators acting in liaison with the universities. Others, while subscribing to the principle of freedom in research, believed it to be unrealistic to expect that funders would be prepared to provide unlimited resources to allow uncontrolled expansion of research in every area of endeavour.

Several delegates from developing countries explained that the immediate needs of their own communities for speedy technology transfer to solve urgent problems, and the low level of research activity resulting from shortage of funds, produced great pressure for concentration on applicable research. One pointed out that a special problem was that industrial and commercial organizations, which might be seen as potential sources of research funding, were often branches of international groups which were not interested in local problems whose solution did not bring short-term profit.

A delegate invited the group to consider the appropriateness to current needs of traditional PhD training, which was seen to be both a means of equipping individuals with the techniques necessary to increase knowledge through research, and, at the same time, through collaboration with established research workers, itself a means of increasing knowledge. While it had always been assumed that such training was of great value to the outside community, the increasing tendency of good bachelor-level students in some areas to take employment without proceeding to a PhD, and the value placed on them by employers, should lead us to question whether the value added to a bachelor's degree through PhD training was commensurate with the costs in time and money. If a university were a knowledge factory, then it was time to assess its products in terms of the market. If the PhD graduate was to be accepted as of special value to industry and commerce, then the training should inculcate broad and applicable skills as well as those required for the effective pursuit of knowledge for its own sake.

After this preliminary discussion largely relating to the need for, and means of assuring, a high level of research activity across a wide spectrum, through the dissemination of information demonstrating its many-faceted value, the group considered how the ensuing fruits might be appropriately disseminated according to different needs.

It was traditionally accepted that an important means of disseminating the fruits of research was through the teaching of undergraduate and postgraduate students, and that the hall-mark of university teaching was that it was done by people who were themselves involved in learning through their scholarship and research, so facilitating immediate transfer of new knowledge to students who, in turn, would disseminate it widely. While most of those who spoke believed that the nexus between research and teaching was essential, some suggested that the important relationship was between scholarship in general and teaching, and that encouragement of academics to maintain a high level of scholarship, rather than require all of them to engage in some narrow area of research, would increase the effectiveness of knowledge transfer and bring enhanced economic and cultural benefits.

While the continuing importance of refereed journals and international conferences as a means of disseminating the fruits of research was generally acknowledged, speakers from countries which were crying out for the early solution of critical and pressing problems urged those from more developed countries to consider means of making necessary research findings and technological developments immediately available to them. Several ways were identified of giving immediacy to the transmission of results of research to those who needed them urgently. Among these were:

- the formation of liaison groups between researchers in universities and groups or individuals in the community with special need;
- acceptance and encouragement of popularizing journalism which was able to make difficult concepts accessible to non-specialists;
- the employment by universities themselves of liaison officers with the job of being completely familiar with what was going on in the university and what was needed by potential users, and facilitating the necessary contacts to ensure direct transfer of knowledge in the shortest possible time;
- secondments, study leave arrangements, release of staff for overseas appointments, exchanges and consultancies, under conditions which encouraged participation by ensuring that those involved did not suffer material or career disadvantages;
- increased use of university companies to ensure that knowledge, techniques and patentable inventions were exploited;
- accelerated development of the use of modern information technology in the dissemination and transfer of knowledge;
- willingness on the part of universities, not only but especially in developing countries, to exchange knowledge with their different communities and to examine traditional and folk methods of solving problems to see whether they might be improved, or even provide insights which could influence the directions and progress of research. Such effective acknowledgement by universities of the fact that they share the capacity for wisdom, knowledge and innovation with all

SUB-TOPIC 2 (c): THE FRUITS OF RESEARCH

communities, and people in all regions, occupations and economic circumstances, would not only bring immediate practical benefits to the world but, because of the necessary accompanying interaction with those outside the universities, bring them closer to and make them part of the communities on whom they depended ultimately for support;
- constant examination of methods and outcomes of teaching in the knowledge that the graduates of our universities are a very significant and continuing means, throughout their lives, of disseminating knowledge throughout the community, combined with the provision of continuing education to ensure that graduates' knowledge is kept up to date;
- ensuring that dissemination of knowledge within and between universities is facilitated by adequate support for libraries, and electronic and other means of technology and information transfer which, compared to the large salary cost of university research workers, represents a relatively small proportion of recurrent outlays;
- encouragement of desk-top publishing, so that individuals may make the results of research available to the community in the shortest possible time.

The important thing to remember was that no single means of knowledge dissemination suited all audiences, all circumstances and all needs. The message that came through strongly was that it was a prime responsibility of universities not only to be involved in teaching and research but to make themselves aware of the many different needs for, and possible uses of, the fruits of their scholarship and research; and to be assiduous, vigorous, innovative and imaginative in developing and utilising means of knowledge dissemination appropriate to the world's many short- and long-term needs.

In brief, the old adage might usefully be re-written to read: 'research not appropriately disseminated is research not done'.

Sub-Topic 2(d)

THE POTENTIAL FOR FURTHER INTERNATIONAL CO-OPERATION OF UNIVERSITIES IN RESEARCH

Tuesday, 9 February

Professor L. S. SRINATH (*Director, Indian Institute of Technology, Madras*): Co-operation, both national and international, in all those activities that are beneficial to mankind is highly desirable. Many national and international organizations exist to promote such endeavours not only in general activities but also in research activities. These organizations have been functioning for many years with good service records. While these world organizations are primarily promoting and managing agencies, the real active research work gets done, by and large, at the level of individuals and groups of individuals. While dissemination of knowledge is taking place in a variety of modes, real co-operation in active research is beset with many difficulties. Let me cite an example. I will be focusing my attention and emphasis on collaborative research programmes.

The Indian Institute of Technology, Madras (IIT-M) was established about 26 years ago, as a joint venture between the government of India and the government of the Federal Republic of Germany. During the last eight years IIT-M has been associating with a few selected German universities in a large number of joint research programmes. Each joint research programme involves two investigators—one from IIT-M and the other from one of the universities in Germany. A problem of common interest is identified, on which investigations get carried out at both places. The results of these investigations are shared for mutual benefit. The project provides opportunities for brief visits of the investigators concerned to each other's laboratories. One would think that such a programme would be an ideal example of international co-operation or collaboration in research. But a detailed examination reveals that the results of these joint research programmes are not

SUB-TOPIC 2 (D): INTERNATIONAL CO-OPERATION [Srinath]

as exciting as one would have hoped or liked to see. It is against this background that I would like to make the following remarks.

Research, to me, is a highly personalized or individualistic activity. For persons working in academic institutions, success in research means some kind of ego satisfaction, recognition through publications in refereed journals, through presentation of research findings in national and international conferences, etc. Career advancement, future opportunities in administrative cadres, etc., are also involved.

In the universities one of the common methods of getting research activities done is through research students who have registered for degree programmes. This factor imposes some serious constraints on the types of problems chosen. In order that one research worker may collaborate with another, it is necessary that a need should exist for active and voluntary collaboration. Some of the needs are obvious. These are:

- common problems or areas of investigation;
- desire to share results for mutual benefit;
- optimum utilisation of time and effort without much duplication;
- optimum utilisation of resources at one's disposal; etc.

Unfortunately research as a highly personalized or individualistic activity with ego satisfaction cannot easily accommodate these requirements. This is particularly so in the field of science and technology. Of course in those areas of research work which involve national security, product or market competition, etc., free and active collaborations at international levels are not at all possible. Such topics are not being discussed in this presentation.

In the example cited, *i.e.* joint Indo-German research, though the problems that were identified for joint investigations were of common interest, the nature of these problems did not much lend themselves to exciting results. Consequently over a period of time the interest in them gradually waned. In addition, as the research work involved students who were anxious about their research degrees, the nature of problems got changed to meet institutional and other degree requirements. An added complication was that the research investigators in both universities became engaged more and more in those problems which were funded through their own several national funding agencies. Consequently there was no common pace of progress in the areas that were initially identified. Very few publications based on the joint research activities have appeared. However the research investigators have been actively engaged in various other research problems. Of course there were a few notable exceptions; but what we thought was an ideal set-up did not function. Another interesting aspect was the following. At the initial stages there were considerable interests for the professors from the German universities to come and spend considerably long periods of time in India. Over the years this interest waned and the same professors started travelling to China and a few other South Asian countries. India, as a country of tourist and other interests, was replaced by China as a new venture place.

An analysis of those research problems which could be considered as reasonably successful for co-operation shows that they belonged to either humanities and social sciences or those areas dealing with agricultural sciences, low-cost housing, pest control, etc. There were no problems which one would classify as belonging to hi-tech or to frontiers of science.

Having made these statements, let me start once again from the beginning. First, about the need.

We all agree that there definitely exists a need for international co-operation in research; particularly when research deals with knowledge—I mean knowledge in the true sense, when the knowledge is for the betterment of mankind and the world that mankind lives in. But we all know that this is as unrealistic a notion as the new economic order. In reality there are severe constraints and restrictions for international co-operation in research. We can appreciate these constraints when we realize how research work gets done in the universities. In these activities either individuals or small groups of individuals are involved. Further, by and large, most of the research activities are not *de novo* activities. This is revealed by the way the research papers appear in journals. Each paper is an extension of earlier ones, as given in the references cited. Dissemination of knowledge and generation of new papers through such publications is one of the commonest methods in the international scene. Now, for two individual research workers from two different countries to come to an agreement to carry out joint or collaborative investigations, several conditions have to be satisfied.

- There should exist a common desire for collaboration.
- The problem chosen should be broad enough, so that the results of the two investigations are complementary or reinforcing and not merely duplication.
- There should be no communication barrier, either in the language or in sharing fully the results of the investigations.
- The level of competence of the two investigators must be comparable.
- The resources available, financial as well as facilities, should

be adequate in both the countries.
- Exchange of information should be fairly frequent.
- The efforts of each investigator should be capable of being assessed independently.
- The results of investigation should provide opportunities for the ego satisfaction and recognition of both partners. It should at the same time provide opportunities for their individual growth and career opportunities in their respective institutions.
- The problems chosen should not be in conflict with their respective national security or other protective national interests.

One can certainly think of a few more constraints of the above types. If one were to meet all the above-mentioned constraints, the room within which to find a solution is naturally extremely small. The categories of problems on which international co-operation is possible will therefore be very limited. Problems in the areas of hi-tech are definitely out of the picture. Problems dealing with national security and defence are also out. Under these circumstances, what kinds of problems lend themselves either for co-operative research or for sharing of information?

- Problems in the area of humanities and social sciences are possible; agriculture, animal husbandry, health, family planning, are possible.
- Low-cost housing, appropriate technology developments; certain types of alternative sources of energy like windmill, biogas, wave energy; epidemic disease control; are also possible areas.
- Fundamental research investigations whose results are not immediately known or cannot be visualized yet are also possible.

One can enumerate a list of such problems or problem areas on which international co-operation and collaboration is possible. But one common characteristic of a large majority of such problems is that the interest in their solutions will be one-sided. For example, in the case of low-cost housing or low-cost construction materials, more interest will be shown from the developing countries; so also in the case of appropriate technologies, family planning, etc. This raises an interesting question, *i.e.* whether co-operation is not possible among the universities in developing countries themselves, since they apparently share common problems. Unfortunately the number of such ventures is rather limited. This may be due to large variations in the quality and standards among the research investigators, capability of resource mobilization, and a few other incompatible and disparate factors that exist among the developing countries. Further, resources—particularly financial resources—being a constraining factor among the developing countries, the potentiality for collaboration does not appear to be high. An interesting paradox is the following. Let me state it without bringing in too many complexities.

I started with the premise that for co-operation and collaboration in research to take place there should exist a need or a desire among the research workers for such collaboration. If such a desire were to be mainly towards knowledge sharing and knowledge dissemination, and totally directed towards the betterment of mankind, it is obvious that there should be no hesitation for co-operation. Further, if one were to identify a class of problems that is common to a group of countries, then it is advantageous if these countries could share the knowledge among themselves for their mutual benefit. Unfortunately these kinds of co-operation do not take place naturally, unless deliberate attempts are made to promote them. Even in these cases very few success stories exist. The so-called dedicated or committed research workers belonging to this category are very small in number. The so-called active research worker wants to shine by himself. He desires recognition. So he focuses his attention towards the activities of the world outside his own country. This is one of the reasons for the frequent statements made that many of the research activities carried out in developing countries are irrelevant to their needs. Very few instances exist where a worker from India or Pakistan desires recognition in Sri Lanka, or a research worker from Sri Lanka desires recognition in the West Indies, or a research worker from the West Indies seeks recognition in one of the African countries. The attention, by and large, is focused towards advanced or developed countries.

Under these circumstances what kinds of international co-operation in research can one think of? If by co-operation in research we merely restrict ourselves to dissemination and sharing of knowledge, then one can say that this has been going on fairly successfully in several modes, particularly when this knowledge pertains to unclassified categories. Improvements are possible, but these will bring only marginal changes. To me, what is important is active collaboration in research, because in this process

- problems of mutual interest are identified,
- experts are identified,
- efforts are made to provide enough resources and facilities based on the project requirements,
- there is some sort of time constraint,
- efforts and results are complementary;

and, more than anything else, it brings a sense of participation and commitment.

SUB-TOPIC 2 (D): INTERNATIONAL CO-OPERATION [Srinath]

While universities are the real sources of wealth and reservoir of intellectual power, at the same time the elements of these systems are so individualistic that it is difficult to bring a degree of coherence into those elements for effective co-operation. Hence a deliberate attempt should be made to bring these elements together. I would like to cite two proposals which are under our consideration, wherein the graduate students play the role of bridging elements.

The first one concerns a joint PhD guidance programme between IIT-M and a few selected universities in Germany. Under this programme a research student has two guides, one from IIT-M and the other from a German university. A common research topic is identified and the student carries out the investigation initially in one of the institutions. A year later he moves to the other institution and spends about a year under the supervision of the joint guide. The degree awarded comes from the institution to which the principal guide belongs. The important point to appreciate is that there is a joint responsibility between the two guides coming from two different institutions, with time constraint built in. An interesting and at the same time a paradoxical thing that makes this kind of joint collaborative project successful at international level is the following. In India, just as in many developing countries, industry-funded research is fairly small. Most of the research funds come from the government and government agencies. In recent years the funds available for research are substantial. Consequently, not only have the research topics tended towards basic research, but also the sources of these problems have been external to the country. Hence it has always been possible to find problems of common interest, but not of much relevance to the needs of the country.

The second proposal deals with a recent offer that has come from one of the universities in Canada. This university wants a selected number of students who have registered themselves for a degree to undergo all the course requirements at IIT-M and then go to Canada to complete the dissertation requirements. The research students obtain the degrees awarded by the particular Canadian university. While this scheme is quite attractive from the students' point of view it reduces IIT-M to merely a teaching institution. This scheme is still under discussion for possible modification.

The third scheme that we plan to initiate soon involves industry as the bridging element. We recently acquired a main-frame computer from the Siemens company in Germany. In this process we have come to an understanding that the computer softwares that Siemens sells to various industries and other establishments will be developed jointly by IIT-M, the University in Aachen and the University of Kaiserslautern. In this the Siemens Computer Corporation is the bridging element between these academic institutions. This particular scheme with suitable modifications can be copied advantageously by the universities in Commonwealth countries and multi-national industrial set-ups with their bases in those countries. International consultancy, joint product developments, developments of new technologies on a co-operative basis, are some of the possibilities.

Professor G. BENNEH (*Pro-Vice-Chancellor, University of Ghana*): Universities in Africa are expected to play a major role in the development of their respective countries by undertaking research into the many problems which confront the communities of which they are a part and by producing skilled manpower to harness their natural resources. However, many African universities are seriously handicapped by inadequate resources—skilled manpower, funding and equipment—to discharge these functions. African universities have, therefore, generally welcomed opportunities for international co-operation in research and staff development. But fruitful co-operation is possible only if there is sound basis for it. Otherwise the advantages to be gained from such co-operation may be one-sided.

Thus before identifying areas for further co-operation in research, it is necessary to discuss briefly some of the problems which African universities face, and how these can be resolved to ensure that the agreements they reach with other universities, especially those of the North, for collaborative research will be of mutual benefit.

Research Capacity

African universities have yet to develop strong research capacities. This is not surprising because to do so requires trained researchers, adequate equipment, facilities and a congenial research environment. It is necessarily a slow process, although it is a prerequisite for any meaningful international co-operation in research. Adzei Bekoe lists some of the key elements of research capacity as follows:

(*a*) the ability to analyse productivity and the problems of human existence and welfare and to identify important bottlenecks and areas;

(*b*) the ability to find solutions to these problems through the adaptation of known technologies and through research and development;

(*c*) the ability to explore new processes, new relationships and new products for which there is demand and for which a demand can be created;

(*d*) the ability to undertake an ongoing review of the science and technology scene, to recognise principles and innovations likely to be of importance in economic activity; and

(*e*) the ability to confront new challenges that are likely to occur in the future.

According to the report of the conference of African ministers responsible for the application of science and technology, 'African development in every area—agriculture, industry, infrastructure, health, education—demands not only the development of local technologies but also the importations of new technologies in order to ensure economic growth and social changes'. There has, however, been scant recognition of the fact that transfer of technologies does not lead to technology transfer unless one has the capacity to understand fully the knowledge and skills behind the techniques. In other words, there must be a scientific base for a successful transfer of technology.

Trained Manpower

Although data on scientists at post in institutions in African countries is not readily available, it is generally conceded that specialists in many research fields are so few that there is often no opportunity for consultation and for local collaborative research in many African countries. In countries such as Ghana, where there could have been a critical mass of scientists and technologists to formulate and execute research programmes, there has been such a steady migration of skilled manpower, for a variety of reasons, that the overall situation is not considerably better than in other countries. According to a World Bank estimate, about 7% of the total professional manpower leaves the African continent every year.

Many leave for lack of job satisfaction. Facilities for work, for communicating through journals and for attending professional meetings are far below their expectations, especially in the case of those who had part of their training in institutions in developed countries. Many professional journals in Africa have not appeared on the shelves for a long time, owing mainly to lack of funding.

Funding

Although African governments have generally acknowledged the importance of research as an instrument for solving Africa's problems, research is poorly funded. It is, for example, estimated that 1%-2% of agricultural GDP should be spent on research for the desired input into agricultural productivity. But the average in a recent survey of 36 African countries was 0.5%, with only a third of countries spending above 1%. In some countries it is not unusual for governments to pay salaries of researchers while not voting enough funds for research projects.

Towards Successful International Co-operation in Research

It is against this background of rather weak research capacity, poor funding of research and an uncongenial research environment that African universities have entered into agreements with universities in the developed countries for collaborative research. Since these agreements have often resulted in the transfer of resources, manpower, equipment and facilities from the institutions in the developed countries to those in Africa, they have not always been scrutinized as carefully as they should have been by African institutions, to ensure that the agreements are of mutual benefit. It has not been unknown in the past for data collected in a developing country to have been sent away for analysis in a developed country without the institutions in the developing country, which collaborated in the research, having access to the new data. On the other hand, co-operation between institutions in the third world may come up against problems of having no access to resources at all. Lack of research facilities and of research funds are perennial features of the academic life of third-world countries.

In order to ensure that international co-operation in research is of mutual benefit to the institutions concerned, the institutions must agree on a research agenda, the modes of co-operation which have a good chance of success within the prevailing and future financial environment, and to agree on the training implications of a research project.

Research Agenda

Given the myriad problems Africa faces, any attempt to draw up a general research agenda is bound to be a crowded one. It is best to leave the choice of research agenda to the collaborating institutions. This has to be drawn up in the context of the pressing problems which need to be researched into by the host institution and taking into consideration the strengths and weaknesses of the collaborating institutions. Thus, in the general area of development policy studies, there are centres of excellence in the North where much work has been done, albeit some is of a theoretical nature. There is a need for empirical research in the South to provide theorists with the data for testing and choosing among conflicting hypotheses.

There are some development policy issues that lend themselves to collaborative research between universities in the North and those of the South, and indeed between those of the South, because of their global dimensions. Among these one may include the unequal terms of trade; the debt crisis; the role of international financial and development organizations, such as the International Monetary Fund and the World Bank, in the development of the economies of third-world countries; and the impact of regional economic integration on national development.

The world economy has not favoured Africa. The real prices of most of her commodity exports—minerals and cash crops—have fallen for more than two decades. Meanwhile the prices of Africa's imports of manufactures and of oil have been rising, so her terms of trade have deteriorated. In 27 out of 32 African countries surveyed by the World Bank, a given quantity of exports bought fewer imports in 1983 than in 1970.

In addition to these grave concerns there are the pressing African problems of malnutrition, hunger, land degradation, desertification, disease and the impact of rapid population growth on resources, which clearly should engage the serious attention of researchers. For the decade of the 1970s, when the African population was expanding at an average annual rate of about 2.8%, total food production in the continent was rising by no more than 1.5%. The number of severely hungry and malnourished people is estimated to have increased from almost 80 million in 1972-74 to as many as 100 million in 1984. African countries have had to resort to borrowing to meet their commitments. Sub-Saharan Africa's debts soared from $17.8 billion in 1976 to $43.6 billion in 1980, a growth rate of 25% a year. Meanwhile the cost of servicing the debt has been growing even faster than the debt itself; between 1978 and 1983 the cost of interest and capital repayment almost trebled, reaching $8 billion in 1984. This burden of debt service has eaten up a fair share of the export earnings of African countries.

These problems cut across African boundaries. No research

centre, university or for that matter country has the resources to tackle them successfully. Africa needs to learn from countries, especially in the South, which have solved some of these problems. Recent advances at the new frontiers of science and technology must be harnessed to upgrade traditional skills and occupations, as some third-world countries have been able to achieve.

In addition to the above conventional fields of research, which focus on the basic needs of the poor majority in African countries, there are new research frontiers such as molecular biology, biotechnology, micro-electronics and information sciences for which Africa needs to have research capacity in order to make a contribution.

Types of International Co-operation in Research

The success of international co-operation in research depends to a large extent on the individual qualities of researchers in the collaborating institutions. Nonetheless it will be useful to examine some of the models of co-operation against the background of some of the critical problems which African universities face. The examples are drawn from the University of Ghana.

Creation of centres of excellence. One way of helping to build research capacity in developing countries and to create a congenial research environment is the establishment of centres of excellence. An example of this is the Noguchi Memorial Institute for Medical Research of the University of Ghana. This was established as a result of collaborative research between the University of Ghana Medical School and the Fukushima Medical College which began in 1969. With the expansion of the programme, scientists from both sides agreed to a need to establish a permanent centre for its continuation, and in November 1979 the centre was formally established. Today the Noguchi Memorial Medical Institute is a well-equipped medical research centre with both Ghanaian and Japanese scientists carrying out research into some of the more pressing health problems of the country.

Establishing a network of researchers; the Kellog International Fellowship Programme. This programme awards fellowships to researchers studying food systems. The fellowship administered by the Michigan State University aims, in respect of Ghana, at reviewing critically the processing of cereals and legumes in order to identify innovative and simple techniques which can be subject to technological improvement. It also aims at assisting the recipient institution to set up model improved traditional food processing units for teaching, research and extension. Kellog International Fellows meet often to share ideas and discuss research results in the different participating institutions around the world.

Collaboration with research institute in Nigeria. The question of post-harvest losses and the preservation of foodstuffs is of major concern to most African countries. In a recent collaborative effort between the Institute of Tropical Agriculture in Ibadan and the home science unit of the University of Ghana's faculty of agriculture, research has been carried out on simple preservative methods for use by farmers and consumers.

Split-site courses. In order to strengthen the graduate programme in the University of Ghana, in spite of lack of resources—equipment and current literature—arrangements have been made for postgraduate students who are enrolled for higher degrees in the University to spend part of their training in universities in the North, where they work under supervision in order to avail themselves of the excellent opportunities for research which exist in these institutions. An added advantage of these split-site courses is that the postgraduate students do return home to complete their degrees and subsequently take up jobs in the University, instead of being attracted to stay in the developed countries as they might have been if they had enrolled for full-time courses there.

While the contribution of research in Africa's development is not in doubt, it will be dangerous to oversell research as a way out of Africa's present dilemmas. The promotion of orderly change in a disorderly world will long remain as much an art as a science. There is, however, the need for improvement in the lives of people to be introduced as soon as the state of knowledge and the skill of practitioners permit.

REFERENCES

Abdus Salam: Opening Address. Conference on South-South and South-North Co-operation in Sciences, Third World Academy of Sciences, 5-9 July 1985, Trieste.

Bekoe, D. A.: 'Regional Co-operation in Science and Education for Development'. Keynote Address, The Joint 13 Biennial Conference of the West African Science Association, August 1987, Accra.

Benneh, G.: 'The Need for Centres of Excellence in International Policy Research to aid Policy Formulations and Implementations in Africa'. IDEP Workshop on Capacity Building in International Economics in Sub-Saharan Africa, 3-5 November 1986, Dakar.

Benneh, G.: 'University of Ghana's Experience with International Links for Higher Education'. International Links in Higher Education in Developing Countries of Africa, A Pan African Commonwealth Experts Meeting, 23-26 June 1986, Harare.

Harrison, P.: *The Greening of Africa*. Paladin Grafton Books, London, 1987.

Kwapong, A. A.: 'The Crisis of Development: Education and Identity'. Keynote Address, Fifth International Congress of African Studies, 16-21 December 1985, Ibadan.

DISCUSSION

(*Rapporteur*: Ms. Christine Shervington, Archivist, University of Western Australia)

Professor E. P. Bachelard (Australian National) opened discussion by drawing attention to the fact that Pro-Vice-Chancellor George Benneh had ignored one of the main constraints to international co-operation in research, that is, political constraint. He pointed out that often researchers go to a country only to be frustrated in their research by local politicians and bureaucrats. In response Professor Benneh agreed that there is a need in the host country to inform their politicians of the need and benefit of such research before agreements are entered into. In his experience politicians are, first, impatient with researchers because they want to implement their results immediately, and, secondly, sensitive about the research emanating from the universities, as they believe universities in Africa have too much influence on society.

Professor J. M. Ashworth (Salford) proposed the model 'research—development—demonstration' and gave the example of a co-operative programme between his university and the National Chemical Laboratory at Poona involving heat technology. This was economically unattractive to Britain because of her cheap north sea gas resource, but attractive to India. In the programme one institution took responsibility for research, the other for the demonstration or operation of the final results. He believes this type of co-operative programme is more hopeful and more fruitful than some others. Salford retained the right to re-import the process to the United Kingdom if it became economically more attractive in the future, and Professor Ashworth stressed later in the discussion the need to incorporate such terms in the original contract.

Professor C. K. Kao (Chinese U. of Hong Kong) commented on Professor L. S. Srinath's point that the purpose of research was a personalized activity, and stated that he believed this was the wrong basis on which to create collaborative projects. Emphasis should be on international agencies to collaborate the research and its implementation.

Dr. D. Harrison (Exeter) commended the example given by Professor Srinath of students working in two countries, *e.g.* India and Germany, as a realistic and pragmatic example of co-operation.

SUB-TROPIC 2 (D): INTERNATIONAL CO-OPERATION

Professor P. L. Wahi (Postgraduate Institute of Medical Education & Research) gave the example of his institution having discussions about co-operating on a research programme with the NIH (National Institutes of Health) relating to an experiment using monkeys. Because of lack of resources in India the NIH wished the monkeys to be transferred to their own country. He raised this as a representative problem for countries with research facilities which are not as developed as in the co-operating country. This can lead to mistrust and parochialism.

Mr. Justice R. E. McGarvie (La Trobe) told the meeting of a programme set up at La Trobe University to: (i) bring together African literature; (ii) conduct research on Africa; (iii) promote trade between Australia and Africa. He stated his concern as to the best way to undertake this research and requested any interested African delegates to contact him.

Professor (Mrs.) K. Rajya Lakshmi (Sri Padmavati Mahila) stated that her institution has the manpower and research material or projects; the need is for money for equipment which can be shared—not only on an interdisciplinary basis but on a multi-centric basis.

Professor M. G. Pitman (CSIRO, Australia) commented on the fact that technology exchange is not aid driven, and that exchange between industries as well as researchers in universities should be encouraged. He wanted to hear of collaboration in this area.

Professor Sir John Butterfield (Cambridge) warned of the danger of modern intellectual colonialism occurring if research is not undertaken at a local level by local universities because an international funding agency, *e.g.* WHO, is undertaking research in that country.

Thursday, 11 February

DISCUSSION (continued)

In the continuation of the discussion on sub-topic 2(d), which preceded the Topic's summing up session, Professor J. Manrakhan (Mauritius) described various collaborative links between Mauritius and other countries, including the French-speaking world. Collaborative groups were set up with programmes on energy and load-bearing materials. One example was a link between the Australian National University, Canberra, and Mauritius on energy research. They also set up networks, including a study of coral reefs. Others were a link with the University of Paris VI and work on a low-frequency radio telescope in Mauritius in association with India. There had been cultural links through UNESCO and an industrial link involving the University of Mauritius, ICI and a Mauritian firm. These various examples indicated that international co-operation could be very efficient.

TOPIC 2: A KNOWLEDGE FACTORY

Mrs. Stella Clarke (Bristol) asked whether the Association of Commonwealth Universities was a motivating force in international collaboration in research, or were the initiatives simply those of individual universities? She could understand funding bodies questioning the justification for spending grants on apparently useless research and looking for accountability. She suggested that, as early retirements freed much useful experience and special skills, it should be made widely known that some universities in developing countries abroad could use the staff concerned.

Professor Sir John Butterfield (Cambridge) said the Committee for International Co-operation in Higher Education arranged such placements. Professor G. Benneh (U. of Ghana) said that the main need in developing countries was expertise in research, and visiting experts would be welcome.

Professor L. S. Srinath (IIT, Madras) said that India was not part of any large multi-national bloc and therefore tried to be self-reliant. Hence it was the national prerogative to determine what projects to pursue.

Dr. D. Harrison (Exeter) also took up Mrs. Clarke's point and said that the higher education division of the British Council encouraged visits of experts to countries in need of their advice or skills. The practical means took various forms and there were diverse types of link. There was usually benefit to both sides and there should be a systematic approach to the task of relating offers to needs.

The Topic Chairman said that the point should be brought to the attention of the ACU officers.

Topic 2

FINAL SESSION

Thursday, 11 February

In the final review and summary session it was agreed to continue investigating the balance between teaching and research which had emerged as a central issue throughout much of the group's discussion.

Professor G. P. McNicol (Aberdeen) said that universities were often failing to project their aims to graduates who would be active in their professional careers well into the twenty-first century. They needed the capacity and motivation for a life-time of continuing education and could acquire it best in a research environment concerned with the assimilation and processing of knowledge. Mr. J. R. S. Morris (Loughborough) referred to the differing abilities of students and staff. All should be engaged in scholarship but not all were fitted for research. Dr. G. J. Hills (Strathclyde) referred to teaching and research as a seamless robe, not to be treated as separate entities. He contested Professor Don Aitkin's view that researchers need not teach and stressed that technology transfer required teaching skills.

Mr. R. M. Mawditt (Bath) said that universities should not undervalue market factors. They should use the basic research to advance applied research and improve their influence in the community through partnership with industry.

Other speakers supported the interlinking of teaching and research and Dr. Chia-Wei Woo (Hong Kong U. of Science and Technology) said that even the institutions in the USA alleged to be solely concerned with teaching in fact collaborated in research.

Professor Aitkin replied that the issue was becoming one of semantics and that if teaching and research were inseparable then a duty to carry out research should be part of the contract of every university teacher. Governments did not interpret research so widely and they demanded accountability for the large funds attributed to research which were also in competition with claims for other activities.

Professor D. G. Penington (Melbourne) referred to the wide

spectrum of higher education institutions. It was possible to teach without doing research but it would be a different sort of teaching. The advancement of knowledge was a university commitment and students were deprived if they were not taught in an environment in which theories were tested and revised or discarded. Professor Sir David Smith (Edinburgh) reaffirmed his view that teaching and research were inseparably linked. It was helpful to think of the process of learning rather than teaching and students would learn best from staff who were also learning. This process ensured continuous advancement of knowledge and it was important to foster it by freeing funds for investment in very bright people.

Professor L. S. Srinath (IIT, Madras) also supported the dual role. Teaching activity was recognised principally on campus while research activity was principally recognised off campus and this made the latter more likely to be rewarding in career terms.

Dr R. C. Atkinson (California, San Diego) said that the USA had no rational policy for science and technology but great attention was paid to setting of priorities. The question was who set priorities, rather than how they were set. He referred to a number of projects which had received 'Golden Fleece' awards by the media as being foolish projects but which had proved in later years to have valid applications. He agreed that teaching and research must be linked but not every college expected every faculty member to do both. Summing up the position in California, he said that the University of California judged faculty on both teaching and research, other universities and colleges laid the emphasis on teaching and some institutions confined themselves to teaching. This spectrum was related to the fact that in California 55% of high-school graduates went on to higher education.

In a subsequent note to the Chief Rapporteur reflecting on the final discussion, Professor Sir John Butterfield (Cambridge) contrasted the 55% in California, and high percentages in some Commonwealth countries, with the 9% of school-leavers going on to universities in the UK. Whereas the high percentage countries needed to cover a wider spectrum of abilities the highly selective UK system produced a concentration of the abler students who were likely to be more demanding of their university teacher's intellectual qualities. This made it more necessary to have teachers who were research-inspired. Sir John also referred to the seminal influence in the development of higher education of the Socratic type of enquiry, drawing out and building upon the intrinsic knowledge of the student. Students were eager for contact with good teachers who stimulated the learning process because they

FINAL SESSION

were themselves involved in it as active researchers. Governments and legislators should consider well the value of investing resources in the development of individual creativity which was fostered best and most efficiently in autonomous universities.

Topic 2

THE UNIVERSITY AS A KNOWLEDGE FACTORY

The Role of Universities as Centres for the Advance and Dissemination of Knowledge and for its application in support of National Development

CHAIRMAN'S REPORT ON THE GROUP'S DISCUSSIONS

Second Plenary Session
Friday, 12 February

Sir JOHN KINGMAN (*Vice-Chancellor, University of Bristol*): The topic for which I have been responsible was concerned, within the overall theme of national development, with research in its broadest sense, with the acquisition and advancement of knowledge, its subjection to critical judgement, its refinement and codification, and with its dissemination and application. Many wise things have been said about the way in which such research can be managed, and resources properly allocated, with the light touch necessary to encourage individual creativity. Much has been said about the increasingly important interplay of central planning and market forces, about the establishment of priorities, about international collaboration and so on, which it would be impertinent and futile for me to try to summarize.

But one issue kept recurring, that of the place of, and the justification for, research in the university. It has been perhaps the most characteristic single feature of the English-speaking university over the 75 years of the ACU that it offers education in a research environment. Not because every teacher produces original research of great note, but because each department of the university has a commitment to its subject, to the advancement of knowledge within its borders, which gives a quite different quality

CHAIRMAN'S REPORT　　　　　　　　　　　　　　　　　　[*Kingman*]

to the educational experience. Teacher and pupil are both, in their different ways, learning new things.

This central role of research and scholarship in the university is now being questioned. This is partly because some research is becoming so expensive that equipment and facilities need to be concentrated in a few centres, but partly because universities are being compared with other degree-level institutions which, without a research commitment, can achieve lower unit costs. The proper reaction to such questioning is not to pull up the drawbridge and defend the status quo, nor even to mount campaigns of lobbying and public relations, but to think; to think through why we see the advancement of knowledge as an essential part of the fabric of education at the highest levels.

In such consideration an important factor is the long-term nature of university education. It is a preparation for a world which will change out of all recognition during the lifetime of the graduate, who must not only adapt to such changes but must profit by and play his or her part in leading them. For it is the future leaders of the community whom the university is educating, and training for short-term purposes will not meet the case.

If university teachers are to be effective in helping their students not only to a deep understanding of their disciplines but to the habits of independent critical thought and responsiveness to change, they must themselves display these qualities. They will also be much more effective teachers if their own knowledge is not second-hand, if they have in their bones the feel of doing the thing they teach.

It is in this spirit that we welcome the increasing involvement of universities with their communities. So long as they avoid the merely routine, applied research can be just as much an intellectual challenge as basic, and greater awareness of the real problems of the world is likely to make for more effective graduates. But in the old phrase universities must be in the world without being of the world; they must resist the easy slide into short-term expediency and must retain that long view which is their special responsibility.

This will not be easy. As in so many of our countries resources become scarcer, the pressure is on to separate teaching from research, to fund teaching on a student numbers basis with little concern for the quality of education and to support research largely in terms of its immediate applicability. There will be much talk of selectivity and concentration, fine for big scientific facilities but bad for those who struggle to keep a research commitment in the average university department. We must learn again how to do good research on a limited budget (as Rutherford said: there is no money, we shall have to think). We must find other sources of research funding, which may very well be for particular applied purposes but which allow some headroom for basic research. Above all we must argue the case for research as a key factor in maintaining the vitality and cutting edge of our courses, and their relevance to long-term applications.

I think I speak for most, if not all, the members of the group when I say that, to educate the leaders of tomorrow, we need to do so in an environment of intellectual enquiry and rigorous scrutiny such as our tradition of the research university provides. It is a precious tradition, and one which still has much to offer a changing world. And if we do not defend it, you may be sure that no-one else will.

Group Discussions

Topic 3

UNIVERSITIES AND CONTINUING EDUCATION

The Responsibility of Universities to make provision for Continuing Education

Chairman: Dr. J. S. DANIEL
President of Laurentian University of Sudbury

Chief Rapporteur: Mr. D. J. CLINCH
Secretary of the Open University (UK)

		Page
Sub-Topic 3(a)	NEEDS, PROBLEMS AND POSSIBLE SOLUTIONS	
	Speakers	
	Dr. J. H. Horlock (paper read by Professor D. J. Murray)	175
	Professor P. N. Srivastava	180
	Discussion	184
Sub-Topic 3(b)	RECENT DEVELOPMENTS IN INDUSTRALIZED COUNTRIES	
	Speakers	
	Dr. J. S. Daniel	187
	Professor M. Skilbeck	192
	Discussion	199
Sub-Topic 3(c)	RECENT DEVELOPMENTS IN NEWLY INDUSTRIALIZED AND DEVELOPING COUNTRIES	
	Speakers	
	Professor A. O. Adesola	204
	Mrs. Kamalini H. Bhansali	210
	Discussion	219

		Page
Sub-Topic 3(d)	THE SPECIAL CONTRIBUTIONS OF DISTANCE EDUCATION AND EDUCATIONAL TECHNOLOGIES IN CONTINUING EDUCATION	
	Speakers	
	Dr. T. R. Morrison	222
	Professor D. S. Wijeyesekera	237
	Discussion	243
Final Session	Mr. B. R. H. Monks	247
CHAIRMAN'S REPORT ON THE GROUP'S DISCUSSIONS		251

For index to names, see p. 533

Sub-Topic 3(a)
NEEDS, PROBLEMS AND POSSIBLE SOLUTIONS

Monday, 8 February

*Dr. J. H. HORLOCK (*Vice-Chancellor, The Open University*):

CONTINUING EDUCATION: THE ACADEMIC CHALLENGE

1. *Introduction*

Definitions of continuing education (CE) are many and varied. A simple definition is post-formal or post-full-time education, but a wider definition used by a working party of the UK University Grants Committee (UGC) is 'any form of education whether vocational or general that is resumed after an interval following the end of continuous initial education'. To put it more simply—continuing education is education through life.

An excellent statement on the roles of continuing education by the UGC and the National Advisory Body for Local Authority Higher Education (NAB) is as follows:

'Continuing education needs to be fostered not only for its essential role in promoting economic prosperity but also for its contribution to personal development and social progress. It can renew personal confidence, regenerate the human spirit, and restore a sense of purpose to people's lives through the cultivation of new interests. In short, both effective economic performance and harmonious social relationships depend on our ability to deal successfully with the changes and uncertainties which are ever present in our personal and working lives'.

Thus continuing education serves two groups of adults—those who have ended their formal education early, and graduates well after they have obtained their degrees.

* Dr. Horlock having been at the last moment unable to attend the Congress, his paper was read by Professor D. J. Murray (Pro-Vice-Chancellor (Degree Studies), The Open University).

2. The Provision of Continuing Education

If the needs for continuing education are recognised in both developed and developing countries, how is CE to be provided? We must use all the educational resources available—including the conventional universities and the distance teaching institutions. But the latter have a major role to play because distance teaching matches the requirements of mature students so well.

New technological developments can assist in the provision of CE particularly through distance teaching. There is an impressive array of new technology becoming available—television by satellite and cable, video cassettes and video discs, teleconferencing and telewriting, micros for computer-aided learning. But we must beware of their associated costs, and there is a need for discrimination in the use of the media. The technology used has to be matched to the nature of the course, to the needs and capabilities of the students, and to the infrastructure available in a country (*e.g.* the reliability and penetration of public services such as postal services, electricity supply and broadcasting). Simple, accessible and easily available technology must be used first (such as radio and radio cassettes); above all the printed word is the principal and least dispensable form of communication for distance teaching/CE.

3. The Responsibility for Continuing Education

Who then should be responsible for the important area of continuing education? Obviously the conventional universities, with their academic expertise, teaching experience and traditional concern with adult education, have a role to play. There is an important and continuing task for extra-mural departments in the general area of adult education and in the provision of 'awareness' courses within the vocational area. Existing discipline-based departments have a bigger role to play in the vocational area, particularly in providing broadening and updating courses in specialist fields, often through short courses. This new role was well put by the Massachusetts Institute of Technology electrical engineering department at the time of its centenary (1982). Here was one of the leading engineering departments in the world stating that it accepted an obligation to provide the necessary updating for its graduates at the later stages in their careers. All MIT graduates will thus have the opportunity of going back to the Institute to 'retread' or to start on a new career in electrical engineering.

A new picture of conventional university departments in the

year 2000 A.D. can therefore be envisaged, with equal commitments to degree teaching, to postgraduate training and research, and to CE. In addition it does now appear from the experience of many countries, starting with the UK, that a separate national university specializing in distance education and co-operating with other educational establishments is required to meet national needs for continuing education.

The organization of continuing education in conventional universities is a difficult task. A separate academic department of CE is not the right answer since its members cannot hope to cover all the academic subjects involved in a comprehensive continuing education programme. Many existing discipline-based departments have to be involved, and this means that academic staff not previously involved must develop a new commitment to a form of teaching with which they have not hitherto been concerned. However it is usually necessary to establish an administrative unit, headed by a senior university officer, to organize the overall programme and to provide the academic leadership and drive for the programme.

In distance teaching universities, in spite of their commitment to continuing education in the widest sense, the problem of the balance between first degree teaching, research and CE is still a difficult one, and a separate administrative unit, possibly with small special academic units, is also required.

I conclude that continuing education thus poses a major academic and administrative challenge for all our universities in the twenty-first century.

4. *Experience of Continuing Education in the UK*

As indicated in the introduction, continuing education serves two groups of adults—those who have ended formal education early, and graduates well after they have obtained their degrees.

4.1 *The Open University.* The Open University of the UK (OU) was founded primarily to meet the needs of the first group, to provide university-level education for those who had either not obtained sufficient qualification for entry to conventional universities or had obtained those qualifications but had not proceeded to university for a variety of reasons (*e.g.* domestic, financial, etc.). The OU has been incredibly successful in meeting that need.

But the OU has also now developed continuing education outside and beyond its first degree programme. This role embraces not only the traditional 'extra-mural'-type short courses for adults (*e.g.* in community education and health education) but also post-experience vocational education, for teachers, for managers, scientists and engineers in industry or commerce. In the explosion of our student numbers on the latter courses during the past five years are included many graduates who find the distance teaching method offered by the Open University to be ideally suited to their requirements—'open learning which enables people to learn at the time, place and pace which meets their needs and their requirements' (a definition due to Holland).

The first degree programme of the OU posed the tremendous problem of bringing people up to degree standard from an academic base below that of the normal entry level for conventional universities. To do that it devised a unique method of teaching embracing many different components (print, audio and video material, experimental kits, residential schools, correspondence and face-to-face tutorials). The more recent extension of the OU's work into the area of post-experience and postgraduate education has provided yet another academic challenge. It was thought that the graduate student would find distance learning relatively easy, but this has not always proved to be so, and we are still seeking the best ways to teach at a higher level at a distance.

The Open University could not have provided continuing education so successfully without the help from many other universities and institutions of higher education in the UK. This co-operation takes several forms—but mainly through assistance in course production, presentation, assessment and examination. In course production many outside consultants are involved. (In the postgraduate courses they play an even greater role.) In any one year the OU employs some 800–1000 consultants. The assessment of course material before it is used has been a vital feature of Open University practice. In any one year, in which perhaps 15 new courses are completed, some 150 assessors will be employed. In course presentation, involving substantial tutorial provision, over 5000 people are involved both in teaching and examining.

An important link with other universities has been established through the movement of students to and from the OU and this occurs in a number of ways. At first degree level a credit scheme has operated for many years with 16 universities and all the polytechnics. Students may transfer from one institution to another, taking with them credit towards the degree in the second institution associated with work successfully completed in the first. In addition many graduates from other universities have taken a second degree at the OU. Recently collaborative schemes have enabled OU students to study full-time or part-time elsewhere (*e.g.* at Warwick and Cardiff universities), gaining credit towards their OU degrees.

Finally many thousands of OU graduates have moved on to postgraduate study. It is estimated that about 10% of the OU's 80,000 graduates have now gone on to master's or PhD degrees.

4.2 *The conventional universities.* Substantial provision for continuing education is now being made in the conventional universities of the UK. In addition to the long-standing education of some professionals (*e.g.* teachers and doctors) traditional extra-mural departments have for many years provided courses for adults (but not usually at professional level). There is now a growing activity in post-experience vocational education. Full-time master's courses have not proved universally successful, for a variety of reasons, but primarily because mature adults do not find it easy, for financial and domestic reasons, to take up long residential courses. Greater emphasis is now therefore being placed on short courses, and on part-time modular courses which may be 'stacked up' into a master's qualification.

With the prospect of diminishing numbers of 18-year-old students at entry, the conventional universities are being encouraged to use their resources to provide continuing education not only for the post-experience professionals but also to widen access to their first degree courses for older people without the usual entry qualifications. Thus the conventional universities will also be meeting the needs of the two groups of people who need continuing education—the early leavers and the post-experience professionals.

5. *Conclusion*

The academic challenge of continuing education—for non-graduates and graduates—is a stimulating one. In the UK no new providers are required as long as the existing institutions undertake continuing education with a will, but they do need financial incentive. More needs to be done to match MIT's commitment to continuing education as the third role for universities. But with current government funding policy, universities are struggling to meet their first two commitments (to first degree teaching and to research and scholarship) and many conventional universities are therefore hesitant about taking on additional responsibilities without further financial support.

The single most effective stimulus to continuing education would be the recognition by funding bodies that life-long continuing education merits a substantial degree of financial support, parallel to that provided for conventional first degree teaching and research.

On the international scene co-operation between the Commonwealth's distance teaching institutions through the new Commonwealth open university may lead to major steps forward in continuing education. We can hope to see courses prepared in one country used in another, and we may also see students working towards qualifications using a variety of courses through credit transfer. The founding of the Commonwealth open university is well-timed to match the growing demand for continuing education at levels ranging from sub-degree, through first degree, to post-graduate and post-experience level.

Professor P. N. SRIVASTAVA (*Member, Planning Commission, India, and formerly Vice-Chancellor, Jawaharlal Nehru University*):

CONTINUING EDUCATION WITH SPECIAL REFERENCE TO SCIENCE AND TECHNOLOGY

In the history of mankind, education has formed a continuum and a basis for the development of human society. Through development of attitudes, values, capabilities both of knowledge and skills, education provides strength and resilience to people to respond to changing situations and enables them to cause and contribute to societal development. It is only education that can imbue people with the knowledge, the sense of purpose and confidence essential for building a dynamic, vibrant and cohesive society capable of providing its people with the wherewithal for creating a better, fuller and more purposeful life.

Higher education is meant to provide ideas and men to sustain development of any nation or society. No programme of high-quality education can be implemented if the faculty themselves are not creative or are devoid of the excitement of innovation. With the explosion of knowledge, changes in curricula, etc., will have to continue to be very frequent. A teacher himself will have to remain a student to be up to date, for which he will have to learn continuously. In science and technology things are developing and changing very fast and if a person does not resort to continuing education he will be nowhere within no time.

It is very hard for developing countries in particular that even before they could cope with the first industrial revolution of the

SUB-TOPIC 3 (A): NEEDS, PROBLEMS, SOLUTIONS   [*Srivastava*]

nineteenth-century they were faced with the challenges of chemical technology, followed by micro-chip technology, biotechnology and the forthcoming technology of superconductors. The task has become very difficult because there has been a tremendous shortening of the time between the development of an idea and its useful application industrially. The time-lag between the development of the principles underlying the combustion engine and their application in automobiles was relatively long. The time-lag between the publication of Einstein's papers (1905) and the development of atomic energy was about four decades. But the period required for the advancement of electronic computing from idea into a major industry has been much shorter. Scientific principles and ideas are now moving to useful applications in only a few years and to product manufacture in only a few years more. It was only 14 years back that Stanley Cohen and Herbert Boyer, the Californian scientists, discovered restriction enzymes to cut the DNA and DNA ligase to join them in 1973 and we have already produced industrially Humulin (to replace insulin), human growth factor, several interferons, monoclonal antibodies, in the market for a few years now. At the moment biotechnology is being presented as potential cornucopia and the individual countries must provide backing to compete and to stay competitive. The possibilities which will be practical within a few decades in the areas of health and medicine, food and agriculture, energy, raw materials, chemicals and environmental management are unlimited and unbelievable.

During the last ten years or so the entry of computers into the ordinary house in developed countries has sustained one of the fastest growing consumer markets. Their use is limitless. They replace the telephone directory, give scientific, political, business, sports information, etc. You ask for any information and the computer will provide the data. All these applications arise from the extremely low cost of microprocessors—electronic circuits providing in a tiny volume the basic logical functions of a computer. The processing power of these components is constantly being increased, while at the same time their cost and size plunge down. Today we see before us the information revolution and the coming of an information society. Information and communication technology make it possible to strengthen man's intellectual ability in a way that other revolutions could not accomplish. In the years to come, however, software will prove to be an even more important problem. Software is in effect 'intangible material' and software technology will be crucially important to the information revolution. The maxim: 'Those who dominate materials, dominate the technology' is being changed to: 'Those who dominate software will dominate the world'.

It is hard to believe, but it is true, that it is only a year and a half since we first heard news of the startling breakthrough in superconductivity by two German scientists (Bednorz, J. G. and Muller, K. A.) working in the IBM's laboratories in Zurich. It is extremely rare for the Nobel Committee to recognise the event so fast and award the Nobel Prize to the two scientists within one year of their achievement. Breakthroughs in superconductivity bring us up to the threshold of a new age. We must recognise that recent breakthroughs in superconductivity have outrun existing theories and brought us to the threshold of a new world of opportunities. The world around us is in the process of a radical transformation, a revolution of shattered paradigms and long-held certainties. This transformation is opening for us new horizons of possibility. Some future superconductor applications include ultrafast shoe-box-size computers; smaller and cheaper medical scanners and magnetic resonance imaging machines; sensors to analyse the earth's magnetic field to find oil and mineral deposits; magnetic 'bottles' that store electricity indefinitely; power lines that transmit electricity with no loss of energy (conventional loss of energy being up to 25%); high-speed trains being levitated above the tracks; etc.

We are increasingly moving, and moving faster and faster, from an age of things to an age of thoughts, an age of mind over matter. In this new age it is the mind of man, free to invent, free to experiment, free to dream, that is our most precious resource. The value of a silicon chip does not lie in the sand from which it comes, but it is in the microscopic architecture engraved upon it by ingenious human minds. The most promising superconductors are made from ceramics—their value does not come from their material but from the brilliant inspiration of a few scientists. It is human imagination that is going to build the twenty-first century out of sand and clay.

The world of tomorrow, which would usher in an information-rich and technology-intensive society, calls for new approaches to learning. Developing the capacity to learn would be more important than what is learnt. Lifelong and recurrent education will have to be the order of the day. Herein lies the true importance of continuing education which will have to play a greater and more important a role in future. It is rather unfortunate that most of the universities have not yet realized the intensity of its importance and that is why perhaps greater attention is not being paid to this. The facilities for continuing education will have to be provided for working personnel in most of the universities and technical institutions. At present they are almost non-existent.

For continuing education, communication technology will have to be profitably used for instructional purposes. The development of new softwares will also have to be very fast, which should compare well with the fast developments in science and technology. It has already been demonstrated that, given a reasonably favourable situation, people will learn from any medium—television, radio, programmed instruction, film strips, tape recording or others. In general the things that control the amount of learning from the teacher face-to-face also control the amount of learning from educational media. What is necessary and important is individual abilities and motivation to learn. Choice of instructional media, therefore, depends on socio-economic and geographical factors, accessibility, convenience, etc., of the students.

In this respect universities which have better facilities have to help and assist universities which lack them. Similarly universities of the developed and advanced countries should assist others in the developing and less advanced countries. It is imperative that co-operation at least amongst the universities of Commonwealth countries should be started, the earlier the better.

It is very timely and heartening that one of the decisions taken at the last Vancouver (Canada) summit of the Commonwealth heads of state was to set up a Commonwealth university and college network for promoting distance education co-operation among Commonwealth countries. This decision is based on the Lord Briggs committee appointed in 1985. The university envisaged by the expert committee is not a degree-giving institution; it is in the form of a resource centre for distance education institutions throughout the Commonwealth, facilitating exchange of programmes, transfer of students, mutual recognition, etc. The offer made by the government of Canada is to set up a network which may in course of time become the University of the Commonwealth for co-operation in Distance Education. It may also be desirable to develop linkages with the United Nations University in Japan. The proposed network will have its headquarters in Canada with various regional units in Britain, the Mediterranean, the Caribbean, Eastern and Southern Africa, West Africa, South Asia and the Pacific, etc. Canada has already offered funds to the extent of £2 million towards capital cost and an additional £4 million towards recurring cost over a period of five years. India too has offered £1 million and Nigeria £1.5 million over a five-year period. Additional funding is expected from other Commonwealth countries such as Britain, Australia, New Zealand, and other countries from Africa and the West Indies. It is a development in the right direction and the Association of Commonwealth Universities should make the best use of it.

DISCUSSION

(*Rapporteur:* Mr. N. J. GILLANDERS, Registrar, University of Hong Kong)

Continuing Education: the Academic Challenge

The ambiguities of policy in most countries with regard to the financing of post-secondary education attracted considerable attention; governments generally appeared to be willing to accept responsibility for funding full-time education of school-leavers to degree level but were reluctant to finance to the same extent continuing education work—whether in the form of professional updating courses or of courses for adults embarking late in life on first degree work. In consequence all universities engaged in continuing education faced difficult problems of resource allocation. The UK government's apparent unwillingness to fund updating courses in engineering and science was however contrasted with the extent of the influence on the establishment of the Open University exerted by the government's own special interest in upgrading the qualifications of in-service teachers in its schools.

Initiatives by the private sector to provide alternative funding sources were rare. A Canadian contributor referred to the dangers of state funding leading eventually to state interference and suggested that the state might play a less obstrusive, but nonetheless effective, role through such policy initiatives as the granting of tax credits to successful continuing education students and the negotiation, in labour contracts, of provisions for granting to workers rights to paid educational leave.

On the interrelationship of the Open University and the Open College in the United Kingdom, Professor D. J. Murray (Open) explained that whilst there was no formal institutional connection there was an element of cross-membership in the governing bodies of the institutions, as well as considerable informal consultations between their academic staff members. The government's intention in creating the Open College had been to develop courses of a technical nature at a sub-degree level, exploiting the technologies of distance learning which had been introduced in the Open University. It also wished, however, to experiment with new organizational forms as alternatives to the somewhat centralized format of the Open University, including in particular the 'contracting out' to external agencies of certain services such as warehousing, computer systems and so on.

One of the Indian delegates stressed the increasing difficulty, with the acceleration in technological change, of attempting to confine the whole educational process within the hitherto conventional timescale of some

SUB-TOPIC 3 (A): NEEDS, PROBLEMS, SOLUTIONS

15 or 16 years, and the consequent need for universities and their teachers to be ready to contribute up-to-date skills over a longer time-span to individual students, through whatever systems of delivery of continuing education might be adopted. He felt this challenge must be met, notwithstanding fears sometimes expressed of resultant increased numbers of unemployed in the ranks of the educated workforce.

Attention was drawn to the practical problems in the UK context of engaging the interest of teachers in the traditional universities in continuing education work. If these institutions were to make significantly greater contributions in the future, means would have to be found not only for ensuring reasonable levels of financial incentives to encourage work beyond normally expected workloads, but also for achieving a fair apportionment of the total input to be made by university teachers to continuing education programmes. He felt that viable incentives, including profit-sharing schemes, could be evolved but agreed, in response to a question, that there were grave practical difficulties in evaluating the relative standing of continuing education teaching work. A solution to this was vital in the situation which currently existed, in which staff promotions ordinarily were heavily influenced by research and publication records and in which, in consequence, there was reluctance by some gifted academic staff to undertake continuing education teaching.

There was general recognition that, where the target clients of continuing education programmes were small in number and/or scattered in distribution, the costs of delivery of programmes could be prohibitively high. Professor Murray suggested the thorough examination of the feasibility of alternative delivery systems involving conventional institutions if at all possible; but concurred in the view that considerations of social policy would sometimes override cost-effectiveness criteria where the fulfillment of the aspirations of students concerned rested solely on the possibilities offered by distance learning techniques.

Continuing Education with special reference to Science and Technology

There was a general appreciation of the special problems which continuing education would face arising from the increasingly rapid developmental cycle of new science and technology to which Professor Srivastava had referred. Attention was drawn to the need to maximize the use of sophisticated and expensive laboratories in existing universities. This suggested that the most effective approach, at least initially, might be the concentration of higher-level work through the existing institutions. There still remained, however, difficulties of funding what were often quite expensive courses. The UK Open University's experience in the production of science courses was that distance education could be effective but that the costs of both production and delivery were high. The experience in the UK was a reluctance of industry, in some fields, to help with these expenditures, if some degree of control was not retained by the sponsors in the use of teaching materials derived from the funding provided. The new Commonwealth distance education initiative was seen

TOPIC 3: CONTINUING EDUCATION

as possibly facilitating the sharing of the costs of developing sophisticated teaching materials for advanced updating professional courses.

Finally the group was reminded that the challenges facing continuing education in relation to science and technology teaching were not confined to keeping pace with quickening scientific advance; if courses were not to become excessively specialized and overnarrow, concentrating solely on training in scientific techniques, thought would also have to be given to education in the moral, political, environmental, aesthetic and other social consequences which flowed from the application of these advances in technology.

Sub-Topic 3(b)

RECENT DEVELOPMENTS IN INDUSTRIALIZED COUNTRIES

Tuesday, 9 February

Dr. J. S. DANIEL (*President, Laurentian University of Sudbury*):

TRENDS IN UNIVERSITY CONTINUING EDUCATION IN THE INDUSTRIALIZED COUNTRIES

Education and the Economy

The belief that training and educating people is the best investment a society can make, known as the human capital theory, inspired the rapid expansion of post-secondary education systems that occurred in the industrialized countries a generation ago. During the period of economic difficulty experienced for a few years before and after 1980 education fell somewhat out of favour as greater attention was accorded to the other ingredients of economic success. But after a decade that has seen the balance of commercial and industrial power swing sharply towards Japan, education has regained its primacy as an economic predictor. Japan is successful, according to Ford (1987), because it is a learning society to a greater degree than other industrialized countries.

This re-emergence of education as a heavily weighted factor in the economic equation has been accompanied by attempts, notably at the OECD, to discover which parts of the overall educational endeavour have the strongest correlations with prosperity. These studies (*The Economist*, 1986) have found two measures that predict economic success more accurately than simple aggregate indicators such as per capita expenditure on education. The two best educational indicators are: (1) the proportion of young people pursuing full-time education after the end of compulsory schooling and how long they do so, and (2) the proportion of young workers (25–35) improving their training through part-time university study.

We do not, of course, suggest that the steady expansion of university continuing education in the last generation has been driven by government and institutional policies reflecting the economic importance of part-time study to the state. The driving force has been individuals, particularly women, who have found continuing education to be of personal benefit and have created a demand for it. Governments have responded to this phenomenon in some countries, notably by the establishment of distance education projects and open universities. Distance education has also been used to augment opportunities for full-time study by young undergraduates. Indeed most of the world's distance education students are enrolled in open universities in countries such as China, the Soviet Union, Korea and Thailand which cater to young, full-time students.

The response of many institutions to the growing demand for continuing education has been much more timid. The slogan that 'more means worse' trips easily from the lips of academics even if it is only a polite paraphrase for 'inconvenient to us means undesirable for society'. Even the laudable efforts devoted to demonstrating the economic benefits of basic and curiosity-oriented research sometimes reflect resistance, within the academy, to the trends toward lifelong learning and easy access to universities.

This is perhaps the most serious ideological challenge facing the world's universities. If they refuse to admit that technology can improve and extend teaching they will be condemned to the old zero-sum game between quality and accessibility. Like cottage industries overwhelmed by quality products from Japanese factories, universities are in danger of losing market share to educational enterprises that have adapted to changing circumstances and understood the potential of new technologies. Fortunately some universities have organized themselves to respond to the new needs. We shall examine some of their responses.

Credentials for Lifelong Learning

Since universities define themselves by the diplomas and degrees they award the creation of a new credential is the most radical response to the demand for lifelong learning. Only the USA has done this in a systematic way (although the notion of credits within degree programmes was a radical innovation in the UK when the Open University introduced it). The US response is the continuing education unit (CEU). These are now awarded by an array of institutions in numerous disciplines and professional fields. The award of a CEU simply attests that a student has devoted a certain number of hours to the study of the field in question. Some Canadian universities, such as McGill, have been authorized to award CEUs since they are more conveniently located for some US professionals than their own universities. The idea has not caught on in Canada generally and this has led some professions (*e.g.* banking) to begin their own work on credentialling for continuing education.

Experiential Learning and Challenge Examinations

Giving credit for knowledge gained through employment or home responsibilities, rather than through formal instruction, is another practice that has been adopted fairly widely in the USA but is less common elsewhere. It is an indirect descendant of the challenge examination system operated for external students by the University of London. The London external degree was, however, almost phased out in recent years. In general it is no easier—and may even be harder—for a student to gain credit from a university without enrolling in that university's own courses than it was ten years ago. In Canada, for example, Athabasca is still the only university to offer a degree that has no residence requirement, *i.e.* to which any number of credits from recognized universities can be applied. It is perhaps in this respect that the new Commonwealth university and college network for distance education, created at the 1987 meeting of the Commonwealth Heads of Government, has the greatest potential for good and will meet its biggest challenge. Its declared aim is that 'any learner anywhere in the Commonwealth shall be able to study any distance-teaching programme available from any bona fide college or university in the Commonwealth'.

Changing Demand for Subjects

Continuing education is mostly education for change so subjects grow and decline in popularity. Computers, for example, have opened up an entirely new field of training, first in programming but now in the application of software packages. Managers had to become computer literate but are now called on to automate office operations, a challenge for which study of the nature and organization of work is probably more relevant than a knowledge of Fortran.

A review conducted in Canada (Bélanger and Omiecinski, 1987) reveals how the demand to study various subjects part-time changed from 1975 to 1985. Arts and science declined by one third, to 20% of enrolments; business increased by the same amount to just over 20%; humanities remained steady at 8%; mathematics and physical sciences increased three times but from a small base, still only accounting for 6% of enrolments. Many of these changes reflect the choices made by women. 60% of part-time students in Canada are female and they have moved strongly into areas that used to attract few women. Now women make up the majority of part-time students in all subject areas except engineering and mathematical/physical sciences.

The Growth of Company Universities

The creation of post-secondary educational institutions within large companies is not new. The General Motors Institute at Flint, Michigan, dates back to 1926 and has graduated 18,000 engineers. Now the commitment to in-house training is probably increasing faster than the commitment to training generally. According to Eurich (1985), by 1984 the combined training budgets of US business and industry were as large as the combined budgets of all that country's colleges and universities. Eighteen corporations, including of course McDonald's, have degree-granting institutions in house (Amos, 1987). There are good reasons for companies to do some training themselves. With the current emphasis on 'corporate culture' it may be more culturally appropriate. Universities should ask themselves, however, whether the trend to in-company training does not reflect shortcomings on their part which could and should be corrected. At a time when large companies are following the Japanese example and contracting out operations wherever possible there is no reason why they should have to adopt the opposite policy for education and training.

The scope for university-industry partnerships is large and, thanks to studies such as that of the Université de Montréal (1985), the dos and don'ts of successful collaboration are beginning to be identified. Productive partnerships require institutional will and flexibility on both sides (Maxwell and Currin, 1984).

Summer Schools

In many industrialized countries university summer schools were an attractive opportunity for teachers to speed up the obtention of their degrees by intensive study. In recent years the number of practising teachers enrolled in universities has declined, causing a reassessment of summer schools in particular. The results show that universities are quite capable of imagination and flexibility. Institutions have discovered that the condensed schedule of summer session can be an advantage, not a handicap. It lends itself well, for example, to intensive language training. Combinations of study and travel have applications in this and other subject areas.

There is also an interesting trend for high school students to seek special courses during the long summer holidays. Last year Laurentian University ran six-week 'summer schools for excellence in science' for 120 students who had one more year to go in high school. Quite apart from being one of the most intrinsically successful courses our University has ever run, we are sure the experience increased the pupils' educational ambitions and will generate additional applications to our university programmes in future.

Distance Education

Distance education is a growing component of continuing education in industrialized countries and of regular university study in some newly industrialized and industrializing countries such as Thailand, China and India. Distance education lends itself well to policy initiatives by governments and must adapt to the communications infrastructure of each country, so generalizations across countries are hazardous. Britain, for example, created a single open university (thereby, some would argue, closing all the others). Canada and Australia have encouraged an institutional free-for-all with some government incentives to create an environment in which the Darwinian selection of the fittest can take place. Probably the major weakness of present patterns of distance education is that, with a few exceptions, some subject areas are oversupplied while in others, usually the contemporary and technical ones, there is not much on offer. It will be a key objective of the Commonwealth distance education initiative, which we mentioned earlier, to develop collaboratively courses and programmes in high demand.

Conclusion

The trends in university continuing education in industrialized countries that we have examined share the characteristic of mirroring trends in society at large. Through the continuing education function universities can demonstrate their responsiveness to the needs of the society to which they are accountable and test different approaches to new challenges. It goes without saying that continuing education units cannot meet this challenge unaided. Unless the whole institution is imbued with the commitment of putting knowledge to the service of people the continuing education unit will not be able to do its job and the quality of the university will suffer.

REFERENCES

Amos, S. (1987): *Learning from Each Other: University Industry Collaboration in the Continuing Education of Scientists and Engineers.* Proceedings of a workshop held November 24 and 25, 1986, in Toronto, Ontario. Science Council of Canada.

Bélanger, R. and Omiecinski, T. (1987): Canadian Social Trends—Summer 1987, p. 22. Statistics Canada, Ottawa.

Eurich, N. P. (1985): *Corporate Classrooms. The Learning Business.* Princeton: Carnegie Foundation for the Advancement of Business.

Ford, W. (1987): 'A learning society: Japan through Australian eyes', in J. Twining et al., eds., *World Yearbook of Education:* Vocational Education. Kogan Page, London.

Maxwell, J. and Currie, S. (1984): *Partnership for Growth: Corporate-University Cooperation in Canada.* Montreal, P.Q.: Corporate-Higher Education Forum.

The Economist (1986): 'Training for Work'. December 20, p. 93.

Université de Montréal (1985), Services Coopératives de développement des ressources humaines: *L'An II. Bilan et perspectives.* Montréal.

Professor M. SKILBECK (*Vice-Chancellor and Principal, Deakin University*):

THE ROLE OF THE UNIVERSITY IN CONTINUING EDUCATION: THE DISTANCE MODE

1. *The Scope and Diversity of Continuing Education*

By 'continuing education', in the most general sense, is meant the education of adults, whether at an elementary or advanced stage but building on their skills and experience, whether vocational or general and more broadly cultural, and whether for the sake of professional advancement or personal interest. Clearly such a wide definition obliges us to consider closely the precise role of the university since ours is but one of the many agencies and institutions with a part to play in a comprehensive provision of continuing education in the modern world.

Postgraduate education in the university setting cannot be overlooked if we adopt the broad definition I have proposed, if only because programmes are now being structured in such a way that the same course may either be taken for credit or be free standing, that is, 'non-award'. Continuing education also includes, in the university setting, advanced specialized diplomas.

First degree courses are also a form of adult education and therefore 'continuing' in that sense. On the other hand, in Australian universities continuing education departments, divisions or centres normally provide a wide range of short courses, workshops, seminars, field trips and conferences which are not related to advanced qualifications. This indicates that the field of continuing education, even in the university, is quite diverse. It is an aspect of the modern university where pluralism and diversity can denote a high degree of flexibility and responsiveness to social and personal demand.

Whereas the major award-bearing programmes in the university are highly structured by required curricula, assessments, degree requirements and so on, many forms of continuing education can be provided on a needs basis and without the inevitable delays and administrative complexities of degree programmes. Non-award continuing education in the university is also characterized by much greater flexibility in relation to academic prerequisites than is to be found in the mainstream degree programmes. Clearly we must, in using the term 'continuing education', keep in mind both the overall scope and the differences between the award and non-award approaches.

Continuing education, even in the more limited non-award sense, has become a significant part of the contemporary Australian university. There is, moreover, a long history of external studies in this country, including part-time degree programmes which have enabled particular professional groups to upgrade their qualifications through evening study. Whilst most universities have provided this on campus, during the past decade there has been a substantial expansion of off-campus provision. Much of our present continuing education in the university sector is therefore to be found in part-time degree programmes taken in the distance education mode. Five major university providers (Deakin, Macquarie, Murdoch, Queensland, University of New England) have formed a consortium to enable students to take each other's courses and there has recently been a proposal for such co-operation amongst the colleges of advanced education. As I have already indicated, there is also a substantial provision of non-award courses in which every university participates.

2. *The Range of Provision*

The range of Australian provision is, in the words of Johnson and Hinton (1987), 'as wide as the range of human interests'. These authors classify those interests into: (1) vocational; (2) general; (3) special needs. It is particularly in the first two of these categories, that is the vocational and the general, that universities have been most active. The vocational theme is now much more firmly linked with commerce and industry and their declared needs than hitherto. This reflects on our economic preoccupations and the very strong current drive to put higher education to the service of national economic development. As for the 'general' area, the most significant developments appear to be the growing overlap between the traditional form of non-award adult education and the award courses. Universities are increasingly widening access to adult students who are not formally qualified on the old entry rules, but are given bridging courses and granted credit for professional experience and personal maturity. The growth of modular courses also facilitates a merging of non-award and award programmes. Distance education is particularly relevant here, given its concentration on mature students and its adoption of course modules in degree programmes. The third category, special needs, particularly of disadvantaged groups, is of growing importance in our universities. Intensive specially-funded programmes, for example for Aboriginal students, and bridging studies for school-leavers from schools which are formally classified as 'disadvantaged', are indicative. As a consequence of government social policies in the domains of equity and social justice, doors once closed or scarcely ajar are opening. The universities have shown a very considerable responsiveness to these policies, as to the economic development initiatives to which I have alluded. It is particularly in such programmes that we find examples of innovative teaching including problem-centred experiential learning (Boud, 1986).

3. *A Policy Vacuum?*

Notwithstanding these and other developments, continuing education in the universities is in a state of some uncertainty and still lacks a rigorous policy framework. Far too much has been left to the interests and initiatives of individual staff members and departments within universities. Admirable as these initiatives have been, they do not and cannot match the requirements of our society for a comprehensive programme of continuing education focused on both social and personal needs. If we take seriously the arguments being put forward by scientists, technologists, policy analysts, economic and social commentators, that our world is undergoing rapid and radical change owing to the transformations of knowledge in every field, the need for high-level continuing education for large sectors of our population is obvious.

All of the industrialized economies of the world, including Australia, are engaged in a highly competitive quest for new knowledge-based industries, and the wide-spread application of technologies to all major sectors of economic activity. The accelerating growth of the service sector and the rapidity of change in the industrial and agricultural sectors require new levels of skill and new kinds of knowledge which cannot adequately be provided in our universities through traditional undergraduate and end-on postgraduate courses. Provision must focus much more closely on the real situations of the adult workforce both in terms of their knowledge and skill requirements and their work and general living circumstances. As already indicated in this Congress, part-time study through flexible modular courses and using the distance education mode is the direction in which we should be going and much more rapidly than at present.

There is a temptation to concentrate new developments along the lines I have indicated in the fields of science, technology, commerce, business administration, computing and other areas of what I shall call manifest economic development. But economic activity is not an end in itself, nor can these fields of knowledge and activity be isolated from a wider social and cultural context. It is already perfectly obvious that new technologies such as genetic engineering raise fundamental moral issues which call for moral knowledge and understanding of a high order in our community. The introduction of new technologies into the workplace raises industrial issues whose understanding and management call for other kinds of social and political knowledge. Agricultural and industrial technologies have complicated environmental and social consequences which must be carefully analysed and understood using interdisciplinary research models and theories. The rapid urbanization of the world poses the most complex questions and raises aesthetic and spiritual as well as more material considerations.

These and other elements which might be adduced do indeed

pose a crisis in modern culture, a turning-point in our civilization. It is not enough to refer to them as the third industrial revolution unless at the same time we are prepared to extend the idea of the industrial revolution to the whole of life. Our policies and practices of continuing education in the university must address the scale and complexity of these issues and our programmes must rise to meet the demands they pose. It is only in the university that the range and depth of knowledge and understanding that are required can be mobilized. I do not mean to suggest by this that it is only in the university that the requisite knowledge and skills reside. That is far from being the case, since it is particularly in the domain of continuing education that we must be ready to draw upon the resources of the whole community. But the university is quite central to the changing knowledge base of our society and it is there that the strategies and instruments for knowledge development and utilisation can be most comprehensively developed. Unfortunately the potential of the university in this regard is not always recognised either by its own members or by the wider community. And we have much work to do in building up this understanding within and outside our institutions.

4. *The Task for the University*

This understanding, these relationships, are not a matter of words and declarations, but action. My proposition is that the university can rapidly establish or re-establish its central role as the principal instrument of advanced knowledge in our society by two means. The first is better articulated and more co-ordinated research including large-scale co-operative research and development. Important as this is, it is not our primary focus in this part of the Congress. The second way in which the university can demonstrate its understanding of the ways in which knowledge is transforming our society is through continuing education. I believe we need to bring to this area models of lifelong or recurrent education which are focused on the lifespan of individuals and their changing and evolving needs for knowledge and understanding. Such models would complement the individualistic and *ad hoc* approaches that are common at present. They still have their place, but it must not be an exclusive one. We must also build up a research base and develop better theories of continuing education and ensure that policy discussions are focused on it. We must also examine the conditions within our own institutions which tend to depress or marginalize continuing education. For example, continuing education needs to be brought more centrally into the concept of the academic career and, as we have already seen in this Congress, conditions of service will have to be renegotiated so that teaching contributions are properly recognised.

We cannot treat continuing education in the university in isolation, however, from the educational system as a whole. I have already suggested that the specific role of the university derives from its central role in the processes of discovery, development, dissemination and utilisation of knowledge of the most advanced kind. While many other things may be included in university continuing education programmes this must surely be the focus of our efforts. Other providers are there to meet other needs.

The approach I have proposed also requires a rethinking of undergraduate degree programmes and upper secondary schooling. Such rethinking is, of course, a continuing process, but I am not convinced that the kinds of issues that I have attempted to raise are being sufficiently thought about in school and undergraduate reform programmes. If continuing education is to be properly understood and developed it must be seen as part of a comprehensive educational process whose foundations are laid in the schools and in the undergraduate years. The better the quality of general education in these years and the more emphasis is given to the processes of learning, values, interests, commitments and motivation in learners, the more able will we be to erect the continuing education structures that are needed. For this purpose learning itself needs to be perceived as a fundamental, lifelong human activity and the dominant force in social development.

5. *The Place of Distance Education*

In conclusion I would like to say that, as with so many other reforms in higher education in Australia, there is a potential for really significant development in continuing education which has been only partially realized. This potential is the instrument of distance education. While distance education exists on a large scale in Australia and has been practised throughout practically the whole of the twentieth century in both university and school sectors, we are at present faced with some major unresolved difficulties. We have achieved a great deal, but still not enough.

There is, on the whole, an unco-ordinated proliferation of courses through distance education within Australia. We are not getting the essential economies of scale without which distance education is an expensive indulgence. Whilst real student needs are being met, the price of meeting them is far too high. Thus, while we have more than 40 providers of courses leading to degrees, etc., we lack a co-ordinated network of study centres. The individual institutions cannot afford to maintain such a network, and there is no national or state-wide provision for it in either the university or the college of advanced education sectors. Library services and facilities are inadequate or, where they are provided on an ambitious scale, as in my own university, they are expensive. Our arrangements for contracting, cross-crediting, split-site teaching, co-operative planning and development are rudimentary and piece-meal, although both the university and the college sectors have made or are making modest moves to improve the situation.

We have an opportunity during 1988, as a consequence of the federal government's recent Green Paper on higher education, to address such problems and to bring distance education quite centrally into consideration as a primary means of expanding continuing education along the lines I have indicated. This will call for the most determined government action at both state and federal levels with constructive co-operation amongst the present providers. The current Green Paper debate in Australia is not focused on continuing education, but there is no doubt that both state and federal governments are looking to the universities to strengthen their contribution to national development including economic development. This seems to me to provide an opportunity for the universities, all of which are being required to prepare institutional profiles in order to participate in the so-called unified national system, to demonstrate that in the late twentieth century the continuing high-level education of the populace is as important to the nation as was universal elementary education in the nineteenth century.

REFERENCES

Anwyl, J., Powles, M. and Patrick, K.: *Who Uses External Studies? Who Should?* University of Melbourne, 1987.

Boud, D.: 'Facilitating learning in continuing education: some important sources'. *Studies in Higher Education*, vol. 11, no. 3, 1986, pp. 237–247.

Johnson, R. and Hinton, H.: 'It's human nature: non-award adult and continuing education in Australia'. A discussion paper prepared for the consideration of the Commonwealth Tertiary Education Commission; July 1986.

Ministerial Review of Adult Education in Victoria: *Focus on Adults. Towards a Productive Learning Culture.* Victoria, Ministry of Education, July 1987.

Neumann, R. and Lindsay, A.: 'The Johnson-Hinton report on continuing education: some implications for higher education'. *Australian Universities Review*, no. 2, 1986, pp. 45–7.

SUB-TOPIC 3(B): IN INDUSTRIALIZED COUNTRIES

Smith, B.: *A Review of Continuing Education by the Australian Universities.* Department of Community Programmes, University of Newcastle, 1984.

Smith, B. W.: 'The financing of adult education in Australia: a view from the perspective of recurrent education'. An unpublished paper, 1987.

University of New South Wales: 'Continuing Education Activities 1986'. 26th *Annual Report.*

University of Queensland: 'Continuing Education' (Guide). February 1987.

Ward, J.: 'Comment. The Centre for Continuing Education?' *The University of Sydney News*, vol. 19, no. 20, 28 July 1987.

West, L. H. T. et al.: 'The Impact of Higher Education on Mature Age Students'. Canberra: Commonwealth Tertiary Education Commission, 1986.

DISCUSSION

(*Rapporteur*: Mr. R. H. ELLIOTT,
University Secretary, Deakin University)

A. *Trends in University Continuing Education in the Industrialized Countries*

After presenting his paper on this subject Dr. Daniel gave an account of events leading to the proposal to establish an institution to foster Commonwealth co-operation in distance education. Discussion following his presentation was, for convenience, separated into these two topic areas.

(i) *Trends in university continuing education in industrialized countries.* Several questions were raised regarding the involvement of universities in continuing education activities leading, in some cases, to the award of continuing education unit (CEU) credits. Issues arising from the award of such units include: under what circumstances is it appropriate that those units be counted for credit towards award-bearing programmes offered by universities? The fact that the CEU is awarded for simply attending a course of study and not on the basis of any assessment of mastery of the course content makes it difficult to have credit given towards the satisfaction of degree requirements. There is also the difficulty that the content and orientation of CE courses is quite likely to have been determined by a company or professional association for a purpose bearing little relation to that of degree courses offered by universities. The calibre of the staff offering the CE course is also a consideration.

Should a university be offering CE courses in particular areas of study? In some areas it is clear that universities are very well placed to offer CE courses which may or may not be suitable for subsequent crediting towards a degree programme. In others, however, it may well be that they are not as well placed as a commercial or industrial organization.

Consideration needs to be given to expertise and facilities required for particular CE courses and if these are not available within the university, nor can they be bought in conveniently, it may well be better to leave the area to a more appropriately equipped organization.

The development of company universities suggests that for several reasons, including but not restricted to the availability of facilities and expertise, some companies believe that they are better placed to offer initial training and CE than universities. In response to a question about the status of company universities in the United States, Dr. Daniel explained that there was a considerable variation in the level of academic work undertaken by them. While some were clearly not of university level, some very good work was being undertaken in the training and research sections of corporations such as IBM and Xerox. In the USA the Boeing Corporation operated its own PhD programme using academic staff of US universities to ensure that appropriate standards were maintained. The question of the limited ability of universities to offer useful courses in some state-of-the-art and sensitive research areas was raised. It was noted however that there seems to be an increasing tendency for companies and other organizations to contract out to universities for some at least of their training and staff development needs.

Several participants commented that a number of Australian universities were providing CE courses on behalf of professional bodies such as the Society of Accountants. Bodies such as this now require members to engage annually in approved CE activities as a condition of continuing membership. Similar requirements appear to be developing in engineering and computing. In these instances, where universities have the necessary expertise and facilities and are well placed to contribute to the design and development of appropriate updating courses, it was thought appropriate that they should be involved. The trend towards contracting universities to undertake such teaching does raise some matters for them to consider, however; for example, the consistency of this activity with university objectives—entry to courses offered on this basis is outside the university's control as is the specification of course content. There are, however, offsetting benefits to consider. The income generated expands the resource base of the university and its ability to pursue its general objectives. The involvement of staff with the commercial and industrial world also has a number of benefits, including the possibility of extending the knowledge of staff and increasing the value of universities in the eyes of those sponsoring these courses.

Information was sought on the extent to which Commonwealth universities are prepared to give credit for CE courses, for experiential learning and for work undertaken at other institutions. It was noted that very little credit is given for experiential learning. In most industrialized countries there is now a general willingness to recognise work undertaken at other universities within the country. Almost all universities, however, have an upper limit to the proportion of a degree that can be granted on this basis. Athabasca University is an exception where there is no such stipulation.

SUB-TOPIC 3(B): IN INDUSTRIALIZED COUNTRIES

The view was expressed that universities should look closely at challenge examinations and other means of assessing the worth of work done by prospective degree students in the continuing education area, as it was likely that more students undertaking these courses would wish to receive credit for them in future.

(ii) *Commonwealth co-operation in distance education.* Dr. Daniel's description of events leading to the proposal to establish in Canada an institution to facilitate Commonwealth co-operation in distance education gave rise to a discussion of organizational issues and of the differing purposes to which distance education was put in Commonwealth countries.

One participant suggested that a regional approach to co-operation would be more effective than a single institution attempting to meet the needs of all regions. Dr. Daniel explained that although the proposal was to have an operational headquarters in Canada there would be a network of agencies linked with this. It was thought essential that accreditation matters be handled centrally but this would not prevent the development of bilateral or regional co-operative arrangements.

The use of distance education as a means of providing access to higher education for those who have just completed secondary schooling was a topic raised by several participants. It was noted that on a world-wide basis the majority of students studying at university level by distance education were in the 18-22-year-old age group and that in quite a number of countries distance education was being used as a means of expanding access to higher education where demand exceeded the capacity of conventional institutions. In other countries however the majority of distance education students are older and usually study part-time. These students often chose to study by distance education for reasons of convenience rather than as a result of their inability to gain a place in a conventional university. In these countries the provision of distance education study opportunities can lead to competition with conventional forms of university study and there has been a tendency to exclude the 18-20-year-old group from access to distance education programmes. The experience of the Open University was that in the UK there was relatively little interest from this age group in studying part-time by distance education. The level of performance of those who did enrol was inferior to that of older students studying by this method.

Mr. P. R. C. Williams (Commonwealth Secretariat) mentioned that in planning for the establishment of a Commonwealth distance education institution it was hoped that smaller existing universities in some countries might be able to make use of distance education materials for on-campus teaching. This would enable them to provide a wider range of study options and to offer courses in specialist areas where local resources did not justify the development of such courses. At the University of Malta distance education materials had been in use for some time for this purpose.

TOPIC 3: CONTINUING EDUCATION

B. *The Role of the University in Continuing Education: the Distance Mode*

A point made by Professor Skilbeck on the need for a co-ordinated network of study centres to support distance education activities was taken up, and Professor Skilbeck explained that in Australia, at least, there was a variety of possibilities. One possibility which was favoured by the Commonwealth Tertiary Education Commission (CTEC) would be to have centres established and operated by colleges of technical and further education. These colleges are more widely distributed throughout Australia than colleges of advanced education or universities and, in some states at least, already provide a network of study centres for teaching at the technical and further education level. Existing universities and colleges could be part of a network as could existing adult learning and teacher education centres. Professor Skilbeck suggested that what was needed first was a policy framework for the provision of a national system of study centres and the agreement of the federal government to fund such a system. This would allow individual institutions to determine the form of their distance education activities with a much clearer knowledge of support facilities available to students.

The staffing of study centres and of continuing education courses is apparently an industrial issue in several countries. In Botswana the university has difficulty in obtaining staff to run evening classes and in some instances it is necessary to offer additional payment to staff to take these classes. It was noted that in Australia the usual pattern is that staff are paid extra for CE activities and that this practice will be accentuated by the development of a more rigid industrial context. From the United Kingdom the view was expressed that the case for CE being seen as part of the mainstream activity of universities was weakened if additional payments were made to the staff involved. It was suggested that it was preferable to include participation in such activities as part of the normal teaching duties of staff and to pay extra only if the total volume of teaching duties exceeds that covered by any teaching agreement or contract.

Professor Skilbeck indicated that in Australia there was a considerable variation in both the level of fee charged and in who pays. If a full cost recovery fee is not charged then the cost is being shared between the university and the client—be it company or individual. Professor Skilbeck commented that more and more Australian institutions are moving towards a full cost recovery approach to continuing education. There was not a standard approach to staff payment for continuing education work: some incentive may be necessary. One contributor from the UK suggested that although universities should be charging the full cost of mounting CE courses, to ensure that these costs did not distort overhead costs in other areas, such an approach can lead to customer resistance. In some instances individual members of staff have been hired to conduct in-house courses at a lower cost to the company than that proposed by the university for it to mount the course.

The development of institutional profiles mentioned in Professor Skilbeck's presentation was one of the proposals made in the Australian

SUB-TOPIC 3(B): IN INDUSTRIALIZED COUNTRIES

government Green Paper on higher education of 1987. Professor Skilbeck explained that under the unified national system of higher education proposed in the Green Paper each university will be required to negotiate its role with the federal government. This will include the nomination of areas in which each university will specialize, enrolment levels, modes of teaching, provision of research funds, etc., and may also involve negotiation of performance levels in various areas. It was pointed out that the information available to universities on the form the profile might take made no provision for reference to the CE activities in which universities may wish to engage. It was also noted that the Green Paper made no comment on the role of universities in CE and that this was consistent with the absence of any statement by the Commonwealth Tertiary Education Commission or federal government policy in this area.

In relation to credit transfer and student mobility an Indian contributor pointed to the problems of language and structural rigidity in Indian higher education and sought information on credit transfer arrangements between Australian universities. Professor Skilbeck provided details of the consortium operated by the five Australian universities offering distance education programmes (Deakin, Macquarie, Murdoch, New England and Queensland). An external studies consortium being developed within the college of advanced education sector in Australia was also described. This will operate on a different basis with distance education teaching materials being sold between member institutions and the purchasing institution assuming responsibility for teaching the course. Under both the universities' and the colleges' consortium arrangements co-operation has led to the identification of gaps in distance education provision and to the joint development of courses to fill these gaps.

The group noted that in Australian and most other universities there is no distinction on academic awards or transcripts as to whether students have studied by distance education or attended classes on campus. In relation to the prospect of using distance education materials developed at one institution in other institutions, and perhaps in other countries, it was mentioned that copyright arrangements needed careful attention. Agreements with staff and with agencies from which teaching material might be drawn are important considerations in containing costs in the development of courses destined for use outside one's own institution.

Sub-Topic 3 (c)

RECENT DEVELOPMENTS IN NEWLY INDUSTRIALIZED AND DEVELOPING COUNTRIES

Tuesday, 9 February

Professor A. O. ADESOLA (*Vice-Chancellor, University of Lagos*):

THE NIGERIAN EXPERIENCE

Continuing education has been used within higher educational institutions interchangeably with terminologies such as adult education, further education, lifelong education, extra-mural studies and outreach programme. The choice of nomenclature often depends on the perspective of the individual. In discussing any aspect of continuing education, therefore, one initial problem is that of definition, or of scope. Practitioners within the university system often limit themselves to outreach or community-based programmes operated by universities as against programmes run for regular or resident students; thus continuing education is regarded as a means of extending university-type education to the general public. Other practitioners outside the university, particularly policy-makers within a ministry of education, would more likely consider any post-literacy programme carried out outside the regular school system as falling within the general term of continuing education. This paper will look beyond the four walls of the university in assessing recent developments in continuing education in Nigeria.

Constitutional Framework

Successive constitutions in Nigeria have always provided for shared responsibility for education at all levels. In practice, however, regional/state governments have shown greater prominence in secondary and primary education, while the federal government has operated predominantly at the tertiary level with only a token input at the secondary level. The very limited resources of local and state governments have therefore always meant inadequate attention to both the primary and secondary education, with consequent high illiteracy rate put at between 70%–80%. Ironically the non-formal type of education has not received so much attention either. By the principle of shared responsibility, adult literacy education, post-literacy and remedial education have been taken care of by the state and local governments. The federal government participation as usual is very minimal.

Private Sector Participation

Remedial post-primary education was for long outside governments' attention. In the early forties and fifties prospective candidates looked towards correspondence tuition houses in England, with Wolsey Hall and Rapid Results College being in the forefront. Beneficiaries were usually those who for one reason or the other did not have the opportunity of school education or could not complete the course. For various reasons private correspondence establishments in Nigeria soon took over from the overseas tuition houses. The private sector participation in continuing education can be classified broadly into two, namely:

(i) vocational studies which help to prepare individuals for external examinations such as Pitman's, City and Guilds, and similar other professional external examinations;

(ii) remedial academic studies leading to School Certificate, the General Certificate of Education and the Joint Admission and Matriculation Examination for university applicants.

Government Participation

Recently both federal and state governments have made some forays into vocational and remedial studies within and outside the normal school system. In the vocational areas ministries of establishments have opened establishment schools for training of professional secretaries and typists from among secondary and primary school-leavers while ministries of trade in the states operate co-operative colleges to train co-operative secretaries and inspectors. Trade centres have also been opened to train various categories of technicians.

Both the federal and state governments as a matter of government policy have also gone into providing remedial education for school-leavers or drop-outs. For example, the Federal School of Arts and Science was intended to provide tuition for School Certificate holders in arts subjects aspiring to do science subjects in the university while providing remedial work in both the arts and the sciences. Many state governments also run similar schools in various parts of the country to provide qualified candidates to fill allotted places in tertiary institutions and establishments such as the armed forces, the police, etc. The Schools of Arts and Science, sometimes called the School of Basic Studies, provide remedial tuition of one to two years' duration.

Foundation of University Participation in Continuing Education

University participation in continuing education practice has always been based on policy decisions and recommendations which gave birth to these institutions. The Asquith Commission, appointed by the British government in 1943 to work out modalities for university education in the colonies, recommended: ' . . . in every colony served by a University there should certainly be one centre for extra-mural studies and . . . there should be similar centres whenever urban or industrialised locations provide opportunities for part-time study'. The Elliot Commission, appointed by the British government in 1943 on the establishment of a university in West Africa, made similar recommendation: ' . . . an extra-mural department should enable the University maintain a direct contact with the community, preventing its students from becoming a separate class'. Similarly, the national policy on education launched by the federal government in 1981 devoted much attention to 'Adult and Non-Formal Education' which should 'provide in-service, on-the-job, vocational and professional training for different categories of workers and professionals in order to improve their skills . . . '.

The University of Lagos Act also provides for an 'Extra-Mural Department' in line with the UNESCO Advisory Commission on the establishment of the university which stated that the University should ' . . . offer continuing professional education in business and industry and to meet the general needs of the country by offering specialised courses, seminars and conferences on appropriate subjects for large groups of people who may be able to benefit thereby'.

SUB-TOPIC 3(c): IN DEVELOPING COUNTRIES   [*Adesola*]

Scope of University Participation in Continuing Education

The scope of university participation in continuing education in the country is as varied as the number of universities. However, we would examine briefly three of the universities which could give a reasonable spectrum of continuing education practice in Nigerian universities.

University of Ibadan. The University started in 1949 an extension department targeted at providing remedial studies for primary school-leavers, secondary school drop-outs and primary school-teachers who wanted to obtain the requisite university admission qualification. Centres were created in the major cities around the country, and qualified teachers appointed to provide face-to-face teaching. By 1964 the department of extra-mural studies was integrated with the faculty of education, which provides a number of intra-mural credit or certificate programmes ranging from one-year certificate course in trade unionism and industrial relations, and two-year diploma in adult education and community development, to various degree and higher degree programmes, and some experimental adult literacy classes organized in conjunction with the Oyo state government.

Recently the University, which had to scale down its original nation-wide extra-mural studies, has introduced some form of distance education programme which would enable working-class people in and around Ibadan to read for various degrees while still in employment.

University of Lagos. Again, as indicated earlier, part of the underlying philosophy of the University of Lagos is the provision of part-time studies for the working-class people of the city of Lagos and its environs. Hence the University's tradition of extra-mural studies is as old as the University itself. The University has had such programmes in the faculties of business administration, law, arts, social sciences (now discontinued), education and science.

While some of these faculties provide such services direct to their clientele, others perform similar functions through our Correspondence and Open Studies Institute which adopts the distance education strategies in its operations, and with study centres in several states of the federation. Until a year or so ago the University also had a Continuing Education Centre which provided tailor-made non-credit courses for government ministries and parastatals and the private sector; these activities have been taken over by the faculty of business administration in conjunction with the University of Lagos Consultancy Services Unit, which ensures that such services are provided on strictly commercial basis in view of the excrutiating finances of the University. The Institute of Education provides 'sandwich' or 'summer' programmes for the advancement of serving teachers, while the department of adult education provides training at undergraduate and postgraduate levels for policy-makers in the area of adult education and mass literacy.

Ahmadu Bello University, Zaria. At the inception of the University it 'acquired' a number of autonomous centres and institutes already performing large-scale extension services in various areas of community life. Hence the extra-mural programmes of Ahmadu Bello University appear much more diverse than those of any of the other universities, and the establishment in 1971 of the Adult Education and General Extension Services Unit was intended to provide a co-ordinating body rather than new services. The collaborative services now provided include: (i) educational broadcasting and public enlightenment; and (ii) evening classes for a wide spectrum of candidates.

In some ways like Lagos, the Institute of Education at the Ahmadu Bello University provides a variety of sandwich long-vacation programmes for teachers.

Also the Ahmadu Bello University provides remedial courses in its School of Basic Studies for prospective university entrants without requisite qualifications.

General Assessment

A number of writers, including Renee and William Petersen in their book, *University Adult Education: A Guide to Policy*, advocate that university participation in adult education should be at the level or standard appropriate to a university, or what they describe as 'College level'. Similarly S. G. Raybould in his *Adult Education at a Tropical University*, which is an assessment of extra-mural work at the University of Ibadan, felt that the extra-mural work below the university normal academic programme should best be handled by agencies outside the university. Similar view is held by a number of Nigerian adult educators. Whatever position one holds, it is pertinent to consider here a quote from Dr. Kwame Nkrumah, a one-time President of the Republic of Ghana, which states in part: 'A University does not exist in vacuum or in the outer space. It exists in the context of a society and it is there that its proper place is'.

The issue of determining appropriate level and scope of continuing education for the universities in developing countries is very debatable. It would be safe to conclude, however, that the nature and scope of societal needs, and the expertise available within a given university relative to facilities available in other institutions, may very well be used as the yardstick for determining the scope of its activities in this important area of providing service.

Other Participants in Continuing Education

That both governments and private institutions have come to realize the importance of lifelong education for the acquisition of new skills, retraining old hands and attitudinal adjustment is manifested in the establishment of institutions such as Administrative and Staff College of Nigeria (ASCON) which provides in-service training for civil and public servants in administration. In collaboration with the University of Lagos ASCON now offers a master's degree programme to some of its graduate participants. Also assuming greater importance is the Centre for Management Development (CMD), which could be described as the private sector equivalent of ASCON, and the Industrial Training Fund (ITF) which provides a variety of training programmes to lower and intermediate staff of industries and companies. By the law establishing it the ITF is sustained with funds contributed by the various organizations it serves. In line with the above, there are now more specialized bodies providing continuing education of a specialized nature. For example the Institute of Journalism, Lagos, provides further education for journalists in the print media, while the Television Production Institute in Jos provides similar training for those in the television houses. The number of such bodies could be listed *ad infinitum*.

The cry of unemployment within the country which has been caused by mass retrenchment of workers both in government and private establishments, the freezing of vacancies in most establishments, has led the federal government into current mode of participation in further education. In order to provide self-employment for retrenched workers, and unemployed school and university graduates, government has embarked on massive retraining programmes. The objective is to turn the unskilled potential workforce which forms the bulk of the unemployed into productive hands with specialized vocations that could generate employment. Such retrained hands are then given loans to start trades of their own.

The threat of retrenchment and redundancies due to government economic policies has given way to a general feeling of insecurity of tenure. Consequently hundreds of unskilled workers at all levels voluntarily seek retraining opportunities in the professions which they could practise to sustain independent livelihood. The most frequently sought after professions are law, accountancy, business administration and computer science. It is not therefore surprising that most universities now run part-time/evening programmes for working executives and for which appropriate economic fees are charged to boost university financing. For example, at the University of Lagos convocation held in January, 1988, out of a total of 538 graduates produced by our faculty of business administration 306 belong to the category of working executives who obtained their degrees through our Correspondence and Open Studies Institute (COSIT)—a distance education programme.

Conclusion

The scramble for educational opportunities and the inadequacies of various governments at local, state and federal levels to satisfy this need, the current economic downturn which has led to various economic policies aimed at revamping the economy but with the attendant side effects manifesting in massive retrenchment, unemployment and job insecurity, have given a new dimension to practice and scope of continuing education in Nigeria. Provision of vocational and professional training opportunities has now become a new industry within the economy. The universities have not been left out; they have responded to the need through the expansion of their further education facilities and part-time programmes, thus generating additional revenue for the institutions. This, no doubt, is a welcome development in view of the funding problems facing the universities. Considering the magnitude of the continuing education activities going on at various levels, university participation, significant though it is, could only be regarded as a drop in the ocean.

Mrs. KAMALINI H. BHANSALI (*Vice-Chancellor, SNDT Women's University*):

Background

For this paper I have taken India as a model of an industrializing and developing country and I propose to emphasize the sociological constraints and the need for new strategies and techniques.

A developing country from the economic standpoint is one in which there is enough potential for economic growth if the available natural resources are optimally utilised, the economic measures of such development being the rise in *per capita* income over a period of time. Developing countries have generally to contend with excessive growth of population, lack of savings and a low rate of capital formation accompanied by imbalance between the different sectors of the society, and India is no exception to these characteristics. Thus, even while granting the growth that we have achieved so far and a good deal of progress that we have made over three decades of planning, the basic problem of population explosion on the one hand and the chronic shortage of capital on the other still persists. To achieve the desired developmental planning India naturally aims to foster industrialization through promotion of an efficient industrial structure with emphasis on cost reduction, quality improvement and upgradation of technology.

One must not lose sight of the fact that economic development by itself does not constitute total development of a society. There are other vital dimensions which need to be considered when we speak of national development. Factors such as economic, political, social, religious, ethical, all go to make an integrated identity of a nation. Politically India is lauded by the world as the biggest democracy. The two important tenets of a social democracy, equality and social justice, pose a difficult task. To meet this need India has the largest programme of upliftment of the conditions of the weaker sections and has emphasized the role attributed to women towards gaining equality through empowerment. The Indian society faces a dichotomy of traditionalism and modernity. This has resulted in diversity between the different social groups towards their attitudes to life styles and towards their requirements in skill and knowledge. India has a total population of 685 millions with a literacy rate at 36%. To meet this challenge the Indian economy has to achieve a balanced growth of all its sectors, and industrialization is the prime key to it. Such industrialization requires a high rate of capital formation.

Since savings are low in a poor country, it has to make the best of its available capital resources. It is in this sense that human resources development assumes considerable importance. Recognising the importance of this facet a central ministry with the designation of Human Resource Development (HRD) has been created. It is accepted that one of the primary tasks of the nation is to harness the country's human resources and improve their capabilities for development with equity. Programmes for alleviation of poverty, improving health programmes, control of demographic trends, reduction of economic and social inequalities through legislative measures and social welfare and improving productivity should be integrated with educational development, as these are indicators related to the progress of the nation. The programmes would particularly focus upon women, youth and economically weaker groups to enable them to make increasing contribution to the socio-economic development of the country.

Education can be formal or non-formal. Formal higher education is entrusted to the universities and, with the emerging needs of development, there has been a tremendous expansion of the formal systems of education. In 1985–86 the higher education system had a complex of 149 universities; 5723 educational institutions; 50,000 teachers; and 35·70 lakhs* students. Recipients under the formal educational system have an ultimate objective of employment. However, mass social requirements of such an education demand increasing efforts for non-formal education. It is in this context that the vast complex of formal reservoir of human resource can be best utilised.

Extension as Third Role of University System

The multi-dimensional concept of continuing education includes adult education, lifelong education, substitute education, second-chance education, further education and so on. In spite of this wide diversity of terminology the distinguishing feature of the different terms has a common core, namely, non-formal approach and non-formal process. For an individual, continuing education is a non-formal mode of learning that continues throughout life; for an institution it is an offering of a multi-faceted lifelong educational service.

The concept of continuing education is not new to India but institutionalization of the concept is of recent origin. It was as far back as 1970 that the University Grants Commission (UGC) initiated the programme of continuing education. Today over 90 universities and 2000 colleges in the country are involved in adult education, of which 30 universities and 50 colleges offer continuing education programmes. The UGC, in its policy frame in 1978, accepted the concept of extension as an equally important function of higher education, in addition to teaching and research; thus giving an opportunity to universities and colleges to promote increasing participation in a dynamic way. In order to have a comprehensive and integrated approach, various facets of education such as continuing education, adult education, population edu-

---

*1 lakh = 100,000

cation, legal literacy, science for the people, planning forums, were aggregated under one single umbrella of extension.

Happily the UGC in less than two decades has made far-reaching strides to concretize extension as the third function of universities. A review undertaken has pointed out that there have been positive gains, such as making the system flexible and open, reflection of relevancy in restructured courses, change in attitude towards obligation to society through a two-way process, programme expansion and emergence of adult education as a discipline.

The thrust areas under continuing education include:
- development of vocational skills and professional competence among technical, managerial, industrial and office workers, entrepreneurs and unemployed youth
- remedial or bridge courses
- promotion of activities for self-employment and self-reliance
- need-based programmes for community development, and for particularly less privileged sections of society
- training and extension packages for functionaries of various social development
- human resource development in the field.

The main target groups would be women, workers including slum-dwellers and migrant workers, school drop-outs and unemployed youth, professionals and para-professionals, business executives and the citizens, as per the demands.

Operational Approach

The operational approach for continuing education needs an analytical definition and here I would like to refer to the one given by International Commission on Development Education:

'There are many possible definitions of *adult education*. For a large number of adults today, it is *a substitute* for the basic education they missed. For the many individuals who received only a very incomplete education, it is the *complement* to elementary or professional education. For those whom it helps to respond to new demands which their environment makes on them, it is the *prolongation* of education. It offers *further* education to those who have already received high level training; and it is a means of *individual development for everybody*. One or the other of these aspects may be more important in one country than in another, but they will have their validity'.

Substitute education. In the Indian context the first function relates to making illiterate adults literate. Nearly 50% of the world's population is illiterate and one third of that is in India. Leadership in India has accepted adult education as a national movement and the government launched the National Adult Education Programme (NAEP) in 1978, followed by a comprehensive revised programme in 1983 comprising the Adult Education Programme (AEP), with a focus on universalization of elementary education for those in the age group 6-14 years, and the programme of eradication of illiteracy for those in the age group 15-35 years through a centre-based approach. The AEP dealt with literacy, social awareness and functional development through literacy, post-literacy, continuing education, and mass programme of functional literacy (MPFL).

Prime Minister Rajiv Gandhi has identified eradication of illiteracy as one of the five missions. The Technology Mission for Eradication of Illiteracy (TMEI) is set up to mobilize social focus for raising the quality of life of the people. Continuing education under the Literacy Mission will be achieved through Jana Shikshan Nilayam (JSN) or community centres to serve clusters of 4-5 villages with a population of 5000, through evening classes, library services, short duration training courses, recreational and cultural activities and setting up of communication centres. Likewise the new education policy of the government of India has also emphasized adult education and extension work.

Universities and colleges, as per the direction of the University Grants Commission, will adopt an area development approach wherein total learning needs of the area would be responded to through a process of providing multiple inputs and multiple strategies including MPFL and centre-based approach. JSN will also be used as one such strategy. UGC, through the above approach, will provide universities and colleges with an integrated package of programmes including adult education, continuing education, population education, legal literacy and so on.

The contribution of Indian Universities Association of Continuing Education (IUACE) is crucial in promotional and co-ordinating roles through a series of workshops bringing personnel in the field on a common platform.

Second chance education. The problem of drop-outs leading to educational wastage is an immense one, second to that of illiteracy in its intensity. Adult education provides a second chance and has proved a useful complement to education. Time is not far when it will become an important alternative to the formal school system. The 'open university' system is a very bold step in this direction. The Central Board of Secondary Education (CBSE) provided an alternative to the formal school for out-of-school learners, working adults, housewives and others, through bridge courses to enable learner aspirants to take up later on secondary-level courses through the open school. Condensed courses is another such programme of education designed for women by the Central Social Welfare Board.

The SNDT Women's University pioneered in 1974 its 'open university programme' providing opportunity to women who are 21 years of age and above, irrespective of their academic qualifications, to join the university mainstream of formal education after undergoing a specially devised bridge course operated through distance education.

The Indira Gandhi National Open University (IGNOU) is the most recent experiment of open learning through distance education techniques designed to provide educational opportunities for adults in their own homes and in their own time and thus enable them to further their knowledge leading to formal programmes or credit courses of a non-formal nature. Other experiments include those by the Mysore, Madurai-Kamaraj and Andhra Pradesh open universities.

Supplementary education. The third aspect, prolongation or extended education, was given a shape through evening classes, adult schools, Shramik Vidyapeeths (institutions devoted to workers), people's universities assisting adults in extending the education acquired by them in their youth and thus equipping them to fulfil the multifaceted acquisitions expected of them in the organized and unorganized sectors. This area of extension work has been successfully undertaken by universities and colleges, voluntary organizations and government-sponsored programmes.

Further education. Further education or education for enrichment, the fourth factor, implies deepening of knowledge and furtherance of education through in-service training courses and updating of professional knowledge and skills. With the strides that knowledge is making this need is increasingly felt. The newest experiment in this direction, as envisaged by the New Education Policy, is the setting up of the academic staff colleges by the University Grants Commission to give orientation to newly appointed college teachers in the technology of teaching and setting up of district-level training institutes.

Linkages within curriculum have been established on various fronts, through involvement of students in field activity, through projects, curricular restructuring and offering training programmes for manpower development.

Women and continuing education. The aim of a learning society should be to make education accessible to everyone through a variety of different paths as may be appropriate to the age of the aspirant. This is applicable more sharply to women as they, as a group, form a disadvantaged section of society and have to face the pressures of dual or multiple roles. Women as a class comprise nearly half of the total manpower resources and, owing to this nature of composition, they suffer most from the ills of illiteracy, ill-health and social injustice. Moreover women form a substantial segment of the labour force in both rural and urban areas. The role of women's universities is particularly crucial in this respect. They should provide leadership to women. They should also work for educating women in a manner that will make women conscious of increasing opportunities to acquire equality in social status. University education must enhance women's capabilities for empowerment, failing which the continuation of the inferior position assigned to women will jeopardize the future of Indian society. The New Education Policy of the government amply substantiates this.

The SNDT Women's University in this resepct, over the years, has organized programmes with different orientations under the continuing education process. The first is the academic orientation which facilitates recipients to receive the degree of the University through the bridge course of its 'open university programme'. Culturally focused programmes are specifically oriented for women to develop appreciative attitudes towards the performing arts and appreciation of the country's cultural ethos. Socially oriented courses bring about awareness of socio-psychological issues surrounding women even with respect to their legal position in their life cycle.

Self-employment oriented courses have been taken advantage of by a number of women to utilise gainfully their leisure time, thus relieving the economic stress on the family. The SNDT University thus provides the type of extension education and community action programmes through its diverse dimensions which do not consider women only at the receiving end but also help in developing their self-confidence and self-reliance. The various departments of the University are also working as a transferring belt of knowledge by giving the role of providers to women. Further, the University has developed models through which women assume the role of change agents.

Programmes within the System and Outside

The Indian scene presents a complex panorama of multi-faceted educational activities. This covers programmes within the tertiary system which can be classified at three levels, namely the high professional level, the middle level and the grass-roots level. In addition there are several agencies and organizations outside the educational system offering continuing education programmes, maybe on a much larger scale. These, however, are limited to top-level training of the highest quality for specialized groups.

In a modern society, to meet fast developing needs, a stronger and closer linkage between institutions within the educational system and outside that system needs to be built up so as to enable both to share the responsibility to create a learning society. Both developed and developing countries are at grips with the transition taking place in the changed social order. Margaret Mead's words describe this situation realistically: 'No one will live all his life in the world in which he was born, and no one will die in the world in which he worked during his maturity'. All the scientific and technological developments must be harnessed through the agency of continuing education for the purposes of bridging this gap between the cradle and the coffin.

The Challenge

The challenge before us is to innovate and offer the last aspect of the definition, the individual development of the recipient, without which all the previous formal or non-formal educational offerings will spell failure. Individual development in a technological age comprises two facets: scientific attitude, and value orientation. Why is it that man who walks bouncingly on the surface of the moon walks hesitantly on his planet? This hesitancy may be due to a lack of critical aspects of this development. It is recognised that the implantation of both attitude and values cannot be achieved either by formal lecturing or by correspondence packages and set books of the open university.

Aldous Huxley gives three dimensions of an educated person. The first 'verbal', the second 'symbolic' and the third 'non-verbal'. The first two can be achieved by continuing education. What is 'non-verbal' education? Wordsworth gives the meaning of 'non-verbal' education as:
'Enough of Science and Art
Close up these barren leaves
Come forth and bring with you a heart
That watches and receives'.

Developed and developing countries have this challenge to meet by structuring strategies for the 'non-verbal' education by unique value-creating pedagogy.

REFERENCES

1. Ansari, N. A.: *Adult Education in India.* New Delhi: S. Chand & Co. Ltd., 1984.
2. Bhatia, S. C.: *Development oriented adult education.* New Delhi: Indian University Association for Continuing Education, 1986.
3. Bhatia, S. C.: *Environmental consciousness and adult education.* Delhi: University of Delhi, 1983.
4. Bhatia, S. C. and Patil, B. R.: *Research in adult education*—proceedings of national seminar 1982. New Delhi: Indian Adult Education Association, 1982.
5. Bordia, A.: *Adult education in India.* New Delhi: Indian Adult Education Association, 1973.
6. Bhansali, K. H.: *Signposts for a learning society.* Nasik: Gokhale Education Society, 1984.
7. Chandra, A. and Shah, A.: *Non-formal education for all.* New Delhi: Sterling Publishers, 1987.
8. Date, S.: *Technical education of women: an assessment.* Bombay: SNDT Women's University's Research Centre for Women's Studies, 1985.
9. Deshmukh, L.: *Women and continuing education programme of SNDT Women's University.* Bombay: SNDT Women's University's Research Centre for Women's Studies, 1981.
10. *Encyclopaedia of Social Work in India,* vols. two and four. New Delhi: Ministry of Welfare, Government of India, Directorate of Publication Division, 1987.
11. Faure, E.: *Learning to be: the world of education today and tomorrow.* Paris: UNESCO, 1972.
12. Illich, I. D.: *Deschooling Society.* New York: Harper & Row, 1973.
13. India, Ministry of Human Resource Development Department of Education: National literacy mission. New Delhi, 1987.
14. Jayagopal, R.: *Adult learning, a psycho-social analysis in the Indian context.* Madras; Department of Adult and Continuing Education, University of Madras, 1981.
15. Kundu, C. L.; *Adult Education principles and practice.* New Delhi: Sterling, 1986.
16. Ministry of Human Resource Development: *Annual Report 1986-87,* part I. Department of Education, Government of India, 1987.
17. Naik, J. P.: *Some perspectives of non-formal education.* New Delhi: Allied Publishers, 1977.
18. Reddy, V. I.: *Generative sources of disadvantage: the role of adult education.* Hyderabad: State Resource Centre, 1985.
19. Reddy, V. I.: *Lifelong learning operational concepts.* Hyderabad: Osmania University, 1983.
20. Sharma, I. P.: *Adult education in India.* New Delhi; N.B.O. Publishers, 1985.
21. Shukla, P. D.: *Lifelong education.* New Delhi: Orient Longmans, 1971.
22. Singh, R. P.: *Non-formal education an alternative approach.* New Delhi: Sterling Publishers, 1987.

SUB-TOPIC 3(c): IN DEVELOPING COUNTRIES

23. Trivedi, J. H.: *New Directions in Higher Education*. Bombay: SNDT Women's University, 1986.
24. UNESCO: *The development of adult education: aspects and trends*; report of fourth international conference on adult education. Paris: UNESCO, 1985.
25. University Grants Commission: *University system and extension as the third dimension*. New Delhi: UGC, 1987.
26. University Grants Commission: *Report 1985-86*. New Delhi: UGC.
27. University Grants Commission: *Guidelines on Adult, Continuing and Extension Education*. New Delhi: UGC, 1982.

Journals and Newsletters

1. *Newsletters* of Indian University Association for Continuing Education (IUACE), New Delhi; Directorate of Adult Education (DAE), Ministry of Education, New Delhi; Indian Adult Education Association (IAEA), New Delhi.
2. *Indian Journal of Adult Education*. New Delhi.
3. *Prasar*. Department of Adult Education, University of Rajasthan, Jaipur.

DISCUSSION

(*Rapporteur*: Mr. A. C. MARSHALL,
Vice-Chancellor's Office, Murdoch University)

A. In the discussion following the presentation of his paper Professor Adesola made the point that the development of the new continuing education programmes and the structures associated with them had been an evolutionary process, and that the pattern established in Nigeria could be expected to happen, over time, elsewhere in Africa.

The pattern involved economic upheaval and pressures which led to an increased demand for continuing education programmes for retraining and providing options for unemployed or retrenched workers to enter or re-enter the workforce. The significant demand for continuing education and the nature of the demand had led to the involvement of federal and state authorities, the professions and private organizations in addition to the universities.

The changes in demand have seen continuing education move from the responsibility of a separate unit within universities, catering for limited numbers of students funded by the UGC, to a separate institution outside the university, but allied to it, operated by a mix of part-time staff, staff from the professions and academic faculty members, on a cost-recovery basis. The demand from students has been for business studies, accountancy, law, etc., rather than the traditional emphasis in continuing education on teacher education. The requirements of teacher education are now readily met via the colleges of education.

The pressure of demand has forced the universities to accommodate to the new programmes or find themselves relegated to a subsidiary and irrelevant role in continuing education. In the event the diversified system has remained closely allied with the universities. Continuing education is now taken seriously as an important area in its own right by the university, related in part to the level of demand but also to the fact that the programmes are sustainable financially.

In the discussion particular interest was expressed in the financial arrangements and the links between the traditional university structures and the new self-funding continuing education programmes. It was reported that the University of Lagos operated the continuing education programmes as a separate unit on a separate budget. In fact it was UGC policy that all income-generating units should be treated differently. The emphasis was on cost recovery and there was no view to subsidizing other operations of the university.

In effect the operation of the new programmes and institutes occurred with the close involvement of the relevant university which monitored the programmes and awarded the degrees. It was a collaborative venture which involved a wide range of staff from outside the university in addition to the academic faculty, who may work a certain percentage of their time within the institute and the balance within their faculty. If additional work was required of staff over a normal workload it would be necessary to maintain incentive by paying some form of salary loading.

It was noted while the question of teaching the new continuing education programmes in affiliated institutes was well established the question of transfer of credit between different institutions had not been faced successfully. One move in the right direction was the recent policy decision that all Nigerian universities move to a semester system which was expected to help facilitate credit transfer.

The issue of the difference in various countries' history and experience in continuing education and the problem of the use of terminology was noted. All Nigerian universities were involved in aspects of continuing education though there were some centres of concentration or excellence in the national system. It was argued that the demands posed by the evolution of society in the third world made the provision of some form of continuing education essential, though the method of delivery, *e.g.* distance education, and the nature of programmes would differ between institutions.

It was seen as important that the emphasis should be on what was appropriate to the specific local conditions and what was likely to succeed. Professor Adesola stressed that if the basic problem was mass illiteracy then clearly it was necessary to tackle that in the first instance, in whatever way would be successful. A strong commitment was needed. It was emphasized that a country should not attempt to move too fast. Certainly a country should learn from others' experiences but developments in other countries should not be allowed to deflect a country from tackling effectively such basic issues as illiteracy.

SUB-TOPIC 3(c): IN DEVELOPING COUNTRIES

B. The discussion of Mrs. Bhansali's paper centred on the challenges posed by the need to increase the participation of women at all levels of education in India. In line with other countries, the participation rate of women in Indian universities is rising and women are increasingly entering traditionally male areas such as engineering and the sciences as well as into developing fields of study such as computer science. While increasing in numbers, the proportion of women in most fields of study is still small except in areas such as medicine where 35-40% of the university places are reserved for women.

The special problem of India, however, is the low level of literacy. Whereas 47% of males are literate only 25% of females are, and therefore tackling the problem via adult literacy programmes is seen as especially important for women. To improve the literacy level of women it was seen as necessary to link literacy programmes to development programmes which provided avenues for gainful employment such as teaching specific skills, etc.

Apart from improving literacy a major educational problem is the drop-out rate from education. Adult education provides a second chance for working adults, unemployed and women to enter mainstream education.

Although women take advantage of these adult education programmes there are still fewer women than men involved owing to the various constraints—financial, marital, family—that women face. To try to counteract these constraints attention has been given by the SNDT Women's University to special condensed bridging courses to allow women to complete schooling quickly. These bridging courses are mainly correspondence-based, relying on printed matter and audio cassettes. These courses provide a major resource for women wishing to continue their education and many women who enter higher education this way are successful, particularly due to their high motivation.

India had established, through 1978 legislation, extension education as a primary aim of universities and colleges. To raise the quality of teaching and increase awareness of new developments, academic staff development colleges were being established throughout India.

Sub-Topic 3(d)
THE SPECIAL CONTRIBUTIONS OF DISTANCE EDUCATION AND EDUCATIONAL TECHNOLOGIES IN CONTINUING EDUCATION

Thursday, 11 February

Dr. T. R. MORRISON (*President, Athabasca University*):

LEARNING CONTINUOUSLY THROUGH DISTANCE EDUCATION

Continuing education is increasingly seen to be a necessary ingredient in an individual's lifelong learning path and a critical element in national development. Learning has become a lifelong necessity but there is a basic incongruence between that fact and public and institutional policies in education. Nowadays the phrase 'lifelong learning' is used as a rationale for a wide spectrum of proposals for reform. Moreover, the phrase is used with such off-handed ease that I think we have lulled ourselves into believing that it is a living reality within our institutions. But is it?

The concept of lifelong learning was injected into public consciousness through a 1972 UNESCO report entitled *Learning To Be*.[1] This concept is a revolutionary one, perhaps the only significant educational idea of this century. Those advocating it are arguing in favour of the implementation, on a system-wide basis, of certain subsidiary ideas: accessibility, institutional openness, needs-based learning, competency-based education, co-operative education, mastery learning, paid educational leave and credit for prior learning. To talk about developing educational institutions as centres for lifelong learning is to pose fundamental change. If the primary imperative of an institution is the control of, rather than the liberation of, people, it may be a false hope to assume that any institution *per se* can be founded upon lifelong learning principles. But a learning system can, since it has an effect greater than the sum of its parts.

In this context, then, what we are experiencing today is a pressure against the internal and external boundaries of our formal learning system brought about not by creative educational or policy thinking but by the aspirations and actions of people themselves. If this pressure continues, as I believe it will, then one can argue that we will witness either an accommodation within or a basic reconfiguration of our learning system. The shape, structure and degree of openness of our learning system, not, as many argue, the financing of it, will be the policy issue of the future. Till now, leaders in higher education have focused on the level of financing without realizing that this has energized an even more intriguing feedback loop: financing what?

Distance education systems provide one expression of the principles underpinning lifelong learning. These systems have risen to prominence, moreover, because of their potential to effect basic changes in the social and economic context of higher education. Distance education is, first, an alternative system for the provision of learning opportunities. It is a process innovation. The blurring of roles and functions amongst the providers of learning services, secondly, allows distance learning systems, through flexible networks, to link students to diverse learning opportunities. Distance learning systems, thirdly, are designed to accommodate the varying time and space realities facing part-time adult learners. Fourthly, as a process-based learning system, distance education is not bound by time, age or location and can provide lifelong learning opportunities, in the real sense. Lastly, distance education, of all areas in education, uses various ways to transmit information, most of which are independent of face-to-face teaching and which are increasingly mediated by tele-computing technologies.

Because of the discontinuity of societal trends with traditional educational systems, and the growing cost-consciousness of funding agencies, distance education has found that it is increasingly legitimate. Broadening the idea of distance to include cultural, social and economic distance from the mainstream of society, as well as geographic distance from the source of teaching, adds further to its appeal. Till now most of the thrust behind the development of distance education systems has been to extend opportunities to those geographically distant from, or culturally marginal to, formal learning. In this, distance education systems have achieved remarkable success in increasing accessibility and at reasonable cost.

Parallel to this core activity, attention is being turned by distance learning systems to continuing education with the encouragement of governments and employers. Unlike conventional universities distance education institutions do not usually have a governing model for continuing education or a tradition of involvement in it, and they have therefore a unique opportunity to assess past practice and to develop an innovative approach.

In higher education there are several different frameworks or models which guide theory and practice in continuing education. They are discussed below. Within each framework continuing education is seen as providing a service to institutions or learners. This segmented approach to continuing education, more than any single factor, explains both its triumphs and tragedies. If continuing education implies lifelong learning, and if, as one of its goals, distance education is concerned with overcoming barriers to the integration of life and learning, then such integration must be at the heart of continuing education through distance learning. The purpose of this paper is to establish some educational signposts to help us, through distance education, to transcend segmentalist thinking.

Let me now turn to the frameworks.

Continuing Education as Business Enterprise

Within this model objectives and programme mix are driven by the forces of the market and stress needs that can be met at a profit. This business model has been required in many universities since continuing education units are either placed on a cost-recovery basis or are expected to generate 'net revenue' for the institution. The entrepreneurial instinct of continuing educators has added further impetus to revenue-seeking. This model, where ability to pay is the main entrance requirement, leads to the development of such corporate strategies as market analysis and segmentation, sophisticated advertising, matrix management systems, 'star' recruitment and a concentration on the business and corporate community as preferred 'clients'.

There is no doubt that continuing education programmes within a business model can be self-sustaining and attractive in net revenue terms. But there are problems. The first is that such programmes lead to a skewing of educational service to those who already have, a 'second creaming' of the chosen crop. Continuing education, rather than providing a second chance to close the learning gap between classes, occupations and groups, would actually widen it.

The 'continuing education as business' model can also engender a cultural conflict within the university. The ethics of business are not necessarily synchronous with the values of the university. Profit alone does not translate into quality learning or academic excellence. Moreover, universities tend to focus on developing of a critical intelligence or habit of mind among their students. Even where ideological frameworks are used they are usually balanced by the injection of countervailing systems of thought. Within most 'continuing education as business' programmes, though, the 'client' is usually interested only in skills and knowledge within a prevailing paradigm, not an analysis of the assumptions of the paradigm itself.

A final problem with this model is that success often brings charges, from the private sector, of 'unfair competition'. Since most universities are seen to be supported by government grants, with major infrastructure costs being covered through subsidy, the costs of university continuing education programmes are seen to be either unrealistically low or their profit margins unfairly high. It is not uncommon for the very same members of the business community who accuse universities of being divorced from the reality of the market to protest vigorously when universities aggressively penetrate that market.

Continuing Education as Brokerage

In this model credits are dispensed through continuing education in exchange for fees or enrolment. The credit currency of the university is used to ascribe status to another agency or institution. There are many examples of such brokering arrangements: from professional associations which negotiate university credit for 'their' courses to various schemes of mandatory continuing education. From a university perspective a brokerage model has some attraction. For very little expenditure of resources universities can reap fee and enrolment credit while building linkages to a host of organizations and agencies. The reverse brokerage model can also be developed through such arrangements: universities can negotiate their courses as integral parts of the certification process of outside bodies, thus increasing demand and status.

But there are serious difficulties with this model too. The value of anything is, in part, related to its scarcity and the effort required to obtain it. Widespread and casual credit dispensing, through a brokerage model, can lead to a devaluation of the credit itself. Effective quality control standards and monitoring procedures have to be developed.

Brokerage models can also pose problems for university autonomy and control of the learning experience. Universities may discover that major curricular decisions about programmes are made by agencies beyond their walls and the reputation of the university used to legitimate the results. So, too, university courses can become entangled in a web of external programmes from which, for financial or political reasons, it is difficult to extract the institution.

Continuing Education as Public Relations

Continuing education programmes are often seen as a way to sway public and governmental opinion in favour of the relevance and values of the publicly funded university. Such programmes can offer the university a potential means of quickly meeting the urgent and fashionable needs of society, and doing so in a flexible way, seen to be free from the cumbersome and time-consuming collegial decision-making processes of the academy.

The difficulty with a purely public relations model is that programming can become guided not by 'what is good' but by what 'looks good'. This model confuses advertising with learning.

Continuing Education as Vocational Training

It has been argued that continuing education should, somehow, be exclusively tied to meeting the needs of people for jobs, careers and professional training and retraining. Tied to labour market forecasts, continuing education programmes would provide a firm bridge between the learner and a job. Programmes would be skill- and competency-based in design and substance. In the area of retraining such continuing education programmes would be buttressed by paid educational leave schemes. Types of knowledge not clearly linked to vocational aspirations or requirements would be absent from curricular offerings; they would be 'nice to know' rather than 'need to know'.

The 'continuing education as vocational training' model, however, contains several questionable assumptions. The model itself hinges upon the accuracy or validity of labour market forecasting. To design programmes within this framework requires clear and unequivocal data not only on employment demand by job type but also on skill needs by job type. The history of demand-supply analysis in the labour market, however, is riddled with errors of gross proportions.[2]

Tying continuing education to vocational objectives assumes too that unemployment and productivity issues can be solved through educational policy.[3] Universities which accept this framework must be willing to be judged by results in the world beyond the academy. Employment may be affected by education but it is not a function of it. Nor is economic growth.

The vocational model faces the university with a confused array of goals and expectations in which earning outweighs learning.

Continuing Education as Personal and Civic Development

In this model continuing education is seen as an extension of the role that the university has always played in developing personal and civic competence, with the university curriculum being transmitted, using adult education techniques, to a new group of consumers. The university is thus extended further into society: hence '*extension* education'.

No doubt there is value in this model. But it, too, can be questioned. The idea of adults or community groups actively participating, not only in expressing their needs or how they wish to learn, is anathema to this model. Experience suggests that if there is one thing adult learners display in continuing education it is impatience with irrelevance.

The extension model has been influenced recently by theory and research in adult education. Within this variant of the model the adult learner is placed at centre stage and the guiding principle is the process of human development. Within this framework the content and delivery modes for continuing education are to reflect the unfolding needs, interests and capabilities of the individual as he or she moves through the various 'stages' of development.[4] The model has produced an array of programmes targeted at particular developmental cohorts, *e.g.* youth, the aged, those in mid-life, single parents and other groups who are in 'developmental transitions'. In these programmes attention is paid to 'how adults learn' and to the unique crises or questions that face particular groups.

While all this has increased our awareness of how adults learn, and the role of life experience in programme design, this very awareness has generated unanticipated consequences. The first difficulty relates to what is called 'stage typing'. Much of the developmental research into adulthood has been conducted within an *a priori* stage model of development and there is a danger that a prescriptive conversion of descriptive tendencies may produce a misguided form of developmental stereotyping.[5]

A second difficulty arising from a developmental model is that it may not deal with the question of the direction of development or the type of development a society wishes to foster. Development of what capacities for what purposes? These are political, cultural and value-laden questions which cannot be resolved through empiricism.

From a university perspective, then, the developmental model of continuing education is problematic since it artificially separates process from substance in learning.

Towards a Model of Continuing Education for Distance Education

These various frameworks all pose problems. To import these models into the distance education context, given the absence of a face-to-face adjustment mechanism, would only intensify the problems. Continuing education within a distance education mode, therefore, requires its own framework—one suited to the goals, constraints, context and opportunities of distance education itself.

The starting-point in the development of a model of continuing education sensitive to the uniqueness of distance education must be the purpose of the enterprise itself. For most distance education institutions and systems the guiding purpose is to increase accessibility to learning for those who, for geographic or social factors, are remote from opportunity. This is not to say that all distance learning systems have been successful in doing this, particularly on the social dimension, but it remains the guiding principle.

Education is considered by most people to offer a means of improvement for the individual and society. The purpose of continuing education within a distance education mode is to develop a learning system in which fair access to this means of improvement is continuously available. This requires a commitment not only to lifelong learning but also to equality in the pursuit of that learning.[6]

The design of continuing education in a distance education mode must be influenced by an awareness not only of models of continuing education but also of the inequity in a given setting and of the barriers preventing learning. Continuing education in a distance mode, therefore requires an explicit concept of fairness and a model of learning which is sensitive to and promotes fairness. This principle of fairness in distance education closely approximates to what the philosopher Amy Guttman has called a democratic theory of education.[7] In it the importance is recognised of empowering citizens to make educational policy and of constraining their choices in accordance with the twin principles of non-repression and non-discrimination. These two principles preserve the intellectual and social foundations of democratic deliberations. The procedural link between the goal of empowerment and the structural principles of non-discrimination and non-repression rests with the process of learning and the way it is thought of. An approach to learning, within distance education, which has empowerment as its goal must transcend textual design, communications systems, production functions, tutorial supports, and begin with the life context of the learner, using it as the basic organizing principle for the design of distance education.

Experiential learning models, in this respect, offer an innovative approach to the design of distance-based continuing education. They provide a fundamentally different view of the learning process from those which currently dominate the distance education field: behaviourism and rationalism. Experiential learning models differ from rationalist models of learning which tend to give primary emphasis to the acquisition, manipulation and recall of abstract symbols, and from behavioural theories, which deny any role for consciousness and subjective experience in the learning process. Indeed, as the model below outlines, experiential learning is integrative, combining within it experience, perception, cognition and behaviour.[8]

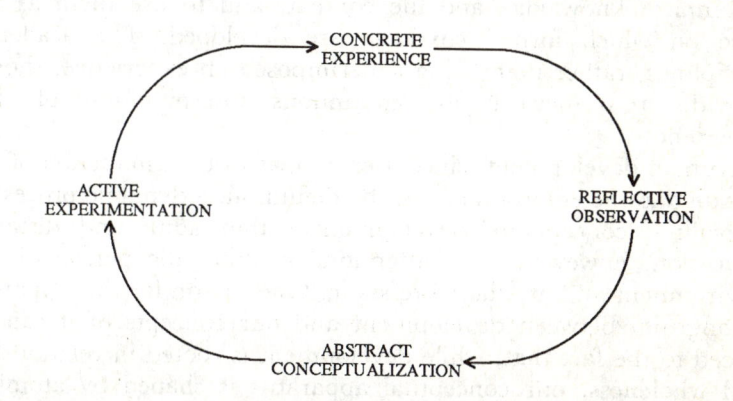

```
              CONCRETE
              EXPERIENCE
            ↗           ↘
    ACTIVE                REFLECTIVE
 EXPERIMENTATION          OBSERVATION
            ↖           ↙
              ABSTRACT
           CONCEPTUALIZATION
```

THE PROCESS OF EXPERIENTIAL LEARNING, from D. Kolb: *Experiential Learning*.

Underpinning experiential learning theory are principles which, when used as guides to programme design and delivery, make continuing education through distance education an empowering device.

Learning is Best Conceived as a Process not in Terms of Outcomes

Within experiential learning ideas are not seen as fixed or immutable but are formed and reformed through experience. Learning is therefore a process through which new ideas are derived from and modified by experience. To define learning in terms of outcomes is therefore maladaptive since it denies continuous change.

If learning is a continuous process then any continuing education programme through distance education must be designed to facilitate a process of on-going change in the learner. This requires that a distance-based continuing education system provide for a high degree of interaction between teacher and learner. Newer telecomputing technologies offer distance education tremendous opportunities in facilitating this interactive process.

Learning is a Continuous Process Grounded in Experience

Knowledge is continuously derived from and tested out in the experience of the learner. This implies, first, that all learning is relearning.[9] The challenge for continuing education in distance education is to tap the experience of the learner, the problems, incomplete knowledge and life context, and to use them as the base on which formal curricula are developed. The academic disciplines, rather than being superimposed on experience, should provide a framework for continuous interpretation of that experience.

Human development, since it encompasses the interaction of the person and the environment, is, by definition, a dynamic process.[10] Prevailing concepts of development within adult and distance education, however, focus attention on either the person or the environment and are therefore static. One reason for this apparent incongruity between development and our concepts of it can be traced to the fact that, while development is rooted in relationship and wholeness, our conceptual apparatus is shaped by atomism and fragmentation.[11] We tend to think in 'either or' terms when what is required is a grasp of the totality of experience.

Until recently, in fact, distance educators have not formulated in any conscious way an image of development unfolding within the context of the environment. Substantial cross-cultural research exists to document how large socio-cultural environments shape human development. This research shows, among other things, that patterns of thought develop differently in different cultural contexts. The role of cultural experience in shaping cognitive patterns, however, has been repeatedly confused with human capacity. Michael Cole and his colleagues have recently proposed the concept of a situational code as a way of clarifying this confusion. To Cole, cognitive processes and cognitive content, contrary to the view of most developmentalists, are intimately intertwined rather than discrete. Most measured differences between people, or the cultural groupings to which they belong, reside more in the situations to which particular cognitive processes are applied than in the existence of a process in one cultural group and its absence in another. What is actually being measured in most adult and distance education research, then, is a situational code; a code that determines the cognitive process used in a given circumstance, making process, content, capacity and experience inseparable.

The concept of situational code poses several implications for distance education, particularly in light of the future. *First* differences in the apparent capacities of individuals within the same culture may be, as the more recognised differences between people from different cultures, in fact manifestations of different cultural codes. Most developmental assessments, then, are really, at root, *a priori* cultural evaluations which are then applied through a ranking process to individuals.

Secondly the concept of situational code suggests the need to uncover those intellectual and other developmental capacities which are nested in various settings, and the degree of congruence between various people and these settings. Substantial research has recently, in this regard, unearthed the situational code of the school and charted the degree of congruence between these codes and 'types' of student. A fruitful direction for research in distance education would be to examine the learning codes of the various non-formal settings in which adults participate, most importantly work and the family. Facilitating development for the diverse individuals who inhabit these settings may require a modification of settings as much as they do changing people.

Thirdly the concept of situational code and its relation to development makes the social structures in our society the basic problematic for distance education. In times of social stasis, an ideal type in any event, this problematic is less pressing. Today, however, various settings in our culture are being dramatically altered. New situational codes are being born out of the daily impact caused by such dynamic processes as technological change, new communication modes and demographic transitions. In fact one could argue that essentially new types of people are being created in these settings. The irony is that distance education, by and large, still utilises the institutional code as the primary basis upon which to chart and assess student growth and understanding.

Lastly the concept of situational code presents us with the need seriously to question our tendency to stereotype people and their capacities by the behaviour they exhibit in particular situations. It requires, in particular, that we realize the tentative nature of our knowledge of any one person at any point in time or in any particular setting. A more holistic and inquisitive approach to the person is urgently demanded; one which is open to discovering new capacities, particularly those blinded to our consciousness by the settings in which we observe people.

If development is rooted in situations and their codes what, then, does this suggest for distance education? Obviously educational institutions, and people within them, must be more outwardly sensitive to the emergent structures within which people, in our culture, find themselves as they are growing and developing. This demands a degree of cultural sensitivity not often characteristic of formal educational institutions which, by and large, still define their own particular settings as master contexts for human development. The growing decentralization in the accessibility of the populace to knowledge and information, and the various settings within which this knowledge can be accessed, makes clear that the dominance of formal institutions in this area may be fast disappearing.

Rather than formal educational institutions teaching the current or next generation, they may have to learn from it. The schools and universities, as other educational institutions, have traditionally been storehouses of knowledge to be transmitted across the generations. In future, if these institutions are to retain their educative roles, they must become places to which people come to share the knowledge they have acquired in other settings. In this context educational institutions become less storehouses and transmitters and more synthesizers and interpreters of that which is known.

Distance education institutions, if they are to fulfil the role of cultural interpreter, will, of necessity, have to rethink many aspects of their current structure and process: the focus on knowledge transmission, age segregation, professional exclusion and isolation from the culture. More importantly, the staff within these institutions must acquire an openness of mind toward the fundamental processes of societal learning with all its diversity and unpredictability.[12]

If the foregoing argument concerning an imminent change in the social location and function of educational institutions has validity—that is, involving a shift from warehousing and transmitting roles to those of synthesis and interpretation—then it follows that a priority for distance education research should be to address, in an imaginative way, the structural factors and psycho-cultural processes which mediate the relationship between educational institutions and their evolving reality.

The Process of Learning Involves Conscious Social Reproduction

Models of learning, whether implicit or explicit, present ways in which people adapt to the world around them. Within experiential learning there is deliberate intention to empower the learner, to involve him or her in conscious social reproduction, to induct him or her into the ways in which citizens are or should be empowered to influence the education that in turn shapes the political values and attitudes and modes of behaviour of future citizens.

Experiential learning as a model for continuing education through distance education is a tension-filled process. It involves the design of programmes which develop four different kinds of abilities, each reflective of a mode of adapting to the world. Learners must be allowed to involve themselves fully, openly and without bias to new experiences. They must reflect on and observe their experiences from many perspectives. They must be able to create concepts that integrate their observations into logically bound theories. They must be able to use these theories to make decisions and solve problems.

Yet this is a difficult ideal to achieve. How can one act and reflect at the same time? How can one be concrete and theoretical? It is not that one can do these simultaneously, but a distance education system must be designed to allow the learner to move in varying degrees from actor to observer, and from specific involvement to general analytic detachment.

Learning is the Process of Creating Knowledge

Knowledge is the result of the transactions between social knowledge and personal knowledge, between objective and subjective experiences, in a process called learning. All learners know something before they enter a new learning situation and this knowledge was actively created by them. Continuing education through distance education should be designed with these principles in mind. Indeed this knowledge should and can be recognised in such programmes. At Athabasca University, for example, we are experimenting with a prior learning assessment technique in which learners can receive credit for their prior knowledge.

The above principles derived from experiential learning theory, and the principle of fair access, together suggest an innovative image for continuing education through distance education. Continuing education, when provided through distance education, should be designed as an interface linkage in the cycle of experiential learning. In this model, distance-based continuing education has three paramount roles. Its first role is to provide multiple access points and feedback mechanisms for a person in the process of experiential learning. Its second role is not only to help a person create knowledge but also to test that knowledge. Its third role is to provide that person, over time, with the experiential learning skills through which he or she can understand, transform and improve upon his or her life circumstances.

Until recently, the possibility of serving learners simultaneously, on both an individual and a social basis, was a faint hope. The challenge has been to find a way of meeting simultaneously the learning needs of people both as individuals and as members of various social groupings. It is what Arthur Koestler has called the Janus principle: treating people as whole parts of a whole.[13] Newer technologies, and most particularly their tendencies toward the integration of voice, image, text and data, offer the distance educator a unique enabling device. These newer technologies now deal with differentiated parts of the wholes they are part of. They are able to get specific about parts that earlier technologies had to leave undifferentiated. In addition they operate as such fast speeds that we may consider their treatment of parts simultaneously. Speed and specificity are the hallmarks of these new technologies and the foundation for the next stage in the development of distance learning: what can be called the mass customizing of distance education.[14]

Consider, as an example of the potential of integrating speed, specificity, mass and customization, the current developments in tele-training. Teleconferencing technology and tele-training systems now exist which enhance two-way audio with two-way video, two-way tele-writing, and individualized computer communication. Voice, image and data are combined in one interactive system. This technology enables one to teach across a wide geographic area and to do so on a group and individual basis, or a combined group-individual format simultaneously.

If one returns to the experiential learning model for distance education, tele-training and other such interactive and convergent technologies allow intervention, at various points in the learning cycle, through distance education linkages. Each person, theoretically, is at a different stage in the learning cycle and functioning as an individual, or member of a larger group, or both. This is the context which generates both the need and possibility for mass customizing in distance education. Add to this the variations in time (when to know) and learning need (need to know) demanded in a continuing education context and mass customizing becomes ever more important.

How can we approach the issue of mass customizing distance education within a continuing education context? Given that new technologies enable the mass customization of distance education, all distance education programmes, institutions and systems exist somewhere on the mass customized continuum. Moreover, various components of their systems also exist on this continuum.

As the chart below shows, it is possible to have a range of relationships, or programme mixes, between the strategic focus of an institution and the context of the learner. One can have, as the symbols indicate, a standardized course or learning programme with customized services and delivery systems focused upon a target segment. Or one can have a customized product with mass services, markets and delivery systems. There are many possibilities.

A mass customized approach to distance education, particularly within a continuing education context, empowers people both as individuals and as members of social and cultural groupings. It avoids the trap of confusing sameness with equality: a logical fault in the assumptions which underpin most educational efforts to reduce inequity. The mass dimension speaks to the non-discrimination principle, while the customized dimension allows one to address non-repression. The mass customization approach, finally,

DISTANCE EDUCATION MASS CUSTOMIZATION MATRIX

Strategic focus \ Learning context	Mass	Customized
Product	X	
Services		X
Market		X
Delivery system		X

allows the design of programmes which address the life context of the learner and to do so in a way which is sensitive to the differentiated experience of people in the learning cycle. And it is the appropriate application of new, more integrated and interactive, technologies, which enables this mass customization to be a reality in distance education.

The distance education mass customization matrix allows one to assess the current pattern, in an institution's programme, between strategic focus and learning context. Based upon this pattern, and measured against both existing incongruities and future objectives, the matrix provides a way of conceptualizing a new configuration in the provision of learning. With the new configuration outlined, various enabling technologies can be assessed for the degree to which they 'fit' the configuration. This style of thinking places technology at the service of education, not, as is too often the case, having education the handmaiden of technology.

Conclusion

The style of strategic thinking which is at the heart of an experiential model for distance education, and its potential through enabling technology for mass customizing, make time and space resources for, rather than obstacles to, learning. It calls for both differentiated and holistic thinking and planning. It forces both organizations and individuals to learn on an on-going basis. It is the continuing education of distance education.

REFERENCES

1. E. Faure: *Learning To Be*. Geneva: UNESCO, 1972.
2. See J. Ganaty: *Unemployment In History*. NY: Harper, 1978.
3. See M. Piore and C. Sobel: *The Second Industrial Divide*. NY: Basic Books, 1984.
4. See Allan Knox: *Adult Learning and Development*. San Francisco: Jossey Ross, 1980.
5. For a critical approach to these same themes, see Howard Gardner: *Frames of Mind*. NY: Basic Books, 1985.
6. See M. Apple: *Teachers and Texts*. London: Routledge and Kegan Paul, 1987.
7. Amy Guttman: *Democratic Education*. Princeton: Princeton University Press, 1987.
8. David Kolb: *Experiential Learning*. NY: Prentice-Hall, 1985.
9. See James O'Toole: *Work, Learning and The American Future*. San Francisco: Jossey Ross, 1979.

10. This point is made forcefully in a recent study of development in a cross-cultural context. See David Guthman: *Reclaimed Powers: Toward A New Psychology of Man and Women in Later Life*. NY: Basic Books, 1987.

11. See D. Bohm: *Wholeness and The Duplicate Order*; London: Cambridge University, 1983; and R. M. Kanten: *The Change Masters*; NY: Harper, 1983.

12. See D. Michael: *On Learning To Plan: On Planning to Learn*. San Francisco: Jossey Ross, 1979.

13. A. Koestler: *Janus*. NY: Abacus, 1980.

14. See S. Davis: *Future Perfect*. NY: Addison-Wesley, 1987, pp. 138–191.

Professor D. S. WIJEYESEKERA (*Vice-Chancellor, Open University of Sri Lanka*):

1. *The Need for Continuing Education*

Education is often referred to as the joint process or the partnership of teaching and learning. While teaching means facilitation of learning, the process of intentional, individual activity is considered learning.

The continuing process of education which should be an essential component in the lifelong development of any person, or the career development of any professional, should aim at one or more goals, such as:

(*a*) further acquisition of professional, formal competence or acquiring of further qualifications; or

(*b*) continuing a purely academic pursuit (for those with an intent on critical problem learning); or

(*c*) to focus on the intellectual and emotional growth and development of the learner.

Once a professional obtains his qualification to enable him to secure employment, it may be necessary for him to acquire further qualifications in order to obtain promotions and thereby receive salary increases. The valuable experience he would have gained during the employment alone may not be sufficient, according to the regulations prevailing in the establishment, for the promotions and the consequent wage increases. This requirement has long been in existence in the teaching profession both in schools and in universities and is now being adopted in various other professions as well.

The process of continuous learning is in-built among research workers who, in their purely academic pursuit, are continuously learning whilst receiving the minimal quantum of teaching.

Apart from aiming at the above goals for professional or occupational reasons, both professionals and even non-professionals would desire to focus on intellectual and emotional growth and development through the process of continuing education.

Hence opportunities for the achievement of these goals would undoubtedly elevate and assist in the development of any society. The process of continuing education has formally and conventionally been available through various types of courses of study, but alternative non-conventional forms have to be considered for those who are unable to (or prefer not to) pursue the traditional forms already in existence.

2. *Avenues Available for Continuing Education*

The traditional continuing education programmes of study to achieve the earlier mentioned goals could be sought through:

(*a*) part-time courses of study either during weekends and/or week-evenings and/or on a day-release basis from the place of work; or

(*b*) short-duration intensive courses or refresher courses during block periods conducted at regular intervals, if necessary; or

(*c*) long-duration postgraduate courses of study leading to postgraduate qualifications; or

(*d*) research studies leading to academic qualifications or research work as part of one's occupation.

In order to fit into any of the above avenues of continuing education there has to be a certain amount of compromise and adjustment on the part of the employers and also the students, to ensure that there would be the least possible disruption to work schedules at the place of employment. Some employers consider it an advantage to encourage, promote and even sponsor their employees to pursue such programmes of continuing education, probably because it could in return bring benefits to the establishment. But very often employers may not be in a position to release their staff to undertake such programmes of study, owing to the possible disruption to work schedules. Also there may be instances when the students who are not being sponsored by their employers (or any other organization) find it financially difficult to pursue such courses by obtaining leave of absence without pay from their work place. In such instances the role of distance education for continuing education programmes becomes very relevant and necessary for the achievement of the stated goals.

3. *Role of Distance Education in Continuing Education*

Distance education has been often referred to as the process of study at different levels which are not under the continuous, immediate supervision of teachers present with their students in lecture rooms or physically in the same premises, but which nevertheless benefit by the careful planning, guidance and academic instruction of an academic organization. Distance must be viewed as geographical as well as psychological and both types contribute to isolation. Both create distance between learning resources and learners. Whatever the cause or condition of isolation, it will influence the motivation to learn as well as the mode and frequency of the delivery of educational services. Distance education is also expected to offer students a measure of flexibility and autonomy to study the programme of their choice when and where they wish at a place to suit their circumstances.

Continuing education through distance education has a valuable role to play under varying circumstances, such as in the case of those:

(i) who are unable to obtain release from their employment to pursue full-time, short- or long-duration courses of study, and also those who are unable to support themselves on no-pay leave and hence unable to bear the additional cost of financing a course of study;

(ii) who have to travel great distances from where they live or work to the nearest educational institution, or would have to be re-located in the vicinity of such an institution to receive the continuing education on a full-time conventional basis;

(iii) who, because of their commitments or responsibilities at the work place (*e.g.* those who are self-employed), would not find it possible to be physically away from their place of work for such a period.

There are also those who are not employed but for their own personal development wish to undertake continuing education programmes of study and cannot take conventional courses because of transport difficulties, infirmities, advanced age, etc.

However, although there are many good reasons for planning continuing education programmes through distance education, the inherent problems among adult students, whatever form of education they want to pursue, have to be borne in mind. Adult students usually have considerable professional, social and family commitments which make it unreasonable to expect them to give very high priority to their studies. Instead they have to adapt their study periods to suit their living and working conditions. They may have to travel extensively on work for certain periods, which may preclude study during such journeys. Also they may find it difficult to find time for concentrated study.

4. *The Need for Educational Technology*

Out of a number of definitions of educational technology put forward by different bodies and organizations, that of the Commission of Instructional Technology, USA, can be considered the best: 'a systematic way of designing, implementing and evaluating the total process of learning and teaching in terms of specific objectives, based on research in human learning and communication and employing a combination of human and non-human resources to bring about more effective instruction'.

Once this is ascertained, it would be necessary to consider the role that educational technology plays in a distance learning system such as that available at an open university. In the context of this paper, and as adopted in the Open University of Sri Lanka, educational technology comprises four major areas.

(*a*) Preparation, development and review of printed course materials starting from the deliberations at the course team level, where the representative(s) from the educational technology board participate, up to the point when the material is ready for printing.

(*b*) Development and production of audio and video materials to supplement the printed course material and also in the preparation of such material for 'public education programmes'.

(*c*) Research studies into the development and evaluation of existing programmes of study and feasibility studies to be conducted to ascertain whether new programmes of study should be commenced or not.

(*d*) Staff development on distance teaching, conducted through workshops, seminars, etc.

5. *Educational Technologies to be Adopted*

The distance education methodologies to be adopted would largely depend on the objective of the programmes of study envisaged. These could be either 'public education programmes,' or programmes of study for associate students, or programmes for fully registered students.

SUB-TOPIC 3(D): DISTANCE EDUCATION [*Wijeyesekera*]

When courses are conducted only through the mass media registrations may not be necessary and such programmes could be considered as 'public education programmes'. But when students have to receive facilities at the centres, or supplementary course material in addition to whatever may be transmitted through the mass media, such students need to be registered and categorized as 'associate students'. If the programme of study is merely to upgrade the students' knowledge without leading to a qualification, such students could also be classed as associate students when they have to be registered with a university or an educational institute.

However for students who pursue programmes of study in order to receive a formal qualification, to meet one of the goals indicated earlier, the methodologies which need to be adopted have to be formal in order to evaluate and assess the suitability of the students for the award of a certificate, diploma, degree or postgraduate qualification. Such students have to be registered as 'students' at the educational institute in order to enjoy the facilities of the institute and to be assessed for the award of the qualifications.

Public education programmes. Distance education institutions should try continuously to educate the public at large on topics of general interest and on recent developments of interest to the general public. These programmes would have to be conducted through the mass media, *i.e.* radio, television, newspapers, journals, etc.

Programmes for associate students. Since the mass media may not always be accessible to every individual for geographical, financial or other reasons, it may be necessary, even for public education programmes, to make facilities for listening, viewing and reading public education material available at various centres of a distance education institute or university distributed within the country. Even when the listening, viewing or reading of public education material is being done in one's own home environment, the material may have to be supplemented with additional reading material or audio/video cassettes. Therefore to obtain such additional facilities interested members of the public could be registered as 'associate students'. Furthermore, there may be certain other programmes of study for which facilities such as computers and other apparatus are necessary. There may also be programmes of study in which large numbers of students would seek to be enrolled at different centres, and since such students' attainment and progress are not evaluated they would not receive a qualification. Such students, too, could be categorised as 'associate students'.

Students who receive qualifications. Students enrolled and registered for courses of study in order to obtain a qualification would have to be recognised differently, as in any other educational institute. The educational technologies to be adopted would vary, depending on the discipline of study. Components such as face-to-face sessions, laboratory work, discussion-type sessions, home experimentation kits, etc., seem to vary a great deal from one open university to another. However the model which should be adopted for the purpose of continuing education need not vary so much, as it is expected that such students would be pursuing courses of study for continuing education in the areas relevant to their occupation. They could use the necessary practical exposure from the work place to supplement the theoretical inputs provided by educational institutes.

However, as distance teaching institutes are now launching into new fields such as science and technology in providing continuing education, the education technologies which should be adopted have to be carefully planned, bearing in mind the target group of the students, financial resources available to allow for non-conventional methodologies, and above all the maintenance of the requisite academic standards, comparable to those at conventional institutes conducting similar programmes of study. If qualifications are to be credible, this will be essential.

Furthermore, for continuing education in the fields of science and technology through distance education methodologies, it is most advantageous if the students have jobs in relevant fields of study. This would mean that the practical training they get in their occupations would contribute to the practical component and training required in science and technological programmes of study. However, in order to maintain a uniform minimum training for all the students these facilities would have to be provided by the education institutes concerned. In providing these facilities different methodologies are being adopted at various distance education institutions. For example, in certain developed countries home-based laboratory kits are provided to each individual student, delivered to their homes for use during the period of study and then to be returned. In the Open University of Sri Lanka, for science and technology programmes, a certain amount of laboratory practical work in the earlier years of study is conducted at the centres in the regions; whereas for practical classes in the latter years the students are brought from the regions to the central campus for block periods of practical work. Another methodology for imparting this training has been to provide the video materials to the students either for them to purchase or to be viewed at the centres.

Continuing education courses of study at postgraduate diploma

SUB-TOPIC 3(D): DISTANCE EDUCATION

level (such as for practising engineers) have been identified as feasible, owing to the difficulties encountered in seeking full-time release by such personnel to follow such courses at conventional universities. Moreover fields such as construction management and agricultural engineering are areas of study where hardly any laboratory facilities are required, since most of the work is in the field in the students' own places of work. So as to update the theoretical knowledge of such personnel in these specialized fields, regular day schools at the centres in the regions, accompanied by video material to supplement the printed course material which forms the main self-study component, provide a useful avenue of continuing education for technological study.

Furthermore, the educational technologist should co-ordinate the primary move in deciding whether a programme of study should be implemented or not. This has to be done along with the subject specialists by carrying out a survey among the public, employers, academics and also the decision-makers, together with a cost analysis, to ensure the feasibility of initiating such a course. The resource persons available locally or internationally, on a full or part-time basis, have also to be determined. Dialogue should be established with academics of other conventional institutes to ensure that the academic standards of the course envisaged are comparable.

Finally, the educational technologists should regularly be involved in the development of the academic staff on distance teaching methodologies. This has to be done in connection with the preparation of printed material, production of audio and video material, and also on the non-conventional face-to-face sessions which have to be conducted. Since the continuous assessment of the students plays an important role in these self-study courses through distance education techniques, proper development and implementation of study of such assessments and evaluations should form an important component of the continuous staff development programmes for academic staff at the distance teaching institutes.

DISCUSSION

(*Rapporteur*: Mr. B. R. H. MONKS, Registrar, Massey University)

A. Dr. Morrison made the following points.

1. *The setting*. Athabasca University is purpose built for the sole function of distance education. It is Canada's only open university, it serves the

entire country, and currently has an enrolment of approximately 15,000 students. There are no internal students. The teaching function is achieved via a staff of about 70 full-time academics and about 250 part-time tutors across Canada. A very extensive system of cross-crediting permits Athabasca students to build upon their qualifications from other institutions. A process of continual enrolment is followed which permits students the flexibility of commencing studies at twelve points during the year. Tuition is not bilingual.

2. *The objectives*. Analysis of the national educational needs which led to the creation of Athabasca capabilities in distance education concentrated upon the shape, structure and operation required to meet the needs of the market, rather than merely the finance required. The investigation confirmed the need for a major change in approach. The pressure for change was coming from the public, rather than the universities at large or the government. Conclusions reached included: (*a*) the need to meet increased opportunities for access, including the factors of educational background, culture, age, geographic, employment and financial limitations; (*b*) that courses and qualifications had to relate fully to the market and be 'needs based'; (*c*) a process of incremental progress via 'mastery level' checks; (*d*) that extensive credit for external qualification and prior experience should be a corner-stone of the system.

3. *Implementation*. In introducing and operating this concept of distance education, Athabasca University quite obviously made best use of the advantages of a comparatively high standard of national primary and secondary education, national and individual financial capacity, and the advantages of a sophisticated national communication system and general infrastructure. Additional points included recognition of:

(*a*) the distance education system relating to modern demand for access to a lifelong learning opportunity;

(*b*) the model presently used by Athabasca stresses the need for process innovation in course development, delivery, quality control and operation;

(*c*) the blurring of distinctions between conventional academic institutions and the vast growth in business and professional training now being undertaken by business houses and major corporations;

(*d*) the scope and place of technology in meeting the limitations of students who must study via the distance education mode; that the operation is process-based, not limited by time, age, geographic spread; and that there are numerous ways of transmitting the material;

(*e*) that credibility and student satisfaction would be highly dependent upon the means by which learning is assessed.

4. *Discussion*. In response to questions and observations put to Dr. Morrison, the following aspects were outlined:

(*a*) the widespread application of telephone conferencing system implemented by AT&T in 330 different centres and progress in computer-assisted learning as a distance education tool; however there is a limit to resources and the cultural context within which the technology can be applied;

SUB-TOPIC 3(D): DISTANCE EDUCATION

(*b*) the imbalance between the technical expectations of institutions and the ability of individual students or government subsidy to meet the true cost;

(*c*) the need for a more structured approach to the marketing of courses;

(*d*) the realization of the need for a variable package of development and delivery, including the concept that access should be more dependent upon capability and less on prior qualification, the need to equip graduates with abilities to handle a variety of jobs, and the importance of close integration of university academic planning and professional/business input.

B. Professor Wijeyesekera presented a very detailed description of the origins and operation of the comparatively recently established Open University of Sri Lanka. The presentation was followed by a video tape outlining the university and its role in the Sri Lankan education scene. Some key points were:

(*a*) that the Open University is tailored for a national role and currently serves 15,000 students;

(*b*) the institution is purpose-built and was established after rigorous study and advice; national and international subsidy has kept the cost to students low and has permitted the introduction of significant levels of technology;

(*c*) the operation includes a high component of face-to-face contact with students for teaching and counselling services; a network of regional support bases exists throughout the country;

(*d*) the University tends to concentrate on the provision of certificate, diploma and degree courses for the vocational and professional market, teachers, and the applied sciences; delivery systems are required to meet the three-language criteria for Sri Lanka.

C. *General Discussions*

Delegates and speakers raised a number of general issues regarding the application of technology to distance education and its contribution to the overall concept and aims of continuing education. Discussion acknowledged that technology for instructional purposes involved a systematic way of designing, implementing and evaluating the total process of imparting knowledge and skill. Caution was expressed regarding the direct and indirect costs of the introduction of technological innovations for teaching purposes. Efforts and expenditure, particularly on sophisticated hardware, needed close examination for relevance to the national support infrastructure, the needs and capabilities of students, and the attitudes of staff.

It was also noted that distance education as an overall concept for teaching required a comprehensive staff development programme for the teachers and administrators involved. Although there are special needs that must be satisfied for effective distance learning delivery systems some of the techniques can also be transferred to conventional teaching.

TOPIC 3: CONTINUING EDUCATION

Comment was made on the need to ensure an appropriate integration and acceptability of distance education institutions and programmes whose materials may be used in conventional universities, the staff of which may in turn have contributed to the design of distance education courses. Programmes for continuing education needed to be complementary, overlaps and duplication needed to be identified and avoided, and standards needed to be rigorously enforced. Credit recognition, particularly with the growth of experiential measures of attainment, required very careful consideration and application.

Some doubts were expressed about the means for assessing experiential learning for credit purposes.

Delegates also noted that very considerable experience had been built up by certain Commonwealth universities in various aspects of distance education. There is a variety of modes with varying advantages and disadvantages. The current initiative towards a Commonwealth of Learning can provide a means by which this experience can be shared.

Topic 3

FINAL SESSION

Thursday, 11 February

Mr. B. R. H. Monks (Registrar, Massey University) gave a brief presentation on the New Zealand perspective on distance education. Massey University is the main provider of distance education in New Zealand with some 14,500 external students. The same academic and administrative staff look after the needs of both internal and external students, and all faculties and departments are involved except veterinary science. Co-ordination is provided through an extra-mural planning group chaired by the vice-chancellor and through a co-ordinating unit under a director. Most of the provision is at first degree level but there is also a small number of diploma and taught master's courses. Print is the main medium of instruction. Students typically complete 10-12 assignments for marking during the year and sit the same examination as internal students. Students can attend regional centres during the year and seminars during the university vacations. The range of courses is wide (some 400 courses), and may be reduced on grounds of cost. The model had evolved to meet New Zealand conditions and was felt to be appropriate to the country's circumstances.

The session dealt with the three related aspects of the previous discussion sessions, namely continuing education, distance education and the Commonwealth initiative on distance education. The summary on each which follows draws on points raised in the earlier sessions and points made during the review.

Continuing Education

Continuing education (CE) was defined as the provision of any form of education after an interval following the end of continuous initial education. It was seen as a necessary and essential role for universities to embrace alongside traditional undergraduate teaching and research. Continuing education includes part-time first degrees and various forms of professional, vocational and personal updating at sub-degree, degree and postgraduate levels. Universities had a long tradition of these roles in relation to the updating of teachers but the need now was to establish the universities as the pre-eminent knowledge base for all aspects of continuing education.

The development of CE faces a number of problems and challenges. The group considered a number of these.

(1) The attitudes of government to the funding the CE, which often saw the activity as marginal and to be paid for by its clients.

(2) The need for CE to reflect the needs of students as individuals and of society. Women were a particular priority because they were under-represented in terms of educational attainment and frequently opportunity.

(3) The development of schemes of credit transfer so that students were not disadvantaged through changes of institution and of country.

(4) The emphasis on client or market needs which had to be balanced against the possible erosion of institutional autonomy and standards.

(5) The requirement for collaboration with professional and other bodies.

(6) The means of delivering CE to students, which needed to be based on pedagogic, cost and social considerations rather than technology. Distance education was seen as an appropriate means in certain circumstances, particularly where large numbers of students were to be involved and/or students were dispersed geographically.

(7) Research and development about CE, which was in its infancy. There was an urgent need to increase the body of knowledge about the content and methods of CE programmes.

(8) Within institutions structures for CE had to be established which involved all staff and departments but also provided a client-related organizational focus so that these remained paramount. This was often achieved by establishing a CE, extra-mural or extension department.

(9) Academic staff development programmes to familiarize staff with the needs of CE. Changes to contracts of employment so that staff should have a responsibility for CE work as well as traditional teaching and research were also needed. CE should be recognised for promotion purposes and incentives at the departmental and individual level may be necessary.

FINAL SESSION

Distance Education

Distance education is a term used to describe the means of bringing learning to students in their homes or localities, which can overcome problems of geography and time. It allows the student greater independence as a learner. It was not synonymous with continuing education but in the view of several speakers distance education provided the best means of making lifelong continuing education available. Distance education had at its core specially prepared printed materials, the marking of written assignments during the course and, where an award is to be made at end of course, examination taken under secure conditions. Personal contact with a tutor was usually a feature of distance education either face to face at a local centre (or by telephone) and/or at a short residential seminar during the course. Video and audio tapes or television and radio broadcasts may be used to reinforce the written word or for awareness programmes where the cost and infrastructure make this possible. For practical subjects video or TV can be used for observational experiments but for 'hands-on' practical skills the facilities of local centres or existing colleges/universities in the evenings, weekends or vacation periods were necessary. Only in developed countries is the cost of loaning experimental equipment to students seen as being possible financially. Many contributors argued that new communication and computer technologies should be harnessed for distance education but others expressed caution on grounds of cost, appropriateness and robustness.

Flexibility for the student in terms of minimum and maximum periods of study over which a qualification could be obtained, and the modularization of courses, were identified as important components of distance education, although these features were of importance more generally in continuing education. Distance education institutions and projects had been initiated in many countries of the Commonwealth, developed and developing, and the Commonwealth Heads of Government initiative provided the opportunity of capitalizing on these experiences. Distance education was characterized by high development and production costs but, provided there were large numbers of students, unit costs were often lower than those of conventional universities.

The Commonwealth Initiative

The decision of Heads of Government to create a Commonwealth institution to promote co-operation in distance education was widely welcomed and supported. The group had the benefit of advice and information from Professor A. O. Adesola (Lagos), a member of the Briggs group, and Mr. P. R. C. Williams (Commonwealth Secretariat), and welcomed the appointment of Dr. J. Daniel (Laurentian) as chairman of the working group 'to develop financial and organisational framework, establish appropriate guidelines and set priorities for the institution with a view to ensuring the relevance of programmes and the appropriateness of educational technologies to countries' particular situations and needs'.

In discussion three major priorities were identified for the working group: (1) making available existing teaching materials between countries and developing new materials co-operatively, recognising that problems of culture, staff attitudes and copyright would have to be overcome; (2) the mutual recognition of student credit (credit transfer) in order to provide for student mobility; (3) the development and exchange of information concerning the methodologies of distance education.

Although there were many practical problems to be overcome in achieving these aims the enthusiasm and experience of the ACU and its member institutions should be a major driving force for their successful implementation.

Topic 3

UNIVERSITIES AND CONTINUING EDUCATION

The Responsibility of Universities to make provision for Continuing Education

CHAIRMAN'S REPORT ON THE GROUP'S DISCUSSIONS

Second Plenary Session
Friday, 12 February

Dr. J. S. DANIEL (*President, Laurentian University of Sudbury*): The Topic 3 group, which devoted its attention to the theme 'Universities and Continuing Education' was privileged to hear an excellent series of presentations. Discussion never flagged during our three days of meetings. As a topic chairman who was recruited at the last minute I am especially grateful to Vice-Chancellor Ram Reddy, who organized these sessions even though he could not be here himself; to our eight speakers for their interesting papers and their very professional presentations; to the assiduous group of between 30 and 50 delegates who made the discussions topical and lively; and to our diligent team of rapporteurs led by Mr. Joe Clinch.

We found that at the present time the continuing education function is at the leading edge of the evolution of our universities. This is encouraging, since we also found that continuing education may well be the most important contribution to national development that universities can make. Finally we found that continuing education is at the threshold of a major international initiative, what Sonny Ramphal has called potentially the most important development in the modern Commonwealth, namely the decision of our Heads of Government to create a new multilaterally-governed institution for co-operation in distance education.

Let me amplify briefly on our conclusion about the leading role of continuing education at these three levels: first in the university itself, second for national development and third in international co-operation.

Regarding the role of continuing education in the evolution of our universities, one of our speakers took us back to the Unesco Report of Edgar Faure entitled *Learning to Be* which was published in 1972 and which introduced the concept of lifelong learning. But we were reminded that our concept and practice of lifelong learning still falls far short of the radical set of principles by which the Faure report defined it. Nevertheless, what one speaker called a 'fundamental reconfiguration' of learning systems is now taking place in reponse to the growing personal ambitions of individual members of society, the increasing array of personal technologies to which they have access, and the diversification of lifestyles.

A time of fundamental change is a time of both danger and opportunity. As the continuing education function of our universities explores this new world and tests responses to its challenges, it is vital that the rest of the university integrate continuing education fully into its image of itself. Changing times bring out all kinds of charlatans with nostrums for personal advancement. If university continuing education does not have the full credibility of the university behind it, as it attempts authentic responses to the retraining needs of society, then the credibility of the university as a whole will eventually suffer.

A difficult question that we discussed is how we select among the many demands made on us for continuing education services. Because of the talent and organization that they bring together, universities can tackle a host of educational and developmental challenges in the community. In the industrialized countries universities believe they should pick and choose rather carefully, making sure other providers such as colleges and school systems are not in fact better equipped to respond to some demands. We must also be careful that the university does not devote its energies excessively to certain privileged groups, whether they be teachers, employees of a particular company or members of a particular profession, just because such groups are ready to pay the marginal costs of obtaining continuing education from the university.

In the developing and newly industrialized countries there was much less hesitation in affirming that universities should, within reason, attempt to respond to all the educational demands made by the community. Impressive testimony from Nigeria, India and Sri Lanka showed us how deeply universities in those countries can be involved in every aspect of community development.

The importance of continuing education to national development is underscored by recent OECD studies. These showed that one of the two types of educational expenditure that correlate most strongly with national economic strength is the proportion of working people in their 20s and 30s who return to university on a part-time basis to improve their skills. Much of our discussion on the service that we provide to these people centred on the burgeoning provision of distance education. But we also noted that distance education is increasingly linked to the other strong educational predictor of economic growth, namely the proportion of young people who stay in full-time education after the period of compulsory schooling. In several newly industrialized countries very large numbers of young full-time students are obtaining their degrees at a distance. We usually think of distance education as a tool of continuing education but for millions of students it is now the vehicle for the most traditional function of universities, the teaching of young undergraduates.

We were most impressed with the effective and sophisticated manner in which distance education is being carried out around the Commonwealth. Of particular note in our sessions was the extensive programming offered in Sri Lanka where a blend of media and technologies is used to serve students in three languages. The close relations between the Open University of Sri Lanka and the traditional universities of that country seemed admirable.

This sort of expertise, which now exists in both developed and developing countries, provides a good springboard for greater international co-operation in making distance education widely available. Some members of our sessions had been part of the expert group under Lord Briggs that produced last year the report *Towards a Commonwealth of Learning*. That report led the Heads of Government at their recent meeting in Vancouver to ask that a Commonwealth institution be established to promote the mobility of distance education courses as part of the overall objective of student mobility within the Commonwealth.

Planning for this Commonwealth of Learning begins at the end of this month. Those at the Congress who will be involved in developing the blueprint for this exciting initiative were very encouraged by the enthusiasm shown by our Topic group, for we returned to this project frequently during our discussions. Most felt that we were now ready for much greater mobility of learning materials. Furthermore, the obstacles of accreditation, residence requirements and credit transfer, which have made student mobility within and between countries so difficult, are beginning to break up. In other words the group felt that this was a most propitious time to give a new impetus to the ideal of a Commonwealth of Learning. We shall be most interested to see what it has achieved when we meet in Swansea in five years' time.

Group Discussions

TOPIC 4

UNIVERSITIES AND NATIONAL ADMINISTRATION

The Contribution of Universities to the Government and Administration of their Countries

Chairman: Professor P. J. BOYCE
Vice-Chancellor of Murdoch University

Chief Rapporteur: Mr. I. R. WAY
Deputy Principal and Registrar of the University of New South Wales

		Page
Sub-Topics 4(a) and (b)	(a) UNIVERSITIES AND CONSENSUS BUILDING IN THIRD-WORLD COUNTRIES	
	Speaker Professor I. A. Abdulkadir	256
	(b) PROBLEMS OF ACCOUNTABILITY IN PUBLICLY FUNDED UNIVERSITIES IN THE LIGHT OF THE CARIBBEAN EXPERIENCE	
	Speaker Professor G. M. Richards	264
	Discussion	272
Sub-Topic 4(c)	MASTER'S DEGREES FOR MANDARINS: HAVE TAUGHT HIGHER DEGREES A VALUE FOR PUBLIC SERVANTS?	
	Speaker Professor D. J. Murray	276
	Discussion	282
Final Session		284
CHAIRMAN'S REPORT ON THE GROUP'S DISCUSSIONS		286

For index to names, see p 533

Sub-Topics 4(a) and (b)

Tuesday, 9 February

(a) UNIVERSITIES AND CONSENSUS BUILDING IN THIRD-WORLD COUNTRIES

Professor I. A. ABDULKADIR (*Executive Secretary, National Universities Commission, Lagos*):

THE NIGERIAN EXPERIENCE

Consensus means the practice of basing policies on what will gain wide or popular support. In this paper I discuss how the universities in the third world influence formulation of policies that will gain wide or popular support within the country of their location. To do so one has to examine the historical development of universities within the third world—countries that are industrially less developed or to whom the concept of western education with its attendant science and technological developments have come onto the scene relatively recently.

It is therefore safe to say that the university in the third world is a very recent development. Almost all countries grouped under the concept of third world in central and south America, Africa, Near and Far East have at one time or another been subject to either colonial subjugation or total settlement by the European explorers. The colonial master's introduction of western education to the indigenes had been largely just to produce manpower that would satisfy the needs of the colonial master at a junior and intermediate level only. This was particularly true within Africa. Consequently, university education among the indigenes of the third world started almost invariably before universities became established in their own countries. This was fortunate because the few indigenes that were able to get away to European and American universities contributed in no small way to awakening their fellow

SUB-TOPIC 4(A): CONSENSUS BUILDING [Abdulkadir]

men to rise and fight for their rights, especially for the right to govern themselves.

Within the African continent British colonization appeared in two versions. In East and Central Africa the British actually settled, while in West Africa they contented themselves with being colonial masters only until independence. University development of these colonies followed the pattern I mentioned earlier, namely, the indigenes began to get university education long before universities were actually established in their countries. Nigeria, which became a nation in its present form in 1914, saw the missionaries as the first western educators. The educational institutions established by these missionaries did not, however, go beyond secondary schools. British administration also maintained these concepts until about 1934 when the first tertiary institution, the Yaba College of Technology, was established. By this time many Nigerians had already received university education elsewhere, were already on the scene and were collaborating with some of their colleagues in West Africa to start agitating for education beyond that level. The opening of this school started a spate of public controversy and criticism and the British government eventually started conceding to this agitation. A university college was established in Ibadan in 1948 under what was called a 'special arrangement' with the University of London whereby graduates of the college would receive degrees of University of London while their training was done either completely in Nigeria or partly so. In medicine, for instance, in the early years, the college was training students for pre-clinical years only and the students then had to go to London to finish the MB BS of London University. The college in Ibadan continued in that status until 1962. In the meantime Nigerians educated in Europe and America and other parts of the world at university level, as well as those with secondary school education, eventually began to close ranks and put pressure on the colonial masters for political and economic independence. In the early and mid fifities, as a result of these pressures, the British increased the number of tertiary institutions by establishing three colleges of arts, science and technology in Nigeria, and one at Legon in what was then called the Gold Coast (now Ghana). These colleges trained students in arts, science and technology to the equivalent of 'A'-level, in other words for qualifications preparatory to university education.

In 1960 the first full-fledged university was established in Nigeria. It was called University of Nigeria, Nsukka, which was in the then Eastern Region. Immediately thereafter a wave of establishing regional universities spread across the nation. Not only had the University College at Ibadan been converted into a full-fledged university by the end of 1962, but the year also saw the establishment of regional universities at Zaria for the Northern Region and at Ife for the Western Region. At this time the federal government itself also decided to accept the recommendation of the Ashby report and established its first full-fledged metropolitan university, the University of Lagos. With these developments university graduates began to become a common phenomenon throughout the country. Hitherto a graduate was somebody special, particularly in the north. This development had an effect on the social, economic and political development of the nation.

These regional universities continued until 1975 when the federal government decided to take over the running of them and eventually created seven more; so that within 27 years a country that had had only one university college now had 13 universities. The student enrolment within the 27-year period rose from 50 in 1948 to 32,000 in the 1975.76 session. One must add that this was also the period of great economic boom arising from the discovery of the 'black gold' then being exported in large quantities. After that the country shifted gear and began to consider creating specialized universities. By 1981 seven universities of technology were established, all by federal government. These universities were in full swing by 1982. However in 1984 it was felt that establishing too many universities within too short a time had its shortcomings, and it was decided that four of the universities of technology should be converted to campuses of other universities. But as at January 1, 1988, these campuses regained their full autonomous status as full-fledged universities, two of them becoming universities of agriculture and two remaining as universities of technology.

Between 1979 to 1984 much was happening in the political scene that influenced university development. October 1, 1979, ushered in the second republic in Nigeria with a brand new constitution which put the establishment of universities under the concurrent list. This meant that the federal government did not have the sole right to establish universities. The state governments and individuals or groups of individuals could also establish a university. (This was how it was during the first republic, but the first military regime changed it.) With this new dispensation, within four years Nigeria, with its population of about 100 million, witnessed the establishment of eight state universities and 24 private universities.

In 1984, however, the military regime that deposed the second republic not only converted four of the federal universities into campuses but also banned all 24 of the privately-owned universities, so that as at January 1, 1988, Nigeria had 13 conventional universities, five universities of technology, two universities of agriculture, one university for the new Federal Capital Territory at Abuja, and one military university. All of these were financed directly by the federal government. In addition, the eight state universities created between 1979 and 1984 have also continued, so today there are 30 universities with a total student enrolment of about 130,000.

Since the establishment of the regional universities in 1962 it became obvious to federal government that there was a need to create an organization that would centrally co-ordinate university development. The organization, of which I now have the privilege of being chief executive, came into existence in that year. It was a department in the cabinet office until 1974, when the then military regime formulated a decree which gave the organization statutory status with full powers to co-ordinate the academic and physical development of all universities in the country. It is also responsible for budgeting, receiving funds from government and disbursing to all federal universities except the military university. All the 21 federal government universities are accountable to federal government through this organization in all their financial management as well as their academic and physical developments.

Today federal government alone budgets over ₦600 million for capital and recurrent expenditure for the universities. This accounts for nearly 8% of the total national budget. If one takes into consideration the grants to the eight state universities from their respective states, this comes to nearly 10%. What then are the benefits or otherwise accrued from this heavy investment in university education to the government and people of the Federal Republic of Nigeria?

The problem which faced the nation after independence was that of lack of political stability due primarily to tribalism, sectionalism, religious differences and lack of understanding between the regions. During this period one witnessed the existing university staff (now becoming more Nigerianized) and students being dragged into politics with all its attending tribalistic and religious overtones. This was between 1960 and 1966. The dominant issue of the day was regional strength and autonomy versus the existence of the nation as an entity. If the universities built consensus on any issues in those days they did so within the framework of the existing political and tribal persuasions in the regions. The interest of the nation as a whole and the existence of the federation were at peril. The interest in federal government *per se* was reduced to that of the big brother holding the main bag from which to dole out funds to the regions. The struggle to get to control the central government was seen primarily from the viewpoint of power and money. Such was the state of affairs which made the universities as national consensus builders virtually redundant; not that there were no instances occasioning some muscle-flexing on campus against government policies, but outcomes were largely innocuous.

In Nigeria, universities did not really start flexing their muscles and voicing their opinions on national and international issues until from about the mid-1960s. This period coincided with the beginning of the first military regime, which brought the first republic to an end before that republic could bring to an end the existence of an entity called Nigeria. It cost the nation a civil war with all its attendant cost of men and material for 30 months before the federation could be saved.

During the period of the war, 1967–70, the Nigerian university students and staff within or outside Nigeria contributed in no small measure towards moulding public opinion about the war. Without doubt the foundation of Nigerian universities as consensus builders was laid during the period up to 1970, but the expression of it did not become manifest until after 1970. During the 18 years thereafter the universities not only grew in number and enrolment but also developed into a formidable force in moulding public opinion for or against government's national and international policies. A lot happened during this period and some highlights are given here.

Immediately after the war there was a period of reconciliation, reconstruction and rehabilitation of the war-affected areas and of their people as well as the nation at large. Thanks to oil the resources to do so were there. That was the period when the National Youth Service Corps was introduced. Both staff and students protested, but the military government was adamant. The universities all came under federal control and the National Universities Commission was made a statutory body. Student unrest became common for reasons from poor accommodation to poor food and fees. The students' unions became increasingly powerful. The most powerful was the National Association of Nigerian Students. Many violent demonstrations occurred, akin to those of students in Europe and America at the time. Several students lost their lives. The public became disenchanted because universities were becoming a source of sorrow to the community where they were located, with campus demonstrations spilling over into the surrounding community with regrettable consequences. But the relationship between the students and the university administration, though it had been rough, was also productive. It helped to change the role of students in policy formulation and implementation, especially on matters directly affecting them—a far cry from the colonial days when they virtually had no say. In 1972 the academic staff formed a union called the Academic Staff Union of Universities. This union had it rough with various governments of the day on national and international issues; often the effectiveness of its arguments with government was marred by the fact that the Union tended to rise to the occasion a shade too late. In addition, the union was often left in the hands of confrontation-happy militants who were prepared to threaten national peace and harmony to make their point.

In order to ensure that the universities were effectively controlled in terms of financing, and to prevent their uncontrolled proliferation, they were in 1975 all centralized, and establishing universities anywhere in the country became the exclusive preserve of the federal government. Arising from this centralization of control of universities was the issue of admission to them. The Regions, when they existed, were at different levels of development with regard to western education, and this imbalance had continued. Given the high regard that the nation has had for university education, it followed that in the interest of national unity something had to be done to ensure that admission to the universities reflected federal character. Consequently in 1977 a Joint Admission and Matriculation Board (JAMB) was set up to do just that, among other things. This was not quietly received but, after the dust settled, JAMB stayed. It is today very functional.

The military administrators of this period were confronted with the various turmoils on the campuses which were developing with far-reaching implications within the immediate communities and the nation at large. The head of state was forced to cry out. In 1976 while addressing the vice-chancellors he said, *inter alia*: 'Government is anxious to see that they [the Universities] are well equipped to meet the expectations of the people of this country. Government on its part attaches great importance to the contribution of the Universities outside pure development of manpower resources. The Universities should be a vehicle for the promotion of national consciousness, unity, understanding and peace . . . '. University education was experiencing a crisis which had disrupted national peace and harmony, but fortunately not national unity.

Before the military regime handed over power to the civilian regime in October 1979 it had to contend with another serious crisis in the universities, in March of that year. This time it was

[1] Aminu, J.M. (1979): 'The University as an Instrument for National Unity'. Guest speaker lecture delivered at the 2nd annual seminar of the Committee of Vice-Chancellors of Nigerian Universities, Calabar; June 30, 1979.

over admission. The situation and its implication were most aptly described by Aminu (1979)[1] when he said:

'The crisis brought out the problems of University education and National Unity very clearly. There were misconceptions as to where the blame lay or should lie. Most seriously the crisis demonstrated the serious intolerance and narrow mindedness that afflict the elite of the country—whether it is the Universities, the press or any other sector. It was one of the instances where a person's views can be accurately forecast by looking at his name. To that extent, it was no credit to the country and we must all work to ensure that it does not repeat itself ever . . . '.

Hence the problems during the first republic of sectionalism, tribalism and imbalances were carried over into the military regime, and since there was a ban on political parties these elements which threatened the survival of the first republic simply crept into the campuses and ensured that they made their presence known on any university or university-related issues. They always manifest themselves in one form or another during any campus crisis.

Such was the climate in the universities when the second republic came into being. Its new constitution had a very heavy input by individual university academic staff. This participation foretold what was to come, namely, that university staff would participate strongly in the politics of the day. This they did. Some went into party politics as full participants in the formation of political parties and of their manifestos, while others actually stood for elected offices (despite stringent laws on that) for which they lost heavily. The majority, however, participated in the government of second republic through political appointment by parties in power to which the academics had contributed in one form or another. It was a meeting point between political theory, theory of government, ideology and the realities of life. Unfortunately the theoreticians did not fare very well; in fact it was a disastrous venture for most of them, who were forced to run back to campus. From this viewpoint the universities failed to lead in building consensus during the second republic. The students did not fare better.

The combination of gross mismanagement of resources, intensification of tribal and sectional sentiments in the body politic of the day, and failure of some state governments to function harmoniously with federal government, made the military intervene again. Soon after the second election of the second republic, having observed the way that election was conducted and how the first budget after the election was being manipulated, and having looked at the list of the newly appointed federal ministers, the military took over in December 1983. The military continues in government

SUB-TOPIC 4(A): CONSENSUS BUILDING [Abdulkadir]

to date, though the machinery has been set in motion to effect a gradual handover of power to politicians once again; an exercise which will be completed by 1992.

Since the end of the second republic the military has been involving the academics in the direct business of governing. This time around, because due care has been taken in selecting the participants, most have developed into the pride of the government and the nation in terms of their performance. They are helping to restore the very badly shattered image of university staff in the art and science of governing, including the politics of it all.

This regime has not been without its own share of crisis on the campus. It has had to introduce some drastic measures which only a firm military regime could get away with. It has for instance decided that feeding students would no longer be the business of the university itself. This potentially volatile issue was forced upon the universities and it has come to be accepted as part of life on campus. One of the ugliest student crises in the university system, which nearly spread throughout the country, occurred in May 1986. Tragically several lives were lost. It took military firmness to end it and to establish peace. The episode did not threaten national unity, but it threatened national peace.

There is no doubt that the Nigerian university system, through thick and thin, has contributed immensely to the manpower development of the nation, forged national unity, helped to influence policies in both military and civilian regimes, and participated actively in the art and science of governing in what is called the third world. All these have, however, not been easily achieved. In the process the universities went through a serious erosion of the special positions they held in their earlier days. There is no doubt that the series of constitutional changes in ownership weakened their positions. The nature of military rule and its attendant emphasis on discipline, and less tolerance of 'irritating' dissents, also made the ivory tower appear shorter. The future of Nigerian universities and their role as consensus builders in the development of the nation and in formulating national and international policies is, however, not in doubt. The road is very rough though. The universities will have to deal with many problems all at once.

As third-world universities, the first struggle is to develop themselves into truly academic establishments of national and international repute in research and other academic pursuits. Secondly, to do so the universities will have to struggle to obtain a more stable source of funding, which as of now fluctuates a lot due to the very heavy dependence on government funding. Thirdly, the universities will have to establish their credibility as consensus builders within their immediate communities and the nation as a whole. The academic staff in the third world are still not sure whether or not they should remain academics for life. The conditions of service, among other things, are still not attractive enough to ensure this. Fourthly, there is still an element of competition between the academics and the civil servants, especially in the area of conditions of service and the positive role each is seen to be playing in the overall issue of promoting national unity. However, with all the experiences over the past 40 years, I believe that the Nigerian university system will overcome all these problems and forge ahead as the main builder of national consensus—and as an example to the third world.

(b) PROBLEMS OF ACCOUNTABILITY IN PUBLICLY FUNDED UNIVERSITIES IN THE LIGHT OF THE CARIBBEAN EXPERIENCE

Professor G. M. RICHARDS (*Pro-Vice-Chancellor, University of the West Indies, and Principal, St. Augustine Campus*):

The University of the West Indies—A Case Study

The pattern of relationship between universities and countries is, generally speaking, 'many to one'. In some instances this becomes 'one to one'. However, with the possible exception of the University of the South Pacific, the University of the West Indies (UWI) is unique in having a 'one to many' relationship with the countries, 14 in all, which it serves. These states are geographically scattered—from Belize in Central America to Trinidad and Tobago lying just off the coast of Venezuela, economically disparate and politically diverse, but have a common heritage in their colonial link with Britain. Among the 14 states, 11 are independent while the others are still colonies. All, however, regard the University as an important instrument of development, and the University, which draws most of its revenue from them, sees their needs and aspirations as paramount.

Since its establishment 40 years ago the UWI has become the cornerstone of higher education in the English-speaking Caribbean. It has become a large, complex, decentralized institution with activities dispersed throughout the entire region. It has achieved a high reputation for academic excellence and integrity and its graduates play key roles throughout the region in the professions and the public service. Some have become prime ministers and ministers in several governments. As a regional institution it operates in a complex political, economic, social, cultural and physical environment that is rapidly changing.

Constitution and Relationship with the Governments

Within the terms of its charter the University has, on paper, considerable autonomy and nowhere in the charter is state support implied. We are, however, heavily dependent upon funding from the governments.

Government ministers of the supporting countries sit on the university and campus councils. The governments are also represented on the University Grants Committee (UGC) and the campus grants committees (CGCs). The UGC and its campus counterparts provide recurrent expenditure through triennial block grants. Implicit in the financial arrangements is a recognition of the autonomy of the University.

The University has recently (1984) completed a major restructuring exercise touching upon not only its academic and administrative organization but also its method of financing. The emphasis was on greater devolution of authority to the campuses, whilst attempting to retain a strong regional commitment. Much of the pressure came from the twin prongs of access and cost. Campus territory governments felt that there would be better response from the University if the campuses had more autonomy. They also felt that costs would be under greater control if the finances were dealt with on a campus-by-campus basis.

The UWI remains relatively free of legal control by the parliaments of the various contributing territories. This is in part due to the existence of the charter and also to the buffer provided by the large number of states involved. Like many of the other Commonwealth universities in the developing world, however, the fees payable by students and endowments together represent a relatively small portion of our income. While, therefore, there is no formal legal relationship with the states, there is a strong financial relationship.

Generally speaking, university autonomy from parliamentary interference has been preserved. This applies also to parliamentary audit where so far the accounts of the University are not subject to parliamentary scrutiny, the Public Accounts Committee or the Auditor General.

The Changing Face of the University/Government Relationship

We will now consider some of the ways in which strains in the relationship between governments and the University have developed. The grave economic crisis facing most of the Caribbean territories has resulted in a situation where the integrity of the approved triennial budgets has been lost and the University has now become dependent on sporadic releases of funds at the whims and fancies of the political directorate. We have therefore become particularly vulnerable. We are now in a situation in which we live hand-to-mouth, subject to the arbitrariness of spasmodic releases.

Capital grants, never at a level which would make proper provision for our needs, have, by and large, become a thing of the past. Neither have we been given, over the past three triennia, adequate compensation for inflationary increases in our costs. It has become abundantly clear that governments expect to have university education on the cheap.

There is, in addition, a perception that the University is inefficient, inward-looking and self-satisfied. Indeed it has been said that the University is the only agency which has not heeded the call for 'national reconstruction' and that it has distanced itself from the problems of the society. This despite any evidence to the contrary. Committees have been set up by two of the campus governments to undertake comprehensive reviews of the operations of the University. Our third campus is under threat of a similar enquiry. It was widely expected that such committees would point to areas of inefficiency and waste and the possibility of cuts in funding. The University has, however, emerged unscathed and indeed complimented.

I believe that most of us are agreed that universities are intended for the creation, interpretation, dissemination and application of knowledge. Indeed the rationale for the UWI is reflected in its objectives and is stated in its charter thus: '. . . to secure the advancement of knowledge and the diffusion and extension of arts, science and learning through the Contributing Countries'. Within this neat framework widely differing emphases have long found a place—whether it is the primacy of teaching over research and vice versa, or the assertion of the principle of knowledge for its own sake (the autonomous tradition) over the service function of the university expressed in a commitment to relevance, utility and responsiveness to societal needs.

Related to this is the fact that universities are often unfairly condemned by their communities because it is in their nature and essence to pursue values and programmes that are very often not readily perceived as being convergent with community needs and interests. The 'ivory tower' image and the complaint that universities are out of touch with their communities are universal.

We may also reflect upon the political forces which militate against the autonomous claims of the university or which apply pressure on the institution to function in the national interest or in the interest of professional and vocational needs associated with economic growth and recovery or, by implication, in the interest of our political masters. Universities in their present form, it has to be admitted, are not vote-catchers and the politics is usually hidden behind the economics. The shortage of funds consequent upon the deterioration of national economies has therefore now emerged as the main obstacle facing the majority of universities the world over, although the backgrounds against which such a shortage exists may differ. For the political ideology in certain developed countries like the United States or Britain, for example, renders public spending increasingly illegitimate. Universities as public enterprises have fallen under the monetarist axe and their vulnerability stems largely from the fact that they are public enterprises of an eleemosynary character and therefore widely perceived as being non-productive. The argument develops that it is easier to train fewer engineers, teachers or doctors and to do less pure and applied research than to allow a productive economic enterprise to founder. The implication here is that a university is not productive and is therefore expendable.

In the developing countries, however, the university has had to be taken seriously by the governments as an instrument of national development, whatever the risks. In such countries it cannot be sensible (even if easy) to train fewer professionals and it would clearly be downright suicidal not to engage in serious research so as to develop indigenous capabilities. Moreover, most developing-country governments have achieved power on nationalist platforms of self-determination and independence.

One of the political dimensions of the university's problem is frequently expressed in the often ill-founded charge that universities are inefficient in organization and performance. Hence the need, goes the argument, for universities to effect or be *forced* to effect rationalization of structures and economies of scale.

Certain assumptions of the university's role and function invite political responses as well. The autonomous principle logically gives to the individual academic the right to opt out of any obligation that he might be expected to have to the service principle. This has been seen by some, especially by political leaders in developing countries, as a revolutionary threat to the political status quo, since the right to think freely and to pursue truth wherever it leads may indeed lead to founts of knowledge that flow counter to the pet policies, programmes and ideologies of those in power. Such politicians, faced with the crisis of balancing their budgets, will naturally wish to have the universities which they fund subject themselves as well to budgetary discipline. In this, university grants committees are being surreptitiously transformed from the buffers between universities and the political masters that they should be into bearers of sad tidings of budget cuts and impending penury.

The suggested and attempted solutions in turn present further problems. For example, the rise in students' fees and the limitation of student intake both have political repercussions. The question of elitism versus the commitment to democratic mass education immediately comes to mind. Budgetary constraints constitute an economic factor which carries far-reaching implications for teaching, research and outreach work in any university anywhere today. The situation in the developing world is exacerbated by the fact that the fall in market prices for primary agricultural and mineral produce, the increasing burdens of debt repayment and the policing powers of the International Monetary Fund have all forced policies of draconian cutback on public sector expenditure. This leads inevitably to the general degeneration of intellectual and educational activity.

Increasingly the output of the universities is expected to possess the attitudes, knowledge and skills needed by society, and particularly by the economy, before the system is deemed to be efficient. This concept of efficiency turns on cost-benefit analysis, quantifiable variables indicating the clear and immediate usefulness of the university to society, on straight manpower questions of how many engineers, teachers, agriculturists, doctors, etc., are to be supplied to service the nutrition, food and agriculture sectors of the economy, or to provide good health care delivery systems, and of how many managers may be needed for industry, commerce and the production process. Most often, and especially in the developing countries, the needs and desires are eloquently articulated but usually without the appropriate budgetary support for their realization.

Some General Thoughts on Financial and Social Accountability

There are possibly at least two shades of meaning to the concept of 'financial accountability', viz.—

(1) Ensuring propriety in the use of funds—however, the requirement for and the provision of audited accounts would normally provide a sufficient guarantee. This is therefore not normally a source of friction.

(2) Ensuring financial efficiency—in this context, the institution's objectives are not under scrutiny. The concern here is whether or not those objectives are being pursued at the lowest possible cost.

Examples of some questions which may be posed are:

(*a*) Are staff being remunerated too generously? Can they be recruited and retained at lower cost?

(*b*) Is the university purchasing non-labour inputs economically? Should its procedures and controls be the same as those which apply in the public sector?

(*c*) Can economies be achieved by changing teaching methods? Are class sizes optimal? Should the number of student contact hours per staff member be increased? Is the university at the minimum point on its cost curve? Indeed, is such a point feasible or realizable in the context of the overall budgetary constraints?

For several reasons these and related questions are not easily answered by those seeking to hold the university financially accountable since:

(*a*) They cannot be properly addressed without reference to the university's objectives which are hard to pin down. 'Quality education', for example, is a great 'fudge factor'. Knowledge generation also represents another source of difficulty.

(*b*) The market for academic labour services is more international (or at least less domestic) than other markets and is therefore not strictly comparable with them.

(*c*) The public sector control agencies have little experience and expertise in university evaluation.

(*d*) There are often no other institutions readily usable as standards of comparison.

Social accountability is even more diffuse and subject to argument and differing opinions. In this context, questions which might arise are:

(*a*) Is the university making an appropriate and sufficient contribution to society? Is the type of education being provided 'relevant'?

(*b*) What is the relative importance being attached to research as opposed to teaching?

Governments as possible control agencies tend to have an extremely myopic and short-term view of these matters occasioned by the very nature of electoral and budgetary cycles. Any policies that they may wish to establish are more volatile and short-term than would ideally be required in the interests of a long-term and broader view of development. Governments are also often unwilling to tolerate much freedom of thought and expression. This is an enduring tension. Moreover, a university operating within the confines of a small society finds that its role assumes a much greater prominence. This again could be a source of tension.

The Contemporary University

Universities are facing new challenges as a result of the changing relationship with the government and also because the nature and the importance of knowledge in modern society are changing both qualitatively and quantitatively. Politicians and the public are becoming increasingly hostile to the concept of university autonomy. The increasing financial pressures and general shortage of resources, the rapid socio-economic and political changes and the major scientific and technological advances have all led to a shift of emphasis. It seems clear, therefore, that a wide range of factors has highlighted the need for a re-ordering of priorities for our universities leading to a broader definition of their role and function and to a new relationship with the governments.

The new conception of the university extends well beyond the traditional model of the 'research' university that has dominated the academic world's rhetoric over the past few decades. In order to be responsive to current conditions and needs, and to meet the formidable challenges of the late twentieth century, universities must substantially expand the traditional definition of their scholarly role. They should be clearly seen as development resources for the communities in which they are located. In teaching, as well as in research, the university needs to forge a closer relationship with the world beyond the campus. The basic challenge faced by universities today is to make their intellectual resources more widely available to external constituencies.

Universities are subject to changing societal circumstances and demands. Some of these challenges can only be met by fundamentally affecting the way institutions define and carry out their mission. It is increasingly important that the modern university extend its scholarly activities beyond basic research to include a wide range of applied work, technical assistance, interpretation and dissemination. Such projects are inherently problem-oriented and cut across disciplinary lines.

The changed perception of a university with closer links with the real world beyond the campus differs markedly from the classical vision of an 'ivory tower', an isolated, internally oriented institution engaged in pursuing knowledge for its own sake. Instead it engages in close and continuous two-way interaction with the environment in which it finds itself. Scholarship, instruction and professional service all find an equal place. Theory is related to practice; basic research is linked to its applications; questions posed by practical situations generate new research initiatives. This model of the extended contemporary university is in many respects a modernized version of the US land-grant and state university tradition, where the institution as a whole is dedicated to a broadly defined utilitarian, instrumental purpose. The model of the extended university therefore subsumes a great variety of instructional and professional tasks. In the peculiar context of one university serving 14 different countries, or even a single-country institution, this university has to become involved in the entire span of activities. It has to be all things to all people, stretching its limited resources.

It has to be admitted that very little structural or pedagogical change has yet taken place in either undergraduate or postgraduate education in response to changing needs and mounting external criticisms (often valid) of universities. Employers are dissatisfied with the preparation of newly recruited graduates. They also find most universities rigid, slow and unresponsive. Furthermore faculty values, incentives and reward systems have so far remained substantially unchanged. Without a substantial adaptation of the faculty reward system, all efforts at greater university outreach and expanded faculty activities will continue to be what they have been in the majority of institutions: a matter of well-intended but ineffective rhetoric. Universities therefore need to develop appropriate methods of documenting and evaluating the broader professional activities of their teaching staff and must ensure that quality performance in these areas is as highly regarded and rewarded as achievement in the more traditional areas of faculty responsibility such as basic research that leads to publication in refereed, scholarly journals. Without such a revision of the reward system the faculty will not place any value on outreach activities and will continue to denigrate them as 'public service'.

As we move towards greater involvement in external activities, the university will be in some danger of losing its sense of detachment. Universities constitute the principal societal mechanism for objective analysis and critique of societal activities. They are not social agencies, but rather instruments of society that cannot remain isolated, as in the past they have tended to be, but must instead maintain a measure of detachment and autonomy.

This is possible in the extended university, but will require ongoing vigilance and clear criteria as to the appropriate limit of activities. As long as these limits are maintained greater university involvement in external activities can, in fact, make the institutions much more effective in their critical role. The extended university is likely to be a more useful and responsive institution and is also likely to be a more exciting, a more effective and a more rewarding place to teach, to learn and to be educated.

DISCUSSION

(*Rapporteur:* Mr. D. NEAVE, Secretary-General and Registrar, Brunel University)

The principal preoccupations of universities inevitably change as the pressures upon them, both internal and external, change. In 1988 accountability emerged as a common theme which concerned all of the participants in this session, irrespective of their national background. That notion of accountability embraced not only what we did and how effectively we used resources in doing it, but also to whom we were accountable. Since universities derived the larger part of their funding from governments, accountability to those governments, who were taking an increasingly closer interest in the way in which universities used that money, was seen as important. But so were accountability within institutions and accountability to the community at large.

Accountability to government on the one hand and to parliament on the other was viewed differently. So far as governments were concerned, although the extent of the accountability and the mechanisms used to bring it about differed, the concomitant of increased government control of universities was seen by many as an unwelcome and potentially unhealthy development. Of the countries and regions represented, it was in the West Indies that the explicit involvement of the participating funding governments was perhaps least developed, and the autonomy of the university best preserved. But that situation was changing, not least as a result of the economic difficulties being experienced by many of the Caribbean territories. In Australia and in the UK university autonomy was now under considerable threat. The right of the state auditor-general to 'examine the books' was well established. But in Australia the federal government was now requiring individual institutions to produce 'research management plans' since 30% of the cost of salaries was intended to fund staff effort in research. There was a fear that the federal government

SUB-TOPIC 4(B): ACCOUNTABILITY

might seek to reallocate some or all of this 'research funding' without regard to the existence of the 'binary line' between university and polytechnic institutions. A similar government-backed redistribution of research resources might well occur in the UK in order to establish well-funded 'centres of research excellence' at the expense of others. This redistribution of scarce resources was of less significance in Nigeria and the West Indies, but only because government was not a principal provider of research funding in the first place.

But accountability for use of funds was not only a *post hoc* matter. Increasingly, universities were required to produce development plans which were the subject of discussion between government, or government-created agencies, and the universities. Where civil servants represented government in such discussions, as in the West Indies and Nigeria, there was concern that their analysis and conclusions might well be deficient, if only through lack of understanding. Nor did approval of a plan or of a set of estimates imply that the funds would then be made available. Nonetheless, participation in a planning process, whatever its final outcome, was seen to be preferable to the absence of any planning at all and its possible consequence of 'funding at whim' by governments.

If there was to be accountability it was thought that accountability through parliament was preferable to accountability direct to government (indeed in the UK the experience of such accountability to parliament had proved positively beneficial to the Open University). In the same way accountability through a 'buffer body' such as a university grants committee was to be preferred (the recent removal of such a buffer body by the Australian federal government was causing considerable difficulties for universities). But if there was a 'buffer body' it had to be, and to be seen to be, impartial.

It had to be recognised, however, that ministers and their civil servants were themselves accountable, and it was not necessarily unreasonable, therefore, that they in turn should seek some measure of accountability from the universities. Universities themselves had a duty to ensure that their resources were applied effectively and efficiently. That was particularly the case where the use of staff time was concerned. Were staff adequately carrying out the full range of duties entrusted to them (*e.g.* teaching, research administration, public service)? What was to be done about a member of staff who shone in some aspects and failed in others? Could a brilliant researcher but poor teacher have his teaching load shifted to other members of staff? And how would we deal with the probable resultant tensions that would create? Clearly performance assessment had to become an increasingly important feature of university life.

Whilst much of the criticism of universities emanated from governments and politicians, to an extent they mirrored concerns in the community. In Nigeria academic staff received higher basic pay than civil servants, to reflect their multifaceted role, but it was difficult for a member of staff always to find the time to meet his obligations both to the university and to the community. Whilst the Nigerian community tended to be supportive of universities, at least until it became apparent that not all qualified students could be admitted, the media were less so. The Singapore government had taken a direct hand in forcing universities to fulfil some of their perceived community obligations by appointing, without consultation, university staff to public offices. In general, direct involvement of the Singapore government in the running of individual institutions appeared to be considerable.

The role of universities as catalysts of national unity was interestingly tested in Nigeria by the existence of state and federal universities alongside each other. State universities could operate discriminatory admissions policies by favouring applicants from particular groups or regions. But through its funding of state governments, and its requirement that students at state universities paid fees whilst those at federal universities did not, the federal government exercised a considerable moderating influence. In the UK, universities in Scotland, Wales and Northern Ireland were not above playing the 'regional card' with government when it suited their purpose. And Australian states periodically established state institutions without federal consent and then sought federal funding.

The expression of dissatisfaction by governments, by politicians, by the media and by the public at large was common. But lay members of council could do much to dispel the ignorance upon which that dissatisfaction was often based, by becoming informed as to the part their universities were really playing and then using their influence and knowledge to present the universities' case to the world at large. Their role, in these uncertain times, was critical.

Sub-Topic 4(c)

MASTER'S DEGREES FOR MANDARINS: HAVE TAUGHT HIGHER DEGREES A VALUE FOR PUBLIC SERVANTS?

Thursday, 11 February

In order to provide a framework for this session the Topic Chairman (Professor P. J. Boyce) gave the following brief summary of notes that had been prepared by Professor J. G. A. DAVIS (Director, Australian Graduate School of Management, University of New South Wales) on 'Supplying the Personnel for Government; Education or Training?' This was to have been the subject of a separate Sub-Topic with Professor Davis as speaker, but he was at the last moment unable to attend the Congress.

Professor Davis, comparing the Australian situation with the UK position, contended that:
- tertiary education caters to a 'middle-income society'
- tertiary education is, however, as accessible as in the UK
- in Australia there is a bias towards specific professional courses even when there is a drop in recruitment to the public service
- with regard to postgraduate education, Australia has not made a distinction between business and public administration in the Kennedy school style, providing MBA or MPA, and as a result public sector personnel, too, join the business course at master's level.

The Topic Chairman raised the fundamental question: should universities give particular attention to public service needs, or continue to impart a general liberal education only?

[Murray]   TOPIC 4: NATIONAL ADMINISTRATION

Professor D. J. MURRAY (*Pro-Vice-Chancellor (Degree Studies)*, *Open University (UK)*):

The Opportunities

In Britain during 1987 a major report on *The Making of British Managers*[1] proposed new directions for management education and a new scale of effort. The report was founded on inquiries into staff development practices and surveys of attitudes and expectations of employers and employees. These had revealed that there were large gaps in the education of managers. There was also widespread support for a sharp increase in management education. The report recommended that this education should be a career-long process and that universities and other institutions of higher education should contribute to it on a much enlarged scale by providing programmes leading to awards. In particular managers should expect to take a master's degree in business administration in their late twenties or early thirties.

This report forms part of moves towards a new and enlarged place for British universities in the career development of managers. As mid-career education receives increasing emphasis and post-school education is recognised not as the terminal point in education but as a stage leading on to continuing education, there is the prospect of universities, in general, widening their sphere and contributing through taught master's degrees and other award programmes to the education and training managers in the public as well as private sectors. At present the accepted order, particularly in the public sector, is different. Thus for the generalist administrative service in the civil service universities provide a pool of high-flying graduates for entry to a fast track and other graduates to less exalted positions in that service. The civil service has then sought to select the best talent available for the administrative cadre. To limit this pool to those who have studied public administration or management is accepted as an unnecessary constraint. Universities produce graduates with educated minds. Appropriate training is a matter for the civil service. The distinction between education and training has been a useful one.

The civil service career structure and staff development activities have hitherto aimed to equip and motivate officials through their working lives. In a career service portable qualifications can be treated as unnecessary. Diplomas, degrees and forms of professional recognition are not essential to the management of a career service. What counts is performance and potential as revealed in current performance. Conversely for those managing the service qualifications may create complications as officials secure advancement outside the civil service.

Such, however, is only one perspective. To generalist administrators qualifications enhance opportunities in the wider labour market.

There has nevertheless been a change in assessment of qualifications in Britain and this is indicated by the report to which I have referred. The reasons for this are three. The performance of enterprises is affected by their managers and managers' effectiveness is influenced by their education and training; continuing education in Britain is judged to be inadequate and it is not sufficiently widely accepted by managers as a career-long process; and qualifications are a necessary incentive for changing attitudes and securing the effort needed. 'Individual employees, while interested in obtaining skills, also wish to acquire qualifications which increase their opportunity within [the managerial labour] market.'[2] As a result of this same perspective in one central government service in Britain, it is proposed for managers that there should be an award 'which would have sufficient status to be recognised and accepted nationally both inside the . . . service and outside it'.

The MBA degree has a particular significance. As a qualification it is increasingly a unit of currency internationally and the importance of the degree is associated with a developing sense of management as a career with attributes of a profession. This applies to administrators and managers in the public sector as to ones in the private sector. The commitment in Britain to privatizing parts of the public service, introducing competition in the provision of public services and promoting the market as a decentralized form of administration, and hence stressing the importance of management in a market economy, have each encouraged increased interest in management education and in the MBA degree.

I have sketched the British background in order to provide a context for comment on three broad issues.

Appropriate Academic Expertise

First, what sort of academic expertise is needed in order to offer a master's degree intended for mid-career administrators and managers? Are universities well set to provide what is needed? Universities have been at the heart of the educational system but this does not mean that the academic fields as currently established have the most relevant concerns and expertise. Nor are universities inherently well equipped for all forms of education including mid-career staff development. The form of such education may need, to take one example, to be significantly different from that for post-school students.

Generalizations on such a big question are likely to constitute a distortion but nevertheless let me venture on some sweeping observations relevant to that issue. First, a comment on the state of knowledge and understanding in the relevant fields of public administration and management. Public administration has long sat somewhat uncomfortably as a subdivision of the social sciences, but there, nevertheless, it is commonly located. With a focus on the institutions of executive government or the processes of public administration, a range of disciplinary bodies of knowledge or modes of enquiry are appropriate. To understand and explain health service administration or the management of public finance requires the application of methods and insights from psychology, sociology, economics, political science and information science, among other fields. In practice public administration has tended to occupy a niche within political science to some extent blocked in by other social sciences and law as fields of knowledge have become increasingly specialist. Management, on the other hand, is more eclectic. It does draw on the social sciences and other fields and applies relevant methods, insights and knowledge to aspects of the function of managing. Management, indeed, may best be conceived in terms of a three-dimensional matrix: bodies of knowledge (*e.g.* psychology) applied to management functions (personnel) in a particular sector (*e.g.* retailing or industrial production). Partly, however, because of the existence of public administration, management has focused more on profit-making organizations. Some greater accommodation is now in process and public sector management in a market-orientated economy is emerging. As this happens universities are becoming increasingly well-equipped with knowledge to teach management skills and knowledge in a form that is relevant to governmental administration, and its teaching is informed by appropriate understanding.

Yet the state of knowledge is probably less significant than curriculum design and pedagogy for effective master's degrees. Continuing education as part of career development requires attention to what constitutes a useful programme of learning and the best way to study. Indeed I would suggest that establishing master's degrees as a recognisably valuable part of the mid-career development of administrators and managers means re-emphasizing the central importance of teaching and learning rather than the production of knowledge. Creating a new field of public sector management is not a necessary precondition for establishing a master's programme. What is necessary is to identify the skills and knowledge needed by officials at a particular point in their careers and provide an effective way of developing and practising them. Beyond this, effective mid-career education means creating the conditions for reflecting on individual experience and learning from it; and assisting officials to engage in critical thinking, including about their own assumptions and values. Much attention is needed, in other words, to be given to curriculum design. This may require an important change of attitude. In terms of the analysis in Peter Scott's book *The Crisis of the University*, a characteristic of the liberal university, rather than what he terms the modern university, has to be re-emphasized. It means countering what he describes as a prevailing academicism: 'The discovery and codification of (mainly theoretical) knowledge . . . as the core preoccupation of the University'.[3] If this is indeed the prevailing priority it implies an unhelpful conception of what is needed from a master's degree. Distilling new knowledge and pouring it down eager throats to give necessary sustenance will not bring credit on universities' offerings.

In their experience of pedagogy those teaching public administration and management have, in crude terms, a distinguishable experience. Public administration, particularly in the first world, has commonly been taught as part of a broad education. The main attention has been to what the Robbins report expressed as its second objective—teaching 'in such a way as to promote the general powers of the mind'.[4] To a greater extent the teaching of management has been more instrumental: equipping students with skills and knowledge relevant to an area of employment. There is more emphasis, in other words, on Robbins' first objective: 'instruction in skills to play a part in the general division of labour'.[5] As a result there has been more attention in general to the development of relevant and effective pedagogy. However much of this attention has been given outside universities. The syndicate method and other techniques associated with administrative staff colleges, for instance, are one indication of an area of pedagogical expertise that by-passed universities. Universities need to attend to the process of learning and then to see how to accommodate this with the assessment and evaluation necessary in a master's degree programme.

The Significance of a Master's Degree

A second issue is what a master's award signifies and, related to this, what part should different learning experiences contribute? Does a master's degree depend on formal study, or what balance is appropriate between formal study, in-service training and experiential learning? In one conception a master's degree marks the satisfactory completion of a prescribed programme of study within a specified period, undertaken in the university that awards the degree. There are here two components: study in a prescribed programme and the assessment and certification of performance.

A different conception is that a master's degree is a measure of a person's competence, however this is gained and whether or not it includes formal study. In this conception a master's degree assesses whether a person has developed and possesses sufficient skills, knowledge, appropriate attitudes and experience to perform successfully in defined administrative or managerial roles. Such a conception is based, first, on the idea that people develop skills and knowledge in a variety of ways during their lives and careers. In particular there is experiential learning narrowly conceived—'learning through experience rather than through study or formal instruction'[6], but there is also study which is not certificated. There is, further, the idea that career development is best advanced by building on what has already been achieved. In terms of this conception it becomes relevant to ask whether it is not appropriate that those with the necessary level of knowledge, skills and experience should be able to have this assessed and, as a result, secure the MBA degree as an indication of their competence, even if this involves no additional formal study?

The issue of what a master's degree signifies becomes particularly pertinent if master's degrees are constructed on a modular basis in a way that is particularly suitable for mid-career officials. Where there are modules, credit transfer arrangements are facilitated, allowing for study elsewhere to count towards the requirements of a degree. If, in addition, for the degree and its component modules, educational aims and objectives are elaborated, there is a basis for comparing different forms of previous learning. It is difficult then to provide any convincing rationale for allowing credit only for formal study undertaken in a university.

In the Open University we seek to steer a middle way between the alternatives I have sketched. This represents a compromise. Its justification rests on a judgement about what is acceptable in a British educational context. We recognise that in some fields—for example, in-service professional development for teachers—we are regarded as cautious, in others we may be thought to be generous. We see a measure of consistency across the University and across higher education as a whole as the primary guide to where to draw the limits. In taught master's degrees, however, there are considerable differences in current practice. The danger here is that at a time when the MBA is achieving an international currency and creating an opportunity for universities to extend their contribution to the education of managers and administrators in the private and public sectors, diverse judgements about what the degree signifies may curtail its value.

Institutional Framework

A third issue concerns the form of relationship between universities and those that a master's degree serves. For mid-career administrators and managers this means, among others, public and private sector employers as well as mid-career officials. Universities have experience of three broadly distinguishable institutional arrangements. They operate in a market framework offering graduate degrees, attracting students, and promoting recognition of the resulting graduates and the qualification they hold. Universities are familiar, secondly, with a consultative framework in which representatives of external bodies influence without controlling universities' contribution to the market. Outside the sphere of private or public sector management education, universities have experience also of a tighter structure imposed by a chartered professional body—and the creation of such a one for chartered managers has been floated in Britain.

Universities may have least experience of a fourth framework— one in which a university contracts to provide specified forms of education leading to a qualification. As an example, one part of central government seeks tenders for offering an award programme. The structure of the programme is specified. The syllabus is laid down—expressed in terms of behavioural outputs. ('Managers should be able to organise people—establish an appropriate organisational structure in their own department, define responsibilities clearly, establish accountability and reporting requirements . . . ') Inputs are defined in terms of the technical skills and knowledge to be taught and the attitudes and values inculcated. ('They will promote and encourage the adoption of . . . a full acceptance of responsibility, a participative approach to management . . .') Those tendering have in addition to specify the award to be given.

May I simply pose the question: would this example of a contractual relationship between a university and government employer be acceptable? And if not, why not?

Conclusion

The comments I have made have reflected one conception of the responsibility of universities in providing master's degrees for mandarins. I am critical of academicist trends. You will have noted a belief in some of the attributes of the liberal university—first, a degree of autonomy for the institution and for teachers within it, as a way both of facilitating a critical spirit of inquiry and of encouraging balance and a measure of detachment in its teaching. And, second, a commitment to the advancement of understanding as part of the process of education. Yet while implicitly adopting these values you will have noted also support for an instrumental role for universities in contributing to staff development. If universities are going to occupy a dominant position in this new landscape by contributing more to the continuing education of public and private sector managers, and at the same time safeguard their autonomy, there will need to be a general recognition in society of where universities do stand, and they may need to project more clearly what they stand for.

REFERENCES

1. Constable, J. and McCormick, R.: *The Making of British Managers*. A Report for the BIM and CBI into Management Training, Education and Development, London, 1987.
2. *Ibid.*, p.13.
3. Scott, P.: *The Crisis of the University*. London: Croom Helm, 1984, p.6.
4. Committee on Higher Education (Chairman, Lord Robbins): Higher Education Report. Cmnd. 2154, London, 1963, p.6.
5. *Ibid.*
6. Evans, N.: *Assessing Experiential Learning: A Review of Progress and Practice*. London: Longman, 1987, p.1.

DISCUSSION

(*Rapporteur:* Mr. V. N. SIVARAJAH,
Secretary, Committee of Vice-Chancellors and Directors, Sri Lanka)

During the discussion Dr. J. A. Mitchell (Stirling) called for greater collaboration and appropriate placement of students after proper job evaluation.

Some of the other points that emerged during the discussion are:
● that the academics could be criticized as too theoretical unless they recognise that people at middle levels of their career have acquired skills and knowledge, *i.e.* unless they adopt a change of approach from that used with young students

SUB-TOPIC 4(c): TAUGHT HIGHER DEGREES

- that the new situation may bring about a greater reliance on guest lecturers, creating problems of pensions, etc.
- that one should be very cautious in adopting evaluation and validation of experience and learning on the job, so as to ensure that there is no dilution of academic standards
- that professional people are too busy or involved with the political situation and cannot fully understand long-term issues, underlying philosophies, ethical issues and general trends unless they closely collaborate with universities.

The consensus of the session could be summarized as being that universities should recognise

(*a*) the need to be more involved, widen their role and come to practical terms

(*b*) that their role is teaching and not validating

(*c*) that what is required is greater communication.

Topic 4

FINAL SESSION

Thursday, 11 February

Introducing the summary session, the Topic Chairman (Professor P. J. Boyce) observed that a key issue emerging from the several papers and the following discussions was that related to government's perceptions of the national interest, this being not necessarily consonant with universities' interpretations of their roles in national affairs.

Points from the discussion
- Potential exists for conflict between the university as an objective critic of, and commentator on, society and as a claimant for government funding.
- Government's implied contract with its electorate cannot be ignored by universities. Problem of knowing where to draw the line between government directions and university autonomy in knowledge formation and dissemination. Often the case that university communities don't know where the line should be drawn, but have a distinct feeling of knowing when it has been transgressed. Despite misgivings, if universities are to remain an influence in the community, they must be responsive to government and community aspirations. This does not imply blind subservience. There may be a need for the academic profession to review its traditional views and values to accommodate the new, co-operative, directions.
- In the first world it is legitimate for governments to set priorities, with universities then having the freedom to pursue a different course. But no longer can full funding be expected for such independent directions. Not necessarily so in third world where governments may tend to be much more interventionist and directive to universities.
- Practical problem of government's expecting universities to follow guidelines for national benefit, but with market forces working in other directions (*e.g.* engineering in Australia). Problem of balance in government engineering its national

FINAL SESSION

outcomes by fully funding its priority courses, leaving others to find alternative funding.
- In Nigeria government has intervened in setting broad academic priorities; also in matters of detail such as student laboratory requirements, etc. This was seen as necessary to set and maintain expected university-level standards (especially in some newer private universities).
- In India national needs led to a massive increase in the number of universities and students. There followed some over-supply of graduates, leading to disillusionment. Hence need for manpower planning (to use a sexist expression!).
- Problem of universities asked to be mere validating agencies for externally-run courses and programmes. Universities are primarily *teaching* institutions, not validators of others' efforts.
- Australian experience of serving two political masters (state and federal) mirrors the problems elsewhere. State's requirements may not be in accord with national objectives.
- Importance of buffer bodies between universities and political/government agencies.

Topic 4

UNIVERSITIES AND NATIONAL ADMINISTRATION

The Contribution of Universities to the Government and Administration of their Countries

CHAIRMAN'S REPORT ON THE GROUP'S DISCUSSIONS

Second Plenary Session
Friday, 12 February

Professor P. J. BOYCE (*Vice-Chancellor, Murdoch University*): It became necessary to reduce the number of sessions in Topic 4 because of last-minute withdrawals by two paper-givers. This will excuse me, I hope, for being a little briefer in my presentation than are my colleagues. I think, too, I need to be a little more descriptive than is customary in identifying particular papers. I hope that won't be thought of as cheating, but it has been rather difficult for me to synthesize the discussion or bring the threads together. We were covering disparate topics. In some instances we were focusing almost exclusively on third-world problems. In a latter part of our session we were focusing on questions which embraced or were relevant to both third-world and first-world university systems. I think, too, that some of the Sub-Topics we were looking at could have been just as well subsumed in other Topics. In other words it was a very difficult Topic on which to present any kind of unified response.

In his paper on the role of universities and consensus building in third-world countries, Professor Abdulkadir quite properly focused on Nigeria's own quite turbulent political experience as an example of the difficulties posed for universities in servicing government and helping government set national policies or forge a sense of national unity. After all, in that country 30 federal or state

CHAIRMAN'S REPORT [*Boyce*]

universities have been established within 40 years, and yet 20 of those 40 years have witnessed severe political turbulence, civil war, a series of military coups and so forth. Therefore the challenges to universities in a system like that would be rather different from the challenges that one would expect the Canadian, British or Australian universities to be facing. But he also claimed that there had been an erosion of public confidence in universities, caused partly by that political turbulence but also by some of the economic and social factors which are common, I think, right across the Commonwealth.

Group 4 then proceeded to consider the problems of accountability in publicly funded universities, and Professor George Richards presented his thoughts in the light of another national or regional experience, that of the University of the West Indies. The University of the West Indies faces the usual problems of accountability but these are compounded by the fact that it is answerable to 14 countries, 11 of them sovereign states and three of them still colonies. The only parallel situation which any of us could recall was that of the University of the South Pacific. Despite, or because of, this complexity, the UWI has remained relatively free of legal control by the parliaments, and of political interference generally, all the more surprising and gratifying because of the very heavy dependence of that university on public funding. Indeed in this respect the University of the West Indies is perhaps reminiscent more of a first-world university than a third-world one, and of course it has not been subjected to the same political turbulence or pressures, although some member states of the consortium which sponsors that university have suffered their own political dramas in the last few years.

In the University of the West Indies, we were surprised to hear, even its accounts are not subject to the same sort of scrutiny that we would expect in most western parliamentary systems. There is no scrutiny, for example, by a parliamentary public accounts committee or even an auditor-general. Nevertheless the institution is subject to the vagaries of government willingness to pour money into a university system. 'We are now in a situation in which we live hand to mouth', said Professor Richards, subject to the arbitrary, spasmodic releases of funds, indeed 20% cuts within one year, and a complete departure from or abandonment of controlled triennial planning. This represents, he argued, a real threat to the university's efficiency, its standing and the quality of its academic activities. Furthermore in the West Indies, as in several other countries, buffer bodies have either been drastically weakened or removed altogether. The foreshadowed loss of a powerful federal buffer body in Australian higher education was compared with that of the West Indies in our discussion.

In discussion, as in the paper itself, it was noted that the situation in the developing world for universities is exacerbated by the fall in market prices for primary commodities, with increasing burdens of debt repayment for governments which fund universities. This leads inevitably to a general degeneration of intellectual and educational activity in these countries. There was in discussion a measure of agreement that one of the prescriptions must be that universities expand the traditional definition of their scholarly role to allow themselves to be seen as development resources for their national and regional communities. Scholarship, instruction and professional service all find, or should find, an equal place, but the reward system must then be revised internally. Again this prescription applies to some extent also to the first-world universities.

Discussion focused on social accountability as much as on financial accountability and the emerging importance of performance indicators was recognised. Problems of universities in federal states were also taken into account and the Australian experience of universities having to serve two masters, one the Commonwealth government as paymaster and the other the state government as the source of constitutional power, was seen to be quite important. Throughout the discussion on every Sub-Topic the importance of buffer bodies was acknowledged by representatives of universities in third-world countries and in the more developed countries. It was also recognised that closer links with industry and commerce must be forged and a better and more serious attempt made to explain the purpose of universities and their distinctive features.

Professor David Murray's paper focused on the importance of postgraduate education and opportunities presented to universities to help mid-career development of public sector employees. Before hearing Professor Murray's paper I was able to summarize some notes which had been sent by Professor Jeremy Davis, who was originally scheduled to speak on the role of universities in either training or educating people for government employment. Both Davis and Professor Murray were in general sympathy with the British (I suppose now Commonwealth-wide) tradition of preferring specialist training for government employees at the postgraduate level except for those undertaking professional tasks within government employment such as engineers and social workers, and there seemed to be a general belief among the audience that we should be looking more carefully at the kinds of postgraduate training, using that word advisedly, which we could provide, retaining the

CHAIRMAN'S REPORT   [Boyce]

best of the liberal tradition in undergraduate education.

Murray argued that if universities expand their master's degree programmes as part of career development they are recovering a more commanding position in the educational system, but such programmes could bring in their train serious threats to university autonomy and academic integrity. Clear and unambiguous answers needed to be given to government, business and the broader community to three fundamental questions. What kind of expertise is needed for teaching government employees in mid-career by university people? What does a master's degree signify? What forms of institutional relationship should link universities with employers?

As to the first question, on the kind of expertise needed, I think most of us agreed that there's too much academicism (a word that Professor Murray used), and we agreed with him that there is a tendency within universities to allow academics simply to indulge themselves in their own research specialisms in the way they handle courses for government servants in mid-career. As to what a master's degree should signify, Murray wondered whether we should be recognising past professional experience or acknowledging merely academic performance—performance within university-sponsored programmes. With regard to the preferred forms of institutional relationship between universities and employers, the speaker argued that there should be no undue reliance on outside expertise or the specification of goals by outside bodies. We generally agreed.

The final discussion focused on several elements in the new tension which we discerned between government and universities throughout the Commonwealth. Governments are seeking to harness universities into more direct and immediate service of what they, governments, perceive as their national interests, and this in a time of drastically reduced or threatened public funding and apparently widespread public disaffection with universities. We agreed that at a time like this 'buffer' bodies were desperately needed and should be retained. We agreed that there needed to be closer links with industry and commerce, and in this context I must say that the senior lay members of university councils who participated in our discussions were very helpful indeed. We agreed that there needed to be changes to the internal structures of universities, their management and their reward systems, and we agreed that there needed to be a redefinition of a university, one which did not disregard the traditional primary purposes and objectives of university education, but one which also recognised that publicly funded universities were servants of the state. On the other hand, the privilege and responsibility of redefining the university should not belong exclusively to government.

Group Discussions

TOPIC 5

UNIVERSITIES AND CULTURE

The Relationship between Universities and Culture, and Problems of Cultural Pluralism

Chairman: Professor L. C. Holborow
Vice-Chancellor of the Victoria University of Wellington

Chief Rapporteur: Professor C. W. Dearden
Chairperson, Department of Classics, Victoria University of Wellington

		Page
Sub-Topic 5(a)	CULTURE IN THE COMMONWEALTH: DEFINITION AND HISTORY	
	Speakers	
	Professor T. H. B. Symons	293
	Professor N. S. Bose	299
	Discussion	301
Sub-Topic 5(b)	THE ROLE OF THE UNIVERSITY IN RELATION TO INDIGENOUS CULTURE	
	Speakers	
	Professor E. Willmot	303
	Professor W. Abimbola (paper read by Professor C. Ikoku)	309
	Discussion	313
Sub-Topic 5(c)	CULTURE WITHIN THE CURRICULUM	
	Speakers	
	Professor Tan Sri Dato' Awang Had Salleh	317
	Professor Margaret M. Manion	322
	Discussion	328

		Page
Sub-Topic 5(d)	THE PROVISION OF CULTURAL FACILITIES AND EXTRA-CURRICULAR ACTIVITIES	
	Speakers	
	Professor K. R. McKinnon	330
	Professor D. Tunley	337
	Discussion	342
Sub-Topic 5(e)	THE PROBLEM OF THE BI- OR MULTI-LINGUAL UNIVERSITY	
	Speakers	
	Dr. J. S. Daniel and Dr. C. H. Bélanger	346
	Professor Bh. Krishnamurti	354
	Discussion	362
CHAIRMAN'S REPORT ON THE GROUP'S DISCUSSIONS		364

For index to names, see p 533

Sub-Topic 5(a)

CULTURE IN THE COMMONWEALTH: DEFINITION AND HISTORY

Monday, 8 February

Professor T. H. B. SYMONS (*Vanier Professor, Trent University*):

SOME QUESTIONS ABOUT THE DEFINITION, VARIETY AND DIVERSITY OF CULTURE, AND THE RELATIONSHIP OF CULTURE TO EDUCATION

In this opening paper I have been asked to discuss culture in the Commonwealth in broad introductory terms. In doing so I thought it might be helpful to consider several definitions of culture, to explore at least something of the variety and diversity of cultures, and then to suggest the need for a renewed and more deliberate attention to culture in the work of the post-secondary institutions of the Commonwealth.

First, may I say a word about the nature of culture itself. There are some difficult problems of definition. What is culture? This question needs to be sorted out before one can discuss, in a useful way, the role of culture and its relationship to education.

There are many definitions of culture, as many as there are people and/or groups of people because culture is a rather personal thing. What it is is what you yourself see or decide. It is in the eye of the beholder. I, for one, am not troubled by this. The great diversity of definitions and descriptions of culture seems natural to me; in fact, desirable. It is an expression of our individual values, an affirmation of our differing heritages and points of view.

Thus, in my country, culture is one thing to a French-speaking Canadian, another to an Albertan of Ukrainian descent, another to a Newfoundland outport fisherman, something else again to a Toronto businessman, and still something else to a Saskatchewan wheat farmer or to an Inuit living at Tuktoyaktuk.

Similarly, in the Commonwealth, culture is one thing to a Londoner, something else to a Highland Scot, something else again to an Indian from the north-east hill states, and still something else to an Australian sheep farmer or a West Indian merchant or a Cape Coast fisherman. All have different perceptions of culture based on their different experiences, heritages and environments—not to mention the diversity of their individual personalities. And all these differing perceptions of culture are valid. All are expressing the personal dimension and the personal definition of culture. Indeed, these differences are not only valid, they are the heart of culture. They are the nature of culture itself.

There are, of course, other more comprehensive and perhaps more pat definitions of culture: as, for example, the totality of language, heritage and belief; or, even, the sum total of how one lives and what one values. Then there is the perhaps more conventional and familiar definition of culture as being the arts and letters of society: its music, dance, theatre, painting, writing, sculpture, handcrafts, and so on—all the fine and performing arts. This is the definition of culture that might be used by national granting councils to support the arts, such as the Canada Council, the Australia Council, and the Arts Council of Great Britain. There are many more ways of defining culture. But whatever way one does—as something highly personal and individual; or, very broadly, as the totality of language, heritage and belief; or, simply, as the arts and letters of a society—it is obviously an immense and fundamental part of our personal life. It is also a pervasive and very sensitive part of our communal lives.

Consequently, public policies and actions that affect culture—in effect, cultural policies—including, in particular, the cultural role of education, need to be very carefully thought through and very carefully applied. Any government, in any country, that gets its cultural policy wrong for any length of time is likely to find itself in serious trouble. This is perhaps even truer within the Commonwealth, given the great variety and diversity of the cultures within its member states, than for most of the rest of the world. Certainly, it is true, for example, of my country, Canada.

Canada is a country of remarkable cultural diversity—more so than most Canadians realize—and it has been so from earliest times. The indigenous peoples, who lived in what is now Canada at the time the first Europeans came, spoke many different languages and had, of course, a great variety of cultures. These languages and cultures were in some cases more distinct from one another than were the different languages and cultures of Europe. Some of the languages spoken by the Indians at the time the

SUB-TOPIC 5(A): CULTURE IN THE COMMONWEALTH [*Symons*]

Europeans first came have unfortunately disappeared. But even today the Indian peoples across Canada speak 10 different languages and 58 dialects. This indigenous cultural pluralism was, in turn, affirmed by the coming of French-speaking and English-speaking settlement, and it was re-confirmed, and greatly broadened, by the waves of immigration that came to Canada from all over Europe in the nineteenth and early twentieth centuries, and from all around the globe in the years since 1945.

The outcome of this process through the centuries has been the creation of a society in Canada that is characterized by a profound cultural pluralism. For example, Ontario's population includes some 90 linguistic and ethnic groups, in addition to people of French and British descent and the native peoples. Nova Scotia, a much smaller and more homogeneous province, has identified 73 national groups in its population. And this pattern exists in virtually every province. The findings of the most recent census, published just a few weeks ago, indicate clearly the broadening pattern of cultural pluralism in Canada. In these census returns nearly 30% of Canadians, about seven million people, report an ethnic background that includes more than one ethnic origin. One-quarter of all Canadians have ethnic origins that do not include any French or British ancestry. Out of a total population of some 25 million people, nearly three-quarters of a million Canadians have some aboriginal ancestry.

In addition to the large French, British and aboriginal populations, the Canadian community includes populations of German and Ukrainian descent that in each case are approaching a million, and a dozen other ethnic groups whose numbers exceed 100,000, including those of Dutch, Scandinavian, Polish, Hungarian, Greek, Italian, Portuguese, South Asian, Chinese, Caribbean and African ancestry. There are also significant and growing elements in the population from Malta and from the Pacific islands, amongst many other places in the Commonwealth.

The effects of this cultural diversity are becoming steadily more evident in the educational system. Today, Manitoba schools are testing in 66 languages. In Ontario 90,000 elementary school students are studying 50 different languages. In Quebec more than 18,000 students are studying 39 languages, as part of that province's ethnic languages programme. This extraordinary diversity caused the late British economist, Barbara Ward, to describe Canada as 'the world's first international nation', and it necessitated the invention of a new word, multiculturalism, a term devised by Canadians to describe their own condition. Although not a particularly felicitous term, it is a useful one.

Like Australia, New Zealand and some other parts of the Commonwealth, Canada is a 'settler society', one in which waves of immigration have come to lands that often already had indigenous populations. It is not surprising that these societies have developed considerable cultural diversity. Indeed, cultural pluralism is their hallmark, though recognition of this fact has been slow in coming.

But it is also true that many—indeed, nearly all—of the Commonwealth countries that were peopled in earlier times have culturally diverse populations, too. Certainly this is the case in India with its rich array of cultures and languages, and so it is to varying degrees in, for example, Sri Lanka, Malaysia, the South Pacific, Papua New Guinea, Nigeria, Zimbabwe and the Commonwealth Caribbean. Multiculturalism is a condition prevalent, to a greater or lesser extent, in almost every country of the Commonwealth—not excluding the United Kingdom. Indeed, perhaps paradoxically, it is one of the common bonds, arising from shared experiences, that unite the Commonwealth.

Multiculturalism can, of course, be a mixed blessing, sometimes giving rise to mistrust, tensions, factionalism, and even physical strife. But these consequences need not ensue. They are nearly always the result of ignorance, intolerance and mutual prejudice—conditions that can be dispelled by knowledge and addressed through the educational system. This may be no easy task, but it is one that must be taken up.

It is an area in which there is much to be gained by co-operation amongst the countries of the Commonwealth, and an area in which we have much to learn from one another. If we can learn, in the laboratory of the Commonwealth, how to handle creatively and well the pressures and dynamics of cultural pluralism, it will be an immense contribution not only to our own well-being but also to humankind in the wider world. Properly handled—with understanding, knowledge, care and respect—cultural pluralism offers tremendous opportunities and advantages. For example, the extensive cultural pluralism that I have described in Canada offers to Canadians, I think, and perhaps similarly in varying degrees to all of us in our respective multicultural countries, the chance to build an unusual nation—a new kind of country—one with links outwards to almost all the cultures of the world, and enriched by a multitude of heritages.

Nearly a century ago the then Prime Minister of Canada, Sir Wilfrid Laurier, caught a glimpse of this potential:

'I have visited in England', he declared, 'one of those models of Gothic architecture which the hand of genius, guided by an unerring faith, has molded into a harmonious whole. This cathedral is made of marble, oak and granite. It is the image of the nation I would like to see Canada become. For here, I want the marble to remain marble; the granite to remain granite; the oak to remain oak; and out of all these elements I would build a nation great among the nations of the world.'

A handsome vision, perhaps. But the political path to achieving it is, as we all know, fantastically twisting and difficult. This path, which is cultural policy, is full of land-mines whether one is dealing with questions of cultural policy on the full scale of multiculturalism or with such policy in the more limited, but still complex, sense of public policy relating to the arts and letters which give form and expression to the cultural nature of a society.

I would, in fact, like to suggest to you that most of the great and fundamental problems in our society often have far more to do with cultural affairs, than with the state of the economy, or the constitution, or the armed forces. Although this is perhaps not immediately obvious, reflection and research will suggest, I think, that economic, social and political problems are deeply rooted in cultural issues and differences. For this reason, as well as because of the intrinsic value and importance of culture, we need, I believe, to devote more time and attention to questions about the nature of culture and cultural policy, and, in particular, to the relationship of culture to education.

I spoke at the outset of this paper of three alternative basic definitions of culture: the highly personal and individual definition; the broad definition, as the totality of language, heritage and belief; and the more familiar definition as the arts and letters of a society. But there is a fourth definition, one that relates culture more closely and directly to education. It is this definition, I confess, which is closest to my heart. It is the definition of culture given by the Oxford dictionary as 'improvement by training' or 'intellectual development', that is the development of the sensibilities, the understanding, the knowledge and the critical faculties that can enable us to live a fuller and richer life. In this meaning of culture, education plays a fundamental and pervasive role. Indeed one may argue that this is the principal responsibility of education and that it has been neglected.

May I suggest just a few examples of the themes and areas, at the juncture of culture and education, that merit more attention. These may, in turn, suggest many others for possible consideration. First of these, I would put the problem of cultural amnesia—the fact that, through lack of knowledge of their own society and its heritage, increasing numbers of people seem not to know who they are. This observation leads then to the Greek dictum about education: that it is important to know ourselves—to know who we are; to know about our society, both historical and contemporary; to know the institutions, customs and culture of our society; and to know, also, the physical environment and terrain that we inhabit and for which we have, therefore, some measure of responsibility.

There should be nothing inward-looking or parochial about this educational goal of knowing oneself. On the contrary, to know oneself one must know others. One must know and understand the cultures of other societies as well as one's own. Moreover, it is often the case that one can make a fuller and more useful contribution to the international pool of knowledge when one is really knowledgeable and well-informed about one's own society.

At the heart of cultural pluralism there will often be linguistic pluralism. There is a clear need for our educational systems to give far more attention to language education and to the complex interrelationships of language and culture. Language needs to be studied as the vehicle and transmitter of culture as well as a means of communication.

Similarly, in a discussion of ethnicity and multiculturalism, reference must be made, in many Commonwealth countries, to the aboriginal peoples. It is surely time for the culture, heritage and rights of these peoples to receive more attention at the post-secondary level. It is a regrettable fact, for example, that in Canada, where three-quarters of a million people have some native ancestry, the first university department of native studies was begun less than 20 years ago. And surely this can be done without an overdose of the *mea culpa* syndrome which makes objective scholarship at least as difficult as did the earlier postures of indifference.

Let us not overlook the need and opportunity for more attention to the fine and performing arts in the curriculum and in research. It is surely time to bring them in from the extra-curricular periphery to the centre of our academic programmes where they belong. Nor should the narrow definitions of culture as something restricted to the humanities and social sciences be allowed to stand. Both the natural and applied sciences are, of course, vital parts of the culture of a society, shaping and contributing to it, and also drawing from it and influenced by it to a greater extent than scientists are wont to recognise.

Then, and no light matter, there is the role played by culture and education in promoting consideration and standards of behaviour. Professor Harry Arthurs of York University did higher education a service by calling, in his remarkable inaugural address, for a rediscovery of the place of civility and amenity in the conduct of university affairs.

Much more could be suggested about the definition, the variety and the diversity of culture, and about its manifold relationships to education. But, in the brief time available, perhaps that is enough. It is, no doubt, the bias of my vocation, but I continue to believe that education has the key role to play in the resolution of issues and in the enhancement of the quality of life. It is in this spirit that I would call for a renewed, and more deliberate, attention to culture in the work of our post-secondary institutions.

Professor N. S. BOSE (*Vice-Chancellor, Visva-Bharati*):

CULTURAL DIMENSIONS OF THE MAKING OF MODERN INDIA: A HISTORICAL PERSPECTIVE AND THEIR WIDER REVELANCE

Long historical traditions, the British Indian administrative system, legal and political institutions and the directional trends of the Indian national movement laid the foundations on which the future independent state of India was to be built up. The series of constitutional reforms spasmodically introduced in the years preceding independence had prepared the way for a parliamentary democracy, an independent judiciary, local self-government and an administration resting heavily on British tradition of legal bureaucratic authority. India, like many other Commonwealth countries, had inherited from the British some of their institutions and certain aspects of political life and belief. No proper understanding of the dilemmas which countries like Canada, Nigeria, India, or for that matter the United Kingdom, face today is possible without some consideration of the 'imperial dimension'.

The British conquest of India was essentially political, not cultural. Yet the challenge of the western Christian culture and civilization led to interaction, assimilation and synthesis which were characteristic features of the Indian renaissance or awakening. The capacity for absorption and accommodation had always been a conspicuous character of Indian life. Thus the western values such as liberty, equality, democracy or human rights found a congenial soil and environment to grow and expand in India, so long as they did not seem to threaten the basic structure of social life. In this respect the history of India in the modern period has been strikingly different from many Afro-Asian countries which joined the Commonwealth. Explanation and the roots of Indian democracy and secularism are to be found, along with other factors, in the nature of the British impact on the sub-continent.

The most important agency of westernization or modernization was English education. It has been acknowledged as the lever which moved the medieval Indian world after centuries of inertia. The introduction and spread of English education, especially since the foundation of the universities in 1857, had far-reaching effects on every sphere of life and thought in India, including the struggle for freedom. Most of the reformers, religious leaders and nationalist leaders were deeply influenced by the new education while drawing sustenance from the rich cultural heritage of the country. At the same time the creation of a small English-educated class, and the continued importance given to the English language on the one hand and the steady overall decline in the teaching of English at school and college levels, have created complex socio-economic problems. It is a major dilemma in modern India.

A comparative study of the situations in India and Africa, or India and third-world countries, underlines the tremendous importance of historical traditions—political, religious, social and cultural. The pattern of developments in India has been very different—not simply because the colonial rule in India was of a different sort but also because her long history, her religion and her heritage had made India a very different land. All great Indian thinkers and leaders of the modern period, from Rammohan Roy to Rabindranath Tagore, Bankimchandra to Vivekananda, Gandhiji to Jawaharlal Nehru and Indira Gandhi, drank deep from the nation's ideological and cultural reservoir. It will be impossible to realize why India chose to be a secular democratic state with an independent judiciary and self-government at the Panchayat level, unless the inner personalities and the mental make-up of such men are taken into consideration.

It is also in the above context that the evolution of education and the formulation of the new education policy in India is to be understood and assessed. Historically, India has the tradition of encouraging a global perspective in education imparted in the educational institutions, especially at the university level. Tagore had once regretted that there were scientists who took pride in their knowledge of 'human facts, without taking the trouble to know the man himself'. Swami Vivekananda's vision of education as an instrument of man-making or Gandhiji's concept of basic

SUB-TOPIC 5(A): CULTURE IN THE COMMONWEALTH

education as a religion of service have hardly materialized in the field of education either in India or abroad. Yet the emphasis on man and the lofty universal aspect of their educational ideas continue to have a strong grip on our minds. The new educational policy also has this as one of its goals. The Commonwealth or the Association of Commonwealth Universities and similar international bodies are also motivated by such ideas. Hence the Indian historical experience is of great relevance to other countries.

The relation between education and culture and the role of the universities in disseminating culture and functioning as custodian of culture pose serious questions. Rabindranath Tagore said: 'Education is diamond, its glow is culture'. Does the education that is being given in the universities conform to this ideal? The Indian universities, in general, have not been able to play their expected role in the field of culture. This is true of most universities in many other countries. A fuller analysis and debate on these issues should be encouraged by the universities.

DISCUSSION

(*Rapporteur*: Mr. F. J. O'NEILL, Registrar, University of Adelaide)

Both papers explored definitions of culture and aspects of multiculturalism, drawing on experiences of Canada in the case of Professor Symons and on experiences of India in the case of Professor Bose. A lively discussion ensued and following are the main points emerging therefrom.

Professor S. K. Verma (Central Institute of English & Foreign Languages) maintained that it was difficult to define culture rigorously. Culture is a multidimensional concept involving societal, national and global perspectives, and man's experiences in the world around him and his religious beliefs and values. He maintained that there was a distinct national Indian culture based on a distinctive pattern or way of life, and that this provided 'the unity in diversity' of the regional Indian cultures. These underlying general properties and notion of human values should be built into the curriculum so that the entire system of education is organized to focus on these values.

Professor H. J. Hanham (Lancaster) drew attention to the universality of English as the communication language for science and to the problems this international language domination posed for the development of a balanced curriculum; pushing literary, philosophical and ethical subjects into a 'ghetto' status since they would continue to be dealt with using regional languages. Professor Bose maintained that individuals are able to recognise elements of a world culture which crosses language barriers because of its excellence while at the same time maintaining an ethnic

TOPIC 5: UNIVERSITIES AND CULTURE

cultural integrity; in addition to science other examples could be cited in the areas of dance, music or art. Professor Symons on the other hand drew attention to the particular difficulties experienced by immigrant ethnic societies, but said that tele-links to their country of origin might alleviate some of their cultural isolation.

Dr. J. Ritchie (Waikato) raised the political dimensions for developing public policy in the area of multiculturalism. Professor Bose drew on the experiences of India and the challenge to national unity posed by allowing small groups to maintain a tribal cultural identity outside the influences of mainstream Indian life. There was no doubt that difficult cultural questions needed to be reconciled with political issues.

Dr. L. Barber (Regina) maintained that, just as the homogenization of culture had depended on world trade routes in the past, multinational corporations through their world-wide activities, especially in such fields as sport groups, rock singers and blue jeans, would have more impact on the development of a world culture than the purveyors of higher intellectual pursuits. Professor S. Agesthialingom (Tamil) responded by pointing out that the universities had played an important role in the development of science and technology on a world-wide basis and that they must now play a vital role in developing a world culture based on common human values. This would leave ethnic cultures intact.

Dr. B. H. Bennett (Western Australia) was interested in the Canadian and Indian experiences since he had recently been involved in developing policy for Australia. The preferred outcome there was one of permeation whereby the curriculum is informed by examples of Australian achievement or experiences. Dr. J. W. Berry (Association of Universities & Colleges of Canada) pointed to the interaction of culture, language and cognition and drew on examples from Africa and India. He emphasized the need for the curriculum to take into account these aspects of culture. Although the discussion ended with some issues unresolved the expectation was expressed that many of the issues raised could be picked up during sessions later in the series.

Sub-Topic 5(b)

THE ROLE OF THE UNIVERSITY IN RELATION TO INDIGENOUS CULTURE

Tuesday, 9 February

Professor E. WILLMOT (*Chief Education Officer, ACT Schools Authority*):

THE HIDDEN CARGO

Twenty-five years ago an old man watched me carefully while I explained the process of schooling and my new conceptions of human learning. He was an Aboriginal man steeped in the intellectual and cultural traditions of Australia's first human society. I was a young newly educated teacher. This old man considered my wisdom carefully and then he said to me: 'Why do you want to spend so much time doing this to these children? Why don't you just give them the thing you have in your head?'

Some five years later in New Guinea another old man and I were encouraging his son to continue his schooling with me. He said: 'This man will give you the power when it is time'. I tried to explain that my kind of education was not some kind of cargo. It was simply a body of knowledge and skills and a process of learning. It was not something that I could bestow.

The twentieth century has seen a rapid decline of remaining first human societies. For some of these societies, such as the Eora and other Aboriginal groups on the south-east coast of Australia, it has meant almost complete extinction of their social orders. Others such as the Inuit of Northern Canada have suffered an enormous social shift fully or partly into second human societies. The problem of change goes beyond cultural assimilation because of the extreme social models of first and second humanity. First human societies were virtually all based on a fairly strict nature model. This means that they enshrined the form (and perfection) of nature in their own societies. This usually demanded using nature's methods to achieve the image. Such societies often had to accept infanticide and, in general, ridding themselves of genetically inferior individuals, for instance. Modern second world societies have tended to move to the other extreme in this area, and often regard the approach to the way we deal with the disabled as a measure of the quality of the society. And rather than make use of a modified nature model we have tended to adopt an anti-nature position.

This anti-nature position has been based on the ability of the new societies to oppose nature. Two problems have emerged from this. First, we have not been able to cope with some of the outcomes such as our present population levels. Secondly, we have not been as capable as we first thought in dealing with nature. We have created new problems in the process such as desertification of large areas of the earth and even damage to our planetary atmosphere.

At one level, the first human societies that have been forced into intimate contact with modern societies face the problems of these second societies without the means or social organization to cope with them. This is particularly true in regard to virulent diseases, diet and other health problems. The processes of cultural and racial mixing associated with modern polygenesis[1] has also been devastating to these societies. But perhaps the most disabling part of the contact has been the cost of acquiring the intellectual devices of the anti-nature societies or the power to influence them, apart from simple physical coercive devices like terrorism.

In almost all cases these first and second societies were set apart by the possession of literacy. The lack of this special tool was also noted as characterizing other powerless groups. It will probably never be possible to say with any certainty why some societies became literate and this is illustrated by conflicting views of modern scholars. Various writers such as Gough[2] took the view that literacy was an enabling device, and I am personally inclined to favour this position, though not necessarily that postulated by Gough. To develop a conceptual base leading to understanding both the reasons for societies to adopt literacy and something of the consequences, we should develop a different view of the place of literacy in human social development.

I think the first and most devastating discovery by first human societies is that technical literacy (decoding language into written symbols) does not create the required change, nor is it sufficient to gain significantly from education. Unless people become 'culturally literate' (have their behaviour significantly changed by becoming literate) access to useful tertiary education is virtually denied.

SUB-TOPIC 5(B): INDIGENOUS CULTURE   [*Willmot*]

I believe that literacy goes over beyond culture into the actual nature of the intellectual and, hence, cognitive base of a society. Both first and second human societies explore reality to limits sometimes beyond the evidence of our senses. But if a society is to hold itself together in any sort of viable intellectual situation, then there are certain pre-set rational domains which must not be exceeded. This is not to say that in some societies people do not exceed these limits, and the pressure to try to do this is probably the basic force that has created the world's religions.

The devices societies like ours use to extend reality vary, but the two principal ones that can be observed in action are language and mathematics. The interesting thing about language is that literacy tends to force it to a situation where it can no longer be used efficiently for this purpose. We see this exhibited among novelists for instance, such as David Ireland.[3] In his novel *Woman of the Future* he passes an edge of reality, and, because of the literate nature of English, reaches a sharp hard limit past which he cannot easily proceed. He solves this by stepping into surrealism. Surrealism of course breaches the rules of sense-wise reality, but it happens to be a socially acceptable literary device and so it is used.

Languages that have not had literacy imposed upon them, however, are much more versatile and allow us to extend minds beyond bounds of our other physical senses. Let me give you an example of this. I will refer to traditional Australian society, to a Nunggabuyu myth which is described by Van der Leeden.[4] This myth relates to two spirit characters, or at least what is commonly called dreamtime characters: the emu and the thundering gecko. The story recounts a legend where these two figures live together, one representing a particular moiety of the society and the other being the opposite. These are described by Van der Leeden as Duha and Yirritja. Traditional Aboriginal society is at once concerned with duality and its rationalization into simple reality and into regions of thought which deny reality. The emu traverses a plain—in the case of the myth, it consists of river flats, physically a planar region—the emu kidnaps a human child. His companion, the gecko, is very concerned about this and decides to arrange the child's escape. In order to make certain that the child is able to escape the gecko must release him from the dimension of surveillance of the emu. To do this he makes a hole and the child escapes through this hole using a rope. It is never clear in the English translation of the myth what the hole means or what it pierces. But the hole must have a fundamental orthogonality in relation to the emu's domain. Now this is, of course, a great problem in

English but no problem in the Nunggabuyu language. This confusion of reality has been a constant problem within the relationship of Aboriginal and non-Aboriginal people in this country. English speakers are likely to interpret the Aboriginal expansion of reality as nonsense, superstition, and all of the things that are cast against Aboriginal understanding of this reality.

This, of course, is not true at the highest levels of European scholarship, and scholars such as Stanner[5] and Hiatt[6] have little difficulty in understanding this principle of expanded reality. Linguists involved with Australian languages do use literacy as a tool in understanding them, but they create an orthography which allows the language to be recorded for their use in a way that detracts as little as possible from the nature of the language. Unfortunately these orthographies are seldom practical, and, if the languages are reduced to some simple device such as the Latin alphabet, then the cost of the cognitive incremental step in the expansion of Aboriginal reality is completely lost; or, worse still, is reinterpreted in a simplistic, nonsensical way.

It should be understood that all human societies have a need of another sort to expand reality beyond the senses, and this need is not simply an intellectual one but something forced upon them by the physical universe. If we rely entirely upon our senses, then the world about us appears to have a finite nature and it seems to exclude infinite things, and yet we have examples where the infinite and the finite become connected within a single continuum. For instance, if I have a ballbearing, and I allow it to fall upon a steel surface, and the characteristics of this fall are such that the object will rebound at each fall half its original fall, then clearly this object travels one unit of displacement in its first fall, one half of that in its second, and a quarter in its third, and an eighth in its next fall, then a sixteenth, a thirty-second, a sixty-fourth and so on. In fact, if I attempt to write down all these fractions, I find that there is an infinite number of them. This seems to mean that the ball will bounce forever. There is no way in the finite universe of our senses that this seems possible. If, on the other hand, we use a very simple mathematical device, arithmetic, and add up these fractions, we shall find that no matter how many of them might be present they will never add up to anything more than two units of displacement. Hence the infinite nature is bounded by a finite end, and contained within the natural world. This is known in mathematics as a convergent sequence.

There is no way that these convergent sequences can be understood in any kind of picture in the mind. It is beyond that kind or that level of perceivable reality. Its reality can nevertheless be

SUB-TOPIC 5(B): INDIGENOUS CULTURE [*Willmot*]

accepted in the terms portrayed by the highly sophisticated language known as mathematics.

Non-literate languages, such as those used by the original Australians, are quite able to comprehend and cope with the expansion of reality which was sought by first human society. The problem with alphabetical literacy is that it is a very blunt instrument, and immediately it is applied to a language the extent of meaning of the language is lost, and any attempt to use simpler literate languages to describe an expanded reality assumes the character of nonsense.

This constricting character of literacy is even more pronounced when the language or the object of alphabetic literacy is a pidgin-like English. The problem of course is immediately overcome for at least the first language English-speaking intellectual elite, because they are offered a package deal which can include the highly refined second language of mathematics. While I believe mathematics is certainly the ultimate extra element of such a package, there are other varieties of the package which include extended literacy in the discourse sense in a language even like English. For members of a non-literate society, however, the total package is never fully realized or, indeed, even offered at any level of awareness.

Gavin Seagram's definitive work with Aranda people in the Northern Territory[7] carried this sort of thinking much further. He was able to demonstrate that Aranda children brought up in a traditional cultural setting did not respond in the expected characteristic ways to the progress of cognitive development postulated by Piaget. In fact, in Piagettian terms, the form and structure of cognitive processes of adult Aranda people are not understandable, and yet clearly these people become intellectually competent human beings. Seagram used a control group as part of his work, and these were Aranda children who had been placed in some kind of an intervention situation, that is, adopted into non-Aboriginal families or placed in institutions of one sort or another. These children showed no significant difference in cognitive development from what one would expect of European children. They were the products of, and embedded in, a culturally literate society, and not only did their behaviour indicate this, but the nature of their intellect also bore witness to this situation. They were not aware of the cost, except perhaps to feel that they were profoundly different from the society from which they had descended. This was the cost of moving from a first to a second human society. These children were the changelings between the two human worlds. They could profit from the same education system that I have. More importantly, I realized that it was not so much what they learned but that there was something quite special about the process. They could inherit the empowerment that I did. If I had the opportunity to teach them I could indeed bestow what I have become on them.

After 25 years I understand what the old men had said to me. I realize that they and those who still live in first human societies understood something about education which took me 25 years to learn. There is a component of education which is indeed bestowed. It is human empowerment; that special capacity to influence others so that they can act autonomously to set goals and achieve them. The real art of the second human world lies hidden in all of our roots in first humanity. The responsibility of universities must be to provide a bridge between the two human worlds. If they fail to do this, then those societies which carry the burden of protecting the genetic material of human culture will become extinct.

Literacy is only the simple understandable mechanism that lies at the base of our kind of humanity. Literacy is the power that lies behind modern cultural institutions. Non-literate societies depend on both oral traditions and community continuity to maintain and develop culture. Impinging literate cultural institutions, particularly religion, will continually undermine them unless we can find another way to empower them. In this day and age that may be possible.

Technical alphabetic literacy is after all only a tool. Cultural literacy is the empowering device. It may be that advancing technology may well provide us with other forms of literacy. These new forms may be even more empowering than the alphabetic form. It is clear now that the combination of visual and audio imagery which is provided by television, and is supported by the major area of technological advance in the information sciences, may well lead to another approach or form of literacy which may allow a second pathway into the literate world for members of non-literate societies. But even this is bound to have some sort of hidden costs. The only solution to this is the development of first human scholarship within modern universities. It is only the people from these societies who can protect themselves from intellectual extinction and preserve for the future the first human wisdom.

REFERENCES

1. Willmot, Eric: *Australia, the Last Experiment*. The Boyer Lectures, ABC, 1986.

2. Willmot, Eric: *The Cultural Literacy*, Aborigines and Schooling, Texts in Humanities, Adelaide College of the Arts and Education, 1981.

SUB-TOPIC 5(B): INDIGENOUS CULTURE [*Abimbola*]

3. Ireland, David: *Woman of the Future*. Penguin, 1980.
4. Van der Leeden, A. C.: *Thundering Gecko and Emu: Mythological Structuring of Nunggabuyu Patrimoieties*. AIAS, Canberra, 1945.
5. Emeritus Professor W. E. A. Stanner (late), Australian National University.
6. Hiatt, L. R., Reader, Sydney University.
7. Seagram, G.: *Furnishing the Mind*. Academic Press, Sydney, 1980.

*Professor W. ABIMBOLA (*Vice-Chancellor, Obafemi Awolowo University*): When a university is located in an area, whether in an urban or a rural setting, it is an opportunity to develop the area. Of the different kinds of development which can occur as a result of siting a university in any place, the most important are physical development of the area, intellectual growth of the community as a result of the presence of many scholars in the locality, and the use of the latter to develop the indigenous culture of the area. This short paper is concerned with the benefits which an indigenous culture can and should derive from the presence in its midst of a community of intellectuals known as the university.

To start with, we should emphasize the fact that there should be a close collaboration between the two communities mentioned above—the host community usually referred to as 'town' and the university community known as 'gown'. No university can survive unless it enjoys the co-operation and understanding of its host community. The best way to foster this close relationship is by encouraging mutual participation in the affairs of the two communities. There is indeed a compelling reason why an academic community must promote such an understanding. As a community of scholars, the teachers, researchers and students in the university must take an interest in research into aspects of the indigenous culture of the area in which their university is located. It is an important function of the university community to make sure that they employ all the intellectual tools at their disposal to study the history, culture and technology of their immediate environment. But they cannot do this successfully unless there exists a close collaboration and mutual understanding between themselves and their host community.

Having secured the interest and understanding of the local community in their activities, the scholars of the academic com-

---

*Professor Abimbola having been at the last moment unable to attend the Congress, his paper was read by Professor C. Ikoku (Vice-Chancellor, University of Nigeria).

munity should move forward to study, promote and disseminate aspects of the indigenous culture of their area of location.

We will now illustrate by concrete examples the kind of academic interest which the university community should take in the indigenous culture of its area of location. Many areas of research readily come to one's mind. For example, studies must be made in the areas of languages, religion, anthropology, sociology, music, fine arts, history and archaeology. But studies should not be limited to the humanistic disciplines alone. Much work can be done in the fields of science and applied science as well. For example, studies should be made of the flora and fauna of the area. Some of these researches need to be carried out as urgently as possible since the development which the university brings into its location usually leads to rapid changes which may adversely affect the vegetation and the animal life of the area. Of interest also are studies in the fields of traditional medicine and pharmacopœia. Other possible fields of study should include applied chemistry, traditional architecture and building styles, as well as methods of agriculture and land tenure peculiar to the area.

While we are busy pursuing researches into various fields of indigenous culture we must not forget the question of promotion of culture. There are some academics who believe that this is an activity which should not interest them. They argue that promotion of culture is, strictly speaking, not an academic endeavour and as such it should be left to the local people and government departments set up for that purpose. But we hold the view that promotion of culture should be an important function of the university, largely because of the benefits which such an enterprise will bring into the university community.

No university should be a cultural desert. A university must reflect the culture to which it belongs while at the same time promoting the cultures of other parts of the world. Those who have lived in large university campuses which are residences of many staff and students know how easily such academic communities can be separated from the larger community to which they belong. Children born and bred in such environments soon become victims of the mass media and cheap popular films which they are exposed to in the cinema theatres and on television screens. Such children soon grow up without sharing the values of any particular culture. The psychological and mental effects of such influences can be damaging both to the individual and the community at large. This is one reason behind our belief that promotion of culture should be a sacred duty of any university. After all, an academic community is a community of human beings, and as such it cannot exist in a cultural vacuum. We do, however, share the view that promotion of culture should not be undertaken at the expense or to the exclusion of the other primary functions of the university, *i.e.* teaching and research.

The university should therefore encourage relevant departments and faculties to organize exhibitions, plays, musical performances, dances and lectures on cultural subjects. A great deal of these activities should be devoted to the promotion of the indigenous culture of the area. But we should not limit ourselves to the local area alone. The indigenous and modern cultures of other areas of the country or other parts of the world should also be exhibited and promoted. That way we can develop a comparative approach which will deeply enrich the university community.

To achieve the objectives mentioned above the university needs to establish very early in its life theatres and exhibition halls where all these activities will be carried out. The university also needs to train people whose duty it would be to carry out this important task of promotion of culture. In other words the university should take up the task of promotion of culture as a serious assignment which will be organized on an orderly basis. As mentioned above, cross-cultural activities should be encouraged, such that the university will become at the same time a centre for the promotion of indigenous culture and a centre where the cultures of other parts of the world are also actively encouraged. The university must live up to its reputation as an international centre while at the same time promoting and participating in local, indigenous culture.

In order to make possible the objectives outlined above the university should create a centre which will co-ordinate its activities of research and promotion of culture. Such a centre, which may be called an institute of cultural studies, should be well equipped for the two important tasks of research and promotion of culture already described. The kind of institute we have in mind should not have more than a handful of professors and research fellows of its own; but it should encourage staff from all departments in the university to come in to make use of its facilities and personnel to pursue well-defined research projects for which the institute can also provide moderate finance.

One reason some academics have frowned at setting up institutes of cultural studies in the university system is the fear that such centres often duplicate research which can be easily carried out in the teaching departments. In my University, for example, the Institute of African Studies founded at the inception of the University in 1962 was dissolved by the vice-chancellor in 1975 on the argument that the whole of the University of Ife* should be an Institute of African Studies. In other words, every department in the University should carry out research and teach courses relevant to Africa. But our experience after about seven years soon convinced us that a university of the size and reputation of our own cannot do without a separate unit devoted to research and promotion of African culture. We therefore decided to set up an Institute of Cultural Studies in 1983. The only academic permanent staff of this Institute is its director. The others are visiting professors and research fellows from within or outside our University, who have come into the Institute to make use of its facilities. Of course there are several cultural and technical officers as well as administrative support staff who assist the researchers to carry out the research work, which they must have defined in detail for the approval of the Institute.

It should be an important objective of the institute of cultural studies to encourage local artists to come in and make use of its facilities for artistic expression and creative work of different dimensions. In this way the institute will become an important link between town and gown. The institute should also arrange for visiting artists, lecturers and researchers from other parts of the world to come in and deliver lectures on their own cultural areas and undertake research of a comparative nature. This will greatly enrich the staff and students of the university. An institute of cultural studies which in a sense is an area studies institute, devoted to the study and promotion of the indigenous culture of its own area or country, then at the same time becomes an international centre. The point is that our interest in the study and promotion of our own culture should lead us to a keen interest in the study and understanding of other cultures of the world.

We mentioned above that the presence of a university community in an area should bring some benefits in terms of development. We must warn that there are possible negative effects as well, especially in an indigenous cultural setting. The study of an indigenous culture may sometimes be harmful to that culture, in that the values which inform such a study may be alien to the indigenous culture, thus leading to judgements and evaluations which are not sympathetic to the cause of the indigenous culture concerned. Perhaps one way of minimizing such harmful consequences is by training members of the indigenous culture to acquire the tools of academic analysis so that they can participate in the study of their own culture. This may help to carry out studies of

---

*Obafemi Awolowo University was, until May 1987, known as the University of Ife.

SUB-TOPIC 5(B): INDIGENOUS CULTURE

the indigenous culture from a more sympathetic view-point. But, as often occurs, the would-be scholar of his own culture, once he has passed through the school system and entered the world of the university system, both of which are alien to his own culture, often becomes alienated from his own culture to such an extent that he unconsciously shares the prejudices imposed on that culture by other scholars coming from the outside.

DISCUSSION

(*Rapporteur:* Mr. S. R. BOSWORTH, Registrar, University of Salford)

The discussion of the issues outlined in the presented papers centred around three main groups of ideas: (i) the problems of 'cultural' transition for individuals and minority groups and the consequences of successful transition; (ii) the special role of designated provision for the support of indigenous culture where that culture is now a minority culture; and (iii) the complex spread of inter-related consequences of policies designed to recognise in everyday situations the equal value of the cultures of minority indigenous groups or peoples.

Exploring the notion of 'empowerment', the discussion focused on the inevitable consequences of the 'cultural' transition which Aboriginal people faced in equipping themselves to function effectively in an alien society (Professor E. Willmot, ACT Schools Authority). Various support methods had been tested for this transition from an indigenous society (a society with only one source of race memories) to a polygeneric society (a society with more than one source of race memories). Many indigenous societies had died out not only because of alien imported diseases, conquest, systematic displacement from their homelands, etc., but also because members of those societies were not able to acquire the means of influencing the more powerful culture through the acquisition of language, modes of thought and action, through a cultural literacy which would have enabled them to exert influence and power not only over their own lives but additionally on behalf of the indigenous peoples of whom they were a part.

One of the most important consequences of this 'cultural' transition is the clear risk of the total destruction of the original culture.

Aboriginals were now aware, even if they had not been before, of the notion of losing something to gain something else—an idea of the cost of wisdom, a concept which applied to other forms of learning (Professor Margaret M. Manion, Melbourne). In seeking an alternative to the present choice between 'empowering' all Aboriginals to function in a non-indigenous society, with the consequent destruction of all Aboriginal culture, or preserving the Aboriginal culture at a high price to some Aboriginals, the possibilities opened up by the concept of the 'native

TOPIC 5: UNIVERSITIES AND CULTURE

scholar' working in a structured environment in a university seemed to be a logical and necessary development.

It was important, however, in the context of any discussion of the role of universities in relation to indigenous culture, to pay attention to the place of any minority group in the nation state and to its ability and power to influence the policies and practices of the dominant polygeneric society (Professor R. Tonkinson, Western Australia); *e.g.* Australian Aboriginals who were not a monolithic society but a society and culture of great variety and geographical spread despite their small numbers (some 300,000 in all Australia) (Sister Deirdre F. Jordan, Flinders). It was clear that in this context (Professor Willmot) a potent source of Aboriginal power and influence would be the 1000 graduates whom the special programmes initiated some years ago would ensure emerged from Australian universities by the end of the century. While these graduates would be a source of the 'native scholars' so vital to the successful preservation of Aboriginal culture, it was already clear that not all would return to their own societies to work in schools. They were attractive employees to the public service, to business, commerce and industry as well as to the universities.

Some Aboriginal societies (Sister Jordan) have sought to accept what was best from western thought and to preserve their own culture and knowledge, and were thus seeking to live in two domains. Such an attempt nevertheless (Professor Willmot) involved losing something from both domains. However the problems of cultural transition, of living in two domains, could be described as a failure of synthesis (Professor Subramani, South Pacific), nor was it obvious that literacy of the kind described by Professor Willmot was as powerful an agent of profound change as had been implied. The present retreat into a fundamentalist, narcissistic mode was a dangerous move and represented a failure of the kind of synthesis which was necessary for the successful development of minority indigenous peoples.

The second theme in the discussion related to the nature of the special provision made for the support of indigenous peoples and their culture. Typical of the efforts made and one which had been outstandingly successful was the Aboriginal Enclave Programme (Professor Willmot), developed in the late 1970s from an attempt to obtain an Aboriginal presence in schools through the use of Aboriginals as aides. With the support of the Australian Education Commission the idea had been further developed and universities and colleges had become involved in the training of the Aborigines who were to perform this role. The essence of the scheme was that a special unit with its own designated facilities and space operated in each department to provide a physical focus where tutors could offer academic and social support and counselling to Aboriginal students. Other modes of support for Aboriginal students and scholars were identified. The provision in a Canadian university of an American-Indian-run unit, well-resourced and able to use those resources with a degree of freedom, and not as strictly subject as others to the full weight of the constraints imposed by the academic rules of the university

SUB-TOPIC 5(B): INDIGENOUS CULTURE

(Dr. L. Barber, Regina), was noted as an example of the kind of provision made where a university was seeking to offer a genuinely bi-cultural education, and to provide special support for students meeting for the first time the concepts of science, mathematics, computer science, etc. The unit also offered a special role to the elders of the North American Indian people for whom the unit was provided.

The role of the Australian National Institute for Aboriginal Studies was noted (Professor T. H. B. Symons, Trent), as were its origins. The Institute had been created to preserve the ideas, culture, etc., of the Australian Aboriginals and to undertake specialized research. It now possessed extensive holdings (in print, on film, in various art forms and artefacts) which formed probably the best collection in the world on a single cultural group. It has funded research by home and overseas scholars, and initiated academic posts in other institutions through start-up grants (Professor Willmot).

The intellectual and artistic renaissance in the South Pacific through the bringing together, under the auspices of the University of the South Pacific, of the best writers and scholars and artists in the Pacific islands was noted. As a result the University was now examining more formally the relationship between oral culture and literacy (Professor Subramani).

University approaches to the provision for Maori peoples in New Zealand were explored. One university provided for the appointment of a Maori counsellor for Maori students, a new dedicated building, an active languages and culture department and teaching and examining in the Maori language (Dr. J. Ritchie, Waikato). In particular there was a Maori studies centre started in the 1970s which had an action-orientated framework for its research. Other provision (Professor L. C. Holborow, Victoria, Wellington) included the creation of dedicated space where indigenous customs and formalities were the dominant ones in the conduct of the business of the users of the space. Additionally, staff had been appointed to develop Maori curriculum material in a number of departments/schools of study outside the department of Maori studies. In this overview of developments in New Zealand, the establishment of Te Whananga O Rankawa on the marae of the Ngati Rankawa people at Otaki is significant for a number of reasons (Professor G. S. Fraser, Massey). First, it is an expression of Maori sovereignty which the university system must relate to in a spirit of mutual respect. Second, it provides an opportunity for members of the Ngati Rankawa to study traditional fields of knowledge including language and philosophy in a manner that is consistent with ancient norms and values. Third, it is able to offer courses incorporating taha Maori in fields as diverse as health care, commerce and community development—areas of service delivery critical to the well-being of Maori people. Finally, Te Whananga O Rankawa has been developed largely out of the resources of the Ngati Rankawa. In this respect it provides a novel illustration of the principles now paramount in university systems in the Commonwealth: self-help, income generation and accountability.

A Maori perspective was introduced (Judge M. J. A. Brown, Auckland) with the entering of a number of caveats about the present enthusiasm for multi-cultural societies. In Maori eyes the prime need was to establish first the bi-cultural society. Indigenous minorities no longer welcomed without reservation research and investigation into their cultures and ways of life. 'Cultural studies' were often seen by the objects of study as superficial. There was resentment at past treatment of indigenous cultures, rituals and beliefs. Universities had an especial obligation to offer something in return. The idea of 'the native scholar' needs careful handling, for it demanded a departure from the colonial mimicry of present approaches. Conventional criteria were not appropriate and new flexible and innovative approaches were needed to provide appropriate definitions of scholarship and criteria for assessment. Devoting favourable levels of support to their provision for indigenous peoples, universities had a place as a sanctuary, a facilitator, a communicator and a promoter of indigenous cultures. Universities and indigenous peoples can work together successfully and excitingly provided they are prepared to answer fully and honestly the question: 'What happens when indigenous peoples are no longer a fashion?'

The third theme was illustrated by a description (Professor Holborow) of the care and sensitivity needed for the successful incorporation into the life of the university of the outward expressions of an indigenous culture; for this required modifications to graduation ceremonies to accommodate the aspirations of Maori students and to avoid separatism and strife, adjustments to admissions procedures and to procedures for selection to academic posts, modifications to criteria for appointment and to the rigid use of objective intellectual standards for appointment. These problems were now being addressed—they had not yet been solved.

In general African experience had been of a different kind (Professor C. Ikoku, U. of Nigeria), for there the indigenous people were in a majority. The African problem was that of sifting, *i.e.* of choosing what was useful and helpful from other cultures and incorporating them into their own.

The complexity and scale of the Indian experience was outlined (Professor Bh. Krishnamurti, Hyderabad), involving as it did some 3%–4% of the total population of India, hundreds of languages and cultures, populations of 100,000 to 1 million (some 35–40 million people in total), and constitutional guarantees about teaching in each minority language up to the end of primary stage in education. In a brief coda to the discussion, interesting parallels were drawn between concepts current in the field of feminist studies and in Aboriginal studies (Dr. Susan Mann-Trofimenkoff, Ottawa).

Sub-Topic 5(c)

CULTURE WITHIN THE CURRICULUM

Tuesday, 9 February

Professor Tan Sri Dato' AWANG HAD SALLEH (*Vice-Chancellor, Northern University of Malaysia*):

1. Introduction

Historically universities started off as institutions of higher learning, with a philosophical stand that their function must be above the preoccupations of practical day-to-day welfare of society. Their aloofness to things of practical importance, however, did not imply that they did not at all engage themselves in the study of culture.

Culture has been variously defined; but it is generally taken to mean a way of life, consisting of values, beliefs, customs, arts, scholarship, institutions and artefacts of a society. Universities, in those days, indulged themselves in the study of philosophy, arts, languages. In other words they only studied higher forms of culture. It therefore remains true that they stood detached from, and uninvolved in, the culture and the affairs of the citizenry.

Contemporary universities, however, have come a long way from that position. From an obsession with philosophy we have now come to accept medicine, engineering, accountancy, and give them a respectable place in our curricula. And, presently, universities have even come to recognise and accept the responsibility of providing studies of indigenous cultures and problems associated with minority cultural groups, leading to the introduction of courses such as the black studies, the culturally deprived, multi-cultural and multi-lingual education, etc. Universities, therefore, have already descended from the ivory tower where they once sat (majestically, if I may add); but the questions before us still remain: (1) have we come down far enough? (2) have we got close enough to come to grips with cultural and social realities? In what follows attempts will be made to clarify these points.

2. *The Current State*

Culture is included in most university curricula for three different objectives. First, culture is taught as an academic discipline for academic interest. It includes subjects such as anthropology, sociology, literature, history of civilization, etc. These subjects may be seen as instances of humanities and social sciences with their respective theoretical frameworks, methodologies and bodies of literature.

Secondly, culture is taught as skills. This is typified by subjects that emphasize mastery of cultural forms, such as creative writing, music, painting, etc. However the training for pure skill-mastery of art forms is usually the function of the academy of arts or conservatoire of music. If taught at universities, usually, skill-training is only part of larger study programmes which may include subjects of higher 'academic content', such as history of art/music, literary history, literary criticism, art and society, etc.

Thirdly, culture is presented as a form of universities' hidden curriculum. This is done by universities through their co-curricular programmes (*e.g.* brass bands, literary clubs, symphony orchestra, indigenous music/art groups, etc.) and through common facilities such as campus museum, art gallery, library's special collections and music-listening room, educational film shows, etc.

Universities deal with culture as an object to know about, and its forms of expression as sets of skills to master. Universities do not participate in the making of a culture—in the aculturation or socialization of their students to their respective societal norms and values. This is quite justifiable, especially in the West where universities exist in a culture that has already gone through a historically long process of evolution. Culture is, of course, dynamic, or else it will remain unchanged and inflexible, resulting in it becoming a mere object of study of the past in human history. Culture in the West, no doubt, still continues to undergo changes, but such changes are incidental rather than planned, and evolutionary rather than revolutionary. Such being the case, universities there do not have to play an active role in moulding a society, and in helping deliberately to enrich its culture. In such a context it makes very little sense for the university directly and deliberately to involve itself in the planning of a national culture and promoting national unity through conscious efforts of inculcating common values and ideals in its students.

3. *New Universities in New Nations*

New nations emerging in the last four decades seem to share some characteristics that have bearings on our present discussion. For fear of over-generalization may I confine this observation to those nations within the Commonwealth. It appears to me that the common features shared by these nations are as follows.

(1) Nationally, there is a pressing need to rebuild the nation by unifying its peoples hitherto divided as a consequence of the colonial policy of divide-and-rule.

(2) There is a felt need to foster a national identity, normally consisting of a national language, a national culture, a national philosophy, a national education policy, a national education system.

(3) There is a crucial need for the modernization of the people so as to make them more responsive to modern technology in national development efforts.

(4) There is a sense of urgency prevailing among these countries. In the first place, these nations feel that they have to work hard in order to redeem the 'lost' time. In the second place, present-day technology has made it possible for them to move at a faster rate giving them a new sense and perception of time.

(5) There is a concern among these nations that modern technological advancement has made the development of their people lopsided: their youths are getting to be more and more materialistic and less and less spiritualistic or religious.

4. *Nation Building*

All these new nations naturally place great importance on nation-building, now that they have achieved independence from their colonial masters. Sadly, though, nation building has come to be associated largely with economic and physical development of a country. A nation, after all, consists of two elements, namely the land and the people. There is no doubt that the land must be appropriately developed so as to make it economically productive to support the populace. But then the people too must be developed lest they become the cause of the downfall of their newly-achieved independence for which they had fought so hard before.

These nations, therefore, have to take the necessary steps to make their people united. National unity and inter-ethnic and inter-regional solidarity are uppermost in their national development agenda. National strife, communal conflict, racial biases and prejudices, ignorance, national and regional disintegration, injustices and negative discriminations, uncaring and disrespectful, moral bankruptcy, are real threats to the wellbeing of a nation. Hence the importance of people-development efforts to these new nations.

5. *The Choice of Approach*

Two alternatives are open to these nations. First, they have to recognise that a culture evolves and that it takes time. The western model of cultural evolution is applicable here. Secondly, they also have to recognise the important role of cultural or societal engineering in nation building. The latter presumes that though a culture evolves it is nevertheless directable and teachable. To adopt the first model would mean to allow a culture to develop in a *laissez-faire* fashion. These nations cannot afford to go slow and wait patiently for their culture to develop naturally in the face of the extreme rapidity with which economic and technological development takes place. To do so would mean to leave things to nature and to hope for the best. To do so would also mean that these nations lack a sense of purpose and political will to change.

It may be argued that it is well and good for these nations to plan the development of their culture; but must universities be involved in it? Is it not true that universities are merely critical and analytical observers but not policy-makers, nor policy implementers? Is it not sufficient to leave the task of aculturating and socializing the young to the elementary and secondary schools?

6. *Culture at University*

Universities in these nations inherit university tradition from the West. All the three modes of inclusion of 'culture' in the university curricula of advanced countries are also found in the university curricula of these new nations. Culture as an academic discipline—which includes anthropology, sociology, linguistics, literature, etc.—is provided for in their curricula. Art, music and literary clubs are established in these universities. Library, museum, auditorium, art gallery, are established on campus. In a sense, then, these new universities do not differ, in respect of culture in their curricula, from universities in the West.

As reviewed earlier in this paper, there seem to be three foci of culture in university curricula. They are: knowledge acquisition (theory or cognitive orientation); skill acquisition (practice or psychomotor orientation); and attitude formation (emotion or affective orientation). Universities in the West evidently provide

SUB-TOPIC 5(c): IN THE CURRICULUM   [Awang Had]

their students with the first two orientations, namely, knowledge and skill. Universities in the new nations, on the other hand, must place equal if not greater emphasis on the third orientation, which is the attitude formation.

Universities of the new nations could achieve the above objective in many ways. I am, of course, least qualified to speak for all these universities. That being my limitation, allow me to use examples that I am more familiar with, namely the experiences of Malaysian universities.

7. *The Case of Malaysia*

The following are some of the characteristic features of our curricula vis-à-vis the 'culture' education.

(1) 'Bahasa Malaysia' (the Malaysian language) and English language are provided for in the curricula. The former is our national language—the language for national unity and solidarity. The latter is the world language—the language for international communication and co-operation. Students are required to master these two languages. The medium of instruction for the non-language subjects is 'Bahasa Malaysia'. English is compulsory, but differs among universities in the method of implementation. Other languages are provided for as options.

(2) 'Kenegaraan Malaysia' (Malaysia—the nation, or Malaysian studies) is also provided for in the curricula. The course content includes a brief history of the nation, the constitution, the unique national population composition and its implications on national policies, nation-building strategies and their rationale. The course title, number of credit hours accorded, compulsory/non-compulsory status, vary among universities.

(3) In Malaysia Islam is the official religion of the federation. Being universalistic in its orientation, the study of Islamic values—as opposed to the study of Islamic theological practices—has applicability to all Malaysians. It is only fair, therefore, that the would-be leaders that universities are now preparing know and appreciate these universal values through the study of Islamic civilization, as opposed to Islamic religion. The implementation of this study varies among universities—from being a compulsory course for all students to being an elective.

(4) In one of our universities, three 'studies' that reflect the three major 'cultures' in Malaysia are available to students wishing either to major or to minor in any one or more of them. These are Malay studies, Chinese studies and Indian studies.

[*Manion*] TOPIC 5: UNIVERSITIES AND CULTURE

(5) Other courses of study in the way of 'culture' education consist of subjects that constitute part of larger social science and humanities disciplines, such as race or ethnic relations in Malaysia, the 'Wayang Kulit' and other traditional art forms in Malaysia, etc.

(6) Outside the formal curricula universities provide co-curricular programmes, some of which may foster a sense of comradeship, provide an experience in inter- and multi-ethnic relationship, sharpen students' sensitivity to rural poverty, increase students' awareness and appreciation of health and nutritional problems prevailing in the low-income sectors of the population.

8. *Other Possibilities*

There are other possibilities, of course, that should be explored. My own personal views are—

(1) Universities should strive to prepare their students to be adequate and effective in the art of human relations, intergroup relations, and inter-cultural relations; and at both levels, intra- and inter-national, in both theory and practice.

(2) Universities must prepare their students to be knowledgeable about and appreciative of problems associated with ethnic and racial prejudices, wars and human sufferings, racism and disregard for human dignity and human rights, poverty in both material and spiritual forms, etc.

I suppose the point I am trying to make is merely that universities must participate actively in striving to lessen and minimize human sufferings and unhappiness, nationally and the world over. To do this universities must make their graduates culturally literate so that they know who they are, in terms of their national and cultural identity, and how to relate to and communicate with other peoples and other cultures, aware and conscious all the time that poverty, social injustice, societal inequity, war and racism know no national boundaries. They are the greatest threats to our human civilization.

Professor MARGARET M. MANION (*Herald Professor of Fine Arts, University of Melbourne*): The relationship between the visionary imagination and learning, between the creative artist and the scholar, critic or researcher, has always involved certain tensions. Let me begin our discussion of this issue by reading a poem of W. B. Yeats, a poem which will be familiar to many of you.

SUB-TOPIC 5(c): IN THE CURRICULUM [Manion]

'*The Scholars*

Bald heads, forgetful of their sins,
Old, learned, respectable bald heads
Edit and annotate the lines
That young men, tossing on their beds
Rhymed out in love's despair
To flatter beauty's ignorant ear.

'All shuffle there; all cough in ink;
All wear the carpet with their shoes;
All think what other people think,
All know the man their neighbour knows
Lord, what would they say
Did their Catullus walk that way?'

The challenge of this poem lies in the question of its final lines: 'Lord, what would the scholars say/Did their Catullus walk that way?' How far removed are they in fact from the poet, or from appreciating his work. Though in some sense their role is taken to task, what alternative is suggested? Certainly Yeats' basic intent is clear—learning and scholarship should never become so turned in on themselves that they obscure the object of their study. But if art, music and literature are to flourish, then the works of earlier generations must be conserved for those who follow, and they must continually be assessed, reflected upon and criticized by fresh comers to the field. To be sure, the store must also be added to, if we are to continue to live rich and fully human lives.

Where does the university fit in all this? It is commonly held that universities should foster, develop and conserve culture within the community as well as advancing knowledge. But how exactly this should be done today is problematic. Is it the university's responsibility to produce the creative artist? I think the answer to that is no—at least, that is not its direct and immediate task. Whose responsibility then is it? The answer is a paradox—everyone's and no-one's. Creativity is not taught. We speak of imaginative and creative gifts, and some human beings are more particularly gifted in this way than others. We cannot say, as with economists, lawyers, doctors, etc., that since we need more artists, the establishment of this or that particular course will produce them. Artists, truly imaginative creative poets, writers, thinkers, painters, etc., will spring up from all sorts of unexpected corners and in all sorts of unpredictable ways. It is not the business of the universities to shape their curricula to this end.

In another sense, we are all responsible for fostering and developing the creative gifts of the artist, which need to be recognised, nurtured, encouraged and responded to. The idea of artistic patronage is valid, over and above any material sense, and it is possible, indeed desirable, for artists to emerge from the university as well as from a host of other places—a point to which we shall return later.

Most of the arts, especially those on which I concentrate in this paper, rely to some extent on the acquisition of a craft or practical expertise. It is not simply the painter's or the writer's creativity which we revere, it is the way in which their fresh imaginative commentary on human experience and on the mysteries of the world in which we live is expressed through certain skills which involve hands, eyes, ears, etc. But the teaching of such practical crafts has not traditionally been the preoccupation of universities. In the past it was more usual, certainly in the British and Australian systems, for this kind of training to be carried out in technical colleges or in specialized academies of music, art, etc.

I shall return at the conclusion of this paper to make some brief comments on the present situation in Australia in regard to this division of labour. I wish now to focus on what might be viewed as the main business of a university with respect to the arts, namely 'critique', the provision of an on-going evaluative and intellectual response to the thrust and penetration of the creative artist—and, I would venture to add, of the specialist researcher.

This task of evaluation or critique is essential for the development of culture. It is, furthermore, central to all the *humanities*—not only to the disciplines of literature, art history and musicology, but also to areas such as history, philosophy and sociology, etc.; and its very practice involves creativity and imagination, since it must be infused with the energetic and zestful pursuit of the spiritual force present within the material forms of our universe.

All works of art require a response from the reader, the viewer or the audience. Otherwise they are quite valueless. This, of course, is what education is all about. All of us require education in both doing and responding. A society in which everyone is specializing in his or her own thing and where there is no capacity to evaluate or appreciate anything beyond one's own expertise is a travesty of human values. In this era which is known for its specialization—and in so many cases this is something of which we can be justly proud—there is a greater need than ever to recognise the importance of education in interpretation and communication, in audience evaluation and response. These elements are critical for the integration of knowledge and the development of culture.

How can the humanities departments and faculties best do this?

SUB-TOPIC 5(c): IN THE CURRICULUM [Manion]

I suggest a few basic principles which you may wish later to debate or discuss. First, it is essential to turn the spotlight on the works of art themselves. The link with creative artists in a literature course should, I believe, be chiefly through reading their works. It is nevertheless of great benefit when there are distinguished poets, novelists and critics, etc., on the staff of literature departments, who can teach not simply their own work but offer valuable insights into others. Poetry readings, dramatic performances, engagement with writers-in-residence, have all proved effective ways of helping to bridge the gap between creative initiative and imaginative response. Creative writers within academic departments also act as role models; but many are rightly wary of teaching too specifically their own craft, for fear of encouraging mindless imitation.

Contrary to those who favour a deconstructionalist approach, I believe that certain kinds of literature and particular works are of heightened artistic value, and warrant being singled out for study. Of course the canon should not remain invariable from age to age, and new cultures and local cultures warrant special attention. This is not to deny, however, the possibility of our recognising and responding to greatness achieved in a particular artistic form in another age or another country.

Bound up with the study of literature and of critical evaluation is the growth and development not simply of the skill of reading but also of the use of language in writing and speaking. This, too, is the business of universities, and is all the more important today as the language develops with a vast array of specialist usages. Thinking, and imagining, are bound up with expression and will affect every branch of learning. In a more specialized sense, harking back to Yeats' *Scholars*, training in publishing and editing skills which are able to meet the increasingly complex demands in this field should also be a concern of university education.

With regard to the visual arts or art history and their place in the university curriculum, it is perhaps more difficult to negotiate a satisfactory blend of the critical and artistic. Art history is a relative newcomer to the academic disciplines. Although at the time of the Renaissance there was laid the basis for a critical philosophy of the visual arts by practising artists and theorists such as Leonardo Battisto Alberti and Georgio Vasari, it was not really until the late nineteenth and early twentieth centuries, largely through the work of German and Austrian scholars, that art history or Kunstgeschichte emerged as a fully-fledged academic discipline, with sound roots in archaeology and museology as well as in connoisseurship and aesthetics. Since then it has seen an extraordinary growth, particularly in European and American universities, and in more specialized but no less impressive ways in the United Kingdom. The first chair in art history in Australia was founded 40 years ago. Most universities in the country now teach the discipline in some form. As with literature, I believe the basic requisite is familiarity with the works of art themselves, and much of the teacher's energies must go to cultivating the act of looking, of seeing what is there, as well as reading what others have recorded, seen or deduced.

There is no gainsaying the power of the object—the importance of originals. Art history departments must work closely with art museums and galleries, and to some degree with artists. Fortunately, in the age in which we live, certain properties of the object can be extended to us through photographs and slides, and this visual material is not a poor second-best. Used judiciously and imaginatively, especially in association with the written or spoken word, it can communicate aspects of the work which are otherwise inaccessible; and it helps us to unite across the ages and the continents in probing and responding to the original creative vision of the artist.

One of the very fruitful ways of studying art today is by exploring the relationship between images and words, between the visual and the literary. This, of course, has always been a valid pursuit; but more than ever it is dangerous to erect too definitive barriers between the arts. Literary works are full of images—associations provoked by words. Paintings, sculpture, architecture, often rely on a literary conceit, a story, a comment, etc., in order to be fully understood. Through my studies in medieval art I have developed a particular interest in the power of the illustrated or illuminated book throughout the centuries, and so I find it particularly interesting to see the preoccupation with the power of the word and the visual symbol returning in modern approaches to art and literature. Moreover, books are central to the study of both art and literature at the university. This is not something for which we must apologize—rather it is our glory. We must never forget the place of the library in a university education.

How much should students and teachers of art history be actively involved in drawing, painting, sculpting, etc., themselves? Essentially, I do not believe that this is required for university education, although I hasten to add that it is highly desirable for all students and staff to be confident of a basic ability to draw and to handle paint, to understand what it is to mix colours, create particular tonal values, etc. Ideally this should be learnt at school. Workshops and studios where such knowledge can be acquired and built on, and familiarity gained with other processes such as those of print-making, photography or film-making, not necessarily for credit, are also highly desirable. But I have rather strong reservations about the practicality of trying to train artists and arts graduates or art historians simultaneously. The concentration and application of skills required are too demanding for both to be encompassed satisfactorily within the programme.

One further comment may be pertinent to the curriculum of art history. The visual arts today have been hailed as an attractive teaching tool for a variety of purposes—for history, sociology, the study of patronage and social theory, etc. All this is fine, but it is the responsibility of the art historian to see that works of art are experienced, enjoyed and reflected on directly, with specific reference to the individuality of the artist's contribution and to his or her *comment* on the human condition.

Music is in one sense the art with the strongest academic ties; through theory it is linked with the ancient study of mathematics and philosophy; yet the necessary emphasis on performance makes it difficult to achieve a balance within the university curriculum. The objectives of particular courses need to be clearly stated and courses designed accordingly—for performers and composers, for musicologists, or as part of a general and liberal education.

Finally, relatively recent areas of the arts such as film and photography require the building of new bridges between the training in techniques and basic critique.

In conclusion I return to a point made earlier in this paper. Here in Australia we are seeing dramatic changes in the organization of the tertiary educational systems, but the current definitions and distinctions of 'research' and 'teaching', of relevance and irrelevance, as a rationale for this re-ordering are inadequate. Universities may and do teach a variety of skills. There have long been faculties of medicine and law and, more recently, of science, agriculture, commerce, etc., and we are not unfamiliar with universities of technology. I am also aware that some universities have fully-fledged art, music or drama schools; there is no reason why they should not be extended and why some of the activities currently grouped in technical colleges should not be incorporated in universities, *provided* that they are able to perform their basic and essential task of intellectual evaluation and reflection, and that this task in some way permeates every part of the university's activity. This is what the oft-stated goal of the pursuit of learning and the preservation of knowledge is all about. The integration of knowledge—what in an earlier period was understood by the term research and scholarship, and which was envisaged as taking place in a community in which all were looked on as both teachers and students—a society of scholars—is still the essential goal of a university. Basic to this is a vigorous and lively relationship between the disciplines of the humanities and the creative arts.

DISCUSSION

(*Rapporteur:* Mr. J. B. POTTER, Registrar, University of Melbourne)

For convenience, the discussion is recorded here as two distinct themes. The first relates to that of Professor Awang Had's paper.

A. Professor S. K. Verma (Central Institute of English & Foreign Languages) noted that the objectives of courses in culture, the amount of the teaching that should be provided, and the scope of such courses and who should determine the value system used, had not been discussed by the papers presented. Should only local cultures be considered or national and international cultures also? Professor R. Tonkinson (Western Australia) contrasted the approach taken in the paper with that in other areas where students are asked to challenge society's values and to assess critically the changes which should be made. It was also suggested that institutions should be instruments of change where the needs of society have changed.

Professor E. Willmot (Schools Authority, Australian Capital Territory) noted the danger inherent in a culture being imposed on a people—who is to decide what it is to be?—while Professor K. Koso-Thomas (Sierra Leone) raised the issue of teaching those aspects of the culture which were more difficult to define but important to professionals trained to work in the real world. In reply Professor Awang Had stressed that the culture being taught was a national culture based on Islamic values, agreed to by the major ethnic groups and intended to create integration and stability within the nation; that the cultures of groups and individuals were not being destroyed; that once stability and integration had been achieved the process of change through critical review of the culture could commence; and that while he had concentrated on tangible aspects of culture, such as language, in his paper other aspects were included in teaching students in professional areas. He noted that language as a window on the culture was, in any case, very important.

The question of separating the teaching of Islamic values from teaching the faith itself was raised by Professor B. R. Morris (St. David's University College, Lampeter) but, apart from noting the intention to teach values only, remained unresolved.

B. Discussion of Professor Manion's paper centred largely on what the role of a university should be relative to the teaching of skills, the release of creativity and the use of the creative arts in teaching to enhance other subject areas, such as science and economics, by providing a cultural setting.

SUB-TOPIC 5(c): IN THE CURRICULUM

Professor T. H. B. Symons (Trent) noted that while there appear to be sufficient facilities to support the arts emphasis on the liberation of creativity was now needed. Since creativity was more caught than taught, how did a university get the right people onto its staff when conventional criteria were not perhaps appropriate? Professor Manion agreed that fostering creativity was important, and a proper part of the arts curriculum was the development of attitudes supporting creativity. Teaching methodologies sometimes militate against such development. It is also necessary to have some skills to be able to innovate. However the other skills necessary for a university teacher, such as communication and scholarship, must be looked for as well as creativity and skill in the particular art area.

Professor L. C. Holborow (Victoria, Wellington) extended this discussion to music, noting that to play a piano required not just technical skills but interpretive skills also, and the latter are important where a university is involved. Professor E. Willmot (Schools Authority, Australian Capital Territory) raised the problem of the separation between skills and appreciation more generally in the context of secondary education, noting particularly the temptation to use pop art to gain the attention of children, their ready acceptance of skills, and the conflict which often occurs when appreciation of art and technology may be in conflict. In this context it was noted that it is a demanding exercise to reflect on art; that the basic intention, even at tertiary level, is to enrich lives rather than to train for employment; and that skills learned earlier often provide the means of later development of appreciation. Nonetheless it is possible to use art in other areas of study at school to provide some appreciation activity, but this requires teachers who have a respect for art irrespective of their own discipline. To produce such teachers is a duty of universities. That teaching in the arts requires time for reflection, compared with the apparent pressure approach taken in other areas, was acknowledged as a major problem in providing the arts training identified as essential.

Sub-Topic 5(d)

THE PROVISION OF CULTURAL FACILITIES AND EXTRA-CURRICULAR ACTIVITIES

Thursday, 11 February

Professor K. R. McKinnon (*Vice-Chancellor, University of Wollongong*): There are probably nearly as many models of what a university should be as there are vice-chancellors. I do not see any end to the healthy debate about the degree to which theoretical and practical studies should be combined, nor the on-going debate about the role of the university in national development, particularly economic development. The same is true of the role of universities in cultural activities. The requirements will differ, of course. Universities in those countries in which there is rich diversity of cultural institutions will be under much less pressure than in countries where universities have to take on an important role as conservators of old traditions and facilitators of modern forms of expression. I argue that cultural activities are among the key priorities of all universities, for valid educational reasons, and that as a consequence appropriate facilities ought to be provided. At the same time I argue for assessments of need and effectiveness to be just as rigorous as for other aspects of university activities.

The Narrow View

Many universities interpret their task in narrow terms, confining their effort to the formal teaching and the research carried on within the institution. Especially in countries with many cultures, these universities may disavow any role in culturally shaping students and pretend that it is possible to be culturally neutral. Worse, they may even believe that there is a 'university culture', which, despite differences in institutional practices and requirements, is everywhere very beneficial in its effects and of unchanging value. That being so, they do not need to examine consciously the impact of university facilities and organization on student 'formation', on their cultural values and attitudes.

In the press of other priorities it is easy for vice-chancellors to be only partially conscious of the cultural dimension of university life: it is easy to put off tough-minded examination of this dimension and its needs when other needs seem obviously to be of the highest priority. It is easy to trivialize the question into one of the priority to be accorded to theatres, museums and extra-curricular activities and to go on to classify these as optional extras, rather than, as I argue, to assert the centrality of cultural values in education, with the provision of the required facilities a consequential matter.

Changing Perspectives

It is only in the late twentieth century that any university would even conceive of its role as being culturally neutral and not directly related to national values and aspirations. In the nineteenth century universities and colleges as a matter of course sought to inculcate accepted values and codes of behaviour. In the late twentieth century many universities have collectively abdicated this field, narrowing their objectives to the teaching of content and the skills of scholarship and research, often at the expense of clear values.

As a consequence of the lower priority given to the cultural formation of students, modern universities often put provision of those facilities and services that relate to cultural activities low down on the priority list. Some of the doubts and reluctance stem from reliance on public funding sources. Treasury officials involved in the allocation of funds for universities may raise so many questions about cultural facilities, inferring improper expense, as to make administrators wary of taking too strong a line. But whenever universities fail to examine explicitly and to provide for the cultural needs of young people in universities, blind to the negative impact of the absence of appropriate opportunities, there almost certainly will be unintended consequences.

Special Needs in Developing Countries

In developing countries intellectual colonialism has often persisted well beyond the time of liberation, with detriment to indigenous culture. For example, only certain fields of study, primarily those that have a long ancestry in the western intellectual tradition, may be regarded as respectable. The study of that country's own cultural traditions, institutions and practices may not be regarded as meriting the creation of a department and the establishment of a chair. In the absence of a literature and of persons who have studied that literature in a disciplined way in other universities, it is often assumed that there would be no one capable of being appointed to such a chair. A wise, learned, but non-university-credentialled citizen would not be regarded as having sufficient standing, certainly not the same standing as professors appointed to more traditional disciplines.

National cultural traditions and practices in forming the pattern of organization and functioning of the whole university equally have been casualties of this type of intellectual colonialism. A good example is Australia, where, 200 years after its colonization, the Australian government is only now promoting with vigour, over significant academic opposition and scepticism, the concept of Australian studies and values as desirably permeating the whole of the curriculum; imported organizational practices have persisted in Australian universities.

The University of Papua New Guinea was the direct stimulus, upon its founding in 1966, for the first books written by Papua New Guineans and for the first plays which reinterpreted ancient cultural traditions in fresh ways. These developments illuminated the dilemmas of modern life in that country. The University was the essential element in stimulating efforts to record rich cultural traditions and have these available for later generations. The University was an indispensable agent both for conserving the old and for providing a means of expressing Papua New Guinean values in a changing society. Without the presence of these cultural concerns in the educational offerings of the University, the cultural roots would have been lacking. The mapping of new onto old, of bringing order out of otherwise insuperable complexity, already a major problem in a country changing rapidly, would have been an impossible problem.

Cultural teaching and the provision of cultural facilities in a university cannot be optional extras. Pluralism, including concern for minority values, complicates decisions about what and how to foster cultural programmes. It is not true, however, that the inescapable consequence of the complexity of modern nation-states is a necessary neutrality, an absence of common values and cultural interests among university-educated persons. Rather the reverse: pluralism and modernism both demand cultural evolution, cultural development, the blending of old, diverse values with new values and modes of expression. Nowhere is this more important than among those with a university education. The need is particularly acute in developing countries, where the paucity of other possibilities for relevant cultural experience makes provision of such programmes and facilities indispensable.

Regional and Urban Needs

In any country there will be a difference between what is necessary for universities in urban areas and for those in regional or rural areas. Large, urban, commuter universities have problems of coherence as institutions, as well as those of achieving cultural coherence. They mostly are situated in the midst of a plethora of other cultural opportunities, whereas regional universities much more often must necessarily take a lead or provide the community focus for such activities. Moreover, because academics can organize their own time and are in any case often active in cultural matters and prominent in the locality, they are in a good position to take on regional leadership roles. Regional universities are often the only bodies able to provide that indispensable logistical back-up and support for cultural ventures which will bring dreams to reality. A regional university situated in the midst of a minority language and culture, for example, may be the only possible source of activity devoted to preservation and development of that culture. If the local university is unwilling to take on the role of conserver and developer no one else has the resources.

Public and Private Universities

The difficulties of making adequate cultural provisions in public universities are obvious. University grant bodies customarily link grants to the precise number of students to be enrolled, and to the required laboratories and other teaching facilities. They are not usually easily persuaded of the need for cultural facilities.

Private universities have an easier task. Because they have fees income and benefactors they are able to allocate funds as they choose. The best private universities constitute models, demonstrating not only that cultural facilities have a general educational effect but also that such facilities may provide student experience which could lead directly into employment. At Harvard, for example, experience in working on the *Harvard Crimson* is recognised as providing first-class training for journalism.

Priorities

Given the low resource situation of publicly funded universities, particularly those in countries that are not rich, how are the decisions to be made about the range of cultural facilities and activities to be supported? I can only give a personal response, which has as its base the broad educational perspective that nearly all universities of the Commonwealth tradition over-emphasize critical skills at the expense of creative skills. They do not attend enough to the fostering of creativity in art, literature, drama and music within the university. Why is a good short story or a new play less acceptable as an assignment than a critical essay? If the educational focus of many courses was to be balanced more towards the development of creativity and cultural skills, and if there were facilities within the university which allowed the production and/or performance of creative works, in exactly the same way as scientists can rely on the presence of experimental laboratories to test the correctness of their theories, the educational programme would be more balanced.

The critical tradition is an overly narrow interpretation of the role of universities. The discipline and skills involved in creating new works and in interpreting those works, live or through electronic media, call for high levels of knowledge, intellect and practical skills, including adequate historical knowledge. The results are educationally important, immeasurably valuable for the individual and beneficial for the nation.

Given such an educational perspective, expenditure of resources for television studios, the purchase of fine musical instruments, the accumulation of an art collection, and the setting up of art studios, becomes a priority or priorities equal in rank with the provision of science laboratories. Similarly, provision of the attendant technical staff necessary to support the infrastructure within which cultural activity can take place, while giving the arts a cost structure similar to that of science-based education, is essential.

In short, as far as provisions for students are concerned, there is every reason to provide a wide range of cultural facilities and to use them to facilitate creative expression. Just as one would hope that in the training of scientists students would go beyond their required hours in the laboratory, so one would expect that culturally inclined students would spend a great deal of their free time in writing books, plays and poetry, or painting and sculpture, or composing music, or planning theatrical productions, and readying these, where appropriate, for publication, showing or performance.

Universities as Providers for the Community

Turning to their broader public role in relation to the wider community in which they are situated, most of the older-established

SUB-TOPIC 5(D): EXTRA-CURRICULAR ACTIVITIES [*McKinnon*]

universities have long been active in cultural activities for the general public. Many of the great museum collections, in both the natural and physical sciences, began in universities and were supported as part of the teaching resources of the university. A high proportion continue that way, whereas others have been passed over to public authorities because of the expense of their upkeep. The trend toward handing such facilities over to public authorities for cost reasons is inexorable. Universities which have accepted bequests for major theatre complexes (*e.g.* the Seymour Centre at Sydney University) frequently find that the upkeep is a continuing drain on the university's general resources. Where a community radio station or television station is sponsored by a university, without revenue generated by advertisements, the cost implications for the university will be high enough (especially for television) and obvious enough to generate heavy criticism of the balance of spending priorities within the university.

The opportunity cost, on account of the lost academic effort of those who have put their energies into such activities, must be weighed against the value of the same effort applied to the basic teaching programme. Even if the university can assess accurately the community benefits of the public cultural activities role, the relative importance of that role compared with the enrolment of more students or the provision of more research facilities will be hotly debated.

Of course in developed countries there are many publishers of books and newspapers and multiple radio and television outlets for those academics who are able to provide notes on the news, interpret cultural events, or write or perform creative material for drama and entertainment programmes. The vice-chancellor does not have to feel a heavy responsibility for public cultural activity, or even have to choose between impossibly difficult spending priorities. There may be pressures to curb the off-campus cultural activities of particular individuals, in the interests of those individuals undertaking a fairer share of the total teaching load, or because senior academics with a narrow view of the role of universities frown on such activities, but by and large the pressures are manageable.

Thus in most metropolitan universities it is not necessary to strive to provide public cultural facilities. It remains essential to provide reasonable facilities for students, but these can be built or acquired over time rather than in a rush at great expense. The main objective will be to meet the cultural objectives of the undergraduate educational programme. A more expansive role should be undertaken only if sufficient resources are available.

I would have a more positive view of university sponsorship of television and even radio facilities if that university had a responsibility in the distance education area. The infrastructure needed for distance education courses is of course equally useful for cultural communication; the two roles undertaken together might result in very cost-effective cultural facilities.

The convergence of communication technology also means that enriched teaching presentations could be made on a common basis across universities, electronically, and that there could be student/staff interaction and distance sharing of resources among institutions. The East-West Centre in Hawaii has done a little of this. Any university equipped to use communication technology to the full will have a potentially strong role in dissemination of cultural events at a marginal, or at least manageable, cost.

The Regional Problem

Given the regional role outlined earlier, should regional universities also limit their public cultural activities? Frequently they are expected to take a prominent role. They may even be the only potential point of stimulus for sophisticated cultural activities. They may have to take on the role of facilitator or animateur, with different responsibilities at different times, depending on the stage of cultural evolution of the region. In my university a subsidy was given for the establishment of a regional professional theatre company for some years, even though the university has had an increasingly stringent general policy of 'user pays'. We try not to let such a policy prevent start-up initiatives. We have been able to decrease the subsidy progressively, as the company has become better established, and as some of the support role has been taken over by the community and by government bodies; but university staff provided the main initial impetus and the continuing drive to keep the company alive. A fine professional repertory theatre company, which takes its responsibility to the region and to Australian drama seriously, would not have been able to start, let alone survive, without the help of the university.

Equally the university has seen it as appropriate to assist a community group to establish an FM community radio station, within the proviso that over a period of time the university commitment can be scaled down.

SUB-TOPIC 5(D): EXTRA-CURRICULAR ACTIVITIES [*Tunley*]

Professor D. TUNLEY (*Head, Department of Music, University of Western Australia*):

THE UNIVERSITY AS PATRON OF THE ARTS

My talk is concerned essentially with the idea of university as patron of the arts rather than a consideration of the arts as academic pursuits. Nevertheless, I should state my own view at the outset: that the arts flourish most vigorously in universities which do have a commitment to their academic and professional study, even though there are excellent examples in Australia where, for instance, art collections have been built up without the support of a department of fine arts, and where performance societies have flourished before the creation of a faculty or department of music. The success of such ventures has, indeed, often encouraged the establishment of music and the fine arts as academic disciplines within those universities.

Fortunately, the days seem to have gone when music and the fine arts were looked upon with an academic frown in Australia, and I suspect that it is more a matter of financial and practical considerations rather than philosophical doubts which has discouraged the establishment of such courses in those universities which lack them at present. All Australian universities do have a commitment to the arts in some way or another. Naturally the level of support varies greatly. As I see it, to qualify for the accolade 'patron of the arts' an institution must be prepared to put some of its own funds towards them, and not merely act as a clearing house for bequests and gifts. In the latter case the real patron of the arts is the donor. Thus, this paper will emphasize those artistic developments which universities have initiated and funded either by themselves or (more usually) with the help of outside funds.

The collecting of works of art, including their commissioning, has been undertaken by the older Australian universities from the time they were established in the late nineteenth century. What emerges from the information I have been sent is the distinct impression that the more recently established universities and those in the smaller capital cities and elsewhere appear to have taken a leading role in their community in the commissioning and purchase of works of art by local and leading artists. Thus Monash University's art collection which began in 1961 has over the years developed into a significant public collection of mainly contemporary painting and sculpture. The collection at Western Australia's

Curtin University (until recently the Western Australian Institute of Technology) was the first public collection in this state to support local emerging artists as a matter of policy, covering all media including limited edition prints, ceramics, jewellery, textiles and industrial design.

The University of Adelaide works of art fund is created entirely by voluntary donations from members of the staff of the University, and has been especially active in commissioning works from young local artists. A similar situation is found at the University of New South Wales where works of art are purchased by a university art committee and the Monomeeth Association through their own funds and through donations. Some universities provide funds for acquisitions from their recurrent grant; some from an annual senate grant. At least one (Deakin) purchases works of art from a small fixed percentage of the cost of all new buildings. In a paper as short as this it would be impossible to list the works of art acquired through university patronage. Put together they would make a magnificent touring collection. Perhaps this could be a tercentenary project!

Only seven universities appear to have art galleries in which to house part of their collections. Most universities rely on various spaces available for display and for exhibitions. While this may have the advantage of often spreading the collections widely over the campus for the enjoyment of many people, nevertheless the security and welfare of the most prized works offered by a temperature-controlled gallery obviously weigh strongly in the latter's favour.

Several Australian universities have developed, or are currently considering developing, centres or institutes for the arts, as at the University of Tasmania. In its multiple-facility complex are included: four lecture theatres, separated by soundproof partitions which can be removed to produce one large auditorium seating 800, and suitable for concerts and chamber music; the John Elliott Classics Museum, a university-owned collection of antiquities said to be the most comprehensive in Australia after the Nicholson Museum in the University of Sydney; a studio theatre and a fine arts gallery. This university arts centre has been developed in a number of stages through university capital programmes, public appeals and donations. It is administered directly by the University and the staff are on the normal university payroll.

A community-based centre for the arts is to be found at Deakin University in the Queensland Film and Drama Centre based on the campus. It was established in 1977 and its aims are far broader than the name of the centre would suggest. They include the following: to promote, foster and practise the production and appreciation of film, drama, the visual and plastic arts and related activities; to provide the opportunity for adults, young people and children to participate in the practice and presentation of the respective arts and to provide community access to the arts. Over more than half the costs of the centre are borne by the University. Deakin University is currently considering the establishment of an institute for the arts.

Undoubtedly the most frequently encountered arts facility on campus is the university theatre, very often run by the students' union or guild. Although not always specifically designed for theatrical performance, theatres of some kind or another are found at all Australian universities. I don't think it would be parochial of me to point to the University of Western Australia as possessing the most outstanding array of theatre venues on any Australian campus: the Octagon, with its thrust-stage designed by Sir Tyrone Guthrie; the New Fortune, based upon a design of Elizabethan days; the Dolphin, an experimental theatre, funded by the student guild; and the two open-air theatres, the Sunken Gardens and the Somerville Auditorium. The latter, although now primarily used for the film festival, was for many years the venue for opera and ballet. As at most other universities, profits from renting the theatres go towards their administration, and at the University of Western Australia they also go to the performing arts committee which re-cycles this money in the form of grants and subsidies to university performance groups. It goes without saying that the existence of so many fine venues contributes to the success of the annual festival of Perth which is under the aegis of the University. The University of Western Australia's expenditure on the festival of Perth alone warrants the accolade of 'university patron of the arts'.

During the last decade a feature of many Australian university campuses has been the presence of artists-in-residence, be they musicians, visual artists or writers. As far as music is concerned, it was at the University of Western Australia where the artist-in-residence scheme was first established on a regular, on-going basis. In 1974 the department of music invited the Alberni String Quartet from Britain and the celebrated violinist Alfredo Campoli, to join its staff, each for a term. Since that time there has been an unbroken succession of distinguished musicians from abroad and from Australia, funded partly by the University, partly by bequests, as well as, until recently, by the music board of the Australia Council. It was in fact the Australia Council which helped spread the concept of artist-in-residence throughout the country. The

Australia Council, the federal government's statutory authority for the arts, was established in 1973 and its various boards, such as the music board, visual arts board and literature board, have helped tertiary institutions as well as community groups to enjoy the stimulus of having recognised exponents of their particular art form placed in residence, sometimes to teach, sometimes to give themselves over entirely to the practice of their art. It would be difficult to overestimate the influence such schemes have had on Australian universities and elsewhere during the past decade. One can only regret that the recent reorganization of the Australia Council appears to have downgraded those programmes of assistance which made the schemes so successful. Thus the future is not as bright as the immediate past, but I note from my survey that there are a few universities which have on-going schemes which are already funded primarily from university sources, such as at New South Wales, New England, Tasmania, La Trobe, Macquarie, Adelaide and Western Australia.

Undoubtedly one of the most impressive artist-in-residence schemes is at the University of New South Wales which has been the patron of the Australia Ensemble for over a decade. Professional chamber music ensembles have been established at a few universities in the past: the University of New England Ensemble, the Mayne Trio at Queensland and the Cristofori Trio at Western Australia, for example. What distinguishes the Australia Ensemble from the others is that the six members have no teaching commitments at the University, for the department of music there does not offer performance in its degree. The musicians are appointed primarily to rehearse and to perform. That the Australia Ensemble has become the country's leading chamber music group with an ever-growing international reputation must be a source of much pride to the University of New South Wales, which has made the existence and the success of this group possible by providing the musicians with a regular income, and its own concert manager, and of course a fine place for its rehearsals and concerts. The accolade 'patron of the arts' is richly-deserved by the University of New South Wales on that score alone. In addition the same institution is the primary supporter of the University of New South Wales Opera which, established in 1966, specializes in the production of new Australian or less well-known seventeenth- and eighteenth-century works.

With the increasing frequency of musical events on campus, such as regular lunch-time concerts and those given by musicians-in-residence and visiting musicians and so forth, it is not surprising that their organization goes beyond what could be attempted by the academic staff of a department of music. A number of universities, aware that such events provide some of the best links with the community, have funded the appointment of either full-time or part-time 'activities officers' or 'concert organizers', as at Queensland, Griffith, Adelaide, La Trobe and the University of Western Australia. Similarly the existence of art collections and valuable holdings in the many departmental and university museums has necessitated the appointment to university staff of specialist curators too numerous to mention in a paper as brief as this.

Stripped then of those things which might otherwise confuse the issue we see that Australian universities are, on the whole, modest patrons of the arts, some taking the role more seriously than others, particularly those universities which believe they have a role in the community that goes beyond traditional academic responsibilities. It is my belief that university patronage of the arts can forge some of the strongest links with the community, and in this day and age (perhaps as never before) the university needs the community as much as the community needs the university. The performing, visual and plastic arts can fill a vital role in the life of the modern university.

This was certainly recognised when the University of Adelaide established its University Foundation in 1980 to support, promote and enrich the general intellectual and cultural life of the University and thereby the excellence of its graduates. The range of activities which the Foundation supports includes writers, artists, producers and musicians-in-residence; lectures by outstanding public figures and leading scholars within and beyond Australia; facilities for university activities to have a significant impact on the community, as in theatre, musical performance and radio; activities encouraging community links with ethnic communities in an increasingly multicultural Australian society. Funding for the Foundation comes from the University's recurrent grant, membership donations, the alumni association and from donations over and above the member donations.

In these days of reduced funding it would be naive to imagine that universities will be able to increase their patronage of the arts from recurrent grants. It is more likely that extra-mural cultural activities and art acquisitions will have to depend increasingly upon arts patrons out there in the community to even keep pace with what has happened in the past. But if the experience of the department of music at this University is anything to go by, then it would seem that the more the community is involved with arts activities at the university the greater is the chance that private

TOPIC 5: UNIVERSITIES AND CULTURE

individuals will donate generously to these very activities. In a word, a benign circle! Obviously the more this benign circle can include co-operation and collaboration with other institutions and business firms the more powerful is its impetus.

It was suggested by the organizers of this conference that this session could involve an element of performance. I welcome this because it provides an opportunity to demonstrate the points that I have just made. We are going to see three short extracts from a videotape produced by the media services of this University of an important French opera produced in the Octagon Theatre in September 1986 and released internationally last year to mark the tercentenary of the composer's death. Jean-Baptiste Lully was born in 1632 and died in 1687. He was court-composer to Louis XIV and his music is the very embodiment of the French classical style. He created French opera (called *tragédie-lyrique*) and his *Armide*, which was performed in the second last year of his life, is generally regarded as his greatest work in this genre. Because the department of music at the University of Western Australia is, through its research, closely identified with French baroque music, it was only natural that we should wish to be associated with the Lully tercentenary year, not only with publications but also with performances. The making of the video (which, incidentally, is the only one ever made of a full-length production of a Lully opera) has helped turn a local celebration into one with a potential international audience and a degree of permanency.

I strongly believe that this is the kind of activity that a university should be involved in. The preservation and interpretation of the great achievements of the past being part of the cultural responsibility of universities, it is left to them to bring to life those masterpieces which the commercial companies would not risk presenting.

DISCUSSION

(*Rapporteur:* Mr. K. L. JENNINGS, Registrar and Deputy Principal, University of Sydney)

In the discussion of the papers presented by Professor David Tunley and Professor Ken McKinnon the main issues which arose were:
1. The provision of resources for the performing and visual arts
2. The increasing degree of specialization in bachelor degree programmes

SUB-TOPIC 5(D): EXTRA-CURRICULAR ACTIVITIES

   3. The role of performance in music and visual arts studies
   4. University culture
   5. Community relations and involvement in the arts
   6. The critical versus the creative mind
   7. Quality control

1. Concern was expressed about the vulnerability of the arts in these times of reduction of resources in real terms. How does one gain a university-wide appreciation of the value of the arts in a university education? Several speakers referred to the success story of the Australian Ensemble resident at the University of New South Wales. The Chancellor of that University, Justice Gordon Samuels, outlined the history of the Ensemble, which had its birth some eight years ago following an approach by a musician about the possibility of a chamber music group providing the University with a first call on its services in return for financial and general support assistance. The University agreed to pay fees to the six core players in return for first call on their services for a series of subscription concerts, workshops and free lunch-hour concerts, and to play in the orchestra for the University's opera group. The standing of the Ensemble is such that there has never been any real opposition to it within the University. It has provided excellent publicity for the University and a link with the community. There is an advisory committee chaired by Justice Samuels which determines its own membership, does not report to any other body and plays little part in determining the artistic policy of the Ensemble. Justice Samuels mentioned one problem at the outset, when the group was titled the University of New South Wales Ensemble and booking agents regarded it as a group of students. The change of title avoids this assumption, not only by agents but by the public.

Professor Tunley commented on the need for community involvement, not only because he saw such links as an essential part of the role of a university but also because it gained community support for arts activities in the university. The community could become an influential lobby group. Its members may also be a source of bequests and benefactions if involved in such activities as choral groups. In response to a question asked by Dr. C. H. Bélanger (Laurentian) about the problems of justifying funds for museums, Professor Tunley suggested that universities should not reject the imposition of an entrance fee to museums and galleries as a means of earning revenue.

2. Professor N. S. Bose (Visva-Bharati) asked delegates to consider the practical world facing students with an aptitude for the performing arts. Such aptitude does not reside solely with those enrolled in, say, the bachelor of music course. Provision should be made for those with talent to undertake some studies in music while enrolled in medical sciences or the technologies. Where is the encouragement for this? How do we give the student the opportunity to develop this potential in our highly specialized degree programmes? Professor Tunley suggested the requirement to include some humanities courses as part of the degree programme of science-based courses, but Professor McKinnon stated that unfortu-

TOPIC 5: UNIVERSITIES AND CULTURE

nately the pressure is in the other direction. We were in a world of specialization and his experience was one of specialists in universities wanting still more specialization. We are moving away from the traditional role of universities to turn out the 'whole' person, and both he and Professor Tunley expressed their concern about current attitudes towards specialization. Professor Bose proposed a quinquennial festival of the performing arts for students as an activity worthy of ACU consideration. While there was general support for this proposal, the cost and organizational difficulties of such a project were recognised.

3. The Topic Chairman asked Professor Tunley to expand on his support for performance studies in music as part of degree requirements and to comment on the establishment of creative work for artists and sculptors as part of a university programme. The study of, say, the training of an artist, as against art history, does not appear to have a place in a university. Professor Tunley saw no difficulty in justifying performance studies in music. Performance and composition went hand in hand with the study of music; music was an interdisciplinary study within itself. The feature that distinguishes music from the visual arts is that it is a written art and can be studied from the literature. The research committee of the University of Western Australia accepted quality performance as research output, as a form of publication. He stressed that a university should have nothing to do with the performance of music unless standards of excellence were maintained. Because of the isolation of Perth from the rest of the world, Professor Tunley believed his university had a particular role to fill in the provision of the arts to the community.

Professor McKinnon did not share the lack of support which Professor Tunley, and to a lesser extent perhaps the Topic Chairman, had for the place of creativity studies in the visual arts in university courses. He did not believe a distinction could be made between the performance of music and that of the visual arts.

4. The failure to develop a university culture was seen by Professor McKinnon as partly related to the degree of specialization which takes place. There is little that characterizes a graduate as a graduate of a particular institution. Most are anxious to complete their studies as quickly as possible and get out into the workforce. The institution plays little part in attempting to shape the values of its students. Other than in the development of skills in the area of specialized studies, we are not interested in the kind of product being produced. The Australian attitude appears to be to criticize everything but not to co-operate. There are some values which are important and universities should be working to preserve these. Professor R. Tonkinson (Western Australia) referred to the apathetic attitude that students have to the campus environment: little regard for the property, for preserving the buildings and keeping the place clean—some-one else can clean up the mess.

5. University resources are in the main provided by the taxpayer and students and staff need to exhibit some appreciation of this. Public performances by music groups and welcoming the community were seen

SUB-TOPIC 5(D): EXTRA-CURRICULAR ACTIVITIES

as ways of doing so. Reference has been made above to the need to gain community support in general and the scope which exists for benefactions and bequests from those who have been brought within the university fold.

6. Professor McKinnon in his discussion of the place for creative studies in the visual arts brought out the need to develop creative thinking in our students. He sees an over-emphasis on the development of critical skills. More effort must be put into what it takes to make people creative. This has been a neglected area for too long.

7. Dr. Bélanger saw difficulty in determining excellence in performance studies. He asked how one created quality control. There was little difficulty in the traditional areas of western music, suggested Professor Tunley, but universities had to consider all types of music and, while there was some risk with standards in branching out into the unusual, we have to reach out into new areas. In the performance of non-western music the University of Western Australia has sought to bring overseas specialists as artists in residence and he cited an example with Indonesian music. One has to accept the advice of others in identifying such people. The Topic Chairman mentioned the embassies as a source of such advice when moving outside our culture.

In their closing remarks at the end of the session, both speakers stressed the need for cultural activities as an essential part of university education—the need to turn out the 'whole' person. Universities must give priority to the development of a cultural environment for their students.

Sub-Topic 5(e)

THE PROBLEMS OF THE BI- OR MULTI-LINGUAL UNIVERSITY

Thursday, 11 February

Dr. J. S. DANIEL and Dr. C. H. BÉLANGER (respectively *President* and *Vice-President, Academic, Laurentian University of Sudbury*):

CHALLENGES OF THE BILINGUAL (MULTI-LINGUAL) UNIVERSITY

Languages in Commonwealth Universities

The Commonwealth's membership represents about a quarter of the world's population and about the third of the membership of the United Nations. Although the Commonwealth embraces all the diversity that those figures imply, its members also have a shared heritage of law, language and literature which translates into some similarities of current practice in administrative, legal, governmental and educational matters. In earlier days considerable idealism was invested in the role of the English language as a bond between nations. Winston Churchill, speaking at Harvard University 45 years ago, hailed basic English as 'the head stream of what might well be a mighty fertilizing and health-giving river . . . an advantage to many races, an aid to the building up of our new structure for preserving peace' (Beaty). Today English speakers are more diffident about vaunting the civilizing influence of their language. It takes a francophone, d'Iberville Fortier (1988), to evoke the 'subtle but important association between the English language, those nobler human values with which it is best associated and the principles of internationalism and negotiation which inspire the modern Commonwealth'.

Whether we believe that English has been a force for peace and noble values or not, its emergence since world war II as the

SUB-TOPIC 5(E): BI-/MULTI-LINGUAL UNIVERSITIES   [Daniel/Bélanger]

international lingua franca is undeniable. Churchill himself would probably be surprised at the extent of its use. For English to become the international language was predictable; less predictable was its adoption as an official language by multi-lingual states in Africa and South Asia, even in cases such as the Philippines where it was not the colonial language. No doubt the international status of English was a big attraction. India, for example, might have worked harder to remove the official status of English had it been perceived simply as the colonial language.

It is natural that at a congress of Commonwealth universities we should rejoice in the academic links that the use of English makes possible. Indeed it may be considered in poor taste, at such a forum, to talk about the use of other languages in our institutions. However, a Congress theme is culture and cultural pluralism. Language is the most fundamental and emotive means by which we each identify with a cultural community, and most Commonwealth universities serve communities whose first language is not English. If a main function of universities is to preserve and communicate the cultural heritage they must take into account the language that goes with the culture.

Our purpose in this paper is to explore the special challenges facing universities that offer academic programmes and services in more than one language. We are not referring to the teaching of languages *per se* but to the languages of instruction used for the range of degree courses/programmes on offer by the university. In order to identify such universities we wrote to all national university associations and to a number of individual universities. As university administrators ourselves, and therefore the target of frequent surveys, we are especially grateful to those who responded. As academics in a bilingual university, and therefore aware of the sensitivity of language issues, we understand the delicacy of those who responded guardedly or not at all. We hope that the discussion of bilingualism at this Congress will provide information to allow us to explore this fascinating question more fully in a future article.

The Extent of Bilingualism and Multi-lingualism

Before looking more closely at patterns of bilingualism it will be useful to summarize briefly the results of the survey and offer some comments.

1. *Where bilingualism (multi-lingualism) is not an issue.* Responses indicate that bilingualism (multi-lingualism) is not an issue for universities in Australia, England, the West Indies and Scotland, where English is the first language of the overwhelming majority

of the population. Whether this turns out to be an asset is less sure since illiteracy today is more frequently being defined as the inability to communicate in a language other than a mother tongue. In that connection, the mother tongue is the cultural language whereas other languages are the window on the world.

2. *Universities in highly multi-lingual societies.* According to our respondents English is the universal language of instruction in the universities of the Commonwealth countries of Africa. This is not the place to examine in any detail the tremendous challenge language presents in Africa, where an uneducated person may speak several non-literary languages and an educated individual half a dozen. In some countries the majority do not even have the national language (*e.g.* Kiswahili in Tanzania) as a mother tongue, so English as used in the universities is at least the third language for many students and faculty. The ability of succeeding generations of faculty to be able to teach in English, at a time when fewer African graduate students are being trained in overseas Commonwealth countries, is cause for concern. The alternatives to the use of English seem, however, to be even more problematic.

India presents a complex linguistic diversity with its 15 national/official languages. While English is present as a medium of instruction in nearly all Indian universities, we were informed that at least 21 of them offer courses in one or more Indian languages. Table 1, below, gives some examples.

TABLE 1: EXAMPLES OF THE USE OF LOCAL LANGUAGES IN INDIAN UNIVERSITIES

University	Majority language and proportion of students speaking it	% enrolments in courses taught in different languages	% of faculty able to teach in English and majority language
Gujarat	Gujarati (nearly all)	Most courses taught in Gujarati; English and Hindi also permitted	N/a
Madras	Tamil (80%)	Tamil 13% English 87%	Nearly all
Madurai-Kamaraj	Tamil (80%)	Tamil 11% English 89%	Nearly all
Nagpur	Marathi (80%)	English 34% Marathi } 66% Hindi	90%
Rajasthan	Hindi (80% +)	Most courses taught in Hindi	50%

SUB-TOPIC 5(E): BI-/MULTI-LINGUAL UNIVERSITIES [Daniel/Bélanger]

Singapore is an example of a small multi-lingual and multi-racial society. In this case, as in Africa, English is the language of higher education.

3. *Where there is a revival of a native language.* The best examples in this category are New Zealand and Wales. In New Zealand, outside the universities, there is now a strong current of interest and growing practice in bilingual education using the Maori language. There is also one very small private university which offers a bilingual (Maori/English) approach at the tertiary level. Bilingualism is a growing issue in the country's universities and the October 1987 report of the New Zealand Universities Review Committee recommended that 'the universities encourage the use of the Maori language where appropriate on ceremonial occasions, provide dedicated space for Maori purposes . . ., ensure teaching staff pronounce Maori words accurately and also consult local Maori communities on student admission procedures, appointments and courses where appropriate'.

Wales has also seen a revival of interest in the Welsh language and an increased provision of TV programmes in Welsh. We were informed that the university colleges of Wales in Aberystwyth and Bangor offer selected courses in English and Welsh, but have been unable to obtain further details about how these courses are selected or about policies on language use in administration and governance.

4. *Countries using two or three major languages in higher education.* Between the linguistic diversity of Africa and India and the countries that are unilingually English are a group of Commonwealth countries where two or three languages are used at the national level and in higher education. These jurisdictions, which are the main focus of interest of this paper, include Canada, Hong Kong, Malaysia, Mauritius and Sri Lanka. Obviously they present some very different situations.

CANADA is an officially bilingual country (English/French). However of the 85 university institutions that make up the national Association of Universities and Colleges of Canada (AUCC) only a small number reflect the country's bilingualism. Sixty-three teach almost exclusively in English and 20 in French. The only officially bilingual universities are the University of Ottawa and Laurentian University, although three other institutions have bilingual or French colleges (Alberta, Manitoba, York).

HONG KONG will end its colonial status in 1997. English and Chinese are the languages in use. In principle the University of Hong Kong operates in English and the Chinese University of Hong Kong in Chinese. However, because the population is overwhelmingly Cantonese-speaking and Hong Kong is one of the great international cities both universities are bilingual to a considerable degree.

MALAYSIA has a policy of affirming the Malay language throughout its public institutions. We did not obtain information on the day-to-day reality of language use in Malaysian universities. Large numbers of Chinese Malaysians pursue their higher education outside the country.

MAURITIUS was successively a French and a British colony before independence. The University of Mauritius uses both languages although English has primacy in examinations, etc.

SRI LANKA has a Sinhala-speaking majority and a Tamil-speaking minority. Both languages, as well as English, are used extensively in the universities. Table 2, below, was drawn up from data supplied by the universities of Sri Lanka.

Language Competency

Today all universities, be they unilingual, bilingual or multilingual, claim that the linguistic competency of their students leaves something to be desired. If there is a problem for students using their mother tongue we might expect students operating in a second or third language to experience even greater difficulty.

Some relief for the universities can be obtained by pressuring the secondary schools to do a better job of language teaching. Even if such pressure gives results, however, universities should remember the principle 'use it or lose it' and insist on greater use of language in assignments. Emphasis on the use of language across the whole curriculum is more effective than concentrating efforts to develop writing skills in a few courses.

Language and Institutional Management in Canada

If more than one language is commonly used, either within a university or in its surrounding milieu, there is usually an impact on the operation of the institution in areas such as appointments policy, governance structure and decision-making processes. We shall illustrate these effects with Canadian examples which have parallels in some other Commonwealth countries.

At a first level of linguistic complexity a university may have a single language of instruction and internal communication but exist in a milieu or jurisdiction where the majority language is different. The English-language universities of Quebec (Bishop's,

SUB-TOPIC 5(E): BI-/MULTI-LINGUAL UNIVERSITIES [Daniel/Bélanger]

TABLE 2: LANGUAGE PATTERNS IN SRI LANKAN UNIVERSITIES

University	No. of programmes in each language (% enrolments)	Languages of student services	Mother tongue of students	% of bilingual faculty
Jaffna				
Arts	English 3 (5) Tamil all others (95)	Tamil/English	Tamil 80%+	60
Sciences	English 2 (60) Tamil 1 (40)	Tamil/English	Tamil 80%+	80
Medicine	English 1 (100)	Tamil/English	Tamil 80%+	n/a
Kelaniya	Sinhala 22 (78) English 14 (5) Sinhala/English 6 (17)	Sinhala/English	Sinhala 80%	65
Moratuwa	English all (100)	English/Sinhala/Tamil	Sinhala 85% Tamil 15%	100
Open	Sinhala 7 (n/a) Tamil 5 (n/a) English 8 (n/a)	English/Sinhala/Tamil	Sinhala 80%	100
Peradeniya	English 7 (55) Sinhala 3 (28) Tamil 3 (17)	English/Sinhala/Tamil	Sinhala 70% Tamil 30%	70
Ruhuna	Sinhala 6 (100)	Sinhala/English	Sinhala 90% Tamil or } 10% English	90
Sri Jayewardenepura	Sinhala 11 (96) English 2 (4)	Sinhala/English	Sinhala 98% Tamil 2%	85

Concordia and McGill) are a good example. They teach and operate in English but deal with the provincial government and much of the public in French. At a minimum such universities must appoint bilingual people to all positions that have an external relations component. In practice the trend towards greater inter-university co-operation and joint research creates a growing need and corresponding opportunities for bilingual staff and faculty in all parts of the institution.

The other side of the coin, of course, is that in such an environment staff who speak the language of the institution but not the language of the milieu will find themselves effectively barred from some key positions. Such staff resent this, a resentment sometimes shared by unilingual members of search committees who would rather not accept the need for bilingualism in these externally-oriented but internally-influential positions.

This feature of Quebec's English universities is experienced, to a much smaller degree, by all Canada's French universities. While they deal with the Quebec government and public in French, their senior officials, who must also operate in the wider North American environment, find a knowledge of English important. We imagine there are variations of this phenomenon in all universities that operate in English in milieus which have a different everyday language (*e.g.* Africa, Hong Kong, India).

Universities that use two languages internally face more complex challenges. They need a much higher proportion of bilingual staff. In these universities it is not just external relations but also contact with the students and staff at large that requires a bilingual capability. The situation is further complicated if one of the languages is a minority language in the region where the university is located. Bilingual staff are then harder to find and the linguistic minority tends to be over-represented in jobs involving internal communication or contact with students (*e.g.* registrarial and student services staff, departmental secretaries). These are not necessarily high-status positions and it is natural for these bilingual staff to feel that they are in fact 'covering' the language challenge for the less bilingual and better-paid faculty or professionals to whom they report.

More difficult still, however, are the two other challenges that bilingual universities face if they serve a linguistic minority as well as a majority using another language. These challenges are to promote the minority culture and to give the minority more control over its own destiny. The two are linked but we shall address them separately. While the cultural challenge can be partly met by administrative action the practices of the administration may be perceived by the minority as the key obstacle to greater control of destiny.

A linguistic minority is more conscious of the link between language and culture than the majority. Promoting the culture means living in the language as well as studying in it (Parker and Bélanger, 1987). The larger the size of the minority group on campus the easier this is. University authorities can help by providing the linguistic minority with its own space—both literally and figuratively. French students at Laurentian, for example, have their own lounge in which they discourage the speaking of English. Student associations, newspapers, drama and cultural events initiated by the minority should be strongly supported. This support may be criticized by unilingual members of the majority group claiming that the university should foster integration and bilingualism instead of separation. The reply is that linguistic minorities are already well-integrated. For them assimilation is a greater danger than isolation. Unless the minority has the opportunity to do its own thing part of the time, the cultural richness of bilingual regions will be lost.

Logically, of course, another important way for the minority to do its own thing is for it to control the programmes and services offered by the university in the minority language. This is easier said than done. It is easy enough, at least in principle, to create a separate university for the minority or to split an existing university in two, as was done with Belgium's University of Leuven/Louvain. But if there is a desire to maintain a bilingual university, both for idealistic reasons of promoting national unity and practical reasons of achieving the critical academic mass in a good range of disciplines, giving the minority control over its affairs is difficult. It is not simply a question of good will. Many academics put their allegiance to their discipline group above their allegiance to their language group—majority or minority. Even those who do not mostly agree that the social work curriculum should be overseen by social work faculty, the biology curriculum by biology faculty, etc. The result of this is that the linguistic minority may find itself in a minority at every level of the institution's process for academic decision-making: departmental assembly, faculty council, senate.

We are not aware of any university that has solved this problem in a thoroughly satisfactory way. Recent legislation by the Ontario government, aimed at expanding French-language services and giving the francophone minority greater control of those services, has now given that province's bilingual universities an incentive to find better solutions. One avenue, for example, could be a matrix structure that distinguished clearly between the management of academic staff (the departments) and the management of instructional activities (programmes/courses). This would provide greater autonomy to the minority in operating its programmes and also give it greater parity in the university-wide processes for making decisions about programmes.

Conclusion

In view of the linguistic complexity of the societies served by the universities of the Commonwealth it is at first surprising that there are not more bilingual universities. It becomes less surprising when we find that bilingualism poses a direct challenge to traditional structures of academic governance. We believe that the special cultural and political traditions that bilingual universities can generate make it worthwhile to take up that challenge. The reconciliation between the affirmation of the English language as the international language of business and the growing desire to preserve cultural minorities will take nurturing.

REFERENCES

Beaty, S. (1987): 'The Commonwealth Idea' in *Language and Society* 21, pp. 37-38.

D'Iberville Fortier (1987): *ibid.*, p. 34.

New Zealand Universities Review Committee (1987): *New Zealand's Universities: Partners in National Development.*

Parker, D. H. and Bélanger, C. H. (1987): 'A Challenge for Canadian Universities: Bilingual Students' in *Canadian Modern Language Review* (March 1987), vol. 43, no. 3, pp. 538-547.

Professor BH. KRISHNAMURTI (*Vice-Chancellor, University of Hyderabad*):

THE REGIONAL LANGAUGE *VIS-À-VIS* ENGLISH AS THE MEDIUM OF INSTRUCTION IN HIGHER EDUCATION: THE INDIAN DILEMMA

1. *Assumptions about Language Development*

As a linguist and as a sociologist of language, I would like to present certain assumptions about language development which are either tested or testable with empirical data from ancient or modern societies.

(i) There are primitive societies but no primitive languages. Almost all languages are equipped with necessary structures optimal to handle any domain of human communication.

(ii) A language, besides being a vehicle of communication, is also a cultural institution which is an integral part of the social, emotional and intellectual life of its speakers. Living languages with centuries-old literary traditions cannot easily be relegated to a secondary status by other languages in a given society.

(iii) A language develops appropriate registers (*i.e.* styles and terminologies) in new domains, if its speakers make an effort in an appropriate manner. Language development and language use go hand in hand; one does not precede or follow the other. A language is as good or as bad as its users make it to be.

(iv) Language development in new domains occurs if and only if necessary and sufficient conditions are created (by planners and policymakers) for its uninhibited use (by its speakers) for a considerable period of time. This means that any normative measures taken for language development turn out to be counterproductive.

(v) Standardization of styles and terminology should follow and not precede the extensive use of a language in domains in which it has not been used earlier.

(vi) Language development and vitality are measured in terms of the range of domains in which it can be used effectively, *viz.* socialization, education, government, courts, trade, industry, defence, managerial decision-making, etc. Such domains can be covered by more than one language used complementarily.

(vii) Language development is central to educational advancement on a mass scale. Educational development is central to economic, cultural and political development. Language development, therefore, is a corollary to national development.

(viii) There is hardly a nation which is economically and industrially advanced based on education imparted exclusively through the medium of a foreign language.

2. *Language Medium in Education in India till 1947*

By the time India became independent in 1947, the question of the medium of instruction was resolved and a state of stability had prevailed for at least three decades. Except for a very few schools (meant for the English nationals and wealthy Indians), the medium of instruction was the dominant regional language/mother tongue from the primary to the high school level. English was taught as a subject from standards V or VI. At the levels of the intermediate, the degree college and the university, English was the medium of instruction for all subjects except for modern Indian languages or classical languages taught as subjects. A century-long controversy which started in the early nineteenth century ended with the above scheme emerging as the most satisfactory model by the 1920s. This was further stabilized during the period of diarchy and the provincial autonomy (1920–47).

A brief review of the controversy would be interesting and revealing. The orientalists wanted the revival and improvement of oriental learning through the medium of classical languages, Sanskrit and Persian. The anglicists wanted the European knowledge of science, letters and philosophy taught to the natives in English. The vernacularists claimed the rightful place for vernacular languages as the media of instruction so that modern knowledge could reach the masses. A great social reformer and an oriental scholar, Raja Ram Mohan Roy (1824), supported the dissemination of European knowledge through English. The anglicists won the day when Lord William Bentinck issued his resolution on March 7, 1835, that all funds be utilised only on English education, based on the celebrated minute of Thomas Babington Macaulay (on February 2, 1835). Brian Houghton Hodgson, a civil servant of the East India Company, supported by John Wilson, a great missionary scholar of Bombay, championed the cause of the vernacular languages. The controversy continued until the education dispatch of 1854 sent from the Company's court of directors to the Governor General of India and named after Sir Charles Wood, the president of the board of control. The dispatch forcefully directed the government to promote the use of vernacular languages as media of instruction in education to cater to the middle and lower strata of the society. This dispatch is a landmark in the use of vernacular languages in education. However, the recommendations were not implemented with sincerity for the next seven decades.

After the mutiny of 1857 the administration of India was transferred to the British Crown. Even by 1882, over 60% of primary schools still had English as the medium of instruction. It was Lord Curzon's (1898–1905) educational policy, coupled with the national movement, that brought about sweeping changes in the medium of education in the early part of this century. The resolution on the educational policy of the government of India (February 21, 1913) was a significant pronouncement which led to the establishment of vernacular schools from primary to the secondary level. A commission under the chairmanship of Sir Michael Sadler was

SUB-TOPIC 5(E): BI-/MULTI-LINGUAL UNIVERSITIES [*Krishnamurti*]

set up in 1917 to inquire into the affairs of the Calcutta University in particular, and the crucial problems of education in general. The report gave serious thought to the medium problem and resulted in the restricting of the medium of English only to the college and university stage from 1920s onwards throughout the country.

3. *Post-1947 Scenario of the Medium of Instruction*

When the colonial countries became independent a major problem that they had to tackle was finding a national language both as a symbol of national spirit and solidarity and also as a *lingua franca*. While it was easier for smaller nation states to find such a language (*e.g.* Pakistan, Burma and Sri Lanka), in countries with diverse ethnic populations of sizeable numbers, with different languages, the problem became quite difficult and complex. It is not possible to compare any two countries in the complexity of their problems. The African states and India have multi-lingual and multi-ethnic populations which cannot be served by a single language as a *lingua franca*. The situation in India was easier since it had 14 major modern Indian languages, most of which were spoken in different geographical regions whose boundaries can be marked.

The constitution of India, adopted in 1950, recognises 15 languages as the languages of India included in the VIII Schedule (14 modern Indian languages and Sanskrit, a classical language). English continues as an associate official language, along with Hindi. The major Indian languages are spoken by 87% of the population (according to the 1971 census). Linguistic states were formed in 1956. The University Education Commission report of 1949 suggested, among other things, that 'English be replaced, as early as practicable, by an Indian language as the medium of instruction of higher education' (Naik & Nurullah: 434). The Education Commission (1964–66), in no uncertain terms, discussed the medium question and proposed that the mother tongue (regional language) should be used up to the highest level for instruction and examination, but English should be taught both as a subject and as a library language at higher levels.

The above policy was implemented in a haphazard manner, with many states adopting the regional language as an optional medium beside English up to the undergraduate level in arts and sciences; but professional courses (engineering, medicine, etc.) continue to be in English at all levels. The optionality of medium gave rise to two streams of students, those with the English medium having a definite advantage over the regional language medium students, both in employment and in postgraduate education. Students from regional language medium have found it difficult to switch over to English at the postgraduate level. Therefore instead of becoming an advantage the regional language medium in almost all cases became a handicap to those who had opted for it. This trend has led to a greater importance being given to English medium right from the primary stage. The trend during the past two decades has tilted in favour of English and English medium primary schools have cropped up as mushrooms in both urban and rural areas with inadequately prepared teachers. Children coming out of such schools have a poorer knowledge of and exposure to the mother tongue, and this has made them culturally alienated and their cognitive development is also stunted.

The *Commonwealth Universities Yearbook* 1987 (vol. 3) provides information about the medium of instruction for only some universities. Of the 154 Indian institutions listed in the *Yearbook*, there are 8 central universities, 5 Indian institutes of technology, 25 professional (agriculture, technology, etc.) universities/institutes, 20 'deemed to be universities' and institutions of national importance, and 96 multifaculty universities. The medium of instruction as could be gathered from the *Yearbook* for each group of institutions is as follows:

Institutions	No.	Medium of instruction
(1) Central universities	8	English[1]
(2) Indian institutes of technology	5	English
(3) Professional universities/institutions—		
Agriculture universities	22	Not stated for most[2]
Gujarat Ayurved Univ.	1	
J.N. Technological Univ.	1	
Indira Kala Sangit Univ.	1	
(4) 'Deemed to be universities'	20	English (for professional institutions); Sanskrit, Hindi, English (for language institutions)[3]
(5) Multi-faculty universities	96	English at postgraduate level; regional language as optional medium at undergraduate level
Total	154	

[1] In Visva-Bharati, Bengali is an optional medium in postgraduate non-professional courses.
[2] Agricultural universities have generally English as the medium of instruction.
[3] Gujarat Vidyapeeth has Gujarati, English and Hindi.

SUB-TOPIC 5(E): BI-/MULTI-LINGUAL UNIVERSITIES [Krishnamurti]

Out of the 96 of the last category the *Yearbook* has no information on the medium of instruction for 33 universities.

In its introduction on India the *Commonwealth Universities Yearbook* summarizes the medium of instruction question as follows:

'The issue of the medium of instruction was settled in favour of English, as explained earlier, by the time the first three universities were established in 1857. With the growth of the national movement, however, a good deal of emphasis was put on the development of Indian languages. When the Indian constitution was adopted in 1950, it provided that Hindi should be the official language of the country. For the first 15 years, however, English also was to continue as an official language. When in the mid-sixties those 15 years expired, there was virulent anti-Hindi agitation in Tamil Nadu. Consequently both Hindi and English continue to be official languages of the country today and there is little prospect of any major change occurring in the next few years.

'In the university world, however, there has been some change. About three-quarters of the universities in the Hindi-speaking belt spread over five Indian states have switched to Hindi as the medium of instruction. This pattern has been followed with one or two other Indian languages too but the bulk of the universities continue to have English as the medium of instruction with an option given to students to use their own language also.

'Most of what is said above relates to undergraduate courses. To a lesser extent it applies also to postgraduate courses, but in professional courses English continues to be the medium of instruction as in the past. Of books written in English and published in India, about 8000–10,000 titles a year are published. Three-quarters of them are textbooks while the remaining quarter or even less are either general books or scholarly books. On the whole, English is more popular in India today than it was in 1947.'

It is true that there is a great demand for the study of English at all levels and, by the same token (the demand is outstripped by supply of qualified teachers), the standard of English has been declining at an alarming rate. Particularly 'bad English' acquired in childhood is more difficult to unlearn than at the post-secondary level.

The pre-60s situation was decidely better when the switch from the regional language to English at the initial stage of the tertiary level for all or most of the students gave them adequate preparation of four years before they entered the postgraduate courses. All this confusion has led to the expansion of higher education without a sense of direction. The major employers are industry, banks and government. No preference is given to language medium graduates over the English medium ones. This had a backlash effect on the whole structure of education right from the primary level.

4. *Suggestions*

A proper planning should have led to the following alternatives: (i) ideally, to extend the regional language medium to all levels of education including professional courses—at the same time stepping up the knowledge of English for spoken and written purposes as the students moved higher up the education ladder; (ii) to go back to the pre-60s model, imparting education through the mother tongue/regional language only up to the higher secondary level and retaining English at all tertiary levels. This would naturally restrict the benefit of higher education to a small segment of the population and the gap between the elite and the masses could never be bridged.

A great deal of time was wasted on such questions as the preparation of textbooks and terminologies before the regional language medium was extended to all levels of higher education. As a linguist I can say that this was putting the cart before the horse. A language grows in a given domain of knowledge when it is used by its participants. It is not the terminology that offers the greatest hurdle in learning English; it is the grammar and the idiom of English.

Soon after independence the regional languages should have been extended as instructional media progressively, keeping the textbooks in English. Over the next two decades teachers who had received their education through the English medium could have used the syntax of the regional language with a free admixture of English/international terminology. They would have thereby developed styles suitable to teach different subjects—particularly those of science and technology. The preparation of textbooks and standardization of terms should have followed in due course after employing styles involving free code switching in the classroom for at least one decade. Prescribing norms of style and compulsion to use the terms prepared by scholars have slowed down language development. Certain agencies like the textbook academies monopolizing preparation of the textbooks have curtailed the creative participation of competent writers who could have prepared texts on different subjects with the users' market ultimately determining the coverage and quality of the textbooks, as happened between 1920 and 1947.

5. *Steps to Reverse the Present Situation*

(i) Extending the regional language media to all levels without insistence on the preparation of textbooks and terminologies.

(ii) Allowing teachers and students to use their language freely for acquiring modern knowledge through the mother tongue/regional language, thus creating conditions for different styles and terms to evolve through borrowing, semantic extension, fresh coining, etc.

(iii) Standard English textbooks should continue to be the sources of knowledge.

(iv) Specialized courses have to be developed to familiarize scientific English relating to different fields.

(v) After at least a decade of such experimental classroom preparation, teachers with the experience of teaching different subjects should write books and there should be a free market for such books to compete for quality.

(vi) Committees for standardization of terminology should come as the last step when, for a given international concept, certain criteria of usage would be available to guide in the process of standardization.

REFERENCES

Baman-Behram, B. K. (1943): *Educational Controversies in India.* Bombay: D. P. Taraporevala Sons & Co.

Commonwealth Universities Yearbook 1987 (vol. 3). London: the Association of Commonwealth Universities.

Ferguson, Charles A. and Anwar S. Dil (1979): 'Universals of language planning in national development' in William C. McCormack and Stephen A. Wurm, pp. 693-702.

Kanungo, Gostha Behari (1962): *The Language Controversy in Indian Education: An Historical Study.* Chicago: The University of Chicago, Camparative Education Center.

Krishnamurti, Bh. (1979): 'Problems of language standarization in India', in William C. McCormack and Stephen A. Wurm, pp. 673-692.

Mahmood, Syed (1895): *A History of English Education in India (1781 to 1893).* Aligarh: Honorary Secretary of the MAO College.

McCormack, William C. and Stephen A. Wurm (1979): *Language and Society: Anthropological Issues.* The Hague: Mouton.

Nagarajan, S. (1984): *Children of Macaulay.* New Quest, 46, 207-220.

TOPIC 5: UNIVERSITIES AND CULTURE

Naik, J.P. and Syed Nurullah (1985)(6th edn. revised): *A Student History of Education in India 1800–1973*. New Delhi: Macmillan India Ltd.

National Policy on Education 1986: Programme of Action (1986). New Delhi: Government of India (Ministry of Human Resource Development, Department of Education).

Report of the Education Commission 1964–66: *Education and National Development*. New Delhi: Ministry of Education, Government of India.

West, Michael (1926): 'Bilingualism'. Bureau of Education (India): Occasional Reports No. 13. Calcutta: Government of India.

DISCUSSION

(*Rapporteur*: Mr. D. J. FOSTER, Registrar, University of York)

In contrast to the first four sessions of this theme, sub-topic (e) prompted few questions and in consequence the discussion was relatively brief.

Professor S. K. Verma (Central Institute of English & Foreign Languages), commenting on Professor Krishnamurti's paper, referred to a notion of a number of national languages in India, Hindi being the official national language and English the 'associate' official national language. At international level English was the language which provided the 'window on the world', as well as being the normal medium of communication between state governments and central government. He also referred to a widely-held perception of English as the language of opportunity and of mobility; and described a number of lexical innovations in the use of English.

Responding to Professor Verma's remarks, Professor Krishnamurti referred to what he described as a craze for English in India, reminiscent of the early part of the nineteenth century and which in his view had reached crisis proportions. As regards a solution, he suggested that the initiative for change lay with the policy-makers at national level and, in particular, with employers, rather than with the universities. He also felt that change could only be accomplished by the extension of regional languages to the highest levels.

Responding to another question, Professor Krishnamurti and Professor Verma said that only about 2.5% of students entering Indian universities were fluent in English. On the other hand, Professor Verma said that within his own institution remedial teaching in English had to be provided at every level. This theme was echoed by other speakers who referred to declining standards of linguistic competence in their own countries and to measures being adopted to remedy the situation.

Professor N. S. Bose (Visva-Bharati) said that in order to understand the problem of English in India it was necessary to examine the historical background. Standards of proficiency and competence in English had declined significantly since 1947 due to a variety of factors, some of them

SUB-TOPIC 5(E): BI-/MULTI-LINGUAL UNIVERSITIES

political. At the same time a decline in standards in Indian languages, including Hindi, was also discernible. The mistakes which had been made had now been realized but the damage had been done. Professor Bose also questioned whether the development and extension of regional languages might have an inhibiting effect on academic mobility, to the extent that those with competence in only one regional language might be unable to study at an academic institution where another regional language was in use. He recognised that the issue was a complex one to which there was no easy solution, except through the acquisition of two or three other languages.

Professor Subramani (South Pacific) asked which language was most commonly used by creative writers in India. In reply Professor Krishnamurti said that the most common practice was for writers to use their own language. He also noted that there were currently some powerful writers working in India. In connection with a point raised in Dr. Daniel's and Dr. Bélanger's paper, Professor Verma observed with regard to the situation in Singapore that English was the effective language of communication.

Topic 5

UNIVERSITIES AND CULTURE

The Relationship between Universities and Culture, and Problems of Cultural Pluralism

CHAIRMAN'S REPORT ON THE GROUP'S
DISCUSSIONS

Second Plenary Session
Friday, 12 February

Professor L. C. HOLBOROW (*Vice-Chancellor, Victoria University of Wellington*): The Topic addressed in group 5 was expected to be complex and challenging. This expectation was certainly borne out. It is however gratifying to report that the sessions exhibited a high degree of internal coherence and that there was much illuminating interconnection of major themes across the sub-topics. This report will therefore be thematic rather than chronological.

The first source of complexity in our Topic was the term 'culture' itself. The speakers at our opening session greatly assisted the group by analysing and illustrating its diverse but connected uses. In some contexts 'culture' refers to the totality of language, heritage and belief characteristic of a society of civilization. Culture in this wide sense includes scientific theory. When, however, we speak of *cultural* activities we single out the arts and literature—the products of the creative imagination. When we focus on *cultural* pluralism, as our group was asked to spend some time doing, the term 'cultural' evokes those differences in belief and practice which distinguish different ethnic groups—differences which can be a source of richness, or of conflict.

We were increasingly made aware as the sessions progressed of the cultural richness and diversity of the Commonwealth itself, as well as of the similarity of the issues which arise in different countries despite the many different social contexts. This richness is dynamic and involves anxiously debated questions of national cultural identity. No one doubted that the university had a most important role in seeking to conserve the indigenous or minority cultures of its region, although some scepticism and concern was expressed about its ability to prevail in the face of pervasive elements of popular culture, frequently promoted for purely commercial reasons. At the worst, the university might act as a genetic bank preserving rare species of culture.

We were told how in a developing country such as Malaysia the universities are regarded as having a positive obligation to assist in moulding and developing a national culture as part of the task of fostering a sense of national identity. It was readily conceded that a more detached and critical attitude to the well-formed and established culture of an older western democracy might be appropriate.

This contrast did not go unchallenged, for it raised several questions. First, who was to decide what should be included in such a national culture? The view that the principal task of the university in a developed country was to act as a critic was also challenged in a later session. Immigration on the scale recently experienced in Australia raises questions of Australian cultural identity to which scholars in universities might be expected to make a constructively creative, rather than just constructively critical, contribution. Canada has its own distinctive problems.

More broadly, the point was made that we do in any event influence the attitudes and values of our students. Should we not be more prepared than we are to subject this process to scrutiny and ask whether some of the attitudes we encounter are really consistent with university values. Should we do more to foster co-operative attitudes to work? (If this suggestion seems to threaten the notion of freedom of enquiry by proposing that we take a particular moral stand, we need to reflect that many of us do not regard it as inconsistent with proper freedom of enquiry to introduce regulations to combat plagiarism or sexual harassment).

The matter of whether there is or should be a university culture needs more debate: a debate which would soon lead us into some of the political territory canvassed in Topic group 1. Should we promote entrepreneurial attitudes if that is what our economy needs? Or is it sufficient that it happens in our increasingly emphasized schools of management?

It was also put to us that the aim of producing cultured persons, in the sense of persons of developed intellect and sensibility, was a proper university objective which needed more emphasis. It includes as a leading component the development of the critical faculties, but two presentations argued that the university also has a role in developing the *attitudes* which are part of artistic appreciation, as well as more purely cognitive abilities. We had some discussion about whether our attitude to the inclusion of performing arts in the curriculum was too exclusive, even if music performance was accepted. Despite some unresolved disagreements here, it was common ground that the study of the arts required a close integration of the critical faculties with the visionary practice of the artist if genuine appreciation is to occur. It followed that cultural activities had a place in the university not just as a pleasant diversion but as activities closely connected with one of its central intellectual tasks. We were privileged to see and hear excerpts from a video of an opera produced on this campus which had involved much planning, co-operation with other institutions, and financial sponsorship. The effect of excellent events of this sort on the university's reputation in the community was stressed and their effect on fund-raising was also mentioned.

Further confirmation of the view that the creative imagination had a place in the curriculum was seen in the increasing use of techniques drawn from drama in disciplines such as psychology, history, political science (and, one might add with some emphasis in the light of concerns current in some of our countries, also in management education).

One interesting measure of the extent of *cultural pluralism* within Commonwealth countries is the diversity of languages employed. Several speakers gave some startling statistics, such as the 90 ethnic and linguistic groups in Ontario, and the existence of 14 major languages and approximately 1000 dialects in India—nearly as numerous as the varieties of curry, as one of our Indian speakers told us. One presentation reported on a systematic survey of the language of instruction used in a range of countries. While English has had an influential role on the educational and political development of most countries, the survey revealed that there is much use of other languages. In several countries, including Canada, there are bilingual institutions; in Sri Lanka and India a significant number of institutions employ *three* languages. The problems which this generates for staffing policies and administration were thought to explain why this pattern was not even more pervasive. A paper tracing the development of the policy of employing regional languages in India argued for a mixed approach, partly to allow regional languages to adapt naturally to new needs.

Some of these problems of accommodation also arise when universities seek to conserve and to understand indigenous cultures. One of our most fascinating sessions was devoted to the exploration of this topic. Presentations prepared by a leading Nigerian academic and one of the most influential spokesmen for the Australian Aboriginal people nicely contrasted the situations of a majority indigenous group and a much-threatened minority. Contributions from other participants about developments in New Zealand represented an intermediate case. (Maori people constitute more than 12% of population and also have a treaty which implies partnership in development.) Several New Zealand universities have marae on their campuses and have incorporated Maori ceremonies into occasions such as graduations. We were advised that Nigerian experience supported the wisdom of establishing a modestly staffed institute to co-ordinate the tasks of research and promotion of culture, even though the substantive departments of the university should also be much involved. Just leaving the matter to these departments had not worked.

But in the case of Australian Aboriginal culture we were warned that the cultural gap was extremely difficult to bridge without causing irreparable damage to the distinctive features of the earlier culture. Our speaker confessed that he had belatedly been persuaded of the validity of a conception of what education means for the members of a 'first human society' such as that of the Aboriginal people. The acquisition through education of a modern western culture constitutes a sudden *empowerment*. The acquisition of literacy brings with it new cognitive abilities, just as learning mathematics gives a person a new means of thinking and coping with reality. But it was claimed that the acquisition of these new powers involved a loss. At first it appeared that the loss might be irretrievable, but further exploration of the point in discussion suggested that it was probably more a question of the difficulty that any one individual faces in combining in a single life two demanding ways of thinking, and of formulating objectives and goals. It is difficult, after all, to pursue excellence both in science or mathematics and in another domain of human intellectual endeavour as well. Spreading oneself always involves some loss, and problems of keeping oneself together as an integrated person come to the fore when it is a matter of combining radically difficult cultures. In any event it was argued that the distance between Aboriginal and modern western culture was sufficiently great that the university needed to treat it with care—to provide a sanctuary for the native scholar without forcing a premature literacy in place of the methods of an oral tradition and the surprisingly rich resources of an oral tradition and language. The argument was complex and contested by some, but it carried sufficient conviction for the president of one pioneering Canadian university to state that it provided an intellectual framework justifying the establishment of relatively autonomous centres or institutes, which had proved successful. It also lay behind the form of Aboriginal advancement programmes—the enclave—which has proved to be the most successful arrangement in Australian tertiary institutions.

If this has seemed a densely packed report, I can only plead in mitigation that it reflects in a much-abbreviated way the richness of our presentations and discussions. I have had to omit some interesting themes, such as the notion of *world culture* which appealed to some speakers. I can think of no more appropriate way of ending than to repeat a quotation from Tagore used by one of our Indian speakers: 'Education is a diamond, and culture the glow of the diamond'.

Group Discussions

TOPIC 6
UNIVERSITIES AND THE SOCIAL IMPACT OF TECHNOLOGY

The Role of Universities in Contributing to the Understanding of the Social Impact of Technology

Chairman: Dr. J. Downey
President of the University of New Brunswick

Chief Rapporteur: Mr. D. W. Girvan
Registrar of the University of Otago

			Page
Sub-Topic 6(a)	(i)	THE ROLE OF THE UNIVERSITIES IN CONTRIBUTING TO AN UNDERSTANDING OF THE EMPLOYEE RELATIONS IMPLICATIONS OF TECHNOLOGICAL CHANGE	
		Speaker Professor Dianne Yerbury	372
		Discussion	377
	(ii)	THE ROLE OF UNIVERSITIES IN ASSESSING THE IMPACT OF TECHNOLOGY UPON EMPLOYMENT	
		Speaker Dr. G. J. Hills	379
		Discussion	382

		Page
Sub-Topic 6(b)	**THE ROLE OF UNIVERSITIES IN UNDERSTANDING THE IMPACT OF SOCIETY UPON TECHNOLOGY**	
	Speakers	
	Professor K. B. Dickson	385
	Discussion	390
	Professor R. S. Turner	392
	Discussion	397
Sub-Topic 6(c)	**THE ROLE OF UNIVERSITIES IN UNDERSTANDING THE IMPACT OF TECHNOLOGY UPON EDUCATION AND TRAINING**	
	Speakers	
	Professor K. R. McKinnon	399
	Discussion	405
	Professor C. Ann Cameron	408
	Discussion	414
Sub-Topic 6(d)	**THE ROLE OF UNIVERSITIES IN UNDERSTANDING THE ETHICAL ISSUES INVOLVED IN TECHNOLOGICAL CHANGE**	
	Speakers	
	Dr. A. Naimark	416
	Professor Lydia P. Makhubu	422
	Lord Chilver	427
	Discussion	431
	Paper by Professor S. J. S. Cookey	432
Sub-Topic 6(e)	**THE ROLE OF UNIVERSITIES IN ASSESSING THE IMPACT OF TECHNOLOGY UPON THE ENVIRONMENT**	
	Speaker	
	Professor B. L. Clarkson	437
	Discussion	441
	Paper by Lord Chilver	443

	Page
CHAIRMAN'S REPORT ON THE GROUP'S DISCUSSIONS	448
Other Contributions	453

For index to names, see p 533

Sub-Topic 6(a)

Monday, 8 February

(i) THE ROLE OF THE UNIVERSITIES IN CONTRIBUTING TO AN UNDERSTANDING OF THE EMPLOYEE RELATIONS IMPLICATIONS OF TECHNOLOGICAL CHANGE

Professor DIANNE YERBURY (*Vice-Chancellor, Macquarie University*):

PART 1: *The Relevance of the Issue and its Dimensions in Knowledge Acquisition*

Wherever you find the following circumstances at play, namely, that:
  (1) industrial relations is a key dimension of economic life;
  (2) technological change and the development of technological capacity in the workforce rank high on the politico-economic agenda; and
  (3) the university sector is expected to play a significant role in translating economic and technological goals into reality;
then you may expect to find also that the industrial and employee responses to technological change necessarily comprise a highly topical and relevant field of study. Achieving a technologically competitive edge and developing the necessary skills in the labour force are aspects which other speakers are addressing. These are only part of the challenge, however, that faces most industrial nations (and certainly Australia).

Given the fast-changing nature of technology, its impact on work and (in many economies, at least) the need to achieve employee co-operation for strategies involving technological innovation to be put into effect satisfactorily, we cannot afford to underplay the importance in the pursuit of national economic priorities of employee responses to technological change. Not infrequently this is the area most fraught with uncertainty and most vulnerable to costly delays—often with far-reaching economic implications. It is to be expected that this is one research topic for which there will continue to be funding available from various sources, including the main government funding bodies.

As for why technological change is such a key issue in employment relationships, we need to bear in mind that transition—the sheer fact of change—is often a painful process, whatever the final outcome. Inevitably, technological change has the potential for industrial conflict. The expression and intensity of that conflict depend on many variables, including the state of industrial relationships, the effectiveness of the channels existing or brought into action for processing the conflict, and the advantages and disadvantages to staff of the proposed changes; but the potential for conflict is inherent in the mere fact that changed circumstances mean that decisions affecting employment relationships have to be made.

There is a likelihood of differing interests, conflicting viewpoints and emotional resistance to change, regardless of whether the final outcome is likely to be beneficial or costly to the employees concerned. This may arise out of the need to deal with alterations to work content and procedures, status, qualifications and skills, organizational structure (and, very often, redeployment and/or relocation), promotion opportunities, work value and relativities, the position of work groups *vis-à-vis* other work groups, and management *vis-à-vis* other management and, importantly, job prospects and job security.

Just to list all these impacts on the job and on the work relationship that may result from even one significant technological change in the workplace is to make it clear that the subject we are dealing with is both complex and multi-dimensional. There is no one discipline or field of study which deals with it adequately and comprehensively. That is not to say that the issues involved do not benefit from single-disciplinary consideration. Clearly they can and do. Valuable contributions are made—

- from the relevant technological fields;
- from the professions (such as labour law, or the occupational health and safety side of medicine);
- from the social sciences (for instance, the sociology and psychology of work, labour economics, political science, etc.);
- from the humanities (for example, labour history);
- and from commerce and management subjects (including industrial relations, organizational behaviour, strategic planning and decision-making in relation to both public and private sector employment).

There is also, however, very particular benefit to be gained from multi-disciplinary and interdisciplinary studies of technological change. But it is difficult even in management schools and labour relations programmes, which are inherently multi-disciplinary, to amass adequate breadth and depth of specialization. To bring together the necessary critical mass often requires a formal or informal centre, drawing on academics from different parts of the university. However such complex, flexible, multi-disciplinary linkages tend to be institutionally clumsy in terms of funding, workloads, student units and accountability—which are characteristics not destined to endear them to university administrators (unless they are very successful indeed in pulling in large institutional grants). Nonetheless I anticipate that this is the sort of flexibility that administrators will increasingly have to find ways to accommodate.

Another institutional development we can expect to see more of is collaborative activity across institutions in order to garner sufficient resources for a major teaching and/or research programme on technological change.

We should also encourage the teaching of industrial relations and related subjects to engineering and applied science students. Indeed I think this is crucial if we are to avoid a repetition of some of the industrially disastrous work innovations we have seen too often in the past.

PART 2: *Examples of Knowledge Transfer*

Universities have a crucial role to play in knowledge transfer, of which the conventional (and still the most major) manifestations are teaching at both undergraduate and postgraduate levels, PhD supervision and scholarly publications. The performance of these responsibilities can benefit considerably from the advice of practitioners; and industrial relations schools, management schools and labour-management programmes—certainly in my own university—have set up advisory boards comprising practitioners from management, union and often government ranks, both to ensure continued relevance and also to rally support for the programmes. In Australia a large proportion of new industrial relations practitioners, whether in industry, commerce, unions or governments, are the graduates of such programmes, and this is one of the most useful contributions that universities make in the area.

A much more extensive and varied role in dissemination of scholarship is possible and desirable, however—and indeed this is already happening in Australia and in several other countries. For instance, insights and knowledge can be made generally available by publishing in practitioner-oriented journals, handbooks, etc., as well as in refereed journals. This tends not to be highly regarded for promotion purposes—and that is fair enough. But it does nonetheless have a valid role to play in universities' interaction with industry and unions. So too does dissemination at practitioner-oriented conferences and seminars, such as those run by the industrial relations societies in Australia, which is one of the several ways in which academics participate in public debate on the often controversial issue of technological change.

Academics also design and mount courses for management in the private and public sectors, for union representatives and for government policy-makers and bureaucrats. There are both 'open entry' courses and 'in-house' programmes which are designed for a particular organization or industry and dovetailed to its particular needs, priorities and problems. These courses may be provided on either an individual or institutional contract basis, or may form part of the university's continuing education programme. It is not uncommon for scholarships to be provided to union representatives who might otherwise be unable to participate.

Colleagues and I in one university also maintained a data bank that we made freely available. (In today's conditions such a service might well be provided on a paid basis.) Many academics act as consultants to governments, management and/or unions, helping to develop and implement strategies in this area. Or we may be called upon to act as 'change agents', working with the parties in an atmosphere of mutuality to try to facilitate agreed change. A lot of academics also enter into 'contract research' of a mission-oriented nature, trying to find solutions to problems.

Most Australian universities now have organizations such as Unisearch, which assist in the marketing of research and consultancy services to industry. At Macquarie University, also, we find considerable benefit in the Marcquarie Park Club, which we set up last year to promote interaction with the organizations in the high-technology industrial park in our vicinity. Over 70 companies and government organizations have already joined and there are numerous instances of collaboration.

Like many other universities in Australia, Macquarie has introduced more accommodating guidelines for outside earnings, which put limits on the amount of time an academic spends on consultancy rather than on the quantum of earnings. Moreover most Australian universities are more receptive nowadays to requests for academics to hold directorships in public and private organizations which are compatible with their scholarly work: I happen to be a part-time director of Australia Post, an organization which is introducing a sweeping programme of technological change. An invitation I had to decline because of other commitments at the time was membership of the Australian Science and Technology Council, the independent commission which advises the prime minister on science and technology. It is important that academics do sit on such bodies and that the scientists and technologists who make up that distinguished group include in their midst a social scientist who specializes in the employment and industrial implications.

Another relevant experience was secondment to the federal Department of Labour to set up a national industrial relations division which included work on technological change and redundancy. Most Australian universities now try to assist governments with appropriate secondments, which of course have a two-way benefit (although they are certainly not without their costs to the institution).

In the early eighties the distinguished Vice-Chancellor of the time of the University of New South Wales, Sir Rupert Myers, was invited to chair a committee of inquiry into technological change in Australia and a most important report resulted. Academics, for their part, were able to contribute their expertise in the form of submissions to, or research projects for, the review; and naturally their research was a crucial base for the inquiry.

I spent a sabbatical leave working with the committee of review of the Australian Broadcasting Commission and writing an extensive report, including detailed work on industrial disputes which had been holding back the introduction of proposed technological change for some years. In one such dispute the parties presented part of the report to the Australian Conciliation and Arbitration Commission as a joint submission. Scholarly works have been used in other cases before industrial tribunals on technological change and academics have the opportunity to assist parties in the preparation of the cases, or by advocacy, or by giving evidence as expert witnesses.

Four more personal examples may be worth mentioning as illustrative of the range of interactions in this area in Australia: a review I conducted for the New South Wales Public Service Board on the handling of personnel management, including technological change, in state departments and authorities; my one-time membership of the administrative review committee set up by that Board to advise on its policies and research papers; advice to the state government on the introduction of legislation on technological change; and membership of the New South Wales Privacy Com-

SUB-TOPIC 6(A): EFFECTS ON EMPLOYMENT

mittee which prepared guidelines on, and handled grievances about, privacy issues including the implications for employees of such technological change such as the automatic recording of telephone numbers dialled in the workplace.

There are other examples of involvement by my colleagues which I could give; but the ones I have mentioned do illustrate a number of ways in which universities and their staff can play a role in disseminating their research and scholarship on the employee aspects of technological change through the teaching of students and practitioners; through publications (scholarly and practitioner-oriented); through participation in public debate; through contract research for and assistance to the parties; and through work in connection with government inquiries and tribunal hearings.

DISCUSSION

(*Rapporteur:* Mr. B. J. SPENCER, Registrar, Macquarie University)

Professor Yerbury's paper stimulated a number of questions.

One questioner asked if trade unions tended to be sceptical of the capacity of university people to provide objective advice to employees in the process of managing technological change. Professor Yerbury noted that, while this remained a problem, it was now less so than it had been in the 1960s. Many officers and leaders in union affairs were now university graduates who were aware of sources of reliable advice in the universities. 'Living together has broken down much of the suspicion which was formerly evident', she added. It was now commonplace to invite prominent union leaders to participate fully in industrial relations inquiries, including those into the implications of technological change. Co-operation between interested parties and the involvement of university people had increased.

Asked about the influence of political policy on problems of adaption to technological change, Professor Yerbury observed that in Australia, while there was a political will to deal more sensitively with these problems, the political mechanisms to achieve this objective remained inadequate. The government sought solutions from the interaction of the parties concerned or depended on the intervention of the Australian Conciliation and Arbitration Commission. Some problems remained intractable.

It was acknowledged that there may be greater acceptance by industry of the role of university experts in this process in developed countries than in developing countries.

It was reported that in India there is evidence of strong and explicit opposition by unions to the introduction of technological change, in the belief that it would reduce the demand for labour. Professor Yerbury acknowledged that there remained real fears about the displacement of labour. A recent inquiry into technological change in Australia forecast that many more employment opportunities would be created in the wake of technological change than without it. Such a view would not have gained acceptance without the involvement of a senior union official in the committee which conducted the inquiry. While it is unrealistic not to expect resistance to technological change, it is essential to cushion employees with social support mechanisms to manage redundancy. While the previous Australian government had encouraged technological change, it had been slow to instal mechanisms to provide a social welfare 'safety net'.

Another speaker referred to the importance of changing attitudes of employees. Union representatives now realized that they needed to become well-informed about the impact of technological change, so as to be in a position to assess its implications independently, rather than resorting to uninformed opposition.

In response to another question Professor Yerbury confirmed her view that there are opportunities for academics to contribute to understanding of the implications of technological change for employees (in the ways she had described) in all Commonwealth countries, despite the wide range of social and economic circumstances which prevails within them.

The capacity of academics to predict and to assist employees to prepare for large-scale unemployment created by technological change was questioned. Professor Yerbury noted that many unions had previously tended to wait until their members were faced with redundancy before seeking protection. Attempts to persuade unions to include protective arrangements in awards had been resisted in some cases on the grounds that it amounted to an admission that redundancy was possible and thereby weakened industrial conditions. But the realization that many people are hurt by the absence of protective provisions had stimulated the introduction of standard arrangements which afford employees a measure of protection against the impact of redundancy. Nevertheless, Professor Yerbury acknowledged that the record of predicting manpower needs in Australia had not been a successful one.

Another speaker noted that the contributions by practitioners like Professor Yerbury in this field were uniquely personal and could not be regarded as institutional responses unless there was some formal mechanism to recognise them. Professor Yerbury reported that she had published accounts of her work in refereed journals and other accepted vehicles in the normal way. Such scholarly activity provided a basis for recognition and career development. These days there is much more acceptance (particularly in the industrial relations and management schools) of the kind of applied work she had described, including recognition for the purposes of career advancement.

(ii) THE ROLE OF UNIVERSITIES IN ASSESSING THE IMPACT OF TECHNOLOGY UPON EMPLOYMENT

Dr. G. J. HILLS (*Principal and Vice-Chancellor, University of Strathclyde*):

THE IMPACT OF TECHNOLOGY UPON EMPLOYMENT: THE ROLE OF THE UNIVERSITY

The thesis of my paper is that universities have a vital and unsurplantable role in the continued development of society and especially in the development of its knowledge, technology and skills bases. The future is said to be knowledge-based, the implication being that the third industrial revolution through which we are now living is largely concerned with intellectual development, *i.e.*, as Tofler will have it, with the extension of our brain power. Certainly the IT (Information Technology) revolution has only just begun and the application of artificial intelligence to manufacture, to organizational systems and to communications seems likely to strike at many of the foundations of our present society. Already nationhood is being challenged (or ignored) by the multinational companies. From the viewpoint of industry and commerce, national boundaries are already of small significance. Transnational market forces will impose international standards onto all trading nations: first the metric system of measurement, then the standard operating voltages, frequencies, communication channels, computer and human languages, currencies, levels of taxation, commercial and civil laws, and even university courses. In Europe the European Economic Community is steadily imposing these standards on the community states. What started out as a political ideal will become a reality largely as the result of high-speed communications and the development of international hardware and software standards.

The knowledge-base underlying these developments requires intelligent inputs from a wide variety of people, *all of them graduates*. Some will be graduates researching inside universities. Most, for the time being at least, will be graduates researching outside them, in industry or commerce, many of them in dedicated R&D centres. The rate of further progress will then depend on the rate of technology transfer from the various innovation centres to the market-driven manufacturing or service outlets. The efficiency with which different countries or, failing that, different parts of the world respond to the challenges of technology transfer and skills transfer is likely to determine the level of difficulty with which their peoples will confront the social and industrial changes imposed upon them by their vulnerability to changes elsewhere. It will remain true that those best able to cope with change are those who are already at its leading edge. That is not just because they are culturally prepared for change and confident in their ability to deal with it but because they will also be in a position to steer it. Under these circumstances the feedback is positive and success breeds success. By the same token those left behind by change risk becoming ever more obsolescent. This is the way of the poor becoming poorer and the road to high structural unemployment. The traditional solution to this chronic malaise is migration. It is still the solution for many in the third world and their universities have an ever greater responsibility to educate and train graduates to seize opportunities thrown up by rapid changes in industry. That it can be done is plainly evident in the burgeoning successes of Korea and Indonesia, both able to challenge the United States.

It will, of course, be argued that industrial reconstruction and technology transfer will also be constrained by the rate of investment. That may be true. All inventors and all new-company protagonists soon find out that it is the anticipated satisfaction of the market rather than the quality of the invention that will determine the level of investment in a new product or in a new process. However as the future becomes more knowledge-based the investment will increasingly be that of intelligence, *i.e.* of brainy people. The universities are again the only significant source of such people and, at that level, it is likely that all countries will be competing or collaborating on nearly equal terms.

It is therefore an axiom of this paper that the rate of industrial development will depend more than ever before on the rate of knowledge transfer and technology transfer. It has to be stressed that the knowledge, the technologies and the skills are by no means confined to science or engineering. Indeed, as computer hardware and software take over many of the programmable, rules-based tasks, it may well be that human intelligence will be increasingly deployed in the as yet unsystematized areas of knowledge such as politics and behaviour.

Whatever the form of the knowledge, attention will need to be paid to how that knowledge is acquired, stored, packaged and then down-loaded or transmitted. The creation and acquisition of new knowledge is the fruit of a range of R&D activities, all at different levels of complexity and difficulty. The most important characteristic of the new knowledge is likely to be its short shelf life. Rapid change implies rapid obsolescence. Research and scholarship which is too intensely dedicated to too-particular ends may well be the quickest route to obscurity. The forgetting curve will then assume the same importance as the learning curve. That apart, the efficiency with which the new knowledge is taken up will depend on the knowledge-base of those searching for it. In other words the enquirer needs to be at the same intellectual level as the producer. Old knowledge will not only be unsaleable, its possession may be intellectual luggage in the way of the new ideas. If this is so, then two implications follow. The first is that R&D, innovation and knowledge transfer will prosper most effectively in impermanent, undedicated and unstructured organizations. The second is that easily the greatest repositories of impermanent, undedicated and unstructured intelligences are the universities.

The greater the rate of change the greater the danger that commitment to today's problems will hamper the consideration of tomorrow's. This in turn implies that large, semi-permanent collections of researchers will either rapidly become out of date or need to be regularly re-educated and retrained, in or by those equipped for this task, namely the universities. Hence the world-wide re-examination of the industrial research function and the world-wide concern in industry for updating courses of all kinds.

The creation of additional vehicles for innovation is a natural extension of the university function. SRI at Stanford was the first (or among the first) to set up clusters of independent semi-autonomous research centres, research units and incubation centres contiguous with the university and in which university-based people could direct the studies of university graduates in an inexpensive, flexible way. Researches, even profound researches, can then be entered and exited in a low-cost way which encourages their promotion and their constant reformulation. Under these circumstances the universities come into their own.

It has been argued that a necessary corollary of rapid growth of the knowledge base is the growth in importance of organizations loosely dedicated to the acquisition, understanding, storing, repackaging and down-loading of knowledge. Those organizations already exist. They are called universities. Their staff consist of people trained in these tasks and the products of their training are twofold: (1) the new knowledge itself, in the form of books, papers and, increasingly, interactive data banks and tutored video presentations; and (2) bright people in full possession of the latest knowledge, technology and skills.

TOPIC 6: SOCIAL IMPACT OF TECHNOLOGY

The definition of universities as necessary agents of knowledge transfer (KT), technology transfer (TT) and skills transfer (ST) is not new, although the terminology may be. We need to believe that prowess in KT, TT and ST are the ingredients *sine qua non* for the society of the future. It is prowess which is invaluable and therefore highly saleable to governments, students, industries and to anyone else who wishes to make an effective contribution to our collective future.

As I said in my abstract: the data bases of knowledge, skills and technologies must be value-neutral and automatically accessible at the right price and by the informed enquirer. The custom and attitudes of academic freedom at this point are essential. Universities will therefore become the value-neutral information nodes or neurones, computer networked by satellite connections. Their role will be constantly to evaluate and repackage new knowledge by means of their research training programmes. Their intelligence status will depend on their research effectiveness in specific disciplines, and on their capacity to integrate new knowledge in fitness-for-purpose modes. Their incomes will be derived from the downloading of new skills and new technologies, mainly in the form of trained individuals.

These are the essential skills of knowledge transfer and technology transfer which of necessity will be university-based. The level of employment will then be directly dependent on the level of investment, public and private, in our universities.

DISCUSSION

(*Rapporteur:* Mr. B. J. SPENCER, Registrar, Macquarie University)

Dr. Hills' paper was followed by a lively discussion of his views of the 'essential cycle' of university research involving the acquisition and transfer of knowledge.

Dr. Hills' vision of the data bases of knowledge, skills and technologies as 'value neutral' was challenged as optimistic. It was suggested that the demands of industry were now a dominating influence on the transfer cycle. Dr. Hills responded by claiming that independence is the primary factor which attracts academics to work in universities. A commitment to independence reinforces their 'value neutral' role. However the major problem faced by university staff is not the undue influence of industry but the failure of government to fulfil its social contract to support research. Dr. Hills confirmed his optimism and declared his preparedness to resist overtures from industry if he saw them leading in undesirable directions.

SUB-TOPIC 6(A): EFFECTS ON EMPLOYMENT

Questioned further about the notion of a 'value-neutral' role, Dr. Hills said it raised the question of the essential purpose of a university which was not simply limited to the function of technology transfer. He emphasized that his description of the cycle of technology and knowledge transfer was not a model which may suit all universities. In addition, successful handling of the transfer process may have no implications for a university's approach to undergraduate teaching. An essential element of the model is for the university to be in command of its own destiny.

Dr. Hills had asserted that knowledge now has a very short 'shelf life', but he acknowledged that this view did not have universal application. Clearly much knowledge is of enduring value. But universities must be conscious of their responsibility to contribute useful information and to provide solutions to contemporary economic problems on both local and national scales.

The capacity to advise and to stimulate confidence in the future will certainly involve recourse to shared information. However, today's skill is not to carry knowledge, much of which may be of limited utility, but to be able to access needed information.

In Britain, as in other countries, government is espousing the notion of an 'enterprise culture'. Universities had responded by attempting to be enterprising, for example, through company formation and the establishment of incubation centres. These activities are important not only as a means of raising revenue but by creating a feeling of usefulness which staff and students found attractive. However participation in these activities would always remain on a voluntary basis.

It was suggested that the important responsibility of universities to produce leaders should not be overlooked. Unless universities take care to train 'leaders of technology' (as they have done traditionally for the professions) there was a concern that the self-degenerative approaches of industry could have a deadening effect on universities which, in turn, risked becoming the vehicles of industrial decline. Dr. Hills expressed confidence in the capacity of universities to guard their own future. There was a need to refresh industrial effort through the introduction of new industries. While there is a sense of excitement in working on the threshold of knowledge in the pure sense, there is a need to identify an appropriate mix of research effort.

Reference was made to the impact of the cycle of research and technology transfer which Dr. Hills had described on the level of unemployment. The cycle is based on knowledge and skills acquisition and inevitably there would remain a substantial pool of people who could not take part in the cycle. Dr. Hills acknowledged that the process of high technology acquisition and transfer does not create jobs. Instead it creates wealth and wealth creates new service industries. High technology industries are engaged essentially in labour unintensive activities.

A question was raised about possible mechanisms to involve developing nations in technological change. Two possibilities were mentioned. First, a process by which untrained populations might be excluded from developmental activities and, secondly, the relocation of capable people in a

TOPIC 6: SOCIAL IMPACT OF TECHNOLOGY

number of world zones which would concentrate on high technology development. If such changes were to occur it was likely that very little high technology development would be located in the southern hemisphere. One outcome might be the emergence of discrimination based on intelligence rather than on colour. In response to these views Dr. Hills acknowledged that barriers to investment and to human mobility were barriers to development. But these are political questions which are not likely to be resolved within universities.

Sub-Topic 6(b)

THE ROLE OF THE UNIVERSITIES IN UNDERSTANDING THE IMPACT OF SOCIETY UPON TECHNOLOGY

Tuesday, 9 February

Professor K. B. DICKSON (*Vice-Chancellor University of Cape Coast*):

THE ROLE OF UNIVERSITIES IN PROMOTING UNDERSTANDING OF THE IMPACT OF SOCIETY ON TECHNOLOGY

Introduction

It is usual to speak of the impact of technology on society, and for good reason. Perceptions, mental attitudes, space relations, histories of societies, have been known to change drastically under the influence of technological change. Societies in western Europe were never the same during and after the industrial revolution. In Africa the persistent infiltration of the Bantu from their original homeland in the Cameroons area eastward and southward since about the fifth or sixth century A.D. cannot be understood except with reference to the development of an iron technology which resulted in the development of a terrible weapon, the iron spear, as well as the development of more effective agricultural tools, especially the hoe, which increased the possibility of bringing larger areas of land under cultivation. Today, if there is this stark and frightening contrast between the more developed and the less developed countries of the world—a contrast that is frightening because of its implications for global power politics—it is basically attributable to the differences in the rates and levels of technological development.

Technology and Technique

All this is rather obvious. But it also makes a great deal of sense to think in terms of impact of society on technology; it is arguable that this way of looking at the matter may even be more relevant for countries of the less developed world. This viewpoint is based on definition of the concept 'technology'. I define technology as an integrated set of techniques pertaining to modes of living and mediating between society and environment, with the latter including everything that impinges on the life of society. Technology represents the sum total of what society knows how to do; it is part of society's total culture. Thus, as far as I am concerned, the term technology is meaningless except in the context of a cultural assumption.

By contrast is the term 'technique' which refers to a prescribed way of doing a particular thing or of handling a particular situation. In the simplest sense technique points to the use of a tool or to the application of a method. From the viewpoint of the thing or the situation to be handled, a technique may be judged to be efficient or effective or otherwise. In the case of technology it may be judged to be alien or 'belonging', to be a superimposition or assimilated and part of the local cultural matrix.

A technique of foreign origin must be suitably 'interpreted' for it to become a part of local technology; and the interpretation may well result in the technique being applied in ways which its inventor never dreamt of. In the early years of this century the Public Works Department in the Gold Coast (now Ghana) introduced the wheelbarrow for road works. It was recognised as a means of conveyance, except that after being loaded it was carried on the head and taken that way to the work site. This was understandable: head porterage was the general mode of transportation of men and goods in the country. The British colonial administration, in its turn, realizing that techniques familiar to them and imported from home were apt to be 'reinterpreted', set about inventing techniques that they thought were suitably adapted to the local cultural situation. It was recognised that boots were needed in the Gold Coast by public road construction workers, and the colonial administration decided that it would be much more suitable to paint the soles of the workers' feet with a thick coating of coal tar, the argument being that coal tar would afford excellent protection for the feet while also being a good antiseptic. This mode of protecting the feet certainly was not, and could not become, part of the local technology. It was soon rejected!

SUB-TOPIC 6(B): SOCIETY'S IMPACT [*Dickson*]

Society and Technology

It should now be easy to see why there is everything to be said for paying as much attention to impact of society on technology as to impact of technology on society. A brief clarification is necessary of what is meant here by the notion of impact of society on technology. The use of the word impact, whether of technology on society or the other way round, must be seen as connoting the idea of change in society or technology. There would not be much point in studying the interrelations of society and technology if the idea of change in one or the other was not implicit, unless one would be content with establishing correlations between access to superior techniques, and therefore to natural resources, and social structure or organization, as has been done for example in the case of the so-called hydraulic civilizations.

There are two ways of looking at the question of impact of society on technology. One, the more common, is to assume the inevitability of technological change and consider how society can make sure that whatever changes are occurring in technology will be for the better and not prove to be destructive and thus ultimately to the detriment of society. This way of looking at the matter may seem illogical, if one granted the definition of technology given earlier; but it is valid in so far as it recognises the fact that major changes in a host of major techniques, which come to add up to technological change, are usually brought about by a minority within a society, and that the rest of society may then become concerned over the direction of technological change and seek to discourage it or to have it re-oriented.

The other way of looking at the question is to see society in a much more positive, decision-making and initiatory role in the matter of technological change. This has the support of history. Technological change then becomes a deliberate, conscious act by society and is usually in the name of accelerated development. Countries of the less developed world are understandably attracted to this way of looking at the question of the impact of society on technology.

For society to be able to initiate or encourage technological change in the desired direction, at least four conditions must be fulfilled:

(i) society must have the right sort of leadership, one that is totally committed to society's general welfare and not to its own selfish and parasitic interest;

(ii) society as a whole must become conscious of the need for technological change;

(iii) it must be made fully aware of the implications for its structure and organization of the technological change; finally

(iv) society must deliberately encourage innovation from within, a process that need not exclude deliberate borrowing of techniques from elsewhere and their adaptation or 're-interpretation' for purposes of making them culturally assimilable and thus capable of being developed and managed locally.

The relevance of these prerequisites is fully illustrated by experience with the development of the palm oil manufacturing industry in Ghana, which is the most important rural *manufacturing* activity in the southern half of the country. It is also illustrated by the attempts to propagate large-scale commercial farming throughout the country. Both illustrations are essentially of a major ailment which faces Ghana, as well as similar countries, as it seeks to leap-frog into the twenty-first century, namely, the technique-, worse still, technology-importation syndrome, and how it is now realized that technological development must be by a people and not for a people by someone else.

Role of the University

The preceding points to certain challenges which universities, especially those in the less developed countries of the world, cannot but accept. But first of all universities must themselves reappraise their nature and function. For less developed countries universities are imported 'technologies', and there is the assumption, certainly in much of tropical Africa, that there is a clearly defined university tradition that ought to be followed. This assumption is unwarranted; it tends to have a stultifying effect. The point cannot be made too strongly that what is believed to be university culture or tradition cannot be anything but an abstraction from the experiences of universities throughout the world, more accurately of the older universities in Europe which have been in business for over half a millenium, and of the much younger but powerful ones in North America. This culture or tradition cannot be considered to be fixed and compelling. If they were there could not have been such exciting changes in the role of universities in development in the United States of America after 1862 or in India since about the early 1960s.

It is legitimate to expect universities in at least tropical Africa, where they have almost all been created and are still maintained by government or society, to be an important component of the cutting edge of the development process. In the crucial matter of promoting understanding of the impact of society on technology, the universities must be sure to undertake at least the following.

First, universities in developing countries especially should make it their business to take an inventory of present, known techniques relating to the major aspects of living. Although it is desirable to have such an inventory for its own sake, the paramount objective should be that of researching into ways of making these known techniques more efficient and effective. In this effort society will necessarily be involved not only in the matter of identifying techniques for purposes of an inventory but also in the process of testing and validating research results.

Second, the universities could work directly with tradesmen and artisans in the so-called informal industrial sector. Such tradesmen, artisans, etc., constitute, in Ghana, about 95% of the total number of persons who are classed as working in manufacturing industry. Every household in Ghana relies far more on the skills of such persons than on those of formally educated technicians in the formal manufacturing industrial sector. The role of the universities with regard to these 'technicians' in the informal industrial sector could very usefully be that of helping the latter to acquire scientific explanation of the operations that they undertake and that they would have learnt by imitation.

Third, as an extension of the second point, universities could launch a deliberate programme of working with communities, especially rural in the case of less developed countries, on the management of improved techniques of making a living. There should not be the need to elaborate this point. Fourth, universities in less developed countries of the world would do well to be involved in adult education, not just literacy, programmes, a major part of whose objective should be that of drawing attention to and explaining the possible role of society in effecting technological change.

Finally, universities should be in regular and serious dialogue with government over the issue of the nature, objective and mode of technological innovation. The universities should encourage government to work towards a policy of technological innovation, certainly in countries of the less developed world. This need not evoke the spectre of university's academic activities being forced into a straightjacket.

In making these suggestions I am fully aware of the fact that some may think that some of the activities named are best left to polytechnics and the like, and that they are, strictly speaking, not the business of a university. In reaction I would refer to my earlier remarks on university tradition or culture, so called. A university represents a level, the highest in an institutionalized sense, of academic and intellectual endeavour, and whatever is identified by society as being crucial to its progress—with due regard to the issue of ethics—should be researched and advanced to the highest possible level and propagated. This means that universities must also recognise the possible impact on themselves of this attitude and make suitable adjustments to their academic priorities, and especially to the criteria for professional advancement of their staff.

Conclusion

The issue of impact of society on technology is one of extraordinary importance and not simply of academic interest. It is in the interest of the less developed countries of the world to consider seriously the question of impact of society on technology, in the sense of how society may have a determinative effect on technology. In this endeavour the universities in the less developed countries have a special role to play, for obvious reasons, and in working out modalities the universities should in no way feel constrained by tradition. They should feel free to innovate, both in their external and internal functioning.

DISCUSSION

(*Rapporteur*: Mr. D. W. J. MORRELL, Registrar and Secretary, University of Strathclyde)

The Topic Chairman (Dr. J. Downey) drew attention to two arresting notions: (*a*) that the universities themselves are alien technologies, and (*b*) that the priority should be for appropriate technology rather than high technology.

Two speakers questioned the mechanism and the priority in choosing research emphases. Professor Dickson made it clear that his emphasis upon appropriate technology was an institutional emphasis and that it by no means excluded high technology work by individuals within the appropriate international context.

A speaker from a small university in a small country expressed fear that the social emphasis in research might lead on to greater government expectation and domination. Professor Dickson said that, while the dangers could be seen, given the Ghanaian context, in which the university representatives sat with government representatives on a national council to determine priorities, he would have no fears.

A speaker from Zambia drew attention to the tendency of governments in developing countries to import consultants without reference to local

SUB-TOPIC 6(B): SOCIETY'S IMPACT

expertise. This led to mention of other problems, such as the prohibitive cost of maintaining highly sophisticated equipment, and to Professor Dickson re-emphasizing the need for developing countries to build on their own techniques, from the original inventory, and to provide thereby the infrastructure for secure research development.

Speakers from industrialized countries drew attention to the co-existence of many levels of technology. Japan, having built up a sound base of technological industry, was now believed to be spending much more on basic research to provide for the longer term. It was suggested that technology transfer was naturally slow and needed to be market driven, with developing countries being prepared to leap-frog stages in the earlier history of technological development. Professor Dickson accepted that technology must be borrowed but emphasized that it must also be appropriately re-interpreted to local conditions, with an eye to the dangers of becoming dependent upon external agency.

Two other speakers drew attention to the importance of the appropriateness of technology in the industrialized countries, where all levels of technology were to be found but high technology solutions were sometimes applied inappropriately. Appropriate did not necessarily mean simple. There are many small industries, started by enterprising individuals without much knowledge, which have a critical need for the input of appropriate technology at the appropriate stage. Indeed perhaps it could be said that in some industries 'invention had become the mother of necessity' because of market needs as the outlet for new technology.

A last speaker reminded the group that advice and technology were not the main products. The education of bright people in a way appropriate to their social and technological environment was the most important product of universities. This point was highlighted by final comments upon the inadequate research base of many management schools today and upon the graduates who, although highly acceptable to professional colleagues, could prove to be less than useful in the context of their own every-day society.

Professor Dickson accepted the importance of the production of people who think, who are independent and pursue excellence. But the university was not simply responsible for producing gentlemen; the graduates must be people who are aware of the local environment and have a sense of social responsibility. The universities must communicate more effectively to society their capacity and desire to be useful through explaining technology, starting from what is already known.

[Turner] TOPIC 6: SOCIAL IMPACT OF TECHNOLOGY

Professor R. S. Turner (*Department of History, University of New Brunswick*):

THE ROLE OF UNIVERSITIES IN UNDERSTANDING THE IMPACT OF TECHNOLOGY ON SOCIETY

'The Role of Universities in Understanding the Impact of Society on Technology': the very title of this session is an incongruity. It jars against our conventional perception of 'society' as the passive object of technological change. While most observers disclaim hard theories of technological determinism today, we nevertheless persistently cast 'technology' into the role of independent variable in the complex equation between technological and social change. We commonly equate technological change to rationalization in general, and we frequently espy behind that change an autonomous logic of technological development. So acute an observer as historian Robert L. Heilbroner spoke of technological advances arising 'not by chance but . . . as the next stage in a technological conquest of nature that follows one and only one grand avenue of advance'.[1] Indeed, one might go further and see this implicit acceptance of the large-scale autonomy of technological development as one of the most wide-spread ideologies of our times. It cuts across all the spectra which divide people in the world today: socialists and free-marketeers, realists and romantics, citizens of developed and developing nations.

During the last 15 years, however, a strong new literature has emerged which provides empirical evidence for a very different vision of technology. This literature consists mostly of closely-detailed case studies of technological innovations and the circumstances which give rise to them, and it reveals the processes of technological change and innovation to be far more contingent, more varied, and more unpredictable than conventional wisdom has suggested. These studies indicate that technology is powerfully shaped by contingent social forces, the action of which we retrospectively—and often falsely—attribute to an underlying technological rationality.[2]

This new literature analyses the role of social contingencies in the action of some of the specific forces which *do* direct the course of technological development. Chief among these, at least for the twentieth century, is the role of *science*. Our common belief that science shapes technology usually carries with it the assumption that science is an on-going exploration of objective reality unaffected, except in matters of rate and direction, by the society in which it is conducted. This view, however, has been widely challenged by various new studies which argue for the social shaping of the very content of science itself. They suggest as well that the process by which new technology 'grows out of' new science is little understood. It may be as accurate to claim that science 'grows out of technology', since scientific reasoning consists so exclusively of chains of assumptions and results based upon complex instrumentation.

A second answer to the question 'what shapes technology?' is that *technology* shapes technology. Nathan Rosenberg, among other writers, has emphasized the accretional nature of technological innovation, the importance of the learning curve, and the powerful influence of central technological models or 'paradigms' which come to dominate the direction of future development for long periods. Technology increasingly takes the form of *systems*, which once in place dictate and constrain the nature of future developments. Traditional analyses, however, often attribute the effects of this system of constraints to some inner logic of technological rationality, rather than seeing them as contingent products of prior choices made between formerly-available technological options.

Especially interesting have been recent studies on the economic determinants of technological change. To the considerable extent to which modern technology is deployed in competitive market systems, technological decisions are also economic decisions, addressed to the economic goals of reducing costs and increasing revenues. Again, in retrospect we often confuse economic rationality with an inherent technological rationality. In an intriguing recent study American historian Ruth Cowan has argued that the triumph of the electric refrigerator over its gas-powered rival followed primarily from the heavy capitalization and aggressive marketing techniques available to the General Electric Corporation, rather than from any intrinsic superiority or promise of electric over gas design. In its initial commitment to the electric refrigerator GE was explicitly seeking a design which would maximize profits accruing to electrical utilities, one of its major customers. Even the economic rationality underlying the technological choice, Cowan suggests, was an economic rationality relevant to a single firm operating within an oligopolistic market.

To what extent do the economic pressures underlying technological choice reflect larger, ostensibly non-economic forces? Joseph Schumpeter was the first to argue that important aspects of innovation go beyond, and cannot be explained in terms of, rational economic calculation. More recent studies of innovation and diffusion have been addressed to the question of whether these processes can empirically be shown to conform to neo-classical assumptions, and a lively and still inconclusive debate is taking place.[3] All parties agree that the growing dependence of many enterprises on complex technologies with short performance track records and long lead-times for development has sharpened the uncertainty about future costs and future markets and enhanced the importance of accurate prediction and long-term planning. Some claim that these technological imperatives have invalidated neo-classical assumptions about the behaviour of firms.

In economic systems less directly constrained by market forces, the calculation of economic rationality and its subsequent impact on technological deployment reflect social and political realities much more directly. Amit Bhaduri has argued in a controversial work that landowners in eastern India found it rational to resist technological innovation which would increase peasant agricultural productivity. Although such innovation would increase their revenue from crop-shares, it would indirectly alter the power relationships between landlord and peasant farmer and reduce the landlords' traditional income from usury and the debt-bondage of peasants. Other recent studies have shown that the reward-system to Soviet managers works to discourage certain forms of technological innovation in production but encourage other forms. Even where good approximations to classical markets prevail, different societies experience radically different factor-costs, which in turn can lead to very different patterns of technological change. H. J. Habakkuk has argued that the sharp divergence of American and British production technologies during the nineteenth century had its roots in the availability, and hence cost, of skilled labour in these two economies.

Using quasi-Marxist assumptions, several recent studies have examined the ostensible role of technological innovation as a vehicle for reducing labour costs. David Noble in his study of machine tool automation has argued that the choice of technologies in this field was dictated by management's wish to minimize or eliminate worker control on the shop floor, and not by economic rationality *per se*, *i.e.* the desire to reduce costs. To Noble, and historians writing in similar veins, considerations of economic rationality, and the technological imperatives which ostensibly flow from it, can never be wholly separated from the issue of power relationships in the production process.

The final answer to the question 'What shapes technology?' is that *the state* shapes technology, and this often in more far-reaching ways than through explicit policy. Historians have traced the

'American system' of mass production and the technologies of interchangeable parts to their roots in government arsenals and small-arms contract-manufacture in the middle nineteenth century; the organizational and managerial techniques which later informed industry in the age of mass production have been traced down relentlessly to their theoretical origins in the military academies of the nineteenth century. Students of weapons-systems development in the contemporary world increasingly cast their analyses into a *bureaucratic politics* model. Here competition between organizations rather than scientific advances, technological rationality, or policy challenge and response, is explicitly identified as the leading causal agent in the changing technology of modern weaponry.

My object here is neither to review the new literature on the social studies of technology nor to discuss its specific (and sometimes controversial) findings. My object is rather to emphasize how radically new is the vision of technological change embodied in this scattered, still little-systematized body of literature. It is a vision of a technology profoundly affected by contingent social forces, in which traditional attribution to an inherent technological rationale is shown to reflect either ideological assumptions or an ignorance of underlying social determinants. I predict that when this literature is better systematized and more widely diffused it will produce sweeping changes in both popular and scholarly perceptions of the relationship between technology and society. It will, I believe, make feasible more intelligent national policies for the promotion of science and technology, wiser choices concerning the directions of technological change, and a new sense of understanding and control over this most powerful of all the forces which shape our lives.

What role must universities assume in the unfolding of this important new vision of the relationship between technology and society? The question has already been answered. The hard empirical research illuminating this relationship has overwhelmingly been done by university scholars, working in the traditional disciplines of history, economics, sociology, political science, and increasingly in new interdisciplinary programmes for the social study of science and technology. As such it points an old moral. The business of universities is not just research, but *critical* research, research that relentlessly examines the starting points of what we think we know. Universities, like individuals, find it hard to do this, and the research embodying such attempts is likely to appear to us as eccentric, perverse, peripheral, and sometimes subversive. Often it is.

This consideration leads directly to another, harder moral. To the extent that it has been done within set disciplinary frameworks at all, the research into the social determinants of technology which I have been discussing has often lain at the periphery of the disciplinary interests. Scholars who have pursued it have run the risk of intellectual and institutional marginality. The courses in which the findings of this research are communicated to students fit peripherally or not at all into established programmes of study. This is perhaps doubly true for the activities of the new interdisciplinary programmes, which have increasingly taken on the role of synthesizing and communicating the findings of research in technology studies.

In an emerging era of budget constraints and academic conservatism, the areas of research and teaching most immediately affected will be those existing precariously in the hinterland between the citadels of established disciplines. Within those citadels the affected areas will be those ostensibly most peripheral to the central commitments and interests of the discipline. But, as the emerging revision of our conception of the impact of society on technology attests, it is precisely in research areas of this kind that the most original and the most powerful challenges to our traditional beliefs are to be found. It is precisely these areas that must be pursued and encouraged if our universities are to play their high critical function.

In his autobiography, the famous pianist-accompanist Gerald Moore relates the story of an irate fellow accompanist who, at the interval of a concert, confronted a soprano who had persisted in singing slightly off key. 'Madam', he protested, 'I have tried playing for you on the white notes, I have tried playing for you on the black notes, but I simply cannot play in the cracks'. We as university administrators and professors are not so fortunate. If our universities are to perform their high critical function we *must* play in the cracks. We must pursue and encourage areas of research which lie in the interstices of the established disciplines and upon their periphery. New and valuable perspectives on the impact of society upon technology are but some of the insights which can be expected to flow from that commitment.

REFERENCES

1. Robert L. Heilbroner: 'Do Machines Make History?' *Technology and Culture*, *8*, (July 1967), 335–345.

2. This discussion draws heavily upon Donald MacKenzie and Judy Wajcman, eds.: *The Social Shaping of Technology. How the Refrigerator Got Its Hum* (Philadelphia: Open University Press, 1985), especially pp. 2–24,

SUB-TOPIC 6(B): SOCIETY'S IMPACT

68–74. Their fine bibliography (pp. 308–322) references all the works cited here and many other relevant items.

3. Nathan Rosenberg: *Inside the Black Box: Technology and Economics* (Cambridge: Cambridge University Press, 1982), pp. 3–33.

DISCUSSION

(*Rapporteur*: Mr. D. W. J. MORRELL, Registrar and Secretary, University of Strathclyde)

The first speaker was intrigued by the notion of a range of factors affecting technological change and asked for further comment. In response Professor Turner questioned the assumption that current technological change was vastly faster in rate or greater in impact than before. Toffler had suggested that today's shock was much gentler than that of the industrial revolution. It was therefore interesting to question our current preoccupation with technological change and it might be asserted that the need for change was conceived as a concept rather than driven by named factors.

The technology of innovation is now conscious and promotes change in itself. The level of wealth has allowed the concept of economic obsolescence, rapid substitution of new models is possible. The universities are playing a part in these factors promoting a faster rate of change. Technological universities developed spontaneously in a number of countries early in the nineteenth century, often reponding to the need felt in developing countries today to explain to those who know how to do things why their methods are correct—to back practice with theory.

Another speaker was interested in the suggestion that technology promoted scientific progress. Many able scientists employed in very applied jobs during the war brought feedback from technology to science when the war ended. Primitive laboratory equipment began to be replaced by industrially produced sophisticated instrumentation. Society can react quickly to technological disasters, insisting upon new research being funded in particular instances. However industry is often not very responsive to the results of research. It is usually our own graduates, employed in industry, who give us this response. Where have we gone wrong?

Another speaker referred again to the impact of war upon technology. In his view this impact had been underestimated. He explained how the invention of penicillin led to a large new industry concerned with big-scale fermentation technology. Radar and its war-time success had led to a bias in favour of investment in research in big science after the war. Attention was drawn to the vast increase in research funding by the U.S. in the war-time period. The current analogy was 'star wars' research.

TOPIC 6: SOCIAL IMPACT OF TECHNOLOGY

Multinational competition in research and development might be considered as the successor to war in the stimulation of technological change. However if this was so it was likely to be planned and stimulated on the short-term basis which was normal in industry, and this short-term view was affecting government attitudes and government-funded research also.

The notion of competition promoted thoughts on the ownership of new knowledge. It was suggested that the pace of change made ownership less relevant. What mattered more was the capacity to innovate which provided a state with technological sovereignty, or at least the minimum capacity to maintain its place in the world economy.

It was noted that social and government pressures had encouraged the European Economic Community to maintain an independence from the US and the USSR, to develop its own space research programme.

A final speaker invited Professor Turner to 'unpack' his ideas further and build on the interpretations he had made. He explained that the research was continuing. He doubted whether the social study of technology would assist directly with future planning but expressed the belief that it would bring some reality and demystification to the background thinking.

Sub-Topic 6(c)

THE ROLE OF UNIVERSITIES IN UNDERSTANDING THE IMPACT OF TECHNOLOGY UPON EDUCATION AND TRAINING

Thursday, 9 February

Professor K. R. McKinnon *(Vice-Chancellor, University of Wollongong)*

THE EDUCATION AND TRAINING ROLE OF UNIVERSITIES IN CONTRIBUTING TO AN UNDERSTANDING OF THE SOCIAL IMPACT OF TECHNOLOGY*

The Setting

Within the framework of world-wide change, often characterized as the transition from industrial to post-industrial society, the basis of the Australian economy and the characteristics of its region are undergoing profound change. As in other countries, major social, economic and technological changes are affecting Australia with increasing intensity. Some features of the picture of change are:
- increasing integration of the world economy, yet concurrently a tendency for competitive fragmentation between nation states;
- the central role of information and communications technology as an agent for social change, as a means of integration and as a national resource of increasing value;
- the erosion of national powers to restrict flows of information—whether representing communication or money—as they move across national borders;

*I am pleased to acknowledge the assistance of Associate Professor J. Falk of the Department of Science and Technology Studies, University of Wollongong, in the preparation of this paper.

- the growth of importance of trans-national organizations such as the International Monetary Fund;
- the prominence of structural unemployment, especially in advanced industrial countries as their economies increasingly reshape in a direction made possible by sophisticated automation technology;
- the growth of importance of service industries;
- the impending decline of the office or factory as the place of work;
- the fragmentation and shortening of the working life; and
- the sheer rapidity of technological and institutional change made possible by global economic and technological reorganisation.

Within this broader picture Australia's role is changing with:
- the decline of its agricultural sector;
- the desperate search for economic initiatives within which to gain comparative advantage;
- the increasing economic importance of the Pacific combined with the increasingly vigorous presence of and competition from newly industrialized countries such as Taiwan and Korea;
- the increasing importance of knowledge-led industry, services and innovation to Australian competitiveness; and
- the consequent increasing importance of education and information as economic resources.

Governments everywhere, including Australia, are responding in two ways. On the one hand they are putting universities under scrutiny as to both their mission and their internal efficiency. On the other hand they are realizing that universities are a precious resource and are seeking to enlist them in the service of national objectives.

If universities are perceived to be irrelevant to national needs they may well suffer, with governments neglecting them and initiating other institutions which will do what governments see as necessary. Alternatively, if universities merely react supinely in deterministic ways, as if change always will be unmanageable and as if their role necessarily will be to react, they will not be playing a worth-while role. They do have a choice; they certainly can play an important role, becoming a resource for change, and a means of facilitating change which meets social needs and values.

Coping with Technology

Universities need to provide leadership in technological literacy, social literacy and perspective. Coping with technological change requires an ability for individuals to acquire relevant technological skills, to understand macroscopic trends enough to initiate change successfully (in their own lives or in the management of social institutions) and to comprehend the bigger picture of the implications of individual and institutional actions.

Technological literacy envisages the capacity to take advantage of one's personal options, requiring technological skills such as high-level numeracy, ability to communicate technical ideas and practice in learning in new technical areas, as well as the flexibility to 'unlearn' obsolete skills.

Social literacy involves effective use of such skills as working together, the building of coalitions for political action, and the capacity to resolve conflict, because technological change involves restructured living and working conditions which are unlikely to be achieved without the effective application of such skills. At a time when technological competition has been raised to become a central focus, it is easy to lose sight of the importance of these skills, as well as the ultimate subservience of technological advance to human needs.

Universities have a special responsibility to foster perspective, the capability within students of seeing how and in what direction society and the quality of life are moving, and how their skills and actions in particular disciplines relate to that development. Maintaining the 'big picture' in a time of increasing specialization, complexity and 'data overload' is a fundamental educational objective without which students will be left uncomprehending and incapable of full participation as citizens in shaping their own society.

Educational Implications

The implications are for action to achieve better combinations of specific expertise and broader literacy, achieved best possibly by lengthening undergraduate courses but in part at least by building broader social perspectives into training for particular technological disciplines—and the reverse. The concept of a liberal education is far from dead; rather a new version of it is needed, one which envisages competent professionals with sufficient insight, adaptability and vision to cope with social and technological change.

Rather than simply attempting to provide uniform training throughout the university, it may well be most effective to build the bridges from within disciplines to broader perspectives, *i.e.* to develop a liberal understanding through the technical and social expertise which is developed in tackling the problems of discipline.

For example, the modern engineer now often works as a planner, an executive, a communicator, and/or a political lobbyist, rather than solely as a technically capable person. As we move further into the future, and as industrial production depends increasingly on a growing information sector, the broader social understanding aspect of the engineer's role is likely to increase. Yet the current training of engineers is deficient in preparation for these roles. Engineer educators apparently still believe that all of the available time is needed for the technological content of the curriculum. The same is true of medical and legal education, to name but two others. New hybrid course combinations such as science-law and commerce-law, which are beginning to emerge, comprise one type of response to the new needs of technological change.

Do the new needs require a longer period of tertiary training? They may well, as is already evident in the new course combinations. More generally, it is possible that at the very time that working life is being shortened, owing to technological change, the educational period of life should be lengthened. Alternatively, as demands will change over a working lifetime, paid provision for periodic return to university to acquire new specialist skills and broader perspectives may be necessary. The problem cannot conveniently be postponed by pretending such needs can be covered by voluntary and sporadic continuing education.

Never has there been a better time than now to institute a process of reconsideration of the content and approach to professional training, whether in engineering, medicine, architecture or law, and to consider at the same time the relationship of initial courses to continuing and postgraduate education.

Changes in Universities

University education must be reshaped to fit a world in which demands on individuals and nations may change rapidly. Particular skills may need to be learned and 'unlearned' several times during a person's life. The basic preparation should fit people for periodic return to acquire new specialist skills. How will university staff themselves keep up to date with advances in methodology and technique, especially since the quarter from which these advances might come in future will not necessarily be other universities exclusively? University researchers also will have to accept the need to update frequently in skills and knowledge; they may not be able to learn all they need on the job and may need to retrain via advanced courses. The university will need, for its part, to support them in such activities. Such retraining may be offered in other universities but it is equally likely to come through joint university-industry or university-government co-operation. The presumption that the most advanced research work always will be found in universities is now obviously not universally correct.

Not only has knowledge in particular discipline areas increased quickly, but also the divisions between disciplines have eroded to such an extent that professions often need an extremely broad range of skills. Some analysts claim that the new skills required are so fusing of old, separate disciplines that there really are new disciplines; 'mectronics', for instance, fusing mechanical engineering and electronics. Whether or not these are really new disciplines, it is undeniable that technologies are converging and that the pervasive effect of some types of discoveries are posing problems of keeping abreast of new knowledge, let alone contributing positively to it. There are related organizational challenges. One is to devise academic structures which are open enough to encourage cross-disciplinary scholarship and research, and yet sharp enough to give academics a sense of belonging to a coherent social group.

Postgraduate training arrangements will be transformed. In team settings, teams comprising postgraduate students and staff of varying disciplinary backgrounds, it will be possible to escape the limits which training in individual disciplines sometimes imposes, thereby developing research activity which meets emerging technological and social needs. More varied postgraduate opportunities, including variations ranging from short intensive courses, through modular courses taken one module at a time for an eventual award, to a more varied range of full-time doctoral-level degree programmes, may have to be developed. In any case the recently published Green Paper, which threatens to cut off finance for research from some departments, will no doubt hasten the development of postgraduate schools which cross disciplinary boundaries.

Research Implications

One central implication of the increasing integration, size and global reach of enterprises, and the increasing emphasis on knowledge as an economic resource, is an erosion of the distinction between 'pure', 'basic' and 'strategic' research. In a world where research is not only crucial, but the dynamics of bringing it from conceptual to finally marketed form determines its competitiveness, the usefulness of research not envisaging at least some applications ultimately will be increasingly challenged.

Awareness is increasing that the assumed boundary between fundamental and applied research, in areas such as genetic engineering and information technology, is neither real nor helpful. Modern research in these areas is often possible only as a co-operative endeavour, involving many researchers organized in a series of groups and involving substantial co-operation between different types of institutions (including universities but also a host of industrial and other organizations). It also involves co-operation between those responsible for the product and those at the more theoretical end of the spectrum, since solutions to user problems may involve high value-added intellectual effort.

In short, the establishment required for research and development will increasingly be seen as an integrated system in which universities are a crucial co-operating component. If universities are to be seen to succeed in this new world they must at the minimum be capable of fully understanding and planning their role in the continuum of pure-applied-product-oriented research. Irrespective of preferences for pure research and the continuing value of that research, there will be an increasing need for universities to study and rethink their role in a 'research system' which is seen to produce competitive benefits for the nation.

National Research and Development

Despite considerable current rhetoric to the contrary, national planning of research is likely to be needed more rather than less as we go further into the future. Major research planning in Japan (MITI and the Fifth Generation project), America (SDI), Europe (ESPRIT) and England (Alvey) is the order of the day, its urgency made greater by the clear benefits (*e.g.* Japan) of national co-operation. Universities have a role to play not merely in reacting to or exploiting a national research plan but also in assisting to form it. The formulation of national strategic initiatives and their management to bring about effective results in ways which satisfy political and intellectual values, is an important and novel task in which universities might well participate.

The Relevance of the Traditional University Role

All this having been said, it is crucial to note that there is also a need for universities to play a role in ensuring that not every social value is measured in terms of technological achievement and the relative place of the nation on a notional ladder of competitiveness. The traditional role of universities in examining philosophical and ethical questions, in critical analysis of the social order, and in fostering artistic expression, must be re-endorsed at the same time

SUB-TOPIC 6(c): EDUCATION AND TRAINING

as universities take on enhanced roles in orienting and training students for knowledge-based economic development.

Some philosophic questions cannot be handled within the scientific tradition and require examination of ethical and normative issues. Critical analyses of the social order must not only be retained but strengthened, in an atmosphere in which these achievements could easily be devalued. What we must all accept, I think, is that universities will have their opportunities to contribute in this traditional role curtailed unless they are seen to be succeeding in areas of national priority.

Neither a focus solely on the traditions of the past nor merely reacting to what is perceived to be changing demands on universities will be enough. In the end a more radical role must be carved out in which universities structure and reposition themselves thoughtfully enough to be able to play an effective role in the eyes of the communities which support them.

DISCUSSION

(*Rapporteur*: Mr. A. O. DE SOUSA, Academic Registrar, Curtin University of Technology)

A delegate from the UK inquired as to what sort of preparation there was in schools in Australia, particularly in areas of technological awareness. As a supplementary to this question he inquired whether teachers were being adequately prepared in this area. From his own observation in the UK much remained to be done. Professor McKinnon explained that each state in Australia determined its own educational system. In New South Wales an education department looks after the school system whereas a separate technical and further education authority looks after technical education. In that state cross-institutional structures were being developed whereby Higher School Certificate pupils could take school as well as technical (TAFE) subjects. In this way secondary students were being introduced to technological subjects. Other than this development, all states in Australia had introduced computer courses in schools, some with considerable investment in computers. Professor McKinnon's personal view was that much more needed to be done in the area of general technological preparation of teachers.

Another participant from Australia informed the group of the recent move by the commission on tertiary education in allowing universities to introduce bridging courses. This, together with the lengthening of degree programmes and increasing evidence of students slowing their pace of studies towards graduation by taking additional courses, all pointed to

TOPIC 6: SOCIAL IMPACT OF TECHNOLOGY

some of the responses to the era of technological change. He asked Professor McKinnon what he felt was the place of communication skills within the total educational package.

Professor McKinnon supported the observations from the delegate and explained that Australia had a long tradition of part-time students—students who not only chose to study less than full-time but who attended classes after working hours, bringing with them a wealth of relevant technological work experience. New degrees had recently been established in environmental sciences and in information sciences, in partnership with and with sponsorship from industry. Such programmes were designed in a co-operative education or sandwich mode. All these were examples of the sort of community responses to the technological era. He agreed wholeheartedly with the previous speaker on the importance of communication skills. In his experience he had come across a number of obstacles from those preparing students in professional courses. Such faculty have always felt that any space vacated in the curriculum could and should be filled with more technological knowledge courses, rather than imparting the sorts of perspectives he had outlined in his paper. Given this difficulty, he felt that students should be required to undertake the courses in literacy and critical analysis, not as part of the credit requirements but as a check list towards graduation.

One delegate from the UK sensed that the motivation for change in Australia was from the top handed down to universities, and asked for an elucidation on the planning process. Professor McKinnon explained that, so far as the national apparatus was concerned, a commission on tertiary education (CTEC) with advisory councils on universities, colleges and technical colleges has, up till now, had the responsibility of advising the Australian government on resources for higher education. When government made its decisions these were enshrined in legislation, known as 'states grants' legislation because technically these were grants to the states who in turn provided them to the universities. In this sense one could construe that planning was from the top down. More importantly the system developed within universities a 'dependence mentality'. Within universities Professor McKinnon identified a committee structure for the allocation of resources although a number of universities had efficient management structures. It was pointed out that new degree proposals and new initiatives of this kind were often planned at departmental level and moved upwards in the planning process. Some executive officers are in a position to provide seeding monies for such initiatives.

A faculty delegate from Ontario observed that he was no longer sure what computer literacy meant. He explained the experience of students buying and bringing with them their own computers; this in turn meant the need to provide terminal outlets. In his experience arts faculty students quickly acquired skills in the use of computers with access to a variety of software. As a teacher his task had become much more interesting in that he could return to and concentrate on the basics, conceptualizing the issues and concentrating on critical analysis and philosophies. Students had become proficient in numerical analysis, presentation of assignments

SUB-TOPIC 6(c): EDUCATION AND TRAINING

and structure. As a teacher, more attention could now be focused on output quality.

Professor McKinnon felt that Australia was just beginning to feel the same way about students. As a vice-chancellor the previous speaker had highlighted the need for people in his position to be (*a*) a *risk broker*, where decisions have to be made on the application of technological strategies, and (*b*) a *banker*, where initiatives such as these could be supported, cashed into, invested, and the returns from which could be used more wisely.

A delegate from New Brunswick asked Professor McKinnon to explain the multi-disciplinary developments in Australia. Professor McKinnon explained that at the University of Wollongong the department of science and technology studies was part of the faculty of arts. Faculty had expertise in the history of science, philosophy of science and in science, technology and public policy. The professor in the area eventually hived off with the establishment a centre for science and technology. From a budget of around $80,000 he had developed an operation of around $650,000 through very successful marketing. From a nucleus of government advisory functions the centre had become an important training ground which got industry and unions together.

A Ghanaian delegate observed that lengthening of courses could be an expensive way of addressing the problem. He wondered to what extent the problem was not embedded in existing structures of departments and units. Professor McKinnon agreed with the proposition that lengthening of courses was expensive but said that in Australia, until recently, there were no fees and charges to students. However extension of courses would probably be resisted by government as it is a cost to the community. To some extent the problem had been in the course schemes. In his experience he had had considerable difficulty in getting faculty to displace or replace technical subjects. On the other hand in some universities departments were interdisciplinary in themselves and therefore more capable of providing integrated curricula.

In answer to another question from a representative from Canada, Professor McKinnon admitted that faculties or colleges of education had not always been in the forefront in promoting computer literacy. Many of the initiatives had been undertaken by ministries of education who had outstripped the supply of adequate teachers.

In conclusion the chairman of the Topic group (Dr. J. Downey) stated that so much of the discussion on technological change depended on what happened in schools. The issue then became one of status of the teacher as an agent for social change and the status of the teacher in that society. Until society was able to attract to teacher education people of the highest quality, society would continue to be handicapped in the achievement of these goals.

Professor C. Ann Cameron (*Professor of Psychology, University of New Brunswick*): Because we cannot know in advance how new technology will affect education and training, the role of universities in understanding technological impacts—personal, social, or cultural—must be via their research enterprises. A programme of inquiry into such a question will require time and long-range perspectives; it needs to be absolutely independent of commercial interests; and it requires committed interdisciplinary efforts. Not only do universities have a unique stake in understanding the educational implications of technology, but they are ideally suited to the task because they are uniquely situated to provide these four requirements for such inquiry. Academics are knowledge generators as well as knowledge transmitters, especially about the learning process, and this generation of knowledge as well as its transmission is mediated by technological advances. Academic researchers are insulated from many social and economic pressures in order to engage in long-term research projects, and questions involving technological implications sometimes require lengthy time-frames. Academics are permitted to operate independently of proprietary interests. Further, the university environment can facilitate a collaborative context which is favourable to interdisciplinary work, and there seem few technology-education intersections which do not require interdisciplinary efforts for the full realization of these potentials. And finally we might bear in mind the fact that there are reciprocal influences between developments in education and developments in technology. Educational advances can stimulate technology just as technology can stimulate educational thinking.

Today's schools and training centres are nineteenth-century institutions designed to serve the interests of industrial society. We have been relatively successful in instituting mass educational techniques, and might be excused for being tempted to consider using technology to improve the efficiency of the present model. But current institutional structures may be a bad fit for an 'information' or 'knowledge society' of the twenty-first century—one in which individual learning would be both possible and desirable. We might see a knowledge society as one in which mass indoctrination and subject segregation are, although eminently feasible, quite inappropriate. Although we might sometimes perceive the urgency of the need to take charge of the events surrounding current rapid societal changes, it is the opinion of many careful observers (Plowright, forthcoming) that we have several decades to acquire the understanding which will allow us to make informed educational decisions regarding the implications of communications technology and education. Whereas the time-frames of business and government are constrained either by the competitor or the next election, universities have both the time and the appropriate context to do the necessary research. We need not only to look at technological changes themselves, but also—and perhaps more important—to continue to extend our understanding of the educational context into which they are being introduced, and beyond that at the implications of that introduction for individuals.

Although technology is value-neutral in itself it has the potential to alter in a transformative fashion the social structures into which it is introduced. Technology is transformative in that it seems to modulate both individual perspectives and organizational dynamics in rather unexpected ways. Computer networks, facsimile transmission and other telecommunications advances, for example, have modified our perceptions of time and distance.

Does mere rapid change in the techniques for the transmission of information or knowledge make for a revolution? Whether or not we call this kind of change revolutionary, it is clear that there has been in our lifetime a vast acceleration in communication possibilities. An upcoming report of the Science Council of Canada (Cordell, forthcoming) tells us that if we describe the last 50,000 years of human life on earth in lifetimes, we can call those 50,000 years about 800 lifetimes. Of those 800 lives, only the last 70 had truly effective means of communication, only the last 6 were likely to see a printed word, and the vast majority of technological advances which preoccupy us today were developed during the most recent lifetime. Their appropriate adaptations for education will take generations.

Our understanding of learning processes has increased significantly over the last 30 years, and this understanding has been generated by university scholars. At last we are recovering from the excessive simplicity of earlier attempts to understand the acquisition of knowledge. Furthermore, educators and cognitive scientists are at last talking to one another. The 'cognitive revolution' has had beneficial effects on all of social science. Reciprocally, the field of cognitive science has profited from the influence of anthropology, computer science, education, engineering, linguistics, psychology, sociology and more.

In the course of all this progress we have been reminded of the importance of procedural knowledge. Procedural knowledge is 'understanding how' as opposed to the 'understanding that' of declarative knowledge (Winograd, 1975). One might even suggest there is a traditional relationship between declarative knowledge and 'mass education' on the one hand, and procedural knowledge and 'individual learning' on the other. In any case, with the advent of a 'post-industrial' society, there is more need than ever to rethink the manner in which procedural and declarative knowledge are integrated, and the balance struck between them. One transformative aspect of information technology and its influence on education is the opportunity it offers to move procedural knowledge to the fore.

In 1980 Taylor explored potential education roles of computers—as 'tutors', as 'tutees' and as 'tools', asking whether these machines are best used as teachers, as receptive media to be manipulated, or simply as means to effect educational goals. We have seen in the last decade that while, in time, computer tutors and tutees might prove viable, those implementations have yet to demonstrate their value, and that the computer's most appropriate role is as a tool, as one means for achieving educational goals.

At the elementary education level the focus in the past has been on development of literacy and numeracy skills. This has perhaps been the case in part because of our assumptions regarding the difficulty of teaching the skills required, and in part owing to our lack of respect for the abilities of young children to benefit from a more cognitively rich educational approach. These assumptions are now under critical examination by researchers (for example, Siegler, 1986) and our explorations of early education are leading us to new perspectives (Brown, Bransford, Ferrara & Campione, 1983). At the secondary level, when children become even more challenging in their capacities for abstract thought, educational stimulation lags far behind young people's capacities. Now skill development is important at all levels, and it might certainly be enhanced by technological educational tools; but the gifted teacher is the one to effect the intelligent integration of declarative and procedural knowledge appropriate to an effective liberal education, which is critical to all disciplines and at all levels.

Likewise, at the post-secondary level, needs for specialization may sometimes be met by technological innovations, thus freeing teachers to do what they do best, that is, teach. Sometime in the future machines may teach, but now phenomenal societal demands on educators require superhuman educational responses, and we can only hope that technology will share some of the load. When we see technology capturing academic attention for its own sake, and if it makes inroads on true educational time, something is probably wrong. We learn by doing; and by using technology experimentally we understand its ramifications. It is a misdirection of energy to learn 'about' technology as, for instance, one usually does in a 'computer literacy' course.

SUB-TOPIC 6(c): EDUCATION AND TRAINING [Cameron]

I recently participated in a working group for the Centre for Educational Research and Innovation (CERI) of the Organization for Economic Co-operation and Development, in which we examined the potential of information technologies to offset our difficulties in conquering problems in basic education and learning. I learned a number of lessons from this two-year experience. First, we learn to write by writing, especially when that writing is supported by wise instructors who help us to write in a stimulating, functionally literate environment. For those tool-use proponents who see technology as helpful only when used functionally, there is an interesting convergence here. The most obvious new writing tool at our disposal is the simple word processor, and its utility is receiving productive exploration in many quarters (CERI, 1987). Thus technology becomes appropriate when it can support valid educational goals in an ecologically valid fashion. Indeed my own research suggests that there are children who might not otherwise write fluently who find writing with a word processor an enjoyable, productive experience (Cameron, 1986; Cameron, Hunt & Linton, 1987).

Theoretical and practical controversies emerged during the meetings of the working groups. Should reading be 'taught' 'bottom up' (with phonetic decoding skills stressed) or 'top-down' (with semantics, or the importance of making sense of a text, emphasized)? How much structure should be included in a mathematics curriculum using the programming language, Logo? And what is considered these days to be the value of 'discovery learning'? These debates focused attention on the importance of identifying educational goals and appropriate approaches before determining the tools that might contribute. The consensus of our final report was that technology, when functionally integrated into educational goals, can be a facilitator in the hands of a good teacher.

Another lesson learned was that non-proprietary considerations are at a premium in the field. Few participants are independent of commerical preferences or constraints. University researchers can have that freedom, if they choose. This seems a rare luxury, but I see it as an intellectual necessity.

The politics of the use of technology in education requires more than merely the identification of pedagogical goals; we often need to evaluate and adapt those goals. Our society's gatekeepers may want to ensure that technology reinforces old goals. Educational leaders and policy-makers may hope that technology will solve current implementation problems by reinforcing traditional values. Developers, like the policy-makers, seem to seek success by using technology to shore up hobbling systems and approaches. On the other hand, many implementers and researchers see technology as a vehicle for subversion of an old educational order. This motivation for introduction of technology in the classroom draws my sympathy, but those proponents of technological innovation who promote its use because they see it as an opportunity for change often have a very different understanding of appropriate goals from that of the developers and decision-makers. These discrepancies can result in confusion at least, and frequently they result in chaos.

It has been interesting to me to observe effects in the educational field similar to those which have been noted in office automation, with school principals acting like the much-reported defensive middle-management—not wanting to be seen to acquire 'keyboard skills' but not wanting to admit lack of involvement either. Why is it the case that educators hesitate to admit that they do not know the value of computers in education? Why do they not refuse to acquiesce to pressures to acquire educational technology until they have good evidence of its educational utility, or at least until they can find ways to engage in actively asking the important questions? Mastery of the knowledge base of our disciplines is crucial to critical and innovative educational decision-making. The entire educational community requires collaborative participation if it is to understand the changes that are pressing themselves upon us. And we have time to do this research. In the meantime, imagine the books that could be bought with the money allocated to microcomputer systems lying unused in so many schools today.

The research which needs doing will engage the full range of research strategies currently available, and then some. We must develop entirely new approaches as well as using tried and true techniques, and thus we need more interdisciplinary work than ever before. I worked on an interdisciplinary team for five years, as chair of a federal committee of the deputy minister of communications, investigating the social implications of information technology. We examined the nature of work and working. We read current research on issues of privacy in an information society. We explored technology issues affecting the young, the elderly, women and handicapped people. We commissioned research on equity of access to information in an 'information age'. We investigated concerns about the potential heterogenization of a multi-cultural society such as Canada. We explored the need for and viability of community data bases. To the chagrin of the then minister of communications we called for a national dialogue, for community participation in the decisions surrounding the introduction of information technology in Canadian society (Social Impacts Subcommittee, 1983).

Our committee consisted of government researchers, industrial players, independent consultants and academics. Our interdisciplinary roots were crucial to our success. The backgrounds of members included economics, education, sociology, home economics/family life studies, psychology, communications studies, computer science, physics and library science. The eclectic constitution of this team ensured that many perspectives were represented and that a full range of methods was considered. Again, academic research models are the appropriate venue because of their potential for interdisciplinary investigation and, furthermore, it is the academics who are free to explore even those options which are unpopular with government.

Universities are obvious community resources for the investigation of technology-education intersections, if they promote a balance between the generation of new knowledge and the transmission of the old; if they tolerate, even encourage, long views; if they protect independent inquiry; and if they kindle opportunities for interdisciplinary research. We need the contributions of scholars in all disciplines from the humanities to the applied sciences. While universities must maintain the right of scholars to pursue their own research questions, they must also seek ways to encourage their members to engage in this vital area of concern so that the old and the new will acquire a creative, balanced accommodation. Universities should not miss the opportunity to have an impact on technology, especially since technology will undoubtedly have its influence on universities. Surely we will want to have our say.

REFERENCES

Brown, A. L., Bransford, J. D., Ferrara, R. A. and Campione, J. C. (1983), in P. H. Mussen (ed.): *Handbook of child psychology*, vol. 3: *Cognitive development*. New York: Wiley.

Cameron, C. A. (1986): 'Children's writing and reasoning: Decontextualized representation using computers.' *CPA Section on Developmental Psychology Newsletter*, 5, 9–14.

Cameron, C. A., Hunt, A. K. and Linton, M. J. (1987): 'Some academic correlates of ambiguity detection in primary school children.' *Proceedings of the Biennial Meeting of the Society for Research in Child Development*, Baltimore, MD.

Centre for Educational Research and Innovation (1987): *Information technologies and basic learning: Reading, writing, science and mathematics*. Organization for Economic Co-operation and Development: Paris.

Cordell, A. C. (1985): *The uneasy eighties: The transition to an information society*. Science Council of Canada, Ottawa: Minister of Supply and Services.

Cordell, A. C. (forthcoming): *Information technology and Canadian society: Choices and tradeoffs*. Science Council of Canada.

Plowright, T. (forthcoming): *Social spaces in an information society*. Ottawa: Minister of Supply and Services.

Science Council of Canada (1982): *Planning now for an information society. Tomorrow is too late*. Ottawa: Minister of Supply and Services.

Siegler, R. S. (1986): *Children's thinking*. New York: Prentice-Hall.

Social Impacts Subcommittee (1983): *Information technology: A call for a national dialogue on the emerging information society*. Fredericton: University of New Brunswick.

Taylor, R. P. (ed.) (1980): *The computer in the school: Tutor, tool, tutee*. New York: Teachers College Press.

Winograd, T. (1975): 'Frame representations and the declarative procedural controversy', in D. G. Bobrow and A. Collins (eds.): *Representation and understanding: Studies in cognitive science*. New York: Academic Press.

DISCUSSION

(*Rapporteur*: Mr. A. O. DE SOUSA, Academic Registrar, Curtin University of Technology)

The Topic Chairman (Dr. J. Downey) in opening remarks observed that whereas some of the previous speakers might have had him examining computer options he was now no longer sure, having heard Professor Cameron.

An Australian delegate observed that some 15 years ago the catch phrase was retraining or continuing education. However present-day discussions were about the out-of-date baggage of knowledge and the need to 'unlearn' obsolete ideas. Consequently he wondered what solutions there were for a person like himself who had been 'programmed' through the years, through experience. Professor Cameron felt that the issue was not about unlearning technology but about the need to acknowledge technology and its place in the scheme of things. When a new generation of school pupils come they will hopefully develop new ways.

A delegate from the UK observed that schools are very different from a generation ago. He enquired whether the widening range of opportunities through computers and similar equipment had meant that a greater depth and variety of talent had been identified. Professor Cameron indicated that there was some evidence to support the hypothesis. However she believed the potential was there to be developed, although educators were not necessarily leading the way.

Another delegate pursued the issue as to whether computers had helped pupils learn where traditional methods had failed. As an example, did computers help speech and reading skills in Down's syndrome children? Professor Cameron re-emphasized that her research indicated that the

SUB-TOPIC 6(c): EDUCATION AND TRAINING

computer was a successful tool. There was evidence that pupils could use word processors to get ideas across better than in any other form. However not much was known at this time on the quality of the improvement.

Sub-Topic 6(d)

THE ROLE OF UNIVERSITIES IN UNDERSTANDING THE ETHICAL ISSUES INVOLVED IN TECHNOLOGICAL CHANGE

Thursday, 11 February

Dr. A. NAIMARK (*President, University of Manitoba*): Even a cursory reading of human history provides ample evidence that technological change can induce profound social transformation. This is, of course, not surprising. Major technological advances amplify human power, and changes in the power relationships among the elements of a society are the most potent cause of social transformation and inevitably bring in their wake new values, new behavioural norms and new challenges to the ethical precepts underlying social interactions. These matters are so obvious that one may ask why they should be given special attention now and, more particularly, why universities should be concerned about them. The answer, I suggest, lies in the emergence of a global technological consciousness, in the tempo of technological change and in the changing perception of the role of universities in social development.

The general context, or *Zeitgeist*, in which the contemporary discourse on the impact of technological change is conducted is conditioned by two antithetical views of the prospects for human progress. On the one hand, according to the 'limits to growth view', the prospect for social and economic development will be limited by the finite capacity of the biosphere and the supply of natural resources. Technological ingenuity, or *hubris*, by bringing us more rapidly to these limits, is inherently perverse and ethically indefensible. On the other hand those who hold the 'no limits to human ingenuity view' dismiss the chorus of environmental and technological Cassandras on two grounds. The first is on the facts which, it is argued, do not support the doom-sayers. The second is that history is replete with examples of man using his imaginative and creative powers to unlock what seemed to be an occluded

SUB-TOPIC 6(D): THE ETHICAL ISSUES [*Naimark*]

frontier. Thus, whatever one's inclination—toward the prophets of doom or the prophets of boom—technology, either as devil or saviour, plays a central role.

Against the backdrop of this political and philosophical dialectic the world is said to be undergoing what some, rather extravagantly, call a second industrial revolution based on powerful new tools made possible by advances in microelectronics, computers, biotechnology, communications and materials science. The use of these new tools has already affected global economic relationships, the pattern of employment, the ability to monitor and control work, telecommunications, the balance of military power, the control of human fertility, the nature of medical care and the ability to alter the human genome. In each of these areas—and the list is by no means exhaustive—one can readily identify profoundly important ethical issues. Let me elaborate on one area to illustrate this point.

For the most part technological advances in the past have been associated with high rates of job creation. A striking feature of the new industrial revolution is that new products incorporating microelectronic devices require less labour and raw material for each unit of added value than the goods or devices they replace. Thus job creation in industries which manufacture novel products and in the service sector is being offset by job losses in primary and secondary manufacturing and in commodity production. The net effects of these countervailing tendencies are the phenomenon of jobless economic growth, the emergence of structural unemployment and underemployment and changes in the balance of leisure and work.

The ethical implications of these developments may be profound. For example, if, as a result of mechanization and automation, employment becomes comparatively scarce, and if work continues to meet psychological and social needs and remains a moral 'good', an ethical dilemma must inevitably emerge. Moreover the use of microprocessors to control production lines and office work leads to reorganization of work around the requirements of the new technology. The relationship of man and machine may change from man as operator or monitor of machine to machine as monitor of man. It is not difficult to discern the ethical dimensions of increased power being placed in the hands of machine owners to monitor and control human activity.

The new technologies are marked not only by their deep impact but also by the speed with which they are diffused and by the increasing rate at which new advances are being generated. Societies are being challenged as never before to adapt quickly to new technology and it is, therefore, not surprising that concerns about the impact and ethical implications of technological change should be a matter of intense current interest. The particular relevance of these concerns to universities derives from three main factors: first is the university's traditional function of seeking understanding, through research, of social phenomena; second is the fact that much new technology springs from basic research conducted in universities; third is the growing role of universities in undertaking applied research on their own or under contract to business and industry.

The latter factor deserves some amplification. It is now widely held that national economic growth depends on an increasing ability to compete successfully on international markets. This depends, in turn, on the development and use of new technology to reduce the cost of production of existing goods and services for which markets exist or can be developed. Many sectors of the wider community have called for increased co-operation among governments, the private sector and the universities in expanding research and development and in increasing the rate of technology transfer. Some contend that such involvement by universities imposes a corresponding measure of direct institutional responsibility for the social impact of technology to the development of which universities have contributed. Others argue that technology is neutral and the responsibility which attaches to its use rests with its users not its creators.

Having identified the factors contributing to the contemporary concerns about the impact of technology let me now turn to the role of universities in contributing to an understanding of the ethical implications of technological change. I have chosen to consider this topic in relation to the primary functions of the university; namely, research and scholarship, teaching and community service, and more particularly to the role of the academic staff as researchers and scholars, as teachers and as commentators or as consultants to the wider community.

Researchers and Scholars

Natural and applied sciences. The ethical issues involved in technological change can only be formulated and put in their proper perspective if the nature of technological change is itself understood; not as an abstraction, but in specific terms. The importance of this may be illustrated by considering the field of molecular biology and genetics. Only a decade or so ago there were many articles in both the popular and professional literature about the prospect of changing human genetic composition. Many ethical issues were raised and heated debate ensued, most of which was wrong-headed or premature. Most reputable university scientists knew that genetic engineering, as conceived in the public mind, was a long way off. They also knew that the prospects for an expanded ability to make accurate genetic diagnosis were far more imminent. Few, if any, raised the ethical issues involved in the application of such techniques—nor did they attempt to define the practical parameters of technological change in a way which could alert the public to the issues of immediate concern. The latter strikes me as a reasonable expectation of university scientists.

Social sciences. The social scientists in universities play a particularly important role because their disciplines involve the modes of enquiry necessary to measure and interpret the effects of technological change on individuals and societies. Anthropologists, sociologists, social psychologists, historians, economists, political scientists—all have special responsibilities to help us understand how emerging technologies affect the power relationships in society, its behavioural norms and its ethical values. Despite a growing sense of importance of the subject it does not yet command a significant amount of scholarly effort on the part of university social scientists. There are no doubt many reasons for this relative lack of attention, including the fact that measuring the social effects of technological change *per se* may be very difficult because they are often confounded by coincident changes induced by a variety of other factors. Effective study of the social impact of technology will require a breadth of approach which, with certain notable exceptions, is still relatively infrequent among university social scientists.

Humanities. Limitation of time does not permit me to describe the major contributions which the study of history and literature can make to the understanding of how individuals and social groups are impacted by their environment and by processes of mechanization and industrialization. I do, however, wish to draw special attention to the contribution to be made by university-based philosophers and in particular the ethicists. Their contribution is twofold. First there is the expertise and logical discipline they bring to the analysis of ideas. This attribute is especially relevant in respect of issues which have significant political or social content, where debate too often turns on unspoken assumptions, confused rhetoric, hidden agendas and logical fallacies. Second is the specific expertise they bring to the discussion of ethical issues. This expertise involves both a diagnostic component (the identification of the ethical content of phenomena) and a formative component (relating ethical choices to the existing values of society). Ethicists can assist in the development of new processes by which individuals and groups can examine ethical issues and arrive at appropriately informed decisions.

Despite the importance of their potential contribution the ethical implications of technological change have not as yet commanded sufficient attention among university-based philosophers. With the possible exception of bioethics, the field of applied ethics is in general poorly developed—in part, perhaps, because the very notion of applied ethics is not readily embraced by purists in university philosophy departments.

Teachers

In the long run the university's most important role in contributing to an understanding of the ethical implications of technological change may well be through its instructional function. The generation of new technology and its application depends to a large extent on the activities of university-trained professionals. It is therefore obvious that, by introducing courses in applied ethics as required elements of programmes leading to professional degrees universities can produce trained professionals whose awareness of the ethical dimensions of their disciplines is enhanced, who are able to engage in moral reasoning and who have the conceptual tools to make choices among technical alternatives which will minimize ethically pernicious effects.

The challenge is not confined to professional or vocational programmes in the natural and applied sciences. There are also imperatives for programmes in the humanities and social sciences. Here the task is to provide courses which will contribute to technological literacy and to an understanding of the role of technology in society and its implications for social values and ethics. Without such a foundation many of the future leaders in politics and government will be ill-equipped to understand the ethical implications of technological change and its relation to social policy.

The methods and educational strategies for incorporating studies in applied ethics into the curriculum are not well developed but it may be of some interest to examine briefly the approaches used in medical education—a field in which I have some personal experience. The rapid advance of medical science which followed world war II provided physicians with unprecedented power to intervene safely to prolong life, to extend useful function, to prevent disease, to control fertility, to transplant organs and to modify behaviour. The ethical issues raised by these developments are characterized

SUB-TOPIC 6(D): THE ETHICAL ISSUES [Naimark]

by a special sense of immediacy since nearly everyone in developed areas comes into direct contact with advanced medical technology. In broad terms issues in medical ethics fall into two categories: the ethics of making decisions for individuals who are unwilling or unable to make decisions for themselves, and the ethics of allocating health care resources.

The intensity of public concern about these matters, the growth of litigiousness amongst disaffected patients, and the increasing involvement of government in financing health services and perforce in rationing resources, resulted in medical schools being challenged to 'do something about ethics'. The response of medical educators consisted, in the first instance, of encouraging the introduction of courses in biomedical ethics into the undergraduate curriculum. As is always the case when what are perceived as fringe areas are added to the curriculum, two things happened. First, the courses were introduced as elective rather than compulsory. Second, the persons asked to organize and deliver the courses were often individuals who were themselves regarded as fringe characters in the *dramatis personae* of the medical school and who were not specifically trained in ethics. Before long it became evident that such half-hearted approaches were not good enough and a more concerted effort was made to establish an effective programme in biomedical ethics as part of the medical curriculum. Experience to date leads to three main conclusions.

(1) Introducing applied ethics early in the curriculum, before students have been exposed to clinical problems, militates against assimilation, and therefore biomedical ethics should be an integral part of the clinical curriculum and made part of the work-up of individual cases.

(2) A two-pronged strategy for staffing biomedical ethics programmes appears to work best. This involves identifying and recruiting first-rate professional ethicists to provide the rigour and discipline necessary to ensure that the ethical content of the programme is soundly based. It also involves the preparation of a cadre of clinical teachers who are prepared to examine and discuss the ethical issues involved in specific clinical situations.

(3) Courses in biomedical ethics should not concentrate unduly on the dramatic high-technology-based clinical situations which are so often the centre-pieces of popular discussion but should emphasize the routine situations with which the ethical domain of most doctors is so densely populated.

Commentators and Consultants

In addition to the contribution the university can make to understanding the ethical implications of technological change by virtue of its educational and research functions, it can also make a direct contribution by its role in community service. This most commonly takes the form of individual members of the university acting as consultants or commentators on the ethical dimensions of technological change in the media or in response to requests from public agencies. This expression of the community service role is common to many aspects of the university's expertise and need not be elaborated further.

Another and perhaps more interesting consideration is the role the university can play in a corporate sense in assisting the wider community to deal with the ethical implications of technological change. Time does not permit me to consider all of the ramifications of this complex matter, but perhaps reference to a particular development will serve to demonstrate that a corporate university initiative in this area is feasible. At the University of Manitoba we have established a small centre for professional and applied ethics. The centre acts as a source of expertise which can be drawn on by the media, by professional associations and a variety of governmental and private entities. It acts both to provide a gateway into the University and to impart a higher profile and more tangible representation of the University's interest in this area than would otherwise be the case. It also can open opportunities for university scholars to learn about the ethical implications of technological change by working directly with people involved in grappling with contemporary problems.

Professor LYDIA P. MAKHUBU (*Acting Vice-Chancellor, University of Swaziland*):

Introduction

Technological change may be initiated in one part of the world but it soon spreads to other parts to influence in a very significant way many aspects of human life. It has also been observed that every change, whether it stems from innovation or technology transfer and regardless of the magnitude of its positive impact on individuals and society, always has an accompanying negative impact[1]. Unfortunately, when the benefits of the technology involved seem to outweigh the risks the tendency is to concentrate on the benefits, especially in developing countries where technological change has often been associated with desired socio-economic transformation and the modernization of society. A comparison has been made between indigenous societies and Europe and technological prescriptions compiled to narrow the differences[2]. After nearly 30 years of this approach in Africa it has become clear that technological development is intricately interwoven with societal considerations, and that those targeted for change must understand the issues involved as these often impinge upon their cultural values and practices.

Institutions of higher learning in Africa are in a unique position to promote this understanding in order to ensure that future citizens and leaders will be better informed about technology and its impact on society.

Technology in Traditional African Society

This brief discussion will outline some characteristics which are known to be common among many societies south of the Sahara, where nearly 80% of the population live in the rural areas. It will serve to demonstrate those socio-cultural issues which are invoked by the modernization process and emphasize the need for sensitivity in those who advocate technology as an agent of change.

All communities used traditional technologies in agriculture, medicine, construction, pottery, etc., long before modern science-based technology ever touched their lives. They also harboured strong beliefs on life and death, many of which patterned their behaviour and attitudes towards the environment and resulted in complex family and community interrelationships. Technology was part of these complex interrelationships and not a separate entity, a means of living[3].

Development as perceived in our times has incorporated modern technology as a major and essential tool for social and economic transformation. While there is no doubt that benefits accrue to those who harness technology, it is also true that for these benefits to be sustained the beneficiaries must integrate technology into their culture and become 'technological societies', as is the case with developed countries. This integration in the societies described above may demand major adjustments in existing cultural patterns and even impinge directly on social norms and values. It is in these circumstances that deliberate efforts to introduce new outlooks and approaches to technology and its applications become necessary in order to facilitate transition from old to new.

The following examples illustrate areas in which the introduction of technology to key areas of social and economic development may disturb social and cultural patterns and invoke ethical concerns.

Modernization of rural areas. In the past 20–30 years in Africa numerous programmes directed to agriculture, health, women, industry, etc., have been designed with the aim of improving the standard of living of people in the rural areas. These programmes have sometimes necessitated the movement and resettlement of families in designated areas, in order to provide all members with essential central services such as schools, clinics and water supplies, and make more land available for stock grazing and agriculture. However, in many societies family land is handed down from generation to generation, a cultural practice which is hard to break. Therefore what may appear an easy and logical move to benefit families may become an intense ethical and political issue if a government ignores cultural sensitivities and insists on the movement, which is often the case.

Different sets of concerns arise when the long-term effects of fertilizers, pesticides and other agricultural inputs on human life and the environment is underplayed in the interest of improved production. Everyone agrees that these are important, but the emphasis is always on the benefits of using them and very little attempt is made to highlight their potential hazardous effects.

Similarly governments will spare no efforts in encouraging investment which will result in the industrialization of rural areas, but in locating these industries it may become necessary to destroy indigenous forests with no accompanying reforestation schemes. Furthermore the by-products of such industries may be well-known pollutants but because many countries have no environmental regulations industries feel no obligation to exercise pollution control procedures in the absence of any government directive.

These examples illustrate the need for education to increase societal awareness of environmental issues, industrial safety standards and other matters related to technology application.

Birth control and culture. Every document on African development expresses alarm at the fast rate of population growth in the continent. Conclusions seem to have been drawn that a large population and technological progress are incompatible and yet children are highly treasured in most societies. Childlessness carries a stigma, especially for the woman. The new techniques of embryo transplantation and the use of sperm from sperm banks on infertile women could have far-reaching societal consequences if used widely in Africa. On the one hand they would assist the childless couples, especially the woman who usually carries the burden of childlessness; on the other hand, in societies which are set in complex family interrelationships, such a technique could lead to disruption and disintegration of the family if used indiscriminately without ensuring a thorough explanation by those administering it. A sensitivity to social and cultural implications would be critical in this case.

New technologies. While the rapid technological advances may be taking place in the developed countries some of them, like the computer technologies, are becoming common features in many countries. There is need for countries either individually or collectively to develop capabilities for understanding the potential impacts of these new advances. What, for instance, will be the effect of wide-scale computerization of certain industries on employment? Can any country afford to invest heavily in the adoption and acquisition of new and emerging technologies when the majority of the population use tradition technologies as a way of life? A continuous process of assessment of the technical suitability of the new technologies is essential, but this must be coupled with a rigorous examination of their impact on society.

The foregoing discussion should not give the impression that African societies do not change and that the old socio-cultural beliefs were all worthy of preservation at any cost. In fact present-day African societies have gone through the rigours of colonization and through the post-independence onslaught of technological experimentation and have thus become a mixture of the old and new. It is at this crossroads where it is imperative to understand the impacts of technology on social norms and values if the appropriate choices are going to be made. This understanding is especially important among the youth whose future will no doubt be dominated or influenced by the new technological advances.

Role of Universities

Universities have a major role to play by incorporating topics which reflect the main characteristics of contemporary times in their teaching and research so that graduates are better prepared to face the world. Technological developments and their impact on society have become a feature of our times and cut across all academic disciplines. Universities are recognised leaders of thought and reflection and are also centres where science, technology, ethics and the social and human sciences are studied as disciplines. What is missing is a merger of ideas and a translation into a programme that will address the ethical issues surrounding the practical applications of science which affect mankind. This kind of exercise by African universities is likely to 'ensure protection of the traditional scientific and technological base without an undue emphasis on the past which will block an appreciation of the need for change'[4].

Many institutions are already pursuing various programmes to address the issues raised above. The following suggestions are made merely as points for discussion, and are directed mainly to the African situation.

(1) University faculties of science, engineering, social and human sciences, etc., should constitute interdisciplinary groups to reflect on the effects of technology on their societies and to assemble material for seminars and open lectures. This may be a difficult step in many universities where activities are often organized along strict disciplinary lines with minimal interdisciplinary interaction.

(2) Technology assessment has been discussed as a necessary tool in the introduction of new technologies[5]. Universities could develop expertise in assessment and become advisers to decision-makers and informers of the public on the ethical and economic issues surrounding the introduction of a new technology.

(3) In view of the rapid technological changes that are taking place in the world, faculties should consider adding courses on science, technology and society in their regular programmes, and not as options, in order to build a foundation for active participation in issues pertaining to technology and its impacts among future citizens.

Finally, it must be acknowledged that there are other issues of global significance, such as nuclear arms, which have been omitted from this discussion. This omission does not in any way minimize their importance.

REFERENCES

1. Harrison, Anna: 'Role of Scientists, Engineers and the Public in the Resolution of Societal Issues'. Paper presented at the ICSU Conference on Science and Technology Education and Future Human Needs, Bangalore (1985).

2. Kingsley, Phillip: 'Adaptation to New Technology. Some Cultural and Psychological issues in Technological Development'. African Social Research 30 (1980).

3. Sempebwa, Joshua W.: 'The African World View. Its Distinguished Characteristics in Relation to Experimental Sciences'. Paper presented

at a Symposium on Science and Technology in Africa in relation to Development. Special Committee on Africa (1985).

4. M'bow, A. M. (former director general of UNESCO): 'The role of the academic community in development' quoted in a document for the Second Conference of Ministers Responsible for the Application of Science and Technology to Development in Africa. Arusha (1987).

5. DSE/UNCSTD: International Workshop on Advanced Technology Alert System, *Final Report*. Berlin West (1985).

LORD CHILVER (*Vice-Chancellor, Cranfield Institute of Technology*): The ethical issues are in my view the most demanding in the field of the interaction of technology and society because they require intellectual standards which we have to advance very much further if we are going to make progress in this field.

How can we provide a context for discussion of these ethical issues? Essentially they are generated in situations in which technological change leads to social impacts which are argued to be undesirable, or potentially undesirable. In looking at the interaction of technology and society for our present purposes (and there are many ways of looking at it, of course) we might analyse it in the following way. We bring into society a whole range of technological ideas, which we reconsider, as time goes by, in terms of their desirable or undesirable impacts, their increasing disadvantages and dangers. One can envisage a sort of axis, starting with technological ideas that appear at present to have no known disadvantages, or dangers; moving on to those which have known disadvantages, although there is some dispute as to how well-known they are; and arriving finally at a whole range of so-called known dangers—for example, where a particular scientist or group of scientists will argue that a new material is very toxic indeed, although others say it is not so. (This, incidentally, is not the whole of technology; it is a selection of those components of technology which can have an impact on society.)

The ethical problems are posed in the following way. We want to grapple with the material and social problems generated by these technologies, and basically we do this by subjecting each of them to ever-increasing regulation and control. Some might be so harmless that we do not subject them to any restraint. If we are rather concerned about the social and material impact of technologies we might begin to regulate them—regulation is the next stage. And if we are very worried we move on to the stage of control. This increasing regulation and control can be undertaken at a whole range of levels: local, regional, national, international. Thus the potential area for grappling with the known disadvantages and increasing dangers of technology is very comprehensive.

Against that very simple description of the scene—which in fact has many much more complex ramifications—let us look at a few examples of how the various problems we have been discussing fit into this picture. First, a few material problems. Imagine that we start with matter—any sort of matter—which is thought to have no technological disadvantages or dangers. We are therefore not alerted to the need for any form of regulation or control. In the fullness of time, however, we identify a possible toxic side effect of that material which forces us to reconsider its use, and to move towards some form of regulation which will temper the effects of the toxicity. If with greater knowledge it transpires that the material is very toxic, we can move on to use that is controlled.

The first point, then, is that the effects of technological changes on society and the environment are not static. They can, over a period of time, alter for a given material. Half a dozen examples come immediately to mind. The concept of using nuclear power to generate electricity looked at first very harmless. Then we were alerted to the possible nuclear hazards; these have escalated; they have been regulated; and now safety considerations have so increased interest in regulation and control that it may be necessary to move on to control at international level. Acid rain is an interesting example. No one would consider rain to be harmful, but once it became involved with technological effluence in electrical power production we had to regulate it within our own countries. We now have to move on to even greater regulation and control between countries. Medicines and drugs are also very interesting. We introduce many medicines with, apparently, no side effects. As our knowledge increases we first regulate the use of those with potential disadvantages, and then go on to rigid control of those that prove to be the most toxic.

Many of the social issues we have been discussing can be shown to follow a similar pattern. Professor Yerbury and Dr. Hills talked about employer relations and the displacement of employment by the introduction of new technology. A new technology may appear initially to be very beneficial for all concerned. But gradually disadvantages become apparent, one of them being, of course, the displacement of employment, with the result that immediately many regulations are brought in—not least the reaction of organized labour to the change. So society, through its own mechanisms, begins to regulate the spread of the new technology, and this process can escalate to the point at which state control has to be

SUB-TOPIC 6(D): THE ETHICAL ISSUES [*Chilver*]

introduced. Eventually, when the dangers are more fully understood and are seen to have serious economic implications, the introduction of that technology can be completely blocked for, say, political reasons. The points that Dr. Naimark made this morning about the dilemmas posed are brought out in this sort of analysis. We are all the time wondering how far we have to go along this axis of regulation and control, and this combination of two factors, a technological factor and a social awareness/action factor, is really the axis of the ethical issues.

These ethical issues occur at almost every stage in the development and exploitation of technology, as the way in which we view the interaction of the technology on society evolves over long periods of time. We are much more fussy today about the toxicity of the materials that we use, about the conditions under which we live. In the post-war period in Britain, for example, there was great interest in high-rise public rented housing, now regarded as dangerous to society. It has moved from the regulation to the danger zone and now all planning authorities have rejected that form of change in the technology of accommodation.

The ethical issues are very diverse in form and in scale. They involve many individuals, groups of individuals, organizations, whole countries and even groups of countries. The scene is enormously complex and the subject is consequently a very challenging one. How can we approach the role of universities in this field? I think that we must first have in our minds a picture of the model of a university which can play an effective role. There are in fact many different types of university, but the model I would adopt for this purpose is: a centre of creative ideas generated by study, scholarship and research, which disseminates those ideas through teaching and through wider publication in society and which—this is the crucial point— does so in ways that preserve the institution's intellectual independence of that society. Much of the research leading to technological inputs is sponsored by companies. This is not in itself harmful, but such sponsors cannot be regarded as unbiased contributors to discussions about the ethical issues that we have to resolve in order to regulate and control that technology sensibly. A university, if it is to be effective, *must* be intellectually independent of any forces that might taint, however slightly, its views on ethical issues.

The second point to make is that this model university does not have a precise structure. It can take many forms. Inputs in this field will come from broadly-based institutions; from specialist institutions; from small, from large; from undergraduate institutions, postgraduate institutions and those in which both levels are combined; from institutions predominantly based on the sciences, those in which the humanities predominate, and those that are mixtures of both. Indeed it is the diversity of the institutions having a common theme of independent intellectual pursuit that gives us the capability to solve some of the problems in the area we are discussing. There is a grave danger that by miming the ways in which we work throughout the system we shall deprive ourselves of the advantages that diversity affords.

One area that is evolving and still has a long way to go is that of intellectual debate about how the regulatory/control processes are developed. This is really what organizations throughout the world want to get right in their societies, and it is in this field that new ground will be made in the universities—those with real intellectual independence—in the future, because at the moment the bodies that have to carry out the regulation and control have very few general concepts which they can apply. This is the greatest area of potential for the universities: greater understanding and definition of the ethical issues involved, and the influence that such thinking can have on the regulatory and control bodies themselves, in whichever state, country or region they operate.

There is also a desperate need to develop a recognisable body of knowledge of the regulatory and control situation; and coupled with that a very important need for high-level teaching, by universities, of the producers of technology. The larger organizations who genuinely want their technology to make a positive contribution to the world say that they get little help from the academic community on the question of the range of issues they will face in introducing new technology. This is such an important deficiency. Very small studies could have a profound and far-reaching effect because the products of these organizations will penetrate very large areas of the world, particularly if the organizations have anticipated the problems of regulation and control that will arise as the impact of their technology escalates.

Another category for which high-level—very high-level—teaching is needed is those who are responsible for control and regulatory work—the people in governments and in public agencies. They too have at the moment no centres to which they look for creative ideas on really large-scale problems, on how to grapple with the incorporation, in sensible ways, of the technologies that have an impact on society.

SUB-TOPIC 6(D): THE ETHICAL ISSUES

DISCUSSION

(*Rapporteur*: Mr. V. J. CARNEY, Registrar, University College of Swansea)

The discussion was divided into two parts: (1) on Professor Makhubu's submission; (2) on the submissions by Dr. Naimark and Lord Chilver.

(1) *Comments on Professor Makhubu's presentation*
It was suggested that, if a university properly and successfully pursued its role as an ethical critic of technological developments, this could lead to increasing tensions with the government—in the majority of cases its cash provider. Professor Makhubu contended that universities always 'walked this tightrope' and should not shirk from making the community aware of the impact of technical change. A questioner drew attention to the difference between various parts of the same country in the introduction of new technology, and hoped that this would not mean that the pace of implementation might be that of the least developed area. Professor Makhubu agreed that this should not be so, and was supported by Professor K. B. Dickson (Cape Coast). He and other speakers endorsed the view that developing countries should 'borrow' the technology of developed economies and adapt it to their own local needs. Some speakers expressed the view that by pressing the ethical problems too strongly countries would impede development. However Professor Makhubu, while appreciating the point, warned that underdeveloped economies should not 'let technology walk all over you'—there was a need for balance. Responding to a suggestion that technological change had helped to improve the status of women, particularly in the developing world, Professor Makhubu said that in her view there had been a move away from 'feminist liberation philosophy' to a more practical and economic ethos based on the income generation motive. Opportunities for women to work and more training had improved their position but the universities had played little or no part in this.

In a final comment Professor Makhubu said that in her country, as in many other African states, only very slow progress was being made to establish a cohort of university staff in all the relevant disciplines who could give ethical guidance on technological changes.

(2) *Comments arising from the presentations of Dr. Naimark and Lord Chilver* (who, with Professor K. B. Dickson, formed a panel to take questions and to make comments on matters raised)
One topic considered by the panel was whether universities should be involved in research that leads to the manufacture of weapons of destruction. There was a general view that it was not always possible to disentangle weapons research from basic technological research in large schemes such as the 'star wars' programme. There was general consensus that universities should only undertake weapons research if it was part of a university research programme and should be carefully evaluated to ensure that the university was not compromised.

Consideration was given to the need for financial support to establish independent units to monitor ethical considerations. In some areas such as biomedical ethics and environmental ethics funds would often flow from central government agencies. In more difficult areas such as engineering and business studies there was little likelihood of resources being found. However it was suggested that funds might be obtained 'on the back' of other and wider resources distinct from government or industry, so as to maintain independence from one over-mighty sponsor. At present criticism of the ethical implications came from small vocal groups outside the university system.

Much discussion took place on the role of undergraduate teaching and the temptation to make ethical matters an 'elective' rather than an integral part of the curriculum. The panel agreed that there seemed to be little enthusiasm from students, who tended to think of it as a peripheral part of their teaching programme. Some thought might be given, however, to appealing to the 'media interest' in ethical matters, to present the problem on a much larger platform.

The panel concluded the session by stressing that society and the universities must encourage people to think about the social implications of technological innovation and try to measure the true cost to the community as well as the economic benefit from future technical changes.

Note.—The author of the following paper, who was also to have spoken on Sub-Topic 6(d), was at the last moment unable to attend the Congress but has provided his text for inclusion in the Report of Proceedings.

Professor S. J. S. COOKEY (*Vice-Chancellor, University of Port Harcourt*): In recent years universities, while pursuing their traditional mission of research, have helped in accelerating the pace of scientific and technological change which is now universally perceptible. The change has brought undoubted benefits to man by increasing food production, prolonging life and relieving drudgery, among others. There have also been resultant dangers arising, for example, from the pollution of the environment and the threat to the very survival of the planet. Modern society, as never before, has come to rely on the new science and advanced technology so much that calls have been made for revised social philosophy to save man from his own creations. Whether universities should be concerned by the ethical implications of these developments has inevitably given birth to a dilemma on the responsibilities which universities bear under the present circumstances.

The principal aspects of this dilemma have been reviewed recently as it relates to American academia, though having significant reference for other parts of the globe.[1] They can be traced to the secularization of the universities which eclipsed the stamp of religion on any moral issues that confronted them. In the absence, apparently, of an ideological commitment imposed by the state which could substitute for religion, the universities have found themselves today searching for answers on how to respond to or reconcile evidently conflicting interests which stem from their service to knowledge and society.

One solution to the dilemma could be for the university to reclaim its heritage and accept a religious or political creed either of which would ensure strict adherence to clearly defined ethical principles. However this backward-looking strategy is clearly antithetical to the scientific spirit and hardly practicable. Another approach is to deny the need for the university to interest itself in issues of morality, in the confidence that its actions must inevitably be socially good. Neither solution, in fact, has much relevance to reality viewed from both the universalistic and the nationalistic character evinced by every modern university. One is inclined to accept, in the final analysis, that although each university aspires to be ruled by cognitive rationality as advocated by Parsons and Weber its activities are, to an important extent, ideological and, indirectly, political. Science and political debates cohabit within the walls of the academy and reflect the desires as well as the cultural imperatives of the society outside.

A similar point has been made from a different perspective by Paul Camerisch, who argues that, since universities are created by societies and the latter emerge from 'some consensus of fundamental values', the former can ultimately only reflect those values in the process of achieving their mission.[2] In that context the universities, as human learning institutions, assume a moral obligation to clarify, direct and provide a focus on ethical issues within the parameters of the agreed societal values. Furthermore, he argues, the process of educating students, the future leaders or members of the society, involves also the dissemination of values which would ensure human well-being as perceived by the society. Finally the universities, by their nature, are both part of and critics of societies. In playing their traditional roles, therefore, they have the capacity to state ethical issues within a dialectic which constantly advances societal understanding and comprehension of already accepted values.

Consequently it must clearly be emphasized that knowledge, from an empirical standpoint, is contextual and society-bound rather than neutral. In particular, the specific aspect of knowledge which impinges on life must of necessity evoke ethical considerations. It compels the universities, then, to join in exploring the ethical issues raised by their activities and ensuring that these are not ignored by the larger society. Thus the problem becomes one of identifying the role which universities could play rather than whether it should assume a role.

One obvious line of action which readily presents itself lies in the policy which the university, as individual researchers or as a corporate body, adopts towards its research activities. While in the past universities have relied mainly on themselves and governments to finance their research activities, some have more recently entered into joint ventures with industrial/commercial firms to undertake research. In a number of cases universities have even established private firms to exploit the results of their research activities. This fairly recent development, which is governed by the profit motive, undoubtedly risks the danger of curtailing the spirit of disinterested enquiry and free flow of information which has been the hall-mark of the university.

An aspect of this evolving trend towards commercialization which has raised serious ethical issues for universities is that of patenting.[3] Patents, because of their restrictive nature, could potentially suppress or restrict research in order to maximize profit. This detracts from the professional commitment of the academic to open and disinterested inquiry. Although good arguments can be made in favour of patents, there is need for universities to exercise great caution in rationalizing such entrepreneurial endeavours so that their publics become fully aware of the complex considerations which restrictive proprietary rights to knowledge entail.

The larger problem really is how the university, under the circumstance, can maintain its role of society's critic: for example, in correlating technological progress with fundamental values and social justice rather than with profit. For our present purpose it seems that universities engaging in these commercial ventures should exhibit great awareness of the threat to their traditional mission through constant review of their policies and practices in this regard. In the process the university community is better placed to ensure that its research activities remain uncompromised, especially through its well-established system of peer review, while the society benefits from the wisdom of its judgement on such research activities. This ought to ensure that the university continues to be seen as one of the few centres where the exercise of critical participation in society is still being pursued free of restraint or coercion.

A novel approach to generating understanding of the ethical

issues involved in technological change might lie in the way universities undertake their traditional task of educating their students. The university is required by society to train scientists and technologists who, subsequently, are expected to play leadership roles and to determine the future of the society. Clearly, unless these students are made to appreciate and comprehend the moral dilemma involved in the current scientific and technological advances, the future of the society might be endangered. This is by no means a simple task today. In the past, as already observed, such considerations fell within the orbit of religion whose safe anchorage the tidal wave of the scientific revolution has since swept aside. It has been suggested that the universities should develop courses in applied ethics which, while avoiding the smear of indoctrination, would sensitize the student to the need to examine the moral choices surrounding technological advancement. Such a course would recognise that society is dynamic and constantly engaged in re-assessing its moral options, and equip the budding scientist or technologist with the interest and capability to contribute towards the evolution of a moral consensus.

This is not entirely strange. The traditional professions of law and medicine had long maintained and transmitted codes of ethics to regulate the practice of their members. Now, however, the evolution of such fields as biotechnology or genetic engineering and nuclear science compel us to think beyond all former ethics.[4] The student, for example, now has to confront the rationality of some technological changes which could alter the character of some or all men. The challenge for the university is to equip him with the moral knowledge and rational tool to come to terms with such an unprecedented dilemma. Hence the student needs assistance, as part of his education, in clarifying and assessing the values which the society holds as well as in cultivating his sense of moral obligation. Such learning, in order to be relevant and beneficial, must obviously move beyond theoretical formulations, undertaken for the purpose of intellectual satisfaction, to their applications to real-life situations.

In this connection it must be recognised that the society of contemporary scientists and technologists extends far beyond the boundaries of their predecessors. Issues such as the disposal of nuclear waste, for example, or the emission of pollutants which threaten the biosphere impose moral responsibilities that are global in nature. It would appear that the universities have a responsibility to reclaim their earlier universalist tradition and, while minimizing their parochial, societal interests, constantly advocate the universal good.

This is of particular relevance to the well-being of the countries of the developing world who are still largely receivers of technology. As they struggle to escape from a deteriorating standard of living and to come to terms with the spirit of the new age it becomes imperative to ensure that stone, rather than bread, is not placed in their hands. Here the universities could well serve as the watchdogs of our shrinking world through the free flow of information on scientific and technological advances across the development divide.

It is advocated, then, that the university should beware of the dangers inherent in the commercial spirit born of its alliance with industry which might overwhelm its traditional mission. It needs to recognise and emphasize its commitment to protect the public welfare through its traditional openness and the search for truth. It should seize its new opportunities to create and promote a virtue for the technological age which controls change in order to safeguard and preserve man, his society and his environment. In short, the universities have a responsibility to play an active and radical humanistic role. What is being advocated here is not that universities should change those time-worn obligations to teach, undertake research and render public service. The call is for them to re-assess these obligations in the light of contemporary imperatives which, if care is not taken, could endanger their very survival.

REFERENCES

1. Alexander, Jeffery C.: 'The University and Morality: A Revised Approach to University Autonomy and Its Limits'. *Journal of Higher Education*, Vol. 57, No. 5 (September/October 1986).

2. Camerisch, Paul F.: 'Goals of Applied Ethics Courses'. *Ibid*.

3. Goodman, Alan H.: 'Ethical Issues in Proprietary Restrictions on Research Results'. *Science, Technology, and Human Values*, Vol. 12, Issue 1 (Winter 1987).

4. Jones, Hans: *The Imperative of Responsibility*. Chicago (1984, p. 21.)

Sub-Topic 6(e)
THE ROLE OF UNIVERSITIES IN ASSESSING THE IMPACT OF TECHNOLOGY UPON THE ENVIRONMENT

Thursday, 11 February

Professor B. L. CLARKSON (*Vice-Chancellor, University of Wales*):

SOME ENVIRONMENTAL ISSUES IN THE SOCIAL IMPACT OF TECHNOLOGY

1. *Introduction*

By its very nature technological development interferes with our natural environment. In the early stages of development such intrusion can ususally be contained or restricted to very small areas. However as industry develops to become competitive on a world-wide scale the size of production units increases (to reduce the cost per item) and the intrusion can become very serious. The major impact on the environment is the various forms of physical pollution. The incentives to industry to reduce this impact on the environment are usually very small and so, if left to itself, industry will do little. Strong controls linked with incentives are necessary on a world-wide scale if the environment is not to be damaged irreparably. The universities have a very important role to play in this control. Industry itself and also, to a lesser extent, local and national governments have vested interests in the development of industrial wealth. The universities are the major independent force which can be used to minimize the impact. In this paper I shall discuss some of the major problems and indicate the role which the universities can play in developing a sound environmental policy.

2. The Pollution Process

The four main components of the production cycle can be categorized as: extraction and purification; manufacture; distribution; and final disposal. Each of these intrudes on the environment and is a potential visual, physical, chemical or biological polluter. The small-scale integrated village communities with their 'cottage industries' are giving way to large factories which reduce production costs considerably. This concentration leads to a drift of population from the countryside and its self-sufficient economy to large conurbations. This in turn demands major housing development with intrusive distributive systems and gives rise to severe waste disposal problems. In the past the basic extractive industries have been the worst polluters, leaving large holes in the ground and huge mountains of waste. Many of these waste tips continue to pollute rivers by the leaching out of toxic materials over very long periods of time. Metal smelters have been notorious for the toxic fumes emitted during the smelting process.

Waste treatment and control of physical pollution adds a significant cost which in turn usually adds to the price of the product. However, as the larger plants are producing at lower unit cost, part of the gain could be used for pollution control. As the price of raw materials rises recycling and recovery from waste becomes more attractive economically. For example, the rise in the price of oil gave a major impetus to energy saving in factories and the home. The technology is now available to reduce considerably the pollution from modern industrial processes and further improvements could be made. In some cases increased costs may not be incurred if the control is designed into the process from the outset. However, in general, strong incentives are needed which will have to be backed up by international controls.

The incentives to reduce intrusion on the environment are many but most are difficult to quantify economically. At the present time more and more governments are using 'value for money' criteria in assessing developments and thus it is difficult to make a strong case for pollution control in this political climate. Thus the only real lasting incentive must be public pressure expressed through political action leading to legislative control. Ideally this should be at international level if industry in one country is not to be penalized relative to its competitors in other countries.

3. The Role of the Universities

The universities have a most important role to play in the process of reducing the impact on the environment. By its very nature, the problem of control involves many different disciplines and more particularly an independent approach. Other groups have vested interests and even local or national government may have particular priorities which overlook the importance of environmental control. In many cases the damage is long term or geographically distant (acid rain) and so can safely be neglected by representatives who work on a short electoral cycle. However, the increasing emphasis on collaboration between universities and industry and pressures for greater relevance or value for money from governments are eroding the independence of universities. If a significant proportion of a university's income comes from a major industry it may be very difficult for that university to take a stance against the company. However some experience shows that this is not necessarily restrictive, as is shown in an example later. The universities should realize that they are the major independent force to influence public opinion and should take more of a lead rather than leave the matter to individual pressure groups which can easily be discredited or ignored by politicians.

In addition to the important task of influencing public opinion the universities can contribute in the following ways: (1) awareness of long-term environmental changes; (2) development of control methods; (3) schemes for rehabilitation of derelict areas.

3.1 *Awareness and prediction of long-term effects*. Computer-based numerical methods are now being developed which enable global estimates to be made of the effect of the injection of a particular pollutant into the atmosphere or river system. Thus the distribution over a whole continent of, for example, acid rain or the spread of a particular pollutant in the North Sea or Mediterranean can be estimated. Biologists can work with these estimates to predict the effect on plants and mammals. This multi-disciplinary approach, which is the strength of the university system, can thus give early warning of damaging changes. The best impartial information possible should be prepared for use by groups seeking to influence public opinion on these issues.

3.2 *Tools for control*. Traditionally the science and engineering departments of universities have placed greater emphasis on new theories, new developments and new products rather than on the less glamorous area of pollution control. However, much work is now in progress on methods of recovery of waste materials and environmental control. For example, in the area of noise control much work has been done to understand the process of noise production by modern machinery and then to devise methods of reduction at source. In many cases the introduction of control in the initial design does not add significantly to the final cost of the product. The duty of the universities in such cases is to show what can be done and thus make it possible for legislators to insist on best practice. The damaging effect of noise on people is an important environmental hazard in some industries. University work here has shown the long-term damaging potential, developed diagnostic techniques and also palliative and protective measures. In one particular piece of work a company sponsoring the university department did not object to the senior staff member representing an individual claimant against the company. This was because they had confidence that the staff member would give the best impartial evidence and so here company sponsorship did not inhibit independence of action.

3.3 *Rehabilitation*. The universities are in an ideal situation to assemble task forces which can tackle the multi-disciplinary job of rehabilitating areas which have been devastated by industrial processes. One good example of this is the Swansea Valley project. In this case the lower Swansea Valley had been very adversely affected by the intensive smelting activity which peaked at the turn of the century. There were many smelters close to the river. The waste products were dumped in the river and toxic fumes destroyed much of the vegetation on the valley sides. It is best not to contemplate the long-term damaging effects on the workers and their families living in densely-packed housing close to the smelters. The industry declined throughout the twentieth century and ceased completely in the 1950s. A task force conducted a comprehensive survey of the area and proposed a strategy for rehabilitation. Local schools also joined in some of the surveys and later tree planting. The project also covered future social and industrial development as well as improvement of the physical environment. The last waste tip was removed five years ago and the area is now beginning to regenerate. This was an ideal project for a university to undertake. It suited the wide range of skills available, involved the next generation of students and also gave the university a high profile for good in the local community.

Conclusion

I have tried to indicate that the problem of the adverse impact of technology on the environment can be very severe and, in some cases, it is getting worse. However public awareness of the problems

SUB-TOPIC 6(E): THE ENVIRONMENT

is also increasing and methods of control are available. The universities have a very important role to play as the major independent bodies able to give impartial predictions and advice.

DISCUSSION

(*Rapporteur*: Mr. R. M. Raeburn, Secretary Board of Governors, University of Manitoba)

Discussion of Professor Clarkson's paper concentrated on two main points: universities are able to provide an *interdisciplinary* and *independent* approach to the question of reducing the impact of technology on the environment.

While 'universities are ideal places to gather people from different disciplines', there are many examples where universities have failed to deliver interdisciplinary answers to environmental problems. (In fact a theme occurring in virtually all papers presented in this Topic group was the desirability of an interdisciplinary approach to the social impact of technology). In some cases all the disciplines required may not be at a university. But even where all disciplines are represented it is not easy in practical terms to mount an interdisciplinary effort. The discussion group agreed this was a concern and considered ways in which interdisciplinary approaches have been encouraged at universities.

In some respects interdisciplinary groups are regarded by the main disciplines as 'on the fringe'. One way to overcome this attitude is to insure that the group is large enough to develop its own *esprit de corps*. Organization of an institution on the basis of fields of endeavour, rather than a subject approach, also eases the creation of interdisciplinary groups.

Even in universities where curriculum organization is such that students can take a degree across many schools, there are still some difficulties in securing cohesion among the groups. One approach that has been reasonably successful is to establish centres ('a coalition approach'). There is increasing emphasis on this in Australia where the pressure to rationalize has resulted in more centres being established across a university. There is the added incentive that government is encouraging such development by direct funding. Speculation is that government may well look more favourably on centres which are established across more than one university.

Another factor identified to promote the establishment of interdisciplinary groups was the desirability of not appointing faculty exclusively to such groups. While some faculty prefer such appointments, the strength in interdisciplinary groups comes from the fact that members of the group continue to react in their own disciplines. Groups may also come together because of such 'unifying' factors as the cost of sophisticated equipment today. Several disciplines with the need for such equipment are forming

TOPIC 6: SOCIAL IMPACT OF TECHNOLOGY

interdisciplinary groups to share the instrumentation.

Discussion on interdisciplinary approaches ended with the cautionary note that two decades ago several universities aggressively developed interdisciplinary programmes only to discover they did not work. If the interdisciplinary approach is to be emphasized again, as discussion in this Topic group would suggest, there are several people who remember the last experience who will have to be persuaded.

The reference to the independent approach that universities are able to take in matters such as environmental concerns was also a theme that was common to several presentations throughout the week, while others emphasized the need for stronger links with industry and labour. There was some discussion on how to achieve both ends at once. In developing countries input from any source is welcomed. Universities there do not see 'control' that might arise from industrial support as being any more rigid than controls imposed by government. This question has to be considered in the context of the political model of the country.

Recently several changes are taking place in this area in the UK. Industry has become so concerned with the government cuts in university support that it is beginning to 'shout'. Industry is emphasizing the need for highly motivated and trained young people, such that funding from industry now includes support for such general things as scholarships.

Recent changes in Australia at the national level point to government favouring inputs from industry, commerce and unions rather than from universities. This is not to suggest such inputs are not important but there is concern about the quality and depth of informed advice from universities.

One view expressed, but not necessarily supported by all, was that universities should accept research contracts in areas of interest to university professors and that such contracts should be cost recovery. To go further and seek contracts as a source of profit to support other university expenditures begins to compromise universities.

In Canada substantial progress has been made over the past five years in 'building bridges' between business and the academy. Most notable is the Corporate Higher Education Forum which consists of 25 presidents of large universities and 40 chief executive officers of major corporations. The Forum identifies ways in which the two groups can assist each other and has conducted several important studies. However Canada has had little success in improving relations with unions. The UK has also established a similar group, the Council for Industry and Higher Education, which in its $1\frac{1}{2}$ years has been particularly effective in lobbying. Another example raised of an effective link with industry is the Wilson Foundation in the UK which is one of few sources which support 'bricks and mortar'.

The discussion concluded with the observation that some of the most vexatious issues at universities relating to links with industry are not the direct support from industry but the fact that some professors become the exploiters of their inventions—indeed a topic which might well be the subject of a separate session.

SUB-TOPIC 6(E): THE ENVIRONMENT [*Chilver*]

Note.—This paper was prepared for presentation to the Sub-Topic group on the environment, at which Lord Chilver had originally been invited to speak. In the course of the Congress, however, he accepted the Topic Chairman's invitation to speak on ethical issues instead (*see* Sub-Topic 6(d), *above*).

LORD CHILVER (*Vice-Chancellor, Cranfield Institute of Technology*):

TECHNOLOGY, PEOPLE AND THE ENVIRONMENT

Introductory

The subject of 'technology, people and the environment' is a very diverse one. Any discussion of it can touch on almost any area of human interest and endeavour. The roles of universities in this field are also very diverse. There are many areas of university teaching and research which are important to the wide field of technology, people and the environment. Diversity does not, however, detract from the importance of the subject, nor from the importance of the universities in this field. Let us begin by looking at some of the components of the subject.

What do we mean by 'Environment'?

'Environment' can be defined in many different ways. To some the environment is essentially our material surroundings. To them it means the physical appearances of buildings, cities, towns and villages. To others the environment corresponds to our general physical surroundings. This includes natural scenery, which man may decide to 'conserve' in its natural state—as in national parks and green belts. Some such conserved areas may be totally inaccessible to man, while in others access may be more easy.

A related view of environment is of the damage man does—through his many activities—to the land, sea, rivers and the atmosphere. The scale of man's impact may be so great that whole regions are affected deleteriously by his actions. Examples of this are acid rain in northern Europe and—on a wider scale—the possible impact of man-made chemicals on the ozone layer. Such examples fall into a class of problems which are often called 'pollution'.

At another extreme, others associate environment with the 'ambience' of living. They argue that not only are buildings and

443

surroundings important in physical terms, but that it is equally important to understand how the ambience of buildings helps to generate social activities within buildings. Natural surroundings play an important role in this, and it is important to consider how cities and buildings can be created to help man develop within his natural surroundings. Such aspects of the environment are as important in newly developing countries as in addressing problems of urban degeneration which are now occurring in the overcrowded conurbations of the more advanced countries.

The word environment is used in many other ways. In urban development, environment is often very specifically concerned with better living conditions, through better housing and places of employment.

I do not think we should exclude any of these views of environment from our discussions. This is particularly so because all these views of environment include technology and people in varying degrees. Moreover, all these views already attract at least some university interest, and they are vitally important and deserve more of our attention.

Vital Importance of 'Environment' to People

All aspects of the environment are vitally important to people. They can be important to whole nations, to large groups of people and organizations, to smaller groups, and to individuals.

Dwellings, places of work, places for recreation and many other man-made buildings are vitally important to people. At the same time the natural settings in which all these buildings are developed are equally important to people. In the striving of people for better living standards great pressures are generated for the exploitation of environment and many problems arise. It is the understanding of the processes of exploitation of our surroundings, in all their relevant aspects, that is perhaps the central point of our interest in the environment.

It is appropriate to consider some of the forces which drive along this exploitation.

Impact of Technology on People and the Environment

But before attempting that let us look at technology itself. By the word technology we mean—in our present context—the knowledge we have (often in scientific terms) of industrial and practical arts. Many parts of industry and commerce and of the public and military services develop through the exploitation of such technology. This exploitation of technology is one of the most powerful forces in the world scene at the present time. It is sometimes described—in somewhat less emotive terms—as technical innovation. But the term exploitation is a better description of a process which is developed by man for very specific purposes and is pursued with relentless pressure.

Our interest in this process is in both the direct effects of technology and the side effects or the uncalculated effects to which the exploitation of technology can lead. The exploitation of technology is an almost uniquely powerful force in that while it brings immense potential for good—particulary for social well-being—it is at the same time a potential threat to the security of that same well-being. It is not that the threat itself lies in the technology *per se* but rather that its use by people can be destructive. An outstanding example of this in our time is nuclear energy. Indeed, we have only ourselves to blame for the apparent dilemma that technology presents.

The exploitation of technology is now a very powerful force in world economic development. Some economists consider that much of recent world economic development, during the past century or so, has been led effectively by technical change throughout the world.

Most governments of the world—whatever their political leanings—exploit technology for political-social ends. Technology is introduced to solve poverty problems in the less-developed countries. Technology is exploited to improve health and living standards in all countries. Technology is exploited in the world-wide competition to produce consumer materials and goods. It is not at all surprising that technology has a profound impact on environment and people.

Let us look at some of the positive aspects of this impact. Over the millennia man's primary needs have been for food, shelter and defence. We now have a considerable body of knowledge of science and technology to enable us to grow adequate food. At the same time researchers in many aspects of food are ready with many ideas which will progressively improve the quality of food. The technology of shelter—dwellings and buildings of all sorts—is very advanced. In attaining modern 'technological' food and shelter there are many side effects, some of which we do not consider desirable. In our attempts at growing more food we are in danger of polluting our rivers and water supplies with nitrate fertilizers which are washed out of the fields by rain. The rapid building up of cities creates crowded environmental conditions in the centres of cities, along with encroachments on green belts around cities.

The undesirable aspects become most pronounced when we look at the area of 'defence', where the technology of defence is so easily convertible into the technology of attack.

In the modern world man's needs of technology go way beyond these primary needs. We use the most sophisticated forms of technology in transport, communications, health care, education, the arts, to mention only a few.

Let us not underestimate the extent of the power of technological exploitation in the modern world, and particularly its impact on people and the environment. The force of exploitation is of course generated by man. What is a sensible reaction to this powerful force?

The Need to Regulate the Exploitation of Technology

An issue common to most debates about technology, people and the environment is the degree of regulation which must be applied to the exploitation of the environment through technology and people. The magnitudes of the problems of regulation will vary from field to field. We see the problem of regulation in different ways in societies of different cultural backgrounds. We may see them differently from different political and ideological standpoints.

In certain critical areas we will need to regulate at highly international levels. In this debate on regulation technology must be seen as an international currency.

Technology involves powerful creative thinking and the exploitation of empirical knowledge. People will want the greatest possible advantages from the exploitation of technology. Technology and people—coming together—can create either positive or negative impacts on the environment.

Roles of Universities

Against this background, what are the roles of universities? In a liberal-democratic society universities are independent institutions seeking truth and teaching truth. As such independent institutions, universities have crucial roles to play in the field of technology, people and the environment. In particular they can play very important roles in assessing the impact of technology on the environment. This is so because the assessment of this impact requires wide-ranging knowledge and understanding of all the scientific and technological factors involved.

Because of their special positions of independence, a basic role of universities is to disseminate the essential universal knowledge of technology, people and the environment. This involves, first, high standards of intellectual analysis to isolate the basic universal truths of the present situation. It also involves high standards of intellectual discipline to disseminate the truths of environmental issues and not prejudices. The relevant components of basic knowledge are scattered over a wide range of basic disciplines. A vital task for universities is to bring these components together to form a recognisable body of knowledge which can be developed further.

In the future the world will be increasingly concerned with sensible regulation of the exploitation of the environment by technology and people. This leads to the role of universities in developing more profound philosophies of regulation of technology and people in relation to the environment. Technology is always in danger of being exploited in ways which have undesirable side effects. In this situation universities should develop high-level teaching of environmental issues aimed at the 'producers' of technology. At the same time universities should also direct high-level teaching of the potential of technology at 'planners' and 'designers'.

The roles of universities will be greatly enhanced if universities themselves can become more directly involved in the wider debates on technology, people and the environment. This can be helped by developing working centres between universities and other areas of society—public and private—to bring university teaching and research closer to the 'real' problems of the environment.

The environmental field presents many challenges to universities. The unique position of universities—as centres of basic study and understanding—enables them pre-eminently to contribute to both thinking and action in this important field.

Topic 6

UNIVERSITIES AND THE SOCIAL IMPACT OF TECHNOLOGY

The Role of Universities in Contributing to the Understanding of the Social Impact of Technology

CHAIRMAN'S REPORT ON THE GROUP'S DISCUSSIONS

Second Plenary Session
Friday, 12 February

Dr. J. Downey (*President, University of New Brunswick*): I confess I was puzzled about why someone who scarcely knows his microfiche from his microchips had been asked to organize and chair a section of the Congress on the social impact of technology. I am, however, very glad and grateful I accepted to do so. I was impressed equally by the quality of the presentations and the generally upbeat spirit in which they were made and received. There was throughout our proceedings a complete absence of cant—spelled with or without an apostrophe.

As indeed there was throughout the entire Congress. A protracted period of restraint in government support for higher education in many Commonwealth countries had succeeded in concentrating the mind upon the tools and techniques of survival. Recent major reports on the status of tertiary education in the UK, Australia, New Zealand and elsewhere stress the role of universities in serving the economy through the development and transfer of technology together with highly-skilled graduates to make it work.

There are three arguments that have been traditionally used in support of higher education.

(1) That higher education is good in itself: it broadens the mind, quickens the intelligence, refines the sensibilities of those who partake of it; it is a civilizing force that leads to a fuller, more abundant life for the individual and, by extension, for society.

(2) That higher education can be an effective instrument of social equality. It can provide opportunity based upon merit and offset some of the inequitable effects of inheritance. This too, it is assumed, is good for society as well as for those individuals whose own lot in life is improved by virtue of their intelligence and effort.

(3) That higher education is important to a nation's economy, that the knowledge and skills forged and transmitted by universities are essential to industrial competitiveness upon which a country's prosperity depends.

For the most part these arguments are not mutually exclusive; they reinforce each other. From time to time, however, one of them gains ascendancy. In the socially troubled sixties the social equity argument became the strongest—at least with governments, who expanded their university systems while proscribing tuition fees or keeping them to a minimum. The eighties have seen a strong shift towards an economic rationale for higher education. Certain catchphrases have emerged: 'international competitiveness', 'strategic planning', 'performance indicators', 'university-business co-operation', 'efficiency and effectiveness', 'accountability' and of course the ubiquitous 'technology transfer'. All are part of a very powerful social psychology that shapes the public's view of universities—why they exist and what they should be doing.

It was issues such as these that provided the context for some thoughtful presentations and lively discussions in workshop 6. If there was a consensus at the end it was that universities must respond as positively as they can to these new economic challenges without forfeiting or forgetting their essential character of independence and integrity. An obvious consensus perhaps, but still remarkable when one considers the diversity of the institutions and the social and national contexts represented.

Someone has said that university presidents should be optimists even if they must be optimists without hope. Our first two speakers, both of them presidents, were hopeful optimists, and for good reason. In a session which focused on the effects of technology upon the workplace, Professor Dianne Yerbury (of Macquarie University) reported that she and her colleagues have had encouraging responses in Australia to their efforts to study and promote good employment relations. She gave many concrete examples of initiatives which had resulted in effective knowledge transfer. Most encouraging had been the positive response of labour unions whose leadership in Australia is increasingly university-educated and seem to know what advice and information they need and where to look for it.

Graham Hills (of Strathclyde) was positively bullish on the contributions universities can make to the generation of wealth and, by extension, to employment in the long run. 'We need to believe that prowess in knowledge transfer, technology transfer and skills transfer are the ingredients *sine qua non* for the society of the future', he urged.

For a moment as Dr. Hills spoke I had a vision of the future as an endless Australian beach where the warm and beneficial waters of the Third Wave wash over our vitamin-enriched bodies and our computer-assisted minds, and with universities riding the crest. There were, however, doubters in our congregation. Questions were raised about the ability of universities to maintain their 'value-neutral' independence as they draw closer to industry, about the possible distortion of the university's mission, about the relevance of this vision to less developed countries. But Dr. Hills stood his ground, reaffirming his belief in the inevitability of change and the need for universities to take a lead part in directing it, and in their ability to guard their independence while doing so.

At our second session we inverted our topic and examined the impact of society upon technology. Steven Turner (University of New Brunswick) identified some of these contingent social forces that powerfully shape technology: science, the market-place, the state, and technological systems themselves. The role of the university in all this, he argued, is to carry out the empirical research into this complex equation between society and technology and to do it independently, without preconditions, and to mobilize its marginalized interdisciplinary forces in order to find the originality and flexibility needed to address problems that lie in the interstices and at the periphery of knowledge.

Kwamina Dickson (Cape Coast) gave us an African perspective on this symbiosis. He offered some very telling examples of how imported technologies and social norms may collide, such as this one: 'In the early days of this century, the Public Works Department in the Gold Coast (now Ghana) introduced the wheelbarrow for road works. It was recognized as a means of conveyance, except that after being loaded it was carried on the head and taken that way to the work site'. This vignette was an effective reminder that societies, like the people who make them up, have minds of their own, and that the transfer of technology without proper preparation and adaptation may be a feckless or even harmful exercise.

Mediating between technologies and the societies that need or may wish them is an important role for universities, Professor

Dickson contended. To do so effectively in less developed countries, universities may have to recognise that they themselves are imported technologies and need to be sensitive to the character and needs of the societies of which they are part.

In a session devoted to examining the ways universities can assist the educational system in adjusting positively to technological change, Ken McKinnon (of the University of Wollongong) summed up very well the present disposition of governments almost everywhere: 'On the one hand, they are putting universities under scrutiny both as to their mission and their internal efficiency. On the other hand, they are realizing that universities are a precious resource and are seeking to enlist them in the service of national objectives'. Professor McKinnon himself believes that universities should take up the challenge implicit in this ambivalence by providing leadership in giving people the skills—technological, social and personal—to cope with technological change. Like speakers before and after him, he called for a greater measure of multi-disciplinarity in teaching and research.

Increasingly, he argued, universities must become part of research teams, co-operating with other agencies to tackle social and technological challenges that transcend disciplinary and institutional boundaries. Only thus will universities achieve partnership in the planning and development of their nation's economy and culture, and only thus will they be able to protect and enhance their own traditional roles and character.

Ann Cameron (University of New Brunswick) calmly admonished us not to panic and over-react to technological change in education. As she put it: 'If we divide the past 50,000 years into lifetimes, we get about 800. Of those 800 lifetimes, only the last 70 have had truly effective means of communication, only the last six were likely to see a printed word, and the vast majority of technological advances which preoccupy us today were developed during the most recent lifetime. Their appropriate adaptations for education will take generations'. In the meantime we should, she counselled, get on in an independent and interdisciplinary way with the research which will help us to assess the pedagogical efficiency and effectiveness of such technological tools as the personal computer and the word processor

In a session devoted to some ethical questions attendant upon technological change, Arnold Naimark of the University of Manitoba, Lydia Makhubu of the University of Swaziland, and Lord Chilver of the Cranfield Institute of Technology raised cogent and important issues for university research and teaching. The discussion here was perhaps the best we had had and the hardest to summarize. It was my sense that no one thought universities had yet been very successful in addressing the ethical issues thrown up or sharpened by technological development, though perhaps the professional schools (*e.g.* medicine and engineering) were doing a better job of tackling the challenge than faculties of arts and sciences.

Again, nearly everyone agreed that injections of multi-disciplinarity were necessary to counteract the structural arthritis universities sometimes suffer from.

Finally, in a concluding session devoted to environmental impact issues, Brian Clarkson of the University of Wales emphasized nearly all the salient themes heard throughout the week: the need for universities to roll up their sleeves and get involved in their community's technological challenges; the need for institutional independence to give leadership that will earn and keep trust; the need for more cross-disciplinary work. Then he summed up with an account of how, through co-operation with other community agencies, his university had assisted in the recent reclamation of the Swansea Valley from the ravages of last century's industrial revolution. The account was both a paradigm and a parable—a redemptive postscript to *How Green Was My Valley*. And how fitting, though not, I believe, intended as such, that Professor Clarkson should have concluded our sessions with slides of that part of Wales where the next Commonwealth Universities Congress will be held in 1993.

TOPIC 6

Other Contributions

Among the other papers brought to the Congress was the one mentioned below, which related to this Topic.

Dr. K. VENKATASUBRAMANIAN (*Vice-Chancellor, Pondicherry University*), in a short paper entitled 'Science and Technology: its Impact on Society', argued that universities should take a lead in promoting research into the impact of scientific and technological advances upon human society. He noted the major inventions—from the harnessing of energy through steam to the microchip and biotechnology—which have changed, and are continuing to change, society in fundamental ways; and urged that the academic community must undertake responsibility for investigating the social consequences of scientific discoveries, and for finding ways of dealing with whatever potential ill-effects are identified.

Group Discussions

TOPIC 7

UNIVERSITIES AND RURAL DEVELOPMENT

The Role of Universities in the Management of Land Resources and Land Usage for effective rural development

Chairman: Professor D. ODHIAMBO
Vice-Chancellor of Moi University

Chief Rapporteur: Mr. G. A. HAY
Registrar of Lincoln College (New Zealand)

		Page
Sub-Topic 7(a)	THE CHALLENGE OF RURAL DEVELOPMENT SUMMARIZING THE REAL PROBLEMS OF RURAL COMMUNITIES AND EXAMPLES OF HOW UNIVERSITIES HAVE RESPONDED TO THE CHALLENGES	
	Speaker Mr. Devendra Kumar	457
	Discussion	464
Sub-Topic 7(b)	THE DESIGN OF LAND USE AND LAND RESOURCE MANAGEMENT COVERING ANY NEW CONCEPTS AND APPROACHES TO THE PROBLEM	
	Speaker Professor Moonis Raza	466
	Discussion	473

		Page
Sub-Topic 7(c)	THE UNIVERSITIES AS AGENTS OF CHANGE DEALING WITH LINKS BETWEEN UNIVERSITIES AND THE RURAL COMMUNITIES	
	Speakers	
	Mr. K. Kodithuwakku	475
	Professor Dato' Dr. Nayan Ariffin	479
	Discussion	487
Sub Topic 7(d)	STRATEGIES FOR UNIVERSITY PROGRAMMES OF TRAINING, RESEARCH AND EXTENSION WHICH CAN LEAD TO BETTER LAND USE IN THE RURAL AREAS	
	Paper	
	Dr. B. Kayombo	489
Final Session		497
CHAIRMAN'S REPORT ON THE GROUP'S DISCUSSIONS		499
Other Contributions		502

For index to names, see p 533

Sub-Topic 7(a)

THE CHALLENGE OF RURAL DEVELOPMENT SUMMARIZING THE REAL PROBLEMS OF RURAL COMMUNITIES AND EXAMPLES OF HOW UNIVERSITIES HAVE RESPONDED TO THE CHALLENGES

Monday, 8 February

Mr. DEVENDRA KUMAR (*Vice-Chancellor, Gandhigram Rural Institute*):

CHALLENGES OF RURAL DEVELOPMENT AND RESPONSIBILITIES OF UNIVERSITIES

I. *Villages and Universities*

1.1 The 'third world' comprising 141 nations has one thing in common and that is a large rural population. Owing to less industrialization and consequently less urbanization they have a larger proportion of population living in the villages. Three billions—60% of the world population—are living in the villages and out of this 85%, *i.e.* 2.6 billions, live in Asia and Africa. The living standard of the villages is as far behind that of the cities in these countries as their own national income is less than that of the affluent countries. The affluent nations being basically urban and the poorer nations rural, rural development is a critical area to be tackled, in order to bring about a less exploitative and more satisfying system, and the universities must address themselves to it. The universities must bring the academic talents of their faculties and the idealism of their youthful students to bear on the problems of the common people of the land, and not allow themselves to be elitist organizations, deaf to the groanings of the deprived and the suffering.

1.2 Universities are expected to visualize and conceptualize things with a long-range perspective, which capacity neither the political nor the commercial organizations can be expected to possess. For this the universities and the society should have close interaction, as their so-called 'ivory tower' image has become outdated. The areas of interface between the university and rural economy have to increase and be made more intimate in the three dimensions of the university system, viz. teaching, research and extension, which should be geared to rural upliftment.

1.3 Higher education in universities has been found to be out of tune with the reality of the developmental needs of the area. Their structure, courses and disciplines, academic and administrative organization, and the way that they evaluate 'excellence' are on the lines of international academic standards set by richer industrialized nations. Hence their contribution to national/rural development, *i.e.* to the world of the less developed, is very meagre. The universities will do well to address themselves to:

(i) How does the education system relate itself to the needs of the community of its areas? Does it influence the rate, structure and character of economic development? How does the economic development influence the nature of the educational system?

(ii) Do the higher educational system and the general structure of education contribute to or check the growth of economic inequality and poverty?

(iii) How does a university in the third world relate education to rural-urban migration and rural-urban unemployment?

(iv) Does the higher educational system tend to promote or decelerate balanced urban-rural development?

1.4 Some specialized universities like agricultural and other rural universities, are there to help in the rural economy. But this sectoral system is not enough to arrest rural poverty. It is necessary for the total university system to have a larger area of interface with the rural economy. For this the universities, instead of remaining passive symbols of the status quo, will have to develop into active change agents of the society they serve. The layer of insensitivity that seems to be developing between the privileged university set-up and the toiling masses of these countries has to be removed. If the distance between the two goes on increasing, the progressive imbalance may lead to explosive consequences.

Let us now consider the principal challenges of poverty, population, illiteracy and environment which the villages pose for us and for the universities.

II. *Poverty*

2.1 The village becomes deprived of profitable economic activities because of the erosion of occupations and avenues of employment, talents and wealth from the villages to the cities. Poverty has increased as the number of days people in the village are able to get employment in production work has decreased. In India the rough figures are that whereas in 1900 the number of days of availability of work during the year to an average villager was 250, by 1925 it was reduced to 225; by 1950 it was 200 and by 1975 it stood at 175 days in the year. This may have gone down still more during the intervening years. Large numbers of the villagers, therefore, live below the level of subsistence.

To solve this problem the exodus of the villagers to cities is not a relief, because our cities also do not have enough work. We will have to create more jobs in the villages themselves. And as arable land is scarce these jobs should include such as are non-land-based; agriculture alone, even with irrigation and other intensive methods, cannot foot the growing unemployment bill. Unless we push up the number of days of work to some figure near 300 the rural-urban divide will become more acute with time.

2.2 The universities, therefore, owe it to themselves to take up this problem by seeking to evolve an economic model in which the urban system would assist the larger rural economy and *ecologically sound* and *socially just* scientific development can take place in the decentralized units of population that villages are, without taking away their advantages of conviviality amongst their members and their proximity to mother nature. For this the universities will have to evolve in their laboratories technologies that can create new industries which have low capital, low energy, and are adaptable to the conditions of the poor in the villages. In India we have 162 universities and more than 100 specialized national research laboratories under various technological bodies, but except for 22 agricultural universities the contribution of these scientific bodies in solving the problems of the villages has not been as it was expected to be. Universities and these laboratories will have to increase their area of interface with the villages; take up such techniques or processes as fulfil the criteria of appropriateness; and seek to optimize them to suit the conditions of the villages around them, by translating these techniques into trades and professions suitable to employ the rural poor and increase their working days and income.

2.3 One example of techniques which should be made into trades is biogas technology, which is acceptable to the villages, where cowdung is converted into cooking gas and at the same time provides better and more manure. This work, being done through government agencies, is progressing rather slowly. If it is made into a trade for the villages, and a biogas artisan class created, the work will leap forward. Universities taking up this and other similar activities will need technological, academic and managerial skills woven into the effort. In our Institute we have begun this exercise with good results.

III. *Population*

3.1 The second important area of challenge in the villages is the increase in population. In order to overcome this problem investment in education, training and health needs to be promoted, which in turn will slacken reliance on child labour and encourage lower fertility. The universities can do a lot in these respects through creating awareness among the teachers and students as well as in the rural/urban community round about.

3.2 In India, for instance, where urban population continues to swell by 2% per annum besides the onrush of migration from rural areas of the order of another 2% per annum, the University Grants Commission has selected 12 universities as population education resource centres (PERC). Gandhigram is one of them, with an operational spread all over the state of Tamil Nadu in the south except the metropolis of Madras. The PERC is intended to reach three target groups: the teaching faculty; the students; and the community, which specially constitutes its bull's-eye. The prime objects of PERC are to: (1) raise awareness among young people of population growth and its consequences, of the status of women, of fertility, mortality, infant mortality and population planning as components of development: (2) develop leadership qualities among the youth and sensitize every segment of the population to the concept of 'quality of life'; (3) undertake research, training and preparation of learning materials related to population education.

Its field activities include formation of population clubs in colleges/universities, which receive the facility of audio-visual aids such as film strips, slides, video cassettes, etc. These clubs organize seminars, conferences, lectures and discussions on the population problem, evils of dowry, better health and nutrition, status of women, and other related subjects. So far 30 population clubs have been instituted through the Institute's PERC programme.

3.3 The Gandhigram Rural Institute also reaches out to the village adults (men and women) for this programme through the animators of its 120 adult education centres. Thus there are at present 29 adult-education-based population education clubs in the villages. In India the University Grants Commission as well as the Association of Indian Universities has a special section to deal with this area, and many universities have taken up the nearby villages in their vicinity to make people aware of the problem and to find out how to overcome the obstacles. About 5000 villages have been taken up by 63 universities and 1300 colleges under this programme. This is a good beginning and an instance where the university is reacting to the problem of the people.

IV. *Illiteracy*

4.1 We do not know whether poverty generates ignorance or vice-versa but illiteracy and poverty do go together. India has more than 400 million illiterates and has taken up a mission approach on literacy, for adults belonging to the 15–35 age group. 92 universities and 2500 colleges are presently involved in this field and special grants are being provided to the universities for this programme under which some 10,000–12,000 villages are being covered.

4.2 The tempo will show its fuller impact when the voluntary help of the people is generated for this task, because we involve the community, make the people aware of their responsibility and help them to take it up. Good results follow. Those privileged to have attained higher education owe it all the more to themselves and the community to use their knowledge to remove illiteracy. For it is not the individual development of the few but the total development of the community/country that is the area of education.

4.3 The University Grants Commission of India, having recognised extension as the third dimension after teaching and research, and stressing it as an important part of university activities, has encouraged departments of extension in many universities to plan rural-oriented programmes in their area. It is expected that through this programme the various faculties will seek to help find solutions to the critical problems of the local village people.

V. *Environment*

5.1 Environmental awareness is another important area. Whereas in the affluent countries pollution seems to be a problem due to excess industrialization, production and consumption, in the poor countries the pressure of populations—though consuming per capita much less than others—on the meagre resource base of land, water and flora and fauna, creates environmental hazards of a deeper nature. The hills and mountains get denuded of trees, all plain land comes under the plough and erosion takes place both on sloping and plain lands. Excess agriculture leads to loss of soil fertility and scarcity of ground-water resource. All plant and animal life degenerates leading to a vicious cycle of poverty. India has instituted programmes of afforestation in waste lands on the plains and tree plantation on the hills. Under the National Wasteland Board many universities have taken up programmes of afforestation. We, for example, are also undertaking this year through the lab-to-land programme tree-planting schemes in 20 villages.

5.2 Though university courses do not contain much that brings the students closer to the immediate community from which they come, there are extra-curricular activities like the National Service Scheme and the National Cadet Corps whereby students have camps in rural areas and undertake physical labour in civil works for the village communities, *e.g.* making roads, bunds, etc. It is estimated that 1.1 million students are involved in these and such other programmes, which is about 1/3rd of the student population in higher education.

VI. *The Strategy*

6.1 A strategy is suggested here whereby the three wings of the university—extension, teaching and research—can be geared for the purpose of uplifting the society in which they are placed.

6.2 **Step one**: to change the attitude of the students and the faculty members and to do so by creating conditions under which they go to the villages and understand their problems and the strategy of offering alternative models of bringing about structural improvements and consequential changes which can help in bringing about a new order in which the villages will have a due place.

6.3 **Step two**: extension as a third dimension in universities in India is widely recognised and a few universities have full-fledged programmes of extension in the area of adult education, social forestry, transfer of technology, etc. These programmes should be made to involve as many of the faculties and students as possible and not be left to the few who are in the extension department.

6.4 **Step three**: in countries where the vast majority still live in the villages, in the field of teaching too we may have to make great changes, giving a rural orientation to the courses so that the benefits of newer knowledge of ecological living with rising income of the poor become the focus. In the new education policy (NEP 1986) of the government of India the universities are required to restructure the existing curricula so as to foster new interdisciplinary areas of teaching and study which will make education a means of national development at all levels—economic, social and political. The universities also should seek out the majority of the people in rural areas who depend largely on an agriculture-based economy and provide them with an opportunity to understand the significant social, economic, cultural, moral and spiritual issues facing humanity today.

6.5 **Step four**: in the field of research, the kind of topics and problems to be undertaken could be made more society-oriented and rural problems be given greater priority. The universities can also assist public bodies at the block/district/state/national levels in building up a reliable data base on all aspects of rural development, so that planning becomes realistic and result-oriented. Such data may be documented and a constant updating process may be launched so that over a period of time rural change, developments and directions can be systematically measured. A sort of 'social observatory' to watch the changes and ensure regular and systematic documentation may be of help.

6.6 **Step five**: in order to fulfil the objective four major interrelated components for any type of academic exercise towards community action are required.

(i) The universities should fix target groups—the students and teachers, who will be prime movers; the segments of local population to be reached on the basis of resources and needs, for example, the poor, the landless, small/marginal farmers, village artisans, etc., who will be the intermediate target; and the larger community, *viz.* the block, district, state, nation, world, which will form the ultimate target.

(ii) The universities should move on to organize 'development tactics', *i.e.* principles, procedures or techniques to bring about necessary changes in the university administration, in the students and staff, and in areas where they work, through persuasive tactics of logical, emotional, scientific and moral appeals and a re-educative approach to beliefs, the removal of superstition, and value modification.

(iii) The universities should help the government and society to set development goals, which connote the means and ends—the outcome sought or expected results from higher education for action. They may be short-, medium- and long-term goals, which may be basic to the university's hinterland for social and economic action.

(iv) The universities should help locate resources, both physical and human, and find usable methods and techniques to plan, upgrade and deploy human resources in their neighbourhood for

TOPIC 7: RURAL DEVELOPMENT

an egalitarian exploitation of the physical resources and management by the application of a suitable human-faced technology.

DISCUSSION

(*Rapporteur*: Mr. R. G. BOMONT, Secretary, University of Stirling)

(1) The first concern expressed was whether it was legitimate to concentrate on rural development when areas of deprivation, *i.e.* poverty, population, illiteracy and environmental degradation, were also present in urban communities—should the concern of universities not be with all underprivileged? Mr. Kumar agreed that the problems were not restricted to rural populations. However 80% of the population of most third-world countries were resident in villages and it was here that universities should concentrate for maximum impact.

(2) The second discussant stressed the need for rural development to be a measured thrust in national life which must be fully absorbed by higher education. A micro-approach was required with a new system of rural higher education being evolved. This new system required a total curriculum change where knowlege would be acquired from empirical sources, practice would be the basis of theory and the centrality of work rather than books would be emphasized. This new system would have as its major aim the meeting of the needs of country villages—this would be the major aim and not merely an appendage as may be the case with extension studies. Transformation of rural society should be the major goal with the development of human resources its priority aim.

(3) The third discussant asked for details of applied research projects. In response Mr. Kumar stressed the need to establish a rapport with villagers which was based on mutual respect. Self-help and motivation were to be encouraged and assisted. The poor had to be given the confidence to raise themselves above begging and dependence. The aim should be to release latent resources within the village and in doing this the university had to work closely with government and voluntary agencies. A university should look for lessons that can be transferred to other locations, and heighten the awareness of its students by basing 25% of its curriculum on the village—being topical to its location and including elements of rural technology, rural economics, sanitation and health.

Specific examples given of applied projects successfully introduced were:

(*a*) literacy programmes using villagers as the teaching instruments;

(*b*) education programmes in health, sanitation and population with emphasis on faecal-borne diseases and the importance of pure water. Following on from this a programme of introduction of latrines and systems for collecting water and the use of soaking pits;

(*c*) improvement of construction and housing standards by way of fireproofing, making of roof panels and construction of beams;

SUB-TOPIC 7(A): RURAL COMMUNITIES

(*d*) economy in the use of fuel (and thus control of environmental degradation) by improving the design of stoves;

(*e*) biogas tanks for gas and manure production;

(*f*) introduction of new crops, *e.g.* sunflowers, and new techniques, *e.g.* bee-keeping.

The aim of all these projects was to improve the human condition, to redress the balance between urban and rural society and to retain population in rural areas.

(4) The fourth discussant stressed the role of universities as monitoring and evaluation agencies for local schemes and for government and international agencies. In this role the universities would act as a watchdog—an example was given of the lack of knowledge of the future impact of many irrigation schemes.

(5) The fifth discussant put forward the view that the major task was the seeking of a solution to exploding population. This should be tackled through education and literacy programmes—there was a responsibility to illustrate to the villagers the link between population and the degradation of environment and functional roles in modern society. Without a solution of this problem the rest of the rural development programme was ineffectual and this element must be given priority.

(6) The final points raised were the scope for co-operative-type developments and the development of industries in rural areas. Mr. Kumar considered that the co-operative movement was very important. Universities were responding by running courses in co-operation. It was important to link the product with marketing. However there was a problem in wide-scale introduction in that the population was in the main reluctant to lose its individuality.

The introduction of industries into rural communities must at least for the moment, because of educational standards in the villages, be linked with the rural economy and be small and grow out of the general development, *e.g.* food processing and paper-making.

In conclusion it was suggested that universities should form networks for rural development both inside countries and perhaps externally.

Sub-Topic 7(b)

THE DESIGN OF LAND USE AND LAND RESOURCE MANAGEMENT COVERING ANY NEW CONCEPTS AND APPROACHES TO THE PROBLEM

Tuesday, 9 February

Professor MOONIS RAZA (*Vice-Chancellor, University of Delhi*):

LAND USE: CONCEPTS, CLASSIFICATION AND INFORMATION SYSTEM—THE EMERGING SCENARIO IN INDIA

Optimum land use is governed by considerations of land capability. It follows, therefore, that reliable information both on soil potentialities and current land use are needed for planning optimum land use. Land use pattern is dynamic in nature and changes from season to season and year to year unless it is optimized and stabilized under a very sophisticated management system.

Part I: *Towards Perceiving Newly Emerging Concepts: Concept of Dynamics of Land Use*

The term 'dynamics' refers more to the processes of spatial change of land use than to the functioning of land use systems. Some of the particular problems of land use change are those involving the expansion of land uses on the rural fringe, the expansion of small-holdings and disintensification in marginal areas. The IGU working group on the dynamics of land use systems has identified three tasks:

(1) the elaboration of classification of land use systems, hierarchical in nature and capable of being applied at all scales;

(2) the study of spatial change of land use systems and the consequences of such change using clearly defined 'universal' criteria and modern 'data-gathering techniques'; and

(3) the study of the functioning of land use systems as systems.

Land evaluation: land suitability and capability analysis. Considering the increasing competition between different uses of land, such as industrial, recreational and agricultural, a land use pattern based on optimal use of land capability needs to be emphasized. Wasteful use of land needs to be discouraged by adopting a rational policy. Any over-emphasis on one type of land use may cause a chain reaction with adverse effects on the other types of land use. With a view to prevent irrational use of land, an extensive survey is needed to establish the capability of various types of land for optimal uses. Land suitability evaluation is an inseparable part of land use—agricultural, forestry or recreational. This practice was inherently used in crop yield and agricultural land use evaluation by traditional farmers.

Many Indian scholars have in recent years studied land capability and land limitations with the aid of air-photographs. An inventory of capability classes has been prepared depicting physical characteristics, present as well as potential land use, and prevalent hazards and suggested improvements in agricultural land use.

Sustainable land use: measurement through carrying capacity. The concept of sustainable land use may be understood in terms of carrying capacity. The carrying capacity expresses the ability of land to support a population/organisms on a continuing basis. However there is no standard approach to how it should be calculated. The concept is based on the understanding that an ecosystem can tolerate a certain degree of anthropogenetic intervention or human/livestock pressure under normal conditions. Beyond that degradation sets in and sustainable utilisation is retarded. Each piece of land has its own unique productive capacity. No two land units or pastures are exactly alike. This productive capacity—the biotic potential—varies in terms of the quantity of vegetation it can produce as well as in terms of its other qualities. The productive capacity of individual farms varies in space and changes with time. The high productivity of land had attracted settlers to some areas in the past but floods and drought have now reduced crop yield in many such areas. It is imperative that we consider such variations and adjust our populations accordingly.

The state of range lands and tragedy of the commons. Most of the Indian range lands are suffering from threat of desertification. Though unwise attempts to cultivate range lands have led to disastrous results in some cases, overgrazing by domestic animals may be considered to be the main anthropogenetic cause of desertification. The traditional economic and social systems, including systems of land tenure, and the social institutions further complicate the issue. There appears to be an inherent contradiction between private and public interest in the use of communal grazing areas. While livestock belongs to individuals, grazing land is communal property. Individual livestock owners tend to increase the size of their livestock even if such increase damages the interest of communal grazing owing to deterioration of land. Such overgrazing has been termed the 'tragedy of the commons'.

Watershed management: an integrated concept. There is urgent need for wider application of 'watershed' concept to evolve a suitable regional development planning strategy which will make efficient use of a deficient natural resource base. This approach is well suited to warding off natural disasters, *i.e.* floods and droughts, by evolving a comprehensive development plan with a multidisciplinary integrated approach to achieving soil and water conservation and land management. After experimenting with diverse techniques on 40-odd selected watersheds in various parts of the country, the agriculture ministry has decided to launch a nationwide project in each of the 4200 dryland blocks. Each watershed will comprise nearly 2000 ha for integrated development.

Upland watersheds: empirical evidence from Damodar river basin. Through managing upland watersheds, the Damodar river basin has been transformed into a valley of prosperity. Following the example of the Tennessee Valley Authority in the United States this project was started with the aim of bringing the benefits of flood control, irrigation, power for industry and increased employment into the basin as a whole. Field work began in 1951–52 after a preliminary soil survey. Progress has been registered as follows:

(1) reconnaissance soil survey of 1,245,822 ha (69% of the total catchment area of dams);

(2) detailed soil survey of 436,214 ha (24% of the total catchment area of dams);

(3) afforestation of 142,641 ha (75% of the area needing treatment);

(4) soil conservation treatment of 148,526 ha of agricultural land and 106,252 ha of gullied land (54% and 85% respectively of the area found to need treatment);

(5) renovation of 39 old water storage tanks;

(6) establishment of and measurements at 55 sediment observation posts;

(7) a 137-kilometer canal built for irrigation and navigation has

enlarged the annual irrigated area from 89,000 to more than 350,000 ha;

(8) four dams built and floods moderated as documented by records from 1958 to 1982;

(9) reclaiming and irrigating fallow and degraded lands upstream and downstream of the silt-detention check dams;

(10) achieving better productivity from rainfed crops by an estimated 60–100 kg ha through soil conservation work on agricultural lands; and

(11) increasing water supply for people and cattle from water stored in silt detention dams.

Efforts are being made to extend such measures to other watersheds with a view to securing stable and productive land use.

Emerging cash-crop tree farming. Wood has gradually entered into the market economy in many places where tree resources have become scarce. The realization that markets for building poles, fuel-wood and charcoal are quite large, and are expanding, has provided incentive for farmers to take up farm forestry. Gujarat, where markets for construction poles and for fuel-wood have provided a significant incentive for farmers to plant trees, is the most widely reported example. At least 10% of Gujarat's farming population has been involved in farm forestry. More than 150,000 ha had been planted by 1983. An important achievement of this project is the involvement of schools and private farmers in growing seedlings.

Forestry for the landless and life for dying lands. This programme involved the landless by making state-owned lands accessible to them on a leasehold basis. In Gujarat, for example, shifting cultivators have been settled on degraded lands and given land use rights but not given official title deeds. Land preparation is carried out by the forest department, and seedlings and other inputs are provided free to the settlers. People protect and look after the trees and are also paid for 25 days of work per month. Settled families are allowed to collect building material and other forest products. The trees belong to the forest department but the settled families receive 20% of the net profits. About 18,000 ha of degraded forests had already been planted under this scheme in Gujarat by 1982.

The West Bengal social forestry project, aided by the World Bank, was launched in 1981 with the goal of increasing wood and fodder supplies through reforestation of denuded lands owned by the government. In the 1984–85 planting season alone, 24,000 ha of trees were planted by more than 51,000 farmers participating in various types of activities. During the first four years the forestry department was able to replant 14,430 ha of degraded forest and oversee the strip planting of 10,147 ha.

Biosphere reserves: as multiple land use units. Conservation of forest ecosystems depends on having good information available and using this information in land use planning. UNESCO-MAB (programme on Man and the Biosphere) is one of the most ambitious attempts to develop multiple-use planning for protected areas. India is establishing 13 biosphere reserves. These will function as multiple land use units containing environmental centres to encourage the participation of local people in managing the reserves. The reserves represent nine of the 12 major biogeographic provinces in India and will supplement India's 44 national parks and 207 wildlife sanctuaries. The total conservation area comes to 8.7 million ha. The national MAB committee, under the Department of Environment, has identified 12 sites as potential areas for biosphere reserves.

Dryland farming. At present about two-thirds (70%), or about 102 million ha of cultivated area of the country is under dryland conditions (rain-fed). These areas face numerous, varied and intricate problems. It has been estimated that, even if all the available water resources are exploited, about 55% of the country's cropped area will continue to remain under dryland farming for many years to come. At the same time the rain-dependent areas contribute nearly 42% of the total food produced in the country.

Scientific investigation into dryland farming has developed considerably during the last two decades. Soil conservation research centres, all-India co-ordinated projects and pilot development projects in dryland farming have come into operation. The establishment of the International Crops Research Institute of the Semi-Arid Tropics (ICRISAT) at Hyderabad marked a significant step in this direction.

Wetlands inventory. Most of the wetlands are highly productive ecosystems. An inventory of Indian wetlands has been prepared in recent years but information available about them is rather meagre, fragmentary and inadequate, even for the purpose of making broad generalizations. Wetlands have great potential for economic and biological productivity. However, specific research and inventory is needed for value assessment, including evaluation techniques for drinking water, irrigation, aquaculture for food, biofertilizers and nitrogen fixation. Land use management in the entire catchment area is the key to long-term sustainability in the use of wetlands.

SUB-TOPIC 7(B): LAND USE/RESOURCES [*Raza*]

Part II: *Need for More Meaningful Land Use Classification*

The present land use classification is based primarily on whether a particular area is cultivated, grazed, forested or put to non-agricultural uses. It shows mainly the distribution of existing land according to its actual use and not how a particular piece of land can be potentially utilised. Thus the area figure for culturable waste land does not represent the area which is really cultivable, because it may not be possible to bring under cultivation a large part of this area except at a huge cost. Therefore mere collection of statistics under the head 'culturable waste' serves little purpose. Detailed information about types of waste land in each district and state, the ownership of such land, its availability in sizeable block and the cost of reclamation measures should be collected. Similarly considerable portions of Indian forests are such only in name and are subject to various forms of degradation. Unless the area under different types of forest land is known, it will not be possible to plan forest development properly. The same applies to other land use classes also.

To make land use classification more meaningful for planning purposes it should be made more exhaustive. The forest area should be subdivided in relation to intensity of forest cover; cultivated area in relation to number of crops taken in a year, quality of soil and reliability of irrigation facilities; waste land in relation to type and extent of degradation and their suitability for different uses; pasture land in relation to types of grasses, etc. Such classification would also help in integrating land use planning with rural development programmes.

Part III: *Land Use Information System*

Existing land use data base. Many organizations and institutions are involved in the collection of data pertaining to land use, and all the available data is held in files/reports and is scattered in various departments. The National Bureau of Soil Survey and Land Use Planning (NBSSLUP) of the Indian Council of Agricultural Research and the All-India Soil and Land Use Survey of the Department of Agriculture are two organizations in the country with established data bases on land use. The district census publishes land use data at the village level every ten years. The ninefold classification on land utilisation is available at the village level and is published by the Bureau of Economics and Statistics every year. The National Commission on Agriculture (1976) also contained land degradation statistics. There has been overlapping of the areas in various types of land degradation with those in different land utilisation classes.

Status of land use mapping. Land use mapping is often considered synonymous with planning. The Survey of India brings out topographic maps on different scales with the use of ground and aerial surveys and mapping. The Forest Survey of India prepares land use maps of forest areas and monitors the changes every ten years utilising the aerial photographs on 1:50,000 scale. The National Atlas and Thematic Map Organization mapped land use information on 1.1 million scale. The district census, village agricultural census abstract and Bureau of Economics and Statistics have developed their own classification schemes for land use mapping and are limited to their particular areas of interest. The National Remote Sensing Agency has prepared a wastelands map of the country and of the various states based on the visual interpretation of Landsat imagery.

With the help of large-scale topographical maps, air photographs and remote sensing data it is possible to conduct a land resource inventory and to identify and characterize a hierarchic system of land units. This further needs to (i) evaluate the positive and negative aspects of the relationship between environment, existing use and capabilities, and (ii) identify the gap between its present productivity and potential. This gap needs to be narrowed over the years so as to achieve land use specialization and integrated land use in both physical and economic terms at micro-level. To do so requires an institutional set-up equipped with modern techniques. The NRDMS project described below is a good example of what is being attempted in this direction.

Proposed district data base management system. The Department of Science and Technology (DST) has recently launched a comprehensive programme to develop a national resources data management system (NRDMS) by setting up computerised data bases at micro-level, taking the district as the unit. Five experimental district data base centres have already been established during the seventh plan, to work out various management and maintenance procedures before the scheme is put into operation in all the districts.

The emphasis is on integration of conventional land-based and remotely sensed data so as to develop comprehensive data bases in a particular area which can be used for micro-level planning. The system involves two distinct tasks: (i) development of interface technology to link satellite remote sensing to CDDBR; and (ii) adoption of a grid-based geo-coded integrated data system, for both macro- and micro-level analysis and planning purposes.

Each unit would have authentic land use information at three

SUB-TOPIC 7(B): LAND USE/RESOURCES

levels: village, block and district. The principal application areas related to land use are: (1) land use for agricultural development; (2) soil erosion affected area and type of treatment needed in each case; (3) soil and water analysis; (4) estimation of forest cover to plan for forestry/social forestry; (5) location and identification of water resources for various uses; (6) demarcation of flood plain zones; (7) planning watershed catchment in drought-prone areas; (8) location and estimation of biomass; (9) thematic land use mapping; and (10) socio-economic information.

REFERENCES

Bonnet, H. H. (1955): Elements of Soil Conservation. New York, p. 144.

Brij Gopal (1986): Wetland Ecosystems: An Appraisal. Veroff Geobot Inst. ETH Stiftung Rubel, Zurich—87, pp. 362–71.

Dent, D. and Young, A. (1981): *Soil Survey and Land Evaluation.* London: George Allen and Unwin.

Grahm, E. H. (1961): *Natural Principles of Land Use.* New York: Oxford Univ. Press.

Straus, M. W. (1955): *Why not Survive?* New York: Simon and Schuster, pp. 182–83.

Vogt, W. (1948): *Road to Survival.* New York: William Sloane Associates, p. 16.

World Resource Institute (1985): *Tropical Forests: A Call for Action.* Part II, Case Studies, Washington.

DISCUSSION

(*Rapporteur:* Mr. D. C. WILLIAMS, Registrar, University of New England)

By way of background to his paper Professor Moonis Raza stressed that he considered agricultural and industrial development to be two interrelated, rather than separate, halves of rural development. He pointed out that the poor do not live only in rural areas nor the rich only in the cities. He also expressed the view that the university system has a responsibility to be closely involved in the many aspects of rural development. As a concluding personal statement he called for a new monetary measure of agricultural development. He considered that a more appropriate measure would be the ratio of energy in and energy produced.

The following points emerged during disucssion.
- There is an urgent need for data relating to the reclamation of mining land.

TOPIC 7: RURAL DEVELOPMENT

- Because of uncertain climatic conditions it is necessary to have a combination of activities in order to optimize land use.
- While good research work is being undertaken in university laboratories, the results are not being transmitted to the farmers.
- University research should take into account the needs and problems of the people living in the surrounding region.
- The collection of statistics for the purpose of evaluating projects must be undertaken by an independent organization, *e.g.* a university.
- The development of rural people should go beyond economic development and encompass the quality of life of the people.
- Concern was expressed that development would erode the traditional tribal cultures. Other speakers were of the view that the tribal economy could (perhaps should) advance without losing its basic culture.
- Universities should emphasize that land use management is a long-term issue, whereas politicians, who make many of the decisions, see issues from a short-term perspective.
- Because of the sociological issues involved in development, there are problems confronting non-Indian consultants and researchers in giving assistance.
- There was a call for involvement and collaboration of Commonwealth (and world) universities to assist in resolving development problems.
- There is a need to use the whole spectrum of technology to solve what in many cases are elementary problems in achieving development.
- Both primary and secondary industry should be developed at the village level. Industrialization is occurring in India but the tribes are not sharing in it.
- Land production per labour unit must be increased. Production increases achieved merely by more input of labour must be avoided.
- Because of the large percentage of the population that lives in the drylands, there is a need for a dry-crop revolution.
- Water management requires a commonality of catchment and command areas. An index of equity should be developed.
- Ownership of land is an important issue.
- Rural development should be seen in terms of a new world where high technology can be available on a small scale. Rural development programmes must take advantage of this.
- Universities must be involved in all aspects of rural development. They must have a vision for the future, and train people to utilise new technologies in order to improve the quality of life of rural communities.

Sub-Topic 7(c)

THE UNIVERSITIES AS AGENTS OF CHANGE DEALING WITH LINKS BETWEEN UNIVERSITIES AND THE RURAL COMMUNITIES

Tuesday, 9 February

Mr. K. KODITHUWAKKU (*Vice-Chancellor, University of Sri Jayewardenepura, Sri Lanka*): University education in most of the Commonwealth countries, including Sri Lanka, is often modelled after the long-established traditions of higher education in the United Kingdom. The British model of education has been effective in dealing with social and economic problems of the largely metropolitan communities. However the majority of Commonwealth nations are economies based on rural populations and agricultural activities. The British tradition of university education which shaped the concepts and functions of universities in these countries, particularly during their formative years, and which continued after their political independence has produced a mass of graduates basically to run the state administrative machinery. They were the knowledgeable, disciplined and analytical people who were to make impartial and efficient decisions. Unfortunately these administrative and professional roles for university outputs did not produce the kind of results in these economies that were necessary to meet the growing needs and expectations of the majority of people living in rural settings. In more recent decades the scene has changed in many countries, including Sri Lanka.

As a result of the expansion of educational facilities on the one hand, and the improvement in the equality of access to university education on the other, the university population in most developing countries has begun to reflect the relative distribution of population between the urban and rural sectors. Since the 1940s Sri Lanka has made quite a distinctive effort at broad-basing its general education system, and it has subsequently produced a large mass of educated people from all parts of the country. The numbers of students seeking university entrance have nearly doubled in each decade after the second world war. Though the universities have not been able to expand their annual enrolments accordingly, a remarkable shift in the patterns of entrance has taken place, largely as a result of the improvement in the equality of access to university education. In addition to the principle of merit, district of education and the facilities of education available in different areas form the basis of university admissions. Through this policy the proportion of university students with a rural background has increased since the early 1970s, and through this phenomenon a clear and strong relationship between the university and the rural community has already been established in Sri Lanka. The issues revolving around the contribution of universities to rural development, therefore, are closely intertwined with the fact that universities now cater largely to a mass of inputs from the rural community itself.

Traditionally the university graduate would like to work in an urban setting for such reasons as prestige, greater availability of opportunities for advancement, and the so-called push factors operating at the village level. Those graduates who have a rural background find it rather attractive to work in the established administrative settings in urban areas for social and for power-related reasons as well. In the village the power base is diffused among a number of centres of social, economic and religious significance. A graduate whose background does not strictly fit into this system of power distribution, which is often the case, cannot easily become effective in holding a formal position in the institutional set-up operating at the village level. He is often challenged and made dysfunctional. Nevertheless, with increasing unemployment on the one hand and changes in the institutional and social setting at the rural level on the other, the 'rural graduate' is now willing to go back to the village. However, a concerted effort has to be made by the universities and other institutions concerned to link programmes motivating graduates to go back to the village with programmes of rural community development. Some of the findings of a study conducted along the above lines in Sri Lanka are discussed in this paper.

The issues of linking up with rural communities can be grouped into three categories: (*a*) the composition of intake of rural students as to age, experience and maturity; (*b*) adjustment to university education including research to be more relevant to rural development; and (*c*) programming for effective utilisation of graduates in rural development activity. Universities are under pressure to open their doors to persons with rich experiences in rural development, which poses a challenge to the existing policy, and to introduce greater variety of student composition in the university. By increasing the variety of student population, the richness of classroom knowledge and opportunities for experimental learning can be enhanced. Coupled with this, the universities need to introduce a greater emphasis on enhancing social utility rather than mere generation of knowledge and its dissemination. This paper does not intend to discuss these two vital areas of issue, since space is limited, but to note the implications of programming for effective utilisation of graduates in rural development activity as concluded from a case study.

The case study covered a total of 100 university graduates who were trained by the graduates' placement service of the Ministry of Youth Affairs and Employment for the posts of unit manager in the accelerated Mahaweli development project, the largest multi-purpose development programme which intended to settle 125,000 farmer families and to double the hydro-power generation in Sri Lanka. All the graduates were selected from the disciplines of social sciences and agriculture with rural backgrounds, and they were given 12 months special training in agriculture, general management, marketing leadership, communication and community medicine. This training was given by universities, colleges and government departments, and it was organized by the graduates' placement service. The study was conducted after three years of work experience of those unit managers, with a view to finding out: (*a*) employment effectiveness in terms of their ability to work with the institutional system; (*b*) levels of job motivation; (*c*) commitment to work; (*d*) factors of success at work; and (*e*) problems they faced. The job of unit manager covered a wide range of responsibilities, including settlement of farmers, land administration, rural development, irrigation work, agricultural development, administrative and credit and marketing activity. In a more technical sense the job required the managers to act as agricultural extension officers as well. The unit manager was expected to work with divisional managers (the immediate superior), agrarian officers, irrigation engineers, land officers, and other similar officials who normally operate at rural level in the districts. The job of unit manager was necessary for the Mahaweli settlement areas to co-ordinate farmer-level institutional activity resulting from the accelerated project development work.

The study found that these graduate unit managers were much more effective, committed to work and highly motivated than other unit managers, both those who were non-graduates (who were less mature and not concerned much about their responsibilities) and those who were graduates in science disciplines (who were seeking better employment in the urban environment). One of the reasons for the effectiveness seemed to be the ability of the social science graduates to work with rural communities, including the farmers, and that resulted mainly from their rural social background and the specific training given to them. Their job expectations might have been somewhat lower than those of science graduates or they might have been different and closer to rural needs. The non-university graduates probably did not fit themselves into the system and they were not in a position to lead rural farmers. Previous settlement projects which obtained the services of non-university graduates had proved that they were not effective co-ordinators, and therefore most of the projects ended up as failures.

The high degree of commitment of new unit managers was observed on the basis of the number of meetings they attended at rural-level organizations, the training and consultation sessions organized, the number of hours worked per day and the results that they achieved. They also received better appreciation from the politicians at the district level, including district ministers and members of parliament. Their higher performance was observed in the following areas as well:

- achieving the best yield for the unit
- number of additional crops introduced
- popularization of fertilizer among farmers
- number of farmers who became grade 1 farmers during the period
- number of farmers motivated to combine farming with animal husbandry
- starting new small-scale ventures
- setting up model farms.

This case study shows that if universities can co-operate with government institutions in special projects dealing with rural development, the universities can make a significant contribution as agents of change dealing with links between universities and the rural communities. Therefore it seems important that universities work closely with agencies which are responsible for planning and programming for sectoral development. A certain degree of innovative thinking directed to linking up university outputs to real situations in rural communities is essential.

SUB-TOPIC 7(c): AGENTS OF CHANGE

Professor Dato' Dr. NAYAN ARIFFIN (*Vice-Chancellor, University of Agriculture, Malaysia*):

THE UNIVERSITIES AS AGENTS OF CHANGE: THE INTERACTION OF UNIVERSITIES AND RURAL COMMUNITIES

University Change Agent Role and Working with Rural Communities

Universities that support the development of rural communities all have a sound rationale for their involvement. In playing the role of a change agent in rural communities four major reasons are often quoted. The first is to facilitate a holistic and realistic perspective of the country's needs and constraints, thus ensuring that the university's programmes remain relevant. The second is to make better use of the resources in the community and those of the other agencies. The third is to build a co-operative spirit among the development agencies and community members and its groups. And the fourth is to sustain the good rapport with the rural communities as well as guard against misinterpretation of the role of the university activities and programmes in their midst.

Most of these efforts will come under the umbrella of the university's outreach, extension, community development or other similar programmes. As a change agent the university can play several roles in the community. It can conduct research together with the community members and groups, initiate community development programmes, or provide knowledge and educational facilities to initiate and hasten community decision-making processes. In either one or several of these roles the university has to have the content and the effective mechanisms for linking with the communities.

Factors Influencing the Linkage Role

Several factors promote or limit the involvement of the university in rural communities. These can be classified into two major categories—external and internal (Sulaiman et al., 1984).

External factors are those which have to do with situations outside the university system influencing the performance of the university. Taken as a group, they may preclude success in any particular role of the university. External factors can be further divided into five dimensions: (i) public values; (ii) political expectations; (iii) research expectations; (iv) financial support; and (v) centralization and government intervention.

Internal factors are those which operate within the university system itself. They have to do with the character of the university and the people who participate in academic activities. These factors have a more direct bearing on the impact of the university's programmes in rural development. Internal factors can be divided into six dimensions which are found to be directly associated with the effectiveness of universities in performing their roles in rural development: (i) university philosophy; (ii) limits of public service option; (iii) leadership and internal coherence; (iv) trends in developing countries; (v) enthusiasm of academic staff; and (vi) techniques for accountability.

When one examines the above set of dimensions it seems obvious that several of them do directly influence the tendency and capability of the university to link with rural communities. From the external factors, the public values and the centralization and government intervention are the two dimensions that affect the university role.

In terms of public values, the external environment actually dictates the role played by the university. Although a university may offer a wide range of disciplines, specialists and intellectuals, the state of the public enterprise creates a demand for university expertise. This demand may be interpreted as knowledge in marketing, production economics or the transfer of technologies. In this respect a university should be expected to give expert advice rather than to implement projects, which is the bona fide function of development agencies. This expertise is manifested through the provision of continuing education, consultancy, advisory services and extension work.

The centralization and government intervention dimension can also shape a university's role within the rural community. This is especially so where there is a trend towards centralization of university policies and control. In this respect university outreach programmes may be relegated to a poor third as consideration is almost always given to the teaching of students followed by research.

In terms of the internal factors, several dimensions such as the university philosphy, the leadership, the funding, the internal linkages, the academic enthusiasm, the accountability procedures and limits of the public service options will shape the university role. Of all the dimensions of internal factors the university philosophy can perhaps be considered as the single most important dimension. A clear philosophy of seeking relevance in its teaching and research functions and for service of the community will facilitate the growth and acceptance of the public service function. In so doing the university's involvement in rural development is given due consideration in university decision-making.

Staff enthusiasm, the internal linkages and the limits of the public service option work together to some extent in affecting the rural outreach role. The root of these dimensions is the academic specialists available in the university, how they interact across disciplines and whether the disciplines are relevant to the rural problem at hand. In any case a particular rural outreach activity must really be relevant to a particular field in the university, if it is to continue to be in demand and attract specialists' attention.

Funding, leadership and accountability procedures may also be seen as working together. In order to mount an effective outreach or public service programme the university must commit resources to establish the operating unit with adequate facilities. This is where the firmness and foresight of the leadership will be crucial to a university's community linkage and public service programme. The leadership can also further support this function if public service activities of university staff are given appropriate weighting in promotional and accountability exercises and procedures. The latter will serve as the motivator for university staff to spend adequate time in rural outreach activities, which otherwise would be better spent by them on instruction and research.

The Linking Requirements

Keeping the foregoing dimensions of the external and internal factors in perspective, we can now discuss the bare essentials for the linking of the university with the rural community. Among these are goals setting, staff commitment, financial support and the linking approach.

The goals to be set have to be in line with the philosophy of the university (assuming that the university subscribes to the outreach function), understood by members of the community and recognized by the university administrators. The commitment of the staff is certainly the single most important requirement in creating linkages with the rural community. Earlier this has been referred to as staff enthusiasm. Essentially, staff commitment has to be significant to balance between teaching, research and outreach work and to help ascertain the internal mechanisms of planning and co-ordination.

By financial support is meant first, the establishment of a functional unit to facilitate, co-ordinate and actively plan for university involvement with rural communities. University-wide public service activities may be self-sufficient or in the long run help to put the university in better light for more funding, but the initial investment in a public service outfit can be substantial.

The linking approach adopted can take three major forms. First is from the stance that the university offers its useful expertise for the rural community. In this role the university through its staff becomes the facilitator of change in the community (see also Rollings, N. 1987; Sulaiman and Mohd. Fadzillah, 1983). Second is by way of responding to the actual needs of the community, working on the requests from the rural community (Havelock, 1969). In these two approaches the university is often faced with the limitations of staffing, resources, and that it has no direct mandate to be involved in rural development work *per se*. A third approach, which is growing in importance, is by forging mechanisms to collaborate with other development agencies. This is accomplished through memoranda of understanding and the exchange of letters of intent which provide the basic guidelines and scope and mode of co-operation to be fostered.

Modes of Linkage and Useful Experiences

A common mode of linkage that a university often has is through an outreach or extension programme that allows its staff and students to interact with the rural community. The University of Agriculture, Malaysia, for example has a close working relationship with 90 villages in three states. In these villages staff members and students help other development agencies implement community projects, identify training needs and conduct field testing research. Community members are trained at the University and once a year invited to a 'farmers' day' there to foster closer relationships and offer the opportunity to exchange ideas on technical and socio-economic matters. Furthermore, the University reaches farmers indirectly through its co-operation and training programmes involving almost all government development agencies.

Universities in Indonesia promote a programme called *Kuliah Kerja Nyata*, or community practicum, where all students spend a semester living in a rural community with the multiple purposes of absorbing good attitudes, consideration and co-operative spirit (see Abdullah, 1981).

Another common mode of linkage is through co-operation with other institutions working in the community or responsible for the development of a certain geographical area. Memoranda of understanding and letters of intent are often used to facilitate such a linkage. The university may be involved in different kinds of activities as before, with the central concern of supporting its beliefs and answering questions rather than the conduct of operational activities best left to the development agencies themselves. The universities may serve as advisers to projects for beneficiaries that are mutually agreed upon and to work along agreed lines of action. In collaboration with other agencies universities help in trying out new approaches to working with the rural community or in providing the necessary training support and communication materials development.

An interesting project that has resulted in considerable achievement can be found in Khon Kaen University, Thailand. Among others, Khon Kaen University supports an intensive farm training project. It provides comprehensive training for master farmers for a year on the campus farm where the whole farm family stays. At the end of the year 10 farmers' families leave for their villages to provide the secondary linkage between the university and the rural communities (Adul Apinantara, 1981).

Enabling Factors for University-Community Linkage

In this section discussion is posited about the enabling factors that contribute to the success and sustenance of the university-community relationship. This is important in that, as many efforts have been undertaken by many universities, the factors that are most essential can be noted, monitored and nurtured. Table 1 illustrates the dynamics of these factors.

TABLE 1: DYNAMICS OF UNIVERSITY FACTORS INFLUENCING CONDUCT OF RURAL DEVELOPMENT ACTIVITIES

Consideration	*Consequent Action*	*Enabling Factor*
1. Establishment	• Establish mandate for trilogy of functions— teaching, research and extension	University philosophy Public values
	• Accept principles of excellence and relevance in programmes	
	• Design goals for outreach and rural development	

Consideration	Consequent Action	Enabling Factor
2. Administration	• Establish responsible unit for outreach	Leadership and internal coherence Financial support
	• Recognition of staff involvement in outreach activities	Recognition in promotional exercise
3. Organization	• Unit serves as co-ordinator of rural development activities, charged to provide support facilities	Management efficiency Leadership and internal coherence
4. Internal linkages	• Establish university outreach committee, faculty liaison committees, identification of subject-matter specialists	Staff enthusiasm Accountability
5. External linkages	• Establish joint development, training and field research projects with agencies/communities	Scope of public service (as determined by expertise and resources)
	• Joint committees and memoranda of understanding with development agencies	Staff enthusiasm and commitment
6. Research and consultancy	• Conduct joint research and consultancy activities with rural development agencies	Staff enthusiasm Scope of public service Growing research capacities Research expectations from public
7. Community programme	• Institutionalized rural development activities in rural areas	Scope of public service Staff enthusiasm
	• Offer continuing education to agency professionals and take lead in developing and disseminating new technology	Political expectations Financial support

SUB-TOPIC 7(c): AGENTS OF CHANGE [*Nayan*]

To a university administrator charged with the promotion and sustenance of this university role within its outreach or public service function, cognizance of the enabling factors is crucial.

Constraints often Experienced

The constraints most often experienced can usually be traced back to the enabling factors discussed above. Loss of staff enthusiasm and commitment can be a consequence of poor programming or lack of financial support and lead to the eclipse of the public service function. Elsewhere, the Food and Agriculture Organization has labelled these as orientational, organizational and resource constraints (see FAO report, 1985). Among the constraints that often demand greater attention are:

(i) programming—the dynamics and politics of matching rural community objectives with university capacities and mandates;

(ii) participation—a necessary ingredient for programme success, but very much dependent on the quality and extent of such participation;

(iii) problem dynamics—ever-changing range of rural community problems that demand proper monitoring and adaptation of educational efforts; and

(iv) changing technology—causing up-dating of staff competence, community information base development and modification in rural community practices.

Given these constraints, the important principles are still the following. First, university involvement must relate to questions which match its research and teaching functions with community needs. Second, its rural community linkages must be limited in such a way that operational activities are avoided, meaning those under the purview of other agencies in the community are better left for these agencies to accomplish.

Thus, with the two principles in perspective, the need is for a university to deliberate actively in assessing the constraints so that it is better guided in its resources allocation and in pursuing the outcomes in community linkages as expected by the public of its academic leadership status in society.

Implications of University Change Agent Roles

Any university has to be selective in the role it wants to play because it cannot afford to excel in all fields of knowledge. Nevertheless, discussion of university roles will necessarily cover the traditional roles of the acquisition of knowledge, the transmission of culture and the application of knowledge itself.

University's role in teaching. As has been alluded to earlier, several factors will affect the university's role in teaching about rural community linkages and development. Universities do produce trained manpower for rural and community development work, especially in countries where a large proportion of the population reside in the rural areas. When a university believes strongly in relevance, then its activities in outreach and community development may become more visible, as found in most of the ASEAN countries. However, actual interest of the students in rural and community development can only be further enhanced when teaching staff themselves have direct and indirect involvement in off-campus activities.

Research. To advance the rural community linkage endeavour, university researchers must aim to improve the rural community. This requires them to be skilled in local diagnostic research and be open to community participation. The university will then require a system to promote interdisciplinary and collaborative research as demanded by the dynamics of rural community change. Needless to say, the research endeavour needs to be protected from other demands such as heavy schedules of undergraduate teaching, while at the same time being adequately funded.

Public service. The nature and scope of the public service function largely ascertains the university role in affecting university-rural community linkages. Much of this reflects the external environment which demands the university's attention. Other important factors are the university's philosophy on relevance, the sustenance of academic enthusiasm, efficient means to address community problems and the financial and leadership support of such activities. Suffice it to say here that within its public service function, the university-community linkage relationships need to be carefully monitored and assessed as to their contribution to the university ethos and purposes.

Conclusion

Universities in developing countries, if and when considering involvement in rural development, must assess their own situations and the demands that society may place on their shoulders. As and when these demands are accepted by the university community, it must then examine how it can mobilize and allocate its resources to meet such demands and in congruence with the internal coherence thus developed in the university. Again, the major factor here

SUB-TOPIC 7(c): AGENTS OF CHANGE

focuses on the need for enlightened and far-sighted leaders who will have to balance the demands for rural development, and the public recognition that that brings, with available university enthusiasm and expertise, without jeopardizing the university's search for excellence and relevance.

REFERENCES

1. Adul Apinantara (1981): 'Extension Programs In Faculty of Agriculture, Khon Kaen University'. *Asian Seminar Workshop on the Articulation of the Extension Function of Agricultural Colleges and Universities*, Searca, Los Banos.

2. Abdullah Ali (1981): 'The Rural Extension Programs of Syiah Kuala University'. *Ibid.*

3. FAO (1985): *Expert Consultation on Linkages of Agricultural Extension with Research and Agricultural Education*. RAPA, Bangkok.

4. Havelock, R.G. (1969): *Planning for Innovation through Dissemination and Utilization of Knowledge*. Ann Arbor: University of Michigan, Institute of Social Research.

5. Quisumbing, E.C. (1981): 'Establishing Linkages between the Colleges/Universities of Agriculture and Other Agencies'. *Asian Seminar Workshop on the Articulation of the Extension Function of Agricultural Colleges and Universities*, Searca, Los Banos.

6. Rollings, N. (1987): 'Whither Rural Extension'. *Occasional Papers in Rural Extension No. 2*. University of Guelph, Guelph.

7. Sulaiman M. Yassin and Mohd. Fadzillah Kamsah (1983): 'The Need for Information in Effective Community Participation in Implementing Agricultural Programmes', in Oli Mohamed and Wong Tuch Cheong (eds.): *Information for Productivity and Development*. Maruzen Asia Press, Singapore.

8. Sulaiman M. Yassin, Ibrahim Mamat, Saidin Teh and Robert L. Bruce (1984): 'Role of the University in Extension and Rural Development', in Sulaiman M. Yassin, Ibrahim Mamat and Irene Beavers (eds.): *Improving Strategies for Rural Development*. Universiti Pertanian Malaysia Press, Serdang.

DISCUSSION

(*Rapporteur:* Mr. J. D. SMITH, Registrar, James Cook University of North Queensland)

(1) Within the group there was no disagreement about the need for universities to have links with rural communities and to be involved in rural development. There was, however, variation of opinion as to: (*a*)

TOPIC 7: RURAL DEVELOPMENT

just *how* the universities should be involved; and (*b*) what 'rural development' means.

(2) In relation to (*a*) there was some support for the view that universities should be *directly* involved with rural communities, by actually sending staff and students to work in them on projects designed to improve the quality of life for rural dwellers. One speaker went so far as to suggest that universities should recognise a 'third dimension', additional to their teaching and research functions—that of commitment to serve the community; and that they should fulfil this commitment by making a period of rural development instruction and activity a compulsory component of every student's degree programme.

It seemed to be generally accepted, however, that the universities' involvement would be more effective if it were *indirect, i.e.* the universities should work with the personnel of development agencies, and assist them by providing in-service training, refresher courses, etc. Direct involvement would in most cases not be feasible because of inadequate human and financial resources.

(3) In relation to (*b*), the meaning of 'rural development', two important issues were raised.

(i) There is a danger of equating rural development with *agricultural* development, and of assuming that concentration on improving the technical aspects of agricultural production is what is mainly required. But it could be important to develop an extent of rural *industrialization* to reduce the rural area's almost total dependence on agriculture.

(ii) Efforts to improve the quality of rural life may be an *educational* rather than a high-tech problem. In third-world countries there occurs still an enormous number of deaths caused by water-related diseases, and this problem persists because both the rural dwellers themselves and their administrators are poorly educated. The speaker who raised this matter quoted as an example an African community which was given a fine modern clinic to treat its diseases without any attempt being made to modify an unguarded well which was clearly the cause of many of these diseases.

Sub-Topic 7(d)

STRATEGIES FOR UNIVERSITY PROGRAMMES OF TRAINING, RESEARCH AND EXTENSION WHICH CAN LEAD TO BETTER LAND USE IN THE RURAL AREAS

Note.—The author of the following paper, who was to have spoken on Sub-Topic 7(d), was at the last moment unable to attend the Congress but has provided his text for inclusion in the Report of Proceedings.

Dr. B. KAYOMBO (*Department of Agricultural Engineering and Land Planning, Sokoine University of Agriculture*):

THE CASE OF TANZANIA

1. *Introduction*

As universities are among the most important educational institutions, their programmes should be geared to development goals. In Tanzania, and in the developing world in general, the improvement of agricultural production and overall rural development is of great significance. Since agriculture is the most extensive land use activity in Tanzania, land use planning plays a pivotal role, albeit implicitly, in the economy of the country. The function of land use planning is to guide decisions on land use in such a way that the resources of the environment are put to the most beneficial use of man, whilst at the same time conserving those resources for the future. Land evaluation, an important component of the land use planning process, is concerned with the assessment of land performance when used for specified purposes. It involves the execution and interpretation of basic surveys of climate, soils, vegetation and other aspects of land in terms of the requirements of alternative forms of land use (FAO, 1976).

2. Assessment of the Present Situation

2.1 *Training inadequacies.* Success or failure of teaching programmes depends in the first place on the ability and dedication of the teaching staff. The faculty of agriculture of Sokoine University of Agriculture, and the faculty of arts and social sciences and the Institute of Resource Assessment of the University of Dar es Salaam, are in the process of building up qualified permanent staff cadres. This exercise started some 15 years ago and the Institute of Resource Assessment has already filled key positions with nationals; others are striving to achieve this. The average age of the national academic staff is relatively low in the two faculties; some are away following advanced studies, others are ready to go as soon as arrangements for necessary replacements are made. It sometimes occurs, therefore, that important posts remain unfilled for a long period and that the teaching is left to expatriates on short-term assignments or even to teaching assistants. In such circumstances practicals are first to suffer, and if this happens for several subject areas over months the quality of the teaching programmes as a whole may be reduced to a shadow of what it ought to be.

About half of the academic staff cadres have been trained abroad. On returning home the fresh graduates are unable to simulate what they studied in the conditions actually prevailing. This situation is exacerbated by a lack of facilities, which may also hamper the adoption of effective curricula.

There is a strong belief that the teaching of land use planning requires specialized facilities and, as a result, our universities have copied the curricula from universities in developed countries, particularly the United Kingdom. There is thus a persistent lack of flexibility in the curricula to take into account the dynamic local conditions. A very critical aspect of land evaluation is the availability of information about land use requirements (*i.e.* the set of land qualities that determine the production and management conditions of a kind of land use), especially in a developing country such as Tanzania. This information is often very difficult to obtain, and may be incomplete or vague. It is not unusual to find that handbooks on the cultivation of tropical crops give the ideal land conditions, which bear little resemblance to the actual land conditions prevailing in the project area where the suitability needs to be evaluated (Vink, 1985).

2.2 *Lack of research initiatives.* Research funding is inadequate in all activities that use land as a natural resource. In addition there are weaknesses in the management of those scarce funds. Among problems encountered in Tanzania are the fragmentation of

SUB-TOPIC 7(D): TRAINING, RESEARCH, EXTENSION [*Kayombo*]

responsibility among several ministries and excessive dispersion of resources in an attempt to meet all local needs. The situation induces inefficiency in the use of scarce manpower, physical facilities and equipment. The dispersion of responsibility has led to obstacles in adopting an intersectoral approach and the neglect of research on land use systems. It has also made it difficult to curtail the duplication of effort.

The need for training agricultural and land use research managers in developing countries seems to have gone unrecognized until fairly recently. The prevalent practice in most developing countries, including Tanzania, has been to promote senior researchers to administrative positions to manage various agricultural institutions, the criterion for such appointments generally being seniority in service. Consequently research activities have tended to stagnate and in some cases even to deteriorate steadily.

2.3 *Lack of a unified extension service.* During the 1940s and 1950s land use planning and soil conservation were included in the activities of several departments in the then Tanganyika Territory. Although, generally, the advice given by extension workers on soil conservation measures and non-cultivation along water courses and on steeper slopes was well received, in some cases it had to be enforced by administrative measures through local by-laws. In other cases no effort was made by the extension agents to explain the by-laws properly to the farmers. Because of this their implementation was resented and a few ugly incidents were reported (Temple, 1972). The present fragmented responsibility on land use planning among three ministries does not provide an efficient extension service.

In Tanzania, rural communication could be traced to the late 1960s. Two branches of communications and development, radio forums and mass campaigns, began after the Arusha Declaration (Blueprint for Socialism and Self-reliance) in 1967. The radio forums were part of Tanzania's effort to redefine the role of the mass media in the construction of a new socialist society. The mass campaigns, using radio and other means, focused on adult education, health and the co-operative movements. One such mass campaign, conducted in 1973, called 'Mtu ni Afya' (man is health) was rated successful. Reports show, however, that one of the greatest operational problems of the campaign was inadequate training of group leaders (Hall, 1978).

A typical example of the lack of knowledge of the cultural milieu of a population by those who are supposed to help it, and of its subsequent failure, is that of the kind of language sometimes used in radio programmes by extension workers or agronomists when giving explanations to peasant farmers. There are two assumptions which the 'speakers' in the above programmes make about the recipients of the information they are giving. First, they seem to assume that the public they are addressing is versed in land use planning scientific jargon. But the reality is that the majority of the intended recipients are small farmers who have not gone beyond the literacy classes. A second assumption which is connected to the first is the type of language used. Although the sentences do bear the structure of Kiswahili (the national language), the assumption seems to be that the intended public knows English. So there is free use of Swahili-ized English terms even for words which have 'ordinary' equivalents. But worse still is the use of wholesale English words throughout these programmes. It seems, therefore, that technical language is being used by the expert without being properly processed and adapted to suit the level of the people for whom the information is intended (Besha, 1986).

3. Remedial Measures and Future Prospects

3.1 Training initiatives. The University of Dar es Salaam has reviewed the BA degree curriculum and included techniques for assessing and evaluating land resources and land use planning and management in Tanzania (UDSM, 1987). The joint University of Dar es Salaam/Sokoine University of Agriculture BSc(AgricEng) programme includes a 10-week field practical training attachment at the GTZ-assisted soil erosion control and agroforestry project (SECAP) in the Usambaras of north-east Tanzania. The role of SECAP is to restore the ecological balance and halt environmental destruction by implementing agricultural techniques designed to reduce erosion and increase agricultural, livestock and forestry productivity (Scheinman, 1985). Sokoine University of Agriculture will launch an MSc(AgricEng) programme in 1989 with special emphasis in land resource planning and irrigation management training for the SADCC (Southern African Development Co-ordination Conference) countries. Important subjects to be taught include land surveying and aerial photointerpretation, economics of resource management, land resource survey and analysis, soil conservation and reclamation of eroded land, irrigation and drainage management, agricultural extension and research planning and management. Laboratory and field equipment support will be provided by the government of the Federal Republic of Germany through GTZ.

3.2 Provision of research facilities. In Africa success stories of effective agricultural and land use planning research systems could largely be attributed to one or two gifted individuals in the country who provided leadership in organization and management (Anon, 1985). There are also cases in which research systems have begun to deteriorate rapidly on the retirement of one or two individuals who provided the leadership. It is this fragility which strongly argues the case for properly organized programmes for research management training.

At Sokoine University of Agriculture, BSc(Agric) and BSc(Agric-Eng) students do receive a somewhat elementary course in research planning, but they get a better dose of the simulation 'green revolution' game, which gives them an appreciation of the magnitude of planning decisions that a rural land user must take on a given piece of land. Postgraduate students are likely to benefit from the research planning and management course, the four-week field practical group attachment, and from their one-year MSc thesis work. The Institute of Resource Assessment of the University of Dar es Salaam also supervises postgraduate students undertaking research in land use planning. Whereas the Institute of Resource Assessment receives research support from the government of Sweden, Sokoine University of Agriculture will acquire laboratory and field equipment for teaching and research from GTZ.

Land evaluation still relies heavily on data collection, and for practical reasons there is a limit to the number of observations of natural phenomena and experiments that can be made relating to one specific site (Veldkamp, 1979). Making analogues with other areas has been the most common technique for obtaining such additional data (Bennema, 1978). But one cannot always rely on the correlation with analogous areas, since many development situations are characterized by a unique combination of socio-economic and physical constraints and very specific development objectives. As the analysis of physical input/output relations also tends to become more and more complex, system analysis and simulation will need to be increasingly relied upon. Mathematical and analogue models will probably become valuable tools for the study of specific land qualities and land use processes. The use of mathematical models, solely, for simulating all input/output relations influencing the performance of a land use system will probably remain too complex to satisfy practical land evaluation entirely in the immediate future. For a better characterization of the environmental regimes (*i.e.* land qualities), modifications may be required in the data-collecting stage of land evaluation, the methods and density of sampling, the techniques of making land resources maps and the classification of land attributes. More attention should be paid to the study of 'land' and 'landscape' rather than to the study of components only, such as soil, climate, vegetation, hydrology (Zonneveld, 1979).

Land evaluation must compromise between scientific ideals and the limitations set by the availability and reliability of data and the means available for handling these data. Some of the MSc(AgricEng) thesis projects will, in fact, investigate simple but reliable methods of data collection for land evaluation under prevailing local conditions.

3.3 *Training in extension.* Extension work in agriculture and land use planning is important for the successful application of research results. The third-year BSc(Agric) students at Sokoine University of Agriculture receive lectures in extension, and visit neighbouring villages regularly for interviews and discussions on agricultural development activities. However the third-year BSc(AgricEng) students, under the guidance of staff in the department of agricultural engineering and land planning, have had an elaborate extension programme with five neighbouring villages since 1985. The practical aspect of development communication involves going to neighbouring villages to conduct surveys, interviews and discussions about the layout and construction of stormwater drains and channel terraces, tree planting and its significance, the avoidance of burning, preparation of land for contour and tie-ridge cultivation, construction of compost piles, agroforestry and care of water resources and water reserves. These exercises are intended to elicit villagers' attitudes on a wide range of subjects. Students are assisted in preparing audio-visual materials to be used in the discussion with the villagers. For example, charts and cassette recordings were used in discussions about agroforestry and contour-bund cultivation in two villages in 1986. The student teams found that the villagers would be eager to support and sustain the projects if given technical assistance.

The Institute of Continuing Education of Sokoine University of Agriculture is to launch an annual three-month training course in communication skills with special emphasis on land use planning, beginning in July 1989. The entrants for this course will come from the ministries of agriculture and livestock development, lands and natural resources, and water. Training will specifically aim at equipping them with techniques of adapting 'land use planning' language to ordinary usage. For a person to be able to process scientific information for the general public it is necessary for her or him to be very competent in the subject matter. The correct use of the right type of language to the right people is a prerequisite for effective communication in any society.

The department of agricultural engineering and land planning will establish, with financial assistance from the ODA (Overseas Development Administration of the United Kingdom), a demonstration farm in 1990. All important aspects of the whole farming system are to be included, among them mechanized farming, irrigation, soil conservation, land use practices and crop processing and storage. It becomes fairly clear that the best strategy of introducing better land use practices, new technologies or any other innovation is to establish demonstration centres or farms where the target groups can see the practical difference over some time, rather than introducing them through theoretical lectures and crash programmes. Demonstration allows the target groups to study the effects and compare the results of the new ways with those of the old ways of doing certain things.

4. Conclusion

Many developing countries in Africa, Latin America and Asia depend on agriculture for their livelihood. Problems which militate against a better rural land use (*i.e.* lack of adequate training and research facilities and lack of a coherent extension service) are thus not only unique to Tanzania. Universities have an important role to play in redressing the situation through provision of adequate locally-adapted training and research in land use planning and management. Universities should particularly 'go out from the campuses' and 'involve the nearby villages and the countryside in extending new and better land use practices to the farmer'. A demonstration farm (or university farm) should be an important constituent of a developing-country university to demonstrate better land use practices to both the student and the farming community. These are challenges which developing-country universities must strive to achieve.

REFERENCES

Anon, 1985: 'National agricultural research systems: the management factor'. FAO Review Agric. Development, 18 (3): 15-17.

Bennema, J., 1978: 'Land evaluation for agricultural land use planning', in L. D. Swindale (ed.), *Soil-resource data for agricultural development*. Hawaii Agric. Exp. Stat., College of Tropical Agric., Univ. Hawaii, pp. 152-165.

Besha, R. M., 1986: 'Do farmers understand the language used by extension workers?' The Courier, 100: 87-88.

Food and Agricultural Organization of the United Nations (FAO), 1976: 'A framework for land evaluation'. Soils Bull. 32, Rome.

Hall, B. L., 1978: 'Mtu ni Afya: Tanzania's Health Campaign'. Washington, DC: Clearinghouse on Development Communication, 69.

Moormann, F. R. and N. van Breemen, 1978: 'Rice: soil, water, land'. IRRI, Los Banos.

Scheinman, D., 1986: 'Caring for the Land of the Usambaras'. GTZ, Eschborn, West Germany.

Temple, P. H., 1972: 'Soil and water conservation policies in the Uluguru mountains, Tanzania'. Geografiska Annaler, 54A (3-4): 110-123.

University of Dar es Salaam (UDSM), 1987: *The University Calendar*. University Printing Press, Dar es Salaam.

Veldkamp, W. J., 1979: 'Land evaluation of valleys in a tropical rain area—a case study'. PhD thesis, Agric. Univ. Wageningen.

Vink, A. P. A., 1975: 'Land use in advancing agriculture'. Springer Verlag, Berlin, Heidelberg, New York.

Zonneveld, I. S., 1979: 'Land information, ecology and development'. ITC Journal 1979-4, pp. 475-498.

Topic 7

FINAL SESSION

Thursday, 11 February

The group reviewed summaries of discussions it had already had, and went on to talk further about various aspects of the Topic that had been touched upon in previous sessions. The following were among the points made.
- The real problem of the rural poor was not technology transfer as such, but a socio-political problem—how to bring them to accept developmental change despite the element of risk that change always entails. The difficulty lay in the defeatist attitude so frequently engendered by the inability of the poorest members of rural communities to benefit from the changes that they saw taking place around them (*e.g.* the availability of electricity). The emphasis initially should be on new techniques which brought immediate benefits for those who were worst off—not economic benefits, but help with practical aspects of the daily routine (*e.g.* the use of ball bearings to ease the strain of drawing water). However improving the quality of life in this way was not a sufficient end in itself; the structure of society must be changed to enable the poor to escape from their poverty and enjoy economic benefits as well.
- Rural development (or rather re-development) was also becoming important for the western world, in some parts of which changing circumstances were decimating rural communities; and developing countries, while concentrating on rural development, should not neglect the developmental needs of non-rural areas. The paths along which both the developed and the developing countries were moving might be coming closer together, with both leading eventually to the elimination of the present inequities between different sectors of society.
- The part played by women students at one institution in helping to promote the education and welfare of women in rural areas, and in acting as a pressure group on their behalf, was described to illustrate how universities could and should involve themselves in bridging the gap between official implementing agencies and the people for whom benefits were intended.

- Difficulties included the fact that most students were not interested in working in rural areas, where the pay was traditionally poor (though perhaps less so now than in the past) and where, because of the students' entirely different background, they could not even communicate effectively with the rural community. Also scientists were not willing to work on the secondary technologies needed for rural development because peer recognition came only for achievements in fundamental research. In any case, rural communities will not accept and respond to those who come only as 'visitors', and do not live in and identify with the community. However, enthusiastic co-operation is given to those who stay and work alongside the villagers, helping to introduce practically useful technologies that are seen to have immediately beneficial effects.
- A way round these difficulties is to locate higher education institutions, especially those with a scientific/technological emphasis, in the rural areas, where they can attract and educate rural students (who will for the most part remain in their communities thereafter) and can also function more generally as community colleges in the sense of becoming involved in the life of the community as a whole. The curriculum of such institutions must be designed quite differently from the traditional university curriculum, because it has to serve the needs of a population that must work as well as learn.

In bringing the session to a close, the Topic Chairman (Professor D. Odhiambo) commented that the intellectual problems of rural development had been shown to be as interesting and as challenging for universities as any posed in other fields.

Topic 7

UNIVERSITIES AND RURAL DEVELOPMENT

The Role of Universities in the Management of Land Resources and Land Usage for Effective Rural Development

CHAIRMAN'S REPORT ON THE GROUP'S DISCUSSIONS

Second Plenary Session
Friday, 12 February

Professor D. ODHIAMBO (*Vice-Chancellor, Moi University*): Rural development is an integral part of national development. More than 80% of population is in rural areas. If universities are to play a role in national development then they must also be prepared to play a major role in rural development.

Rural development must be seen in the context of transformation of the rural areas in such a manner that the quality of life of the people is raised in all its social, economic, ethical, cultural, aesthetic and physical dimensions. This process of transformation generates many demands and problems which can fully engage the attention of academic staff of any university. All universities in the Commonwealth should therefore make it a point to foster programmes of training and research which are geared towards development of rural areas. It is in the light of this assumption that the three main aspects of the topic were discussed by the group.

The first aspect was the challenges of rural development and responsibilities of universities. The discussion was led by Mr. Devendra Kumar, who emphasized that in the context of improving the quality of life in the rural areas all measures for the amelioration of poverty, illiteracy, overpopulation and environmental degradation had to be addressed. The interface between rural and urban communities was examined. It was pointed out that rural development should not create rural to urban migration, nor should it simply transplant urban conditions to rural areas. Rather there should be an harmonious blend of those urban conditions which improve the quality of life with the general rural matrix.

Emphasis should be given to a micro-approach, including the evolving of new systems of higher education if it is to benefit rural areas. This should involve incorporating into the curriculum the needs of the rural communities.

The importance of universities establishing rapport with the villagers by encouraging self-help activities and generating motivation of the poor to rise above a life of dependence was stressed. Specific examples given were: literacy programmes; education in health and sanitation standards; improved housing construction; fuel use economics; biogas tanks for gas and fertilizer production; and the introduction of new crops such as sunflowers.

The universities must monitor and evaluate the programmes of rural development to ensure that the long-term goals are met. An example was given of irrigation schemes which may in fact have negative effects on land use.

The role of education in checking population growth was emphasized.

The need to develop co-operatives was underlined, although it was also pointed out that the possibilities of co-operatives being controlled by a few richer individuals must be checked and individual initiative fully encouraged.

The second aspect of rural development discussed was the design of land resource management. This discussion was led by Professor Moonis Raza. It was pointed out that there was high diversity in land productivity in different regions of any country. Hence the need for systematic and accurate land assessment for use in regional resource management and development planning. Every effort should be made to adopt land use policies which acknowledge natural endowment of the land and recent advances in technology. It is important therefore that attention be given to the following three tasks: (*a*) classification of land use systems; (*b*) study of spatial changes of land use systems and their consequences; (*c*) study of the functioning of land use systems as systems.

Several points emerged from the discussions of the paper, such as—

(i) the need to collect up-to-date data relating to reclamation of land and climatic conditions, all of which are necessary for maximizing land use;

(ii) good research results emanating from the universities should be made available to farmers; the universities should examine land use management from a long-term perspective and advise as necessary. In this regard rural development should be seen in terms of the development of a new world where high technology will be available on a small-scale basis;

(iii) successful development of the rural areas should be seen in terms of the increase in production per unit of labour applied compared with what it was before in similar enterprises in the rural areas;

(iv) the measurement of rural development in terms of money may conceal other important factors; perhaps the use of energy input and output may be a better indicator of all-embracing development.

Thirdly, the group discussed the universities as agents of change. This discussion was led by Mr. Kodithuwakku and Professor Nayan bin Ariffin.

While it was important that universities should be involved in linkages with rural communities, it was also necessary to work closely with other agencies, government or non-government, involved in the field. The discussions emphasized once again the importance of university and staff commitment to work in the rural areas, and discussed other factors such as those internal and external to universities; modes, constraints; and implications of university linkages with rural communities.

Examples of university linkages with rural communities in Sri Lanka and Malaysia were given. One example indicated the general importance of education in improvement of the quality of life in the rural areas. This was the case of a health clinic being used to treat many patients suffering from waterborne diseases when nearby was an open well from which water, completely contaminated from its surroundings, was being drawn and used by the villagers, leading to their infection with the diseases.

Finally, the dangers of equating rural development with agricultural development were again emphasized. The improvement of cultural, social and other components of life were equally important, and must also be incorporated in the process of development of the rural areas.

Topic 7

OTHER CONTRIBUTIONS

Among the other papers brought to the Congress was the one mentioned below, which related to this Topic.

Professor MOONIS RAZA (*Vice-Chancellor, University of Delhi*), in addition to making his presentation for Sub-Topic 7(b), had prepared a second paper on the 'Role of Agricultural Universities in the Green Revolution: the Indian Experience'. After tracing the development of agricultural education in that country, the paper described in detail the work of one of the universities—Haryana Agricultural—in the three areas of teaching, research and extension. A large part of the paper was devoted to the various services of the directorate of extension education, illustrating the benefits that these services, together with the problem-oriented, location specific, research projects undertaken by the University, have brought to local farming communities.

SECOND PLENARY SESSION AND CLOSING CEREMONY

Friday, 12 February

At the Second Plenary Session the seven Topic Chairmen reported on the week's discussions of their Topics (*see* the separate section for each Topic, *above*).

The Second Plenary Session was followed by a Closing Ceremony at which a message of goodwill from the President of the Republic of Nigeria was delivered by H. R. H. Prince ADO IBRAHIM, who said: I am pleased to have an opportunity to convey to the Association of Commonwealth Universities the good wishes of General Ibrahim Babangida, President and Commander-in-Chief of the Armed Forces of the Federal Republic of Nigeria. My words supplement his goodwill gesture and the support given to ACU* by his government with the co-operation of his Honourable Minister of Education, Professor Jibril Aminu, a former Commonwealth Scholar and a former Vice-Chancellor of the University of Maiduguri.

I particularly want to express my gratitude to the able people who have sustained and strengthened this Association over the years, and to say a special word of thanks to those who invited me to this impressive Congress in this wonderful city of Perth, and provided so much hospitality!

I have been asked by a number of participants where I come from and which university I belong to. My answer has been brief: 'Nigeria, and the Commonwealth universities'. My answer stems from the chance you have given me to participate in the local affairs of this august body, and especially to meet so many distinguished university people.

My impression of the ACU relates not just to the academic support it obviously has but also to the strength which has made the ACU an unofficial Commonwealth union, transcending politics and constituting a world entity in which language is no barrier, fear of expression is non-existent and the acquisition and dissemination of knowledge are unrestricted. I hope and pray that the needle bearing the thread of this common tie will be used at every

---

Editorial note. This relates to a donation to the ACU Endowment Appeal of ₦ = 1 million by the Military Federal Government of Nigeria.

[*Ibrahim*]

available opportunity to connect with the official Commonwealth forum and remind Britain, as the founding mother, of her responsibility to those nations that are her sincere allies and uphold her historical pride.

I also appeal to individual universities, through their vice-chancellors here present, to relate to the private sector in their separate countries so as to generate mutual confidence and ensure private sector contribution to the development of the manpower, research and technological development which buttress the assets of the private sector. I believe that this policy will help to reduce stress in the economy of universities and enhance mutual understanding between all sectors.

My thanks, too, to the Association for the great honour done to Nigeria by the presentation of the coveted Symons Award to Professor Akin Adesola, a former chairman of the ACU and a retiring Vice-Chancellor of the University of Lagos. As an administrator he has been energetic, patient, persevering and purposeful in Nigerian university affairs.

In conclusion may I say that if God offers me the opportunity to attend the 150th Anniversary of the Association in 2063 anywhere in the Western world, I shall welcome it—provided that all of you here present will be there too!

Council of the Association 1987–88

Professor L. M. Birt (New South Wales), *Chairman*
Rt. Hon. Lord Flowers (London), *Vice-Chairman*
Professor T. H. B. Symons (Canada), *Honorary Treasurer*
Professor G. D. Sims (Sheffield), *Honorary Deputy Treasurer*
Professor J. Manrakhan (Mauritius) *Immediate Past Chairman*

Professor M. Ali (Chittagong)
Tan Sri Dato' Professor Awang Had Salleh (Northern, Malaysia)
Dr. G. K. Caston (South Pacific)
Dr. Cham Tao Soon (Nanyang Technological Institute)
Professor B. L. Clarkson (Wales)
Professor G. J. Davies (Liverpool)
Professor T. I. Francis (Federal U. of Technology, Akure)
Dr. D. L. Johnston (McGill)
Dr. A. A. Lee (McMaster)
Dr. W. G. Malcolm (Waikato)
Professor P. M. Mbithi (Nairobi)
Professor A. N. Mohammed (Ahmadu Bello)
Professor K. Mwauluka (Zambia)
Dr. A. Naimark (Manitoba)
Dr. K. L. Ozmon (Saint Mary's)
Professor R. Parikh (Gujarat Vidyapith)
Sir Edward Parkes (Leeds)
Professor Sir Mark Richmond (Manchester)
Professor G. F. A. Sawyerr (Ghana)
Professor J. F. Scott (La Trobe)
Dr. Sukhdev Singh (Punjab Agricultural)
Professor N. M. Swani (Indian Institute of Technology, Delhi)
Dr. K. K. Tiwari (Jiwaji)
Professor S. Vithiananthan (Jaffna)
Professor B. G. Wilson (Queensland)

Dr. A. Christodoulou, *Secretary General*

Members of the Congress

PATRON
The Rt. Hon. Sir Ninian Stephen, Governor-General of Australia

Participants from Member Institutions

AUSTRALIA

ADELAIDE
Professor K. Marjoribanks, Vice-Chancellor
The Hon. Dame Roma Mitchell, Chancellor
Mr. F. J. O'Neill, Registrar
Professor J. R. Prescott, Elder Professor of Physics (Chair, Education Committee)
Mr. J. E. Ridgway, President of Students' Association

AUSTRALIAN NATIONAL
Professor E. P. Bachelard, Chairman of Board of Faculties

BOND
Sir Sydney Schubert, Chancellor
Professor D. W. Watts, President and Vice-Chancellor

CURTIN U. OF TECHNOLOGY
Professor J. R. de Laeter, Acting Vice-Chancellor

DEAKIN
Professor M. J. Charlesworth, Chairman of Academic Board
Mr. R. H. Elliott, University Secretary
Professor M. Skilbeck, Vice-Chancellor and Principal
Mr. G. J. G. Vines, Deputy Chancellor

FLINDERS, SOUTH AUSTRALIA
Mr. H. J. Buchan, Registrar
Dr. N. J. Clark, Chairman of Research Committee
Sister Deirdre F. Jordan, Pro-Chancellor
Professor J. F. Lovering, Vice-Chancellor

GRIFFITH
Professor R. S. Holmes, Dean of School of Science
Mr. Justice J. M. Macrossan, Deputy Chancellor
Mr. J. Topley, Registrar
Professor L. R. Webb, Vice-Chancellor

MEMBERS OF CONGRESS

JAMES COOK, NORTH QUEENSLAND
Professor R. M. Golding, Vice-Chancellor
Professor Rhondda Jones, Chairman of Academic Board
Sir George Kneipp, Chancellor
Mr. J. D. Smith, Registrar

LA TROBE
Professor E. Davies, Pro-Vice-Chancellor
Mr. Justice R. E. McGarvie, Chancellor
Mr. D. D. Neilson, Vice-Principal
Professor J. F. Scott, Vice-Chancellor and Principal

MACQUARIE
Emeritus Professor R. B. Leal, Deputy Vice-Chancellor (Academic)
Mr. B. J. Spencer, Registrar
Professor Dianne Yerbury, Vice-Chancellor

MELBOURNE
Professor Margaret M. Manion, Herald Professor of Fine Arts
Professor D. G. Penington, Vice-Chancellor and Principal
Mr. J. B. Potter, Registrar
Professor Emeritus Sir Douglas Wright, Chancellor

MONASH
Professor M. I. Logan, Vice-Chancellor
Sir George Lush, Chancellor
Professor B. West, Member of Council

MURDOCH
Professor P. J. Boyce, Vice-Chancellor
Mr. D. D. Dunn, Secretary
Mr. D. Fischer, Pro-Chancellor

NEWCASTLE
Professor M. P. Carter, Deputy Chairman, University Senate
Professor K. J. Morgan, Vice-Chancellor and Principal

NEW ENGLAND
Professor L. W. Nichol, Vice-Chancellor
Dr. R. C. Robertson-Cuninghame, Chancellor
Mr. D. C. Williams, Registrar

NEW SOUTH WALES
Professor D. J. Anderson, Chairman of Professorial Board
Professor L. M. Birt, Vice-Chancellor and Principal
Mr. Justice G. J. Samuels, Chancellor
Mr. I. R. Way, Deputy Principal and Registrar

QUEENSLAND
Professor Margaret Bullock, President of Academic Council
Sir James Foots, Chancellor
Mr. D. Porter, Secretary and Registrar
Professor B. G. Wilson, Vice-Chancellor

PARTICIPANTS FROM MEMBER INSTITUTIONS

UNIVERSITY COLLEGE OF THE NORTHERN TERRITORY
Mr. Justice A. Asche, Chairman of Council
Professor J. M. Thomson, Warden

SYDNEY
Professor S. Ball, Chairman of Academic Board
Sir Hermann Black, Chancellor
Mr K. L. Jennings, Registrar and Deputy Principal
Professor J. M. Ward, Vice-Chancellor and Principal

TASMANIA
Sir Guy Green, Chancellor
Professor A. Lazenby, Vice-Chancellor
Professor A. Sale, Chairman of Professorial Board
Professor C. P. Wendell Smith, Deputy Vice-Chancellor

U. OF TECHNOLOGY, SYDNEY
Professor R. D. Guthrie, Vice-Chancellor

WESTERN AUSTRALIA
Mr. D. H. Aitken, Chancellor
Professor P. G. Harris, Professor of Geology
Professor R. H. T. Smith, Vice-Chancellor
Professor R. Tonkinson, Professor of Anthropology

WOLLONGONG
Mr. K. E. Baumber, University Secretary
Professor R. King, Chairman of Academic Senate
Professor K. R. McKinnon, Vice-Chancellor

BOTSWANA

BOTSWANA
Professor T. Tlou, Vice-Chancellor

BRITAIN

ABERDEEN
Professor G. P. McNicol, Principal and Vice-Chancellor

ASTON
Professor Sir Frederick Crawford, Vice-Chancellor

BATH
Mr. R. M. Mawditt, Secretary and Registrar
Professor J. R. Quayle, Vice-Chancellor

QUEEN'S, BELFAST
Dr. G. S. G. Beveridge, President and Vice-Chancellor

MEMBERS OF CONGRESS

BIRMINGHAM
Mr. H. Harris, Secretary of the University
Professor M. W. Thompson, Vice-Chancellor and Principal
Dr. Jean R. F. Wilks, Pro-Chancellor

BRADFORD
Professor J. H. Cairns, Pro-Vice-Chancellor
Mr. R. W. Suddards, Pro-Chancellor
Professor J. C. West, Vice-Chancellor and Principal

BRISTOL
Mrs. Stella Clarke, Chairman of Council
Sir John Kingman, Vice-Chancellor
Mr. E. C. Wright, Registrar and Secretary

BRUNEL
Professor R. E. D. Bishop, Vice-Chancellor and Principal
Mr. D. Neave, Secretary-General and Registrar
Mr. H. W. Try, Chairman of Council

CAMBRIDGE
Professor Sir John Butterfield, Deputy Vice-Chancellor

CITY
Professor L. Finkelstein, Dean, School of Engineering
Professor R. N. Franklin, Vice-Chancellor and Principal
Lord Howie of Troon, Pro-Chancellor
Mr. M. M. O'Hara, Secretary of the University

CRANFIELD INSTITUTE OF TECHNOLOGY
Lord Chilver, Vice-Chancellor

DUNDEE
Professor M. J. Hamlin, Principal and Vice-Chancellor
Mr. R. Seaton, Secretary of the University

DURHAM
Professor F. G. T. Holliday, Vice-Chancellor and Warden
Mr. A. McWilliam, Treasurer

EAST ANGLIA
Colonel G. S. H. Dicker, Pro-Chancellor and Chairman of Council
Mr. M. G. E. Paulson-Ellis, Registrar and Secretary

EDINBURGH
Professor C. P. Brand, Vice-Principal
Mr. A. M. Currie, Secretary to the University
Professor Sir David Smith, Principal and Vice-Chancellor

ESSEX
Professor M. B. Harris, Vice-Chancellor
Mr. E. Newcomb, Registrar

PARTICIPANTS FROM MEMBER INSTITUTIONS

EXETER
Dr. D. Harrison, Vice-Chancellor

GLASGOW
Professor A. S. Skinner, Clerk of Senate
Sir Robert Smith, Chancellor's Assessor
Sir Alwyn Williams, Principal and Vice-Chancellor

HERIOT-WATT
Mr. D. I. Cameron, Secretary of the University
Dr. T. L. Johnston, Principal and Vice-Chancellor

HULL
Dr. W. L. Black, Treasurer
Dr. T. H. F. Farrell, Chairman of Council
Mr. F. T. Mattison, Registrar and Secretary
Professor W. Taylor, Vice-Chancellor

KEELE
Professor B. E. F. Fender, Vice-Chancellor

KENT
Dr. U. H. B. Alexander, Treasurer
Dr. D. J. E. Ingram, Vice-Chancellor

LANCASTER
Professor H. J. Hanham, Vice-Chancellor
Sir Alastair Pilkington, Pro-Chancellor and Chairman of Council
Professor J. H. Shennan, Pro-Vice-Chancellor

LEEDS
Sir Edward Parkes, Vice-Chancellor
Colonel A. C. Roberts, Pro-Chancellor

LEICESTER
Dr. K. J. R. Edwards, Vice-Chancellor
Professor A. R. S. Ponter, Pro-Vice-Chancellor

LIVERPOOL
Professor G. J. Davies, Vice-Chancellor
Mr. R. A. Nind, Registrar
Professor H. R. Perkins, Pro-Vice-Chancellor
Dr. B. L. Rathbone, Pro-Chancellor

LONDON
Rt. Hon. Lord Flowers, Vice-Chancellor
Professor P. G. Moore, Principal, London Business School

INSTITUTE OF EDUCATION
Professor D. Lawton, Director

LONDON SCHOOL OF ECONOMICS AND POLITICAL SCIENCE
Dr. Christine Challis, Secretary

MEMBERS OF CONGRESS

QUEEN MARY COLLEGE
Mr. G. G. Williams, Secretary and Registrar

UNIVERSITY COLLEGE LONDON
Sir James Lighthill, Provost

LOUGHBOROUGH
Mr. H. Brooks, Registrar
Professor F. D. Hales, Acting Vice-Chancellor
Mr. J. R. S. Morris, Chairman of Council

MANCHESTER
Mr. D. K. Redford, Immediate Past Chairman of Council

MANCHESTER, INSTITUTE OF SCIENCE AND TECHNOLOGY
Mr. W. N. Brewood, Chairman of Council
Mr. D. G. Keenleside, Bursar
Professor D. A. Williams, Vice-Principal

NOTTINGHAM
Mr. G. E. Chandler, Registrar
Professor G. B. Warburton, Pro-Vice-Chancellor
Dr. B. C. L. Weedon, Vice-Chancellor

OPEN
Mr. D. J. Clinch, Secretary
Professor D. J. Murray, Pro-Vice-Chancellor (Degree Studies)

OXFORD
Sir Patrick Neill, Vice-Chancellor

READING
Dr. E. S. Page, Vice-Chancellor

SALFORD
Professor J. M. Ashworth, Vice-Chancellor
Mr. S. R. Bosworth, Registrar
Mr. D. W. Hills, Chairman of University Council

SHEFFIELD
Professor R. J. Nicholson, Professor of Econometrics
Professor G. D. Sims, Vice-Chancellor

SOUTHAMPTON
Dr. G. R. Higginson, Vice-Chancellor
Mr. D. A. Schofield, Secretary and Registrar

STIRLING
Mr. R. G. Bomont, University Secretary
Professor A. J. Forty, Principal and Vice-Chancellor
Dr. J. A. Mitchell, Chairman of University Court

PARTICIPANTS FROM MEMBER INSTITUTIONS

STRATHCLYDE
Dr. G. Boyd, Chairman of Court
Dr. G. J. Hills, Principal and Vice-Chancellor
Mr. D. W. J. Morrell, Registrar and Secretary

SURREY
Professor A. Kelly, Vice-Chancellor
Mr. J. F. Whitfield, Chairman of Council

SUSSEX
Dr. G. Lockwood, Registrar and Secretary
The Lord Trafford of Falmer, Chairman of Council and Senior Pro-Chancellor

ULSTER
Professor R. J. Gavin, Pro-Vice-Chancellor

WALES
Professor B. L. Clarkson, Vice-Chancellor, and Principal of University College of Swansea
Mr. A. T. Durbin, Finance Officer
Dr. M. A. R. Kemp, Registrar

UNIVERSITY COLLEGE OF WALES, ABERYSTWYTH
Mr. E. Wynn Jones, Registrar and Secretary
Dr. G. Owen, Principal

UNIVERSITY COLLEGE OF NORTH WALES, BANGOR
Professor G. R. Sagar, Vice-Principal
Professor E. Sunderland, Principal

UNIVERSITY COLLEGE OF SWANSEA
Mr. V. J. Carney, Registrar
Dr. W. Emrys Evans, Chairman of Council

WALES, COLLEGE OF MEDICINE
Dr. A. W. Roberts, Registrar and Secretary

WALES, INSTITUTE OF SCIENCE AND TECHNOLOGY
Professor M. J. Bruton, Deputy Principal and Registrar
Dr. A. F. Trotman-Dickenson, Principal

ST. DAVID'S UNIVERSITY COLLEGE, LAMPETER
Professor B. R. Morris, Principal

WARWICK
Dr. C. L. Brundin, Vice-Chancellor
Professor T. J. Kemp, Pro-Chancellor
Mr. M. L. Shattock, Registrar
Sir Arthur Vick, Pro-Chancellor and Chairman of Council

YORK
Mr. D. J. Foster, Registrar
Professor D. J. Waddington, Pro-Vice-Chancellor

MEMBERS OF CONGRESS

BRUNEI DARUSSALAM

BRUNEI DARUSSALAM
Professor Sharom Ahmat, Academic Adviser
Mr. Mohd. Denis Hj. Roslee, Registrar

CANADA

ALBERTA
Dr. M. Horowitz, President and Vice-Chancellor
Mr. J. L. Schlosser, Chairman of Board of Governors

ATHABASCA
Consul D. Larsen, Chairman of Governing Council
Dr. T. R. Morrison, President

BRITISH COLUMBIA
Dr. D. R. Birch, Academic Vice-President and Provost
Dr. K. D. Srivastava, Vice-President
Dr. D. W. Strangway, President and Vice-Chancellor

BROCK
Professor A. J. Earp, President and Vice-Chancellor
Mr. T. Varcoe, Vice-President, Administration

UNIVERSITY COLLEGE OF CAPE BRETON
Dr. W. M. Reid, President

CARLETON
Dr. W. E. Beckel, President and Vice-Chancellor

CONCORDIA
Dr. P. J. Kenniff, Rector and Vice-Chancellor
Dr. F. R. Whyte, Vice-Rector (Academic)

DALHOUSIE
Dr. H. C. Clark, President and Vice-Chancellor

LAURENTIAN U OF SUDBURY
Dr. C. H. Bélanger, Vice-President, Academic
Dr. J. S. Daniel, President

McGILL
Dr. D. L. Johnston, Principal and Vice-Chancellor

McMASTER
Professor P. J. George, Professor of Economics
Dr. L. J. King, Vice-President (Academic)
Dr. A. A. Lee, President and Vice-Chancellor
Professor S. M. MacLeod, Faculty of Health Sciences

514

PARTICIPANTS FROM MEMBER INSTITUTIONS

MANITOBA
Dr. H. E. Duckworth, Chancellor
Dr. A. Naimark, President and Vice-Chancellor
Mr. R. M. Raeburn, Secretary, Board of Governors

MEMORIAL, NEWFOUNDLAND
Dr. L. Harris, President and Vice-Chancellor

MOUNT SAINT VINCENT
Dr. Naomi Hersom, President and Vice-Chancellor

NEW BRUNSWICK
Lady Violet Aitken, Chancellor
Professor C. Ann Cameron, Department of Psychology
Dr. J. Downey, President and Vice-Chancellor
Dr. C. B. Mackay, President Emeritus
Mr. J. F. O'Sullivan, Vice-President
Professor R. S. Turner, Professor of History
Professor F. R. Wilson, Dean of Engineering

OTTAWA
Dr. J.-M. Beillard, Secretary
Dr. Susan Mann-Trofimenkoff, Vice-Rector, Academic

REGINA
Dr. L. I. Barber, President and Vice-Chancellor

RYERSON POLYTECHNICAL INSTITUTE
Professor T. Grier, Vice-President, Academic
Dr. B. Segal, President

ST. FRANCIS XAVIER
Rev. Dr. G. A. MacKinnon, President and Vice-Chancellor

SAINT MARY'S
Mr. R. J. Downie, Chairman of Board
Dr. K. L. Ozmon, President

SASKATCHEWAN
Professor B. A. Holmlund, Vice-President (Planning and Development)
Mr. D. H. Whiteman, Chairman of Board of Governors

SIMON FRASER
Professor J. W. G. Ivany, Vice-President, Academic and Professor, Faculty of Education
Dr. W. G. Saywell, President and Vice-Chancellor

TORONTO
Professor Joan E. Foley, Vice-President and Provost

TRENT
Dr. J. O. Stubbs, President and Vice-Chancellor
Professor T. H. B. Symons, Vanier Professor

MEMBERS OF CONGRESS

VICTORIA, BRITISH COLUMBIA
Professor H. E. Petch, President and Vice-Chancellor

WATERLOO
Mr. J. Bergsma, Chairman, Board of Governors
Dr. D. T. Wright, President and Vice-Chancellor

WILFRID LAURIER
Dr. J. A. Weir, Vice-Chancellor and President

WINDSOR
Dr. J. F. Leddy, Honorary Professor of Classics

WINNIPEG
Dr. W. J. A. Bulman, Chancellor
Dr. R. H. Farquhar, President and Vice-Chancellor

YORK
Professor H. W. Arthurs, President
Professor K. G. Davey, Vice-President

GHANA

CAPE COAST
Professor K. B. Dickson, Vice-Chancellor

U. OF GHANA
Professor G. Benneh, Pro-Vice-Chancellor
Professor G. F. A. Sawyerr, Vice-Chancellor

KUMASI, U. OF SCIENCE AND TECHNOLOGY
Professor F. O. Kwami, Vice-Chancellor

GUYANA

GUYANA
Dr. G. L. Walcott, Vice-Chancellor

HONG KONG

CHINESE U. OF HONG KONG
Professor C. K. Kao, Vice-Chancellor
Professor Yue-man Yeung, Registrar and Professor of Geography

U. OF HONG KONG
Mr. N. J. Gillanders, Registrar
Mr. V. H. C. Ko, Chairman of Convocation
Dr. Wang Gungwu, Vice-Chancellor
Professor Rosie T. T. Young, Pro-Vice-Chancellor and Professor, Department of Medicine

PARTICIPANTS FROM MEMBER INSTITUTIONS

HONG KONG U. OF SCIENCE AND TECHNOLOGY
Mr. I. F. C. Macpherson, Secretary-General designate
Dr. Chia-Wei Woo, Vice-Chancellor designate

INDIA

ALAGAPPA
Dr. (Mrs.) Radha Thiagarajan, Vice-Chancellor

ALIGARH MUSLIM
Mr. S. H. Ali, Vice-Chancellor

ALLAHABAD
Professor W. U. Malik, Vice-Chancellor

AMRAVATI
Dr. K. G. Deshmukh, Vice-Chancellor

ANNA
Dr. V. C. Kulandaiswamy, Vice-Chancellor

ANNAMALAI
Professor R. M. Sethunarayanan, Vice-Chancellor

AVADH
Professor A. C. Banerjea, Vice-Chancellor

BANGALORE
Dr. D. M. Nanjundappa, Vice-Chancellor

BHAGALPUR
Professor E. B. Singh, Vice-Chancellor

BURDWAN
Professor S. P. Banerjee, Vice-Chancellor

CENTRAL INSTITUTE OF ENGLISH AND FOREIGN LANGUAGES
Professor S. K. Verma, Director

COCHIN U. OF SCIENCE AND TECHNOLOGY
Dr. H. K. Gupta, Vice-Chancellor

DELHI
Professor Moonis Raza, Vice-Chancellor

DEVI AHILYA VISHWAVIDYALAYA
Dr. S. M. Dasgupta, Vice-Chancellor

DIBRUGARH
Mr. K. Bora, Vice-Chancellor
Professor S. M. Dubey, Professor of Arts (Sociology)
Dr. D. H. Goswami, Registrar

MEMBERS OF CONGRESS

DOCTOR HARISINGH GOUR VISHWAVIDYALAYA
Professor P. D. Hajela, Vice-Chancellor

GANDHIGRAM RURAL INSTITUTE
Mr. Devendra Kumar, Vice-Chancellor

GAUHATI
Dr. D. P. Barooah, Vice-Chancellor

GOA
Dr. B. Sheik Ali, Vice-Chancellor

GUJARAT VIDYAPITH
Professor R. Parikh, Vice-Chancellor

GULBARGA
Dr. K. H. Cheluva Raju, Vice-Chancellor

GURU GHASIDAS
Dr. D. N. Tewari, Vice-Chancellor

HIMACHAL PRADESH U.
Professor K. C. Malhotra, Vice-Chancellor

HYDERABAD
Professor Bh. Krishnamurti, Vice-Chancellor

INDIAN INSTITUTE OF TECHNOLOGY, MADRAS
Professor L. S. Srinath, Director

INDIAN SCHOOL OF MINES
Professor D. K. Sinha, Director

JAMIA MILLIA ISLAMIA
Professor A. Ashraf, Vice-Chancellor

JAMMU
Professor M. L. Lakhanpal, Vice-Chancellor

JAWAHARLAL NEHRU U.
Professor M. S. Agwani, Vice-Chancellor

JIWAJI
Dr. K. K. Tiwari, Vice-Chancellor

JODHPUR
Dr. M. L. Mathur, Vice-Chancellor

KAKATIYA
Professor T. Vasudev, Vice-Chancellor

KANPUR
Dr. B. N. Asthana, Vice-Chancellor

PARTICIPANTS FROM MEMBER INSTITUTIONS

KASHMIR
Professor Mushirul Haq, Vice-Chancellor

KERALA
Professor G. B. Thampi, Vice-Chancellor

KURUKSHETRA
Mr. M. K. Miglani, Vice-Chancellor

MADURAI-KAMARAJ
Professor S. Krishnaswamy, Vice-Chancellor

MAGADH
Professor Mangal Dubey, Vice-Chancellor

MANGALORE
Dr. R. M. Pai, Chief Executive, Kasturba Medical College and Hospital
Professor K. M. Safeeulla, Vice-Chancellor

MANIPUR
Professor K. J. Mahale, Vice-Chancellor

MOTHER TERESA WOMEN'S
Dr. (Mrs.) Jaya Kothai Pillai, Vice-Chancellor

MYSORE
Professor Y. P. Rudrappa, Vice-Chancellor

PATNA
Professor S. N. Das, Vice-Chancellor

PONDICHERRY
Dr. K. Venkatasubramanian, Vice-Chancellor

POSTGRADUATE INSTITUTE OF MEDICAL EDUCATION AND RESEARCH
Professor P. L. Wahi, Director

PUNJAB AGRICULTURAL
Dr. Sukhdev Singh, Vice-Chancellor

PUNJABI
Dr. Bhagat Singh, Vice-Chancellor

RAJASTHAN AGRICULTURAL
Dr. K. N. Nag, Vice-Chancellor

U. OF RAJASTHAN
Dr. R. P. Agarwal, Vice-Chancellor

RANCHI
Professor R. Badri Narayan, Pro-Vice-Chancellor

MEMBERS OF CONGRESS

ROHILKHAND
Professor B. B. Singh Bisen, Vice-Chancellor

ROORKEE
Dr. N. C. Mathur, Vice-Chancellor

SARDAR PATEL
Dr. K. C. Patel, Vice-Chancellor
Mr. R. C. Thakkar, Registrar

SAURASHTRA
Professor K. N. Shah, Vice-Chancellor

SHIVAJI
Professor K. B. Powar, Vice-Chancellor

S.N.D.T. WOMEN'S
Mrs. Kamalini H. Bhansali, Vice-Chancellor

SRI PADMAVATI MAHILA VISVAVIDYALAYAM
Professor (Mrs.) K. Rajya Lakshmi, Vice-Chancellor

TAMIL
Professor S. Agesthialingom, Vice-Chancellor

TAMIL NADU AGRICULTURAL
Dr. V. Rajagopalan, Vice-Chancellor

UTKAL
Mr. P. S. Habeeb Mohamed, Vice-Chancellor

VIKRAM
Dr. D. R. Sharma, Vice-Chancellor

VISVA-BHARATI
Professor N. S. Bose, Vice-Chancellor

KENYA

KENYATTA
Professor P. M. Githinji, Vice-Chancellor

MOI
Mr. L. M. Mungai, Chief Administrative Officer
Professor D. Odhiambo, Vice-Chancellor

NAIROBI
Professor F. A. Mutere, Deputy Vice-Chancellor

PARTICIPANTS FROM MEMBER INSTITUTIONS

LESOTHO
NATIONAL U. OF LESOTHO
Dr. L. B. B. J. Machobane, Pro-Vice-Chancellor

MALAWI
MALAWI
Mr. G. G. Chipungu, University Finance Officer
Dr. J. M. Dubbey, Vice-Chancellor

MALAYSIA
U. OF AGRICULTURE, MALAYSIA
Professor Dato' Dr. Nayan Ariffin, Vice-Chancellor

MALAYA
Professor Ishak bin Haron, Dean, Faculty of Education
Professor Khairuddin bin Yusof, Deputy Vice-Chancellor
Professor Tunku Shamsul Bahrin, Department of Geography

NATIONAL U. OF MALAYSIA
Professor Dato' Abdul Hamid Abdul Rahman, Vice-Chancellor

NORTHERN U. OF MALAYSIA
Tan Sri Dato' Professor Awang Had Salleh, Vice-Chancellor

U. OF SCIENCE, MALAYSIA
Datuk Haji Musa bin Mohamad, Vice-Chancellor

MALTA
MALTA
Professor P. Serracino Inglott, Rector
Mr. L. Ellul, Registrar

MAURITIUS
MAURITIUS
Mr. A. K. Gayan, Chairman of Council
Professor J. Manrakhan, Vice-Chancellor
Mr. B. K. Seebaluck, Registrar

MEMBERS OF CONGRESS

NEW ZEALAND

AUCKLAND
Judge M. J. A. Brown, Chancellor
Dr. C. J. Maiden, Vice-Chancellor
Mr. W. B. Nicoll, Registrar
Professor P. N. Tarling, Professor of History and Deputy Vice-Chancellor

CANTERBURY
Mr. R. H. Bowron, Chancellor
Mr. A. W. Hayward, Registrar

LINCOLN COLLEGE
Mr. G. A. Hay, Registrar
Emeritus Professor B. J. Ross, Principal
Sir Allan Wright, Chairman

MASSEY
Mr. J. D. Easton, Chancellor
Professor G. S. Fraser, Assistant Vice-Chancellor
Mr. B. R. H. Monks, Registrar
Dr. T. N. M. Waters, Vice-Chancellor

OTAGO
Mr. D. W. Girvan, Registrar
Dr. R. O. H. Irvine, Vice-Chancellor
Mr. J. A. Valentine, Chancellor

VICTORIA, WELLINGTON
Professor C. W. Dearden, Department of Classics
Professor L. C. Holborow, Vice-Chancellor
Mr. J. J. McGrath, Chancellor

WAIKATO
Mrs. M. Joy Drayton, Pro-Chancellor
Mr. N. W. Kingsbury, Registrar
Dr. W. G. Malcolm, Vice-Chancellor
Dr. Jane Ritchie, Director, Centre for Women's Studies

NIGERIA

AHMADU BELLO
Professor A. N. Mohammed, Vice-Chancellor

ANAMBRA STATE U. OF TECHNOLOGY
Professor C. Ejike, Vice-Chancellor

FEDERAL U. OF TECHNOLOGY, AKURE
Professor T. I. Francis, Vice-Chancellor

PARTICIPANTS FROM MEMBER INSTITUTIONS

JOS
Professor O. C. Onazi, Vice-Chancellor
Ambassador M. A. Sanusi, Pro-Chancellor and Chairman of Council

LAGOS
Professor A. O. Adesola, Vice-Chancellor

U. OF NIGERIA
Mrs. Tejumade Alakija, Pro-Chancellor and Chairman of Council
Professor C. Ikoku, Vice-Chancellor

SIERRA LEONE
SIERRA LEONE
Professor E. T. Bangura, Pro-Vice-Chancellor, and Principal of Njala University College
Professor K. Koso-Thomas, Vice-Chancellor

SINGAPORE
NATIONAL U. OF SINGAPORE
Dr. Cheong Siew Keong, Member of Council
Professor Lim Pin, Vice-Chancellor

NANYANG TECHNOLOGICAL INSTITUTE
Dr. Cham Tao Soon, President

SOUTH PACIFIC
SOUTH PACIFIC
Dr. G. K. Caston, Vice-Chancellor
Professor Subramani, Pro-Vice-Chancellor

SRI LANKA
COLOMBO
Mr. H. M. N. Warakaulle, Registrar
Professor S. Wijesundera, Vice-Chancellor

JAFFNA
Professor S. Vithiananthan, Vice-Chancellor

KELANIYA
Mr. N. B. Amarasinghe, Registrar
Professor M. M. J. Marasinghe, Vice-Chancellor

MORATUWA
Mr. N. W. S. W. S. de Silva, Registrar
Professor M. W. J. G. Mendis, Vice-Chancellor

MEMBERS OF CONGRESS

OPEN
Professor (Mrs.) Nalini B. Ratnasiri, Dean, Faculty of Natural Sciences
Professor D. S. Wijeyesekera, Vice-Chancellor

PERADENIYA
Mr. C. G. Abayakoon, Registrar
Professor R. G. Panabokke, Vice-Chancellor

RUHUNA
Mr. B. Abeysundera, Registrar
Professor G. P. Samarawickrama, Vice-Chancellor

SRI JAYEWARDENEPURA
Mr. M. Abeywardene, Registrar
Mr. K. Kodithuwakku, Vice-Chancellor

SWAZILAND
SWAZILAND
Professor Lydia P. Makhubu, Acting Vice-Chancellor

TANZANIA
DAR ES SALAAM
Mr. N. A. Kuhanga, Vice-Chancellor

UGANDA
MAKERERE
Professor B. G. Kirya, Vice-Chancellor

WEST INDIES
WEST INDIES
Professor G. M. Richards, Pro-Vice-Chancellor of the University and Principal, St. Augustine Campus
Professor L. R. B. Robinson, Acting Vice-Chancellor

ZAMBIA
COPPERBELT
Professor M. E. Kashoki, Vice-Chancellor

ZIMBABWE
ZIMBABWE
Professor W. J. Kamba, Vice-Chancellor

Representatives and Guests

Commonwealth National and Regional Inter-University Bodies

ASSOCIATION OF ATLANTIC UNIVERSITIES
Dr. J. R. Keyston, Executive Director

AUSTRALIAN VICE-CHANCELLORS' COMMITTEE
Mr. T. R. Earle, Assistant Secretary
Mr. F. S. Hambly, Secretary
Dr. V. Massaro, Director, Planning and Development
Ms. Helen M. Trinca, Public Relations Officer

ASSOCIATION OF UNIVERSITIES AND COLLEGES OF CANADA
Dr. J. W. Berry, Director, International Division
Dr. A. K. Gillmore, Executive Director

INTER-UNIVERSITY COUNCIL FOR EAST AFRICA
Mr. E. K. Kigozi, Executive Secretary

COMMITTEE OF VICE-CHANCELLORS OF THE UNIVERSITIES IN GHANA
Mr. P. Effah, Secretary

ASSOCIATION OF INDIAN UNIVERSITIES
Professor S. K. Agrawala, Secretary

NEW ZEALAND VICE-CHANCELLORS' COMMITTEE
Mr. L. S. Taiaroa, Executive Officer

COMMITTEE OF VICE-CHANCELLORS OF NIGERIAN UNIVERSITIES
Chief H. B. Afolabi, Secretary

COUNCIL OF ONTARIO UNIVERSITIES
Dr. E. J. Monahan, Executive Director
Professor M. H. Yeates, Executive Vice-Chairman, Ontario Council on Graduate Studies

COMMITTEE OF VICE-CHANCELLORS AND DIRECTORS (SRI LANKA)
Mr. V. N. Sivarajah, Secretary

COMMITTEE OF VICE-CHANCELLORS AND PRINCIPALS OF THE UNIVERSITIES OF THE UNITED KINGDOM (*see also* p. 528)
Mr. B. H. Taylor, Secretary General

MEMBERS OF CONGRESS

Commonwealth University Grants Committees or Equivalent Bodies

COMMONWEALTH TERTIARY EDUCATION COMMISSION
Professor D. McNicol, Chairman, Universities Advisory Council

UNIVERSITY GRANTS COMMITTEE, BRITAIN
Mr. N. T. Hardyman, Secretary

UNIVERSITY GRANTS COMMITTEE, NEW ZEALAND
Professor D. Hall, Chairman

NATIONAL UNIVERSITIES COMMISSION, NIGERIA
Professor I. A. Abdulkadir, Executive Secretary
Professor E. U. Essien-Udom, Chairman

UNIVERSITY GRANTS COMMISSION, SRI LANKA
Mr. M. D. G. Abeyratne, Secretary
Dr. F. S. C. P. Kalpage, Chairman

Other Organisations within the Commonwealth

ACT SCHOOLS AUTHORITY
Professor E. Willmot, Chief Education Officer

AUSTRALIAN COMMITTEE OF DIRECTORS AND PRINCIPALS
Dr. J. O. Miller, Chairman

AUSTRALIAN RESEARCH COUNCIL
Professor Don Aitkin, Interim Chairman

AUSTRALIAN UNIVERSITIES INDUSTRIAL ASSOCIATION
Mr. A. H. G. Conolly, Executive Director

BRITISH COUNCIL
Mr. R. S. Newberry, Representative in Australia
Mr. S. R. Smith, Controller, Higher Education Division

COMMONWEALTH FOUNDATION
Mr. I. F. Faletau, Director

COMMONWEALTH SCHOLARSHIP COMMISSION IN THE UNITED KINGDOM
Sir Albert Sloman, Deputy Chairman

COMMONWEALTH SCIENTIFIC AND INDUSTRIAL RESEARCH ORGANIZATION (Australia)
Professor M. G. Pitman, Deputy to Chief Executive

REPRESENTATIVES AND GUESTS

COMMONWEALTH SECRETARIAT
Mr. A. Khan, Feature Writer, Information Division
Mrs. Gail Larose, Head, Higher Education Unit
Mr. M. Malhoutra, Assistant Secretary-General
Mr. P. R. C. Williams, Director, Education Programme

DEPARTMENT OF EMPLOYMENT, EDUCATION AND TRAINING (Commonwealth of Australia)
Mr. G. J. Williams, Assistant Secretary, International Division

DEPARTMENT OF SECRETARY OF STATE FOR CANADA
Mr. J. T. Fournier, Under Secretary of State

INTERNATIONAL DEVELOPMENT PROGRAMME OF AUSTRALIAN UNIVERSITIES AND COLLEGES
Professor K. J. C. Back, Executive Director

RHODES TRUST
Dr. R. A. Fletcher, Warden of Rhodes House

WESTERN AUSTRALIAN POST-SECONDARY EDUCATION COMMISSION
Dr. W. A. Pullman, Chairman

ZAMBIAN HIGH COMMISSION (Australia)
H. E. Mr. J. C. Mfula, High Commissioner

Other Organisations

Partial Commonwealth Membership

INTERNATIONAL ASSOCIATION OF UNIVERSITIES
Professor J. Thorens, President

STANDING CONFERENCE OF RECTORS, PRESIDENTS AND VICE-CHANCELLORS OF THE EUROPEAN UNIVERSITIES
Professor G. D. Sims, Member of the Bureau (Vice-Chancellor, University of Sheffield)

UNESCO
Dr. Mary-Louise Kearney, Division of Higher Education and Training of Educational Personnel

Outside the Commonwealth

ASSOCIATION OF AMERICAN UNIVERSITIES
Dr. R. C. Atkinson, Chancellor, University of California, San Diego
Dr. S. O. Ikenberry, President, University of Illinois
Dr. C. E. Young, Chancellor, University of California, Los Angeles

Special Guests of the Association of Commonwealth Universities

H.R.H. Prince Ado Ibrahim
Sir Alec Merrison, Chairman, 13th Commonwealth Universities Congress
H.E. Sir Hugh W. Springer, Governor General of Barbados
Mr. E. E. Temple, former Assistant Secretary General (Commonwealth Scholarships), ACU

Congress Speakers not named elsewhere in these lists

Professor P. N. Srivastava, Member, Planning Commission, Government of India, and former Vice-Chancellor, Jawaharlal Nehru University
Professor D. Tunley, Head, Department of Music, University of Western Australia

Media

Ms. Ngaio Crequer, Education Correspondent, *The Independent*
Mr. P. Scott, Editor, *Times Higher Education Supplement*
Ms. Auriol Stevens, Director, Universities Information Unit, Committee of Vice-Chancellors and Principals of the Universities of the United Kingdom

Congress Committees and Secretariat

ACU CONGRESS ORGANISING COMMITTEE

Professor L. M. Birt, *Chairman*
Professor A. O. Adesola (until 4.11.86)
Mr. F. S. Hambly
Professor J. Manrakhan (from 4.11.86)
Professor Dato' Nayan bin Ariffin (5.11.85 to 3.11.87)
Mr. M. R. Orr
Professor G. D. Sims
Sir Albert Sloman (28.2.85 to 3.11.87)
Professor T. H. B. Symons
Professor S. Wijesundera (until 5.11.85)

Dr. A. Christodoulou, *Secretary General*
Mr. T. Craig, *Deputy Secretary General*
Mrs. Blanche Gubertini, *Personal Assistant to the Secretary General*

AUSTRALIAN ORGANISING COMMITTEE

Professor L. M. Birt, *Chairman*
Professor P. J. Boyce
Mr. F. S. Hambly
Professor R. H. T. Smith

Mr. M. R. Orr, *Secretary*
Mrs. Margaret Shellam-Harper, *Congress Organiser*

ACU CONGRESS SECRETARIAT

Dr. A. Christodoulou, *Secretary General*
Mr. T. Craig, *Deputy Secretary General*
Mr. P. B. Hetherington, *Deputy Secretary General (Commonwealth Awards & Appointments)*
Mr. J. A. Whittingham, *Finance Officer*
Mrs. Blanche Gubertini, *Personal Assistant to the Secretary General*

CONGRESS STAFF

Miss Corinne Clarke	Mrs. Valerie Landgrebe	Mr. A. Baird
Mrs. Nyree Maidenberg	Mrs. Miriam Angus	Mrs. Sue Thom
Miss Jane Wishaw	Mrs. Coral Newton	Mrs. Helen de'Lestang

HOSPITALITY COMMITTEE

Mrs. Margaret Aitken, *Organiser*	Mrs. Mirlwyn Hood	Mrs. Jeanette Orr
Mrs. Judy Bottomley	Mrs. Ros Lindsay	Mrs. Judith Parfitt
Mrs. Barbara Clyde	Mrs. Ann Lourens	Mrs. Elizabeth Smith

APPENDIX

Message from the Director-General of Unesco on the occasion of the 75th Anniversary of the founding of the Association of Commonwealth Universities

May I extend my warmest greetings to the Association of Commonwealth Universities on the occasion of its 75th Anniversary.

As we move towards the twenty-first century, the challenges facing higher education's teaching and research institutions in industrialized and developing countries alike require greatly increased co-operation in order to optimize the use of human and material resources. Therefore, in this ever more complex and interdependent world, and given the magnitude of the problems that have to be tackled, it is essential that academic communities pool their vast reserves of scholarship and intellectual excellence in order to build up a strong partnership with national decision-makers.

The international co-operation, which Unesco is seeking to promote in the field of higher education, aims to provide assistance to national, regional and international initiatives. In this regard, the Organization attaches particular importance to its collaboration with non-governmental organizations. The Association of Commonwealth Universities, the oldest inter-university association in the world, has long been a highly valued partner of Unesco by virtue of its dynamic activities and its diverse membership.

The university must continue to be a place of reflection while at the same time being involved in the major issues of contemporary society, participating in the solution of problems and contributing to both national and international development. In the light of these responsibilities it is clear that Unesco and the Association of Commonwealth Universities have convergent interests in higher education and I look forward to enhancing still further the strong ties of co-operation between our two organizations.

FEDERICO MAYOR
Director-General

NAMES INDEX

Abayakoon, C. G., 524
Abdul Hamid Abdul Rahman, 10, 521
Abdulkadir, I. A., 256, 286, 526
Abeyratne, M. D. G., 526
Abeysundera, B., 524
Abeywardene, M., 524
Abimbola, W., 309
Adesola, A. O., 6, 11, 204, 219, 220, 250, 523, 529
Afolabi, H. B., 525
Agarwal, R. P., 519
Agesthialingom, S., 302, 520
Agrawala, S. K., 525
Agwani, M. S., 518
Aitken, D. H., 13, 14, 17, 509
Aitken, Margaret, 11, 14, 529
Aitken, Lady Violet, 515
Aitkin, D., 129, 133, 167, 526
Alakija, Tejumade, 523
Alexander, U. H. B., 511
Ali, M., 505
Ali, S. H., 517
Amarasinghe, N. B., 523
Anderson, D. J., 508
Angus, Miriam, 529
Archer, Eileen A., 4
Arthurs, H. W., 118, 120, 516
Asche, A., 509
Ashraf, A., 518
Ashworth, J. M., 10, 128, 134, 135, 164, 512
Asthana, B. N., 518
Atkinson, R. C., 128, 168, 528
Awang Had Salleh, 317, 328, 505, 521

Bachelard, E. P., 136, 164, 507
Back, K. J. C., 527
Baird, A., 529
Ball, S., 509
Banerjea, A. C., 517
Banerjee, S. P., 517
Bangura, E. T., 523
Barber, L. I., 302, 315, 515
Barooah, D. P., 518
Baumber, K. E., 509
Beckel, W. E., 514
Beillard, J.-M., 515

Bélanger, C. H., 343, 345, 346, 514
Benneh, G., 158, 164, 166, 516
Bennett, B. H., 302
Bergsma, J., 516
Berry, J. W., 302, 525
Beveridge, G. S. G., 509
Bhansali, Kamalini H., 210, 520
Birch, D. R., 514
Birt, L. M., 6, 11, 12, 13, 14, 17, 28, 29, 33, 505, 508, 529
Bishop, R. E. D., 510
Black, Sir H., 509
Black, W. L., 511
Bomont, R. G., 464, 512
Bora, K., 517
Bose, N. S., 299, 301, 302, 343, 344, 362, 363, 520
Bosworth, S. R., 313, 512
Bottomley, Judy, 529
Bowes, D., 148
Bowron, R. H., 522
Boyce, P. J., 11, 13, 255, 275, 284, 286, 508, 529
Boyd, G., 513
Brand, C. P., 510
Brewood, W. N., 512
Brooks, H., 512
Brown, M. J. A., 315, 522
Brundin, C. L., 513
Bruton, M. J., 513
Buchan, H. J., 507
Bullock, Margaret, 508
Bulman, W. J. A., 516
Butterfield, Sir J., 165, 166, 168, 510

Cairns, J. H., 510
Cameron, C. Ann, 408, 414, 451, 515
Cameron, D. I., 511
Carney, V. J., 431, 513
Carter, M. P., 508
Caston, G. K., 505, 523
Challis, Christine, 511
Cham Tao Soon, 505, 523
Chandler, G. E., 512
Charlesworth, M. J., 507
Cheluva Raju, K. H., 135, 518
Cheong Siew Keong, 523

Chilver, Lord, 427, 431, 443, 451, 510
Chipungu, G. G., 521
Christodoulou, A., 6, 11, 14, 28, 505, 529
Clark, H. C., 514
Clark, N. J., 507
Clarke, Corinne, 529
Clarke, Stella, 166, 510
Clarkson, B. L., 13, 437, 452, 505, 513
Clinch, D. J., 173, 251, 512
Clyde, Barbara, 529
Conolly, A. H. G., 526
Cookey, S. J. S., 432
Craig, T., 4, 6, 11, 529
Crawford, Sir F., 509
Crequer, Ngaio, 528
Currie, A. M., 510

Daniel, J. S., 13, 173, 187, 199, 200, 201, 250, 251, 346, 514
Das, S. N., 519
Dasgupta, S. M., 517
Davey, K. G., 516
Davies, E., 508
Davies, G. J., 10, 505, 511
Davis, J. G. A., 275, 288
Dawkins, J., 14, 27
de Laeter, J. R., 507
de'Lestang, Helen, 529
de Silva, N. W. S. W. S., 523
de Sousa, A. O., 405, 414
Dearden, C. W., 291, 522
Denis Hj. Roslee, M., 514
Deshmukh, K. G., 517
Dicker, G. S. H., 128, 510
Dickson, K. B., 385, 390, 391, 431, 450, 451, 516
Downey, J., 13, 369, 390, 407, 414, 448, 515
Downie, R. J., 515
Drayton, M. Joy, 522
Dubbey, J. M., 120, 521
Dubey, M., 519
Dubey, S. M., 517
Duckworth, H. E., 515
Dunn, D. D., 508
Durbin, A. T., 513

Earle, T. R., 525
Earp, A. J., 10, 514
Easton, J. D., 522

533

NAMES INDEX

Edwards, K. J. R., 511
Effah, P., 525
Ejike, C., 522
Elliott, R. H., 199, 507
Ellul, L., 521
Emrys Evans, W., 513
Essien-Udom, E. U., 526

Faletau, I. F., 526
Farquhar, R. H., 516
Farrell, T. H. F., 511
Fender, B. E. F., 511
Finkelstein, L., 127, 135, 510
Fischer, D., 508
Fletcher, R. A., 527
Flowers, Lord, 48, 505, 511
Foley, Joan E., 134, 515
Foots, Sir J., 508
Forty, A. J., 512
Foster, D. J., 362, 513
Fournier, J. T., 18, 527
Francis, T. I., 505, 522
Franklin, R. N., 510
Fraser, G. S., 315, 522

Gavin, R. J., 513
Gayan, A. K., 521
George, P. J., 514
Gillanders, N. J., 184, 516
Gillmore, A. K., 525
Girvan, D. W., 369, 522
Githinji, P. M., 520
Golding, R. M., 508
Goswami, D. H., 517
Green, Sir G., 509
Grier, T., 515
Gubertini, Blanche, 6, 11, 529
Gupta, H. K., 517
Guthrie, R. D., 509

Habeeb Mohamed, P. S., 520
Hajela, P. D., 135, 518
Hales, F. D., 512
Hall, D., 526
Hambly, F. S., 6, 11, 525, 529
Hamlin, M. J., 510
Hanham, H. J., 10, 301, 511
Haq, M., 519
Hardyman, N. T., 526
Harris, H., 510
Harris, L., 515
Harris, M. B., 510
Harris, P. G., 509
Harrison, D., 128, 164, 166, 511
Hay, G. A., 455, 522
Hayward, A. W., 522

Hersom, Naomi, 515
Hetherington, P. B., 529
Higginson, G. R., 512
Higgott, L. Anne, 86
Hills, D. W., 512
Hills, G. J., 134, 167, 379, 382, 383, 384, 450, 513
Holborow, L. C., 13, 291, 315, 316, 329, 364, 522
Holliday, F. G. T., 510
Holmes, R. S., 507
Holmlund, B. A., 515
Hood, Mirlwyn, 529
Horlock, J. H., 175
Horowitz, M., 128, 135, 514
Howie, Lord, 510

Ibrahim, Prince A., 13, 18, 503, 528
Ikenberry, S. O., 528
Ikoku, C., 10, 309, 316, 523
Ingram, D. J. E., 127, 136, 511
Irvine, R. O. H., 119, 522
Ishak bin Haron, 521
Ivany, J. W. G., 515

Jennings, K. L., 342, 509
Johnston, D. L., 505, 514
Johnston, T. L., 10, 511
Jones, Rhondda, 508
Jordan, Deirdre F., 314, 507

Kalpage, F. S. C. P., 526
Kamba, W. J., 10, 62, 524
Kao, C. K., 118, 128, 164, 516
Kashoki, M. E., 524
Kayombo, B., 489
Kearney, Mary-Louise, 527
Keenleside, D. G., 512
Kelly, A., 513
Kemp, M. A. R., 513
Kemp, T. J., 513
Kenniff, P. J., 118, 514
Keyston, J. R., 525
Khairuddin bin Yusof, 521
Khan, A., 527
Kigozi, E. K., 525
King, L. J., 514
King, R., 509
Kingman, Sir J., 10, 13, 105, 170, 508
Kingsbury, N. W., 58, 522
Kirya, B. G., 524
Kneipp, Sir G., 508
Ko, V. H. C., 516
Kodithuwakku, K., 475, 501, 524
Koso-Thomas, K., 328, 523
Krishnamurti, Bh., 316, 354, 362, 363, 518

Krishnaswamy, S., 519
Kuhanga, N. A., 524
Kulandaiswamy, V. C., 517
Kumar, D., 457, 464, 465, 499, 518
Kwami, F. O., 516

Lakhanpal, M. L., 518
Lakshmi, K. Rajya, 165, 520
Landgrebe, Valerie, 529
Larose, Gail, 527
Larsen, D., 514
Lawton, D., 511
Lazenby, A., 107, 509
Leal, R. B., 508
Leddy, J. F., 516
Lee, A. A., 10, 505, 514
Lighthill, Sir J., 118, 512
Lim Pin, 136, 523
Lindsay, Ros, 529
Lockwood, G., 513
Logan, M. I., 508
Lourens, Ann, 529
Lovering, J. F., 507
Lush, Sir G., 508

McGarvie, R. E., 165, 508
McGrath, J. J., 522
Machobane, L. B. B. J., 521
Mackay, C. B., 515
MacKinnon, G. A., 515
McKinnon, K. R., 330, 343, 344, 345, 399, 405, 406, 407, 451, 509
MacLeod, S. M., 514
McNicol, D., 526
McNicol, G. P., 167, 509
Macpherson, I. F. C., 517
Macrossan, J. M., 507
McWilliam, A., 510
Mahale, K. J., 519
Maiden, C. J., 522
Maidenberg, Nyree, 529
Makhubu, Lydia P., 137, 422, 431, 451, 524
Malcolm, W. G., 10, 505, 522
Malhotra, K. C., 518
Malhoutra, M., 527
Malik, W. U., 517
Manion, Margaret M., 313, 322, 329, 508
Mann-Trofimenkoff, Susan, 316, 515
Manrakhan, J., 6, 11, 13, 27, 165, 505, 521, 529
Marasinghe, M. M. J., 523
Marjoribanks, K., 507
Marshall, A. C., 219
Massaro, V., 525
Mathur, M. L., 518

NAMES INDEX

Mathur, N. C., 520
Mattison, F. T., 98, 511
Mawditt, R. M., 118, 167, 509
Mayor, F., 531
Mbithi, P. M., 505
Mendis, M. W. J. G., 10, 55, 523
Merrison, Sir A., 528
Mfula, J. C., 527
Miglani, M. K., 519
Miller, J. O., 526
Mitchell, J. A., 282, 512
Mitchell, Dame Roma, 507
Mohammed, A. N., 10, 505, 522
Monahan, E. J., 525
Monks, B. R. H., 243, 247, 522
Moore, N., 13
Moore, P. G., 511
Morgan, K. J., 508
Morrell, D. W. J., 390, 397, 513
Morris, B. R., 328, 513
Morris, J. R. S., 167, 512
Morrison, T. R., 222, 243, 244, 514
Mungai, L. M., 520
Murray, D. J., 175, 184, 185, 276, 288, 289, 512
Musa bin Mohamad, 521
Mutere, F. A., 520
Mwauluka, K., 505

Nag, K. N., 519
Naimark, A., 10, 416, 431, 451, 505, 515
Nanjundappa, D. M., 517
Narayan, R. B., 519
Nayan bin Ariffin, 6, 11, 479, 501, 521, 529
Neave, D., 272, 510
Neill, Sir P., 512
Neilson, D. D., 53, 508
Newberry, R. S., 526
Newcomb, E., 510
Newton, Coral, 529
Nichol, L. W., 10, 508
Nicholson, R. J., 512
Nicoll, W. B., 74, 522
Nind, R. A., 511

Odhiambo, D., 13, 455, 498, 499, 520
O'Hara, M. M., 510
Onazi, O. C., 523
O'Neill, F. J., 301, 507
Orr, Jeanette, 14, 529
Orr, M. R., 6, 11, 14, 529
O'Sullivan, J. F., 515
Owen, G., 513
Ozmon, K. L., 505, 515

Page, E. S., 512
Pai, R. M., 519
Panabokke, R. G., 10, 524
Parfitt, Judith, 529
Parikh, R., 505, 518
Parker, D. C., 13, 22, 28
Parkes, Sir E., 127, 505, 511
Patel, K. C., 520
Paulson-Ellis, M. G. E., 510
Pearce, R., 18
Penington, D. G., 118, 128, 167, 508
Perkins, H. R., 511
Petch, H. E., 516
Pilkington, Sir A., 118, 511
Pillai, Jaya K., 519
Pitman, M. G., 120, 134, 165, 526
Ponter, A. R. S., 511
Porter, D., 508
Potter, J. B., 328, 508
Powar, K. B., 520
Prescott, J. R., 507
Pullman, W. A., 129, 527

Quayle, J. R., 509

Raeburn, R. M., 441, 515
Rajagopalan, V., 520
Ram Reddy, G., 13, 251
Rathbone, B. L., 511
Ratnasiri, Nalini B., 524
Raza, M., 10, 466, 473, 500, 502, 517
Redford, D. K., 512
Reid, W. M., 514
Richards, G. M., 264, 287, 524
Richmond, Sir M., 505
Ridgway, J. E., 507
Ritchie, Jane, 302, 315, 522
Roberts, A. C., 511
Roberts, A. W., 133, 513
Robertson-Cuninghame, R. C., 508
Robinson, L. R. B., 120, 524
Rosehart, R. G., 59
Ross, B. J., 142, 522
Rudrappa, Y. P., 519

Safeeulla, K. M., 519
Sagar, G. R., 513
Sale, A., 120, 509
Samarawickrama, G. P., 524
Samuels, G. J., 13, 33, 34, 35, 343, 508
Sanusi, M. A., 523
Sawyerr, G. F. A., 82, 505, 516
Saywell, W. G., 515

Schlosser, J. L., 120, 514
Schofield, D. A., 512
Schubert, Sir S., 507
Scott, J. F., 10, 14, 128, 505, 508
Scott, P., 528
Seaton, R., 510
Seebaluck, B. K., 521
Segal, B., 515
Serracino Inglott, P., 521
Sethunarayanan, R. M., 517
Shah, K. N., 520
Sharma, D. R., 520
Sharom Ahmat, 514
Shattock, M. L., 513
Sheik Ali, B., 518
Shellam-Harper, Margaret, 11, 14, 529
Shennan, J. H., 511
Shervington, Christine, 127, 164
Sims, G. D., 6, 11, 505, 512, 527, 529
Singh, B., 519
Singh, E. B., 517
Singh, S., 505, 519
Singh Bisen, B. B., 520
Sinha, D. K., 518
Sivarajah, V. N., 282, 525
Skilbeck, M., 192, 202, 203, 507
Skinner, A. S., 511
Sloman, Sir A., 6, 11, 526, 529
Smith, Sir D., 112, 119, 135, 168, 510
Smith, Elizabeth, 14, 529
Smith, J. D., 487, 508
Smith, Sir R., 511
Smith, R. H. T., 9, 10, 11, 13, 14, 17, 24, 28, 509, 529
Smith, S. R., 526
Spencer, B. J., 377, 382, 508
Springer, Lady, 18
Springer, Sir H. W., 18, 528
Srinath, L. S., 152, 166, 168, 518
Srivastava, K. D., 514
Srivastava, P. N., 180, 528
Stephen, Lady, 17
Stephen, Sir N., 12, 13, 17, 20, 21, 507
Stevens, Auriol, 528
Strangway, D. W., 93, 514
Stubbs, J. O., 515
Subramani, 314, 315, 363, 523
Suddards, R. W., 510
Sunderland, E., 513
Swani, N. M., 505
Symons, T. H. B., 6, 11, 14, 293, 302, 315, 329, 505, 515, 529

535

NAMES INDEX

Taiaroa, L. S., 525
Tarling, P. N., 68, 522
Taylor, B. H., 525
Taylor, W., 75, 511
Temple, E. E., 528
Tewari, D. N., 518
Thakkar, R. C., 520
Thampi, G. B., 519
Thiagarajan, Radha, 517
Thom, Sue, 529
Thompson, M. W., 118, 510
Thomson, J. M., 509
Thorens, J., 527
Tiwari, K. K., 505, 518
Tlou, T., 509
Tonkinson, R., 314, 328, 344, 509
Topley, J., 507
Trafford, Lord, 513
Trinca, Helen M., 525
Trotman-Dickenson, A. F., 513
Try, H. W., 136, 510
Tunku Shamsul Bahrin, 521
Tunley, D., 337, 343, 344, 345, 528
Turner, R. S., 392, 397, 398, 450, 515

Valentine, J. A., 522
Varcoe, T., 514
Vasudev, T., 518

Venkatasubramanian, K., 453, 519
Verma, S. K., 301, 328, 362, 363, 517
Vick, Sir A., 513
Vines, G. J. G., 135, 507
Vithiananthan, S., 505, 523

Waddington, D. J., 513
Wahi, P. L., 118, 165, 519
Walcott, G. L., 516
Wang Gungwu, 13, 53, 101, 516
Warakaulle, H. M. N., 523
Warburton, G. B., 512
Ward, J. M., 509
Waters, T. N. M., 522
Watts, D. W., 119, 134, 507
Way, I. R., 255, 508
Webb, L. R., 507
Weedon, B. C. L., 512
Weir, J. A., 516
Weller, G. R., 59
Wendell Smith, C. P., 509
West, B., 508
West, J. C., 510
Whiteman, D. H., 515
Whitfield, J. F., 513
Whittingham, J. A., 529
Whyte, F. R., 514
Wijesundera, S., 6, 10, 11, 523, 529

Wijeyesekera, D. S., 237, 245, 524
Wilks, Jean R. F., 510
Williams, Sir A., 119, 134, 136, 511
Williams, D. A., 512
Williams, D. C., 473, 508
Williams, G. G., 118, 512
Williams, G. J., 527
Williams, P. R. C., 201, 250, 527
Willmot, E., 303, 313, 314, 315, 328, 329, 526
Wilson, B. G., 10, 505, 508
Wilson, F. R., 515
Wishaw, Jane, 529
Woo, Chia-Wei, 127, 135, 167, 517
Wright, Sir A., 522
Wright, Sir D., 508
Wright, D. T., 516
Wright, E. C., 105, 510
Wynn Jones, E., 513

Yeates, M. H., 525
Yerbury, Dianne, 372, 377, 378, 449, 508
Yeung, Yue-man, 87, 516
Young, C. E., 127, 528
Young, Rosie T. T., 121, 516